THE

HISTORICAL SHAKSPEARIAN READER:

COMPRISING

THE "HISTORIES," OR, "CHRONICLE PLAYS"

OF

SHAKSPEARE;

CAREFULLY EXPURGATED AND REVISED, WITH

INTRODUCTORY AND EXPLANATORY NOTES.

EXPRESSLY ADAPTED FOR THE USE OF SCHOOLS, COLLEGES, AND THE FAMILY READING CIRCLE.

BY

JOHN W. S. HOWS,

AUTHOR OF THE "SHAKSPEARIAN READER," ETC., ETC.

— "Shakspeare's English Histories *are* the text book of a large portion of English History to all of English blood, and rightly so, because they more than compensate for their slight inaccuracies of detail by the vividness and force with which they give the 'very form and pressure' of those times."

G. C. VERPLANCK.

NEW YORK:
D. APPLETON AND COMPANY,
549 & 551 BROADWAY.
1875.

PREFACE.

MY "Shakspearian Reader" was published sixteen years ago, with the hope of making Shakspeare a "Text Book" for schools. The experiment at that time was considered one of doubtful success: the work however has become a "standard" in educational literature, and a continuation of selections from the Poet's works is now demanded. In preparing a second series, those Plays have been selected that would best subserve my original design. The *Historical, or Chronicle Plays* of Shakspeare seemed expressly adapted for this purpose. The ablest writers have declared them to be invaluable adjuncts to the study of English history, presenting, as they do, a truthful narration of events, drawn from accredited chronicles of the times, and vivid pictures of the manners, habits, and customs of the people. This marvellous power of truthful characterization, with which the poet has invested the leading historical personages, makes them invaluable aids to the youthful student.

The original text of Shakspeare is given as fully as the prescribed limits of this volume would allow;

the continuity of the action is preserved by explanatory notes. Knowing, from long practical experience, that it is impossible to introduce Shakspeare as an educational work, in its original entirety, the same rigid expurgation and revision have been adopted, as were rendered imperative in my first series. This latter portion of my task has been executed, in a due reverential spirit for the purity and integrity of the text.

JNO. W. S. HOWS.

5 Cottage Place, New York,
April 16, 1863.

CONTENTS.

THE LIFE AND DEATH OF

KING JOHN.

KING JOHN stands first in chronological order in the list of "Histories," or "Chronicle Plays," written by Shakspeare, founded on the leading events which marked the reigns of the Kings of England whose lives he selected for dramatic illustration.

The old chroniclers, Hall, Holinshed, Stowe, and others, furnished the Poet ample and reliable materials for his principal Historical facts; and at times the very expression of these authorities is copiously used. In preparing King John, Shakspeare was also largely indebted to a chronicle drama he found upon the stage, entitled "The Troublesome Raigne of King John." But while using this superstructure for his work, he clothes the dry historical details of the chronicler with all the beauty of his own poetic imagination, and invests his characters with a vigor and elevation which give a depth of interest mere dramatic history could not attain. The action of this Play begins at the thirty-fourth year of John's life; it takes in the principal transactions of his reign to the time of his death, being an interval of seventeen years.

The tragic interest of the Play mainly rests in the majesty of maternal grief, as exhibited in the character of Constance, and the innocence and winning affection of her son, young Arthur. They are exquisitely elaborated pictures. The predominant interest thrown around these two characters, seems to have prevented Shakspeare from introducing into this Play John's contest with his Barons, and his final signing of the great "*Magna Charta*" of English liberty. The struggles of the King with the Papal power, his submission to the Pope, his resignation of the crown, and the other main incidents of his troublesome reign, are all depicted with historical accuracy.

PERSONS REPRESENTED.

KING JOHN.
PRINCE HENRY, *his son.*
ARTHUR, *Duke of* Bretagne, *nephew to* King John.
WILLIAM MARESHALL, *Earl of* Pembroke.
GEFFREY FITZ-PETER, *Earl of* Essex, *chief justiciary of* England.

WILLIAM LONGSWORD, *Earl of* Salisbury.
ROBERT BIGOT, *Earl of* Norfolk.
HUBERT DE BURGH, *chamberlain to the* King.
ROBERT FAULCONBRIDGE.
PHILIP FAULCONBRIDGE, *his half-brother.*
JAMES GURNEY, *servant to Lady* Faulconbridge.
PETER OF POMFRET, *a prophet.*
PHILIP, *King of* France.
LEWIS, *the Dauphin.*
ARCHDUKE OF AUSTRIA.
Cardinal PANDULPH, *the Pope's legate.*
MELUN, *a* French *lord.*
CHATILLON, *ambassador from* France.

ELINOR, *widow of* King Henry II., *and mother to* King John.
CONSTANCE, *mother to* Arthur.
BLANCH, *daughter to* Alphonso, *King of* Castile, *and niece to* King John.
LADY FAULCONBRIDGE, *mother to* Robert *and* Philip Faulconbridge.

Lords, Ladies, Citizens of Angiers, *Sheriff, Heralds, Officers, Soldiers, Messengers, and Attendants.*

SCENE,—*Sometimes in* ENGLAND, *and sometimes in* FRANCE.

ACT I.

SCENE I.—Northampton. *A Room of State in the Palace.*

Enter King JOHN, *Queen* ELINOR, PEMBROKE, ESSEX, SALISBURY, *and others, with* CHATILLON.

K. John. Now, say, Chatillon, what would France with us?
Chat. Thus, after greeting, speaks the king of France,
In my behavior, to the majesty,
The borrow'd majesty of England here.
Eli. A strange beginning;—borrow'd majesty!
K. John. Silence, good mother; hear the embassy.
Chat. Philip of France, in right and true behalf
Of thy deceased brother Jeffrey's son,
Arthur Plantagenet, lays most lawful claim
To this fair island and the territories,—
To Ireland, Poictiers, Anjou, Touraine, Maine;
Desiring thee to lay aside the sword
Which sways usurpingly these several titles,
And put the same into young Arthur's hand,
Thy nephew and right royal sovereign.
K. John. What follows, if we disallow of this?
Chat. The proud control of fierce and bloody war,
To enforce these rights so forcibly withheld.

K. John. Here have we war for war, and blood for blood,
Controlment for controlment: so answer France.
Chat. Then take my king's defiance from my mouth,
The farthest limit of my embassy.
K. John. Bear mine to him, and so depart in peace:
Be thou as lightning in the eyes of France;
For ere thou canst report I will be there,
The thunder of my cannon shall be heard:
So, hence! Be thou the trumpet of our wrath,
And sullen presage of your own decay.—
An honorable conduct let him have:—
Pembroke, look to't.—Farewell, Chatillon.
[*Exeunt* CHATILLON *and* PEMBROKE.
Eli. What now, my son! have I not ever said,
How that ambitious Constance would not cease,
Till she had kindled France, and all the world,
Upon the right and party of her son?
K. John. Our strong possession, and our right for us.
Eli. Your strong possession, much more than your right,
Or else it must go wrong with you, and me.
Enter the Sheriff *of* Northamptonshire, *who whispers* ESSEX.
Essex. My liege, here is the strangest controversy,
Come from the country to be judg'd by you,
That e'er I heard: shall I produce the men?
K. John. Let them approach.— [*Exit* Sheriff.
Our abbeys, and our priories shall pay
This expedition's charge.—

Re-enter Sheriff, *with* ROBERT FAULCONBRIDGE, *and* PHILIP, *his half-brother.*

What men are you?
Faul. Your faithful subject I; a gentleman
Born in Northamptonshire, and eldest son,
As I suppose, to Robert Faulconbridge,—
A soldier, by the honor-giving hand
Of Cœur-de-lion knighted in the field.
K. John. What art thou?
Rob. The son and heir to that same Faulconbridge.
K. John. Is that the elder, and art thou the heir?
You came not of one mother, then, it seems.
Faul. Most certain of one mother, mighty king,—
That is well known; and, as I think, one father:
But, for the certain knowledge of that truth,
I put you o'er to heaven, and to my mother;
Of that I doubt.
Eli. Out on thee, rude man! thou dost shame thy mother,
And wound her honor with this diffidence.
Faul. I, madam? no, I have no reason for it,—

That is my brother's plea and none of mine;
The which if he can prove, 'a pops me out
At least from fair five hundred pound a-year:
Heaven guard my mother's honor, and my land!
K. John. A good blunt fellow.—Why, being younger born,
Doth he lay claim to thine inheritance?
Faul. I know not why, except to get the land.
If Sir Robert were our father, and this son like him,
O, old Sir Robert, father, on my knee
I give heaven thanks, I was not like to thee.
K. John. Why, what a madcap hath heaven lent us here!
Eli. He hath a trick of Cœur-de-lion's face;
The accent of his tongue affecteth him:
Do you not read some tokens of my son
In the large composition of this man?
K. John. Mine eye hath well examined his parts,
And finds them perfect Richard.—Sirrah, speak,
What doth move you to claim your brother's land?
Faul. Because he hath a half-face, like my father,
With that half-face would he have all my land:
A half-fac'd groat five hundred pound a-year!
Rob. My gracious liege, when that my father liv'd,
Your brother did employ my father much,—
And once despatch'd him in an embassy
To Germany, there, with the emperor,
To treat of high affairs touching that time.
The advantage of his absence took the king,
And in the mean time sojourn'd at my father's;
Where how he did prevail, I shame to speak,—
But truth is truth:
My father on his death-bed by will bequeath'd
His lands to me; and took it, on his death,
That this, my mother's son, was none of his;
Then, good my liege, let me have what is mine,
My father's land, as was my father's will.
K. John. Sirrah, your brother is legitimate,—
Your father's wife did after wedlock bear him;
Your father's heir must have your father's land.
Eli. (*To* FAULCONBRIDGE.) Whether hadst thou rather be a Faulconbridge,
And like thy brother, to enjoy thy land,
Or the reputed son of Cœur-de-lion,
Lord of thy presence, and no land beside?
Faul. Madam, an if my brother had my shape,
And I had his, Sir Robert his, like him;
And if my limbs were two such riding-rods,
My arms such eel-skins stuff'd; my face so thin,
That in mine ear I durst not stick a rose,

Lest men should say, "Look, where three-farthings goes!"
And, to his shape, were heir to all this land,—
Would I might never stir from off this place,
I'd give it every foot to have this face;
I would not be Sir Nob in any case.
Eli. I like thee well: wilt thou forsake thy fortune,
Bequeath thy land to him, and follow me?
I am a soldier, and now bound to France.
Faul. Brother, take you my land, I'll take my chance:
Your face hath got five hundred pounds a-year;
Yet sell your face for five pence, and 'tis dear.—
Madam, I'll follow you unto the death.
Eli. Nay, I would have you go before me thither.
Faul. Our country manners give our betters way.
K. John. What is thy name?
Faul. Philip, my liege,—so is my name begun,—
Philip, good old Sir Robert's wife's eldest son.
K. John. From henceforth bear his name whose form thou bearest:
Kneel thou down Philip, but arise more great,—
Arise Sir Richard, and Plantagenet.
Faul. Brother, by the mother's side, give me your hand:
My father gave me honour, your's gave land.—
Eli. The very spirit of Plantagenet!
I am thy grandam, Richard; call me so.
Faul. Madam, by chance, but not by truth.
K. John. Go, Faulconbridge: now hast thou thy desire;
A landless knight makes thee a landed 'squire.—
Come, madam,—and come, Richard; we must speed
For France, for France; for it is more than need.
Faul. Bother, adieu: good fortune come to thee!
[*Exeunt all except* FAULCONBRIDGE.
A foot of honor better than I was;
But many a foot of land the worse.
Well, now can I make any Joan a lady:—
"Good den, Sir Richard:"—"God-a-mercy, fellow;"—
And if his name be George, I'll call him Peter;
For new-made honor doth forget men's names,—
'Tis too respective, and too sociable,
For your conversion.
Yet, to avoid deceit, I mean to learn;
For it shall strew the footsteps of my rising. [*Exit.*

ACT II.

SCENE I.—France. *Before the Walls of* Angiers.

Enter, on one side, the Archduke of Austria, *and forces; on the other,* Philip, *King of France and forces;* Lewis, Constance, Arthur, *and* Attendants.

Lew. Before Angiers well met, brave Austria.—
Arthur, that great fore-runner of thy blood,
Richard, that robb'd the lion of his heart,
And fought the holy wars in Palestine,
By this brave duke came early to his grave:
And, for amends to his posterity,
At our importance hither is he come,
To spread his colors, boy, in thy behalf;
And to rebuke the usurpation
Of thy unnatural uncle, English John:
Embrace him, love him, give him welcome hither.
Arth. Heaven shall forgive you Cœur-de-lion's death,
The rather, that you give his offspring life,
Shadowing their right under your wings of war:
I give you welcome with a powerless hand,
But with a heart full of unstained love:
Welcome before the gates of Angiers, duke.
Lew. A noble boy! Who would not do thee right?
Aust. Upon thy cheek lay I this zealous kiss,
As seal to this indenture of my love;—
That to my home I will no more return,
Till Angiers, and the right thou hast in France,
Together with that pale, that white-fac'd shore,
Whose foot spurns back the ocean's roaring tides,
And coops from other lands her islanders,—
Even till that England, hedg'd in with the main,
That water-walled bulwark, still secure
And confident from foreign purposes,—
Even till that utmost corner of the west
Salute thee for her king: till then, fair boy,
Will I not think of home, but follow arms.
Const. O, take his mother's thanks, a widow's thanks,
Till your strong hand shall help to give him strength,
To make a more requital to your love!
Aust. The peace of heaven is theirs that lift their swords
In such a just and charitable war.
K. Phi. Well then, to work: our cannon shall be bent
Against the brows of this resisting town.—
Call for our chiefest men of discipline,

To cull the plots of best advantages:
We'll lay before this town our royal bones,
Wade to the market-place in Frenchmen's blood,
But we will make it subject to this boy.
Const. Stay for an answer to your embassy,
Lest unadvis'd you stain your swords with blood:
My lord Chatillon may from England bring
That right in peace, which here we urge in war;
And then we shall repent each drop of blood,
That hot rash haste so indirectly shed.

Enter CHATILLON.

K. Phi. A wonder, lady!—lo, upon thy wish
Our messenger, Chatillon, is arriv'd.—
What England says, say briefly, gentle lord;
We coldly pause for thee; Chatillon, speak.
Chat. Then turn your forces from this paltry siege,
And stir them up against a mightier task.
England, impatient of your just demands,
Hath put himself in arms: the adverse winds,
Whose leisure I have stay'd, have given him time
To land his legions all as soon as I;
His marches are expedient to this town,
His forces strong, his soldiers confident.
With him along is come the mother-queen,
With her her niece, the lady Blanch of Spain;
And all th' unsettled humors of the land:
Rash, inconsiderate, fiery voluntaries,
With ladies' faces, and fierce dragons' spleens,—
Have sold their fortunes at their native homes,
Bearing their birthrights proudly on their backs,
To make a hazard of new fortunes here:
In brief, a braver choice of dauntless spirits,
Than now the English bottoms have waft o'er,
Did never float upon the swelling tide,
To do offence and scath in Christendom. [*Drums heard within.*
The interruption of their churlish drums
Cuts off more circumstance: they are at hand,
To parley, or to fight; therefore, prepare.
K. Phi. How much unlook'd for is this expedition!
Aust. By how much unexpected, by so much
We must awake endeavor for defence;
For courage mounteth with occasion:
Let them be welcome then; we are prepar'd.

Enter KING JOHN, ELINOR, BLANCH, FAULCONBRIDGE, Lords, *and forces.*

K. John. Peace be to France, if France in peace permit

Our just and lineal entrance to our own!
If not, bleed France, and peace ascend to heaven!
K. Phi. Peace be to England, if that war return
From France to England, there to live in peace!
Look here upon thy brother Geffrey's face;—
[*Leading* ARTHUR *to* JOHN.
These eyes, these brows, were moulded out of his:
This little abstract doth contain that large,
Which died in Geffrey:
That Geffrey was thy elder brother born,
And this his son; England was Geffrey's right,
And this is Geffrey's: in the name of heaven,
How comes it, then, that thou art call'd a king,
When living blood doth in these temples beat,
Which owe the crown that thou o'ermasterest?
K. John. From whom hast thou this great commission, France,
To draw my answer from thy articles?
K. Phi. From that supernal Judge, that stirs good thoughts
In any breast of strong authority,
To look into the blots and stains of right.
That Judge hath made me guardian to this boy:
Under whose warrant I impeach thy wrong;
And by whose help I mean to chastise it.
K. John. Alack, thou dost usurp authority.
K. Phi. Excuse,—it is to beat usurping down.
Eli. Who is it thou dost call usurper, France?
Const. Let me make answer;—thy usurping son.
Aust. Peace!
Faul. Hear the crier.
Aust. What art thou?
Faul. One that will play the mischief, sir, with you,
An 'a may catch your hide and you alone:
You are the hare of whom the proverb goes,
Whose valor plucks dead lions by the beard:
I'll smoke your skin-coat, an I catch you right;
Sirrah, look to't; i' faith, I will, i' faith.
Blanch. O, well did he become that lion's robe,
That did disrobe the lion of that robe!
Faul. It lies as sightly on the back of him,
As great Alcides' shoes upon an ass:—
But, ass, I'll take that burden from your back,
Or lay on that shall make your shoulders crack.
Aust. What cracker is this same, that deafs our ears
With this abundance of superfluous breath?
K. Phi. Lewis, determine what we shall do straight.
Lew. King John, this is the very sum of all,—
England and Ireland, Anjou, Touraine, Maine,

In right of Arthur do I claim of thee:
Wilt thou resign them, and lay down thy arms?
K. John. My life as soon:—I do defy thee, France.—
Arthur of Bretagne, yield thee to my hand;
And, out of my dear love, I'll give thee more
Than e'er the coward hand of France can win:
Submit thee, boy.
Eli. Come to thy grandam, child.
Const. Do, child, go to it' grandam, child:
Give grandam kingdom, and it' grandam will
Give it a plum, a cherry, and a fig:
There's a good grandam.
Arth. Good my mother, peace!
I would that I were low laid in my grave:
I am not worth this coil that's made for me.
Eli. His mother shames him so, poor boy, he weeps.
Const. Now shame upon you, whe'r she does, or no!
His grandam's wrongs, and not his mother's shames,
Draw those heaven-moving pearls from his poor eyes,
Which heaven shall take in nature of a fee;
Ay, with these crystal beads heaven shall be brib'd
To do him justice, and revenge on you.
Eli. Thou monstrous slanderer of heaven and earth!
Const. Thou monstrous injurer of heaven and earth!
Call not me slanderer; thou and thine usurp
The dominions, royalties, and rights,
Of this oppressed boy.
Eli. I can produce
A will, that bars the title of thy son.
Const. Ay, who doubts that? a will! a wicked will;
A woman's will; a canker'd grandam's will!
K. Phi. Peace, lady! pause, or be more temperate:
Some trumpet summon hither to the walls
These men of Angiers: let us hear them speak,
Whose title they admit, Arthur's or John's.

Trumpet sounds. Enter Citizens *upon the walls.*

1 *Cit.* Who is it that hath warn'd us to the walls?
K. Phi. 'Tis France for England.
K. John. England for itself:—
You men of Angiers, and my loving subjects,—
K. Phi. You loving men of Angiers, Arthur's subjects,
Our trumpet call'd you to this gentle parle.
K. John. For our advantage; therefore hear us first.
These flags of France that are advanc'd here
Before the eye and prospect of your town,
Have hither march'd to your endamagement:
All preparation for a bloody siege,

And merciless proceeding by these French,
Confront your city's eyes, your winking gates;
But, on the sight of us, your lawful king,—
Behold, the French, amaz'd, vouchsafe a parle;
And now, instead of bullets wrapp'd in fire,
To make a shaking fever in your walls,
They shoot but calm words, folded up in smoke,
To make a faithless error in your ears:
Which trust accordingly, kind citizens,
And let us in, your king; whose labor'd spirits,
Forwearied in this action of swift speed,
Crave harborage within your city walls.

K. Phi. When I have said, make answer to us both.
Lo, in this right hand, whose protection
Is most divinely vow'd upon the right
Of him it holds, stands young Plantagenet,
Son to the elder brother of this man,
And king o'er him, and all that he enjoys:
For this down-trodden equity, we tread
In warlike march these greens before your town.
'Tis not the roundure of your old-fac'd walls
Can hide you from our messengers of war,
Though all these English, and their discipline,
Were harbor'd in their rude circumference.
Then, tell us, shall your city call us lord,
In that behalf which we have challeng'd it?
Or shall we give the signal to our rage,
And stalk in blood to our possession?

1 *Cit.* In brief, we are the king of England's subjects:
For him, and in his right, we hold this town.

K. John. Acknowledge then the king, and let me in.

1 *Cit.* That can we not; but he that proves the king,
To him will we prove loyal: till that time,
Have we ramm'd up our gates against the world.

K. John. Doth not the crown of England prove the king?
And if not that, I bring you witnesses,
Twice fifteen thousand hearts of England's breed,—
To verify our title with their lives.

K. Phi. As many, and as well-born blood as those,—
Stand in his face to contradict his claim.

1 *Cit.* Till you compound whose right is worthiest,
We for the worthiest hold the right from both.

K. John. Then heaven forgive the sin of all those souls,
That to their everlasting residence,
Before the dew of evening fall, shall fleet,
In dreadful trial of our kingdom's king!

K. Phi. Amen, Amen!—Mount, chevaliers! to arms!

Faul. St. George, that swinged the dragon, and e'er since

Sits on his horseback at mine hostess' door,
Teach us some fence!—[*To* Austria.] Sirrah, were I at home,
At your den, sirrah, with your lioness,
I would set an ox-head to your lion's hide,
And make a monster of you.

Aust. Peace! no more.

Faul. O, tremble, for you hear the lion roar!

K. John. Up higher to the plain; where we'll set forth
In best appointment all our regiments.

Faul. Speed, then, to take advantage of the field.

K. Phi. It shall be so;—[*To* Lewis.] and at the other hill
Command the rest to stand.—God, and our right! [*Exeunt.*

SCENE II.—*The Same.*

Alarums and Excursions; then a Retreat. Enter a French Herald, *with trumpets, to the gates.*

F. Her. You men of Angiers, open wide your gates,
And let young Arthur, duke of Bretagne, in.
Who, by the hand of France, this day hath made
Much work for tears in many an English mother;
And victory, with little loss, doth play
Upon the dancing banners of the French,
Who are at hand, triumphantly display'd,
To enter conquerors, and to proclaim
Arthur of Bretagne, England's king, and yours.

Enter an English Herald, *with trumpets.*

E. Her. Rejoice, you men of Angiers, ring your bells;
King John, your king and England's, doth approach,
Commander of this hot malicious day:
Open your gates, and give the victors way.

1 *Cit.* Heralds, from off our towers we might behold
From first to last, the onset and retire
Of both your armies; whose equality
By our best eyes cannot be censured:
Blood hath bought blood, and blows have answer'd blows;
Strength matched with strength, and power confronted power;
Both are alike; and both alike we like.
One must prove greatest: while they weigh so even,
We hold our town for neither; yet for both.

Enter, at one side, King John, *with his power,* Elinor, Blanch, *and* Faulconbridge; *at the other,* King Philip, Lewis, Austria, *and forces.*

K. John. France, hast thou yet more blood to cast away?
Say, shall the current of our right run on?
Whose passage, vex'd with thy impediment,

Shall leave his native channel, and o'er-swell
With course disturb'd even thy confining shores,
Unless thou let his silver water keep
A peaceful progress to the ocean.
K. Phi. England, thou hast not sav'd one drop of blood,
In this hot trial, more than we of France;
Rather, lost more: and by this hand I swear,
That sways the earth this climate overlooks,
Before we will lay down our just-borne arms,
We'll put thee down, 'gainst whom these arms we bear,
Or add a royal number to the dead,
Gracing the scroll, that tells of this war's loss,
With slaughter coupled to the name of kings.
Faul. Ha, majesty! how high thy glory towers,
When the rich blood of kings is set on fire!
Why stand these royal fronts amazéd thus?
Cry, havock, kings! back to the stainéd field,
You equal potents, fiery-kindled spirits!
Then let confusion of one part confirm
The other's peace; till then, blows, blood, and death!
K. John. Whose party do the townsmen yet admit?
K. Phi. Speak, citizens, for England; who's your king?
1 *Cit.* The king of England, when we know the king.
K. Phi. Know him in us, that here hold up his right.
K. John. In us, that are our own great deputy,
And bear possession of our person here;
Lord of our presence, Angiers, and of you.
1 *Cit.* A greater power than we denies all this;
And, till it be undoubted, we do lock
Our former scruple in our strong-barr'd gates;
King'd of our fears, until our fears, resolv'd,
Be by some certain king purg'd and depos'd.
Faul. By heaven, these scroyles* of Angiers flout you, kings,
And stand securely on their battlements,
As in a theatre, whence they gape and point
At your industrious scenes and acts of death.
Your royal presences be rul'd by me:—
Be friends awhile, and both conjointly bend
Your sharpest deeds of malice on this town:
By east and west let France and England mount
Their battering cannon, charged to the mouths,
Till their soul-fearing clamors have brawl'd down
The flinty ribs of this contemptuous city:
I'd play incessantly upon these jades,
Even till unfenced desolation
Leave them as naked as the vulgar air.
That done, dissever your united strengths,
And part your mingled colors once again;

* Scroyles, mean fellows.

Turn face to face, and bloody point to point;
Then, in a moment, fortune shall cull forth
Out of one side her happy minion,
To whom in favor she shall give the day
And kiss him with a glorious victory.
How like you this wild counsel, mighty states?
Smacks it not something of the policy?
K. John. Now, by the sky that hangs above our heads,
I like it well.—France, shall we knit our powers
And lay this Angiers even with the ground;
Then, after, fight who shall be king of it?
Faul. An if thou hast the mettle of a king,—
Being wrong'd, as we are, by this peevish town,—
Turn thou the mouth of thy artillery,
As we will ours, against these saucy walls;
And when that we have dash'd them to the ground,
Why, then defy each other.
K. Phi. Let it be so.—Say, where will you assault?
K. John. We from the west will send destruction
Into this city's bosom.
Aust. I from the north.
K. Phi. Our thunder from the south,
Shall rain their drift of bullets on this town.
Faul. [*Aside.*] O, prudent discipline! From north to south,
Austria and France shoot in each other's mouth:
I'll stir them to it.—Come, away, away!
1 *Cit.* Hear us, great kings: vouchsafe a while to stay,
And I shall show you peace, and fair-fac'd league;
Win you this city without stroke, or wound;
Rescue those breathing lives to die in beds,
That here come sacrifices for the field:
Persévor not, but hear me, mighty kings.
K. John. Speak on, with favor; we are bent to hear.
Cit. That daughter there of Spain, the lady Blanch,
Is near to England:—look upon the years
Of Lewis the Dauphin, and that lovely maid.
O, two such silver currents, when they join,
Do glorify the banks that bound them in;
And two such shores to two such streams made one,
Two such controlling bounds shall you be, kings,
To these two princes, if you marry them.
This union shall do more than battery can
To our fast-closed gates; for, at this match,
With swifter spleen than powder can enforce,
The mouth of passage shall we fling wide ope,
And give you entrance: but without this match,
The sea enraged is not half so deaf,
Lions more confident, mountains and rocks

More free from motion; no, not death himself
In mortal fury half so peremptory,
As we to keep the city.
Faul. Here's a stay,
That shakes the rotten carcase of old death
Out of his rags! Here's a large mouth, indeed,
That spits forth death and mountains, rocks and seas;
Talks as familiarly of roaring lions,
As maids of thirteen do of puppy-dogs!
What cannoneer father'd this lusty blood?
He speaks plain cannon,—fire and smoke and bounce;
He gives the bastinado with his tongue;
Our ears are cudgell'd; not a word of his,
But buffets better than a fist of France;
Zounds! I was never so bethumped with words,
Since I first called my brother's father dad.
Eli. Son, list to this conjunction, make this match;
Give with our niece a dowry large enough:
For by this knot thou shalt so surely tie
Thy now unsur'd assurance to the crown,
That yond' green boy shall have no sun to ripe
The bloom that promiseth a mighty fruit.
I see a yielding in the looks of France;
Mark, how they whisper: urge them while their souls
Are capable of this ambition,
Lest zeal, now melted by the windy breath
Of soft petitions, pity, and remorse,
Cool and congeal again to what it was.
Cit. Why answer not the double majesties
This friendly treaty of our threaten'd town?
K. Phi. Speak England first, that hath been forward first
To speak unto this city: what say you?
K. John. If that the Dauphin there, thy princely son,
Can in this book of beauty read, "I love,"
Her dowry shall weigh equal with a queen:
For Anjou, and fair Touraine, Maine, Poictiers,
And all that we upon this side the sea
(Except this city now by us besieg'd)
Find liable to our crown and dignity,
Shall gild her bridal bed; and make her rich
In titles, honors, and promotions,
As she in beauty, education, blood,
Holds hand with any princess of the world.
K. Phi. What say'st thou, boy? look in the lady's face.
Lew. I do, my lord; and in her eye I find
A wonder, or a wondrous miracle,
The shadow of myself form'd in her eye;
Which, being but the shadow of your son,

Becomes a sun, and makes your son a shadow;
I do protest, I never lov'd myself,
Till now infixed I beheld myself
Drawn in the flattering table of her eye.
[*Whispers with* BLANCH.

Faul. Drawn in the flattering table of her eye!—
Hang'd in the frowning wrinkle of her brow!—
And quarter'd in her heart!—he doth espy
Himself love's traitor:—this is pity now,
That, hang'd and drawn and quarter'd, there should be,
In such a love, so vile a lout as he.

K. John. What say these young ones?—What say you, my niece?

Blanch. That she is bound in honor still to do
What you in wisdom still vouchsafe to say.

K. John. Speak then, prince Dauphin; can you love this lady?

Lew. Nay, ask me if I can refrain from love;
For I do love her most unfeignedly.

K. John. Philip of France, if thou be pleas'd withal,
Command thy son and daughter to join hands.

K. Phi. It likes us well.—Young princes, close your hands.
Now, citizens of Angiers, ope your gates,
Let in that amity which you have made;
For at saint Mary's chapel presently
The rites of marriage shall be solemnized.—
Is not the lady Constance in this troop?
I know she is not; for this match, made up,
Her presence would have interrupted much:
Where is she and her son? tell me, who knows.

Lew. She is sad and passionate at your highness' tent.

K. Phi. And, by my faith, this league, that we have made,
Will give her sadness very little cure.—
Brother of England, how may we content
This widow lady? In her right we came;
Which we, heaven knows, have turn'd another way,
To our own vantage.

K. John. We will heal up all;
For we'll create young Arthur duke of Bretagne
And earl of Richmond; and this rich fair town
We make him lord of.—Call the lady Constance;
Some speedy messenger bid her repair
To our solemnity:—I trust we shall,
If not fill up the measure of her will,
Yet in some measure satisfy her so,
That we shall stop her exclamation.
Go we, as well as haste will suffer us,
To this unlook'd for unpreparéd pomp.
[*Exeunt all except* FAULCONBRIDGE. *The* Citizens *retire from the walls.*

Faul. Mad world! mad kings! mad composition!
John, to stop Arthur's title in the whole,
Hath willingly departed with a part;
And France, (whose armor conscience buckled on,
Whom zeal and charity brought to the field
As heaven's own soldier,) rounded in the ear
With that same purpose-changer, that sly devil;
That broker, that still breaks the pate of fate;
That daily break-vow; he that wins of all,
Of kings, of beggars, old men, young men; maids,—
That smooth-faced gentleman, tickling commodity,—
Commodity, the bias of the world;
This all-changing word,
Clapp'd on the outward eye of fickle France,
Hath drawn him from his own determin'd aid,
From a resolv'd and honorable war,
To a most base and vile-concluded peace.—
And why rail I on this commodity?
But for because he hath not woo'd me yet:
Not that I have the power to clutch my hand,
When his fair angels would salute my palm;
But for my hand, as unattempted yet,
Like a poor beggar, raileth on the rich.
Well, whiles I am a beggar, I will rail,
And say, There is no sin, but to be rich;
And being rich, my virtue then shall be,
To say, There is no vice, but beggary:
Since kings break faith upon commodity,
Gain, be my lord; for I will worship thee! [*Exit.*

ACT III.

SCENE I.—France. *The French King's Tent.*

Enter CONSTANCE, ARTHUR, *and* SALISBURY.

Const. Gone to be married! gone to swear a peace!
False blood to false blood joined! Gone to be friends!
Shall Lewis have Blanch, and Blanch those provinces?
It is not so; thou hast misspoke, misheard;
I do not believe thee, man;
I have a king's oath to the contrary.
Thou shalt be punished for thus frightening me,
For I am sick, and capable of fears;
Oppress'd with wrongs, and therefore full of fears;
A widow, husbandless, subject to fears;
A woman naturally born to fears.
What dost thou mean by shaking of thy head?
Why dost thou look so sadly on my son?

What means that hand upon that breast of thine?
Why holds thine eye that lamentable rheum,
Like a proud river peering o'er its bounds?
Be these sad signs confirmers of thy words?
Then speak again,—not all thy former tale,
But this one word, whether thy tale be true.
Sal. As true, as I believe you think them false,
That give you cause to prove my saying true.
Const. O, if thou teach me to believe this sorrow,
Teach thou this sorrow how to make me die.
Lewis marry Blanch! O boy, then where art thou?
France friend with England! what becomes of me?—
Fellow, be gone: I cannot brook thy sight;
This news hath made thee a most ugly man.
Sal. What other harm have I, good lady done,
But spoke the harm that is by others done?
Const. Which harm within itself so heinous is,
As it makes harmful all that speak of it.
Arth. I do beseech you, madam, be content.
Const. If thou, that bidd'st me be content, wert grim,
Full of unpleasing blots and sightless stains,
Lame, foolish, crooked, swart, prodigious,
Patch'd with foul moles and eye-offending marks,
I would not care, I then would be content;
For then I should not love thee; no, nor thou
Become thy great birth, nor deserve a crown.
But thou art fair; and at thy birth, dear boy,
Nature and Fortune join'd to make thee great:
Of Nature's gifts thou may'st with lilies boast,
And with the half-blown rose: but Fortune, O!
She is corrupted, chang'd, and won from thee;
She adulterates hourly with thine uncle John;
And with her golden hand hath pluck'd on France
To tread down fair respect of sovereignty.
Tell me, thou fellow, is not France forsworn?
Envenom him with words; or get thee gone,
And leave those woes alone, which I alone
Am bound to under-bear.
Sal. Pardon me, madam,
I may not go without you to the kings.
Const. Thou may'st, thou shalt; I will not go with thee:
I will instruct my sorrows to be proud;
For grief is proud, and makes his owner stoop.
To me, and to the state of my great grief,
Let kings assemble; for my grief's so great,
That no supporter but the huge firm earth
Can hold it up; here I and sorrows sit;
Here is my throne, bid kings come bow to it.
[*She casts herself seated on the ground.*

Enter KING JOHN, KING PHILIP, LEWIS, BLANCH, ELINOR, FAULCONBRIDGE, AUSTRIA, *and* Attendants.

K. Phi. 'Tis true, fair daughter; and this blessed day
Ever in France shall be kept festival:
To solemnize this day the glorious sun
Stays in his course, and plays the alchemist,
Turning, with splendor of his precious eye,
The meagre cloddy earth to glittering gold:
The yearly course, that brings this day about,
Shall never see it but a holiday.
Const. [*Rising.*] A wicked day, and not a holy day!
What hath this day deserv'd? what hath it done,
That it in golden letters should be set,
Among the high tides, in the calendar?
Nay, rather turn this day out of the week,
This day of shame, oppression, perjury:
This day, all things begun come to ill end,—
Yea, faith itself to hollow falsehood change!
K. Phi. By heaven, lady, you shall have no cause
To curse the fair proceedings of this day:
Have I not pawn'd to you my majesty?
Const. You have beguiled me with a counterfeit,
Resembling majesty; which, being touch'd and tried,
Proves valueless: you are forsworn, forsworn;
You came in arms to spill mine enemies' blood,
But now in arms you strengthen it with yours:
The grappling vigor and rough frown of war
Is cold in amity and painted peace,
And our oppression hath made up this league.—
Arm, arm, you heavens, against these perjur'd kings!
A widow cries: be husband to me, heavens!
Let not the hours of this ungodly day
Wear out the day in peace; but, ere sunset,
Set armèd discord 'twixt these perjur'd kings!
Hear me! O, hear me!
Aust. Lady Constance, peace!
Const. War! war! no peace! peace is to me a war.
O, Lymoges! O, Austria! thou dost shame
That bloody spoil; thou slave, thou wretch, thou coward!
Thou little valiant, great in villainy!
Thou ever strong upon the stronger side!
Thou Fortune's champion, that dost never fight
But when her humorous ladyship is by
To teach thee safety! Thou cold-blooded slave,
Hast thou not spoke like thunder on my side?
Been sworn my soldier? bidding me depend
Upon thy stars, thy fortune, and thy strength?

And dost thou now fall over to my foes?
Thou wear a lion's hide! doff it for shame,
And hang a calf's-skin on those recreant limbs.
Aust. O, that a man should speak those words to me!
Faul. And hang a calf's-skin on those recreant limbs.
Aust. Thou dar'st not say so, villain, for thy life.
Faul. And hang a calf's-skin on those recreant limbs.
K. John. We like not this; thou dost forget thyself.
K. Phi. Here comes the holy legate of the pope.

Enter PANDULPH.

Pand. Hail, you anointed deputies of heaven!
To thee, King John, my holy errand is,
I Pandulph, of fair Milan cardinal,
And from Pope Innocent the legate here,
Do in his name religiously demand,
Why thou against the church, our holy mother,
So wilfully dost spurn; and, force perforce,
Keep Stephen Langton, chosen archbishop
Of Canterbury, from that holy see?
This, in our 'foresaid holy father's name,
Pope Innocent, I do demand of thee.
K. John. What earthly name to interrogatories
Can task the free breath of a sacred king?
Thou canst not, cardinal, devise a name
So slight, unworthy, and ridiculous,
To charge me to an answer, as the pope.
Tell him this tale; and from the mouth of England,
Add thus much more,—that no Italian priest
Shall tithe or toll in our dominions;
But, as we under heaven are supreme head,
So, under Him, that great supremacy,
Where we do reign, we will alone uphold,
Without th' assistance of a mortal hand:
So tell the pope; all reverence set apart
To him, and his usurp'd authority.
K. Phi. Brother of England, you blaspheme in this.
K. John. Though you, and all the kings of Christendom,
Are led so grossly by this meddling priest,
Dreading the curse that money may buy out;
And, by the merit of vile gold, dross, dust,
Purchase corrupted pardon of a man,
Who, in that sale, sells pardon from himself;
Though you and all the rest, so grossly led,
This juggling witchcraft with revenue cherish;
Yet I, alone, alone do me oppose
Against the pope, and count his friends my foes.
Pand. Then, by the lawful power that I have,

Thou shalt stand curs'd and excommunicate:
And blessed shall he be that doth revolt
From his allegiance to a heretic;
And meritorious shall that hand be call'd,
Canonized, and worshipp'd as a saint,
That takes away by any secret course
Thy hateful life.
Const. O, lawful let it be
That I have room with Rome to curse awhile!
Good father cardinal, cry thou amen
To my keen curses; for, without my wrong,
There is no tongue hath power to curse him right.
Pand. There's law and warrant, lady, for my curse.
Const. And for mine too: when law can do no right,
Let it be lawful that law bar no wrong;
Law cannot give my child his kingdom here;
For he that holds his kingdom holds the law:
Therefore, since law itself is perfect wrong,
How can the law forbid my tongue to curse?
Pand. Philip of France, on peril of a curse,
Let go the hand of that arch-heretic;
And raise the power of France upon his head,
Unless he do submit himself to Rome.
Eli. Look'st thou pale, France? do not let go thy hand.
Aust. King Philip, listen to the cardinal.
Faul. And hang a calf's-skin on his recreant limbs.
Aust. Well, ruffian, I must pocket up these wrongs.
K. John. Philip, what say'st thou to the cardinal?
K. Phi. Good reverend father, make my person yours,
And tell me how you would bestow yourself.
This royal hand and mine are newly knit,
And shall these hands, so lately purg'd of blood,
So newly join'd in love, so strong in both,
Unyoke this seizure and this kind regret?
O, holy sir,
My reverend father, let it not be so!
Out of your grace, devise, ordain, impose
Some gentle order; and then we shall be bless'd
To do your pleasure, and continue friends.
Pand. All form is formless, order orderless,
Save what is opposite to England's love.
Therefore, to arms! be champion of our church!
Or let the church, our mother, breathe her curse,—
A mother's curse,—on her revolting son.
France, thou may'st hold a serpent by the tongue,
A chafed lion by the mortal paw,
A fasting tiger safer by the tooth,
Than keep in peace that hand which thou dost hold.

K. Phi. I may disjoin my hand, but not my faith.
Pand. So mak'st thou faith an enemy to faith:
O, let thy vow
First made to heaven, first be to heaven perform'd,—
But, if not, then know,
The peril of our curses light on thee,
So heavy, as thou shalt not shake them off,
But in despair die under their black weight.
Aust. Rebellion, flat rebellion!
Faul. Will't not be?
Will not a calf's-skin stop that mouth of thine?
Lew. Father, to arms!
Blanch. Upon thy wedding day?
Against the blood that thou hast married?
O husband, hear me! even for that name,
Which till this time my tongue did ne'er pronounce,
Upon my knee I beg, go not to arms
Against mine uncle.
Const. O, upon my knee,
Made hard with kneeling, I do pray to thee,
Thou virtuous Dauphin, alter not the doom
Fore-thought by heaven.
Blanch. Now shall I see thy love: what motive may
Be stronger with thee than the name of wife?
Const. That which upholdeth him that thee upholds,
His honor:—O, thine honor, Lewis, thine honor!
Lew. I muse your majesty doth seem so cold,
When such profound respects do pull you on.
Pand. I will denounce a curse upon his head.
K. Phi. Thou shalt not need.—England, I'll fall from thee.
Const. O, fair return of banish'd majesty!
Eli. O, foul revolt of French inconstancy!
K. John. France, thou shalt rue this hour within this hour.
Cousin, go draw our puissance together.—
[*Exit* FAULCONBRIDGE.
France, I am burn'd up with inflaming wrath;
A rage whose heat hath this condition,
That nothing can allay, nothing but blood,
The blood, and dearest valu'd blood of France.
K. Phi. Thy rage shall burn thee up, and thou shalt turn
To ashes, ere our blood shall quench that fire:
Look to thyself, thou art in jeopardy.
K. John. No more than he that threats.—To arms let's hie!
[*Exeunt.*

SCENE II.—France. *Plains near* Angiers.

Alarums; Excursions. Enter FAULCONBRIDGE *with* AUSTRIA'S *head.*

Faul. Now, by my life, this day grows wondrous hot;
Some airy devil hovers in the sky,
And pours down mischief. Austria's head, lie there,
While Philip breathes.

Enter KING JOHN, ARTHUR, *and* HUBERT.

K. John. Hubert, keep this boy.—Philip, make up:
My mother is assailed in our tent,
And ta'en, I fear.
Faul. My lord, I rescued her;
Her highness is in safety, fear you not:
But on, my liege; for very little pains
Will bring this labor to a happy end. [*Exeunt.*

SCENE III.—*The Same.*

Alarums; Excursions; Retreat. Enter KING JOHN, ELINOR, ARTHUR, FAULCONBRIDGE, HUBERT, *and* Lords.

K. John. [*To* ELINOR.] So shall it be; your grace shall stay behind,
So strongly guarded.—[*To* ARTHUR.] Cousin, look not sad:
Thy grandam loves thee; and thy uncle will
As dear be to thee as thy father was.
Arth. O, this will make my mother die with grief!
K. John. [*To* FAUL.] Cousin, away for England; haste before:
And, ere our coming, see thou shake the bags
Of hoarding abbots; imprisoned angels
Set at liberty: the fat ribs of peace
Must by the hungry now be fed upon:
Use our commission in its utmost force.
Faul. Bell, book, and candle shall not drive me back,
When gold and silver becks me to come on.
I leave your highness.—Grandam, I will pray
(If ever I remember to be holy,)
For your fair safety; so I kiss your hand.
Eli. Farewell, gentle cousin.
K. John. Coz, farewell.
[*Exit* FAULCONBRIDGE.
Eli. Come hither, little kinsman; hark, a word.
[*She takes* ARTHUR *aside.*
K. John. Come hither, Hubert. O my gentle Hubert,
We owe thee much; within this wall of flesh

There is a soul counts thee her creditor,
And with advantage means to pay thy love:
And, my good friend, thy voluntary oath
Lives in this bosom, dearly cherished.
Give me thy hand. I had a thing to say,—
But I will fit it with some better time,
By heaven, Hubert, I am almost asham'd
To say what good respect I have of thee.
Hub. I am much bounden to your majesty.
K. John. Good friend, thou hast no cause to-say so yet:
But tho shalt have; and creep time ne'er so slow,
Yet it ushall come for me to do thee good.
I had a thing to say,—but let it go:
The sun is in the heaven, and the proud day,
Attended with the pleasures of the world,
Is all too wanton, and too full of gawds,
To give me audience:—if the midnight bell
Did, with his iron tongue and brazen mouth,
Sound one into the drowsy ear of night;
If this same were a churchyard where we stand,
And thou possessèd with a thousand wrongs;
Or if that surly spirit, melancholy,
Had bak'd thy blood, and made it heavy, thick;
(Which else runs tickling up and down the veins,
Making that idiot, laughter, keep men's eyes,
And strain their cheeks to idle merriment,—
A passion hateful to my purposes,)
Or if that thou could'st see me without eyes,
Hear me without thine ears, and make reply
Without a tongue, using conceit alone,
Without eyes, ears, and harmful sound of words;
Then, in despite of brooded watchful day,
I would into thy bosom pour my thoughts:
But ah, I will not:—yet I love thee well;
And, by my troth, I think thou lov'st me well.
Hub. So well, that what you bid me undertake,
Though that my death were adjunct to my act,
By heaven, I would do it.
K. John. Do not I know thou would'st?
Good Hubert, Hubert, Hubert, throw thine eye
On yond' young boy: I'll tell thee what, my friend,
He is a very serpent in my way;
And wheresoe'er this foot of mine doth tread,
He lies before me:—dost thou understand me?
Thou art his keeper.
Hub. And I'll keep him so,
That he shall not offend your majesty.
K. John. Death.

Hub. My lord?
K. John. A grave.
Hub. He shall not live.
K. John. Enough.
I could be merry now. Hubert, I love thee;
Well, I'll not say what I intend for thee:
Remember.—Madam, fare you well:
I'll send those powers o'er to your majesty.
Eli. My blessing go with thee!
K. John. For England, cousin, go:
Hubert shall be your man, attend on you
With all true duty.—On toward Calais, ho! [*Exeunt.*

SCENE IV.—France. *The French King's Tent.*

Enter KING PHILIP, LEWIS, PANDULPH, *and* Attendants.

K. Phi. So, by a roaring tempest on the flood,
A whole armado of convicted sail
Is scatter'd, and disjoin'd from fellowship.
Pand. Courage and comfort! all shall yet go well.
K. Phi. What can go well, when we have run so ill?
Are we not beaten? Is not Angiers lost?
Arthur ta'en prisoner? divers dear friends slain?
And bloody England into England gone,
O'erbearing interruption, spite of France?
Lew. What he hath won, that hath he fortified:
So hot a speed with such advice dispos'd,
Such temperate order in so fierce a cause,
Doth want example: who hath read, or heard,
Of any kindred action like to this?
K. Phi. Well could I bear that England had this praise,
So we could find some pattern of our shame.—
Look, who comes here! a grave unto a soul;
Holding th' eternal spirit, against her will,
In the vile prison of afflicted breath.—

Enter CONSTANCE.

I pr'ythee, lady, go away with me.
Const. Lo, now! now see the issue of your peace!
K. Phi. Patience, good lady! comfort, gentle Constance!
Const. No, I defy all counsel, all redress,
But that which ends all counsel, true redress,
Death, death:—O, amiable lovely death!
Arise forth from the couch of lasting night,
Thou hate and terror to prosperity,
And I will kiss thy détestable bones:
Come, grin on me; and I will think thou smil'st,

And buss thee as thy wife! Misery's love,
O, come to me!
K. Phi. O, fair affliction, peace!
Const. No, no, I will not, having breath to cry:—
O, that my tongue were in the thunder's mouth!
Then with a passion would I shake the world;
And rouse from sleep that fell anatomy,
Which cannot hear a lady's feeble voice,
Which scorns a modern invocation.
Pand. Lady, you utter madness, and not sorrow.
Const. Thou art not holy to belie me so;
I am not mad: this hair I tear is mine;
My name is Constance; I was Geffrey's wife;
Young Arthur is my son, and he is lost:
I am not mad;—I would to heaven I were!
For then 'tis like I should forget myself:
O, if I could, what grief should I forget!—
Preach some philosophy to make me mad,
And thou shalt be canoniz'd, cardinal;
If I were mad, I should forget my son,
I am not mad; too well, too well I feel
The different plague of each calamity.
K. Phi. Bind up those tresses.
Const. Yes, that I will; and wherefore will I do it?
I tore them from their bonds, and cried aloud,
"O, that these hands could so redeem my son:
As they have given these hairs their liberty!"
But now, I envy at their liberty,
And will again commit them to their bonds,
Because my poor child is a prisoner.—
And, father cardinal, I have heard you say
That we shall see and know our friends in heaven:
If that be true, I shall see my boy again;
For, since the birth of Cain, the first male child,
To him that did but yesterday suspire,
There was not such a gracious creature born.
But now will canker sorrow eat my bud,
And chase the native beauty from his cheek,
And he will look as hollow as a ghost,
As dim and meagre as an ague's fit;
And so he'll die; and, rising so again,
When I shall meet him in the court of heaven
I shall not know him: therefore never, never
Must I behold my pretty Arthur more.
Pand. You hold too heinous a respect of grief.
Const. He talks to me, that never had a son.
K. Phi. You are as fond of grief, as of your child.
Const. Grief fills the room up of my absent child,

Lies in his bed, walks up and down with me,
Puts on his pretty looks, repeats his words,
Remembers me of all his gracious parts,
Stuffs out his vacant garments with his form;
Then, have I reason to be fond of grief.
Fare you well: had you such a loss as I,
I could give better comfort than you do.—
I will not keep this form upon my head,
[*Tearing off her head-dress.*
When there is such disorder in my wit.
O Lord! my boy, my Arthur, my fair son!
My life, my joy, my food, my all the world!
My widow-comfort, and my sorrow's cure! [*Exit.*
K. Phi. I fear some outrage, and I'll follow her. [*Exit.*
Lew. There's nothing in this world can make me joy:
Life is as tedious as a twice-told tale,
Vexing the dull ear of a drowsy man;
And bitter shame hath spoil'd the sweet world's taste,
That it yields naught but shame and bitterness.
Pand. Before the curing of a strong disease,
Even in the instant of repair and health,
The fit is strongest; evils that take leave,
On their departure most of all show evil.
What have you lost by losing of this day?
Lew. All days of glory, joy, and happiness,
Pand. If you had won it, certainly you had.
No, no; when Fortune means to men most good,
She looks upon them with a threatening eye.
'Tis strange to think how much king John hath lost
In this which he accounts so clearly won.
Are you not griev'd that Arthur is his prisoner?
Lew. As heartily as he is glad he hath him.
Pand. Your mind is all as youthful as your blood.
Now hear me speak with a prophetic spirit:
John hath seiz'd Arthur; and it cannot be,
That, whiles warm life plays in that infant's veins,
The misplac'd John should entertain an hour,
One minute, nay, one quiet breath of rest.
A sceptre snatch'd with an unruly hand,
Must be as boisterously maintain'd as gain'd;
And he that stands upon a slippery place,
Makes nice of no vile hold to stay him up:
That John may stand, then Arthur needs must fall;
So be it, for it cannot be but so.
Lew. But what shall I gain by young Arthur's fall?
Pand. You, in the right of lady Blanch your wife,
May then make all the claim that Arthur did.
Lew. And lose it, life and all, as Arthur did.

Pand. How green you are, and fresh in this old world!
John lays you plots; the times conspire with you.
Lew. May be, he will not touch young Arthur's life,
But hold himself safe in his prisonment.
Pand. O, sir, when he shall hear of your approach,
If that young Arthur be not gone already,
Even at that news he dies; and then the hearts
Of all his people shall revolt from him.
Go with me to the king: 'tis wonderful
What may be wrought out of their discontent,
Now that their souls are topfull of offence:
For England go:—I will whet on the king.
Lew. Strong reasons make strange actions: let us go:
If you say ay, the king will not say no. [*Exeunt.*

ACT IV.

SCENE I.—Northampton. *A Room in the Castle.*

Enter HUBERT *and two* Attendants.

Hub. Heat me these irons hot; and look thou stand
Within the arras: when I strike my foot
Upon the bosom of the ground, rush forth,
And bind the boy, which you shall find with me,
Fast to the chair: be heedful: hence, and watch.
1 *Attend.* I hope your warrant will bear out the deed.
Hub. Uncleanly scruples! fear not you: look to't.—
[*Exeunt* Attendants.
Young lad, come forth; I have to say with you.

Enter ARTHUR.

Arth. Good morrow, Hubert.
Hub. Good morrow, little prince.
Arth. As little prince (having so great a title
To be more prince,) as may be.—You are sad.
Hub. Indeed, I have been merrier.
Arth. Mercy on me!
Methinks nobody should be sad but I:
Yet, I remember, when I was in France,
Young gentlemen would be as sad as night,
Only for wantonness. By my christendom,
So I were out of prison. and kept sheep,
I should be as merry as the day is long;
And so I would be here, but that I doubt
My uncle practises more harm to me:
He is afraid of me, and I of him:

Is it my fault that I was Geffrey's son?
No, indeed, is't not; and I would to heaven
I were your son, so you would love me, Hubert.
Hub. [*Aside.*] If I talk to him, with his innocent prate
He will awake my mercy, which lies dead:
Therefore I will be sudden, and despatch.
Arth. Are you sick, Hubert? you look pale to-day:
In sooth, I would you were a little sick,
That I might sit all night, and watch with you:
I warrant, I love you more than you do me.
Hub. [*Aside.*] His words do take possession of my bosom.—
Read here, young Arthur. [*Showing a paper*
[*Aside.*] How now, foolish rheum!
I must be brief, lest resolution drop
Out at mine eyes in tender womanish tears.—
Can you not read it? is it not fair writ?
Arth. Too fairly, Hubert, for so foul effect:
Must you with hot irons burn out both mine eyes?
Hub. Young boy, I must.
Arth. And will you?
Hub. And I will.
Arth. Have you the heart? When your head did but ache,
I knit my handkerchief about your brows,
(The best I had, a princess wrought it me,)
And I did never ask it you again;
And with my hand at midnight held your head;
And, like the watchful minutes to the hour,
Still and anon cheer'd up the heavy time,
Saying, "What lack you?" and, "Where lies your grief?"
Or, "What good love may I perform for you?"
Many a poor man's son would have lain still,
And ne'er have spoke a loving word to you;
But you at your sick service had a prince.
Nay, you may think my love was crafty love,
And call it cunning:—do, an if you will:
If heaven be pleas'd that you must use me ill,
Why, then you must.—Will you put out mine eyes?
These eyes that never did, nor never shall
So much as frown on you?
Hub. I have sworn to do it;
And with hot irons must I burn them out.
Arth. An if an angel should have come to me,
And told me Hubert should put out mine eyes,
I would not have believ'd him,—no tongue but Hubert's.
Hub. [*Stamps.*] Come forth.

Re-enter Attendants, *with cord*, *irons*, *&c.*

Do as I bid you do.

Arth. O! save me, Hubert, save me! my eyes are out
Even with the fierce looks of these bloody men.
Hub. Give me the iron, I say, and bind him here.
Arth. Alas! what need you be so boisterous-rough?
I will not struggle, I will stand stone-still.
For heaven's sake, Hubert, let me not be bound!
Nay, hear me, Hubert!—drive these men away,
And I will sit as quiet as a lamb:
I will not stir, nor wince, nor speak a word,
Nor look upon the iron angerly:
Thrust but these men away, and I'll forgive you,
Whatever torment you do put me to.
Hub. Go, stand within; let me alone with him.
1 *Attend.* I am best pleased to be from such a deed.
[*Exeunt* Attendants.
Arth. Alas! I then have chid away my friend:
He hath a stern look, but a gentle heart:—
Let him come back, that his compassion may
Give life to yours.
Hub. Come, boy, prepare yourself.
Arth. Is there no remedy?
Hub. None, but to lose your eyes.
Arth. O heaven!—that there were but a mote in yours,
A grain, a dust, a gnat, a wandering hair,
Any annoyance in that precious sense!
Then, feeling what small things are boisterous there,
Your vile intent must needs seem horrible.
Hub. Is this your promise? go to, hold your tongue.
Arth. Hubert, the utterance of a brace of tongues
Must needs want pleading for a pair of eyes:
Let me not hold my tongue,—let me not, Hubert;
Or, Hubert, if you will, cut out my tongue,
So I may keep mine eyes: O, spare mine eyes,
Though to no use but still to look on you!—
Lo! by my troth, the instrument is cold,
And would not harm me.
Hub. I can heat it, boy.
Arth. No, in good sooth; the fire is dead with grief;
The breath of heaven hath blown his spirit out,
And strew'd repentant ashes on his head.
Hub. But with my breath I can revive it, boy.
Arth. And if you do, you will but make it blush,
And glow with shame of your proceedings, Hubert.
Hub. I will not touch thine eyes
For all the treasure that thine uncle owes.
Arth. O, now you look like Hubert! all this while
You were disguised.
Hub. Peace! no more. Adieu.

Your uncle must not know but you are dead;
I'll fill these dogged spies with false reports:
And, pretty child, sleep doubtless and secure,
That Hubert for the wealth of all the world
Will not offend thee.
Arth. O heaven!—I thank you, Hubert.
Hub. Silence! no more: go closely in with me:
Much danger do I undergo for thee. [*Exeunt.*

SCENE II.—Northampton. *A Room of State in the Palace.*

Enter KING JOHN, *crowned;* PEMBROKE, SALISBURY, *and other* Lords. *The* King *takes his state.*

K. John. Here once again we sit, once again crown'd,
And look'd upon, I hope, with cheerful eyes.
Pem. This "once again," but that your highness pleas'd,
Was once superfluous: you were crown'd before,
And that high royalty was ne'er pluck'd off;
The faiths of men ne'er stainèd with revolt;
Fresh expectation troubled not the land,
With any long'd-for change, or better state.
Sal. Therefore, to be possess'd with double pomp,
To guard a title that was rich before,
To gild refinèd gold, to paint the lily,
To throw a perfume on the violet,
To smooth the ice, or add another hue
Unto the rainbow, or with taper-light
To seek the beauteous eye of heaven to garnish,
Is wasteful, and ridiculous excess.
Pem. But that your royal pleasure must be done,
This act is as an ancient tale new told;
And in the last repeating troublesome,
Being urged at a time unseasonable.
Sal. In this, the antique and well-noted face
Of plain old form is much disfigured;
And, like a shifted wind unto a sail,
It makes the course of thoughts to fetch about;
Startles and frights consideration;
Makes sound opinion sick, and truth suspected,
For putting on so new a fashion'd robe.
Pem. When workmen strive to do better than well,
They do confound their skill in covetousness;
And, oftentimes, excusing of a fault
Doth make the fault the worse by the excuse,—
As patches, set upon a little breach,
Discredit more in hiding of the fault,
Than did the fault before it was so patch'd.

Sal. To this effect, before you were new-crown'd,
We breath'd our counsel: but it pleas'd your highness
To overbear it; and we are all well pleas'd,
Since all and every part of what we would,
Doth make a stand at what your highness will.
K. John. Some reasons of this double coronation
I have possessed you with, and think them strong;
And more, more strong, (when lesser is my fear,)
I shall indue you with: meantime, but ask
What you would have reform'd that is not well,
And well shall you perceive how willingly
I will both hear and grant you your requests.
Pem. Then I, (as one that am the tongue of these,
To sound the purposes of all their hearts,)
Both for myself and them, (but, chief of all,
Your safety, for the which myself and them
Bend their best studies,) heartily request
Th' enfranchisement of Arthur; whose restraint
Doth move the murmuring lips of discontent.
That the time's enemies may not have this
To grace occasions, let it be our suit,
That you have bid us ask his liberty.
K. John. Let it be so: I do commit his youth
To your direction.—

Enter HUBERT.

Hubert, what news with you?
[*Speaks apart with him.*

Pem. This is the man should do the bloody deed;
He show'd his warrant to a friend of mine:
The image of a wicked heinous fault
Lives in his eye; that close aspect of his
Does show the mood of a much-troubled breast;
And I do fearfully believe 'tis done,
What we so fear'd he had a charge to do.
Sal. The color of the king doth come and go
Between his purpose and his conscience,
Like heralds 'twixt two dreadful battles set:
His passion is so ripe, it needs must break.
Pem. And when it breaks, I fear will issue thence
The foul corruption of a sweet child's death.
K. John. We cannot hold mortality's strong hand:—
Good lords, although my will to give is living,
The suit which you demand is gone and dead:
He tells us, Arthur is deceas'd to-night.
Sal. Indeed, we fear'd his sickness was past cure.
Pem. Indeed, we heard how near his death he was,
Before the child himself felt he was sick:

This must be answer'd, either here, or hence.
K. John. Why do you bend such solemn brows on me?
Think you I bear the shears of destiny?
Have I commandment on the pulse of life?
Sal. It is apparent foul-play; and 'tis shame,
That greatness should so grossly offer it:
So thrive it in your game! and so, farewell.
Pem. Stay yet, lord Salisbury; I'll go with thee.
This must not be thus borne: this will break out
To all our sorrows, and ere long, I doubt.
[*Exeunt* Lords.
K. John. They burn in indignation. I repent:
There is no sure foundation set on blood,
No certain life achiev'd by others' death.—

Enter a Messenger.

A fearful eye thou hast: where is that blood
That I have seen inhabit in those cheeks?
So foul a sky clears not without a storm:
Pour down thy weather:—how goes all in France?
Mess. From France to England.—Never such a power
For any foreign preparation
Was levied in the body of a land.
The copy of your speed is learn'd by them;
For, when you should be told they do prepare,
The tidings come that they are all arriv'd.
K. John. O, where hath our intelligence been drunk?
Where hath it slept? Where is my mother's care,
That such an army could be drawn in France,
And she not hear of it?
Mess. My liege, her ear
Is stopp'd with dust; the first of April, died
Your noble mother: and, as I hear, my lord,
The lady Constance in a frenzy died
Three days before.
K. John. Withhold thy speed, dreadful Occasion!
O, make a league with me, till I have pleas'd
My discontented peers!—What! mother dead!
How wildly, then, walks my estate in France!—
Under whose conduct came those powers of France,
That thou for truth giv'st out are landed here?
Mess. Under the Dauphin.
K. John. Thou hast made me giddy
With these ill tidings.—

Enter FAULCONBRIDGE *and* PETER OF POMFRET.

Now, what says the world
To your proceedings? do not seek to stuff

My head with more ill news, for it is full.
Faul. But if you be afeard to hear the worst,
Then let the worst, unheard, fall on your head.
K. John. Bear with me, cousin; for I was amaz'd
Under the tide: but now I breathe again
Aloft the flood; and can give audience
To any tongue, speak it of what it will.
Faul. How I have sped among the clergymen,
The sums I have collected shall express:
But as I travell'd hither through the land,
I find the people strangely fantasied;
Possess'd with rumours, full of idle dreams,
Not knowing what they fear, but full of fear:
And here's a prophet, that I brought with me
From forth the streets of Pomfret, whom I found
With many hundreds treading on his heels;
To whom he sung, in rude harsh-sounding rhymes,
That, ere the next Ascension-day at noon,
Your highness should deliver up your crown.
K. John. Thou idle dreamer, wherefore didst thou so?
Peter. Foreknowing that the truth will fall out so.
K. John. Hubert, away with him; imprison him;
And on that day at noon, whereon, he says,
I shall yield up my crown, let him be hang'd.
Deliver him to safety; and return,
For I must use thee.— [*Exit* HUBERT, *with* PETER.
O my gentle cousin,
Hear'st thou the news abroad, who are arriv'd?
Faul. The French, my lord; men's mouths are full of it:
Besides, I met lord Bigot, and lord Salisbury,
(With eyes as red as new-enkindled fire,)
And others more, going to seek the grave
Of Arthur, who, they say, is kill'd to-night
On your suggestion.
K. John. Gentle kinsman, go,
And thrust thyself into their companies:
I have a way to win their loves again;
Bring them before me.
Faul. I will seek them out.
K. John. Nay, but make haste; the better foot before.
O, let me have no subject enemies,
When adverse foreigners affright my towns
With dreadful pomp of stout invasion!
Be Mercury; set feathers to thy heels,
And fly like thought from them to me again.
Faul. The spirit of the time shall teach me speed.
[*Exit* FAULCONBRIDGE.
K. John. Go after him; for he, perhaps, shall need

Some messenger betwixt me and the peers;
And be thou he.

Mess. With all my heart, my liege. [*Exit.*

K. John. My mother dead!

Re-enter HUBERT.

Hub. My lord, they say, five moons were seen to-night:
Four fixed; and the fifth did whirl about
The other four in wondrous motion.

K. John. Five moons!

Hub. Old men, and beldams, in the streets
Do prophesy upon it dangerously:
Young Arthur's death is common in their mouths:
And when they talk of him, they shake their heads,
And whisper one another in the ear;
And he that speaks, doth gripe the hearer's wrist;
Whilst he that hears, makes fearful action,
With wrinkled brows, with nods, with rolling eyes.
I saw a smith stand with his hammer, thus,
The whilst his iron did on the anvil cool,
With open mouth swallowing a tailor's news;
Who, with his shears and measure in his hand,
Standing on slippers, (which his nimble haste,
Had falsely thrust upon contráry feet,)
Told of a many thousand warlike French,
That were embattailèd and rank'd in Kent:
Another lean unwash'd artificer
Cuts off his tale, and talks of Arthur's death.

K. John. Why seek'st thou to possess me with these fears?
Why urgest thou so oft young Arthur's death?
Thy hand hath murder'd him: I had a mighty cause
To wish him dead, but thou hadst none to kill him.

Hub. Had none, my lord! why, did you not provoke me?

K. John. It is the curse of kings, to be attended
By slaves, that take their humors for a warrant
To break within the bloody house of life;
And, on the winking of authority,
To understand a law; to know the meaning
Of dangerous majesty, when, perchance, it frowns
More upon humour than advis'd respect.

Hub. Here is your hand and seal for what I did.

K. John. O, when the last account 'twixt heaven and earth
Is to be made, then shall this hand and seal
Witness against us to our condemnation!
How oft the sight of means to do ill deeds,
Makes deeds ill done! Had'st not thou been by,
A fellow by the hand of nature mark'd,
Quoted, and sign'd, to do a deed of shame,

This murder had not come into my mind:
But, taking note of thy abhorr'd aspect.
Finding thee fit for bloody villainy,
Apt, liable to be employ'd in danger,
I faintly broke with thee of Arthur's death;
And thou, to be endeared to a king,
Made it no conscience to destroy a prince.
Hub. My lord,—
K. John. Hadst thou but shook thy head, or made a pause,
When I spake darkly what I purposed,
Or turn'd an eye of doubt upon my face,
As bid me tell my tale in express words,
Deep shame had struck me dumb, made me break off,
And those thy fears might have wrought fears in me:
But thou didst understand me by my signs,
And didst in signs again parley with sin;
Yea, without stop, didst let thy heart consent,
And consequently thy rude hand to act
The deed, which both our tongues held vile to name.
Out of my sight, and never see me more!
My nobles leave me: and my state is brav'd,
Even at my gates, with ranks of foreign powers:
Nay, in the body of this fleshly land,
This kingdom, this confine of blood and breath,
Hostility and civil tumult reigns
Between my conscience and my cousin's death.
Hub. Arm you against your other enemies,
I'll make a peace between your soul and you.
Young Arthur is alive: this hand of mine
Is yet a maiden and an innocent hand,
Not painted with the crimson spots of blood.
Within this bosom never enter'd yet
The dreadful motion of a murderous thought;
And you have slander'd nature in my form,—
Which, howsoever rude exteriorly,
Is yet the cover of a fairer mind
Than to be butcher of an innocent child.
K. John. Doth Arthur live? O, haste thee to the peers,
Throw this report on their incensèd rage,
And make them tame to their obedience!
Forgive the comment that my passion made
Upon thy feature; for my rage was blind,
And foul imaginary eyes of blood
Presented thee more hideous than thou art.
O, answer not; but to my closet bring
The angry lords, with all expedient haste! [*Exeunt.*

SCENE III.—Northampton. *Before the Castle.*

Enter ARTHUR, *on the walls.*

Arth. The wall is high; and yet will I leap down:—
Good ground, be pitiful, and hurt me not!— [*Leaps down.*
O me! my uncle's spirit is in these stones:—
Heaven take my soul, and England keep my bones! [*Dies.*

Enter PEMBROKE, SALISBURY, *and* BIGOT.

Sal. Lords, I will meet him at Saint Edmund's-Bury·
It is our safety, and we must embrace
This gentle offer of the perilous time.
Pem. Who brought that letter from the cardinal?
Sal. The count Melun, a noble lord of France;
Whose private with me, of the Dauphin's love,
Is much more general than these lines import.
Big. To-morrow morning let us meet him, then.
Sal. Or rather, then set forward; for 'twill be
Two long days' journey, lords, or e'er we meet.

Enter FAULCONBRIDGE.

Faul. Once more to-day well met, distemper'd lords!
The king by me requests your presence straight.
Sal. The king hath dispossessed himself of us:
We will not line his thin bestained cloak
With our pure honors, nor attend the foot
That leaves the print of blood where'er it walks.
Return, and tell him so: we know the worst.
Faul. Whate'er you think, good words, I think, were best.
Sal. Our griefs, and not our manners, reason now.
Faul. But there is little reason in your grief;
Therefore, 'twere reason you had manners now.
Pem. Sir, sir, impatience hath his privilege.
Faul. 'Tis true,—to hurt his master, no man else.
Sal. This is the prison:—what is he lies here?
[*Seeing* ARTHUR.
Pem. O death, made proud with pure and princely beauty!
The earth had not a hole to hide this deed.
Sal. Murder, as hating what himself hath done,
Doth lay it open to urge on revenge.
Big. Or, when he doom'd this beauty to a grave,
Found it too precious-princely for a grave.
Sal. Sir Richard, what think you?
Faul. It is a hideous and a bloody work;
The graceless action of a heavy hand,—
If that it be the work of any hand.
Sal. If that it be the work of any hand?—

We had a kind of light, what would ensue:
It is the shameful work of Hubert's hand;
The practice, and the purpose, of the king:—
From whose obedience I forbid my soul,
Kneeling before this ruin of sweet life,
And breathing to his breathless excellence
The incense of a vow, a holy vow,
Never to taste the pleasures of the world,
Never to be infected with delight,
Nor conversant with ease and idleness,
Till I have set a glory to this head,
By giving it the worship of revenge.
Pem. Big. Our souls religiously confirm thy words.

Enter HUBERT.

Hub. Lords, I am hot with haste in seeking you:
Arthur doth live; the king hath sent for you.
Sal. O, he is bold, and blushes not at death:—
Avaunt, thou hateful villain, get thee gone!
Hub. I am no villain.
Sal. [*Drawing his sword.*] Must I rob the law?
Faul. Your sword is bright, sir; put it up again.
Sal. Not till I sheathe it in a murderer's skin.
Hub. Stand back, lord Salisbury,—stand back, I say:
By heaven, I think my sword's as sharp as yours:
I would not have you, lord, forget yourself,
Nor tempt the danger of my true defence;
Lest I, by marking of your rage, forget
Your worth, your greatness, and nobility.
Big. Out, villain! dar'st thou brave a nobleman?
Hub. Not for my life: but yet I dare defend
My innocent life against an emperor.
Sal. Thou art a murderer.
Hub. Do not prove me so;
Yet, I am none: whose tongue soe'er speaks false,
Not truly speaks; who speaks not truly, lies.
Pem. Cut him to pieces.
Faul. Keep the peace, I say.
Sal. Stand by, or I shall gall you, Faulconbridge.
Faul. If thou but frown on me, or stir thy foot,
Or teach thy hasty spleen to do me shame,
I'll strike thee dead.
Big. What wilt thou do, renowned Faulconbridge?
Second a villain and a murderer?
Hub. Lord Bigot, I am none.
Big. Who kill'd this prince?
Hub. 'Tis not an hour since I left him well:
I honor'd him, I lov'd him; and will weep

My date of life out for his sweet life's loss.
Sal. Trust not those cunning waters of his eyes,
For villainy is not without such rheum;
And he, long traded in it, makes it seem
Like rivers of remorse and innocency.
Away with me, all you whose souls abhor
Th' uncleanly savors of a slaughter-house;
For I am stifled with this smell of sin.
Big. Away toward Bury, to the Dauphin there!
Pem. There, tell the king, he may enquire us out.
[*Exeunt* Lords.

Faul. Here's a good world!—Knew you of this fair work?
Hub. Do but hear me, sir:—
Faul. Ha! I'll tell thee what;
There is not yet so grim a fiend of darkness
As thou shalt be, if thou didst kill this child.
Hub. Upon my soul,—
Faul. If thou didst but consent
To this most cruel act, do but despair;
And if thou want'st a cord, the smallest thread
That ever spider twisted from herself
Will serve to strangle thee; a rush will be a beam
To hang thee on; or would'st thou drown thyself,
Put but a little water in a spoon,
And it shall be as all the ocean,
Enough to stifle such a villain up.
I do suspect thee very grievously.
Hub. If I in act, consent, or sin of thought,
Be guilty of the stealing that sweet breath
Which was embounded in this beauteous clay,
Let hell want pains enough to torture me!
I left him well.
Faul. Go, bear him in thine arms.—
I am amaz'd, methinks; and lose my way
Among the thorns and dangers of this world.—
How easy dost thou take all England up!
From forth this morsel of dead royalty,
The life, the right, and truth of all this realm
Is fled to heaven.—Bear away that child,
And follow me with speed: I'll to the king:
A thousand businesses are brief in hand,
And heaven itself doth frown upon the land. [*Exeunt.*

ACT V.

SCENE I.—Northampton. *A Room in the Palace.*

Enter KING JOHN, PANDULPH *with the crown, and* Attendants.

K. John. Thus have I yielded up into your hand
The circle of my glory.
Pand. [*Giving* JOHN *the crown.*] Take again
From this my hand, as holding of the pope,
Your sovereign greatness and authority.
K. John. Now keep your holy word: go meet the French;
And from his holiness use all your power
To stop their marches, 'fore we are inflam'd.
Our discontented counties do revolt;
Our people quarrel with obedience;
Swearing allegiance, and the love of soul,
To stranger blood, to foreign royalty.
Pand. It was my breath that blew this tempest up,
Upon your stubborn usage of the pope:
But since you are a gentle convertite,
My tongue shall hush again this storm of war,
And make fair weather in your blustering land.
On this Ascension-day, remember well,
Upon your oath of service to the pope,
Go I to make the French lay down their arms. [*Exit.*
K. John. Is this Ascension-day? Did not the prophet
Say, that before Ascension-day at noon,
My crown I should give off? Even so I have:
I did suppose it should be on constraint;
But, heaven be thank'd, it is but voluntary.

Enter FAULCONBRIDGE.

Faul. All Kent hath yielded; nothing there holds out,
But Dover castle: London hath receiv'd,
Like a kind host, the Dauphin and his powers:
Your nobles will not hear you, but are gone
To offer service to your enemy;
And wild amazement hurries up and down
The little number of your doubtful friends.
K. John. Would not my lords return to me again,
After they heard young Arthur was alive?
Faul. They found him dead, and cast into the streets;
An empty casket, where the jewel of life
By some vile hand was robb'd and ta'en away.
K. John. The villain Hubert told me he did live.
Faul. So, on my soul, he did, for aught he knew.

But wherefore do you droop? why look you sad?
Be great in act, as you have been in thought;
Let not the world see fear, and sad distrust,
Govern the motion of a kingly eye:
Be stirring as the time; be fire with fire;
Threaten the threatener, and outface the brow
Of bragging horror; so shall inferior eyes,
That borrow their behaviors from the great,
Grow great by your example, and put on
The dauntless spirit of resolution.

K. John. The legate of the pope hath been with me,
And I have made a happy peace with him;
And he hath promis'd to dismiss the powers
Led by the Dauphin.

Faul. O inglorious league!
Shall we, upon the footing of our land,
Send fair-play orders, and make compromise,
Insinuation, parley, and base truce,
To arms invasive? shall a beardless boy,
A cocker'd silken wanton, brave our fields,
And flesh his spirit in a warlike soil,
Mocking the air with colors idly spread,
And find no check? Let us, my liege, to arms:
Perchance, the cardinal cannot make your peace;
Or if he do, let it at least be said,
They saw we had a purpose of defence.

K. John. Have thou the ordering of this present time.

Faul. Away then, with good courage! yet, I know,
Our party may well meet a prouder foe. [*Exeunt.*

SCENE II.—*A Plain, near* St. Edmund's-Bury. *The French Camp.*

Enter, in arms, LEWIS, SALISBURY, MELUN, PEMBROKE, BIGOT, *and* Soldiers.

Lew. My lord Melun, let this be copied out,
And keep it safe for our remembrance:
Return the precedent to these lords again;
That, having our fair order written down,
Both they, and we, perusing o'er these notes,
May know wherefore we took the sacrament,
And keep our faiths firm and inviolable.

Sal. Upon our sides it never shall be broken.
And, noble Dauphin, albeit we swear
A voluntary zeal, and unurg'd faith,
To your proceedings; O, it grieves my soul,

That I must draw this metal from my side
To be a widow-maker! O, and there,
Where honorable rescue, and defence,
Cries out upon the name of Salisbury!
Lew. A noble temper dost thou show in this;
Look, where the holy legate comes apace,
To give us warrant from the hand of heaven,
And on our actions set the name of right
With holy breath.

Enter PANDULPH, *attended.*

Pand. Hail, noble prince of France!
The next is this,—king John hath reconcil'd
Himself to Rome;
Therefore, thy threat'ning colors now wind up;
And tame the savage spirit of wild war,
That, like a lion foster'd up at hand,
It may lie gently at the foot of peace,
And be no farther harmful than in show.
Lew. Your grace shall pardon me, I will not back:
I am too high-born to be propertied,
To be a secondary at control,
Or useful serving-man, and instrument,
To any sovereign state throughout the world.
Your breath first kindled the dead coal of wars
Between this chastis'd kingdom and myself.
And come ye now to tell me, John hath made
His peace with Rome? What is that peace to me?
Pand. You look but on the outside of this work.
Lew. Outside or inside, I will not return
Till my attempt be so much glorified,
As to my ample hope was promised. [*Trumpet sounds.*
What lusty trumpet thus doth summon us?

Enter FAULCONBRIDGE, *attended.*

Faul. According to the fair play of the world,
Let me have audience; I am sent to speak:—
My holy lord of Milan, from the king
I come, to learn how you have dealt for him;
And, as you answer, I do know the scope
And warrant limited unto my tongue.
Pand. The Dauphin is too wilful-opposite,
And will not temporize with my entreaties;
He flatly says, he'll not lay down his arms.
Faul. By all the blood that ever fury breath'd,
The youth says well.—Now, hear our English king;
For thus his royalty doth speak in me.
He is prepar'd, and reason too, he should,

To whip this dwarfish war, these pigmy arms,
From out the circle of his territories.
Shall that victorious hand be feebled here,
That in your chambers gave you chastisement?
No! Know, the gallant monarch is in arms;
And like an eagle o'er his eyry towers,
To souse annoyance that comes near his nest.

Lew. There end thy brave, and turn thy face in peace;
We grant thou canst outscold us: fare thee well:
We hold our time too precious to be spent
With such a brabbler.

Pand. Give me leave to speak.

Faul. No, I will speak.

Lew. We will attend to neither.—
Strike up the drums; and let the tongue of war
Plead for our interest, and our being here.

Faul. Indeed, your drums, being beaten, will cry out;
And so shall you, being beaten: do but start
An echo with the clamor of thy drum,
And even at hand a drum is ready brac'd,
That shall reverberate all as loud as thine;
Sound but another, and another shall,
As loud as thine, rattle the welkin's ear,
And mock the deep-mouth'd thunder: for at hand
(Not trusting to this halting legate here,
Whom he hath us'd rather for sport than need)
Is warlike John; and in his forehead sits
A bare-ribb'd death, whose office is this day
To feast upon whole thousands of the French.

Lew. Strike up our drums, to find this danger out.

Faul. And thou shalt find it, Dauphin, do not doubt.
[*Exeunt.*

SCENE III.—*Near* St. Edmund's-Bury. *A Field of Battle.*

Alarums. Enter KING JOHN *and* HUBERT.

K. John. How goes the day with us? O, tell me, Hubert.

Hub. Badly, I fear. How fares your majesty?

K. John. This fever, that hath troubled me so long,
Lies heavy on me;—O, my heart is sick!

Enter a Messenger.

Mess. My lord, your valiant kinsman, Faulconbridge,
Desires your majesty to leave the field,
And send him word by me which way you go.

K. John. Tell him, toward Swinstead, to the abbey there.

Mess. Be ot good comfort; for the great supply,

That was expected by the Dauphin here,
Are wreck'd three nights ago on Goodwin sands.
This news was brought to Richard but even now:
The French fight coldly, and retire themselves.
K. John. Ah me! this tyrant fever burns me up,
And will not let me welcome this good news.
Set on toward Swinstead: to my litter straight;
Weakness possesseth me, and I am faint. [*Exeunt.*

SCENE V.—*Near* St. Edmund's-Bury. *The French Camp.*

Enter LEWIS *and his train.*

Lew. The sun of heaven, methought, was loath to set,
But stay'd, and made the western welkin blush,
When th' English measur'd backward their own ground,
In faint retire. O, bravely came we off,
When with a volley of our needless shot,
After such bloody toil, we bid good night;
And wound our tottering colors clearly up,
Last in the field, and almost lords of it!

Enter a Messenger.

Mess. Where is my prince, the Dauphin?
Lew. Here:—what news?
Mess. The count Melun is slain: the English lords
By his persuasion, are again fallen off;
And your supply, which you have wish'd so long,
Are cast away, and sunk, on Goodwin sands.
Lew. Ah, foul shrewd news!—Beshrew thy very heart!—
I did not think to be so sad to-night,
As this hath made me.—Who was he, that said,
King John did fly an hour or two before
The stumbling night did part our weary powers?
Mess. Whoever spoke it, it is true, my lord.
Lew. Well; keep good quarter, and good care to-night:
The day shall not be up so soon as I,
To try the fair adventure of to-morrow. [*Exeunt.*

SCENE VI.—*An open Place in the Neighborhood of* Swinstead-Abbey.

Enter FAULCONBRIDGE *and* HUBERT, *meeting.*

Hub. Who's there? speak, ho! speak quickly, or I shoot.
Faul. A friend.—What art thou?
Hub. Of the part of England.

Faul. Whither dost thou go?
Hub. What's that to thee? Why may not I demand
Of thine affairs, as well as thou of mine?
Faul. Hubert, I think?
Hub. Thou hast a perfect thought:
I will, upon all hazards, well believe
Thou art my friend, that know'st my tongue so well.
Who art thou?
Faul. Who thou wilt: an if thou please,
Thou may'st befriend me so much as to think
I come one way of the Plantagenets.
Hub. Unkind remembrance! thou, and eyeless night,
Have done me shame:—brave soldier, pardon me,
That any accent breaking from thy tongue
Should 'scape the true acquaintance of mine ear.
Faul. Come, come; sans compliment, what news abroad?
Hub. Why, here walk I, in the black brow of night,
To find you out.
Faul. Brief, then; and what's the news?
Hub. O, my sweet sir, news fitting to the night,—
Black, fearful, comfortless, and horrible.
Faul. Show me the very wound of this ill news:
I am no woman, I'll not swoon at it.
Hub. The king, I fear, is poison'd by a monk:
I left him almost speechless; and broke out
To acquaint you with this evil, that you might
The better arm you to the sudden time,
Than if you had at leisure known of this.
Faul. How did he take it? who did taste to him?
Hub. A monk, I tell you; a resolvèd villain.
The king yet speaks, and, peradventure, may recover.
Faul. Whom didst thou leave to tend his majesty?
Hub. Why, know you not? the lords are all come back,
And brought prince Henry in their company;
At whose request the king hath pardon'd them,
And they are all about his majesty.
Faul. Withhold thine indignation, mighty heaven,
And tempt us not to bear above our power!—
I'll tell thee, Hubert, half my power this night,
Passing these flats, are taken by the tide,—
These Lincoln washes have devoured them;
Myself, well-mounted, hardly have escap'd.
Away, before! conduct me to the king;
I doubt he will be dead or ere I come. [*Exeunt.*

SCENE VII.—*The Orchard of* Swinstead-Abbey.

Enter PRINCE HENRY, SALISBURY, *and* BIGOT.

P. Hen. It is too late: the life of all his blood
Is touch'd corruptibly; and his pure brain
(Which some suppose the soul's frail dwelling-house)
Doth, by the idle comments that it makes,
Foretell the ending of mortality.

Enter PEMBROKE.

Pem. His highness yet doth speak; and holds belief,
That, being brought into the open air,
It would allay the burning quality
Of that fell poison which assaileth him.
P. Hen. Let him be brought into the orchard here.—
[*Exit* BIGOT.
Doth he still rage?
Pem. He is more patient
Than when you left him; even now he sung.
P. Hen. O vanity of sickness! fierce extremes
In their continuance will not feel themselves.
'Tis strange that death should sing.—
I am the cygnet to this pale faint swan,
Who chants a doleful hymn to his own death,
And from the organ-pipe of frailty sings
His soul and body to their lasting rest.
Sal. Be of good comfort, prince; for you are born
To set a form upon that indigest,
Which he hath left so shapeless and so rude.

Re-enter BIGOT *and* Attendants, *who bring in* KING JOHN *in a chair.*

K. John. Ay, marry, now my soul hath elbow-room;
It would not out at windows, nor at doors.
There is so hot a summer in my bosom,
That all my bowels crumble up to dust:
I am a scribbled form, drawn with a pen
Upon a parchment; and against this fire
Do I shrink up.
P. Hen. How fares your majesty?
K. John. Poison'd,—ill fare;—dead, forsook, cast off:
And none of you will bid the winter come,
To thrust his icy fingers in my maw;
Nor let my kingdom's rivers take their course
Through my burn'd bosom; nor entreat the north
To make his bleak winds kiss my parched lips,
And comfort me with cold:—I do not ask you much,

I beg cold comfort; and you are so strait,
And so ingrateful, you deny me that.
P. Hen. O, that there were some virtue in my tears,
That might relieve you!
K. John. The salt in them is hot.—
Within me is a hell; and there the poison
Is, as a fiend, confin'd to tyrannize
On unreprievable condemnèd blood.

Enter FAULCONBRIDGE.

Faul. O, I am scalded with my violent motion,
And spleen of speed to see your majesty.
K. John. O cousin, thou art come to set mine eye:
The tackle of my heart is crack'd and burn'd;
And all the shrouds, wherewith my life should sail,
Are turned to one thread, one little hair:
My heart hath one poor string to stay it by,
Which holds but till thy news be uttered;
And then all this thou seest is but a clod,
And model of confounded royalty.
Faul. The Dauphin is preparing hitherward,
Where, heaven he knows, how we shall answer him;
For, in a night, the best part of my power,
As I upon advantage did remove,
Were in the washes, all unwarily,
Devourèd by the unexpected flood. [*The* KING *dies.*
Sal. You breathe these dead news in as dead an ear.—
My liege! my lord!—But now a king,—now thus.
P. Hen. Even so must I run on, and even so stop.
What surety of the world, what hope, what stay,
When this was now a king, and now is clay?
Faul. Art thou gone so? I do but stay behind
To do the office for thee of revenge,
And then my soul shall wait on thee to heaven,
As it on earth hath been thy servant still.
P. Hen. At Worcester must his body be interr'd;
For so he will'd it.
Faul. Thither shall it, then:
And happily may your sweet self put on
The lineal state and glory of the land!
To whom, with all submission, on my knee,
I do bequeath my faithful services,
And true subjection everlastingly.
Sal. And the like tender of our love we make,
To rest without a spot for evermore.
P. Hen. I have a kind soul that would give you thanks,
And knows not how to do it, but with tears.
Faul. O, let us pay the time but needful woe,

Since it hath been beforehand with our griefs.—
This England never did, nor never shall,
Lie at the proud foot of a conqueror,
But when it first did help to wound itself.
Now these, her princes, are come home again,
Come the three corners of the world in arms,
And we shall shock them: naught shall make us rue,
If England to itself do rest but true. [*Exeunt.*

THE LIFE AND DEATH OF

KING RICHARD II.

For the incidents in the life of Richard II., the "most admirable of all Shakspeare's purely Historical Plays," the Poet was chiefly indebted to Holinshed. It is a vivid and faithful picture of the reign of that unfortunate monarch, whose character is drawn with a fidelity and beauty of execution which renders it invaluable as a mere historical portrait. The other characters are also faithful embodiments, while the real incidents of Richard's eventful life are portrayed with such perfect truth, that the whole Play forms a glowing picture of the most romantic and picturesque period of English History. The Play is the introductory one to the series of dramatic histories of the wars of York and Lancaster, while together they form a faithful narrative of the whole prolonged civil contest.

The history of Richard II., as comprised in this Play, embraces only the last two years of his life, commencing in the year 1398, and ending with the murder of Richard at Pomfret Castle toward the end of the year 1400.

PERSONS REPRESENTED.

King Richard the Second.
Edmund of Langley, *Duke of* York, } *Uncles to the* King.
John of Gaunt, *Duke of* Lancaster, } *Uncles to the* King.
Henry Bolingbroke, *Duke of* Hereford, *son to* John of Gaunt; *afterwards* King Henry IV.
Duke of Aumerle, *son to the Duke of* York.
Thomas Mowbray, *Duke of* Norfolk.
Duke of Surrey.
Earl of Salisbury.
Earl Berkley.
Bushy, } *Creatures to* King Richard.
Bagot, } *Creatures to* King Richard.
Green, } *Creatures to* King Richard.
Earl of Northumberland.
Henry Percy, *his son.*

LORD ROSS.
LORD WILLOUGHBY.
LORD FITZWATER.
BISHOP OF CARLISLE.
ABBOT OF WESTMINSTER.
The Lord Marshal.
Sir PIERCE OF EXTON.
Sir STEPHEN SCROOP.
Captain of a Band of Welshmen.

QUEEN TO KING RICHARD.
DUCHESS OF GLOSTER.
DUCHESS OF YORK.
Lady attending on the Queen.

Lords, Heralds, Officers, Soldiers, Gardeners, Keeper, Messenger, Groom, and other Attendants.

SCENE,—*Dispersedly in* ENGLAND *and* WALES.

ACT I.

SCENE I.—London. *A Room in the Palace.*

Enter KING RICHARD, *attended;* JOHN OF GAUNT, *and other* Nobles.

K. Rich. Old John of Gaunt, time-honor'd Lancaster,
Hast thou, according to thy oath and band,
Brought hither Henry Hereford thy bold son,
Here to make good the boisterous late appeal,
Which then our leisure would not let us hear,
Against the duke of Norfolk, Thomas Mowbray?
Gaunt. I have, my liege.
K. Rich. Tell me, moreover, hast thou sounded him,
If he appeal the duke on ancient malice;
Or worthily, as a good subject should,
On some known ground of treachery in him?
Gaunt. As near as I could sift him on that argument,—
On some apparent danger seen in him,
Aim'd at your highness,—no inveterate malice.
K. Rich. Then call them to our presence: face to face,
And frowning brow to brow, ourselves will hear
Th' accuser, and th' accused, freely speak:—
[*Exeunt some* Attendants.
High-stomach'd are they both, and full of ire,
In rage deaf as the sea, hasty as fire.

Re-enter Attendants *with* BOLINGBROKE *and* NORFOLK.

Boling. Many years of happy days befall
My gracious sovereign, my most loving liege!

Nor. Each day still better other's happiness;
Until the heavens, envying earth's good hap,
Add an immortal title to your crown!
K. Rich. We thank you both: yet one but flatters us,
As well appeareth by the cause you come;
Namely, to appeal each other of high treason.—
Cousin of Hereford, what dost thou object
Against the duke of Norfolk, Thomas Mowbray?
Boling. First, (heaven be the record to my speech!)
In the devotion of a subject's love,
Tendering the precious safety of my prince,
And free from other misbegotten hate,
Come I appellant to this princely presence.—
Now, Thomas Mowbray, do I turn to thee,
And mark my greeting well; for what I speak,
My body shall make good upon this earth,
Or my divine soul answer it in heaven.
Thou art a traitor and a miscreant,
Too good to be so, and too bad to live,—
Once more, the more to aggravate the note,
With a foul traitor's name stuff I thy throat;
And wish, (so please my sovereign) ere I move,
What my tongue speaks, my right-drawn sword may prove.
Nor. Let not my cold words here accuse my zeal:
'Tis not the trial of a woman's war,
The bitter clamor of two eager tongues,
Can arbitrate this cause betwixt us twain;
The blood is hot that must be cool'd for this:
Setting aside his high blood's royalty,
And let him be no kinsman to my liege,
I do defy him, and I spit at him;
Call him a slanderous coward, and a villain:
Which to maintain, I would allow him odds;
And meet him, were I tied to run a-foot
Even to the frozen ridges of the Alps,
Or any other ground inhabitable,
Where ever Englishman durst set his foot.
Meantime, let this defend my loyalty,—
By all my hopes, most falsely doth he lie.
Boling. Pale trembling coward, there I throw my gage,
Disclaiming here the kindred of the king;
And lay aside my high blood's royalty,
Which fear, not reverence, makes thee to except:
If guilty dread have left thee so much strength
As to take up mine honor's pawn, then stoop:
By that and all the rites of knighthood else,
Will I make good against thee, arm to arm,
What I have spoke, or thou canst worse devise.

Nor. I take it up; and by that sword I swear,
Which gently laid my knighthood on my shoulder,
I'll answer thee in any fair degree,
Or chivalrous design of knightly trial:
And when I mount, alive may I not light,
If I be traitor, or unjustly fight!
K. Rich. What doth our cousin lay to Mowbray's charge?
It must be great, that can inherit us
So much as of a thought of ill in him.
Boling. Look, what I speak, my life shall prove it true;—
That Mowbray hath receiv'd eight thousand nobles
In name of lendings for your highness' soldiers,
The which he hath detain'd for lewd employments,
Like a false traitor and injurious villain.
Besides, I say, and will in battle prove,—
Or here, or elsewhere, to the farthest verge
That ever was survey'd by English eye,—
That all the treasons, for these eighteen years
Complotted and contrived in this land,
Fetch from false Mowbray their first head and spring.
Farther, I say,—and farther will maintain
Upon his bad life to make all this good,—
That he did plot the duke of Gloster's death;
Whose blood, like sacrificing Abel's, cries,
Even from the tongueless caverns of the earth,
To me for justice and rough chastisement;
And, by the glorious worth of my descent,
This arm shall do it, or this life be spent.
K. Rich. How high a pitch his resolution soars!—
Thomas of Norfolk, what say'st thou to this?
Nor. O, let my sovereign turn away his face,
And bid his ears a little while be deaf,
Till I have told this slander of his blood,
How God, and good men, hate so foul a liar.
K. Rich. Mowbray, impartial are our eyes and ears:
Were he my brother, nay, my kingdom's heir,
(As he is but my father's brother's son,)
Now, by my sceptre's awe, I make a vow,
Such neighbor nearness to our sacred blood
Should nothing privilege him, nor partialize
The unstooping firmness of my upright soul:
He is our subject, Mowbray, so art thou;
Free speech and fearless, I to thee allow.
Nor. Then, Bolingbroke, as low as to thy heart,
Through the false passage of thy throat, thou liest!
I interchangeably hurl down my gage
Upon this overweening traitor's foot,
To prove myself a loyal gentleman

Even in the best blood chamber'd in his bosom.
In haste whereof, most heartily I pray
Your highness to assign our trial-day.
K. Rich. Wrath-kindled gentlemen, be rul'd by me;
Let's purge this choler without letting blood:
Forget, forgive; conclude, and be agreed;
Good uncle, let this end where it begun;
We'll calm the duke of Norfolk, you your son.
Gaunt. To be a make-peace shall become my age:—
Throw down, my son, the duke of Norfolk's gage.
K. Rich. And, Norfolk, throw down his.
Gaunt. When, Harry? when?
Obedience bids, I should not bid again.
K. Rich. Norfolk, throw down; we bid; there is no boot.
Nor. Myself I throw, dread sovereign, at thy foot.
My life thou shalt command, but not my shame.
K. Rich. Rage must be withstood:—
Give me his gage:—lions make leopards tame.
Nor. Yea, but not change their spots: take but my shame,
And I resign my gage. My dear dear lord,
The purest treasure mortal times afford,
Is spotless reputation; that away,
Men are but gilded loam, or painted clay.
A jewel in a ten times barr'd up chest
Is a bold spirit in a loyal breast.
Mine honor is my life; both grow in one;
Take honor from me, and my life is done:
Then, dear my liege, mine honor let me try;
In that I live, and for that will I die.
K. Rich. Cousin, throw down your gage; do you begin.
Boling. O, heaven defend my soul from such foul sin!
K. Rich. We were not born to sue, but to command;—
Which since we cannot do to make you friends,
Be ready, as your lives shall answer it,
At Coventry, upon Saint Lambert's day:
There shall your swords and lances arbitrate
The swelling difference of your settled hate:
Since we cannot atone you, we shall see
Justice design the victor's chivalry.—
Lord Marshal, command our officers at arms
Be ready to direct these home alarms. [*Exeunt.*

SCENE III.—Gosford Green, *near* Coventry.

Lists set out and a Throne. Heralds, *&c., attending. Enter the* Lord Marshal *and* AUMERLE.

Mar. My lord Aumerle, is Harry Hereford arm'd?
Aum. Yea, at all points; and longs to enter in.
Maa. The duke of Norfolk, sprightfully and bold,
Stays but the summons of the appellant's trumpet.
Aum. Why then, the champions are prepar'd, and stay
For nothing but his majesty's approach.

Flourish of Trumpets. Enter KING RICHARD, *who takes his seat on his Throne;* GAUNT, BUSHY, BAGOT, GREEN, *and others, who take their places. A Trumpet is sounded, and answered by another Trumpet within. Then enter* NORFOLK *in armor, preceded by a Herald.*

K. Rich. Marshal, demand of yonder champion
The cause of his arrival here in arms:
Ask him his name; and orderly proceed
To swear him in the justice of his cause.
Mar. In heaven's name and the king's, say who thou art,
And why thou com'st thus knightly clad in arms;
Against what man thou com'st, and what thy quarrel:
Speak truly, on thy knighthood and thine oath;
As so defend thee heaven and thy valor!
Nor. My name is Thomas Mowbray, duke of Norfolk;
Who hither come engaged by my oath,
Both to defend my loyalty and truth
To God, my king, and his succeeding issue,
Against the duke of Hereford that appeals me;
And, by the grace of Heaven and this mine arm,
To prove him, in defending of myself,
A traitor to my God, my king, and me:
And, as I truly fight, defend me heaven! [*He takes his seat.*

Trumpet sounds. Enter BOLINGBROKE, *in armor, preceded by a Herald.*

K. Rich. Marshal, ask yonder knight in arms,
Both who he is, and why he cometh hither
Thus plated in habiliments of war;
And formally, according to our law,
Depose him in the justice of his cause.
Mar. What is thy name? and wherefore com'st thou hither,
Before king Richard in his royal lists?
Against whom comest thou? and what's thy quarrel?
Speak like a true knight, so defend thee heaven!
Boling. Harry of Hereford, Lancaster, and Derby,

Am I; who ready here do stand in arms,
To prove, by God's grace and my body's valor,
In lists, on Thomas Mowbray, duke of Norfolk,
That he's a traitor, foul and dangerous,
To heaven, king Richard, and to me;
And, as I truly fight, defend me heaven!
Mar. On pain of death, no person be so bold,
Or daring hardy, as to touch the lists;
Except the marshal, and such officers
Appointed to direct these fair designs.
Boling. Lord marshal, let me kiss my sovereign's hand,
And bow my knee before his majesty;
For Mowbray and myself are like two men
That vow a long and weary pilgrimage;
Then let us take a ceremonious leave,
And loving farewell of our several friends.
Mar. The appellant in all duty greets your highness,
And craves to kiss your hand, and take his leave.
K. Rich. [*Descends from his throne.*] We will descend, and fold him in our arms.—
Cousin of Hereford, as thy cause is right,
So be thy fortune in this royal fight!
Farewell, my blood; which if to-day thou shed,
Lament we may, but not revenge thee dead.
Boling. O, let no noble eye profane a tear
For me, if I be gor'd with Mowbray's spear:
As confident as is the falcon's flight
Against a bird, do I with Mowbray fight.—
Gaunt. Heaven in thy good cause make thee prosperous!
Boling. Mine innocency, and Saint George to thrive!
[*He takes his seat.*
Nor. [*Rising.*] However heaven, or fortune, cast my lot,
There lives or dies, true to king Richard's throne,
A loyal, just, and upright gentleman.
K. Rich. Farewell, my lord: securely I espy
Virtue with valor couchèd in thine eye.—
Order the trial, marshal, and begin.
[*The* KING *and the* Lords *return to their seats.*
Mar. Harry of Hereford, Lancaster, and Derby,
Receive thy lance; and God defend the right!
Boling. [*Rising.*] Strong as a tower in hope, I cry, amen.
Mar. [*To an* Officer.] Go bear this lance to Thomas, duke of Norfolk.
1 *Her.* Harry of Hereford, Lancaster, and Derby,
Stands here for heaven, his sovereign, and himself,
On pain to be found false and recreant,
To prove the duke of Norfolk, Thomas Mowbray,

A traitor to his God, his king, and him;
And dares him to set forward to the fight.
2 *Her.* Here standeth Thomas Mowbray, duke of Norfolk,
On pain to be found false and recreant,
Both to defend himself, and to approve
Henry of Hereford, Lancaster, and Derby,
To heaven, his sovereign, and to him, disloyal;
Courageously, and with a free desire,
Attending but the signal to begin.
Mar. Sound, trumpets; and set forward, combatants.
[*A charge sounded.*
Stay, the king hath thrown his warder down.
K. Rich. Let them lay by their helmets and their spears,
And both return back to their chairs again:—
Withdraw with us; and let the trumpets sound,
While we return these dukes what we decree.—
[*A long flourish.*
[*To the Combatants.*] Draw near,
And list, what with our council we have done.
You, cousin Hereford, upon pain of life,
Till twice five summers have enrich'd our fields,
Shall not regreet our fair dominions,
But tread the stranger paths of banishment.
Boling. Your will be done: this must my comfort be,—
That sun that warms you here shall shine on me;
And those his golden beams, to you here lent,
Shall point on me, and gild my banishment.
K. Rich. Norfolk, for thee remains a heavier doom,
Which I with some unwillingness pronounce:
The sly slow hours shall not determinate
The dateless limit of thy dear exile;—
The hopeless word of—" never to return "
Breathe I against thee, upon pain of life.
Nor. A heavy sentence, my most sovereign liege,
And all unlook'd for from your highness' mouth.
Thus I turn me from my country's light,
To dwell in solemn shades of endless night. [*Retiring.*
K. Rich. Return again, and take an oath with thee.
Lay on our royal sword your banish'd hands;
Swear by the duty that you owe to heaven,
To keep the oath that we administer:—
You never shall (so help you truth and God!)
Embrace each other's love in banishment;
Nor never look upon each other's face;
Nor never write, regreet, nor reconcile
This lowering tempest of your home-bred hate;
Nor never by advisèd purpose meet

To plot, contrive, or complot any ill
'Gainst us, our state, our subjects, or our land.
Boling. I swear.
Nor. And I, to keep all this.
Boling. Norfolk, so far, as to mine enemy;—
By this time, had the king permitted us,
One of our souls had wander'd in the air,
Banish'd this frail sepulchre of our flesh,
As now our flesh is banish'd from this land:
Confess thy treasons, ere thou fly the realm;
Since thou hast far to go, bear not along
The clogging burden of a guilty soul.
Nor. No, Bolingbroke: if ever I were traitor,
My name be blotted from the book of life,
And I from heaven banish'd, as from hence!
But what thou art, heaven, thou, and I do know;
And all too soon, I fear, the king shall rue.—
Farewell, my liege.—Now no way can I stray:
Save back to England, all the world's my way. [*Exit.*
K. Rich. Uncle, even in the glasses of thine eyes
I see thy grievèd heart: thy sad aspect
Hath from the number of his banish'd years
Pluck'd four away.—[*To* Boling.] Six frozen winters spent,
Return with welcome home from banishment.
Boling. How long a time lies in one little word!
Four lagging winters, and four wanton springs,
End in a word: such is the breath of kings.
Gaunt. I thank my liege, that in regard of me
He shortens four years of my son's exile:
But little vantage shall I reap thereby;
For, ere the six years that he hath to spend,
Can change their moons and bring their times about,
My oil-dried lamp, and time-bewasted light,
Shall be extinct with age and endless night;
My inch of taper will be burnt and done,
And blindfold death not let me see my son.
K. Rich. Why, uncle, thou hast many years to live.
Gaunt. But not a minute, king, that thou canst give:
Shorten my days thou canst with sullen sorrow,
And pluck nights from me, but not lend a morrow;
Thou canst help time to furrow me with age,
But stop no wrinkle in his pilgrimage;
Thy word is current with him for my death,
But, dead, thy kingdom cannot buy my breath.
K. Rich. Thy son is banish'd upon good advice,
Whereto thy tongue a party verdict gave:
Why at our justice seem'st thou, then, to lower?

Gaunt. Things sweet to taste prove in digestion sour.
You urg'd me as a judge; but I had rather
You would have bid me argue like a father.
K. Rich. Cousin, farewell;—and, uncle, bid him so:
Six years we banish him, and he shall go.
[*Flourish. Exeunt* KING RICHARD *and train.*
Aum. Cousin, farewell: what presence must not know,
From where you do remain, let paper show.
Mar. My lord, no leave take I; for I will ride,
As far as land will let me, by your side.
Gaunt. O! to what purpose dost thou hoard thy words,
That thou return'st no greeting to thy friends?
Boling. I have too few to take my leave of you,
When the tongue's office should be prodigal
To breathe th' abundant dolor of the heart.
Gaunt. Thy grief is but thy absence for a time.
The sullen passage of thy weary steps
Esteem a foil, wherein thou art to set
The precious jewel of thy home-return.
Boling. Nay, rather, every tedious stride I make
Will but remember me, what a deal of world
I wander from the jewels that I love.
Gaunt. All places that the eye of heaven visits,
Are to a wise man ports and happy havens.
Teach thy necessity to reason thus;
There is no virtue like necessity.
Look, what thy soul holds dear, imagine it
To lie that way thou go'st, not whence thou com'st:
Suppose the singing birds musicians,
The grass whereon thou tread'st the presence strew'd,
The flowers fair ladies, and thy steps no more
Than a delightful measure, or a dance;
For gnarling sorrow hath less power to bite
The man that mocks at it, and sets it light.
Boling. O, who can hold a fire in his hand,
By thinking on the frosty Caucasus?
Or cloy the hungry edge of appetite,
By bare imagination of a feast?
Or wallow naked in December snow,
By thinking on fantastic summer's heat?
O, no! the apprehension of the good,
Gives but the greater feeling to the worse:
Fell sorrow's tooth doth never rankle more,
Than when it bites, but lanceth not the sore.
Gaunt. Come, come, my son, I'll bring thee on thy way:
Had I thy youth and cause, I would not stay.
Boling. Then, England's ground, farewell; sweet soil, adieu;
My mother, and my nurse, that bears me yet!

Where'er I wander, boast of this I can,—
Though banish'd, yet a true-born Englishman. [*Exeunt.*

SCENE IV.—*The Court.*

Enter KING RICHARD, BAGOT, *and* GREEN; AUMERLE *following.*

K. Rich. We did observe.—Cousin Aumerle,
How far brought you high Hereford on his way?
Aum. I brought high Hereford, if you call him so,
But to the next highway, and there I left him.
K. Rich. And say, what store of parting tears were shed?
Aum. 'Faith, none for me; except the north-east wind,
Which then blew bitterly against our faces,
Awak'd the sleeping rheum, and so by chance
Did grace our hollow parting with a tear.
K. Rich. What said our cousin, when you parted with him?
Aum. "Farewell": and, for my heart disdainèd that my tongue
Should so profane the word, that taught me craft
To counterfeit oppression of such grief,
That words seem'd buried in my sorrow's grave.
Marry, would the word "farewell" have lengthen'd hours,
And added years to his short banishment,
He should have had a volume of farewells;
But, since it would not, he had none of me.
K. Rich. He is our cousin, cousin; but 'tis doubt,
When time shall call him home from banishment,
Whether our kinsman come to see his friends.
Ourself, and Bushy, Bagot here, and Green,
Observ'd his courtship to the common people;
How he did seem to dive into their hearts
With humble and familiar courtesy;
What reverence he did throw away on slaves;
Wooing poor craftsmen with the craft of smiles,
And patient underbearing of his fortune,
As 'twere to banish their affects with him.
Off goes his bonnet to an oyster-wench;
A brace of draymen bid God speed him well,
And had the tribute of his supple knee,
With—"Thanks, my countrymen, my loving friends;"
As were our England in reversion his,
And he our subjects' next degree in hope.
Green. Well, he is gone; and with him go these thoughts.
Now for the rebels, which stand out in Ireland,—
Expedient manage must be made, my liege,
Ere farther leisure yield them farther means,
For their advantage, and your higness' loss.

K. Rich. We will ourself in person to this war:
And, for our coffers,—with too great a court,
And liberal largess,—are grown somewhat light,
We are enforc'd to farm our royal realm;
The revenue whereof shall furnish us
For our affairs in hand. If that come short,
Our substitutes at home shall have blank charters;
Whereto, when they shall know what men are rich,
They shall subscribe them for large sums of gold,
And send them after to supply our wants:
For we will make for Ireland presently.

Enter BUSHY.

Bushy, what news?
Bushy. Old John of Gaunt is grievous sick, my lord,
Suddenly taken; and hath sent post-haste,
To entreat your majesty to visit him.
K. Rich. Where lies he?
Bushy. At Ely-house.
K. Rich. Now put it, heaven, in his physician's mind,
To help him to his grave immediately!
The lining of his coffers shall make coats
To deck our soldiers for these Irish wars.—
Come, gentlemen, let's all go visit him:
Pray heaven, we may make haste, and come too late! [*Exeunt.*

ACT II.

SCENE I.—London. *An Apartment in* Ely-house.

GAUNT *on a couch; the* DUKE OF YORK, *and others, standing by him.*

Gaunt. Will the king come, that I may breathe my last
In wholesome counsel to his unstaid youth?
York. Vex not yourself, nor strive not with your breath;
For all in vain comes counsel to his ear.
Gaunt. O, but they say, the tongues of dying men
Enforce attention like deep harmony:
Where words are scarce, they are seldom spent in vain;
For they breathe truth that breathe their words in pain.
He that no more must say, is listen'd more,
Than they whom youth and ease have taught to glose:
More are men's ends mark'd, than their lives before:
The setting sun, and music at the close,
As the last taste of sweets, is sweetest last,
Writ in remembrance more than things long past:

Though Richard my life's counsel would not hear,
My death's sad tale may yet undeaf his ear.
York. No; it is stopp'd with other flattering sounds.
Gaunt. Methinks I am a prophet new inspir'd,
And thus, expiring, do foretell of him:
His rash fierce blaze of riot cannot last,
For violent fires soon burn out themselves;
Small showers last long, but sudden storms are short;
He tires betimes, that spurs too fast betimes;
With eager feeding food doth choke the feeder:
Light vanity, insatiate cormorant,
Consuming means, soon preys upon itself.
This royal throne of kings, this scepter'd isle,
Is now leas'd out, (I die pronouncing it,)
Like to a tenement, or pelting farm:
England, bound in with the triumphant sea,
Whose rocky shore beats back the envious siege
Of watery Neptune, is now bound in with shame,
With inky blots, and rotten parchment bonds:
That England, that was wont to conquer others,
Hath made a shameful conquest of itself.
Ah, would the scandal vanish with my life,
How happy then were my ensuing death!

Enter KING RICHARD *and* QUEEN; AUMERLE, BUSHY, GREEN, BAGOT, ROSS, *and* WILLOUGHBY.

York. The king is come: deal mildly with his youth;
For young hot colts, being rag'd, do rage the more.
Queen. How fares our noble uncle, Lancaster?
K. Rich. What comfort, man? How is't with aged Gaunt?
Gaunt. O, how that name befits my composition!
Old Gaunt, indeed; and gaunt in being old:
Gaunt am I for the grave, gaunt as a grave,
Whose hollow vault inherits naught but bones.
K. Rich. Can sick men play so nicely with their names?
Gaunt. No, misery makes sport to mock itself:
Since thou dost seek to kill my name in me,
I mock my name, great king, to flatter thee.
K. Rich. Should dying men flatter with those that live?
Gaunt. No, no, men living flatter those that die.
K. Rich. Thou, now a-dying, say'st thou flatter'st me.
Gaunt. O, no! thou diest, though I the sicker be.
K. Rich, I am in health, I breathe, and see thee ill.
Gaunt. Now, He that made me knows I see thee ill.
O, had thy grandsire, with a prophet's eye,
Seen how his son's son should destroy his sons,
From forth thy reach he would have laid thy shame,
Deposing thee before thou wert possess'd,

Which art possess'd now to depose thyself.
Why, cousin, wert thou regent of the world,
It were a shame to let this land by lease;
But for thy world enjoying but this land,
Is it not more than shame to shame it so?
Landlord of England art thou now, not king:
Thy state of law is bondslave to the law;
And—

K. Rich. And thou a lunatic lean-witted fool,
Presuming on an ague's privilege,
Dar'st with thy frozen admonition
Make pale our cheek, chasing the royal blood
With fury from his native residence.
Now, by my seat's right royal majesty,
Wert thou not brother to great Edward's son,
This tongue that runs so roundly in thy head,
Should run thy head from thy unreverend shoulders.

Gaunt. O, spare me not, my brother Edward's son,
For that I was his father Edward's son;—
That blood already, like the pelican,
Hast thou tapp'd out, and drunkenly carous'd:
My brother Gloster, plain well-meaning soul,
(Whom fair befall in heaven 'mongst happy souls!)
May be a precedent and witness good,
That thou respect'st not spilling Edward's blood:
Join with the present sickness that I have;
And thy unkindness be like crookèd age,
To crop at once a too-long withered flower.
Live in thy shame, but die not shame with thee!—
These words hereafter thy tormentors be!—
Convey me to my bed, then to my grave:
Love they to live, that love and honor have.

[*Exit, borne out by his* Attendants.

K. Rich. And let them die, that age and sullens have;
For both hast thou, and both become the grave.

York. I do beseech your majesty, impute his words
To wayward sickliness and age in him:
He loves you, on my life, and holds you dear
As Harry, duke of Hereford, were he here.

K. Rich. Right, you say true: as Hereford's love, so his;
As theirs, so mine; and all be as it is.

Enter NORTHUMBERLAND.

North. My liege, old Gaunt commends him to your majesty.

K. Rich. What says he?

North. Nay, nothing; all is said.
His tongue is now a stringless instrument:
Words, life, and all, old Lancaster hath spent.

York. Be York the next that must be bankrupt so!
Though death be poor, it ends a mortal woe.
K. Rich. The ripest fruit first falls, and so doth he;
His time is spent, our pilgrimage must be:
So much for that.—Now for our Irish wars:
We must supplant those rough rug-headed kerns,
Which live like venom, where no venom else,
But only they, hath privilege to live.
And for these great affairs do ask some charge,
Towards our assistance we do seize to us
The plate, coin, revenues, and moveables,
Whereof our uncle Gaunt did stand possess'd.
York. How long shall I be patient? Ah, how long
Shall tender duty make me suffer wrong?
K. Rich. Why, uncle, what's the matter?
York. O, my liege!
Pardon me, if you please; if not, I, pleas'd
Not to be pardon'd, am content withal.
Seek you to seize, and gripe into your hands,
The royalties and rights of banish'd Hereford?
Is not Gaunt dead? and doth not Hereford live?
Was not Gaunt just? and is not Harry true?
Did not the one deserve to have an heir?
Is not his heir a well-deserving son?
Take Hereford's rights away, and take from time
His charters and his customary rights;
Let not to-morrow, then, ensue to-day;
Be not thyself; for how art thou a king,
But by fair sequence and succession?
You lose a thousand well-disposed hearts,
And prick my tender patience to those thoughts,
Which honor and allegiance cannot think.
K. Rich. Think what you will: we seize into our hands
His plate, his goods, his money, and his lands.
York. I'll not be by the while. My liege, farewell:
What will ensue hereof, there's none can tell;
But by bad courses may be understood,
That their events can never fall out good. [*Exit.*
K. Rich. Go, Bushy, to the earl of Wiltshire straight:
Bid him repair to us to Ely-house,
To see this business. To-morrow next
We will for Ireland; and 'tis time, I trow:
And we create, in absence of ourself,
Our uncle York lord governor of England;
For he is just, and always lov'd us well.—
Come on, our queen: to-morrow must we part;
Be merry, for our time of stay is short. [*Flourish.*
[*Exeunt* KING, QUEEN, BUSHY, AUMERLE, GREEN, *and* BAGOT.

North. Well, lords, the duke of Lancaster is dead.
Ross. And living too; for now his son is duke.
Willo. Barely in title, not in revenue.
North. Richly in both, if justice had her right.
Ross. My heart is great; but it must break with silence,
Ere't be disburden'd with a liberal tongue.
North. Nay, speak thy mind; and let him ne'er speak more,
That speaks thy words again to do thee harm!
Willo. Tends that thou'dst speak, to the duke of Hereford?
If it be so, out with it boldly, man;
Quick is mine ear to hear of good towards him.
Ross. Be confident to speak, Northumberland:
We three are but thyself; and, speaking so,
Thy words are but as thoughts; therefore, be bold.
North. Then thus:—I have from Port le Blanc, a bay
In Brittany, receiv'd intelligence,
That Harry duke of Hereford, Reignold lord Cobham,
That late broke from the duke of Exeter,
His brother, archbishop late of Canterbury,
Sir Thomas Erpingham, Sir John Ramston,
Sir John Norbery, Sir Robert Waterton, and Francis Quoint,—
All these well furnish'd by the duke of Bretagne,
With eight tall ships, three thousand men of war,
Are making hither with all due expedience,
And shortly mean to touch our northern shore:
Perhaps they had ere this, but that they stay
The first departing of the king for Ireland.
If, then, we shall shake off our slavish yoke,
Imp out our drooping country's broken wing,
Redeem from broking pawn the blemish'd crown,
Wipe off the dust that hides our sceptre's gilt,
And make high majesty look like itself,
Away with me in post to Ravenspurg;
But if you faint, as fearing to do so,
Stay and be secret, and myself will go.
Ross. To horse, to horse! urge doubts to them that fear.
Willo. Hold out my horse, and I will first be there. [*Exeunt.*

SCENE II.—London. *An Apartment in the Palace.*

Enter QUEEN, BUSHY, *and* BAGOT.

Bushy. Madam, your majesty is too much sad:
You promis'd, when you parted with the king,
To lay aside life-harming heaviness,
And entertain a cheerful disposition.
Queen. To please the king, I did; to please myself
I cannot do it; yet I know no cause

Why I should welcome such a guest as grief,
Save bidding farewell to so sweet a guest
As my sweet Richard: yet, again, methinks
Some unborn sorrow, by fortune ripening,
Is coming towards me; and my inward soul
With nothing trembles: at some thing it grieves,
More than with parting from my lord, the king.

Bushy. Each substance of a grief hath twenty shadows,
Which show like grief itself, but are not so;
For sorrow's eye, glazed with blinding tears,
Divides one thing entire to many objects.
Then, thrice-gracious queen,
More than your lord's departure weep not,—more's not seen;
Or if it be, 'tis with false sorrow's eye,
Which for things true weeps things imaginary.

Queen. It may be so; but yet my inward soul
Persuades me it is otherwise: howe'er it be,
I cannot but be sad; so heavy sad,
As,—though, in thinking, on no thought I think,—
Makes me with heavy nothing faint and shrink.

Bushy. 'Tis nothing but conceit, my gracious lady.

Queen. 'Tis nothing less: conceit is still deriv'd
From some forefather grief; mine is not so,
For nothing hath begot my something grief;
Or something hath the nothing that I grieve:
'Tis in reversion that I do possess;
But what it is, that is not yet known; what,
I cannot name: 'tis nameless woe, I wot.

Enter GREEN.

Green. God save your majesty!—and well met, gentlemen:—
I hope the king is not yet shipp'd for Ireland.

Queen. Why hop'st thou so? 'tis better hope he is;
For his designs crave haste, his haste good hope:
Then wherefore dost thou hope he is not shipp'd?

Green. That he, our hope, might have retir'd his power,
And driven into despair an enemy's hope,
Who strongly hath set footing in this land:
The banish'd Bolingbroke repeals himself,
And with uplifted arms is safe arriv'd
At Ravenspurg.

Queen. Now heaven forbid!

Green. O madam, 'tis too true: and that is worse,
The lord Northumberland, his son young Henry Percy,
The lords of Ross, Beaumond, and Willoughby,
With all their powerful friends, are fled to him.

Bushy. Why have you not proclaim'd Northumberland,
And all the rest of the revolted faction, traitors?

Green. We have: whereupon the earl of Worcester
Hath broke his staff, resign'd his stewardship,
And all the household servants fled with him
To Bolingbroke. Here comes the duke of York.
Queen. With signs of war about his aged neck:
O, full of careful business are his looks!—

Enter the DUKE OF YORK.

Uncle, for heaven's sake, speak comfortable words.
York. Should I do so, I should belie my thoughts:
Comfort's in heaven; and we are on the earth,
Where nothing lives but crosses, care, and grief.
Your husband, he is gone to save far off,
Whilst others come to make him lose at home:
Here am I left to underprop his land,
Who, weak with age, cannot support myself:
Now comes the sick hour that his surfeit made;
Now shall he try his friends that flatter'd him.

Enter a Servant.

Serv. My lord, your son was gone before I came.
York. He was?—Why, so!—go all which way it will!—
The nobles they are fled, the commons they are cold,
And will, I fear, revolt on Hereford's side.—
Sirrah, get thee to Plashy, to my sister Gloster;
Bid her send me presently a thousand pound:—
Hold, take my ring.
Serv. My lord, I had forgot to tell your lordship:
To-day, as I came by, I callèd there;—
But I shall grieve you to report the rest.
York. What is't, knave?
Serv. An hour before I came, the duchess died.
York. Heaven for its mercy! what a tide of woes
Comes rushing on this woful land at once!
I know not what to do:—
What, are there no posts despatch'd for Ireland?—
How shall we do for money for these wars?—
Come, sister,—cousin, I would say,—pray, pardon me.—
[*To the* Servant.] Go, fellow, get thee home; provide some carts,
And bring away the armor that is there.— [*Exit* Servant
Gentlemen, will you go muster men?—
And meet me presently at Berkley castle.
I should to Plashy too:—
But time will not permit:—all is uneven,
And every thing is left at six and seven.
[*Exeunt* YORK *and* QUEEN.
Bushy. The wind sits fair for news to go to Ireland,
But none returns. For us to levy power

Proportionable to the enemy,
Is all impossible.
Green. Besides, our nearness to the king in love,
Is near the hate of those love not the king.
Bagot. And that's the wavering commons: for their love
Lies in their purses; and whoso empties them,
By so much fills their hearts with deadly hate.
Bushy. Wherein the king stands generally condemn'd.
Bagot. If judgment lie in them, then so do we,
Because we ever have been near the king.
Green. Well, I'll for refuge straight to Bristol castle:
The earl of Wiltshire is already there.
Bushy. Thither will I with you; for little office
Will the hateful commons perform for us,
Except like curs to tear us all to pieces.—
Will you go along with us?
Bagot. No; I will to Ireland to his majesty.
Farewell: if heart's presages be not vain,
We three here part, that ne'er shall meet again.
Bushy. That's as York thrives to beat back Bolingbroke.
Green. Alas, poor duke! the task he undertakes
Is numbering sands, and drinking oceans dry:
Where one on his side fights, thousands will fly.
Farewell at once,—for once, for all, and ever.
Bushy. Well, we may meet again.
Bagot. I fear me, never. [*Exeunt.*

SCENE III.—*The Wilds in* Glostershire.

Enter BOLINGBROKE *and* NORTHUMBERLAND, *with forces.*

Boling. How far is it, my lord, to Berkley now?
North. Believe me, noble lord,
I am a stranger here in Glostershire.
Boling. Who comes here?
North. It is my son, young Harry Percy,
Sent from my brother Worcester, whencesoever.—

Enter HENRY PERCY.

Harry, how fares your uncle?
Percy. I had thought, my lord, to have learn'd his health of you.
North. Why, is he not with the queen?
Percy. No, my good lord; he hath forsook the court,
Broken his staff of office, and dispers'd
The household of the king.
North. What was his reason?
He was not so resolv'd, when last we spake
Together.

Percy. Because your lordship was proclaimèd traitor.
But he, my lord, is gone to Ravenspurg,
To offer service to the duke of Hereford;
And sent me over by Berkley, to discover
What power the duke of York had levied there;
Then, with direction to repair to Ravenspurg.
North. Have you forgot the duke of Hereford, boy?
Percy. No, my good lord; for that is not forgot,
Which ne'er I did remember: to my knowledge,
I never in my life did look on him.
North. Then learn to know him now; this is the duke.
Percy. My gracious lord, I tender you my service,
Such as it is, being tender, raw, and young;
Which elder days shall ripen, and confirm
To more approvèd service and desert.
Boling. I thank thee, gentle Percy; and be sure,
I count myself in nothing else so happy,
As in a soul remembering my good friends;
And, as my fortune ripens with thy love,
It shall be still thy true love's recompense;
My heart this covenant makes, my hand thus seals it.
North. How far is it to Berkley? And what stir
Keeps good old York there, with his men of war?
Percy. There stands the castle, by yond' tuft of trees,
Mann'd with three hundred men, as I have heard;
And in it are the lords of York, Berkley, and Seymour;
None else of name and noble estimate.
North. Here come the lords of Ross and Willoughby,
Bloody with spurring, fiery-red with haste.

Enter Ross *and* Willoughby.

Boling. Welcome, my lords. I wot, your love pursues
A banish'd traitor: all my treasury
Is yet but unfelt thanks, which, more enrich'd,
Shall be your love and labor's recompense.
Ross. Your presence makes us rich, most noble lord.
Willo. And far surmounts our labor to attain it.
Boling. Evermore thanks, the exchequer of the poor;
Which, till my infant fortune comes to years,
Stands for my bounty.—But who comes here?
North. It is my lord of Berkley, as I guess.

Enter Berkley.

Berk. My lord of Hereford, my message is to you.
Boling. My lord, my answer is—to Lancaster;
And I am come to seek that name in England;
And I must find that title in your tongue,
Before I make reply to aught you say.

Berk. Mistake me not, my lord; 'tis not my meaning,
To raze one title of your honor out:—
To you, my lord, I come, (what lord you will,)
From the most gracious regent of this land,
The duke of York, to know what spurs you on
To take advantage of the absent time,
And fright our native peace with self-born arms.
Boling. I shall not need transport my words by you;
Here comes his grace in person.—

Enter YORK, *attended.*

[*Kneels.*] My noble uncle!
York. Show me thy humble heart, and not thy knee,
Whose duty is deceivable and false.
Boling. My gracious uncle!—
York. Tut, tut! Grace me no grace, nor uncle me no uncle:
I am no traitor's uncle; and that word "grace,"
In an ungracious mouth, is but profane.
Why have those banish'd and forbidden legs
Dar'd once to touch a dust of England's ground?
Com'st thou because th' anointed king is hence?
Why, foolish boy, the king is left behind,
And in my loyal bosom lies his power.
Were I but now the lord of such hot youth,
As when brave Gaunt, thy father, and myself,
Rescued the Black Prince, that young Mars of men,
From forth the ranks of many thousand French,
O, then, how quickly should this arm of mine,
Now prisoner to the palsy, chastise thee,
And minister correction to thy fault!
Boling. My gracious uncle, let me know my fault;
On what condition stands it, and wherein?
York. Even in condition of the worst degree,—
In gross rebellion, and detested treason:
Thou art a banish'd man; and here art come
Before the expiration of thy time,
In braving arms against thy sovereign.
Boling. As I was banish'd, I was banish'd Hereford:
But as I come, I come for Lancaster.
And, noble uncle, I beseech your grace,
Look on my wrongs with an indifferent eye:
You are my father, for methinks in you
I see old Gaunt alive; O, then, my father,
Will you permit that I shall stand condemn'd
A wandering vagabond; my rights and royalties
Pluck'd from my arms perforce, and given away
To upstart unthrifts? Wherefore was I born?
If that my cousin king be king of England,

It must be granted I am duke of Lancaster.
You have a son, Aumerle, my noble kinsman;
Had you first died, and he been thus trod down,
He should have found his uncle Gaunt a father,
To rouse his wrongs, and chase them to the bay.
I am denied to sue my livery here,
And yet my letters patent give me leave:
My father's goods are all distrain'd, and sold;
And these, and all, are all amiss employ'd.
What would you have me do? I am a subject,
And challenge law: attornies are denied me;
And therefore personally I lay my claim
To my inheritance of free descent.

North. The noble duke hath been too much abused.

Ross. It stands your grace upon to do him right.

Willo. Base men by his endowments are made great.

York. My lords of England, let me tell you this:—
I have had feeling of my cousin's wrongs,
And labor'd all I could to do him right;
But in this kind to come, in braving arms,
Be his own carver, and cut out his way,
To find out right with wrong,—it may not be;
And you, that do abet him in this kind,
Cherish rebellion, and are rebels all.

North. The noble duke hath sworn his coming is
But for his own; and for the right of that,
We all have strongly sworn to give him aid;
And let him ne'er see joy that breaks that oath.

York. Well, well, I see the issue of these arms;—
I cannot mend it, I must needs confess,
Because my power is weak, and all ill left:
But if I could, by him that gave me life,
I would attach you all, and make you stoop
Unto the sovereign mercy of the king;
But since I cannot, be it known to you,
I do remain as neuter. So, fare you well;—
Unless you please to enter in the castle,
And there repose you for this night.

Boling. An offer, uncle, that we will accept:
But we must win your grace to go with us
To Bristol castle; which, they say, is held
By Bushy, Bagot, and their complices,
The caterpillars of the commonwealth,
Which I have sworn to weed and pluck away.

York. It may be, I will go with you:—but yet I'll pause;
For I am loath to break our country's laws.
Nor friends, nor foes, to me welcome you are:
Things past redress are now with me past care. [*Exeunt.*

ACT III.

SCENE I.—BOLINGBROKE'S *Camp at* Bristol.

Enter BOLINGBROKE, YORK, NORTHUMBERLAND, PERCY, WILLOUGHBY, ROSS: Officers *behind, with* BUSHY *and* GREEN, *prisoners.*

Boling. Bring forth these men.—
Bushy, and Green, I will not vex your souls,
(Since presently your souls must part your bodies,)
With too much urging your pernicious lives;
For 'twere no charity: yet, to wash your blood
From off my hands, here, in the view of men,
I will unfold some causes of your deaths.
You have misled a prince, a royal king,
A happy gentleman in blood and lineaments,
By you unhappied and disfigur'd clean:
You have, in manner, with your sinful hours,
Made a divorce betwixt his queen and him,
And stain'd the beauty of a fair queen's cheeks
With tears, drawn from her eyes by your foul wrongs.
Myself,—a prince by fortune of my birth,
Near to the king in blood, and near in love,
Till you did make him misinterpret me,—
Have stoop'd my neck under your injuries,
And sigh'd my English breath in foreign clouds,
Eating the bitter bread of banishment;
Whilst you have fed upon my signories,
Dispark'd my parks, and fell'd my forest woods,
From mine own windows torn my household coat,
Raz'd out my impress, leaving me no sign,
Save men's opinions and my living blood,
To show the world I am a gentleman.
This and much more, much more than twice all this,
Condemns you to the death.—See them deliver'd over
To execution and the hand of death.
My lord Northumberland, see them despatch'd.
[*Exeunt* NORTHUMBERLAND *and others, with* BUSHY *and* GREEN.
Uncle, you say the queen is at your house;
For heaven's sake, fairly let her be entreated:
Tell her I send to her my kind commends;
Take special care my greetings be deliver'd.
York. A gentleman of mine I have despatch'd
With letters of your love to her at large.
Boling. Thanks, gentle uncle.—Come, lords, away,

To fight with Glendower and his complices:
A while to work, and after holiday. [*Exeunt.*

SCENE II.—*The Coast of* Wales. *A Castle in view.*

Flourish: Drums and Trumpets. Enter KING RICHARD, *the* BISHOP OF CARLISLE, AUMERLE, *and* Soldiers.

K. Rich. Barkloughly castle call they this at hand?
Aum. Yea, my lord. How brooks your grace the air,
After your late tossing on the breaking seas?
K. Rich. Needs must I like it well: I weep for joy,
To stand upon my kingdom once again.—
Dear earth, I do salute thee with my hand,
Though rebels wound thee with their horses' hoofs:
As a long parted mother with her child
Plays fondly with her tears and smiles in meeting,
So, weeping, smiling, greet I thee, my earth,
And do thee favor with my royal hands.
Feed not thy sovereign's foe, my gentle earth,
Nor with thy sweets comfort his ravenous sense;
But let thy spiders, that suck up thy venom,
And heavy-gaited toads, lie in their way,
Doing annoyance to the treacherous feet,
Which with usurping steps do trample thee.
Yield stinging nettles to mine enemies;
And when they from thy bosom pluck a flower,
Guard it, I pray thee, with a lurking adder,
Whose double tongue may with a mortal touch
Throw death upon thy sovereign's enemies.—
Mock not my senseless conjuration, lords:
This earth shall have a feeling, and these stones
Prove armèd soldiers, ere her native king
Shall falter under foul rebellion's arms.
Bishop. Fear not, my lord: that Power that made you king,
Hath power to keep you king, in spite of all.
The means that heaven yields must be embrac'd,
And not neglected; else, if heaven would,
And we will not, heaven's offer we refuse,
The proffer'd means of succor and redress.
Aum. He means, my lord, that we are too remiss;
Whilst Bolingbroke, through our security,
Grows strong and great in substance, and in friends.
K. Rich. Discomfortable cousin! know'st thou not,
That when the searching eye of heaven is hid
Behind the globe, and lights the lower world,
Then thieves and robbers range abroad unseen,
In murders and in outrage, boldly here;
But when, from under this terrestrial ball,

He fires the proud tops of the eastern pines,
And darts his light through every guilty hole,
Then murders, treasons, and detested sins,
The cloak of night being pluck'd from off their backs,
Stand bare and naked, trembling at themselves?
So when this thief, this traitor, Bolingbroke,—
Who all this while hath revell'd in the night,
Whilst we were wandering with the antipodes,—
Shall see us rising in our throne, the east,
His treasons will sit blushing in his face,
Not able to endure the sight of day,
But, self-affrighted, tremble at his sin.
Not all the water in the rough rude sea
Can wash the balm from an anointed king;
The breath of worldly men cannot depose
The deputy elected by the Lord:
For every man that Bolingbroke hath press'd
To lift shrewd steel against our golden crown,
Heaven for his Richard hath in heavenly pay
A glorious angel: then, if angels fight,
Weak men must fall; for heaven still guards the right.

Enter SALISBURY.

Welcome, my lord: how far off lies your power?
Sal. Nor near, nor farther off, my gracious lord,
Than this weak arm: discomfort guides my tongue,
And bids me speak of nothing but despair.
One day too late, I fear, my noble lord,
Hath clouded all thy happy days on earth.
O, call back yesterday, bid time return,
And thou shalt have twelve thousand fighting men!
To-day, to-day, unhappy day too late,
O'erthrows thy joys, friends, fortune, and thy state;
For all the Welshmen, hearing thou wert dead,
Are gone to Bolingbroke, dispers'd, and fled.
Aum. Comfort, my liege; why looks your grace so pale?
K. Rich. But now, the blood of twenty thousand men
Did triumph in my face, and they are fled;
And, till so much blood thither come again,
Have I not reason to look pale and dead?
All souls that will be safe, fly from my side;
For time hath set a blot upon my pride.
Aum. Comfort, my liege; remember who you are.
K. Rich. I had forgot myself: am I not king?
Awake, thou sluggard majesty! thou sleepest.
Is not the king's name forty thousand names?
Arm, arm, my name! a puny subject strikes
At thy great glory.—Look not to the ground,
Ye favorites of a king: are we not high?

High be our thoughts: I know my uncle York
Hath power enough to serve our turn.—But who comes here!

Enter SCROOP.

Scroop. More health and happiness betide my liege,
Than can my care-tun'd tongue deliver him!
K. Rich. Mine ear is open, and my heart prepar'd:
The worst is worldly loss thou canst unfold.
Say, is my kingdom lost? why, 'twas my care;
And what loss is it to be rid of care?
Strives Bolingbroke to be as great as we?
Greater he shall not be; if he serve heaven,
We'll serve it too, and be his fellow so:
Revolt our subjects? that we cannot mend;
They break their faith to heaven, as well as us:
Cry woe, destruction, ruin, loss, decay;
The worst is death, and death will have his day.
Scroop. Glad am I, that your highness is so arm'd
To bear the tidings of calamity.
White-beards have arm'd their thin and hairless scalps
Against thy majesty; and boys, with women's voices,
Strive to speak big, and clap their female joints
In stiff unwieldy arms against thy crown:
Thy very beadsmen learn to bend their bows
Of double-fatal yew against thy state;
Yea, distaff-women manage rusty bills
Against thy seat: both young and old rebel,
And all goes worse than I have power to tell.
K. Rich. Too well, too well, thou tell'st a tale so ill.
Where is the earl of Wiltshire? where is Bagot?
What is become of Bushy? where is Green?
That they have let the dangerous enemy
Measure our confines with such peaceful steps?
If we prevail, their heads shall pay for it:
I warrant they have made peace with Bolingbroke.
Scroop. Peace have they made with him, indeed, my lord.
K. Rich. O villains, vipers, condemn'd without redemption!
Dogs, easily won to fawn on any man!
Snakes, in my heart-blood warm'd, that sting my heart!
Three Judases, each one thrice worse than Judas!
Scroop. Sweet love, I see, changing his property,
Turns to the sourest and most deadly hate:—
Their peace is made
With heads, and not with hands: those whom you curse,
Have felt the worst of death's destroying wound,
And lie full low, grav'd in the hollow ground.
Aum. Is Bushy, Green, and the earl of Wiltshire, dead?
Scroop. Yea, all of them at Bristol lost their heads.

Aum. Where is the duke, my father, with his power?

K. Rich. No matter where;—of comfort no man speak:
Let's talk of graves, of worms, and epitaphs;
Make dust our paper, and with rainy eyes
Write sorrow on the bosom of the earth.
Let's choose executors, and talk of wills:
And yet not so,—for what can we bequeath,
Save our deposèd bodies to the ground?
Our lands, our lives, and all are Bolingbroke's,
And nothing can we call our own but death,
And that small model of the barren earth,
Which serves as paste and cover to our bones.
For heaven's sake, let us sit upon the ground,
And tell sad stories of the death of kings:—
How some have been depos'd; some slain in war;
Some haunted by the ghosts they have depos'd;
Some poison'd by their wives; some sleeping kill'd;
All murder'd:—for within the hollow crown
That rounds the mortal temples of a king,
Keeps death his court; and there the antick sits,
Scoffing his state, and grinning at his pomp;
Allowing him a breath, a little scene,
To monarchize, be fear'd, and kill with looks;
Infusing him with self and vain conceit,—
As if this flesh, which walls about our life,
Were brass impregnable; and, humor'd thus,
Comes at the last, and with a little pin
Bores through his castle-wall, and—farewell king!
Cover your heads, and mock not flesh and blood
With solemn reverence; throw away respect,
Tradition, form, and ceremonious duty;
For you have but mistook me all this while:
I live with bread like you, feel want,
Taste grief, need friends:—subjected thus,
How can you say to me—I am king?

Bishop. My lord, wise men ne'er sit and wail their woes,
But presently prevent the ways to wail.

K. Rich. Thou chid'st me well.—Proud Bolingbroke, I come
To change blows with thee for our day of doom.
This ague-fit of fear is over-blown;
An easy task it is, to win our own.—
Say, Scroop, where lies our uncle with his power?
Speak sweetly, man, although thy looks be sour.

Scroop. Men judge by the complexion of the sky
The state and inclination of the day
So may you by my dull and heavy eye,
My tongue hath but a heavier tale to say.
I play the torturer, by small and small

To lengthen out the worst that must be spoken:—
Your uncle York is join'd with Bolingbroke;
And all your northern castles yielded up,
And all your southern gentlemen in arms
Upon his party.
K. Rich. Thou hast said enough.—
What comfort have we now?
By heaven, I'll hate him everlastingly,
That bids me be of comfort any more.
Go to Flint castle: there I'll pine away;
A king, woe's slave, shall kingly woe obey.
That power I have, discharge; and let them go
To ear the land that hath some hope to grow,
For I have none: let no man speak again
To alter this, for counsel is but vain.
Aum. My liege, one word.
K. Rich. He does me double wrong,
That wounds me with the flatteries of his tongue.
Discharge my followers: let them hence away,
From Richard's night to Bolingbroke's fair day. [*Exeunt.*

SCENE III.—Wales. *A Plain before* Flint Castle.

Enter, with Drum and Colors, BOLINGBROKE *and forces;* YORK, NORTHUMBERLAND, *and others.*

Boling. So that by this intelligence we learn,
The Welshmen are dispers'd; and Salisbury
Is gone to meet the king, who lately landed
With some few private friends upon this coast.
North. The news is very fair and good, my lord;
Richard, not far from hence, hath hid his head.
York. It would beseem the lord Northumberland
To say, king Richard:—alack, the heavy day,
When such a sacred king should hide his head!
North. Your grace mistakes me; only to be brief,
Left I his title out.
York. The time hath been,
Would you have been so brief with him, he would
Have been so brief with you, to shorten you,
For taking so the head, your whole head's length.
Boling. Mistake not, uncle, farther than you should.
York. Take not, good cousin, farther than you should,
Lest you mistake: the heavens are o'er our heads.
Boling. I know it, uncle: and oppose not myself
Against their will.—But who comes here?

Enter PERCY.

Welcome, Harry: what, will not this castle yield?

Percy. The castle royally is mann'd, my lord,
Against thy entrance.
Boling. Royally!
Why, it contains no king?
Percy. Yes, my good lord,
It doth contain a king; king Richard lies
Within the limits of yond' lime and stone:
And with him are the lord Aumerle, lord Salisbury,
Sir Stephen Scroop; besides a clergyman
Of holy reverence,—who, I cannot learn.
North. O, belike it is the bishop of Carlisle.
Boling. [*To* NORTH.] Noble lord,
Go to the rude ribs of that ancient castle;
Through brazen trumpet send the breath of parle
Into his ruin'd ears, and thus deliver:—
Henry Bolingbroke
On both his knees doth kiss king Richard's hand,
And sends allegiance, and true faith of heart,
To his most royal person; hither come
Even at his feet to lay my arms and power,
Provided that, my banishment repeal'd,
And lands restor'd again, be freely granted:
If not, I'll use th' advantage of my power,
And lay the summer's dust with showers of blood,
Rain'd from the wounds of slaughter'd Englishmen.
Go, signify as much, while here we march
Upon the grassy carpet of this plain.—
[NORTH. *advances to the Castle, with a Trumpet.*
Let's march without the noise of threat'ning drum,
That from the castle's tatter'd battlements
Our fair appointments may be well perus'd.
Methinks king Richard and myself should meet
With no less terror than the elements
Of fire and water, when their thundering shock
At meeting tears the cloudy cheeks of heaven.
Be he the fire, I'll be the yielding water:
The rage be his, while on the earth I rain
My waters,—on the earth, and not on him.—
March on, and mark king Richard how he looks.

A parle sounded, and answered by another Trumpet within. Flourish. Enter on the walls KING RICHARD, *the* BISHOP OF CARLISLE, AUMERLE, SCROOP, *and* SALISBURY.

See, see, king Richard doth himself appear,
As doth the blushing discontented sun
From out the fiery portal of the east,
When he perceives the envious clouds are bent

To dim his glory, and to stain the track
Of his bright passage to the occident.
York. Yet looks he like a king: behold, his eye,
As bright as is the eagle's, lightens forth
Controlling majesty:—alack, alack, for woe,
That any harm should stain so fair a show!
K. Rich. [*To* NORTH.] We are amaz'd; and thus long have we stood
To watch the fearful bending of thy knee,
Because we thought ourself thy lawful king:
And if we be, how dare thy joints forget
To pay their awful duty to our presence?
If we be not, show us the hand of heaven
That hath dismiss'd us from our stewardship;
For well we know, no hand of blood and bone
Can gripe the sacred handle of our sceptre,
Unless he do profane, steal, or usurp.
And though you think that all, as you have done,
Have torn their souls by turning them from us,
And we are barren and bereft of friends;
Yet know,—my master, God omnipotent,
Is mustering in his clouds, on our behalf,
Armies of pestilence; and they shall strike all
That lift their vassal hands against my head,
And threat the glory of my precious crown.
Tell Bolingbroke, (for yond' methinks he is,)
That every stride he makes upon my land
Is dangerous treason: he is come to ope
The purple testament of bleeding war;
But ere the crown he looks for live in peace,
Ten thousand bloody crowns of mothers' sons
Shall ill become the flower of England's face,
Change the complexion of her maid-pale peace
To scarlet indignation, and bedew
Her pastures' grass with faithful English blood.
North. The King of heaven forbid, our lord the king
Should so with civil and uncivil arms
Be rush'd upon! Thy thrice-noble cousin,
Harry Bolingbroke, doth humbly kiss thy hand;
And by the honorable tomb he swears,
That stands upon your royal grandsire's bones,
And by the royalties of both your bloods,
His coming hither hath no farther scope,
Than for his lineal royalties, and to beg
Enfranchisement immediate on his knees:
Which on thy royal party granted once,
His glittering arms he will commend to rust,
His barbèd steeds to stables, and his heart

To faithful service of your majesty.
This swears he, as he is a prince, is just;
And, as I am a gentleman, I credit him.
K. Rich. Northumberland, say,—thus the king returns:—
His noble cousin is right welcome hither;
And all the number of his fair demands
Shall be accomplish'd without contradiction:
With all the gracious utterance thou hast,
Speak to his gentle hearing kind commends.—
[NORTHUMBERLAND *retires to* BOLINGBROKE.
[*To* AUMERLE.] We do debase ourself, cousin, do we not,
To look so poorly, and to speak so fair?
Shall we call back Northumberland, and send
Defiance to the traitor, and so die?
Aum. No, good my lord; let's fight with gentle words
Till time lend friends, and friends their helpful swords.
K. Rich. O heaven! that e'er this tongue of mine,
That laid the sentence of dread banishment
On yond' proud man, should take it off again
With words of sooth! O, that I were as great
As is my grief, or lesser than my name!
Or that I could forget what I have been!
Or not remember what I must be now!
Swell'st thou, proud heart? I'll give thee scope to beat,
Since foes have scope to beat both thee and me.
Aum. Northumberland comes back from Bolingbroke.
K. Rich. What must the king do now? Must he submit?
The king shall do it: must he be deposed?
The king shall be contented: must he lose
The name of king? in heaven's name, let it go:
I'll give my jewels for a set of beads,
My gorgeous palace for a hermitage,
My gay apparel for an alms-man's gown,
My figur'd goblets for a dish of wood,
My sceptre for a palmer's walking-staff,
My subjects for a pair of carved saints,
And my large kingdom for a little grave,
A little little grave, an obscure grave;—
Aumerle, thou weep'st,—my tender-hearted cousin!—
We'll make foul weather with despisèd tears;
Our sighs and they shall lodge the summer corn,
And make a dearth in this revolting land.
Or shall we play the wantons with our woes,
And make some pretty match with shedding tears?
As thus;—to drop them still upon one place,
Till they have fretted us a pair of graves
Within the earth; and, therein laid,—There lies
Two kinsmen digg'd their graves with weeping eyes.

Would not this ill do well?—Well, well, I see
I talk but idly, and you mock at me.—
Most mighty prince, my lord Northumberland,
What says king Bolingbroke? will his majesty
Give Richard leave to live till Richard die?

North. My lord, in the base court he doth attend
To speak with you;—may't please you to come down?

K. Rich. Down, down, I come; like glistering Phæton,
Wanting the manage of unruly jades.

[NORTHUMBERLAND *retires again to* BOLINGBROKE.

In the base court? Base court, where kings grow base,
To come at traitors' calls, and do them grace.
In the base court? Come down? Down, court! down, king!
For night-owls shriek, where mounting larks should sing.

[*Exeunt, from above.*

Boling. What says his majesty?

North. Sorrow and grief of heart
Makes him speak fondly, like a frantic man:
Yet he is come.

Enter KING RICHARD, *and his* Attendants, *below.*

Boling. Stand all apart,
And show fair duty to his majesty.— [*Advances and kneels.*
My gracious lord,—

K. Rich. Fair cousin, you debase your princely knee,
To make the base earth proud with kissing it:
Me rather had, my heart might feel your love,
Than my unpleas'd eye see your courtesy.
Up, cousin, up;—your heart is up, I know,
Thus high at least, [*Touching his own head.*] although your knee be low.

Boling. My gracious lord, I come but for mine own.

K. Rich. Your own is yours, and I am yours, and all.

Boling. So far be mine, my most redoubted lord,
As my true service shall deserve your love.

K. Rich. Well you deserve:—they well deserve to have,
That know the strong'st and surest way to get.—
Uncle, give me your hand: nay, dry your eyes;
Tears show their love, but want their remedies.—
Cousin, I am too young to be your father,
Though you are old enough to be my heir.
What you will have, I'll give, and willing too;
For do we must what force will have us do.—
Set on towards London:—cousin, is it so?

Boling. Yea, my good lord.

K. Rich. Then I must not say no.

[*Flourish. Exeunt.*

SCENE IV.—Langley. *The* DUKE OF YORK'S *Garden.*

Enter the QUEEN *and two* Ladies.

Queen. What sport shall we devise here in this garden,
To drive away the heavy thought of care?
1 *Lady.* Madam, we'll play at bowls.
Queen. 'Twill make me think the world is full of rubs,
And that my fortune runs against the bias.
1 *Lady.* Madam, we'll dance.
Queen. My limbs can keep no measure in delight,
When my poor heart no measure keeps in grief:
Therefore, no dancing, girl; some other sport.
1 *Lady.* Madam, we'll tell tales.
Queen. Of sorrow, or of joy?
1 *Lady.* Of either, madam.
Queen. Of neither, girl:
For if of joy, being altogether wanting,
It doth remember me the more of sorrow;
Or if of grief, being altogether had,
It adds more sorrow to my want of joy:
For what I have, I need not to repeat;
And what I want, it boots not to complain.
1 *Lady.* Madam, I'll sing.
Queen. 'Tis well that thou hast cause;
But thou should'st please me better, would'st thou weep.
1 *Lady.* I could weep, madam, would it do you good.
Queen. And I could weep, would weeping do me good,
And never borrow any tear of thee.—
But stay, here come the gardeners:
Let's step into the shadow of these trees.
My wretchedness unto a row of pins,
They'll talk of state; for every one doth so
Against a change. Woe is forerun with woe.
[QUEEN *and* Ladies *retire.*

Enter a Gardener *and two* Servants.

Gard. Go, bind thou up yond' dangling apricots,
Which, like unruly children, make their sire
Stoop with oppression of their prodigal weight:
Give some supportance to the bending twigs.—
Go thou, and like an executioner,
Cut off the heads of too-fast-growing sprays,
That look too lofty in our commonwealth:
All must be even in our government.—
You thus employ'd, I will go root away
The noisome weeds, that without profit suck
The soil's fertility from wholesome flowers.
1 *Serv.* Why should we, in the compass of a pale,

Keep law, and form, and due proportion,
Showing, as in a model, our firm estate,
When our sea-walled garden, the whole land,
Is full of weeds; her fairest flowers chok'd up,
Her fruit-trees all unprun'd, her hedges ruin'd,
Her knots disorder'd, and her wholesome herbs
Swarming with caterpillars?

Gard. Hold thy peace:—
He that hath suffer'd this disorder'd spring,
Hath now himself met with the fall of leaf:
The weeds that his broad-spreading leaves did shelter,
That seem'd in eating him to hold him up,
Are pluck'd up, root and all, by Bolingbroke,—
I mean, the earl of Wiltshire, Bushy, Green.

1 *Serv.* What, are they dead?

Gard. They are; and Bolingbroke
Hath seiz'd the wasteful king.—O! what pity is it,
That he had not so trimm'd and dress'd his land,
As we this garden! We at time of year
Do wound the bark, the skin of our fruit-trees,
Lest, being over-proud in sap and blood,
With too much riches it confound itself:
Had he done so to great and growing men,
They might have liv'd to bear, and he to taste
Their fruits of duty. Superfluous branches
We lop away, that bearing boughs may live:
Had he done so, himself had borne the crown,
Which waste of idle hours hath quite thrown down.

1 *Serv.* What, think you, then, the king shall be depos'd?

Gard. Depress'd he is already; and depos'd,
'Tis doubt, he will be: letters came last night
To a dear friend of the good duke of York's,
That tell black tidings.

Queen. O, I am press'd to death, through want of speaking!
[*Coming forward, with* Ladies.
Thou, old Adam's likeness, set to dress this garden,
How dares thy harsh rude tongue sound this unpleasing news?
What Eve, what serpent, hath suggested thee
To make a second fall of cursed man?
Why dost thou say king Richard is depos'd?
Dar'st thou, thou little better thing than earth,
Divine his downfall? Say, where, when, and how,
Cam'st thou by these ill tidings? speak, thou wretch.

Gard. Pardon me, madam: little joy have I
To breathe these news; yet what I say is true,
King Richard, he is in the mighty hold
Of Bolingbroke: their fortunes both are weigh'd:
In your lord's scale is nothing but himself,

And some few vanities that make him light;
But in the balance of great Bolingbroke,
Besides himself, are all the English peers,
And with that odds he weighs king Richard down.
Post you to London, and you'll find it so;
I speak no more than every one doth know.
Queen. Nimble mischance, that art so light of foot,
Doth not thy embassage belong to me,
And am I last that knows it? O! thou think'st
To serve me last, that I may longest keep
Thy sorrow in my breast.—Come, ladies, go,
To meet at London London's king in woe.—
What, was I born to this, that my sad look
Should grace the triumph of great Bolingbroke?—
Gardener, for telling me these news of woe,
I would the plants thou graft'st may never grow.
[*Exeunt* QUEEN *and* Ladies.
Gard. Poor queen! so that thy state might be no worse,
I would my skill were subject to thy curse.
Here did she fall a tear; here, in this place,
I'll set a bank of rue, sour herb of grace:
Rue, even for ruth, here shortly shall be seen,
In the remembrance of a weeping queen. [*Exeunt.*

ACT IV.

SCENE I.—London. Westminster Hall.

The Lords spiritual on the right side of the Throne; the Lords temporal on the left; the Commons below. Enter BOLINGBROKE, AUMERLE, SURREY, NORTHUMBERLAND, PERCY, FITZ WATER, *another* Lord, *the* BISHOP OF CARLISLE, *the* ABBOT OF WESTMINSTER, *and* Attendants. Officers *behind with* BAGOT.

Boling. Call forth Bagot.—
Now, Bagot, freely speak thy mind;
What thou dost know of noble Gloster's death,
Who wrought it with the king, and who perform'd
The bloody office of his timeless end.
Bagot. Then set before my face the lord Aumerle.
Boling. Cousin, stand forth, and look upon that man.
Bagot. My lord Aumerle, I know your daring tongue
Scorns to unsay what once it hath deliver'd.
In that dead time when Gloster's death was plotted.
I heard you say,—"Is not my arm of length,
That reacheth from the restful English court
As far as Calais, to my uncle's head?"

Amongst much other talk, that very time,
I heard you say, that you had rather refuse
The offer of a hundred thousand crowns,
Than Bolingbroke's return to England;
Adding withal, how blest this land would be
In this your cousin's death.
Aum. Princes, and noble lords,
What answer shall I make to this base man?
Shall I so much dishonor my fair stars,
On equal terms to give him chastisement?
Either I must, or have mine honor soil'd
With the attainder of his slanderous lips.—
There is my gage, the manual seal of death.
I will maintain what thou hast said is false
In thy heart-blood, though being all too base
To stain the temper of my knightly sword.
Boling. Bagot, forbear; thou shalt not take it up.
Aum. Excepting one, I would he were the best
In all this presence, that hath mov'd me so.
Fitz. If that thy valor stand on sympathy,
There is my gage, Aumerle, in gage to thine:
By that fair sun which shows me where thou stand'st,
I heard thee say, and vauntingly thou spak'st it,
That thou wert cause of noble Gloster's death.
Besides, I heard the banish'd Norfolk say,
That thou, Aumerle, didst send two of thy men
To execute the noble duke at Calais.
Aum. Some honest Christian trust me with a gage:
That Norfolk lies, here do I throw down this,
If he may be repeal'd to try his honor.
Boling. These differences shall all rest under gage,
Till Norfolk be repeal'd: repeal'd he shall be,
And, though mine enemy, restor'd again
To all his lands and signories: when he's return'd,
Against Aumerle we will enforce his trial.
Bishop. That honorable day shall ne'er be seen.
Many a time hath banish'd Norfolk fought
For Jesu Christ in glorious Christian field,
Streaming the ensign of the Christian cross
Against black pagans, Turks, and Saracens;
And toil'd with works of war, retir'd himself
To Italy; and there, at Venice, gave
His body to that pleasant country's earth,
And his pure soul unto his captain Christ,
Under whose colors he had fought so long.
Boling. Why, bishop, is Norfolk dead?
Bishop. As surely as I live, my lord.
Boling. Sweet peace conduct his sweet soul to the bosom

Of good old Abraham!—Lords appellants,
Your differences shall all rest under gage,
Till we assign you to your days of trial.

Enter YORK, *attended.*

York. Great duke of Lancaster, I come to thee
From plume-pluck'd Richard; who with willing soul
Adopts thee heir, and his high sceptre yields
To the possession of thy royal hand.
Ascend his throne, descending now from him,—
And long live Henry, of that name the fourth!
Boling. In heaven's name, I'll ascend the regal throne.
Bishop. Marry, heaven forbid!—
Worst in this royal presence may I speak,
Yet best beseeming me to speak the truth.
Would heaven, that any in this noble presence
Were enough noble to be upright judge
Of noble Richard! then, true nobless would
Learn him forbearance from so foul a wrong.
My lord of Hereford here, whom you call king,
Is a foul traitor to proud Hereford's king;
And if you crown him, let me prophesy,—
The blood of English shall manure the ground,
And future ages groan for this foul act;
Peace shall go sleep with Turks and infidels,
And in this seat of peace tumultuous wars
Shall kin with kin, and kind with kind confound;
Disorder, horror, fear, and mutiny,
Shall here inhabit, and this land be call'd
The field of Golgotha, and dead men's skulls.
O! if you raise this house against this house,
It will the wofullest division prove,
That ever fell upon this cursed earth.
Prevent, resist it, let it not be so,
Lest child, child's children, cry against you—woe!
North. Well have you argu'd, sir; and, for your pains,
Of capital treason we arrest you here.—
My lord of Westminster, be it your charge
To keep him safely till his day of trial.—
May it please you, lords, to grant the commons' suit.
Boling. Fetch hither Richard, that in common view
He may surrender: so we shall proceed
Without suspicion.
York. I will be his conductor. [*Exit.*
Boling. Lords, you that here are under our arrest,
Procure your sureties for your days of answer.—
[*To the* BISHOP.] Little are we beholden to your love,
And little look'd for at your helping hands.

Re-enter YORK, *with* KING RICHARD, *and* Officers *bearing the Crown, &c.*

K. Rich. Alack, why am I sent for to a king,
Before I have shook off the regal thoughts
Wherewith I reign'd? I hardly yet have learn'd
To insinuate, flatter, bow, and bend my limbs:
Give sorrow leave a while to tutor me
To this submission. Yet I well remember
The favors of these men: were they not mine?
Did they not sometime cry, all hail! to me?
God save the king!—Will no man say, amen?
Am I both priest and clerk? well then, amen.
God save the king! although I be not he;
And yet, amen, if heaven do think him me.—
To do what service am I sent for hither?

York. To do that office of thine own good will,
Which tired majesty did make thee offer;
The resignation of thy state and crown
To Henry Bolingbroke.

K. Rich. Give me the crown.—Here, cousin, seize the crown;
On this side my hand, and on that side yours.
Now is this golden crown like a deep well,
That owes two buckets, filling one another;
The emptier ever dancing in the air,
The other down, unseen, and full of water:
That bucket down, and full of tears, am I,
Drinking my griefs, whilst you mount up on high.

Boling. I thought you had been willing to resign.

K. Rich. My crown, I am; but still my griefs are mine:
You may my glories and my state depose,
But not my griefs; still am I king of those.

Boling. Part of your cares you give me with your crown.

K. Rich. Your cares set up, do not pluck my cares down.
My care is, loss of care, by old care done;
Your care is, gain of care, by new care won.
The cares I give, I have, though given away;
They tend the crown, yet still with me they stay.

Boling. Are you contented to resign the crown?

K. Rich. Ay, no;—no, ay;—for I must nothing be;
Therefore no no, for I resign to thee.
Now mark me, how I will undo myself:—
I give this heavy weight from off my head,
And this unwieldy sceptre from my hand,
The pride of kingly sway from out my heart;
With mine own tears I wash away my balm,
With mine own hands I give away my crown,
With mine own tongue deny my sacred state,

With mine own breath release all duteous rites:
All pomp and majesty I do forswear;
My manors, rents, revenues, I forego;
My acts, decrees, and statutes, I deny:
God pardon all oaths that are broke to me!
God keep all vows unbroke that swear to thee!
Make me, that nothing have, with nothing griev'd,
And thou with all pleas'd, that hast all achiev'd!
Long may'st thou live in Richard's seat to sit,
And soon lie Richard in an earthy pit!
God save king Henry, unking'd Richard says,
And send him many years of sunshine days!—
What more remains?
North. [*Offering a paper.*] No more, but that you read
These accusations, and these grievous crimes,
Committed by your person, and your followers,
Against the state and profit of this land;
That, by confessing them, the souls of men
May deem that you are worthily depos'd.
K. Rich. Must I do so? and must I ravel out
My weav'd up follies? Gentle Northumberland,
If thy offences were upon record,
Would it not shame thee, in so fair a troop,
To read a lecture of them? If thou would'st,
There should'st thou find one heinous article,—
Containing the deposing of a king,
And cracking the strong warrant of an oath:—
Nay, all of you, that stand and look upon me,
Whilst that my wretchedness doth bait myself,—
Though some of you, with Pilate, wash your hands,
Showing an outward pity; yet you Pilates
Have here deliver'd me to my sour cross,
And water cannot wash away your sin.
North. My lord, despatch; read o'er these articles.
K. Rich. Mine eyes are full of tears, I cannot see:
And yet salt water blinds them not so much,
But they can see a sort of traitors here.
Nay, if I turn mine eyes upon myself,
I find myself a traitor with the rest;
For I have given here my soul's consent,
To undeck the pompous body of a king;
Made glory base, and sovereignty a slave,
Proud majesty a subject, state a peasant.
North. My lord,—
K. Rich. No lord of thine, thou proud, insulting man,
Nor no man's lord; I have no name, no title,—
No, not that name was given me at the font,—
But 'tis usurp'd:—alack, the heavy day,

That I have worn so many winters out,
And know not now what name to call myself!
O! that I were a mockery king of snow,
Standing before the sun of Bolingbroke,
To melt myself away in water drops!—
Good king,—great king,—(and yet not greatly good,)
And if my word be sterling yet in England,
Let it command a mirror hither straight,
That it may show me what a face I have,
Since it is bankrupt of his majesty.
Boling. Go some of you, and fetch a looking-glass.
[*Exit an* Attendant.
North. Read o'er this paper, while the glass doth come.
K. Rich. Fiend! thou torment'st me!
Boling. Urge it no more, my lord Northumberland.
North. The commons will not then be satisfied.
K. Rich. They shall be satisfied: I'll read enough,
When I do see the very book indeed
Where all my sins are writ, and that's—myself.

Re-enter Attendant, *with a glass.*

Give me the glass, and therein will I read.—
No deeper wrinkles yet? Hath sorrow struck
So many blows upon this face of mine,
And made no deeper wounds?—O, flattering glass!
Like to my followers in prosperity,
Thou dost beguile me. Was this face the face,
That every day under his household roof
Did keep ten thousand men? Was this the face,
That like the sun did make beholders wink?
Was this the face, that fac'd so many follies,
And was at last out-fac'd by Bolingbroke?
A brittle glory shineth in this face:
As brittle as the glory is the face;
[*Dashes the glass against the ground.*
For there it is, crack'd in a hundred shivers.—
Mark, silent king, the moral of this sport,—
How soon my sorrow hath destroy'd my face.
Boling. The shadow of your sorrow hath destroy'd
The shadow of your face.
K. Rich. Say that again.
The shadow of my sorrow? Ha! let's see:—
'Tis very true, my grief lies all within;
And these external manners of lament
Are merely shadows to the unseen grief,
That swells with silence in the tortur'd soul;
There lies the substance: and I thank thee, king,
For thy great bounty, that not only giv'st

Me cause to wail, but teachest me the way
How to lament the cause. I'll beg one boon,
And then be gone and trouble you no more.
Shall I obtain it?
Boling. Name it, fair cousin.
K. Rich. Fair cousin! I am greater than a king:
For when I was a king, my flatterers
Were then but subjects; being now a subject,
I have a king here to my flatterer.
Being so great, I have no need to beg.
Boling. Yet ask.
K. Rich. And shall I have?
Boling. You shall.
R. Rich. Then give me leave to go.
Boling. Whither?
K. Rich. Whither you will, so I were from your sights.
Boling. Go, some of you; convey him to the Tower.
K. Rich. O, good! Convey?—Conveyers are you all,
That rise thus nimbly by a true king's fall.
[*Exeunt* KING RICHARD, *some* Lords, *and a* Guard.
Boling. On Wednesday next we solemnly set down
Our coronation: lords, prepare yourselves. [*Exeunt.*

ACT V.

SCENE I.—London. *A Street leading to the Tower.*

Enter QUEEN *and* Attendants.

Queen. This way the king will come; this is the way
To Julius Cæsar's ill-erected tower,
To whose flint bosom my condemnèd lord
Is doom'd a prisoner by proud Bolingbroke.
Here let us rest, if this rebellious earth
Have any resting for her true king's queen.—
But soft, but see, or rather do not see,
My fair rose wither: yet look up, behold,
That you in pity may dissolve to dew,
And wash him fresh again with true-love tears.—

Enter KING RICHARD *and* Guards.

Ah! thou, the model where old Troy did stand,
Thou map of honor, thou king Richard's tomb,
And not king Richard; thou most beauteous inn,
Why should hard-favor'd grief be lodg'd in thee,
When triumph is become an alehouse guest?

K. Rich. Join not with grief, fair woman, do not so,
To make my end too sudden: learn, good soul,
To think our former state a happy dream;
From which awak'd, the truth of what we are
Shows us but this: I am sworn brother, sweet,
To grim necessity; and he and I
Will keep a league till death. Hie thee to France,
And cloister thee in some religious house:
Our holy lives must win a new world's crown,
Which our profane hours here have stricken down.

Queen. What, is my Richard both in shape and mind
Transform'd and weakened? Hath Bolingbroke
Depos'd thine intellect? hath he been in thy heart?
The lion, dying, thrusteth forth his paw,
And wounds the earth, if nothing else, with rage
To be o'erpower'd; and wilt thou, pupil-like,
Take thy correction mildly, kiss the rod,
And fawn on rage with base humility,
Which art a lion, and a king of beasts?

K. Rich. A king of beasts, indeed; if aught but beasts,
I had been still a happy king of men.
Good sometime queen, prepare thee hence for France:
Think I am dead; and that even here thou tak'st,
As from my death-bed, my last living leave.
In winter's tedious night sit by the fire
With good old folks, and let them tell thee tales
Of woful ages long ago betid;
And ere thou bid good night, to quit their grief,
Tell thou the lamentable tale of me,
And send the hearers weeping to their beds.

Enter NORTHUMBERLAND, *attended.*

North. My lord, the mind of Bolingbroke is chang'd:
You must to Pomfret, not unto the Tower.—
And, madam, there is order ta'en for you;
With all swift speed you must away to France.

K. Rich. Northumberland, thou ladder, wherewithal
The mounting Bolingbroke ascends my throne,
The time shall not be many hours of age
More than it is, ere foul sin gathering head
Shall break into corruption: thou shalt think,
Though he divide the realm, and give thee half,
It is too little, helping him to all;
He shall think, that thou, which know'st the way
To plant unrightful kings, wilt know again,
Being ne'er so little urg'd, another way
To pluck him headlong from the usurpèd throne.
The love of wicked friends converts to fear;

That fear to hate; and hate turns one, or both,
To worthy danger and deservèd death.
North. My guilt be on my head, and there an end.
Take leave, and part; for you must part forthwith.
K. Rich. Doubly divorc'd!—Bad men, ye violate
A twofold marriage,—'twixt my crown and me,
And then, betwixt me and my married wife.—
Let me unkiss the oath 'twixt thee and me;
And yet not so, for with a kiss 'twas made.—
Part us, Northumberland; I towards the north,
Where shivering cold and sickness pines the clime;
My wife to France,—from whence, set forth in pomp,
She came adorned hither like sweet May,
Sent back like Hallowmas, or short'st of day.
Queen. And must we be divided? must we part?
K. Rich. Ay, hand from hand, my love, and heart from heart.
Queen. Banish us both, and send the king with me.
North. That were some love, but little policy.
Queen. Then whither he goes, thither let me go.
K. Rich. So two, together weeping, make one woe.
Weep thou for me in France, I for thee here;
Better far off than—near, be ne'er the near'.
Go, count thy way with sighs, I mine with groans.
Queen. So longest way shall have the longest moans.
K. Rich. Twice for one step I'll groan, the way being short,
And piece the way out with a heavy heart.
Come, come, in wooing sorrow let's be brief,
Since, wedding it, there is such length in grief
One kiss shall stop our mouths, and dumbly part;
Thus give I mine, and thus take I thy heart. [*They kiss.*
Queen. Give me mine own again; 'twere no good part,
To take on me to keep and kill thy heart. [*They kiss again.*
So, now I have mine own again, be gone,
That I may strive to kill it with a groan.
K. Rich. We make woe wanton with this fond delay:
Once more, adieu; the rest let sorrow say. [*Exeunt.*

SCENE II.—London. *A Room in the* DUKE OF YORK'S *Palace.*

Enter YORK *and his* DUCHESS.

Duch. My lord, you told me you would tell the rest,
When weeping made you break the story off,
Of our two cousins coming into London.
York. Where did I leave?
Duch. At that sad stop, my lord,
Where rude misgovern'd hands, from windows' tops,
Threw dust and rubbish on king Richard's head.

York. Then, as I said, the duke, great Bolingbroke,
Mounted upon a hot and fiery steed,
Which his aspiring rider seem'd to know,—
With slow but stately pace kept on his course,
While all tongues cried—"God save thee, Bolingbroke!"
You would have thought the very windows spake,
So many greedy looks of young and old
Through casements darted their desiring eyes
Upon his visage; and that all the walls
With painted imagery had said at once,—
"Heaven preserve thee! welcome, Bolingbroke!"
Whilst he, from one side to the other turning,
Bare-headed, lower than his proud steed's neck,
Bespake them thus,—"I thank you, countrymen:"
And thus still doing, thus he pass'd along.
Duch. Alas, poor Richard! where rode he the while?
York. As in a theatre, the eyes of men,
After a well-grac'd actor leaves the stage,
Are idly bent on him that enters next,
Thinking his prattle to be tedious;
Even so, or with much more contempt, men's eyes
Did scowl on Richard; no man cried, God save him;
No joyful tongue gave him his welcome home:
But dust was thrown upon his sacred head;
Which with such gentle sorrow he shook off,
His face still combating with tears and smiles,
The badges of his grief and patience;—
That had not heaven, for some strong purpose, steel'd
The hearts of men, they must perforce have melted,
And barbarism itself have pitied him.
But heaven hath a hand in these events,
To whose high will we bound our calm contents.
To Bolingbroke are we sworn subjects now,
Whose state and honor I for aye allow.
Duch. Here comes my son Aumerle.
York. Aumerle that was;
But that is lost for being Richard's friend,
And, madam, you must call him Rutland now:
I am in parliament pledge for his truth,
And lasting fealty to the new-made king.

Enter AUMERLE.

Duch. Welcome, my son: who are the violets now,
That strew the green lap of the new-come spring?
Aum. Madam, I know not, nor I greatly care not:
God knows, I had as lief be none as one.
York. Well, bear you well in this new spring of time,

Lest you be cropp'd before you come to prime.
What news from Oxford? hold those jousts and triumphs?
  Aum. For aught I know, my lord, they do.
  York. You will be there, I know.
  Aum. If heaven prevent it not, I purpose so.
  York. What seal is that, that hangs without thy bosom?
Yea, look'st thou pale? let me see the writing.
  Aum. My lord, 'tis nothing.
  York. No matter then who sees it:
I will be satisfied; let me see the writing.
  Aum. I do beseech your grace to pardon me:
It is a matter of small consequence,
Which for some reasons I would not have seen.
  York. Which for some reasons, sir, I mean to see.
I fear, I fear,—
  Duch. What should you fear?
'Tis nothing but some bond he's enter'd into
For gay apparel 'gainst the triumph day.
  York. Bound to himself! what doth he with a bond
That he is bound to? Wife, thou art a fool.—
Boy, let me see the writing.
  Aum. I do beseech you, pardon me; I may not show it.
  York. I will be satisfied; let me see it, I say.
[*Snatches it, and reads.*
Treason! foul treason!—villain! traitor! slave!
  Duch. What is the matter, my lord?
  York. Ho! who is within there?

Enter a Servant.

Saddle my horse.—
Heaven for its mercy, what treachery is here!
  Duch. Why, what is it, my lord?
  York. Give me my boots, I say; saddle my horse.—
Now, by mine honor, by my life, my troth,
I will appeach the villain. [*Exit* Servant.
  Duch. What's the matter?
  York. Peace, foolish woman.
  Duch. I will not peace.—What is the matter, son?
  Aum. Good mother, be content; it is no more
Than my poor life must answer.
  Duch. Thy life answer!
  York. Bring me my boots:—I will unto the king.

Re-enter Servant *with boots.*

  Duch. Strike him, Aumerle.—Poor boy, thou art amaz'd.—
[*To* Servant.] Hence, villain! never more come in my sight.
[*Exit* Servant.
  York. Give me my boots, I say.

Duch. Why, York, what wilt thou do?
Wilt thou not hide the trespass of thine own?
And wilt thou pluck my fair son from mine age,
And rob me of a happy mother's name?
Is he not like thee? is he not thine own?

York. Thou fond mad woman,
Wilt thou conceal this dark conspiracy?
A dozen of them here have ta'en the sacrament,
And interchangeably set down their hands,
To kill the king at Oxford.

Duch. He shall be none;
We'll keep him here: then, what is that to him?

York. Away, fond woman! were he twenty times
My son, I would appeach him. [*Exit.*

Duch. After, Aumerle! Mount thee upon his horse;
Spur, post, and get before him to the king,
And beg thy pardon ere he do accuse thee.
I'll not be long behind; though I be old,
I doubt not but to ride as fast as York:
And never will I rise up from the ground,
Till Bolingbroke have pardon'd thee. Away, be gone!
[*Exeunt.*

SCENE III.—Windsor. *A room in the Castle.*

Enter BOLINGBROKE, *as King;* PERCY, *and other* Lords.

Boling. Can no man tell of my unthrifty son?
'Tis full three months since I did see him last:—
If any plague hang over us, 'tis he.
I would to heaven, my lords, he might be found:
Enquire at London, 'mongst the taverns there;
For there, they say, he daily doth frequent,
With unrestrainèd loose companions,—
Even such, they say, as stand in narrow lanes,
And beat our watch, and rob our passengers;
While he, young, wanton, and effeminate boy,
Takes on the point of honor to support
So dissolute a crew.
As dissolute as desperate; yet, through both
I see some sparkles of a better hope,
Which elder days may happily bring forth.—
But who comes here?

Enter AUMERLE, *hastily.*

Aum. Where is the king?

Boling. What means our cousin, that he stares and looks
So wildly?

Aum. Heaven save your grace! I do beseech your majesty,
To have some conference with your grace alone.
Boling. Withdraw yourselves, and leave us here alone.—
[*Exeunt* PERCY *and* Lords.
What is the matter with our cousin now?
Aum. [*Kneels.*] For ever may my knees grow to the earth,
My tongue cleave to my roof within my mouth,
Unless a pardon, ere I rise or speak.
Boling. Intended, or committed, was this fault?
If on the first, how heinous e'er it be,
To win thy after-love I pardon thee.
Aum. Then give me leave that I may turn the key,
That no man enter till my tale be done.
Boling. Have thy desire. [AUMERLE *locks the door.*
York. [*Within.*] My liege, beware; look to thyself;
Thou hast a traitor in thy presence there.
Boling. [*Drawing.*] Villain, I'll make thee safe.
Aum. Stay thy revengeful hand; thou hast no cause to fear.
York. [*Within.*] Open the door, secure, fool-hardy king:
Shall I, for love, speak treason to thy face?
Open the door, or I will break it open.
[BOLINGBROKE *unlocks the door; and afterwards, relocks it.*

Enter YORK.

Boling. What is the matter, uncle? speak;
Recover breath; tell us how near is danger,
That we may arm us to encounter it.
York. Peruse this writing here, and thou shalt know
The treason that my haste forbids me show.
Aum. Remember, as thou read'st, thy promise past:
I do repent me; read not my name there;
My heart is not confederate with my hand.
York. It was, villain, ere thy hand did set it down.—
I tore it from the traitor's bosom, king;
Fear, and not love, begets his penitence:
Forget to pity him, lest thy pity prove
A serpent that will sting thee to the heart.
Boling. O heinous, strong, and bold conspiracy!—
O loyal father of a treacherous son!
Thou sheer, immaculate, and silver fountain,
From whence this stream through muddy passages
Hath held his current, and defil'd himself!
Thy overflow of good converts to bad;
And thy abundant goodness shall excuse
This deadly blot in thy digressing son.
York. Mine honor lives when his dishonor dies,
Or my sham'd life in his dishonor lies:

Thou kill'st me in his life; giving him breath,
The traitor lives, the true man's put to death.

Duch. [*Within.*] What ho! my liege! for heaven's sake let me in.

Boling. What shrill-voic'd suppliant makes this eager cry?

Duch. [*Within.*] A woman, and thine aunt, great king; 'tis I.
Speak with me, pity me, open the door:
A beggar begs, that never begg'd before.

Boling. Our scene is altered from a serious thing,
And now chang'd to "The Beggar and the King."—
My dangerous cousin, let your mother in:
I know she's come to pray for your foul sin.

[AUMERLE *unlocks the door.*

York. If thou do pardon, whosoever pray,
More sins, for this forgiveness, prosper may.
This fester'd joint cut off, the rest rests sound;
This, let alone, will all the rest confound.

Enter DUCHESS.

Duch. O king, believe not this hard-hearted man!
Love, loving not itself, none other can.

York. Thou frantic woman, what dost thou make here?

Duch. Sweet York, be patient.—[*Kneels.*] Hear me, gentle liege.

Boling. Rise up, good aunt.

Duch. Not yet, I thee beseech:
For ever will I walk upon my knees,
And never see day that the happy sees,
Till thou give joy; until thou bid me joy,
By pardoning Rutland, my transgressing boy.

Aum. [*Kneels.*] Unto my mother's prayers, I bend my knee.

York. [*Kneels.*] Against them both, my true joints bended be.
Ill may'st thou thrive, if thou grant any grace!

Duch. Pleads he in earnest? look upon his face;
His eyes do drop no tears, his prayers are in jest;
His words come from his mouth, ours from our breast:
He prays but faintly, and would be denied;
We pray with heart and soul, and all beside:
His weary joints would gladly rise, I know;
Our knees shall kneel till to the ground they grow:
His prayers are full of false hypocrisy;
Ours of true zeal and deep integrity.
Our prayers do out-pray his; then let them have
That mercy which true prayers ought to have.

Boling. Good aunt, stand up.

Duch. Nay, do not say—"stand up;"
But, "pardon" first, and afterwards, "stand up."
An if I were thy nurse, thy tongue to teach,

"Pardon" should be the first word of thy speech.
I never long'd to hear a word till now;
Say—"pardon," king; let pity teach thee how:
The word is short, but not so short as sweet;
No word like "pardon," for kings' mouths so meet.
Boling. Good aunt, stand up.
Duch. I do not sue to stand;
Pardon is all the suit I have in hand.
Boling. I pardon him, as heaven shall pardon me.
Duch. O happy vantage of a kneeling knee!
Yet am I sick for fear: speak it again;
Twice saying "pardon" doth not pardon twain,
But makes one pardon strong.
Boling. With all my heart
I pardon him.
Duch. A god on earth thou art.
Boling. But for our trusty brother-in-law, and the abbot,
With all the rest of that consorted crew,
Destruction straight shall dog them at the heels.—
Good uncle, help to order several powers
To Oxford, or where'er these traitors are:
They shall not live within this world, I swear,
But I will have them, if I once know where.
Uncle, farewell:—and cousin too, adieu:
Your mother well hath pray'd, and prove you true.
Duch. Come, my old son:—I pray heaven make thee new.
[*Exeunt.*

SCENE IV.—Windsor. *Another room in the Castle.*

Enter SIR PIERCE OF EXTON *and a* Servant.

Exton. Didst thou not mark the king, what words he spake?
"Have I no friend will rid me of this living fear?"
Was it not so?
Serv. Those were his very words.
Exton. "Have I no friend?" quoth he: he spake it twice,
And urg'd it twice together,—did he not?
Serv. He did.
Exton. And speaking it, he wistly look'd on me;
As who should say,—I would thou wert the man
That would divorce this terror from my heart,—
Meaning the king at Pomfret. Come, let's go:
I am the king's friend, and will rid his foe. [*Exeunt.*

SCENE V.—Pomfret. *The Dungeon of the Castle.*

Enter KING RICHARD.

K. Rich. I have been studying how I may compare
This prison, where I live, unto the world:
And, for because the world is populous,
And here is not a creature but myself,
I cannot do it;—yet I'll hammer't out.
Still breeding thoughts people this little world;
In humors, like the people of this world,
For no thought is contented. The better sort,—
As thoughts of things divine,—are intermix'd
With scruples, and do set the word itself
Against the word:
As thus,—"Come, little ones;" and then again,—
"It is as hard to come, as for a camel
To thread the postern of a needle's eye."
Thoughts tending to ambition, they do plot
Unlikely wonders: how these vain weak nails
May tear a passage through the flinty ribs
Of this hard world, my ragged prison walls;
And, for they cannot, die in their own pride.
Thoughts tending to content, flatter themselves
That they are not the first of fortune's slaves,
Nor shall not be the last:
Thus play I, in one person, many people,
And none contented: sometimes am I king;
Then, treason makes me wish myself a beggar,
And so I am: then, crushing penury
Persuades me I was better when a king;
Then, am I king'd again: and, by and by,
Think that I am unking'd by Bolingbroke,
And straight am nothing.—[*Music.*] Music do I hear?
Ha, ha! keep time:—how sour sweet music is,
When time is broke, and no proportion kept!
So is it in the music of men's lives.
And here have I the daintiness of ear
To check time broke in a disorder'd string;
But, for the concord of my state and time,
Had not an ear to hear my true time broke.
I wasted time, and now doth time waste me;
For now hath time made me his numbering clock:
My thoughts are minutes; and, with sighs, they jar
Their watches on unto mine eyes, the outward watch,
Whereto my finger, like a dial's point,
Is pointing still, in cleansing them from tears.
Now, sir, the sounds that tell what hour it is,

Are clamorous groans, that strike upon my heart,
Which is the bell: so sighs, and tears, and groans,
Show minutes, times, and hours:—but my time
Runs posting on in Bolingbroke's proud joy,
While I stand fooling here, his Jack o' the clock.
This music mads me; let it sound no more;
For though it have holp madmen to their wits,
In me, it seems, it will make wise men mad.
Yet, blessing on his heart that gives it me!
For 'tis a sign of love; and love to Richard
Is a strange brooch in this all-hating world.

Enter Groom.

Groom. Hail, royal prince!
K. Rich. Thanks, noble peer;
The cheapest of us is ten groats too dear.
What art thou? and how com'st thou hither,
Where no man ever comes, but that sad dog
That brings me food to make misfortune live?
Groom. I was a poor groom of thy stable, king,
When thou wert king; who, travelling towards York,
With much ado, at length have gotten leave
To look upon my sometime royal master's face.
O, how it yearn'd my heart, when I beheld,
In London streets, that coronation day,
When Bolingbroke rode on roan Barbary!
That horse that thou so often hast bestrid,
That horse that I so carefully have dress'd!
K. Rich. Rode he on Barbary? Tell me, gentle friend,
How went he under him?
Groom. So proudly, as if he disdain'd the ground.
K. Rich. So proud that Bolingbroke was on his back!
That jade hath eat bread from my royal hand;
This hand hath made him proud with clapping him.
Would he not stumble? Would he not fall down,
(Since pride must have a fall) and break the neck
Of that proud man that did usurp his back?
Forgiveness, horse! why do I rail on thee,
Since thou, created to be aw'd by man,
Wast born to bear? I was not made a horse;
And yet I bear a burden like an ass,
Spur-gall'd, and tir'd, by jaunting Bolingbroke.

Enter Keeper, *with a dish.*

Keep. [*To the* Groom.] Fellow, give place; here is no longer stay.
K. Rich. If thou love me, 'tis time thou wert away.
Groom. What my tongue dares not, that my heart shall say.
[*Exit.*

Keep. My lord, will't please you to fall to?
K. Rich. Taste of it first, as thou art wont to do.
Keep. My lord, I dare not: Sir Pierce of Exton, who lately came from the king, commands the contrary.
K. Rich. The foul fiend take Henry of Lancaster, and thee!
Patience is stale, and I am weary of it. [*Strikes the* Keeper.
Keep. Help, help, help!

Enter SIR PIERCE OF EXTON, *and* Servants, *armed.*

K. Rich. How now! what means death in this rude assault?
Villain, thine own hand yields thy death's instrument.
[*Snatching a weapon, and killing one, and then another: then* EXTON *strikes him down,*
That hand shall burn in never-quenching fire,
That staggers thus my person.—Exton, thy fierce hand
Hath with the king's blood stain'd the king's own land.
Mount, mount, my soul! thy seat is up on high;
Whilst my gross flesh sinks downward, here to die. [*Dies.*
Exton. As full of valor, as of royal blood:
Both have I spilt;—O, would the deed were good!
This dead king to the living king I'll bear:—
Take hence the rest, and give them burial here. [*Exeunt.*

SCENE VI.—Windsor. *A Room in the Castle.*

Flourish. Enter BOLINGBROKE *as King,* YORK, Lords, *and* Attendants.

Boling. Kind uncle York, the latest news we hear
Is, that the rebels have consum'd with fire
Our town of Cicester in Glostershire;
But whether they be ta'en, or slain, we hear not.

Enter NORTHUMBERLAND.

Welcome, my lord: what is the news?
North. First, to thy sacred state wish I all happiness.
The next news is,—I have to London sent
The heads of Salisbury, Spencer, Blunt, and Kent:
The manner of their taking may appear
At large discoursèd in this paper here. [*Presenting a paper.*
Boling. We thank thee, gentle Percy, for thy pains;
And to thy worth will add right worthy gains.

Enter FITZWATER.

Fitz. My lord, I have from Oxford sent to London
The heads of Brocas, and Sir Bennet Seely,
Two of the dangerous consorted traitors,
That sought at Oxford thy dire overthrow.
Boling. Thy pains, Fitzwater, shall not be forgot;
Right noble is thy merit, well I wot.

Enter PERCY, *with the* BISHOP OF CARLISLE.

Percy. The grand conspirator, abbot of Westminster,
With clog of conscience and sour melancholy,
Hath yielded up his body to the grave;
But here is Carlisle living, to abide
Thy kingly doom and sentence of his pride.
Boling. Carlisle, this is your doom:—
Choose out some secret place, some reverend room,
More than thou hast, and with it joy thy life;
So, as thou liv'st in peace, die free from strife:
For though mine enemy thou hast ever been,
High sparks of honor in thee have I seen.

Enter EXTON, *with* Attendants *bearing a coffin.*

Exton. Great king, within this coffin I present
Thy buried fear: herein all breathless lies
The mightiest of thy greatest enemies,
Richard of Bourdeaux, by me hither brought.
Boling. Exton, I thank thee not; for thou has wrought
A deed of slander, with thy fatal hand,
Upon my head, and all this famous land.
Exton. From your own mouth, my lord, did I this deed.
Boling. They love not poison that do poison need,
Nor do I thee: though I did wish him dead,
I hate the murderer, love him murderèd.
The guilt of conscience take thou for thy labor,
But neither my good word, nor princely favor:
With Cain go wander through the shade of night,
And never show thy head by day nor night.—
Lords, I protest, my soul is full of woe,
That blood should sprinkle me to make me grow:
Come, mourn with me for that I do lament,
And put on sullen black incontinent:
I'll make a voyage to the Holy Land,
To wash this blood off from my guilty hand:—
March sadly after; grace my mournings here,
In weeping after this untimely bier. [*Exeunt.*

THE HISTORY OF

KING HENRY IV.

PART I.

SHAKSPEARE seems to have designed that the whole series of action, from the beginning of *Richard* II. to the end of *Henry* V. should be considered as one work upon one plan, only broken into parts by the necessity of exhibition. In following out this design, the Poet has drawn largely from "The Chronicles" for his strictly historical characters and incidents; thus exhibiting the men and deeds of the times vividly and impressively, and presenting to the student of History the "truest conceptions of England's feudal ages." In this play Shakspeare has introduced a group of imaginary characters, who, although not strictly historical, are yet faithful types of certain phases of society in the period represented. These fictitious personages are made to surround the young and dissolute Prince Henry, and, with their rich comic humor, serve to make the two parts of Henry IV. the most attractive of the whole historical series. Foremost in this imaginary creation looms the unapproachable *Falstaff*, a character so rich in humor and so lifelike in its embodiment, that we feel it impossible not to conceive him to be as strictly historical in his delineation as Henry IV. himself. In our necessary revision of the humors of the fat knight, we have endeavored *in all earnestness* not to divest him of his inimitable characteristics.

The transactions contained in this Historical Drama are comprised within the period of about ten months, for the action commences with the battle of Halidown Hill, or Holmedon, which was fought on Holy-rood day (the 14th of September), 1402, and it closes with the defeat and death of Hotspur, at Shrewsbury, which engagement happened on Saturday, the 21st July, 1403.

PERSONS REPRESENTED.

KING HENRY THE FOURTH.
HENRY, *Prince of Wales*, } *Sons to the* King.
PRINCE JOHN OF LANCASTER, } *Sons to the* King.
RALPH NEVILLE, *Earl of* Westmoreland.
Sir WALTER BLUNT.
THOMAS PERCY, *Earl of* Worcester.

HENRY PERCY, *Earl of* Northumberland.
HENRY PERCY, *surnamed* HOTSPUR, *his Son.*
EDMUND MORTIMER, *Earl of* March.
SCROOP, *Archbishop of* York.
ARCHIBALD, *Earl of* Douglas.
OWEN GLENDOWER.
Sir RICHARD VERNON.
Sir JOHN FALSTAFF.
Sir MICHAEL, *a Friend of the Archbishop of* York.
POINS.
GADSHILL.
PETO.
BARDOLPH

LADY PERCY, *Wife to* Hotspur, *and Sister to* Mortimer.
LADY MORTIMER, *Daughter to* Glendower, *and Wife to* Mortimer.
Mistress QUICKLY, *Hostess of the* Boar's Head Tavern *in* Eastcheap.

Lords, Officers, Sheriff, Vintner, Chamberlain, Drawers, Carriers, Travellers, and Attendants.

SCENE,—ENGLAND.

ACT I.

SCENE I.—London. *A Room in the Palace.*

Enter KING HENRY, WESTMORELAND, *Sir* WALTER BLUNT, *and others.*

K. Hen. So shaken as we are, so wan with care,
Find we a time for frighted peace to pant,
And breathe short-winded accents of new broils
To be commenc'd in strands afar remote.
No more the thirsty entrance of this soil
Shall daub her lips with her own children's blood;
No more shall trenching war channel her fields,
Nor bruise her flow'rets with the armèd hoofs
Of hostile paces: those opposèd eyes,
Which, like the meteors of a troubled heaven,
All of one nature, of one substance bred,
Did lately meet in the intestine shock
And furious close of civil butchery,
Shall now, in mutual well-beseeming ranks,
March all one way, and be no more oppos'd
Against acquaintance, kindred, and allies:
The edge of war, like an ill-sheathed knife,
No more shall cut his master. Therefore, friends,
As far as to the sepulchre of Christ,
Forthwith a power of English shall we levy;
To chase these pagans, in those holy fields,

Over whose acres walk'd those blessed feet,
Which, fourteen hundred years ago, were nail'd
For our advantage on the bitter cross.
Then, let me hear
Of you, my gentle cousin Westmoreland,
What yesternight our council did decree,
In forwarding this dear expedience.
West. My liege, this haste was hot in question,
And many limits of the charge set down
But yesternight: when, all athwart, there came
A post from Wales loaden with heavy news;
Whose worst was, that the noble Mortimer,
Leading the men of Herefordshire to fight
Against the irregular and wild Glendower,
Was by the rude hands of that Welshman taken,
A thousand of his people butchered.
K. Hen. It seems, then, that the tidings of this broil
Brake off our business for the Holy Land.
West. This, match'd with other, did, my gracious lord;
For more uneven and unwelcome news
Came from the north, and thus it did import:
On Holy-rood day, the gallant Hotspur there,
Young Harry Percy, and brave Archibald,
That ever-valiant and approvèd Scot,
At Holmedon met,
Where they did spend a sad and bloody hour;
As by discharge of their artillery,
And shape of likelihood, the news was told;
For he that brought them, in the very heat
And pride of their contention did take horse,
Uncertain of the issue any way.
K. Hen. Here is a dear, and true-industrious friend,
Sir Walter Blunt, new lighted from his horse,
Stain'd with the variation of each soil
Betwixt that Holmedon and this seat of ours;
And he hath brought us smooth and welcome news.
The earl of Douglas is discomfited:
Ten thousand bold Scots, two and twenty knights,
Balk'd in their own blood, did Sir Walter see
On Holmedon's plains: of prisoners, Hotspur took
Mordake earl of Fife, and eldest son
To beaten Douglas, and the earls of Athol,
Of Murray, Angus, and Menteith:
And is not this an honorable spoil?
A gallant prize? ha, cousin, is it not?
West. In faith,
It is a conquest for a prince to boast of.
K. Hen. Yea, there thou mak'st me sad, and mak'st me sin

In envy that my lord Northumberland
Should be the father to so blest a son,—
A son who is the theme of honor's tongue;
Amongst a grove, the very straightest plant;
Who is sweet Fortune's minion, and her pride:
Whilst I, by looking on the praise of him,
See riot and dishonor stain the brow
Of my young Harry. O that it could be prov'd,
That some night-tripping fairy had exchang'd
In cradle-clothes our children where they lay,
And call'd mine Percy, his Plantagenet!
Then would I have his Harry, and he mine:
But let him from our thoughts.—What think you, coz,
Of this young Percy's pride? the prisoners,
Which he in this adventure hath surpris'd,
To his own use he keeps; and sends me word,
I shall have none but Mordake earl of Fife.
West. This is his uncle's teaching, this is Worcester,
Malevolent to you in all aspécts;
Which makes him prune himself, and bristle up
The crest of youth against your dignity.
K. Hen. But I have sent for him to answer this;
And for this cause awhile we must neglect
Our holy purpose to Jerusalem.
Cousin, on Wednesday next our council we
Will hold at Windsor; so inform the lords:
But come yourself with speed to us again;
For more is to be said, and to be done,
Than out of anger can be uttered.
West. I will, my liege. [*Exeunt.*

SCENE II.—London. *Another Room in the Palace.*

Enter PRINCE HENRY *and* FALSTAFF.

Fal. Now, Hal, what time of day is it, lad?

P. Hen. Thou art so fat-witted, with drinking of old sack, and unbuttoning thee after supper, and sleeping upon benches after noon, that thou hast forgotten to demand that truly, which thou wouldst truly know. What hast thou to do with the time of the day? unless hours were cups of sack, and minutes capons, I see no reason why thou should'st be so superfluous to demand the time of the day.

Fal. Indeed, you come near me now, Hall; for we that take purses, go by the moon and the seven stars, and not by Phœbus,—he, "that wandering knight so fair." And, I pr'ythee, sweet wag, when thou art king,—as, heaven save thy grace, (majesty, I should say, for grace thou wilt have none,)—

P. Hen. What! none?

Fal. No, by my troth; not so much as will serve to be prologue to an egg and butter.

P. Hen. Well, how then? come, roundly, roundly.

Fal. Marry, then, sweet wag, when thou art king, let not us, that are squires of the night's body, be called thieves of the day's beauty: let us be Diana's foresters, gentlemen of the shade, minions of the moon; and let men say, we be men of good government, being governed, as the sea is, by our noble and chaste mistress the moon, under whose countenance we steal.

P. Hen. Thou sayest well, and it holds well, too; for the fortune of us, that are the moon's men, doth ebb and flow like the sea, being governed, as the sea is, by the moon. As for proof, now: a purse of gold most resolutely snatched on Monday night, and most dissolutely spent on Tuesday morning.

Fal. Thou sayest true, lad. And is not my hostess of the tavern a most sweet wench?

P. Hen. As the honey of Hybla, my old lad of the castle. And is not a buff jerkin a most sweet robe of durance?

Fal. How now, how now, mad wag! what, in thy quips, and thy quiddities? what a plague have I to do with a buff jerkin?

P. Hen. Why, what a plague have I to do with my hostess of the tavern?

Fal. Well, thou hast called her to a reckoning many a time and oft.

P. Hen. Did I ever call for thee to pay thy part?

Fal. No; I'll give thee thy due; thou hast paid all there.

P. Hen. Yea, and elsewhere, so far as my coin would stretch; and where it would not, I have used my credit.

Fal. Yea, and so used it, that were it not here apparent that thou art heir apparent,—but, I pr'ythee, sweet wag, shall there be gallows standing in England when thou art king? and resolution thus fobbed, as it is, with the rusty curb of old father antick, the law. Do not thou, when thou art king, hang a thief.

P. Hen. No; thou shalt.

Fal. Shall I? O rare! O, I'll be a brave judge.

P. Hen. Thou judgest false already: I mean, thou shalt have the hanging of the thieves, and so become a rare hangman.

Fal. Well, Hal, well; and in some sort it jumps with my humor, as well as waiting in the court, I can tell you.

P. Hen. For obtaining of suits?

Fal. Yea, for obtaining of suits, whereof the hangman hath no lean wardrobe. I am as melancholy as a gib cat, or a lugged bear.

P. Hen. Or an old lion, or a lover's lute.

Fal. Yea, or the drone of a Lincolnshire bagpipe.

P. Hen. What sayest thou to a hare, or the melancholy of Moor-ditch?

Fal. Thou hast the most unsavory similes, and art, indeed, the most comparative, rascallest,—sweet young prince,—but, Hal, I pr'ythee, trouble me no more with vanity. I would to heaven, thou and I knew where a commodity of good names were to be bought. An old lord of the council rated me the other day in the street about you, sir,—but I marked him not; and yet he talked very wisely,—but I regarded him not; and yet he talked wisely, and in the street too.

P. Hen. Thou didst well; for wisdom cries out in the streets, and no man regards it.

Fal. O, thou hast abominable iteration, and art, indeed, able to corrupt a saint. Thou hast done much harm upon me, Hal, —heaven forgive thee for it! Before I knew thee, Hal, I knew nothing; and now am I, if a man should speak truly, little better than one of the wicked. I must give over this life, and I will give it over; an I do not, I am a villain: I'll be lost for never a king's son in Christendom.

P. Hen. Where shall we take a purse to-morrow, Jack?

Fal. Where thou wilt, lad, I'll make one; an I do not, call me villain, and baffle me.

P. Hen. I see a good amendment of life in thee,—from praying to purse-taking.

Enter POINS, *at a distance.*

Fal. Why, Hal, 'tis my vocation, Hal; 'tis no sin for a man to labor in his vocation. Poins!—Now shall we know if Gadshill have set a match.—This is the most omnipotent villain that ever cried "Stand!" to a true man.

P. Hen. Good morrow, Ned.

Poins. Good morrow, sweet Hal.—What says monsieur Remorse? What says Sir John Sack-and-Sugar? But, my lads, my lads, to-morrow morning, by four o'clock, early at Gadshill! There are pilgrims going to Canterbury with rich offerings, and traders riding to London with fat purses: I have visors for you all, you have horses for yourselves: Gadshill lies to-night in Rochester: I have bespoke supper to-morrow night in Eastcheap: we may do it as secure as sleep. If you will go, I will stuff your purses full of crowns; if you will not, tarry at home and be hanged.

Fal. Hear ye, Yedward; if I tarry at home, and go not, I'll hang you for going.

Poins. You will, chops?

Fal. Hal, wilt thou make one?

P. Hen. Who, I rob? I a thief? not I, by my faith.

Fal. There's neither honesty, manhood, nor good fellowship in thee, nor thou camest not of the blood royal, if thou darest not stand for ten shillings,

P. Hen. Well then, once in my days I'll be a madcap.

Fal. Why that's well said.

P. Hen. Well, come what will, I'll tarry at home.

Fal. I'll be a traitor then, when thou art king.

P. Hen. I care not.

Poins. Sir John, I pr'ythee, leave the prince and me alone: I will lay him down such reasons for this adventure, that he shall go.

Fal. Well, heaven give thee the spirit of persuasion, and him the ears of profiting, that what thou speakest may move, and what he hears may be believed, that the true prince may (for recreation sake) prove a false thief; for the poor abuses of the time want countenance. Farewell: you shall find me in Eastcheap.

P. Hen. Farewell, thou latter spring! Farewell, All-hallown summer! [*Exit* FALSTAFF.

Poins. Now, my good sweet honey lord, ride with us to-morrow: I have a jest to execute, that I cannot manage alone. Falstaff, Bardolf, Peto, and Gadshill, shall rob those men that we have already waylaid; yourself and I will not be there; and when they have the booty, if you and I do not rob them, cut this head from my shoulders.

P. Hen. But how shall we part with them in setting forth?

Poins. Why, we will set forth before or after them, and appoint them a place of meeting, wherein it is at our pleasure to fail; and then will they adventure upon the exploit themselves: which they shall have no sooner achieved, but we'll set upon them.

P. Hen. Ay, but 'tis like that they will know us, by our horses, by our habits, and by every other appointment, to be ourselves.

Poins. Tut! our horses they shall not see,—I'll tie them in the wood; our visors we will change, after we leave them; and, sirrah, I have cases of buckram for the nonce, to immask our noted outward garments.

P. Hen. But I doubt they will be too hard for us.

Poins. Well, for two of them, I know them to be as true-bred cowards as ever turned back; and for the third, if he fight longer than he sees reason, I'll forswear arms. The virtue of this jest will be, the incomprehensible lies that this same fat rogue will tell us, when we meet at supper: how thirty, at least, he fought with; what wards, what blows, what extremities he endured; and in the reproof of this lies the jest.

P. Hen. Well, I'll go with thee: provide us all things necessary, and meet me to-morrow night in Eastcheap; there I'll sup. Farewell.

Poins. Farewell, my lord. [*Exit.*
P. Hen. I know you all, and will a while uphold
The unyok'd humor of your idleness:
Yet herein will I imitate the sun,
Who doth permit the base contagious clouds
To smother up his beauty from the world,
That, when he please again to be himself,
Being wanted, he may be more wonder'd at,
By breaking through the foul and ugly mists
Of vapors, that did seem to strangle him.
If all the year were playing holidays,
To sport would be as tedious as to work;
But when they seldom come, they wish'd-for come,
And nothing pleaseth but rare accidents.
So, when this loose behavior I throw off,
And pay the debt I never promised,
By how much better than my word I am,
By so much shall I falsify men's hopes;
And, like bright metal on a sullen ground,
My reformation, glittering o'er my fault,
Shall show more goodly, and attract more eyes,
Than that which hath no foil to set it off.
I'll so offend, to make offence a skill;
Redeeming time, when men think least I will. [*Exit.*

SCENE III.—London. *Another Room in the Palace.*

Enter KING HENRY, NORTHUMBERLAND, WORCESTER, HOTSPUR, *Sir* WALTER BLUNT, *and others.*

K. Hen. My blood hath been too cold and temperate,
Unapt to stir at these indignities,
And you have found me; for accordingly,
You tread upon my patience: but, be sure,
I will from henceforth rather be myself,
Mighty, and to be fear'd, than my condition;
Which hath been smooth as oil, soft as young down,
And therefore lost that title of respect,
Which the proud soul ne'er pays but to the proud.
Wor. Our house, my sovereign liege, little deserves
The scourge of greatness to be used on it;
And that same greatness, too, which our own hands
Have holp to make so portly.
North. My lord,—
K. Hen. Worcester, get thee gone; for I do see
Danger and disobedience in thine eye: [*Exit* WORCESTER.
[*To* NORTH.] You were about to speak.
North. Yea, my good lord.

Those prisoners in your highness' name demanded,
Which Harry Percy here, at Holmedon took,
Were, as he says, not with such strength denied,
As is deliver'd to your majesty:
Either envy, therefore, or misprision
Is guilty of this fault, and not my son.
Hot. My liege, I did deny no prisoners:
But I remember, when the fight was done,
When I was dry with rage and extreme toil,
Breathless and faint, leaning upon my sword,
Came there a certain lord, neat, trimly dress'd,
Fresh as a bridegroom; and his chin, new reap'd,
Show'd like a stubble-land at harvest-home;
He was perfumed like a milliner;
And 'twixt his finger and his thumb he held
A pouncet-box, which ever and anon
He gave his nose, and took't away again;—
Who, therewith angry, when it next came there,
Took it in snuff:—and still he smil'd and talk'd;
And as the soldiers bore dead bodies by,
He call'd them untaught knaves, unmannerly,
To bring a slovenly unhandsome corse
Betwixt the wind and his nobility.
With many holiday and lady terms
He question'd me; among the rest, demanded
My prisoners in your majesty's behalf.
I then, all smarting, with my wounds being cold,
To be so pester'd with a popinjay,
Out of my grief and my impatience,
Answer'd neglectingly, I know not what,—
He should, or he should not;—for he made me mad
To see him shine so brisk, and smell so sweet,
And talk so like a waiting-gentlewoman,
Of guns, and drums, and wounds,—God save the mark!—
And telling me, the sovereign'st thing on earth
Was parmaceti for an inward bruise;
And that it was great pity, so it was,
This villainous salt-petre should be digg'd
Out of the bowels of the harmless earth,
Which many a good tall fellow had destroy'd
So cowardly; and, but for these vile guns,
He would himself have been a soldier.
This bald unjointed chat of his, my lord,
I answer'd indirectly, as I said;
And I beseech you, let not his report
Come current for an accusation,
Betwixt my love and your high majesty.
Blunt. The circumstance consider'd, good my lord,

Whate'er Lord Harry Percy then had said
To such a person, and in such a place,
At such a time, with all the rest re-told,
May reasonably die, and never rise
To do him wrong, or any way impeach
What then he said, so he unsay it now.
K. Hen. Why, yet he doth deny his prisoners,
But with proviso and exception,—
That we, at our own charge, shall ransom straight
His brother-in-law, the foolish Mortimer;
Who, on my soul, hath wilfully betray'd
The lives of those that he did lead to fight
Against the great magician, curs'd Glendower,
Whose daughter, as we hear, the earl of March
Hath lately married. Shall our coffers, then,
Be emptied to redeem a traitor home?
Shall we buy treason? and indent with fears,
When they have lost and forfeited themselves?
No, on the barren mountains let him starve;
For I shall never hold that man my friend,
Whose tongue shall ask me for one penny cost,
To ransom home revolted Mortimer.
Hot. Revolted Mortimer!
He never did fall off, my sovereign liege,
But by the chance of war:—to prove that true,
Needs no more but one tongue for all those wounds,
Those mouthèd wounds, which valiantly he took,
When on the gentle Severn's sedgy bank,
In single opposition, hand to hand,
He did confound the best part of an hour
In changing hardiment with great Glendower:
Three times they breath'd, and three times did they drink,
Upon agreement, of swift Severn's flood;
Who then, affrighted with their bloody looks,
Ran fearfully among the trembling reeds,
And hid his crisp head in the hollow bank,
Blood-stainèd with these valiant combatants.
Never did base and rotten policy
Color her working with such deadly wounds;
Nor never could the noble Mortimer
Receive so many, and all willingly:
Then, let him not be slander'd with revolt.
K. Hen. Thou dost belie him, Percy, thou dost belie him;
He never did encounter with Glendower.
Art thou not asham'd? But, sirrah, henceforth
Let me not hear you speak of Mortimer:
Send me your prisoners with the speediest means,
Or you shall hear in such a kind from me,

As will displease you.—My lord Northumberland,
We license your departure with your son.—
Send us your prisoners, or you'll hear of it.
[*Exeunt* KING HENRY, BLUNT, *and train.*

Hot. If the foul fiend come and roar for them,
I will not send them:—I will after straight,
And tell him so; for I will ease my heart,
Albeit I make a hazard of my head.

North. What! drunk with choler? stay, and pause awhile:
Here comes your uncle.

Re-enter WORCESTER.

Hot. Speak of Mortimer!
'Zounds! I will speak of him; and let my soul
Want mercy, if I do not join with him:
Yea, on his part, I'll empty all these veins,
And shed my dear blood drop by drop i' the dust,
But I will lift the down-trod Mortimer
As high i' the air as this unthankful king,
As this ingrate and canker'd Bolingbroke.

North. [*To* WOR.] Brother, the king hath made your nephew mad.

Wor. Who struck this heat up after I was gone?

Hot. He will, forsooth, have all my prisoners;
And when I urg'd the ransom once again
Of my wife's brother, then his cheek look'd pale,
And on my face he turn'd an eye of death,
Trembling even at the name of Mortimer.

Wor. I cannot blame him: was he not proclaim'd
By Richard, that dead is, the next of blood?

North. He was; I heard the proclamation:
And then it was when the unhappy king
(Whose wrongs in us heaven pardon!) did set forth
Upon his Irish expedition;
From whence he intercepted did return
To be depos'd, and shortly murdered.

Wor. And for whose death, we in the world's wide mouth
Live scandaliz'd, and foully spoken of.

Hot. But, soft, I pray you, did king Richard then
Proclaim my brother Edmund Mortimer
Heir to the crown?

North. He did; myself did hear it.

Hot. Nay then, I cannot blame his cousin king,
That wish'd him on the barren mountains starve.
But shall it be, that you, that set the crown
Upon the head of this forgetful man,
And for his sake wear the detested blot
Of murd'rous subornation,—shall it be,

That you a world of curses undergo,
Being the agents, or base second means,
The cords, the ladder, or the hangman rather?—
O, pardon me, that I descend so low,
To show the line, and the predicament,
Wherein you range under this subtle king;—
Shall it, for shame, be spoken in these days,
Or fill up chronicles in time to come,
That men of your nobility and power,
Did gage them both in an unjust behalf,—
As both of you, heaven pardon it! have done,—
To put down Richard, that sweet lovely rose,
And plant this thorn, this canker, Bolingbroke?
And shall it, in more shame, be farther spoken,
That you are fool'd, discarded, and shook off
By him, for whom these shames ye underwent?
No; yet time serves, wherein you may redeem
Your banish'd honors, and restore yourselves
Into the good thoughts of the world again;
Revenge the jeering and disdain'd contempt
Of this proud king, who studies day and night
To answer all the debt he owes to you,
Even with the bloody payment of your deaths:
Therefore, I say,—
  Wor. Peace, cousin, say no more:
And now I will unclasp a secret book,
And to your quick-conceiving discontents
I'll read you matter deep and dangerous;
As full of peril and adventurous spirit,
As to o'er-walk a current, roaring loud,
On the unsteadfast footing of a spear.
  Hot. If he fall in, good night!—or sink or swim:—
Send danger from the east unto the west,
So honor cross it from the north to south,
And let them grapple:—O, the blood more stirs
To rouse a lion, than to start a hare.
  North. Imagination of some great exploit
Drives him beyond the bounds of patience.
  Hot. By heaven, methinks, it were an easy leap,
To pluck bright honor from the pale-fac'd moon;
Or dive into the bottom of the deep,
Where fathom-line could never touch the ground,
And pluck up drowned honor by the locks,
So he that doth redeem her thence might wear
Without corrival all her dignities:
But out upon this half-fac'd fellowship!
  Wor. He apprehends a world of figures here,

But not the form of what he should attend.—
Good cousin, give me audience for a while.
  Hot. I cry you mercy.
  Wor. Those same noble Scots,
That are your prisoners,—
  Hot. I'll keep them all;
By heaven, he shall not have a Scot of them;
No, if a Scot would save his soul, he shall not:
I'll keep them, by this hand.
  Wor. You start away,
And lend no ear unto my purposes.—
Those prisoners you shall keep.
  Hot. Nay, I will; that's flat:—
He said, he would not ransom Mortimer;
Forbad my tongue to speak of Mortimer;
But I will find him when he lies asleep,
And in his ear I'll holla—"Mortimer!"
Nay, I'll have a starling shall be taught to speak
Nothing but "Mortimer," and give it him,
To keep his anger still in motion.
  Wor. Hear you, cousin; a word.
  Hot. All studies here I solemnly defy,
Save how to gall and pinch this Bolingbrol
And that same sword-and-buckler prince of Wales,—
But that I think his father loves him not,
And would be glad he met with some mischance,
I would have him poison'd with a pot of ale.
  Wor. Farewell, kinsman: I will talk to you,
When you are better temper'd to attend.
  North. Why, what a wasp-tongue and impatient fool
Art thou to break into this woman's mood,
Tying thine ear to no tongue but thine own!
  Hot. Why, look you, I am whipp'd and scourg'd with rods,
Nettled, and stung with pismires, when I hear
Of this vile politician, Bolingbroke.
In Richard's time,—what do ye call the place?—
A plague upon't—it is in Gloucestershire;—
'Twas where the mad-cap duke his uncle kept,—
His uncle York;—where I first bow'd my knee
Unto this king of smiles, this Bolingbroke,—
When you and he came back from Ravenspurg.
  North. At Berkley castle.
  Hot. You say true:—
Why, what a candy deal of courtesy
This fawing greyhound then did proffer me!
Look,—"when his infant fortune came to age,"
And,—"gentle Harry Percy,"—and, "kind cousin,"—

O, a plague take such cozeners!—
Good uncle, tell your tale; for I have done.
Wor. Nay, if you have not, to't again;
We'll stay your leisure.
Hot. I have done, i' faith.
Wor. Then once more to your Scottish prisoners.
Deliver them up without their ransom straight,
And make the Douglas' son your only mean
For powers in Scotland; which, for divers reasons
Which I shall send you written, be assur'd,
Will easily be granted.—[To NORTH.] You, my lord,
Your son in Scotland being thus employ'd,
Shall secretly into the bosom creep
Of that same noble prelate, well belov'd,
The archbishop.
Hot. Of York, is it not?
Wor. True; who bears hard
His brother's death at Bristol, the lord Scroop.
Hot. I smell it; upon my life, it will do well.
North. Before the game's afoot, thou still let'st slip.
Hot. Why, it cannot choose but be a noble plot:—
And then the power of Scotland, and of York,—
To join with Mortimer, ha?
Wor. And so they shall.
Hot. In faith, it is exceedingly well aim'd.
Wor. And 'tis no little reason bids us speed,
To save our heads by raising of a head;
For, bear ourselves as even as we can,
The king will always think him in our debt,
And think we think ourselves unsatisfied,
Till he hath found a time to pay us home:
And see already how he doth begin
To make us strangers to his looks of love.
Hot. He does, he does: We'll be reveng'd on him.
Wor. Cousin, farewell:—No farther go in this,
Than I by letters shall direct your course.
When time is ripe, (which will be suddenly,)
I'll steal to Glendower and lord Mortimer;
Where you and Douglas, and our powers at once,
(As I will fashion it,) shall happily meet,
To bear our fortunes in our own strong arms,
Which now we hold at much uncertainty.
North. Farewell, good brother: we shall thrive, I trust.
Hot. Uncle, adieu:—O, let the hours be short,
Till fields, and blows, and groans applaud our sport! [*Exeunt.*

ACT II.

SCENE I.—Rochester. *An Inn-Yard.*

Enter a Carrier, *with a lantern in his hand.*

1 *Car.* Heigh ho! An't be not four by the day, I'll be hanged: Charles' wain is over the new chimney, and yet our horse not packed.—What, ostler!

Ost. [*Within.*] Anon, anon.

1 *Car.* I pr'ythee, Tom, beat Cut's saddle, put a few flocks in the point; the poor jade is wrung in the withers out of all cess.

Enter another Carrier

2 *Car.* Peas and beans are as dank here as a dog, and that is the next way to give poor jades the bots: this house is turned upside down, since Robin ostler died.

1 *Car.* Poor fellow! never joyed since the price of oats rose; it was the death of him.

2 *Car.* I think this be the most villainous house in all London road for fleas: I am stung like a tench.

1 *Car.* Like a tench! by the mass, there is ne'er a king in Christendom could be better bit than I have been. What, ostler! come away and be hanged; come away.

2 *Car.* I have a gammon of bacon, and two frails of ginger, to be delivered as far as Charing-cross.

1 *Car.* 'Odsbody! the turkeys in my pannier are quite starved. —What, ostler!—A plague on thee! hast thou never an eye in thy head? canst not hear? An 'twere not as good a deed as drink, to break the pate of thee, I am a very villain.—Come, and be hanged:—hast no faith in thee?

Enter GADSHILL.

Gads. Good morrow, carriers. What's o'clock?

1 *Car.* I think it be two o'clock.

Gads. I pr'ythee, lend me thy lantern, to see my horse in the stable.

1 *Car.* Nay, soft, I pray ye: I know a trick worth two of that, i' faith.

Gads. I pr'ythee, lend me thine.

2 *Car.* Ay, when? canst tell?—Lend me thy lantern, quoth a? marry, I'll see thee hanged first.

Gads. Sirrah carrier, what time do you mean to come to London?

2 *Car.* Time enough to go to bed with a candle, I warrant thee.—Come, neighbor Mugs, we'll call up the gentlemen: they will along with company, for they have great charge.

[*Exeunt* Carriers.

Gads. What, ho! chamberlain!

Cham. [*Within.*] At hand, quoth pick-purse.

Gads. That's even as fair as—at hand, quoth the chamberlain; for thou variest no more from picking of purses, than giving direction doth from laboring; thou layest the plot how.

Enter Chamberlain.

Cham. Good morrow, master Gadshill. It holds current, that I told you yesternight:—there's a franklin in the wild of Kent hath brought three hundred marks with him in gold: I heard him tell it to one of his company, last night at supper; a kind of auditor; one that hath abundance of charge too. They are up already, and call for eggs and butter: they will away presently.

Gads. Sirrah, if they meet not with saint Nicholas' clerks, I'll give thee this neck.

Cham. No, I'll none of it: I pr'ythee, keep that for the hangman; for I know thou worship'st saint Nicholas as truly as a man of falsehood may.

Gads. Give me thy hand: thou shalt have a share in our purchase, as I am a true man.

Cham. Nay, rather let me have it, as you are a false thief.

Gads. Go to; *homo* is a common name to all men. Bid the ostler bring my horse out of the stable. Farewell, you muddy knave. [*Exeunt.*

SCENE II.—*The Road by* Gadshill.

Enter Prince Henry *and* Poins; Bardolph *and* Peto, *at some distance.*

Poins. Come, shelter, shelter: I have removed Falstaff's horse, and he frets like a gummed velvet.

P. Hen. Stand close. [*They retire.*

Enter Falstaff.

Fal. Poins! Poins, and be hanged! Poins!

P. Hen. [*Coming forward.*] Peace, ye fat-kidneyed rascal! What a brawling dost thou keep!

Fal. Where's Poins, Hal?

P. Hen. He is walked up to the top of the hill: I'll go seek him. [*Pretends to seek* Poins, *and retires.*

Fal. I am accursed to rob in that thief's company; the rascal hath removed my horse, and tied him I know not where. If I travel but four foot by the square farther afoot, I shall break my wind. Well, I doubt not but to die a fair death for all this, if I 'scape hanging for killing that rogue. I have forsworn his company hourly any time this two-and-twenty years, and yet I am bewitched with the rogue's company. If the rascal have not given me medicines to make me love him, I'll be hanged; it could not be else; I have drunk medicines.—Poins!—Hal!—a plague upon you both!—Bardolph!—Peto!—I'll starve, ere I'll rob a foot farther. An 'twere not as good a deed as drink, to turn true man, and leave these rogues, I am the veriest varlet that ever chewed with a tooth. Eight yards of uneven ground is three score and ten miles afoot with me; and the stony-hearted villains know it well enough: a plague upon't, when thieves cannot be true one to another! [*They whistle.*] Whew!—a plague upon you all! Give me my horse, you rogues; give me my horse, and be hanged.

P. Hen. [*Coming forward.*] Peace, peace! lie down; lay thine ear close to the ground, and list if thou canst hear the tread of travellers.

Fal. Have you any levers to lift me up again, being down? I'll not bear mine own flesh so far afoot again, for all the coin in thy father's exchequer. I pr'ythee, good prince Hal, help me to my horse, good king's son.

P. Hen. Out, you rogue! shall I be your ostler?

Fal. Go, hang thyself in thine own heir-apparent garters! If I be ta'en, I'll peach for this. An I have not ballads made on you all, and sung to filthy tunes, let a cup of sack be my poison:—when a jest is so forward, and afoot too!—I hate it.

Enter GADSHILL.

Gads. Stand.

Fal. So I do, against my will.

Poins. O, 'tis our setter: I know his voice.

[*Coming forward with* BARDOLPH *and* PETO.

Bard. What news?

Gads. Case ye, case ye; on with your visors: there's money of the king's coming down the hill; 'tis going to the king's exchequer.

Fal. You lie, you rogue; 'tis going to the king's tavern.

Gads. There's enough to make us all.

Fal. To be hanged.

P. Hen. Sirs, you four shall front them in the narrow lane: Ned Poins and I will walk lower: if they 'scape from your encounter, then they light on us.

Peto. How many be there of them?

Gads. Some eight, or ten.

Fal. Zounds! will they not rob us?

P. Hen. What, a coward, Sir John Paunch?

Fal. Indeed, I am not John of Gaunt, your grandfather; but yet no coward, Hal.

P. Hen. Well, we leave that to the proof.

Poins. Sirrah Jack, thy horse stands behind the hedge: when thou needest him, there thou shalt find him. Farewell, and stand fast.

Fal. Now cannot I strike him, if I should be hanged.

P. Hen. [*Aside to* POINS.] Ned, where are our disguises?

Poins. Here, hard by: stand close.

[*Exeunt* P. HENRY *and* POINS.

Fal. Now, my masters, happy man be his dole, say I: every man to his business.

Enter Travellers.

1 *Trav.* Come, neighbor: the boy shall lead our horses down the hill; we'll walk afoot awhile, and ease our legs.

Fal., Gads., &c. Stand!

Travellers. Heaven bless us!

Fal. Strike; down with them; cut the villains' throats:—ah! vile caterpillars! bacon-fed knaves! they hate us youth:—down with them; fleece them.

Travellers. O! we are undone, both we and ours, for ever.

Fal. Hang ye, gorbellied knaves, are ye undone? No, ye fat chuffs; I would your store were here! On, bacons, on! What, ye knaves! young men must live. You are grand-jurors, are ye? We'll jure ye, i' faith.

[*Exeunt* FAL., GADS., *&c. driving the* Travellers *out.*

Re-enter PRINCE HENRY *and* POINS, *in buckram suits.*

P. Hen. The thieves have bound the true men.
Now could thou and I rob the thieves, and go merrily to London, it would be argument for a week, laughter for a month, and a good jest for ever.

Poins. Stand close; I hear them coming. [*They retire.*

Re-enter FALSTAFF, GADSHILL, BARDOLPH, *and* PETO.

Fal. Come, my masters, let us share, and then to horse before day. And the prince and Poins be not two arrant cowards, there's no equity stirring: there's no more valor in that Poins, than in a wild duck.

[*As they are sharing, the* PRINCE *and* POINS *rush out and set upon them.*

P. Hen. Your money!

Poins. Villains!

[GADSHILL, BARDOLPH, *and* PETO *run away; and* FALSTAFF, *after a blow or two, runs away too, leaving the booty behind.*

P. Hen. Got with much ease. Now merrily to horse:
The thieves are scatter'd, and possess'd with fear
So strongly, that they dare not meet each other;
Each takes his fellow for an officer.
Away, good Ned. Falstaff sweats to death,

And lards the lean earth as he walks along:
Wer't not for laughing, I should pity him.
Poins. How the rogue roar'd! [*Exeunt.*

SCENE III.—Warkworth. *A Room in the Castle.*

Enter HOTSPUR, *reading a letter.*

"—*But for mine own part, my lord, I could be well contented to be there, in respect of the love I bear your house.*"—He could be contented,—why is he not, then? In respect of the love he bears our house:—he shows in this, he loves his own barn better than he loves our house. Let me see some more. "*The purpose you undertake, is dangerous:*" Why, that's certain: 'tis dangerous to take a cold, to sleep, to drink; but I tell you, my lord fool, out of this nettle, danger, we pluck this flower, safety. "*The purpose you undertake, is dangerous; the friends you have named, uncertain; the time itself unsorted; and your whole plot too light for the counterpoise of so great an opposition.*"—Say you so, say you so? I say unto you again, you are a shallow, cowardly hind, and you lie. What a lack-brain is this! Our plot is a good plot as ever was laid; our friends true and constant: a good plot, good friends, and full of expectation; an excellent plot, very good friends. What a frosty-spirited rogue is this! Why, my lord of York commends the plot, and the general course of the action. 'Zounds! an I were now by this rascal, I could brain him with his lady's fan. Is there not my father, my uncle, and myself? lord Edmund Mortimer, my lord of York, and Owen Glendower? Is there not, besides, the Douglas? Have I not all their letters, to meet me in arms by the ninth of the next month? and are they not, some of them, set forward already? What a pagan rascal is this! an infidel! Ha! you shall see now, in very sincerity of fear and cold heart, will he to the king, and lay open all our proceedings. O, I could divide myself, and go to buffets, for moving such a dish of skimmed milk with so honorable an action! Hang him! let him tell the king: we are prepared. I will set forward to-night.

Enter LADY PERCY.

How now, Kate! I must leave you within these two hours.
Lady. O, my good lord, why are you thus alone?
Tell me, sweet lord, what is't that takes from thee
Thy stomach, pleasure, and thy golden sleep?
Why dost thou bend thine eyes upon the earth,
And start so often when thou sit'st alone?
Why hast thou lost the fresh blood in thy cheeks;
And given my treasures and my rights of thee,
To thick-ey'd musing and curs'd melancholy?

In thy faint slumbers, I by thee have watch'd,
And heard thee murmur tales of iron war;
Speak terms of manage to thy bounding steed;
Cry, "Courage! to the field!"
O, what portents are these?
Some heavy business hath my lord in hand,
And I must know it, else he loves me not.

Hot. What, ho! [*Enter* Servant.] Is Gilliams with the packet gone?

Serv. He is, my lord, an hour ago.
Hot. Hath Butler brought those horses from the sheriff?
Serv. One horse, my lord, he brought even now.
Hot. What horse? a roan, a crop-ear, is it not?
Serv. It is, my lord.
Hot. That roan shall be my throne.
Well, I will back him straight: O, *esperance!*—
Bid Butler lead him forth into the park. [*Exit* Servant.
Lady. But hear you, my lord.
Hot. What say'st thou, my lady?
Lady. What is it carries you away?
Hot. Why my horse,
My love,—my horse.
Lady. Out, you mad-headed ape!
A weasel hath not such a deal of spleen,
As you are toss'd with. In faith,
I'll know your business, Harry,—that I will.
I fear my brother Mortimer doth stir
About his title, and hath sent for you
To line his enterprise: but if you go,—
Hot. So far afoot, I shall be weary, love.
Lady. Come, come, you paraquito, answer me
Directly unto this question that I ask:
In faith, I'll break thy little finger, Harry,
An if thou wilt not tell me all things true.
Hot. Away,
Away, you trifler!—Love?—I love thee not,
I care not for thee, Kate: this is no world
To play with mammets, and to tilt with lips:
We must have bloody noses and crack'd crowns,
And pass them current too.—Odd's me, my horse!—
What say'st thou, Kate? what would'st thou have with me?
Lady. Do you not love me? do you not, indeed?
Well, do not, then; for since you love me not,
I will not love myself. Do you not love me?
Nay, tell me if you speak in jest or no.
Hot. Come, wilt thou see me ride?
And when I am o' horseback, I will swear
I love thee infinitely. But hark you, Kate;

I must not have you henceforth question me
Whither I go, nor reason whereabout:
Whither I must, I must; and, to conclude,
This evening must I leave you, gentle Kate.
I know you wise; but yet no farther wise
Than Harry Percy's wife: constant you are;
But yet a woman: and for secrecy,
No lady closer; for I well believe
Thou wilt not utter what thou dost not know,—
And so far will I trust thee, gentle Kate.
Lady. How! so far?
Hot. Not an inch farther. But hark you, Kate·
Whither I go, thither shall you go too;
To-day will I set forth, to-morrow you.—
Will this content you, Kate?
Lady. It must, of force. [*Exeunt.*

SCENE IV.—Eastcheap. *A Room in the* Boar's Head Tavern.

Enter PRINCE HENRY.

P. Hen. Ned, pr'ythee, come out of that fat room, and lend me thy hand to laugh a little.

Enter POINS.

Poins. Where hast been, Hal?

P. Hen. With three or four loggerheads, amongst three or four score hogsheads. I have sounded the very base string of humility. Sirrah, I am sworn brother to a leash of drawers; and can call them all by their Christian names, as—Tom, Dick, and Francis. They take it already upon their salvation, that though I be but prince of Wales, yet I am the king of courtesy; and tell me flatly I am no proud Jack, like Falstaff; but a Corinthian, a lad of mettle, a good boy, (so they call me,) and when I am king of England, I shall command all the good lads in Eastcheap. —To conclude, I am so good a proficient in one quarter of an hour, that I can drink with any tinker in his own language during my life. I tell thee, Ned, thou hast lost much honor, that thou wert not with me in this action. But, sweet Ned,—to sweeten which name of Ned, I give thee this pennyworth of sugar, clapped even now into my hand by an under-skinker, one that never spake other English in his life, than—"Eight shillings and sixpence," and—"You are welcome," with this shrill addition,— "Anon, anon, sir! Score a pint of Spanish in the Half-moon," or so:—But, Ned, to drive away the time till Falstaff come, I pr'ythee, do thou stand in some by-room, while I question my puny drawer to what end he gave me the sugar; and do thou never leave calling—"Francis!" that his tale to me may be nothing but—"anon." Step aside, and I'll show thee a precedent.

Poins. [*Going.*] Francis!

P. Hen. Thou art perfect.

Poins. [*Going.*] Francis! [*Exit* POINS.

Enter FRANCIS.

Fran. Anon, anon, sir.—Look down into the Pomegranate, Ralph.

P. Hen. Come hither, Francis.

Fran. My lord?

P. Hen. How long hast thou to serve, Francis?

Fran. Forsooth, five years, and as much as to—

Poins. [*Within.*] Francis!

Fran. Anon, anon, sir.

P. Hen. Five years! by'r lady, a long lease for the clinking of pewter. But, Francis, darest thou be so valiant, as to play the coward with thy indenture, and show it a fair pair of heels and run from it?

Fran. O lord, sir, I'll be sworn upon all the books in England, I could find in my heart—

Poins. [*Within.*] Francis!

Fran. Anon, anon, sir.

P. Hen. How old art thou, Francis?

Fran. Let me see,—about Michaelmas next I shall be—

Poins. [*Within.*] Francis!

Fran. Anon, sir.—Pray you, stay a little, my lord.

P. Hen. Nay, but hark you, Francis: for the sugar thou gavest me,—'twas a pennyworth, was't not?

Fran. O lord, sir, I would it had been two.

P. Hen. I will give thee for it a thousand pound: ask me when thou wilt, and thou shalt have it.

Poins. [*Within.*] Francis!

Fran. Anon, anon.

P. Hen. Anon, Francis? No, Francis; but to-morrow, Francis; or, Francis, on Thursday; or, indeed, Francis, when thou wilt. But, Francis,—

Fran. My lord?

P. Hen. Wilt thou rob this leathern-jerkin, crystal-button, nott-pated, agate-ring, puke-stocking, caddis-garter, smooth-tongue, Spanish-pouch,—

Fran. O lord, sir, who do you mean?

P. Hen. Why then, your brown Spanish is your only drink; for, look you, Francis, your white canvas doublet will sully: in Barbary, sir, it cannot come to so much.

Fran. What, sir?

Poins. [*Within.*] Francis!

P. Hen. Away, you rogue! Dost thou not hear them call?

[*Here they both call him;* FRANCIS *stands amazed, not knowing which way to go.*

Enter Vintner.

Vint. What, standest thou still, and hearest such a calling? Look to the guests within. [*Exit* FRAN.] My lord, old Sir John, with half a dozen more, are at the door: shall I let them in?

P. Hen. Let them alone awhile, and then open the door. [*Exit* Vintner.] Poins!

Re-enter POINS.

Poins. Anon, anon, sir.

P. Hen. Sirrah, Falstaff and the rest of the thieves are at the door; shall we be merry?

Poins. As merry as crickets, my lad. But hark ye; what cunning match have you made with this jest of the drawer? come, what's the issue?

P. Hen. I am now of all humors, that have show'd themselves humors, since the old days of goodman Adam to the pupil age of this present twelve o'clock at midnight. [FRANCIS *crosses the stage, with wine.*] What's o'clock, Francis?

Fran. Anon, anon, sir. [*Exit.*

P. Hen. That ever this fellow should have fewer words than a parrot, and yet the son of a woman! His industry is—up stairs, and down stairs; his eloquence,—the parcel of a reckoning. I am not yet of Percy's mind, the Hotspur of the North; he that kills me some six or seven dozen of Scots at a breakfast, washes his hands, and says to his wife,—"Fie upon this quiet life! I want work." "O my sweet Harry," says she, "how many hast thou killed to-day?" "Give my roan horse a drench," says he; and answers, "Some fourteen," an hour after, —"a trifle, a trifle."—I pr'ythee, call in Falstaff: call in ribs, call in tallow.

Enter FALSTAFF, GADSHILL, BARDOLPH, *and* PETO; *followed by* FRANCIS, *with wine.*

Poins. Welcome, Jack: where hast thou been?

Fal. A plague of all cowards, I say, and a vengeance too! marry, and amen!—Give me a cup of sack, boy.—Ere I lead this life long, I'll sew netherstocks, and mend them, and foot them too. A plague of all cowards!—Give me a cup of sack, rogue.—Is there no virtue extant? [*He drinks.*

P. Hen. Didst thou never see Titan kiss a dish of butter? pitiful-hearted butter, that melted at the sweet tale of the sun! if thou didst, then behold that compound.

Fal. You rogue, here's lime in this sack too: there is nothing but roguery to be found in villanous man: yet a coward is worse than a cup of sack with lime in it,—a villanous coward.—Go thy ways, old Jack; die when thou wilt, if manhood, good manhood, be not forgot upon the face of the earth, then am I a shotten herring. There live not three good men unhanged in England; and one of them is fat, and grows old: heaven help the while! a bad world, I say. I would I were a weaver; I could sing psalms or any thing. A plague of all cowards, I say still.

P. Hen. How now, wool-sack! what mutter you?

Fal. A king's son! If I do not beat thee out of thy kingdom with a dagger of lath, and drive all thy subjects afore thee like a flock of wild geese, I'll never wear hair on my face more. You prince of Wales!

P. Hen. Why, you vile round man, what's the matter?

Fal. Are you not a coward? answer me to that:—and Poins there?

Poins. 'Zounds! ye fat paunch, an ye call me coward, I'll stab thee.

Fal. I call thee coward! I'll see thee hanged ere I'll call thee coward: but I would give a thousand pounds, I could run as fast as thou canst. You are straight enough in the shoulders,—you care not who sees your back: call you that backing of your friends? A plague upon such backing! give me them that will face me.—Give me a cup of sack:—I am a rogue, if I drunk today.

P. Hen. O villain! thy lips are scarce wiped since thou drunkest last.

Fal. All's one for that. [*He drinks.*] A plague of all cowards, still say I.

P. Hen. What's the matter?

Fal. What's the matter! there be four of us here have ta'en a thousand pound this day morning.

P. Hen. Where is it, Jack? where is it?

Fal. Where is it! taken from us it is: a hundred upon poor four of us.

P. Hen. What, a hundred, man?

Fal. I am a rogue, if I were not at half-sword with a dozen of them two hours together. I have 'scap'd by miracle. I am eight times thrust through the doublet, four through the hose; my buckler cut through and through; my sword hacked like a hand-saw,—*ecce signum!* I never dealt better since I was a man: all would not do. A plague of all cowards!—Let them speak: if they speak more or less than truth, they are villains, and the sons of darkness.

P. Hen. Speak, sirs; how was it?

Gads. We four set upon some dozen,—

Fal. Sixteen, at least, my lord.

Gads. And bound them.

Peto. No, no, they were not bound.

Fal. You rogue, they were bound, every man of them; or I am a Jew else, an Ebrew Jew.

Gads. As we were sharing, some six or seven fresh men set upon us,—

Fal. And unbound the rest, and then come in the other.

P. Hen. What, fought ye with them all?

Fal. All! I know not what ye call all; but if I fought not with fifty of them, I am a bunch of radish: if there were not two or three and fifty upon poor old Jack, then am I no two-legged creature.

P. Hen. Pray heaven, you have not murdered some of them.

Fal. Nay, that's past praying for: I have peppered two of them; two, I am sure, I have paid,—two rogues in buckram suits. I tell thee what, Hal,—if I tell thee a lie, spit in my face, and call me horse. Thou knowest my old ward;—here I lay, and thus I bore my point. Four rogues in buckram let drive at me,—

P. Hen. What, four? thou saidst but two even now.

Fal. Four, Hal; I told thee four.

Poins. Ay, ay, he said four.

Fal. These four came all a-front, and mainly thrust at me. I made me no more ado, but took all their seven points in my target, thus.

P. Hen. Seven? why, there were but four even now.

Fal. In buckram.

Poins. Ay, four, in buckram suits.

Fal. Seven, by these hilts, or I am a villain else.

P. Hen. Pr'ythee, let him alone; we shall have more anon.

Fal. Dost thou hear me, Hal?

P. Hen. Ay, and mark thee too, Jack.

Fal. Do so, for it is worth the listening to. These nine buckram, that I told thee of,—

P. Hen. So, two more already.

Fal. Their points being broken, began to give me ground: but I followed me close, came in, foot and hand; and with a thought, seven of the eleven I paid.

P. Hen. O monstrous! eleven buckram men grown out of two!

Fal. But, as ill luck would have it, three misbegotten knaves, in Kendal green, came at my back, and let drive at me;—for it was so dark, Hal, that thou could'st not see thy hand.

P. Hen. These lies are like the father that begets them,—gross as a mountain, open, palpable. Why, thou knotty-pated fool, thou vile, greasy, tallow-keech,—

Fal. What, art thou mad? art thou mad? is not the truth the truth?

P. Hen. Why, how couldst thou know these men in Kendal green, when it was so dark thou could'st not see thy hand? come, tell us your reason: what sayest thou to this?

Poins. Come, your reason, Jack,—your reason.

Fal. What, upon compulsion? No; were I at the strappado, or all the racks in the world, I would not tell you on compulsion. Give you a reason on compulsion! if reasons were as plenty as blackberries, I would give no man a reason upon compulsion, I.

P. Hen. I'll be no longer guilty of this sin; this sanguine coward, this bed-presser, this horse-back-breaker, this huge hill of flesh,—

Fal. Away, you starveling, you elf-skin, you dried neat's-tongue, you stock-fish,—O for breath to utter what is like thee! —you tailor's yard, you sheath, you bow-case, you vile standing tuck,—

P. Hen. Well, breathe awhile, and then to it again: and when thou hast tired thyself in base comparisons, hear me speak but this.

Poins. Mark, Jack.

P. Hen. We two saw you four set on four; you bound them, and were masters of their wealth.—Mark now, how a plain tale shall put you down.—Then did we two set on you four; and, with a word, out-faced you from your prize, and have it; yea, and can show it you here in the house:—and, Falstaff, you carried yourself away as nimbly, with as quick dexterity, and roared for mercy, and still ran and roared, as ever I heard bull-calf. What a slave art thou, to hack thy sword as thou hast done, and then say, it was in fight! What trick, what device, what starting hole, canst thou now find out, to hide thee from this open and apparent shame?

Poins. Come, let's hear, Jack; what trick hast thou now?

Fal. By the Lord, I knew ye, as well as he that made ye. Why, hear ye, my masters: was it for me to kill the heir-apparent? Should I turn upon the true prince? Why, thou knowest I am as valiant as Hercules: but beware instinct; the lion will not touch the true prince. Instinct is a great matter; I was a coward on instinct. I shall think the better of myself and thee, during my life; I for a valiant lion, and thou for a true prince. But, lads, I am glad you have the money.—[*To the* Hostess *within.*] Hostess, clap to the door:—watch to-night, pray to-morrow.—Gallants, lads, boys, hearts of gold, all the titles of good fellowship come to you! What, shall we be merry? shall we have a play extempore?

P. Hen. Content;—and the argument shall be, thy running away.

Fal. Ah, no more of that, Hal, an thou lovest me!

Enter Hostess.

Host. O! My lord the prince,—

P. Hen. How now, my lady the hostess! what sayest thou to me?

Host. Marry, my lord, there is a nobleman of the court at door would speak with you: he says he comes from your father.

P. Hen. Give him as much as will make him a royal man, and send him back again to my mother.

Fal. What manner of man is he?

Host. An old man.

Fal. What doth gravity out of his bed at midnight?—Shall I give him his answer?

P. Hen. Pr'ythee, do, Jack.

Fal. 'Faith, and I'll send him packing. [*Exit.*

P. Hen. Now, sirs:—by'r lady, you fought fair;—so did you, Peto;—so did you, Bardolph: you are lions too, you ran away upon instinct, you will not touch the true prince; no,—fie!

Bard. 'Faith, I ran when I saw others run.

P. Hen. 'Faith, tell me now in earnest,—how came Falstaff's word so hacked?

Peto. Why, he hacked it with his dagger; and said he would swear truth out of England, but he would make you believe it was done in fight; and persuaded us to do the like.

Bard. Yea, and to tickle our noses with spear-grass, to make them bleed; and then to beslubber our garments with it, and to swear it was the blood of true men. I did that I did not this seven year before,—I blushed to hear his monstrous devices.

P. Hen. O villain! thou stolest a cup of sack eighteen years ago, and wert taken with the manner, and ever since thou hast blushed extempore. Thou hadst fire and sword on thy side, and yet thou ran'st away: what instinct hadst thou for it?

Bard. My lord, do you see these meteors? do you behold these exhalations?

P. Hen. I do.

Bard. What think you they portend?

P. Hen. Hot livers and cold purses.

Bard. Choler, my lord, if rightly taken.

P. Hen. No, if rightly taken, halter.—Here comes lean Jack, here comes bare-bone.—[*Re-enter* FALSTAFF.] How now, my sweet creature of bombast! How long is't ago, Jack, since thou sawest thine own knee?

Fal. My own knee! when I was about thy years, Hal, I was not an eagle's talon in the waist; I could have crept into any alderman's thumb-ring: a plague of sighing and grief! it blows a man up like a bladder.—There's villanous news abroad: here was Sir John Bracy from your father; you must to the court in the morning. That same mad fellow of the north, Percy; and he of Wales,—what, a plague, call you him?—

Poins. O, Glendower.

Fal. Owen, Owen,—the same; and his son-in-law, Mortimer;

and old Northumberland; and that sprightly Scot of Scots, Douglas, that runs o' horseback up a hill perpendicular,—

P. Hen. He that rides at high speed, and with his pistol kills a sparrow flying.

Fal. You have hit it.

P. Hen. So did he never the sparrow.

Fal. Well, that rascal hath good mettle in him; he will not run.

P. Hen. Why, what a rascal art thou, then, to praise him so for running.

Fal. O' horseback, ye cuckoo! but, afoot, he will not budge a foot.

P. Hen. Yes, Jack, upon instinct.

Fal. I grant ye, upon instinct.—Well, he is there too, and one Mordake, and a thousand blue-caps more: Worcester is stolen away to-night; thy father's beard is turned white with the news: you may buy land now as cheap as stinking mackarel. But tell me, Hal, art thou not horribly afeard? thou being heir-apparent, could the world pick thee out three such enemies again, as that fiend Douglas, that spirit Percy, and that fiend Glendower? Art thou not horribly afraid? doth not thy blood thrill at it?

P. Hen. Not a whit, i' faith; I lack some of thy instinct.

Fal. Well, thou wilt be horribly chid to-morrow, when thou comest to thy father: if thou love me, practise an answer.

P. Hen. Do thou stand for my father, and examine me upon the particulars of my life.

Fal. Shall I? content:—this chair shall be my state, this dagger my sceptre, and this cushion my crown.

P. Hen. Thy state is taken for a joint-stool, thy golden sceptre for a leaden dagger, and thy precious rich crown for a pitiful bald crown!

Fal. Well, an the fire of grace be not quite out of thee, now shalt thou be moved.—Give me a cup of sack, to make mine eyes look red, that it may be thought I have wept; for I must speak in passion, and I will do it in king Cambyses' vein.

P. Hen. Well, here is my bow.

Fal. And here is my speech.—Stand aside, nobility.

Host. O! this is excellent sport, i' faith!

Fal. Weep not, sweet queen; for trickling tears are vain.

Host. O, the father! How he holds his countenance!

Fal. For heaven's sake, lords, convey my tristful queen;
For tears do stop the flood-gates of her eyes.

Host. O! he doth it as like one of the players as ever I see!

Fal. Peace, good pint-pot! peace, good tickle-brain!—Harry, I do not only marvel where thou spendest thy time, but also how thou art accompanied: for though the camomile, the more it is trodden on, the faster it grows, yet youth, the more it is wasted, the sooner it wears. That thou art my son, I have partly thy mother's word, partly my own opinion; but chiefly, a villanous trick of thine eye, and a foolish hanging of thy nether lip, that doth warrant me. If, then, thou be son to me, here lies the point:—why, being son to me, art thou so pointed at? Shall the blessed sun of heaven prove a micher, and eat blackberries? a question not to be asked. Shall the son of England prove a thief, and take purses? a question to be asked. There is a thing, Harry, which thou hast often heard of, and it is known to many in our land by the name of pitch: this pitch, as ancient writers do report, doth defile; so doth the company thou keepest: for, Harry, now I do not speak to thee in drink, but in tears; not in pleasure, but in passion; not in words only, but in woes also:—and yet there is a virtuous man, whom I have often noted in thy company, but I know not his name.

P. Hen. What manner of man, an it like your majesty?

Fal. A goodly portly man, i' faith, and a corpulent; of a cheerful look, a pleasing eye, and a most noble carriage; and, as I think, his age some fifty, or, by'r lady, inclining to three score; and now I remember me, his name is Falstaff: if that man should be badly given, he deceiveth me; for, Harry, I see virtue in his looks. If, then, the tree may be known by the fruit, as the fruit by the tree, then, peremptorily I speak it, there is virtue in that Falstaff: him keep with, the rest banish. And tell me now, thou naughty varlet, tell me, where hast thou been this month?

P. Hen. Dost thou speak like a king? Do thou stand for me, and I'll play my father.

Fal. Depose me? if thou dost it half so gravely, so majestically, both in word and matter, hang me up by the heels for a rabbit-sucker, or a poulter's hare.

P. Hen. Well, here I am set.

Fal. And here I stand:—judge, my masters.

P. Hen. Now, Harry, whence come you?

Fal. My noble lord, from Eastcheap.

P. Hen. The complaints I hear of thee are grievous.

Fal. My lord, they are false:—nay, I'll tickle ye for a young prince, i' faith.

P. Hen. Thou art violently carried away from grace: there is a demon haunts thee, in the likeness of a fat old man,—a tun of man is thy companion. Why dost thou converse with that trunk of humors, that swoln parcel of dropsies, that huge bombard of sack, that roasted Manningtree ox, that reverent Vice, that grey Iniquity, that father ruffian, that Vanity in years? Wherein is he good, but to taste sack and drink it? wherein neat and cleanly, but to carve a capon and eat it? wherein cunning, but in craft? wherein crafty, but in villany? wherein villanous, but in all things? wherein worthy, but in nothing?

Fal. I would your grace would take me with you: whom means your grace?

P. Hen. That villanous abominable misleader of youth, Falstaff, that old white-bearded Satan.

Fal. My lord, the man I know.

P. Hen. I know thou dost.

Fal. But to say, I know more harm in him than in myself, were to say more than I know. That he is old, (the more the pity,) his white hairs do witness it; but that he is vile, that I utterly deny. If sack and sugar be a fault, heaven help the wicked! If to be old and merry be a sin, then many an old host that I know, is condemned: if to be fat be to be hated, then Pharaoh's lean kine are to be loved. No, my good lord; banish Peto, banish Bardolph, banish Poins: but, for sweet Jack Falstaff, kind Jack Falstaff, true Jack Falstaff, valiant Jack Falstaff, and therefore more valiant, being, as he is, old Jack Falstaff, banish not him thy Harry's company, banish not him thy Harry's company:—banish plump Jack, and banish all the world.

P. Hen. I do, I will. [*A knocking heard.*

[*Exeunt* Hostess, FRANCIS, *and* BARDOLPH.

Re-enter BARDOLPH, *running.*

Bard. O! my lord, my lord! the sheriff, with a most monstrous watch, is at the door.

Fal. Out, you rogue!—Play out the play: I have much to say in the behalf of that Falstaff.

Re-enter Hostess.

Host. O! my lord, my lord!—

P. Hen. Heigh, heigh! what's the matter?

Host. The sheriff and all the watch are at the door: they are come to search the house. Shall I let them in?

Fal. Dost thou hear, Hal? never call a true piece of gold a counterfeit: thou art essentially mad, without seeming so.

P. Hen. And thou a natural coward, without instinct.

Fal. I deny your *major:* if you will deny the sheriff, so; if not, let him enter: if I become not a cart as well as another man, a plague on my bringing up! I hope I shall as soon be strangled with a halter as another.

P. Hen. Go, hide thee behind the arras:—the rest walk up above. Now, my masters, for a true face, and good conscience.

Fal. Both which I have had; but their date is out, and therefore I'll hide me. [*Exeunt all except the* PRINCE *and* POINS.

P. Hen. Call in the sheriff.

Enter Sheriff *and* Carrier.

Now, master sheriff, what's your will with me?

Sher. First, pardon me, my lord. A hue and cry
Hath follow'd certain men unto this house.

P. Hen. What men?

Sher. One of them is well known, my gracious lord,—
A gross fat man.
Car. As fat as butter.
P. Hen. The man, I do assure you, is not here;
For I myself at this time have employ'd him.
And, sheriff, I will engage my word to thee,
That I will, by to-morrow dinner-time,
Send him to answer thee, or any man,
For anything he shall be charg'd withal:
And so, let me entreat you leave the house.
Sher. I will, my lord. There are two gentlemen
Have in this robbery lost three hundred marks.
P. Hen. It may be so: if he have robb'd these men,
He shall be answerable; and so, farewell.
Sher. Good night, my noble lord.
P. Hen. I think it is good morrow, is it not?
Sher. Indeed, my lord, I think it be two o'clock.
[*Exeunt* Sheriff *and* Carrier.

P. Hen. This oily rascal is known as well as Paul's. Go, call him forth.

Poins. Falstaff!—fast asleep behind the arras, and snorting like a horse.

P. Hen. Hark, how hard he fetches breath. Search his pockets. [Poins *searches.*] What hast thou found?

Poins. Nothing but papers, my lord.

P. Hen. Let's see what they be: read them.

Poins. [*Reads.*]
Item, A capon, 2*s.* 2*d.*
Item, Sauce, 4*d.*
Item, Sack, two gallons, 5*s.* 8*d.*
Item, Anchovies, and sack after supper, 2*s.* 6*d.*
Item, Bread, a half-penny.

P. Hen. O monstrous! but one half-pennyworth of bread to this intolerable deal of sack!—What there is else, keep close; we'll read it at more advantage. There let him sleep till day. I'll to the court in the morning: we must all to the wars, and thy place shall be honorable. I'll procure this fat rogue a charge of foot; and, I know, his death will be a march of twelve-score. The money shall be paid back again with advantage. Be with me betimes in the morning; and so good morrow, Poins.

Poins. Good morrow, good my lord. [*Exeunt.*

ACT III.

SCENE I.—Bangor. *A Room in the Archdeacon's House.*

Enter HOTSPUR, WORCESTER, MORTIMER, *and* GLENDOWER.

Mort. These promises are fair, the parties sure,
And our induction full of prosperous hope.
Hot. Lord Mortimer, and cousin Glendower, will you sit down?
—And, uncle Worcester:—a plage upon it! I have forgot the map.
Glend. No, here it is.
Sit, cousin Percy; sit, good cousin Hotspur;
For by that name, as oft as Lancaster
Doth speak of you,
His cheek looks pale, and with a rising sigh,
He wisheth you in heaven.
Hot. And you in hell, as oft as he hears Owen
Glendower spoke of.
Glend. I cannot blame him: at my nativity,
The front of heaven was full of fiery shapes,
Of burning cressets; and at my birth,
The frame and huge foundation of the earth
Shak'd like a coward.
Hot. Why, so it would have done at the same season, if your mother's cat had but kittened, though yourself had never been born.
Glend. I say, the earth did shake when I was born.
Hot. And I say, the earth was not of my mind,
If you suppose as fearing you it shook.
Glend. The heavens were all on fire, the earth did tremble.
Hot. O, then the earth shook to see the heavens on fire,
And not in fear of your nativity.
Diseasèd nature oftentimes breaks forth
In strange eruptions; oft the teeming earth
Is with a kind of colic pinch'd and vex'd,
Which, for enlargement striving,
Shakes the old beldam earth, and topples down
Steeples, and moss-grown towers. At your birth,
Our grandam earth, having this distemperature,
In passion shook.
Glend. Cousin, of many men
I do not bear these crossings. Give me leave
To tell you once again,—that at my birth,
The front of heaven was full of fiery shapes;
The goats ran from the mountains, and the herds
Were strangely clamorous to the frighted fields.

These signs have mark'd me extraordinary;
And all the courses of my life do show,
I am not in the roll of common men.
Where is he living,—clipp'd in with the sea
That chides the banks of England, Scotland, Wales,—
Which calls me pupil, or hath read to me?
And bring him out, that is but woman's son,
Can trace me in the tedious ways of art,
And hold me pace in deep experiments.
Hot. I think there is no man speaks better Welsh.—
I'll to dinner.
Mort. Peace, cousin Percy! you will make him mad.
Glend. I can call spirits from the vasty deep.
Hot. Why, so can I, or so can any man;
But will they come, when you do call for them?
Glend. Why, I can teach thee, cousin, to command the devil.
Hot. And I can teach thee, coz, to shame the devil,
By telling truth: tell truth, and shame the devil.—
If thou have power to raise him, bring him hither,
And I'll be sworn, I have power to shame him hence.
O, while you live, tell truth, and shame the devil!
Mort. Come, come,
No more of this unprofitable chat.
Glend. Three times hath Henry Bolingbroke made head
Against my power; thrice from the banks of Wye,
And sandy-bottom'd Severn, have I sent him
Bootless home, and weather-beaten back.
Hot. Home without boots, and in foul weather too!
How 'scapes he agues?
Glend. Come, here's the map: shall we divide our right,
According to our three-fold order ta'en?
Mort. The archdeacon hath divided it
Into three limits, very equally:—
To-morrow, cousin Percy, you, and I,
And my good lord of Worcester, will set forth
To meet your father and the Scottish power,
As is appointed us, at Shrewsbury.
My father Glendower is not ready yet,
Nor shall we need his help these fourteen days:—
[*To* GLEND.] Within that space you may have drawn together
Your tenants, friends, and neighboring gentlemen.
Glend. A shorter time shall send me to you, lords,
And in my conduct shall your ladies come;
From whom you now must steal, and take no leave;
For there will be a world of water shed,
Upon the parting of your wives and you.
Hot. Methinks my moiety, north from Burton here,
In quantity equals not one of yours.

Glend. I will not have it alter'd.
Hot. Will not you?
Glend. No, nor you shall not.
Hot. Who shall say me nay?
Glend. Why, that will I.
Hot. Let me not understand you, then;
Speak it in Welsh.
Glend. I can speak English, lord, as well as you;
For I was train'd up in the English court;
Where, being but young, I framed to the harp
Many an English ditty, lovely well,
And gave the tongue a helpful ornament,
A virtue that was never seen in you.
Hot. Marry, and I'm glad of it with all my heart:
I had rather be a kitten, and cry mew,
Than one of these same metre ballad-mongers;
I had rather hear a brazen canstick turn'd,
Or a dry wheel grate on the axle-tree;
And that would set my teeth nothing on edge,
Nothing so much as mincing poetry;—
'Tis like the forc'd gait of a shuffling nag.
Glend. Come, you shall have Trent turn'd.
Hot. I do not care:
I'll give thrice so much land to any well-deserving friend;
But in the way of bargain, mark ye me,
I'll cavil on the ninth part of a hair.
Are the indentures drawn? shall we be gone?
Glend. The moon shines fair; you may away by night. [*Exit.*
Mort. Fie, cousin Percy! how you cross my father!
Hot. I cannot choose: sometimes he angers me
With telling me of the moldwarp and the ant,
Of the dreamer Merlin and his prophecies,
And of a dragon and a finless fish,
A clip-wing'd griffin and a moulten raven,
A couching lion and a ramping cat,
And such a deal of skimble-skamble stuff
As puts me from my faith. O, he's as tedious
As a tired horse, a railing wife;
Worse than a smoky house:—I had rather live
With cheese and garlick in a windmill, far,
Than feed on cates, and have him talk to me,
In any summer-house in Christendom.
Mort. In faith, he is a worthy gentleman;
Exceedingly well read, and profited
In strange concealments.
Hot. Well, I am school'd: good manners be your speed!
Here come our wives, and let us take our leave. [*Exeunt.*

SCENE II.—London. *A Room in the Palace.*

Enter KING HENRY, PRINCE HENRY, *and* Lords.

K. Hen. Lords, give us leave; the Prince of Wales and I
Must have some private conference: but be near at hand,
For we shall presently have need of you.— [*Exeunt* Lords.
I know not whether heaven will have it so,
For some displeasing service I have done,
That, in his secret doom, out of my blood
He'll breed revengement and a scourge for me;
But thou dost, in thy passages of life,
Make me believe that thou art only mark'd
For the hot vengeance and the rod of heaven.
To punish my mistreadings. Tell me else,
Could such inordinate and low desires,
Such poor, such bare, such vile, such mean attempts,
Such barren pleasures, rude society,
As thou art match'd withal and grafted to,
Accompany the greatness of thy blood,
And hold their level with thy princely heart?

P. Hen. So please your majesty, I would I could
Quit all offences with as clear excuse,
As well as, I am doubtless, I can purge
Myself of many I am charg'd withal:
Yet such extenuation let me beg,
As, in reproof of many tales devis'd,—
Which oft the ear of greatness needs must hear,—
By smiling pick-thanks and base newsmongers,
I may, for some things true, wherein my youth
Hath faulty wander'd and irregular,
Find pardon on my true submission.

K. Hen. Heaven pardon thee!—yet let me wonder, Harry,
At thy affections, which do hold a wing
Quite from the flight of all thy ancestors.
Thy place in council thou hast rudely lost,
Which by thy younger brother is supplied;
And art almost an alien to the hearts
Of all the court, and princes of my blood:
The hope and expectation of thy time
Is ruin'd; and the soul of every man
Prophetically does forethink thy fall.
Had I so lavish of my presence been,
So common-hackney'd in the eyes of men,
So stale and cheap to vulgar company,—
Opinion, that did help me to the crown,
Had still kept loyal to possession,
And left me in reputeless banishment,

A fellow of no mark nor likelihood.
By being seldom seen, I could not stir,
But, like a comet, I was wonder'd at;
That men would tell their children, "This is he;"
Others would say, "Where? which is Bolingbroke?"
And then I stole all courtesy from heaven,
And dress'd myself in such humility,
That I did pluck allegiance from men's hearts,
Loud shouts and salutations from their mouths,
Even in the presence of the crownèd king.
Thus did I keep my person fresh and new;
My presence, like a robe pontifical,
Ne'er seen but wonder'd at: and so my state,
Seldom, but sumptuous, showed like a feast;
And won, by rareness, such solemnity.
The skipping king, he ambled up and down
With shallow jesters and rash bavin wits,
Soon kindled, and soon burn'd; carded his state;
Mingled his royalty with carping fools;
Had his great name profanèd with their scorns;
Grew a companion to the common streets;
That, being daily swallow'd by men's eyes,
They surfeited with honey, and began
To loathe the taste of sweetness.
So, when he had occasion to be seen,
He was but as the cuckoo is in June,
Heard, not regarded,—seen, but with such eyes,
As, sick and blunted with community,
Afford no extraordinary gaze,
Such as is bent on sun-like majesty,
When it shines seldom in admiring eyes;
But rather drows'd, and hung their eyelids down
Slept in his face, and render'd such aspect
As cloudy men use to their adversaries,
Being with his presence glutted, gorg'd, and full.
And in that very line, Harry, stand'st thou;
For thou hast lost thy princely privilege,
With vile participation: not an eye
But is a-weary of thy common sight,
Save mine, which hath desir'd to see thee more;
Which now doth that I would not have it do,—
Make blind itself with foolish tenderness.

P. Hen. I shall hereafter, my thrice-gracious lord,
Be more myself.

K. Hen. For all the world,
As thou art to this hour, was Richard then,
When I from France set foot at Ravenspurg;
And even as I was then, is Percy now.

Now, by my sceptre, and my soul to boot,
He hath more worthy interest to the state,
Than thou, the shadow of succession:
For, of no right, nor color like to right,
He doth fill fields with harness in the realm;
Turns head against the lion's armèd jaws;
And, being no more in debt to years than thou,
Leads ancient lords and reverend bishops on
To bloody battles, and to bruising arms.
What never-dying honor hath he got
Against renownèd Douglas! whose high deeds,
Whose hot incursions, and great name in arms,
Holds from all soldiers chief majority.
Thrice hath this Hotspur, Mars in swathing clothes,
This infant warrior, in his enterprises
Discomfited great Douglas; ta'en him once,
Enlarged him, and made a friend of him,
To fill the mouth of deep defiance up,
And shake the peace and safety of our throne.
And what say you to this? Percy, Northumberland,
The archbishop's grace of York, Douglas, Mortimer,
Capitulate against us, and are up.
But wherefore do I tell these news to thee?
Why, Harry, do I tell thee of my foes,
Which art my near'st and dearest enemy?
Thou that art like enough,—through vassal fear,
Base inclination, and the start of spleen,—
To fight against me under Percy's pay,
To dog his heels, and court'sy at his frowns,
To show how much thou art degenerate.

P. Hen. Do not think so; you shall not find it so:
And heaven forgive them, that so much have sway'd
Your majesty's good thoughts away from me!
I will redeem all this on Percy's head,
And in the closing of some glorious day,
Be bold to tell you that I am your son;
When I will wear a garment all of blood,
And stain my favors in a bloody mask,
Which, wash'd away, shall scour my shame with it:
And that shall be the day, whene'er it lights,
That this same child of honor and renown,
This gallant Hotspur, this all-praised knight,
And your unthought-of Harry, chance to meet.
For every honor sitting on his helm,
'Would they were multitudes, and on my head
My shames redoubled! for the time will come,
That I shall make this northern youth exchange
His glorious deeds for my indignities.

This, in the name of heaven, I promise here:
And I will die a hundred thousand deaths,
Ere break the smallest parcel of this vow.
K. Hen. A hundred thousand rebels die in this
Thou shalt have charge, and sovereign trust herein.

Enter Sir WALTER BLUNT.

How now, good Blunt! thy looks are full of speed.
Blunt. So hath the business that I come to speak of.
Lord Mortimer of Scotland hath sent word,
That Douglas and the English rebels met,
The eleventh of this month, at Shrewsbury:
A mighty and a fearful head they are,
(If promises be kept on every hand,)
As ever offer'd foul play in a state.
K. Hen. The earl of Westmoreland set forth to-day;
With him my son, lord John of Lancaster;
For this advertisement is five days old:—
On Wednesday next, Harry, you shall set forward;
On Thursday we ourselves will march.
Our hands are full of business: let's away;
Advantage feeds him fat, while men delay. [*Exeunt.*

SCENE III.—Eastcheap. *A Room in the* Boar's Head Tavern.

Enter FALSTAFF *and* BARDOLPH.

Fal. Bardolph, am I not fallen away vilely since this last action? do I not bate? do I not dwindle? Why, my skin hangs about me like an old lady's loose gown; I am wither'd like an old apple-John. Well, I'll repent, and that suddenly, while I am in some liking; I shall be out of heart shortly, and then I shall have no strength to repent. Company, villanous company, hath been the spoil of me.

Bard. Sir John, you are so fretful, you cannot live long.

Fal. Why, there is it:—come, sing me a jovial song; make me merry. I was as virtuously given as a gentleman need to be; virtuous enough; swore little; diced not above seven times a week; paid money that I borrowed—three or four times; lived well, and in good compass: and now I live out of all order, out of all compass.

Bard. Why, you are so fat, Sir John, that you must needs be out of all compass,—out of all reasonable compass, Sir John.

Fal. Do thou amend thy face, and I'll amend my life: thou art our admiral, thou bearest the lantern, but 'tis in the nose of thee: thou art the Knight of the Burning Lamp.

Bard. Why, Sir John, my face does you no harm.

Fal. No, I'll be sworn; I make a good use of it. O, thou art a perpetual triumph, an everlasting bonfire-light! Thou hast saved me a thousand marks in links and torches, walking with thee in the night betwixt tavern and tavern: but the sack that thou hast drunk me, would have brought me lights as good cheap, at the dearest chandler's in Europe. I have maintained that salamander of yours with fire any time this two and thirty years; heaven reward me for it!

Bard. I would my face were in your stomach!

Fal. Heaven have mercy! so should I be sure to be heart-burned.

Enter Hostess.

How now, dame Partlet the hen! have you enquired yet who picked my pocket?

Host. Why, Sir John, what do you think, Sir John? Do you think I keep thieves in my house? I have searched, I have enquired, so has my husband, man by man, boy by boy, servant by servant: the tithe of a hair was never lost in my house before.

Fal. You lie, hostess: Bardolph was shaved, and lost many a hair; and I'll be sworn, my pocket was picked. Go to, you are a woman, go.

Host. Who, I? No; I defy thee: I was never called so in my house before.

Fal. Go to; I know you well enough.

Host. No, Sir John; you do not know me, Sir John: I know you, Sir John: you owe me money, Sir John; and now you pick a quarrel to beguile me of it: I bought you a dozen of shirts to your back.

Fal. Dowlas, filthy dowlas: I have given them away to bakers' wives, and they have made bolters of them.

Host. Now, as I am a true woman, holland of eight shillings an ell. You owe money here besides, Sir John, for your diet, and by-drinkings, and money lent you, four and twenty pound.

Fal. He had his part of it; let him pay.

Host. He? alas! he is poor; he hath nothing.

Fal. How! poor? look upon his face; what call you rich? let them coin his nose, let them coin his cheeks: I'll not pay a denier. What, will you make a younker of me? shall I not take mine ease in mine inn, but I shall have my pocket picked? I have lost a seal-ring of my grandfather's, worth forty mark.

Host. O! I have heard the prince tell him, I know not how oft, that that ring was copper.

Fal. How! the prince is a Jack, a sneak-cup: an he were here, I would cudgel him like a dog, if he would say so.

Enter PRINCE HENRY *and* POINS, *marching.* FALSTAFF *meets the* PRINCE, *playing on his truncheon like a fife.*

Fal. How now, lad! is the wind in that door, i' faith? must we all march?

Bard. Yea, two and two, Newgate-fashion.

Host. My lord, I pray you, hear me.

P. Hen. What sayest thou, mistress Quickly? How does thy husband? I love him well; he is an honest man.

Host. Good my lord, hear me.

Fal. Pr'ythee, let her alone, and list to me.

P. Hen. What sayest thou, Jack?

Fal. The other night I fell asleep here, behind the arras, and had my pocket picked.

P. Hen. What didst thou lose, Jack?

Fal. Wilt thou believe me, Hal? three or four bonds of forty pound a-piece, and a seal-ring of my grandfather's.

P. Hen. A trifle, some eight-penny matter.

Host. So I told him, my lord; and I said I heard your grace say so: and, my lord, he speaks most vilely of you, like a foul-mouthed man as he is; and said, he would cudgel you.

P. Hen. What! he did not?

Host. There's neither faith, truth, nor womanhood in me else.

Fal. There's no more faith in thee than in a stewed prune; nor no more truth in thee, than in a drawn fox.

Host. I am an honest man's wife; and, setting thy knighthood aside, thou art a knave to call me otherwise.

P. Hen. Thou sayest true, hostess; and he slanders thee most grossly.

Host. So he doth you, my lord; and said this other day, you ought him a thousand pound.

P. Hen. Sirrah! do I owe you a thousand pound?

Fal. A thousand pound, Hal! a million: thy love is worth a million; thou owest me thy love.

Host. Nay, my lord, he called you Jack, and said he would cudgel you,

Fal. Did I, Bardolph?

Bard. Indeed, Sir John, you said so.

Fal. Yea,—if he said my ring was copper.

P. Hen. I say, 'tis copper: darest thou be as good as thy word now?

Fal. Why, Hal, thou knowest, as thou art but man, I dare: but as thou art prince, I fear thee, as I fear the roaring of the lion's whelp.

P. Hen. And why not, as the lion?

Fal. The king himself is to be feared as the lion: dost thou think, I'll fear thee as I fear thy father?

P. Hen. Sirrah, there's no room for faith, truth, nor honesty, in this bosom of thine.—Charge an honest woman with picking thy pocket! Why, thou vile, impudent, embossed rascal, if there were any thing in thy pocket but tavern reckonings, memorandums, and one poor pennyworth of sugar-candy to make thee long-winded,—if thy pocket were enriched with any other injuries but these, I am a villain: and yet you will stand to it; you will not pocket up wrong. Art thou not ashamed?

Fal. Dost thou hear, Hal? thou knowest in the state of innocency, Adam fell; and what should poor Jack Falstaff do, in the days of villany? Thou seest, I have more flesh than another man; and therefore more frailty. You confess, then, you picked my pocket?

P. Hen. It appears so by the story.

Fal. Hostess, I forgive thee: go, make ready breakfast; love thy husband, look to thy servants, cherish thy guests: thou shalt find me tractable to any honest reason: thou seest, I am pacified. —Still!—Nay, pr'ythee, begone. [*Exit* Hostess.] Now, Hal, to the news at court: for the robbery, lad,—how is that answered?

P. Hen. O, my sweet beef, I must still be good angel to thee: —the money is paid back again.

Fal. O, I do not like that paying back; 'tis a double labor.

P. Hen. I am good friends with my father, and may do any thing.

Fal. Rob me the exchequer the first thing thou dost, and do it with unwashed hands too.

Bard. Do, my lord.

P. Hen. I have procured thee, Jack, a charge of foot.

Fal. I would it had been of horse. Where shall I find one that can steal well? O for a fine thief, of the age of two and twenty, or thereabouts! I am heinously unprovided. Well, heaven be thanked for these rebels,—they offend none but the virtuous; I laud them, I praise them.

P. Hen. Bardolph,—

Bard. My lord!

P. Hen. Go bear this letter to lord John of Lancaster,
To my brother John; this to my lord of Westmoreland.—
[*Exit* BARDOLPH.
Go, Poins, to horse, to horse; for thou and I
Have thirty miles to ride yet ere dinner time.— [*Exit* POINS.
Jack, meet me to-morrow in the Temple-hall
At two o'clock in the afternoon:
There shalt thou know thy charge; and there receive
Money, and order for their furniture.
The land is burning; Percy stands on high;
And either they, or we, must lower lie. [*Exit.*

Fal. Rare words! brave world!—Hostess, my breakfast; come:—
O, I could wish this tavern were my drum! [*Exit.*

ACT IV.

SCENE I.—*The Rebel Camp near* Shrewsbury.

Enter HOTSPUR, WORCESTER, *and* DOUGLAS.

Hot. Well said, my noble Scot: if speaking truth
In this fine age were not thought flattery,
Such attribution should the Douglas have,
As not a soldier of this season's stamp
Should go so general current through the world.
By heaven, I cannot flatter; I defy
The tongues of soothers; but a braver place
In my heart's love hath no man than yourself:
Nay, task me to my word; approve me, lord.
Doug. Thou art the king of honor:
No man so potent breathes upon the ground,
But I will beard him.
Hot. Do so, and 'tis well.—

Enter a Messenger, *with letters.*

What letters hast thou here?—[*To* DOUGLAS.] I can but thank you.
Mess. These letters come from your father.
Hot. Letters from him! why comes he not himself?
Mess. He cannot come, my lord; he's grievous sick.
Hot. 'Zounds! how has he the leisure to be sick,
In such a justling time? Who leads his power?
Under whose government come they along?
Mess. His letters bear his mind, not I, my lord.
Wor. I pr'ythee, tell me, doth he keep his bed?
Mess. He did, my lord, four days ere I set forth;
And at the time of my departure thence,
He was much fear'd by his physicians.
Wor. I would the state of time had first been whole,
Ere he by sickness had been visited:
His health was never better worth than now.
Hot. Sick now! droop now! this sickness doth infect
The very life-blood of our enterprise;
'Tis catching hither, even to our camp.—
Yet doth he give us bold advertisement,
That with our small conjunction we should on,
To see how fortune is dispos'd to us;
For, as he writes, there is no quailing now,
Because the king is certainly possess'd
Of all our purposes. What say you to it?
Wor. Your father's sickness is a maim to us.

Hot. A perilous gash, a very limb lopp'd off:—
And yet, in faith, 'tis not; his present want
Seems more than we shall find it.
Wor. I would your father had been here.
The quality and hair of our attempt
Brooks no division: it will be thought
By some, that know not why he is away,
That wisdom, loyalty, and mere dislike
Of our proceedings, kept the earl from hence.
Hot. You strain too far.
I, rather, of his absence make this use:—
It lends a lustre, and more great opinion,
A larger dare to our great enterprise,
Than if the earl were here; for men must think,
If we, without his help, can make a head
To push against the kingdom, with his help,
We shall o'erturn it topsy-turvy down.—
Yet all goes well; yet all our joints are whole.
Doug. As heart can think: there is not such a word
Spoke of in Scotland as this term of fear.

Enter Sir RICHARD VERNON.

Hot. My cousin Vernon! welcome, by my soul.
Ver. Pray heaven my news be worth a welcome, lord.
The earl of Westmoreland, seven thousand strong,
Is marching hitherwards; with him, prince John.
Hot. No harm: what more?
Ver. And farther, I have learn'd,
The king himself in person is set forth,
Or hitherwards intended speedily,
With strong and mighty preparation.
Hot. He shall be welcome too. Where is his son,
The nimble-footed mad-cap prince of Wales,
And his comrades, that daff'd the world aside,
And bid it pass?
Ver. All furnish'd, all in arms,
All plum'd like estridges (that with the wind
Bated, like eagles having lately bath'd);
Glittering in golden coats, like images;
As full of spirit as the month of May,
And gorgeous as the sun at midsummer;
Wanton as youthful goats, wild as young bulls.
I saw young Harry,—with his beaver on,
His cuisses on his thighs, gallantly arm'd,—
Rise from the ground like feather'd Mercury,
And vaulted with such ease into his seat,
As if an angel dropp'd down from the clouds,

To turn and wind a fiery Pegasus,
And witch the world with noble horsemanship.
Hot. No more, no more: worse than the sun in March,
This praise doth nourish agues. Let them come.
Come, let me taste my horse,
Who is to bear me like a thunderbolt,
Against the bosom of the prince of Wales:
Harry to Harry shall, hot horse to horse,
Meet, and ne'er part, till one drop down a corse.—
O, that Glendower were come!
Ver. There is more news:
I learn'd in Worcester, as I rode along,
He cannot draw his power this fourteen days.
Doug. That's the worst tidings that I hear of yet.
Wor. Ay, by my faith, that bears a frosty sound.
Hot. What may the king's whole battle reach unto?
Ver. To thirty thousand.
Hot. Forty let it be:
My father and Glendower being both away,
The powers of us may serve so great a day.
Come, let us take a muster speedily:
Doomsday is near; die all, die merrily. [*Exeunt.*

SCENE II.—*A public Road near* Coventry.

Enter FALSTAFF *and* BARDOLPH.

Fal. Bardolph, get thee before to Coventry; fill me a bottle of sack: our soldiers shall march through; we'll to Sutton-Cophill to-night.

Bard. Will you give me money, captain?

Fal. Lay out, lay out.

Bard. This bottle makes an angel.

Fal. An if it do, take it for thy labor; and if it make twenty, take them all; I'll answer the coinage. Bid my lieutenant Peto meet me at the town's end.

Bard. I will, captain: farewell. [*Exit.*

Fal. If I be not ashamed of my soldiers, I am a soused gurnet. I have misused the king's press shamefully. I have got, in exchange of a hundred and fifty soldiers, three hundred and odd pounds. I press me none but good householders, yeomen's sons; enquire me out contracted bachelors, such as had been asked twice on the bans; such a commodity of warm slaves, as had as lief hear the evil one as a drum; such as fear the report of a caliver, worse than a struck fowl, or a hurt wild-duck. I pressed me none but such toasts and butter, with hearts in them no bigger than pins' heads, and they have bought out their services; and now my whole charge consists of ancients, corporals, lieutenants, gentlemen of companies, slaves as ragged as Lazarus in the painted cloth, and such as, indeed, were never soldiers, but discarded unjust serving men, younger sons to younger brothers, revolted tapsters, and ostlers trade-fallen; the cankers of a calm world and a long peace; ten times more dishonorable ragged than an old faced ancient: and such have I, to fill up the rooms of them that have bought out their services, that you would think that I had a hundred and fifty tattered prodigals, lately come from swine-keeping, from eating draff and husks. A mad fellow met me on the way, and told me I had unloaded all the gibbets, and pressed the dead bodies. No eye hath seen such scarecrows. I'll not march through Coventry with them, that's flat:—nay, and the villains march wide betwixt the legs, as if they had gyves on; for, indeed, I had the most of them out of prison.

Enter PRINCE HENRY *and* WESTMORELAND.

P. Hen. How now, blown Jack! how now, quilt!

Fal. What, Hal! How now, mad wag! what dost thou in Warwickshire?—My good lord of Westmoreland, I cry you mercy: I thought your honor had already been at Shrewsbury.

West. 'Faith, Sir John, 'tis more than time that I were there, and you too; but my powers are there already. The king, I can tell you, looks for us all: we must away all night.

Fal. Tut, never fear me: I am as vigilant as a cat to steal cream.

P. Hen. I think, to steal cream, indeed; for thy theft hath already made thee butter. But tell me, Jack, whose fellows are these that come after?

Fal. Mine, Hal, mine.

P. Hen. I did never see such pitiful rascals.

Fal. Tut, tut! good enough to toss; food for powder, food for powder; they'll fill a pit as well as better: tush, man, mortal men, mortal men.

West. Ay, but, Sir John, methinks they are exceeding poor and bare,—too beggarly.

Fal. 'Faith, for their poverty, I know not where they had that; and for their bareness, I am sure, they never learned that of me.

P. Hen. No, I'll be sworn; unless you call three fingers on the ribs, bare. But, sirrah, make haste: Percy is already in the field.

Fal. What, is the king encamped?

West. He is, Sir John: I fear we shall stay too long.

Fal. Well,
To the latter end of a fray, and the beginning of a feast,
Fits a dull fighter, and a keen guest. [*Exeunt.*

SCENE III.—*The Rebel Camp near* Shrewsbury

Enter HOTSPUR, WORCESTER, DOUGLAS, *and* VERNON.

Hot. We'll fight with him to-night.
Wor. Good cousin, be advis'd; stir not to-night.
Ver. Do not, my lord.
Doug. You do not counsel well:
You speak it out of fear, and cold heart.
Ver. Do me no slander, Douglas: by my life,
If well-respected honor bid me on,
I hold as little counsel with weak fear,
As you, my lord, or any Scot that lives
Let it be seen to-morrow in the battle,
Which of us fears.
Doug. Yea, or to-night.
Ver. Content.
Hot. To-night, say I.
Wor. The number of the king exceedeth ours:
For heaven's sake, cousin, stay till all come in.
[*The trumpet sounds a parley.*

Enter Sir WALTER BLUNT.

Blunt. I come with gracious offers from the king,
If you vouchsafe me hearing and respect.
Hot. Welcome, Sir Walter Blunt; and would to God
You were of our determination!
Some of us love you well; and even those some
Envy your great deservings, and good name,
Because you are not of our quality,
But stand against us like an enemy.
Blunt. And heaven defend but still I should stand so,
So long as out of limit and true rule,
You stand against anointed majesty!
But, to my charge.—The king hath sent to know
The nature of your griefs; and whereupon
You conjure from the breast of civil peace
Such bold hostility, teaching his duteous land
Audacious cruelty. If that the king
Have any way your good deserts forgot,—
Which he confesseth to be manifold,—
He bids you name your griefs; and with all speed,
You shall have your desires with interest,
And pardon absolute for yourself, and these,
Herein misled by your suggestion.
Hot. The king is kind; and well we know, the king
Knows at what time to promise, when to pay.
My father, and my uncle, and myself,

Did give him that same royalty he wears;
And when he was not six-and-twenty strong,
Sick in the world's regard, wretched and low,
A poor unminded outlaw sneaking home,
My father gave him welcome to the shore;
And when he heard him swear, and vow to heaven,
He came but to be duke of Lancaster,
To sue his livery and beg his peace,
With tears of innocency and terms of zeal,—
My father, in kind heart and pity mov'd,
Swore him assistance, and perform'd it too.
Now, when the lords and barons of the realm
Perceiv'd Northumberland did lean to him,
The more and less came in with cap and knee;
Met him in boroughs, cities, villages,
Attended him on bridges, stood in lanes,
Laid gifts before him, proffer'd him their oaths,
Gave him their heirs as pages; follow'd him,
Even at the heels, in golden multitudes.
He presently,—as greatness knows itself,—
Steps me a little higher than his vow
Made to my father while his blood was poor,
Upon the naked shore at Ravenspurg;
And now, forsooth, takes on him to reform
Some certain edicts, and some strait decrees,
That lie too heavy on the commonwealth;
Cries out upon abuses, seems to weep
Over his country's wrongs; and by this face,
This seeming brow of justice, did he win
The hearts of all that he did angle for:
Proceeded farther; cut me off the heads
Of all the favorites, that the absent king
In deputation left behind him here,
When he was personal in the Irish war.
Blunt. Tut! I came not to hear this.
Hot. Then, to the point.
In short time after, he depos'd the king;
Soon after that, depriv'd him of his life;
And, in the neck of that, task'd the whole state:
To make that worse, suffer'd his kinsman March
(Who is, if every owner were well plac'd,
Indeed his king) to be engag'd in Wales
There without ransom to lie forfeited;
Disgrac'd me in my happy victories;
Sought to entrap me by intelligence;
Rated my uncle from the council-board;
In rage dismiss'd my father from the court;
Broke oath on oath committed wrong on wrong;

And, in conclusion, drove us to seek out
This head of safety; and withal to pry
Into his title, the which we find
Too indirect for long continuance.
Blunt. Shall I return this answer to the king?
Hot. Not so, Sir Walter: we'll withdraw awhile.
Go to the king; and let there be impawn'd
Some surety for a safe return again,
And in the morning early shall my uncle
Bring him our purposes: and so farewell.
Blunt. I would you would accept of grace and love.
Hot. And, may be, so we shall.
Blunt. 'Pray God you do! [*Exeunt.*

ACT V.

SCENE I.—*The* KING'S *Camp near* Shrewsbury.

Enter KING HENRY, PRINCE HENRY, PRINCE JOHN OF LANCASTER, *Sir* WALTER BLUNT, *and Sir* JOHN FALSTAFF.

K. Hen. How bloodily the sun begins to peer
Above yond' bosky hill! the day looks pale
At his distemperature.
P. Hen. The southern wind
Doth play the trumpet to his purposes;
And by his hollow whistling in the leaves,
Foretels a tempest, and a blustering day.
K. Hen. Then, with the losers let it sympathise,
For nothing can seem foul to those that win.—
[*Trumpet sounds.*

Enter WORCESTER *and* VERNON.

How now, my lord of Worcester! 'tis not well,
That you and I should meet upon such terms
As now we meet. You have deceiv'd our trust,
And made us doff our easy robes of peace,
To crush our old limbs in ungentle steel:
This is not well, my lord, this is not well.
What say you to it? will you again unknit
This churlish knot of all-abhorred war?
Wor. Hear me, my liege.
For mine own part, I could be well content
To entertain the lag-end of my life
With quiet hours; for, I do protest,
I have not sought the day of this dislike.
K. Hen. You have not sought it! how comes it then?

Fal. Rebellion lay in his way, and he found it.
P. Hen. Peace, chewet, peace!
Wor. It pleas'd your majesty to turn your looks
Of favor from myself and all our house;
We were enforc'd, for safety' sake, to fly
Out of your sight, and raise this present head:
Whereby we stand opposèd by such means
As you yourself have forg'd against yourself,
By unkind usage, dangerous countenance,
And violation of all faith and troth
Sworn to us in your younger enterprise.
K. Hen. These things, indeed, you have articulated,
Proclaim'd at market-crosses, read in churches,
To face the garment of rebellion
With some fine color, that may please the eye
Of fickle changelings, and poor discontents,
Which gape, and rub the elbow, at the news
Of hurlyburly innovation.
And never yet did insurrection want
Such water-colors to impaint his cause;
Nor moody beggars, starving for a time
Of pellmell havock and confusion.
P. Hen. In both our armies, there is many a soul
Shall pay full dearly for this encounter,
If once they join in trial.
K. Hen. No, good Worcester, no,
We love our people well; even those we love
That are misled upon your cousin's part;
And, will they take the offer of our grace,
Both he and they, and you, yea, every man
Shall be my friend again, and I'll be his:
So tell your cousin, and bring me word
What he will do: but if he will not yield,
Rebuke and dread correction wait on us,
And they shall do their office. So, be gone;
We will not now be troubled with reply:
We offer fair; take it advisedly.
[*Exeunt* WORCESTER *and* VERNON.
P. Hen. It will not be accepted, on my life:
The Douglas and the Hotspur both together
Are confident against the world in arms.
K. Hen. Hence, therefore, every leader to his charge;
For, on their answer, will we set on them:
And heaven befriend us, as our cause is just!
[*Exeunt* KING, BLUNT *and* PRINCE JOHN.
Fal. Hal, if thou see me down in the battle, and bestride me, so; 'tis a point of friendship.

P. Hen. Nothing but a colossus can do thee that friendship. Say thy prayers, and farewell.

Fal. I would it were bed-time, Hal, and all well.

P. Hen. Why, thou owest heaven a death. [*Exit.*

Fal. 'Tis not due yet; I would be loath to pay him before his day. What need I be so forward with him that calls not on me? Well, 'tis no matter; honor pricks me on. Yea, but how if honor prick me off when I come on? how then? Can honor set to a leg? no: or an arm? no: or take away the grief of a wound? No. Honor hath no skill in surgery, then? no. What is honor? a word. What is that word, honor? air. A trim reckoning!—Who hath it? he that died o' Wednesday. Doth he feel it? no. Doth he hear it? no. Is it insensible, then? yea, to the dead. But will it not live with the living? no. Why? detraction will not suffer it:—therefore, I'll none of it: honor is a mere scutcheon:—and so ends my catechism. [*Exit.*

SCENE III.—*Plain near* Shrewsbury.

Excursions, and Parties fighting. Alarum to the Battle. Then enter DOUGLAS *and* BLUNT, (*who is accoutred like the* KING,) *meeting.*

Blunt. What is thy name, that in the battle thus
Thou crossest me? what honor dost thou seek
Upon my head?

Doug. Know, then, my name is Douglas;
And I do haunt thee in the battle thus,
Because some tell me that thou art a king.

Blunt. They tell thee true.

Doug. The lord of Stafford dear to-day hath bought
Thy likeness; for, instead of thee, king Harry,
This sword hath ended him: so shall it thee,
Unless thou yield thee as my prisoner.

Blunt. I was not born a yielder, thou proud Scot;
And thou shalt find a king that will revenge
Lord Stafford's death. [*They fight, and* BLUNT *is slain.*

Enter HOTSPUR.

Hot. O Douglas! hadst thou fought at Holmedon thus,
I never had triumph'd upon a Scot.

Doug All's done, all's won: here breathless lies the king.

Hot. Where?

Doug. Here.

Hot. This, Douglas? no; I know this face full well:
A gallant knight he was, his name was Blunt;
Semblably furnish'd like the king himself.

Doug. A fool go with thy soul, where'er it goes!

A borrow'd title hast thou bought too dear:
Why didst thou tell me that thou wert a king?

Hot. The king hath many marching in his coats.

Doug. Now, by my sword, I will kill all his coats;
I'll murder all his wardrobe, piece by piece,
Until I meet the king.

Hot. Up, and away!
Our soldiers stand full fairly for the day. [*Exeunt.*

Alarums. Enter FALSTAFF.

Fal. Though I could 'scape shot-free at London, I fear the shot here; here's no scoring, but upon the pate.—Soft! who art thou? Sir Walter Blunt!—there's Honor for you! here's no vanity!—I am as hot as molten lead, and as heavy too: heaven keep lead out of me! I have led my raggamuffins where they are peppered; there's not three of my hundred and fifty left alive; and they are for the town's end, to beg during life.—But who comes here?

Enter PRINCE HENRY.

P. Hen. What! stand'st thou idle here? lend me thy sword:
Many a nobleman lies stark and stiff
Under the hoofs of vaunting enemies,
Whose deaths are unreveng'd. Pr'ythee, lend thy sword.

Fal. O Hal! I pr'ythee, give me leave to breathe a while.—Turk Gregory never did such deeds in arms, as I have done this day. I have paid Percy. I have made him sure.

P. Hen. He is, indeed; and living to kill thee.
I pr'ythee, lend me thy sword.

Fal. Nay, before heaven, Hal, if Percy be alive, thou get'st not my sword; but take my pistol, if thou wilt.

P. Hen. Give it me: what, is it in the case?

Fal. Ay, Hal; 'tis hot, 'tis hot; there's that will sack a city.
[*The* PRINCE *draws out a bottle of sack.*

P. Hen. What! is't a time to jest and dally now?
[*Throws it at him, and exit.*

Fal. Well, if Percy be alive, I'll pierce him. If he do come in my way, so; if he do not, if I come in his, willingly, let him make a carbonado of me. I like not such grinning honor as Sir Walter hath: give me life: which if I can save, so: if not, honor comes unlooked for, and there's an end. [*Exit.*

SCENE IV.—*Another part of the Field.*

Alarums. Excursions. Enter KING HENRY, PRINCE HENRY, PRINCE JOHN, *and* WESTMORELAND.

K. Hen. I pr'ythee,

Harry, withdraw thyself; thou bleed'st too much.—
Lord John of Lancaster, go you with him.
P. John. Not I, my lord, unless I did bleed too.
P. Hen. I beseech your majesty, make up,
Lest your retirement do amaze your friends.
K. Hen. I will do so.—My lord of Westmoreland,
Lead him to his tent.
West. Come, my lord, I'll lead you to your tent.
P. Hen. Lead me, my lord? I do not need your help·
And heaven forbid, a shallow scratch should drive
The prince of Wales from such a field as this,
Where stain'd nobility lies trodden on,
And rebels' arms triumph in massacres!
P. John. We breathe too long:—come, cousin Westmoreland,
Our duty this way lies.
[*Exeunt* PRINCE JOHN *and* WESTMORELAND.
P. Hen. By heaven, thou hast deceiv'd me, Lancaster;
I did not think thee lord of such a spirit:
Before, I lov'd thee as a brother, John;
But now, I do respect thee as my soul.
K. Hen. I saw him hold lord Percy at the point,
With lustier maintenance than I did look for
Of such an ungrown warrior.
P. Hen. O, this boy
Lends mettle to us all! [*Exit.*

Alarums. Enter DOUGLAS.

Doug. Another king! they grow like Hydra's heads:
I am the Douglas, fatal to all those
That wear those colors on them:—what art thou,
That counterfeit'st the person of a king?
K. Hen. The king himself; who, Douglas, grieves at heart,
So many of his shadows thou hast met,
And not the very king. I have two boys
Seek Percy, and thyself, about the field:
But, seeing thou fall'st on me so luckily,
I will assay thee: so, defend thyself.
Doug. I fear thou art another counterfeit;
And yet, in faith, thou bear'st thee like a king:
But mine I am sure thou art, whoe'er thou be,
And thus I win thee.
[*They fight. The* KING *being in danger, re-enter* P. HENRY.
P. Hen. Hold up thy head, vile Scot, or thou art like
Never to hold it up again! the spirits
Of valiant Shirley, Stafford, Blunt, are in my arms:
It is the prince of Wales that threatens thee;

Who never promiseth, but he means to pay.—
[*They fight.* DOUGLAS *flies.*
Cheerly, my lord: how fares your grace?—
Sir Nicholas Gawsey hath for succor sent,
And so hath Clifton: I'll to Clifton straight.
K. Hen. Stay, and breathe a while:—
Thou hast redeem'd thy lost opinion;
And show'd thou mak'st some tender of my life,
In this fair rescue thou hast brought to me.
P. Hen. They did me too much injury,
That ever said I hearken'd for your death.
If it were so, I might have let alone
The insulting hand of Douglas over you;
Which would have been as speedy in your end,
As all the poisonous potions in the world,
And sav'd the treacherous labor of your son.
K. Hen. Make up to Clifton: I'll to Sir Nicholas Gawsey.
[*Exit.*

Enter HOTSPUR.

Hot. If I mistake not, thou art Harry Monmouth.
P. Hen. Thou speak'st as if I would deny my name.
Hot. My name is Harry Percy.
P. Hen. Why, then I see
A very valiant rebel of that name.
I am the prince of Wales; and think not, Percy,
To share with me in glory any more:
Two stars keep not their motion in one sphere;
Nor can one England brook a double reign,
Of Harry Percy, and the prince of Wales.
Hot. Nor shall it, Harry; for the hour is come
To end the one of us; and would to heaven
Thy name in arms were now as great as mine!
P. Hen. I'll make it greater, ere I part from thee,
And all the budding honors on thy crest
I'll crop, to make a garland for my head.
Hot. I can no longer brook thy vanities. [*They fight.*

Enter FALSTAFF.

Fal. Well said, Hal! to it, Hal!—Nay, you shall find no boy's play here, I can tell you.

Re-enter DOUGLAS; *he fights with* FALSTAFF, *who falls down as if he were dead, and exit* DOUGLAS. HOTSPUR *is wounded, and falls.*

Hot. O, Harry, thou hast robb'd me of my youth!
I better brook the loss of brittle life,
Than those proud titles thou hast won of me;

They wound my thoughts worse than thy sword my flesh:—
But thought's the slave of life, and life, time's fool;
And time, that takes survey of all the world,
Must have a stop. O, I could prophesy,
But that the earthy and cold hand of death
Lies on my tongue:—no, Percy, thou art dust,
And food for— [*Dies.*

P. Hen. For worms, brave Percy: fare thee well, great heart!
Ill-weav'd ambition, how much art thou shrunk!
When that this body did contain a spirit,
A kingdom for it was too small a bound;
But now, two paces of the vilest earth
Is room enough:—this earth, that bears thee dead,
Bears not alive so stout a gentleman.
If thou wert sensible of courtesy,
I should not make so dear a show of zeal:
But let my favors hide thy mangled face;
[*Covers* HOTSPUR *with his scarf.*
And, even in thy behalf, I'll thank myself
For doing these fair rites of tenderness.
Adieu, and take thy praise with thee to heaven?
Thy ignomy sleep with thee in the grave,
But not remember'd in thy epitaph!—
[*He sees* FALSTAFF *on the ground.*
What, old acquaintance! Could not all this flesh
Keep in a little life? Poor Jack, farewell!
I could have better spar'd a better man:
O, I should have a heavy miss of thee,
If I were much in love with vanity!
Death hath not struck so fat a deer to-day
Though many dearer, in this bloody fray.
Embowell'd will I see thee by and by;
Till then, in blood by noble Percy lie. [*Exit.*

Fal. [*Rising.*] Embowelled! if thou embowel me to day, I'll give you leave to powder me, and eat me too, to-morrow. 'Twas time to counterfeit, or that hot termagant Scot had paid me scot and lot too. Counterfeit? I lie, I am no counterfeit: to die, is to be a counterfeit; for he is but the counterfeit of a man, who hath not the life of a man: but to counterfeit dying, when a man thereby liveth, is to be no counterfeit, but the true and perfect image of life indeed. The better part of valor is discretion; in the which better part, I have saved my life. 'Zounds! I am afraid of this gunpowder Percy, though he be dead: how, if he should counterfeit too, and rise? by my faith, I am afraid he would prove the better counterfeit. Therefore I'll make him sure; yea, and I'll swear I killed him. Why may not he rise, as well as I? Nothing confutes me but eyes, and nobody sees me: therefore, sirrah, [*Stabbing him.*] with a new wound in you, come you along with me.

[*He takes* HOTSPUR *on his back.*

Re-enter PRINCE HENRY *and* PRINCE JOHN.

P. Hen. Come, brother John; full bravely hast thou flesh'd
Thy maiden sword.

P. John. But soft! whom have we here?
Did you not tell me this fat man was dead?

P. Hen. I did; I saw him dead, breathless, and bleeding
On the ground—
Art thou alive? or is it fantasy
That plays upon our eyesight? I pr'ythee, speak;
We will not trust our eyes, without our ears:—
Thou art not what thou seem'st.

Fal. No, that's certain; I am not a double man: but if I be not Jack Falstaff, then am I a Jack. There is Percy: [*Throwing the body down.*] if your father will do me any honor, so; if not, let him kill the next Percy himself. I look to be either earl or duke, I can assure you.

P. Hen. Why, Percy I killed myself, and saw thee dead.

Fal. Didst thou?—Lord, lord, how this world is given to lying!—I grant you I was down, and out of breath; and so was he: but we rose both at an instant, and fought a long hour by Shrewsbury clock. If I may be believed, so; if not, let them that should reward valor bear the sin upon their own heads. I'll take it upon my death, I gave him this wound: if the man were alive, and would deny it, 'zounds, I would make him eat a piece of my sword.

P. John. This is the strangest tale that e'er I heard.

P. Hen. This is the strangest fellow, brother John.—
Come, bring your luggage nobly on your back:
For my part, if a lie may do thee grace,
I'll gild it with the happiest terms I have. [*A retreat is sounded.*
The trumpet sounds retreat; the day is ours.
Come, brother, let us to the highest of the field,
To see what friends are living, who are dead.

[*Exeunt* PRINCE HENRY *and* PRINCE JOHN.

Fal. I'll follow, as they say, for reward. He that rewards me, heaven reward him! If I do grow great, I'll grow less; for I'll reform, and leave sack, and live cleanly, as a nobleman should do.

[*Exit, bearing off the body.*

SCENE V.—*Another Part of the Field.*

The trumpets sound. Enter KING HENRY, PRINCE HENRY, PRINCE JOHN, WESTMORELAND, *and others, with* WORCESTER *and* VERNON, *prisoners.*

K. Hen. Thus ever did rebellion find rebuke.—
Ill-spirited Worcester! did we not send grace,
Pardon, and terms of love to all of you?
And would'st thou turn our offers contrary?
Wor. What I have done, my safety urg'd me to;
And I embrace this fortune patiently,
Since not to be avoided it falls on me.
K. Hen. Bear Worcester to the death, and Vernon too:
Other offenders we will pause on.—
[*Exeunt* WORCESTER *and* VERNON, *guarded.*
How goes the field?
P. Hen. The noble Scot, lord Douglas, when he saw
The fortune of the day quite turn'd from him,
The noble Percy slain, and all his men
Upon the foot of fear,—fled with the rest;
And falling from a hill, he was so bruis'd,
That the pursuers took him. At my tent
The Douglas is; and I beseech your grace,
I may dispose of him.
K. Hen. With all my heart.
P. Hen. Then, brother John of Lancaster, to you
This honorable bounty shall belong:
Go to the Douglas, and deliver him
Up to his pleasure, ransomless, and free:
His valor, shown upon our crests to-day,
Hath taught us how to cherish such high deeds,
Even in the bosom of our adversaries.
P. John. I thank your grace for this high courtesy,
Which I shall give away immediately.
K. Hen. Then this remains,—that we divide our power.—
You, son John, and my cousin Westmoreland,
Towards York shall bend you, with your dearest speed,
To meet Northumberland, and the prelate Scroop,
Who, as we hear, are busily in arms:
Myself and you, son Harry, will towards Wales,
To fight with Glendower and the earl of March.
Rebellion in this land shall lose his sway,
Meeting the check of such another day:
And since this business so fair is done,
Let us not leave till all our own be won. [*Exeunt.*

THE HISTORY OF

KING HENRY IV.

PART II.

The second portion of the History of Henry the Fourth is not considered equal to the opening part: the same fidelity of delineation in the strictly historical subjects is, however, preserved, as in the first part, and in the comic characters we have a rich addition in Justice Shallow, Silence, and their retainers. As a record of historical events, and in its truthful picture of the manners and habits of the times, the whole drama is, however, worthy of careful study by the youthful readers of Shakspeare. The action of this dramatic history takes up about nine years, commencing with the account of Hotspur's defeat and death at Shrewsbury, 1403, and closing with the death of Henry the Fourth, and the coronation of Henry the Fifth, 1412–13.

PERSONS REPRESENTED.

King Henry the Fourth.
Henry, *Prince of Wales; afterwards K. Hen. V.* } *His Sons.*
Thomas, *Duke of* Clarence, } *His Sons.*
Prince John of Lancaster, } *His Sons.*
Prince Humphrey of Gloster, } *His Sons.*
Earl of Warwick, } *Of the* King's *Party.*
Earl of Westmoreland, } *Of the* King's *Party.*
Earl of Surrey, } *Of the* King's *Party.*
Gower Harcourt, } *Of the* King's *Party.*
Sir William Gascoigne, *Lord Chief Justice of the King's Bench.*
A Gentleman *attending on the Chief Justice.*
Earl of Northumberland, } *Opposites to the* King.
Scroop, *Archbishop of* York. } *Opposites to the* King.
Lord Mowbray, } *Opposites to the* King.
Lord Hastings, } *Opposites to the* King.
Lord Bardolph, } *Opposites to the* King.
Sir John Colevile, } *Opposites to the* King.
Travers *and* Morton, *Retainers of* Northumberland.
Sir John Falstaff.
His Page.
Bardolph.

PISTOL.
POINS.
PETO.
SHALLOW *and* SILENCE, *Country Justices.*
DAVY, *Servant to* SHALLOW.
MOULDY, SHADOW, WART, FEEBLE, *and* BULL-CALF, *Recruits.*
FANG *and* SNARE, *Sheriff's Officers.*
A Porter.

LADY NORTHUMBERLAND.
LADY PERCY.
Hostess QUICKLY.

Lords *and* Attendants; Officers, Soldiers, Messenger, Drawers, Grooms, &c.

SCENE,—ENGLAND.

ACT I.

SCENE I.—*Warkworth Castle.*

Enter LORD BARDOLPH.

L. Bard. Who keeps the gate here? ho!—

Enter Porter *above the gate.*

Where is the earl?

Port. What shall I say you are?
L. Bard. Tell thou the earl,
That the lord Bardolph doth attend him here.
Port. His lordship is walk'd forth into the orchard:
Please it your honor, knock but at the gate,
And he himself will answer.
L. Bard. Here comes the earl.
[*Exit* Porter *above.*

Enter NORTHUMBERLAND.

North. What news, lord Bardolph? every minute now
Should be the father of some stratagem.
The times are wild: contention, like a horse
Full of high feeding, madly hath broke loose,
And bears down all before him.
L. Bard. Noble earl,
I bring you certain news from Shrewsbury.
North. Good, an heaven will!
L. Bard. As good as heart can wish:—
The king is almost wounded to the death;
And, in the fortune of my lord your son,
Prince Harry slain outright. O, such a day,
So fought, so follow'd, and so fairly won,

Came not till now to dignify the times,
Since Cæsar's fortunes!
North. How is this deriv'd?
Saw you the field? came you from Shrewsbury?
L. Bard. I spake with one, my lord, that came from thence;
A gentleman well bred, and of good name,
That freely render'd me these news for true.
North. Here comes my servant, Travers, whom I sent
On Tuesday last to listen after news.
L. Bard. My lord, I over-rode him on the way;
And he is furnish'd with no certainties,
More than he haply may retail from me.

Enter TRAVERS.

North. Now, Travers, what good tidings come with you?
Tra. My lord, Sir John Umfrevile turn'd me back
With joyful tidings; and, being better hors'd,
Out-rode me. After him came spurring hard
A gentleman, almost forspent with speed,
That stopp'd by me to breathe his bloodied horse.
He ask'd the way to Chester; and of him
I did demand, what news from Shrewsbury:
He told me that rebellion had bad luck,
And that young Harry Percy's spur was cold.
North. Ha!—Again:
Said he, young Harry Percy's spur was cold?
Of Hotspur, coldspur? that rebellion
Had met ill luck?
L. Bard. My lord, I'll tell you what;
If my young lord your son have not the day,
Upon mine honor, for a silken point
I'll give my barony: never talk of it.
North. Why should the gentleman, that rode by Travers,
Give, then, such instances of loss?
L. Bard. Who, he?
He was some hilding fellow, that had stolen
The horse he rode on; and, upon my life,
Spoke at a venture.—Look, here comes more news.

Enter MORTON.

North. Yea, this man's brow, like to a title-leaf,
Foretels the nature of a tragic volume:
So looks the strand, whereon th' imperious flood
Hath left a witness'd usurpation.
Say, Morton, didst thou come from Shrewsbury?
Mor. I ran from Shrewsbury, my noble lord;
Where hateful death put on his ugliest mask,
To fright our party.

North. How doth my son and brother?
Thou tremblest; and the whiteness in thy cheek
Is apter than thy tongue to tell thy errand.
Even such a man, so faint, so spiritless,
So dull, so dead in look, so woe-begone,
Drew Priam's curtain in the dead of night,
And would have told him, half his Troy was burn'd;
But Priam found the fire, ere he his tongue,
And I my Percy's death, ere thou report'st it.
This thou would'st say,—Your son did thus, and thus;
Your brother, thus; so fought the noble Douglas;
Stopping my greedy ear with their bold deeds:
But in the end, to stop mine ear indeed,
Thou hast a sigh to blow away this praise,
Ending with—brother, son, and all are dead.
Mor. Douglas is living, and your brother, yet;
But, for my lord your son,—
North. Why, he is dead.—
See, what a ready tongue suspicion hath!
He that but fears the thing he would not know,
Hath, by instinct, knowledge from others' eyes,
That what he fear'd is chanc'd. Yet speak, Morton;
Tell thou thy earl his divination lies,
And I will take it as a sweet disgrace,
And make thee rich for doing me such wrong.
Mor. You are too great to be by me gainsaid:
Your spirit is too true, your fears too certain.
North. Yet, for all this, say not that Percy's dead.—
I see a strange confession in thine eye:
Thou shak'st thy head, and hold'st it fear, or sin,
To speak a truth. If he be slain, say so;
The tongue offends not, that reports his death:
And he doth sin that doth belie the dead;
Not he which says the dead is not alive.
Yet the first bringer of unwelcome news
Hath but a losing office; and his tongue
Sounds ever after as a sullen bell,
Remember'd knolling a departing friend.
L. Bard. I cannot think, my lord, your son is dead.
Mor. I am sorry I should force you to believe
That which I would to heaven I had not seen;
But these mine eyes saw him in bloody state,
Rendering faint quittance, wearied and outbreath'd,
To Harry Monmouth; whose swift wrath beat down
The never-daunted Percy to the earth,
From whence with life he never more sprung up.
In few, his death, (whose spirit lent a fire
Even to the dullest peasant in his camp,)

Being bruited once, took fire and heat away
From the best temper'd courage in his troops;
For from his metal was his party steel'd;
Which once in him abated, all the rest
Turn'd on themselves, like dull and heavy lead.
The sum of all
Is that the king hath won; and hath sent out
A speedy power to encounter you, my lord,
Under the conduct of young Lancaster,
And Westmoreland. This is the news at full.
North. For this I shall have time enough to mourn.
In poison there is physic; and these news,
Having been well, that would have made me sick,
Being sick, have in some measure made me well:
And as the wretch, whose fever-weaken'd joints,
Like strengthless hinges, buckle under life,
Impatient of his fit, breaks like a fire
Out of his keeper's arms; even so my limbs,
Weaken'd with grief, being now enrag'd with grief,
Are thrice themselves.
Now bind my brows with iron; and approach
The ragged'st hour that time and spite dare bring,
To frown upon th' enrag'd Northumberland!
Let heaven kiss earth! now let not nature's hand
Keep the wild flood confin'd! let order die!
And let this world no longer be a stage,
To feed contention in a lingering act;
But let one spirit of the first-born Cain
Reign in all bosoms, that, each heart being set
On bloody courses, the rude scene may end,
And darkness be the burier of the dead!
Tra. This strainèd passion doth you wrong, my lord.
L. Bard. Sweet earl, divorce not wisdom from your honor.
Mor. The lives of all your loving complices
Lean on your health; and which, if you give o'er
To stormy passion, must perforce decay.
L. Bard. We all, that are engagèd to this loss,
Knew that we ventur'd on such dangerous seas,
That if we wrought out life, 'twas ten to one;
And yet we ventur'd, for the gain propos'd
Chok'd the respect of likely peril fear'd;
And since we are o'erset, venture again.
Come, we will all put forth; body, and goods.
Mor. 'Tis more than time: and, my most noble lord,
I hear for certain, and to speak the truth,
The gentle archbishop of York is up,
With well-appointed powers.
And more, and less, do flock to follow him.

North. I knew of this before; but, to speak truth,
This present grief had wip'd it from my mind.
Go in with me; and counsel every man
The aptest way for safety, and revenge:
Get posts and letters, and make friends with speed;
Never so few, and never yet more need. [*Exeunt.*

SCENE II.—London. *A Street.*

Enter Sir JOHN FALSTAFF, *with his* Page *bearing his sword and buckler.*

Fal. Men of all sorts take a pride to gird at me: the brain of this foolish-compounded clay, man, is not able to invent any thing that tends to laughter, more than I invent, or is invented on me: I am not only witty in myself, but the cause that wit is in other men. [*To Page.*] If the prince put thee into my service for any other reason than to set me off, why then, I have no judgment. He may keep his own grace, but he is almost out of mine, I can assure him.—What said master Dumbleton about the satin for my short cloak, and my slops?

Page. He said, sir, you should procure him better assurance than Bardolph: he would not take his bond and yours; he liked not the security.

Fal. Let him be hanged! A vile Achitophel! a rascally yea-forsooth knave! to bear a gentleman in hand, and then stand upon security!—The smooth-pates do now wear nothing but high shoes, and bunches of keys at their girdles; and if a man is thorough with them in honest taking up, then they must stand upon security. I had as lief they would put ratsbane in my mouth, as offer to stop it with security. I looked he should have sent me two and twenty yards of satin, as I am a true knight, and he sends me security. Where's Bardolph?

Page. He's gone into Smithfield, to buy your worship a horse.

Fal. I bought him in Pauls, and he'll buy me a horse in Smithfield.

Page. Sir, here comes the nobleman that committed the prince for striking him about Bardolph.

Fal. Wait close; I will not see him.

Enter the Lord Chief Justice *and an* Attendant.

Ch. Just. What's he that goes there?

Atten. Falstaff, an't please your lordship.

Ch. Just. He that was in question for the robbery?

Atten. He, my lord: but he hath since done good service at Shrewsbury; and, as I hear, is now going with some charge to the lord John of Lancaster.

Ch. Just. What, to York? Call him back again.

Atten. Sir John Falstaff!

Fal. Boy, tell him I am deaf.

Page. You must speak louder; my master is deaf.

Ch. Just. I am sure he is, to the hearing of any thing good.—Go, pluck him by the elbow; I must speak with him.

Atten. Sir John,—

Fal. What! a young knave, and begging? Is there not wars? is there not employment? doth not the king lack subjects? do not the rebels need soldiers? Though it be a shame to be on any side but one, it is worse shame to beg than to be on the worst side, were it worse than the name of rebellion can tell how to make it.

Atten. You mistake me, sir.

Fal. Why, sir, did I say you were an honest man? setting my knighthood and my soldiership aside, I had lied in my throat, if I had said so.

Atten. I pray you, sir, then set your knighthood and your soldiership aside; and give me leave to tell you, you lie in your throat, if you say I am any other than an honest man.

Fal. I give thee leave to tell me so! I lay aside that which grows to me! If thou get'st any leave of me, hang me; if thou takest leave, thou wert better be hanged. Hence! avaunt!

Atten. Sir, my lord would speak with you.

Ch. Just. Sir John Falstaff, a word with you.

Fal. My good lord! heaven give your lordship good time of day. I am glad to see your lordship abroad: I heard say, your lordship was sick: I hope, your lordship goes abroad by advice. Your lordship, though not clean past your youth, hath yet some smack of age in you, some relish of the saltness of time; and I most humbly beseech your lordship to have a reverend care of your health.

Ch. Just. Sir John, I sent for you before your expedition to Shrewsbury.

Fal. An't please your lordship, I hear his majesty is returned with some discomfort from Wales.

Ch. Just. I talk not of his majesty:—you would not come when I sent for you.

Fal. And I hear, moreover, his highness has fallen into this same vile apoplexy.

Ch. Just. Well, heaven mend him!—I pray you, let me speak with you.

Fal. This apoplexy is, as I take it, a kind of lethargy, an't please your lordship; a kind of sleeping in the blood, a sort of tingling.

Ch. Just. What tell you me of it? be it as it is.

Fal. It hath its original from much grief, from study, and perturbation of the brain: I have read the cause of his effects in Galen: it is a kind of deafness.

Ch. Just. I think you are fallen into the disease; for you hear not what I say to you.

Fal. Very well, my lord, very well: rather, an't please you, it is the disease of not listening, the malady of not marking, that I am troubled withal.

Ch. Just. To punish you by the heels, would amend the attention of your ears; and I care not, if I do become your physician.

Fal. I am as poor as Job, my lord, but not so patient: your lordship may minister the potion of imprisonment to me, in respect of poverty; but how I should be your patient to follow your prescriptions, the wise may make some dram of a scruple, or, indeed, a scruple itself.

Ch. Just. I sent for you, when there were matters against you for your life, to come speak with me.

Fal. As I was then advised by my learned counsel in the laws of this land-service, I did not come.

Ch. Just. Well, the truth is, Sir John, you live in great infamy.

Fal. He that buckles him in my belt, cannot live in less.

Ch. Just. Your means are very slender, and your waste is great.

Fal. I would it were otherwise; I would my means were greater, and my waist slenderer.

Ch. Just. You have misled the youthful prince.

Fal. The young prince hath misled me.

Ch. Just. Well, I am loath to gall a new-healed wound: your day's service at Shrewsbury hath a little gilded over your night's exploit on Gadshill: you may thank the unquiet time for your quiet o'erposting that action.

Fal. My lord,—

Ch. Just. But since all is well, keep it so: wake not a sleeping wolf.

Fal. To wake a wolf, is as bad as to smell a fox.

Ch. Just. What! you are as a candle, the better part burnt out.

Fal. A wassail candle, my lord; all tallow: if I did say of wax, my growth would approve the truth.

Ch. Just. There is not a white hair on your face, but should have his effect of gravity. You follow the young prince up and down, like his ill angel.

Fal. Not so, my lord; your ill angel is light; but I hope he that looks upon me, will take me without weighing: and yet, in some respects, I grant, I cannot go,—I cannot tell. Virtue is of so little regard in these coster-monger times, that true valor is turned bear-herd: sharpness is made a tapster, and hath his quick wit wasted in giving reckonings: all the other gifts appertinent to man, as the malice of this age shapes them, are not worth a gooseberry. You, that are old, consider not the capacities of us that are young; you measure the heat of our livers by the bitterness of your galls: and we that are in the vaward of our youth, I must confess, are wags too.

Ch. Just. Do you set down your name in the scroll of youth, that are written down old with all the characters of age? Have you not a moist eye? a dry hand? a yellow cheek? a white beard? a decreasing leg? an increasing stomach? Is not your voice broken? your wind short? your chin double? your wit single? and every part about you touched with antiquity? and will you yet call yourself young? Fie, fie, fie, Sir John!

Fal. My lord, I was born about three of the clock in the afternoon, with a white head, and something of a roundness. For my voice,—I have lost it with hollaing, and singing of anthems. To approve my youth farther, I will not: the truth is, I am only old in judgment and understanding: and he that will caper with me for a thousand marks, let him lend me the money, and have at him. For the box o' the ear that the prince gave you,—he gave it like a rude prince, and you took it like a sensible lord. I have checked him for it; and the young lion repents,—marry, not in ashes and sackcloth, but in new silk and old sack.

Ch. Just. Well, heaven send the prince a better companion!

Fal. Heaven send the companion a better prince! I cannot rid my hands of him.

Ch. Just. Well, the king hath severed you and prince Harry: I hear, you are going with lord John of Lancaster against the archbishop, and the earl of Northumberland.

Fal. Yea; I thank your pretty sweet wit for it. But look you, pray, all you that kiss my lady Peace at home, that our armies join not on a hot day; if it be a hot day, and I brandish any thing but my bottle, I would I might never spit white again. There is not a dangerous action can peep out his head, but I am thrust upon it: well, I cannot last ever: but it was always yet the trick of our English nation, if they have a good thing, to make it too common. If you will needs say I am an old man, you should give me rest. I would to heaven, my name were not so terrible to the enemy as it is: I were better to be eaten to death with rust, than to be scoured to nothing with perpetual motion.

Ch. Just. Well, be honest, be honest; and heaven bless your expedition.

Fal. Will your lordship lend me a thousand pound to furnish me forth?

Ch. Just. Not a penny, not a penny; you are too impatient to bear crosses. Fare you well: commend me to my cousin Westmoreland. [*Exeunt* Chief Justice *and* Attendant.

Fal. If I do, fillip me with a three-man beetle. A man cannot separate age and covetousness. Boy!

Page. Sir?

Fal. What money is in my purse?

Page. Seven groats and two-pence.

Fal. I can get no remedy against this consumption of the purse: borrowing only lingers and lingers it out, but the disease is incurable.—Go bear this letter to my lord of Lancaster; this to the prince; this to the earl of Westmoreland; and this to old mistress Ursula, whom I have weekly sworn to marry since I perceived the first white hair on my chin. About it: you know where to find me. [*Exit* Page.] A murrain on this gout! It plays the rogue with my great toe. It is no matter, if I do halt; I have the wars for my color, and my pension shall seem the more reasonable. A good wit will make use of any thing: I will turn diseases to commodity. [*Exit.*

SCENE III.—York. *A Room in the* Archbishop's *Palace.*

Enter the ARCHBISHOP OF YORK, LORD HASTINGS, LORD MOWBRAY, *and* LORD BARDOLPH.

Arch. Thus have you heard our cause, and known our means;
And, my most noble friends, I pray you all,
Speak plainly your opinions of our hopes:—
And first, lord marshal, what say you to it?

Mowb. I well allow the occasion of our arms;
But gladly would be better satisfied,
How, in our means, we should advance ourselves
To look with forehead bold and big enough
Upon the power and puissance of the king.

Hast. Our present musters grow upon the file
To five and twenty thousand men of choice;
And our supplies live largely in the hope
Of great Northumberland, whose bosom burns
With an incensed fire of injuries.

L. Bard. The question, then, Lord Hastings, standeth thus;—
Whether our present five and twenty thousand
May hold up head without Northumberland.

Hast. With him, we may.

L. Bard. Ay, marry, there's the point:
But if without him we be thought too feeble,
My judgment is, we should not step too far,
Till we had his assistance by the hand.

Arch. 'Tis very true, lord Bardolph; for, indeed,
It was young Hotspur's case at Shrewsbury.

L. Bard. It was, my lord.

Hast. Grant, that our hopes (yet likely of fair birth,)
Should be still-born, and that we now possess'd
The utmost man of expectation;
I think we are a body strong enough,
Even as we are, to equal with the king.

L. Bard. What! is the king but five and twenty thousand?
Hast. To us, no more; nay, not so much, lord Bardolph.
For his divisions, as the time do brawl,
Are in three heads.
Arch. That he should draw his several strengths together,
And come against us in full puissance,
Need not be dreaded.
Hast. If he should do so,
He leaves his back unarm'd, the French and Welsh
Baying him at the heels: never fear that.
L. Bard. Who, is it like, should lead his forces hither?
Hast. The duke of Lancaster, and Westmoreland·
Against the Welsh, himself and Harry Monmouth;
But who is substituted 'gainst the French,
I have no certain notice.
Arch. Let us on,
And publish the occasion of our arms.
What trust is in these times?
They that, when Richard liv'd, would have him die,
Are now become enamor'd on his grave:
Thou, that threw'st dust upon his goodly head,
When through proud London he came sighing on
After th' admired heels of Bolingbroke,
Cry'st now, "O earth, yield us that king again,
And take thou this!" O, thoughts of men accurst!
Past, and to come, seem best; things present, worst.
Mowb. Shall we go draw our numbers, and set on?
Hast. We are time's subjects, and time bids be gone. [*Exeunt.*

ACT II.

SCENE I.—London. *A Street.*

Enter Hostess QUICKLY; FANG, *and his Boy, with her; and* SNARE *following.*

Host. Master Fang, have you entered the action?
Fang. It is entered.
Host. Where's your yeoman? Is it a lusty yeoman? will he stand to't?
Fang. Sirrah, where's Snare?
Host. O lord, ay! good master Snare.
Snare. Here, here.
Fang. Snare, we must arrest Sir John Falstaff.
Host. Yea, good master Snare; I have entered him and all.
Snare. It may chance cost some of us our lives, for he will stab.
Host. Alas the day! take heed of him; he stabbed me in

mine own house: in good faith, he cares not what mischief he doth; he will spare neither man, woman, nor child.

Fang. If I can close with him, I care not for his thrust.

Host. I'll be at your elbow.

Fang. An I but fist him once; an he come but within my vice,—

Host. I am undone by his going; I warrant you, he's an infinitive thing upon my score:—good master Fang, hold him sure. Yonder he comes; and that arrant malmsey-nose knave, Bardolph, with him. Do your offices, do your offices, master Fang and master Snare; do me, do me, do me your offices.

Enter Sir John Falstaff, Page, *and* Bardolph.

Fal. How now! whose mare's dead! what's the matter?

Fang. Sir John, I arrest you at the suit of mistress Quickly.

Fal. Away, varlets!—Draw, Bardolph: cut me off the villain's head; throw the quean in the channel.

Host. Throw me in the channel! I'll throw thee in the channel. Wilt thou? wilt thou?—Murder, murder! O, thou honey-suckle villain! wilt thou kill the king's officers. O, thou honey-seed rogue! thou art a honey-seed, a man-queller, and a woman-queller.

Fal. Keep them off, Bardolph.

Fang. A rescue! a rescue!

Host. Good people, bring a rescue or two!—Thou wo't, wo't thou? thou wo't, wo't thou? do, do, thou rogue! do, thou hemp-seed!

Fal. Away, you scullion! you rampallian! you fustilarian!

Enter the Lord Chief Justice, *attended.*

Ch. Just. What is the matter? keep the peace here, ho!

Host. Good my lord, be good to me! I beseech you, stand to me!

Ch. Just. How now, Sir John! what, are you brawling here?
Doth this become your place, your time, and business?
You should have been well on your way to York.—
Stand from him, fellow: wherefore hang'st upon him?

Host. O, my most worshipful lord, an't please your grace, I am a poor widow of Eastcheap, and he is arrested at my suit.

Ch. Just. For what sum?

Host. It is more than for some, my lord; it is for all, all I have. He hath eaten me out of house and home; he hath put all my substance into that fat stomach of his:—but I will have some of it again.

Ch. Just. How comes this, Sir John? Fie! what man of good temper would endure this tempest of exclamation? Are you not ashamed to enforce a poor widow to so rough a course to come by her own?

Fal. What is the gross sum that I owe thee?

Host. Marry, if thou wert an honest man, thyself, and the money too. Thou didst swear to me upon a parcel-gilt goblet, sitting in my Dolphin-chamber, at the round table, by a sea-coal fire, upon Wednesday in Whitsun week, when the prince broke thy head for liking his father to a singing-man of Windsor; thou didst swear to me then, as I was washing thy wound, to marry me, and make me my lady thy wife. Canst thou deny it? Did not goodwife Keech, the butcher's wife, come in then, and call me gossip Quickly? coming in to borrow a mess of vinegar; telling us, she had a good dish of prawns; whereby thou didst desire to eat some; whereby I told thee, they were ill for a green wound? And didst thou not, when she was gone down stairs, desire me to be no more so familiarity with such poor people; saying, that ere long they should call me madam? And didst thou not kiss me, and bid me fetch thee thirty shillings? I put thee now to thy book-oath: deny it, if thou canst.

Fal. My lord, this is a poor mad soul; and she says, up and down the town, that her eldest son is like you: she hath been in good case, and the truth is, poverty hath distracted her. But for these foolish officers, I beseech you, I may have redress against them.

Ch. Just. Sir John, Sir John, I am well acquainted with your manner of wrenching the true cause the false way. It is not a confident brow, nor the throng of words that come with such more than impudent sauciness from you, can thrust me from a level consideration: you have, as it appears to me, practised upon the easy yielding spirit of this woman.

Host. Yea, in troth, my lord.

Ch. Just. Pr'ythee, peace.—Pay her the debt you owe her, and unpay the villany you have done with her.

Fal. My lord, I will not undergo this sneap without reply. You call honorable boldness, impudent sauciness: if a man will make court'sy, and say nothing, he is virtuous. No, my lord, my humble duty remember'd, I will not be your suitor: I say to you, I do desire deliverance from these officers, being upon hasty employment in the king's affairs.

Ch. Just. You speak as having power to do wrong: but answer in the effect of your reputation, and satisfy the poor woman.

Fal. Come hither, hostess. [*Taking her aside.*

Enter GOWER.

Ch. Just. Now, master Gower,—what news?

Gow. The king, my lord, and Harry prince of Wales
Are near at hand: the rest the paper tells. [*Gives a letter.*

Fal. As I am a gentleman,—

Host. Faith, you said so before.

Fal. As I am a gentleman: come, no more words of it.

Host. By this heavenly ground I tread on, I must be fain to pawn both my plate, and the tapestry of my dining-chambers.

Fal. Glasses, glasses, is the only drinking: and for thy walls, —a pretty slight drollery, or the story of the Prodigal, or the German hunting in water-work, is worth a thousand of these bed-hangings, and these fly-bitten tapestries. Let it be ten pound, if thou canst. Come, an it were not for thy humors, there is not a better woman in England. Go, wash thy face, and draw thy action. Come, thou must not be in this humor with me; dost not know me? Come, come, I know thou wast set on to this.

Host. Pray thee, Sir John, let it be but twenty nobles: i' faith, I am loath to pawn my plate, in good earnest, la.

Fal. Let it alone; I'll make other shift: you'll be a fool still.

Host. Well, you shall have it, though I pawn my gown. I hope, you'll come to supper. You'll pay me all together?

Fal. Will I live?—[*To* BARDOLPH.] Go, with her, with her; hook on, hook on.

[*Exeunt* Hostess, BARDOLPH, Officers, *and Boy.*

Ch. Just. I have heard better news.

Fal. What's the news, my good lord?

Ch. Just. Where lay the king last night?

Gow. At Basingstoke, my lord.

Fal. I hope, my lord, all's well: what is the news, my lord?

Ch. Just. Come all his forces back?

Gow. No; fifteen hundred foot, five hundred horse,
Are march'd up to my lord of Lancaster,
Against Northumberland, and the archbishop.

Fal. Comes the king back from Wales, my noble lord?

Ch. Just. You shall have letters of me presently: come, go along with me, good master Gower.

Fal. My lord!

Ch. Just. What's the matter?

Fal. Master Gower, shall I entreat you with me to dinner?

Gow. I must wait upon my good lord here,—I thank you, good Sir John.

Ch. Just. Sir John, you loiter here too long, being you are to take soldiers up in counties as you go.

Fal. Will you sup with me, master Gower?

Ch. Just. What foolish master taught you these manners, Sir John?

Fal. Master Gower, if they become me not, he was a fool that taught them me.—This is the right fencing grace, my lord; tap for tap, and so part fair.

Ch. Just. Now, the Lord lighten thee! thou art a great fool.

[*Exeunt.*

SCENE II.—London. *Another Street.*

Enter PRINCE HENRY *and* POINS.

P. Hen. Trust me, I am exceeding weary.

Poins. Is it come to that? I had thought, weariness durst not have attached one of so high blood.

P. Hen. 'Faith, it does me; though it discolors the complexion of my greatness to acknowledge it. Doth it not show vilely in me to desire small beer?

Poins. Why, a prince should not be so loosely studied, as to remember so weak a composition.

P. Hen. Belike then, my appetite was not princely got; for, by my troth, I do now remember the poor creature, small beer. But, indeed, these humble considerations make me out of love with my greatness. What a disgrace is it to me, to remember thy name? or to know thy face to-morrow? or to take note how many pair of silk stockings thou hast, *viz.* these, and those that were thy peach-color'd ones? or to bear the inventory of thy linen; as, one for superfluity, and one other for use?

Poins. How ill it follows, after you have labored so hard, you should talk so idly! Tell me, how many good young princes would do so, their fathers being so sick as yours at this time is?

P. Hen. Shall I tell thee one thing, Poins?

Poins. Yes, faith; and let it be an excellent good thing.

P. Hen. Marry, I tell thee,—it is not meet that I should be sad, now my father is sick: albeit I could tell to thee, (as to one it pleases me, for fault of a better, to call my friend) I could be sad, and sad indeed too.

Poins. Very hardly upon such a subject.

P. Hen. By this hand, thou think'st me as far in wickedness, as thou and Falstaff, for obduracy and persistency: let the end try the man. But I tell thee, my heart bleeds inwardly, that my father is so sick: and keeping such vile company as thou art, hath in reason taken from me all ostentation of sorrow.

Poins. The reason?

P. Hen. What would'st thou think of me, if I should weep?

Poins. I would think thee a most princely hypocrite.

P. Hen. It would be every man's thought; and thou art a blessed fellow, to think as every man thinks: never a man's thought in the world keeps the road-way better than thine: every man would think me a hypocrite indeed. And what makes your most worshipful thought to think so?

Poins. Why, because you have been so loose, and so much engraffed to Falstaff.

P. Hen. And to thee.

Poins. By this light, I am well spoken of; I can hear it with mine own ears: the worst that they can say of me is, that I am a second brother, and that I am a proper fellow of my hands; and those two things, I confess, I cannot help. By the mass, here comes Bardolph.

P. Hen. And the boy that I gave Falstaff: he had him from me Christian; and look, if the fat villain have not transformed him ape.

Enter BARDOLPH *and* Page.

Bard. Heaven save your grace!

P. Hen. And yours, most noble Bardolph!

Bard. [*To the* Page.] Come, you bashful fool, must you be blushing? wherefore blush you now?

Page. He called me even now, my lord, through a red lattice, and I could discern no part of his face from the window: at last, I spied his eyes; and methought he had made two holes in the ale-wife's new skirts, and peeped though.

P. Hen. Hath not the boy profited?

Poins. O, that this good blossom could be kept from cankers! —Well, there is sixpence to preserve thee.

Bard. An you do not make him be hanged among you, the gallows shall have wrong.

P. Hen. And how doth thy master, Bardolph?

Bard. Well, my lord. He heard of your grace's coming to town: there's a letter for you.

Poins. Delivered with good respect.—And how doth the martlemas, your master?

Bard. In bodily health, sir.

Poins. Marry, the immortal part needs a physician; but that moves not him: though that be sick, it dies not.

P. Hen. I do allow this wen to be as familiar with me as my dog: and he holds his place; for look you how he writes.

Poins. [*Reads.*] "Sir John Falstaff, knight, to the son of the king, nearest his father, Harry Prince of Wales, greeting."— Why, this is a certificate.

P. Hen. Peace!

Poins. [*Reads.*] "I will imitate the honorable Romans in brevity:"—sure he means brevity in breath, short-winded.— "I commend me to thee, I commend thee, and I leave thee. Be not too familiar with Poins; for he misuses thy favors so much, that he swears thou art to marry his sister Nell. Repent at idle times as thou mayest; and so farewell.

"Thine, by yea and no, (which is as much as to say, as thou usest him,) Jack Falstaff, with my familiars; John, with my brothers and sisters; and Sir John with all Europe."

My lord, I will steep this letter in sack, and make him eat it.

P. Hen. That's to make him eat twenty of his words. But do you use me thus, Ned? must I marry your sister?

Poins. Heaven send the girl no worse fortune! but I never said so.

P. Hen. Well, thus we play the fools with the time; and the spirits of the wise sit in the clouds, and mock us.—Is your master here in London?

Bard. Yes, my lord.

P. Hen. Where sups he? doth the old boar feed in the old frank?

Bard. At the old place, my lord; in Eastcheap.

P. Hen. Shall we steal upon them, Ned, at supper?

Poins. I am your shadow, my lord; I'll follow you.

P. Hen. Sirrah, you boy,—and Bardolph,—no word to your master that I am yet come to town: there's for your silence. [*Gives money.*

Bard. I have no tongue, sir.

Page. And for mine, sir, I will govern it.

P. Hen. Fare ye well; go. [*Exeunt* BARDOLPH *and* Page.

P. Hen. How might we see Falstaff bestow himself to-night in his true colors, and not ourselves be seen?

Poins. Put on two leathern jerkins and aprons, and wait upon him at his table as drawers.

P. Hen. From a prince to a prentice? a low transformation! that shall be mine; for in every thing the purpose must weigh with the folly. Follow me, Ned. [*Exeunt.*

ACT III.

SCENE I.—Westminster. *A Room in the Palace.*

Enter KING HENRY *in his nightgown, with a* Page.

K. Hen. Go, call the earls of Surrey and of Warwick;
But, ere they come, bid them o'er-read these letters,
And well consider of them: make good speed. [*Exit* Page.
How many thousand of my poorest subjects
Are at this hour asleep!—O sleep! O gentle sleep!
Nature's soft nurse, how have I frighted thee,
That thou no more wilt weigh my eyelids down,
And steep my senses in forgetfulness?
Why rather, sleep, liest thou in smoky cribs,
Upon uneasy pallets stretching thee,
And hush'd with buzzing night-flies to thy slumber,
Than in the perfum'd chambers of the great,
Under the canopies of costly state,
And lull'd with sounds of sweetest melody?
O, thou dull god! why liest thou with the vile,
In loathsome beds, and leav'st the kingly couch,

A watch-case, or a common 'larum bell?
Wilt thou upon the high and giddy mast
Seal up the ship-boy's eyes, and rock his brains
In cradle of the rude imperious surge,
And in the visitation of the winds,
Who take the ruffian billows by the top,
Curling their monstrous heads, and hanging them
With deaf'ning clamors in the slippery clouds,
That, with the hurly, death itself awakes?
Canst thou, O partial sleep! give thy repose
To the wet sea-boy in an hour so rude;
And in the calmest and most stillest night,
With all appliances and means to boot,
Deny it to a king? Then, happy low, lie down!
Uneasy lies the head that wears a crown.

Enter WARWICK *and* SURREY.

War. Many good morrows to your majesty!
K. Hen. Is it good morrow, lords?
War. 'Tis one o'clock, and past.
K. Hen. Why then, good morrow to you all, my lords.
Have you read o'er the letters that I sent you?
War. We have, my liege.
K. Hen. Then you perceive, the body of our kingdom,
How foul it is; what rank diseases grow,
And with what danger, near the heart of it.
War. It is but as a body, yet, distemper'd,
Which to his former strength may be restor'd,
With good advice, and little medicine:
My lord Northumberland will soon be cool'd.
K. Hen. O heaven! that one might read the book of fate,
And see the revolution of the times
Make mountains level, and the continent
(Weary of solid firmness,) melt itself
Into the sea! and, other times, to see
The beachy girdle of the ocean
Too wide for Neptune's hips; how chances mock,
And changes fill the cup of alteration
With divers liquors! O, if this were seen,
The happiest youth,—viewing his progress through,
What perils past, what crosses to ensue,
Would shut the book, and sit him down and die.
'Tis not ten years gone,
Since Richard and Northumberland, great friends,
Did feast together, and in two years after
Were they at wars: it is but eight years, since
This Percy was the man nearest my soul;
Who like a brother toil'd in my affairs,

And laid his love and life under my foot;
Yea, for my sake, even to the eyes of Richard,
Gave him defiance. But which of you was by, [*To* WARWICK.
(You, cousin Nevil, as I may remember)
When Richard,—with his eye brimfull of tears,
Then check'd and rated by Northumberland,—
Did speak these words, now prov'd a prophecy?
"Northumberland, thou ladder, by the which
My cousin Bolingbroke ascends my throne;"—
Though then, heaven knows, I had no such intent,
But that necessity so bow'd the state,
That I and greatness were compell'd to kiss:—
"The time shall come," thus did he follow it,
"The time will come, that foul sin, gathering head,
Shall break into corruption:"—so went on,
Foretelling this same time's condition,
And the division of our amity.
War. There is a history in all men's lives,
Figuring the nature of the times deceas'd;
The which observ'd, a man may prophesy,
With a near aim, of the main chance of things.
K. Hen. Are these things, then, necessities?
Then let us meet them like necessities;—
And that same word even now cries out on us;
They say, the bishop and Northumberland
Are fifty thousand strong.
War. It cannot be, my lord;
Rumor doth double, like the voice and echo,
The numbers of the fear'd.—Please it your grace,
To go to bed.
Your majesty hath been this fortnight ill;
And these unseason'd hours, perforce, must add
Unto your sickness.
K. Hen. I will take your counsel:
And were these inward wars once out of hand,
We would, dear lords, unto the Holy Land. [*Exeunt.*

SCENE II.—*Court before Justice* SHALLOW'S *House in* Gloucestershire.

Enter SHALLOW *and* SILENCE, *meeting;* MOULDY, SHADOW, WART, FEEBLE, BULL-CALF, *and* Servants, *behind.*

Shal. Come on, come on, come on, sir; give me your hand, sir, give me your hand, sir: an early stirrer, by the rood. And how doth my good cousin Silence?

Sil. Good morrow, good cousin Shallow.

Shal. And how doth my cousin, your wife? and your fairest daughter, and mine, my god-daughter Ellen?

Sil. Alas, a black ouzel, cousin Shallow!

Shal. By yea and nay, sir, I dare say, my cousin William is become a good scholar: he is at Oxford, still, is he not?

Sil. Indeed, sir, to my cost.

Shal. He must, then, to the inns of court shortly: I was once of Clement's-inn; where, I think, they will talk of mad Shallow yet.

Sil. You were called lusty Shallow then, cousin.

Shal. By the mass, I was called any thing; and I would have done any thing indeed too, and roundly too. There was I, and little John Doit of Staffordshire, and black George Bare, and Francis Pickbone, and Will Squele a Cotswold man; you had not four such swinge bucklers in all the inns of court again. Then was Jack Falstaff, now Sir John, a boy, and page to Thomas Mowbray, duke of Norfolk.

Sil. This Sir John, cousin, that comes hither anon about soldiers?

Shal. The same Sir John, the very same. I saw him break Skogan's head at the court gate, when he was a crack, not thus high: and the very same day did I fight with one Sampson Stockfish, a fruiterer, behind Gray's-inn. O, the mad days that I have spent! and to see how many of mine old acquaintance are dead!

Sil. We shall all follow, cousin.

Shal. Certain, 'tis certain; very sure, very sure: death, as the Psalmist saith, is certain to all; all shall die.—How a good yoke of bullocks at Stamford fair?

Sil. Truly, cousin, I was not there.

Shal. Death is certain.—Is old Double of your town living yet?

Sil. Dead, sir.

Shal. Dead!—See, see!—he drew a good bow;—and dead!—he shot a fine shoot:—John of Gaunt loved him well, and betted much money on his head. Dead!—he would have clapped in the clout at twelve score; and carried you a forehand shaft a fourteen and fourteen and a half, that it would have done a man's heart good to see.—How a score of ewes now?

Sil. Thereafter as they be: a score of good ewes may be worth ten pounds.

Shal. And is old Double dead!

Sil. Here come two of Sir John Falstaff's men, as I think.

Enter BARDOLPH, *and one with him.*

Bard. Good morrow, honest gentlemen. I beseech you, which is justice Shallow?

Shal. I am Robert Shallow, sir; a poor esquire of this county, and one of the king's justices of the peace: what is your good pleasure with me?

Bard. My captain, sir, commends him to you; my captain, Sir John Falstaff,—a tall gentleman, and a most gallant leader.

Shal. He greets me well, sir. I knew him a good backsword man. How doth the good knight? may I ask how my lady his wife doth?

Bard. Sir, pardon; a soldier is better accommodated than with a wife.

Shal. It is well said, in faith, sir; and it is well said indeed too. Better accommodated!—it is good; yea, indeed, is it: good phrases are surely, and ever were, very commendable. Accommodated!—it comes of *accommodo:* very good; a good phrase.

Bard. Pardon me, sir; I have heard the word. Phrase, call you it? By this good day, I know not the phrase; but I will maintain the word with my sword to be a soldier-like word, and a word of exceeding good command, by heaven. Accommodated; that is, when a man is, as they say, accommodated; or, when a man is,—being,—whereby,—he may be thought to be accommodated; which is an excellent thing.

Shal. It is very just.—Look, here comes good Sir John—[*Enter* FALSTAFF.] Give me your good hand, give me your worship's good hand: by my troth, you look well, and bear your years very well: welcome, good Sir John.

Fal. I am glad to see you well, good master Robert Shallow:—Master Sure-card, as I think.

Shal. No, Sir John; it is my cousin Silence, in commission with me.

Fal. Good master Silence, it well befits you should be of the peace.

Sil. Your good worship is welcome.

Fal. Fie! this is hot weather.—Gentlemen, have you provided me here half a dozen sufficient men?

Shal. Marry, have we, sir. Will you sit?

Fal. Let me see them, I beseech you.

Shal. Where's the roll? where's the roll? where's the roll?—Let me see, let me see, let me see. So, so, so, so. Yea, marry, sir:—Ralph Mouldy!—let them appear as I call; let them do so, let them do so.—Let me see; where is Mouldy?

Moul. [*Advancing.*] Here, an't please you.

Shal. What think you, Sir John? a good limbed fellow; young, strong, and of good friends.

Fal. Is thy name Mouldy?

Moul. Yea, an't please you.

Fal. 'Tis the more time thou wert used.

Shal. Ha, ha, ha! most excellent, i' faith! things that are mouldy lack use: very singular good!—In faith, well said, Sir John; very well said.

Fal. [*To* SHALLOW.] Mark him.

Moul. O, my old dame will be undone now, for one to do her husbandry, and her drudgery: you need not to have marked me; there are other men fitter to go out than I.

Fal. Go to; peace, Mouldy! you shall go. Mouldy, it is time you were spent.

Moul. Spent!

Shal. Peace, fellow, peace! stand aside: know you where you are?—For the other, Sir John:—let me see;—Simon Shadow.

Fal. Yea, marry, let me have him to sit under: he's like to be a cold soldier.

Shal. Where's Shadow?

Shad. [*Advancing.*] Here, sir.

Fal. Shadow, whose son art thou?

Shad. My mother's son, sir.

Fal. Thy mother's son! like enough; and thy father's shadow.

Shal. Do you like him, Sir John?

Fal. Shadow will serve for summer,—mark him; for we have a number of shadows to fill up the muster-book.

Shal. Thomas Wart!

Fal. Where's he?

Wart. [*Advancing.*] Here, sir.

Fal. Is thy name Wart?

Wart. Yea, sir.

Fal. Thou art a very ragged wart.

Shal. Shall I mark him, Sir John?

Fal. It were superfluous; for his apparel is built upon his back, and the whole frame stands upon pins: mark him no more.

Shal. Ha, ha, ha!—you can do it, sir; you can do it: I commend you well.—Francis Feeble!

Fee. [*Advancing.*] Here, sir.

Fal. What trade art thou, Feeble?

Fee. A woman's tailor, sir.

Shal. Shall I mark him, sir?

Fal. You may.—Wilt thou make as many holes in an enemy's battle, as thou hast done in a woman's garments?

Fee. I will do my good will, sir: you can have no more.

Fal. Well said, good woman's tailor! well said, courageous Feeble! Thou wilt be as valiant as the wrathful dove, or most magnanimous mouse.

Fee. I would Wart might have gone, sir.

Fal. I would thou wert a man's tailor, that thou might'st mend him, and make him fit to go. I cannot put him to a private soldier, that is the leader of so many thousands: let that suffice, most forcible Feeble.

Fee. It shall suffice, sir.

Fal. I am bound to thee, reverend Feeble.—Who is next?

Shal. Peter Bull-calf of the green!

Fal. Yea, marry, let us see Bull-calf.

Bull. [*Advancing.*] Here, sir.

Fal. 'Fore heaven, a likely fellow!—Come, mark me Bull-calf till he roar again.

Bull. O Lord! good my lord captain,—

Fal. What dost thou roar for?

Ball. O Lord, sir! I am a diseased man.

Fal. What disease hast thou?

Bull. A vile cold, sir,—a cough, sir,—which I caught with ringing in the king's affairs upon his coronation day, sir.

Fal. Come, thou shalt go to the wars in a gown; we will have away thy cold, and I will take such order, that thy friends shall ring for thee.—Is here all?

Shal. Here is two more called than your number; you must have but four here, sir:—and so, I pray you, go in with me to dinner.

Fal. Come, I will go drink with you, but I cannot tarry dinner. I am glad to see you, by my troth, master Shallow.

Shal. O, Sir John, do you remember since we lay all night in the windmill in Saint George's fields?

Fal. No more of that, good master Shallow, no more of that.

Shal. Ha, it was a merry night. Ha, cousin Silence, that thou hadst seen that that this knight and I have seen!—Ha, Sir John, said I well?

Fal. We have heard the chimes at midnight, master Shallow.

Shal. That we have, that we have, that we have; in faith, Sir John, we have: our watch-word was, "Hem, boys!"—Come, let's to dinner; come, let's to dinner.—O, the days that we have seen!—Come, come.

[*Exeunt* FALSTAFF, SHALLOW, *and* SILENCE.

Bull. Good master corporate Bardolph, stand my friend, and here is four Harry ten shillings in French crowns for you. In very truth, sir, I had as lief be hanged, sir, as go: and yet, for mine own part, sir, I do not care; but rather, because I am unwilling, and, for mine own part, have a desire to stay with my friends; else, sir, I did not care, for mine own part, so much.

Bard. Go to; stand aside.

Moul. And, good master corporal captain, for my old dame's sake, stand my friend: she has nobody to do anything about her, when I am gone; and she is old, and cannot help herself: you shall have forty, sir.

Bard. Go to; stand aside.

Fee. By my troth, I care not; a man can die but once;—we owe heaven a death: I'll ne'er bear a base mind:—an't be my destiny, so; an't be not, so: no man's too good to serve his prince; and let it go which way it will, he that dies this year is quit for the next.

Bard. Well said; thou art a good fellow.

Fee. 'Faith, I'll bear no base mind.

Re-enter FALSTAFF, SHALLOW, *and* SILENCE.

Fal. Come, sir, which men shall I have?

Shal. Four, of which you please.

Bard. [*To* FAL.] Sir, a word with you.—[*Aside to him.*] I have three pound to free Mouldy and Bull-calf.

Fal. [*Aside to* BARD.] Go to; well.

Shal. Come, Sir John, which four will you have?

Fal. Do you choose for me.

Shal. Marry, then,—Mouldy, Bull-calf, Feeble, and Shadow.

Fal. Mouldy, and Bull-calf: for you, Mouldy, stay at home till you are past service:—and for your part, Bull-calf, grow till you come unto it:—I will none of you.

Shal. Sir John, Sir John, do not yourself wrong: they are your likeliest men, and I would have you served with the best.

Fal. Will you tell me, master Shallow, how to choose a man? Care I for the limb, the thewes, the stature, bulk, and big assemblance of a man? Give me the spirit, master Shallow.—Here's Wart;—you see what a ragged appearance it is: he shall charge you, and discharge you, with the motion of a pewterer's hammer; come off, and on, swifter than he that gibbets on the brewer's bucket. And this same half-faced fellow, Shadow,—give me this man: he presents no mark to the enemy; the foeman may with as great aim level at the edge of a penknife. And, for a retreat,—how swiftly will this Feeble, the woman's tailor, run off? O, give me the spare men, and spare me the great ones.—Put me a caliver into Wart's hand, Bardolph.

Bard. Hold, Wart, traverse; thus, thus, thus.

Fal. Come, manage me your caliver. So:—very well:—go to:—very good:—exceeding good.—O, give me always a little, lean, old, chapped, bald shot.—Well said, i' faith, Wart; thou'rt a good fellow: hold, there's a tester for thee.

Shal. He is not his craft's master, he doth not do it right. I remember at Mile-end green, (when I lay at Clement's-inn,) I was then Sir Dagonet in Arthur's show,—there was a little quiver fellow, and he would manage you his piece thus; and he would about, and about, and come you in, and come you in: "rah, tah, tah," would he say: "bounce," would he say; and away again would he go, and again would he come:—I shall never see such a fellow.

Fal. These fellows will do well, master Shallow.—Heaven keep you, master Silence: I will not use many words with you.—Fare you well, gentlemen both: I thank you: I must a dozen mile to-night.—Bardolph, give the soldiers coats.

Shal. Sir John, heaven bless you, and prosper your affairs, and send us peace! As you return, visit my house; let our old acquaintance be renewed: peradventure, I will with you to the court.

Fal. I would you would, master Shallow.

Shal. Go to; I have spoke at a word. Fare you well.

Fal. Fare you well, gentle gentlemen.—[*Exeunt* SHALLOW *and* SILENCE.] On, Bardolph; lead the men away. [*Exeunt* BARDOLPH, *Recruits, &c.*] As I return, I will fetch off these justices: I do see the bottom of justice Shallow. Lord, lord, how subject we old men are to this vice of lying! This same starved justice hath done nothing but prate to me of the wildness of his youth, and the feats he hath done about Turnbull-street; and every third word a lie, duer paid to the hearer than the Turk's tribute. I do remember him at Clement's-inn, like a man made after supper of a cheese-paring: he was, for all the world, like a forked radish, with a head fantastically carved upon it with a knife: he was so forlorn, that his dimensions to any thick sight were invisible: he was the very genius of famine. He came ever in the rear-ward of the fashion; and sung those tunes to the over-scutched huswives that he heard the carmen whistle, and sware —they were his fancies, or his good-nights. And now is this Vice's dagger become a squire; and talks as familiarly of John of Gaunt, as if he had been sworn brother to him; and I'll be sworn he never saw him but once in the Tilt-yard,—and then he burst his head, for crowding among the marshal's men. I saw it, and told John of Gaunt he beat his own name; for you might have thrust him, and all his apparel, into an eel-skin; the case of a treble hautboy was a mansion for him, a court:—and now has he land and beeves. Well, I will be acquainted with him, if I return; and it shall go hard, but I will make him a philosopher's stone to me: if the young dace be a bait for the old pike, I see no reason, in the law of nature, but I may snap at him. Let time shape, and there an end. [*Exit.*

ACT IV.

The Archbishop of York, with Mowbray, Hastings, and the rebel forces, take the field near Gaultree Forest in Yorkshire, where they are met by the king's army, led by Prince John of Lancaster, who is commissioned by the king to treat with the Archbishop of York and his followers.

SCENE II.—*A Forest in* Yorkshire.

Enter, from one side, MOWBRAY, *the* ARCHBISHOP, HASTINGS, *and others; from the other side,* PRINCE JOHN OF LANCASTER, WESTMORELAND, Officers, *and* Attendants.

P. John. You are well encounter'd here, my cousin Mowbray:—

Good day to you, gentle lord archbishop;—
And so to you, lord Hastings,—and to all.—
My lord of York, it better show'd with you,
When that your flock, assembled by the bell,
Encircled you to hear with reverence
Your exposition on the holy text,
Than now to see you here an iron man,
Cheering a rout of rebels with your drum,
Turning the word to sword, and life to death.
You have taken up,
Under the counterfeited zeal of heaven,
The subjects of his substitute, my father;
And, both against the peace of heaven and him,
Have here up-swarm'd them.
Arch. Good my lord of Lancaster,
I am not here against your father's peace;
But, as I told my lord of Westmoreland,
The time misorder'd doth, in common sense,
Crowd us and crush us to this monstrous form,
To hold our safety up. I sent your grace
The parcels and particulars of our grief,—
The which hath been with scorn shov'd from the court,—
Whereon this Hydra son of war is born;
Whose dangerous eyes may well be charm'd asleep,
With grant of our most just and right desires,
And true obedience, of this madness cur'd,
Stoop tamely to the foot of majesty.
Mowb. If not, we ready are to try our fortunes
To the last man.
Hast. And though we here fall down,
We have supplies to second our attempt:
If they miscarry, theirs shall second them;
And so success of mischief shall be born,
And heir from heir shall hold this quarrel up,
Whiles England shall have generation.
P. John. You are too shallow, Hastings, much too shallow,
To sound the bottom of the after-times.
West. Pleaseth your grace, to answer them directly,
How far forth you do like their articles.
P. John. I like them all, and do allow them well;
And swear, here, by the honor of my blood,
My father's purposes have been mistook;
And some about him have too lavishly
Wrested his meaning and authority.—
My lord, these griefs shall be with speed redress'd;
Upon my soul, they shall. If this may please you,
Discharge your powers unto their several counties,
As we will ours: and here, between the armies,

Let's drink together friendly, and embrace,
That all their eyes may bear those tokens home,
Of our restored love and amity.

Arch. I take your princely word for these redresses.

P. John. I give it you, and will maintain my word:
And thereupon I drink unto your grace.

Hast. [*To an* Officer.] Go, captain, and deliver to the army
This news of peace: let them have pay, and part:
I know it will well please them. Hie thee, captain.
[*Exit* Officer.

Arch. To you, my noble lord of Westmoreland.

West. I pledge your grace; and, if you know what pains
I have bestow'd to breed this present peace,
You would drink freely: but my love to you
Shall show itself more openly hereafter.

Arch. I do not doubt you.

West. I am glad of it.—
Health to my lord and gentle cousin, Mowbray.

Mowb. You wish me health in very happy season,
For I am, on the sudden, something ill.

Arch. Against ill chances men are ever merry;
But heaviness foreruns the good event.

West. Therefore be merry, coz; since sudden sorrow
Serves to say thus,—some good thing comes to-morrow.

Arch. Believe me, I am passing light in spirit.

Mowb. So much the worse, if your own rule be true.
[*Shouts within.*

P. John. The word of peace is render'd: hark, how they shout!

Mowb. This had been cheerful, after victory.

Arch. A peace is of the nature of a conquest;
For then both parties nobly are subdued,
And neither party loser.

P. John. Go, my lord,
And let our army be dischargèd too.— [*Exit* WESTMORELAND.
And good my lord, so please you, let our trains
March by us, that we may peruse the men
We should have cop'd withal.

Arch. Go, good lord Hastings;
And, ere they be dismiss'd, let them march by. [*Exit* HASTINGS.

P. John. I trust, lords, we shall lie to-night together.—

Re-enter WESTMORELAND.

Now, cousin, wherefore stands our army still?

West. The leaders, having charge from you to stand,
Will not go off until they hear you speak.

P. John. They know their duties.

Re-enter HASTINGS.

Hast. My lord, our army is dispers'd already:
Like youthful steers unyok'd, they take their courses
East, west, north, south; or, like a school broke up,
Each hurries toward his home, and sporting-place.
West. Good tidings, my lord Hastings; for the which
I do arrest thee, traitor, of high treason:—
And you, lord archbishop,—and you, lord Mowbray,—
Of capital treason I attach you both.
Mowb. Is this proceeding just and honorable?
West. Is your assembly so?
Arch. Will you thus break your faith?
P. John. I pawn'd thee none:
I promis'd you redress of these same grievances,
Whereof you did complain; which, by mine honor,
I will perform with a most Christian care.
But for you, rebels,—look to taste the due
Meet for rebellion, and such acts as yours.
Most shallowly did you these arms commence,
Fondly brought here, and foolishly sent hence.—
Strike up our drums, pursue the scatter'd stray;
Heaven, and not we, hath safely fought to-day.—
Some guard these traitors to the block of death,
Treason's true bed, and yielder up of breath. [*Exeunt.*

SCENE III.—*Another Part of the Forest.*

Alarums: Excursions. Enter FALSTAFF *and* COLEVILE, *meeting.*

Fal. What's your name, sir, of what condition are you, and of what place, I pray?

Cole. I am a knight, sir; and my name is Colevile, of the dale.

Fal. Well, then, Colevile is your name, a knight is your degree, and your place, the dale: Colevile shall still be your name, a traitor your degree, and the dungeon your place,—a place deep enough; so shall you be still Colevile of the dale.

Cole. Are not you Sir John Falstaff?

Fal. As good a man as he, sir, whoe'er I am. Do ye yield, sir? or shall I sweat for you? If I do sweat, they are the drops of thy lovers, and they weep for thy death: therefore, rouse up fear and trembling, and do observance to my mercy.

Cole. I think you are Sir John Falstaff; and in that thought yield me.

Fal. I have a whole school of tongues in this stomach of mine; and not a tongue of them all speaks any other word than my name. Here comes our general.

Enter Prince John of Lancaster, Westmoreland, *and others.*

P. John. The heat is past; follow no farther now:—
Call in the powers, good cousin, Westmoreland.— [*Exit* West.
Now, Falstaff, where have you been all this while?
When everything is ended, then you come:
These tardy tricks of yours will, on my life,
One time or other break some gallows' back.

Fal. I would be sorry, my lord, but it should be thus; I never knew yet, but rebuke and check was the reward of valor. Do you think me a swallow, an arrow, or a bullet? have I, in my poor and old motion, the expedition of thought? I have speeded hither with the very extremest inch of possibility; I have foundered nine-score and odd posts: and here, travel-tainted as I am, have, in my pure and immaculate valor, taken Sir John Colevile of the dale, a most furious knight, and valorous enemy. But what of that? he saw me, and yielded; that I may justly say with the hook-nosed fellow of Rome,—I came, saw, and overcame.

P. John. It was more of his courtesy than your deserving.

Fal. I know not:—here he is, and here I yield him: and I beseech your grace, let it be booked with the rest of this day's deeds; or, I will have it in a particular ballad else, with mine own picture on the top of it, Colevile kissing my foot: to the which course if I be enforced, if you do not all show like gilt two-pences to me, and I, in the clear sky of fame, o'ershine you as much as the full moon doth the cinders of the element, which show like pins' heads to her, believe not the words of the noble: therefore let me have right, and let desert mount.

P. John. Thine's too heavy to mount.

Fal. Let it shine then.

P. John. Thine's too thick to shine.

Fal. Let it do something, my good lord, that may do me good, and call it what you will.

P. John. Is thy name Colevile?

Cole. It is, my lord.

P. John. A famous rebel art thou, Colevile.

Fal. And a famous true subject took him.

Cole. I am, my lord, but as my betters are,
That led me hither: had they been rul'd by me,
You should have won them dearer than you have.

Fal. I know not how they sold themselves, but thou, like a kind fellow, gavest thyself away gratis; and I thank thee for thee.

Re-enter Westmoreland.

P. John. Now, have you left pursuit?

West. Retreat is made, and execution stay'd.

P. John. Send Colevile, with his confederates,

To York, to present execution:—
Blunt, lead him hence; and see you guard him sure.
[*Exit* COLEVILE, *guarded.*
And now despatch we toward the court, my lords:
I hear, the king my father is sore sick:
Our news shall go before us to his majesty,—
Which, cousin, you shall bear,—to comfort him;
And we with sober speed will follow you.

Fal. My lord, I beseech you, give me leave to go through Glostershire: and, when you come to court, stand my good lord, pray, in your good report.

P. John. Fare you well, Falstaff: I, in my condition,
Shall better speak of you than you deserve. [*Exit.*

Fal. I would, you had but the wit: 'twere better than your dukedom—Good faith, this same young sober-blooded boy doth not love me; nor a man cannot make him laugh;—but that's no marvel, he drinks no wine. There's never any of these demure boys come to any proof; for thin drink doth over-cool their blood; they are generally fools and cowards. A good sherris-sack hath a two-fold operation in it. It ascends me into the brain; dries me there all the foolish, and dull, and crudy vapors which environ it; makes it apprehensive, quick, forgetive, full of nimble, fiery, and delectable shapes; which, deliver'd o'er to the voice, becomes excellent wit. The second property of your excellent sherris is,—the warming of the blood; which, before cold and settled, left the liver white and pale, which is the badge of pusillanimity and cowardice; but the sherris warms it; it illumineth the face, which, as a beacon, gives warning to all the rest of this little kingdom, man, to arm; and then the vital commoners, and inland petty spirits, muster me all to their captain, the heart, who, great, and puffed up with this retinue, doth any deed of courage: and this valor comes of sherris. So that skill in the weapon is nothing without sack, for that sets it a-work; and learning, a mere hoard of gold kept by a demon, till sack commences it, and sets it in act and use. Hereof comes it, that Prince Harry is valiant; for the cold blood he did naturally inherit of his father, he hath, like lean, sterile, and bare land, manured, husbanded, and tilled, with excellent endeavor of drinking good, and good store of fertile sherris, that he is become very hot and valiant. If I had a thousand sons, the first human principle I would teach them should be,—to forswear thin potations, and to addict themselves to sack. [*Enter* BARDOLPH.] How now, Bardolph!

Bard. The army is discharged all, and gone.

Fal. Let them go. I'll through Glostershire; and there will I visit Master Robert Shallow, esquire: I have him already tempering between my finger and my thumb, and shortly will I seal with him. Come away. [*Exeunt.*

SCENE IV.—Westminster. *A Room in the Palace.*

Enter KING HENRY, CLARENCE, PRINCE HUMPHREY, WARWICK, *and others.*

K. Hen. Now, lords, if heaven doth give successful end
To this debate that bleedeth at our doors,
We will our youth lead on to higher fields,
And draw no swords but what are sanctified.
Our navy is address'd, our power collected,
Our substitutes in absence well invested,
And every thing lies level to our wish:
Only, we want a little personal strength;
And pause us, till these rebels, now afoot,
Come underneath the yoke of government.
War. Both which, we doubt not but your majesty
Shall soon enjoy.
K. Hen. Humphrey, my son of Gloster,
Where is the prince your brother?
P. Humph. I think he's gone to hunt, my lord, at Windsor.
K. Hen. And how accompanied?
P. Humph. I do not know, my lord.
K. Hen. Is not his brother, Thomas of Clarence, with him?
P. Humph. No, my good lord; he is in presence here.
Cla. What would my lord and father?
K. Hen. Nothing but well to thee, Thomas of Clarence.
How chance thou art not with the prince thy brother?
He loves thee, and thou dost neglect him, Thomas;
Thou hast a better place in his affection,
Than all thy brothers: cherish it, my boy;
And noble offices thou may'st effect
Of mediation, after I am dead,
Between his greatness and thy other brethren:
Therefore omit him not; blunt not his love,
Nor lose the good advantage of his grace,
By seeming cold, or careless of his will;
For he is gracious, if he be observ'd:
He hath a tear for pity, and a hand
Open as day for melting charity:
Yet, notwithstanding, being incens'd, he's flint;
As humorous as winter, and as sudden
As flaws congealèd in the spring of day.
His temper, therefore, must be well observ'd:
Chide him for faults, and do it reverently,
When you perceive his blood inclin'd to mirth;
But, being moody, give him line and scope,
Till that his passions, like a whale on ground,
Confound themselves with working. Learn this, Thomas,

And thou shalt prove a shelter to thy friends;
A hoop of gold to bind thy brothers in,
That the united vessel of their blood,
Mingled with venom of suggestion,
Shall never leak, though it do work as strong
As aconitum, or rash gunpowder.
Cla. I shall observe him with all care and love.
K. Hen. Why art thou not at Windsor with him, Thomas?
Cla. He is not there to-day; he dines in London.
K. Hen. And how accompanied? can'st thou tell that?
Cla. With Poins, and other his continual followers.
K. Hen. Most subject is the fattest soil to weeds,
And he, the noble image of my youth,
Is overspread with them: therefore my grief
Stretches itself beyond the hour of death:
The blood weeps from my heart, when I do shape,
In forms imaginary, th' unguided days
And rotten times, that you shall look upon
When I am sleeping with my ancestors.
For when his headstrong riot hath no curb,
When rage and hot blood are his counsellors,
When means and lavish manners meet together,
O, with what wings shall his affections fly
Towards fronting peril and oppos'd decay!
War. My gracious lord, you look beyond him quite:
The prince but studies his companions,
Like a strange tongue; which once attain'd,
Your highness knows, comes to no farther use,
But to be known, and hated. So, like gross terms,
The prince will, in the perfectness of time,
Cast off his followers; and the memory
Shall as a pattern or a measure live,
By which his grace must mete the lives of others,
Turning past evils to advantages.
K. Hen. 'Tis seldom when the bee doth leave her comb
In the dead carrion. Who's here? Westmoreland?

Enter WESTMORELAND.

West. Health to my sovereign, and new happiness
Added to that that I am to deliver!
Prince John, your son, doth kiss your grace's hand:
Mowbray, the bishop Scroop, Hastings, and all,
Are brought to the correction of your law;
There is not now a rebel sword unsheath'd,
But peace puts forth her olive every where:
The manner how this action hath been borne,
Here at more leisure may your highness read,
With every course in his particular.

K. Hen. O Westmoreland, thou art a summer bird,
Which ever in the haunch of winter sings
The lifting up of day. Look, here's more news.

Enter HARCOURT.

Har. From enemies heaven keep your majesty;
And, when they stand against you, may they fall
As those that I am come to tell you of!
The earl Northumberland, and the lord Bardolph,
With a great power of English, and of Scots,
Are by the sheriff of Yorkshire overthrown:
The manner and true order of the fight,
This packet, please it you, contains at large.

K. Hen. And wherefore should these good news make me sick?
Will Fortune never come with both hands full,
But write her fair words still in foulest letters?
She either gives a stomach, and no food,—
Such are the poor, in health; or else a feast,
And takes away the stomach,—such are the rich,
That have abundance, and enjoy it not.
I should rejoice now at this happy news;
And now my sight fails, and my brain is giddy:—
O me! come near me; now I am much ill. [*Swoons.*

P. Humph. Comfort, your majesty!

Cla. O my royal father!

West. My sovereign lord, cheer up yourself, look up!

K. Hen. I pray you take me up, and bear me hence
Into some other chamber: softly, pray.

[*They place the* KING *on a bed in an inner part of the Room.*

Let there be no noise made, my gentle friends;
Unless some dull and favorable hand
Will whisper music to my weary spirit.

War. Call for the music in the other room.

K. Hen. Set me the crown upon my pillow here.

Cla. His eye is hollow, and he changes much.

War. Less noise, less noise!

Enter PRINCE HENRY.

P. Hen. Who saw the duke of Clarence?

Cla. I am here, brother, full of heaviness.

P. Hen. How now! rain within doors, and none abroad!
How doth the king?

P. Humph. Exceeding ill.

P. Hen. Heard he the good news yet?
Tell it him.

P. Humph. He alter'd much upon the hearing it.

P. Hen. If he be sick with joy, he will recover
Without physic.

War. Not so much noise, my lords:—sweet prince, speak low;
The king your father is dispos'd to sleep.
Cla. Let us withdraw into the inner room.
War. Will't please your grace to go along with us?
P. Hen. No; I will sit and watch here by the king.
[*Exeunt all except* PRINCE HENRY.
Why doth the crown lie there upon his pillow,
Being so troublesome a bedfellow?
O polish'd perturbation! golden care!
That keep'st the ports of slumber open wide
To many a watchful night!—sleep with it now!
Yet not so sound, and half so deeply sweet,
As he, whose brow with homely biggin bound,
Snores out the watch of night. O majesty!
When thou dost pinch thy bearer, thou dost sit
Like a rich armor worn in heat of day,
That scalds with safety. By his gates of breath
There lies a downy feather, which stirs not:
Did he suspire, that light and weightless down
Perforce must move.—My gracious lord! my father!—
This sleep is sound indeed; this is a sleep,
That from this golden circle hath divorc'd
So many English kings. Thy due from me
Is tears and heavy sorrows of the blood,
Which nature, love, and filial tenderness,
Shall, O dear father, pay thee plenteously:
My due from thee is this imperial crown,
Which, as immediate from thy place and blood,
Derives itself to me. Lo, here it sits,—
[*Putting it on his head.*
Which heaven shall guard; and put the world's whole strength
Into one giant arm, it shall not force
This lineal honor from me: this from thee
Will I to mine leave, as 'tis left to me. [*Exit.*
K. Hen. Warwick! Gloster! Clarence!

Re-enter WARWICK *and the rest.*

Cla. Doth the king call?
War. What would your majesty? How fares your grace?
K. Hen. Why did you leave me here alone, my lords?
Cla. We left the prince, my brother, here, my liege,
Who undertook to sit and watch by you.
K. Hen. The prince of Wales? Where is he? let me see him:
He is not here.
War. This door is open; he is gone this way.
P. Humph. He came not through the chamber where we stay'd.
K. Hen. Where is the crown? who took it from my pillow?

War. When we withdrew, my liege, we left it here.
K. Hen. The prince hath ta'en it hence :—go, seek him out.
Is he so hasty, that he doth suppose
My sleep my death?—
Find him, my lord of Warwick; chide him hither.
[*Exit* WARWICK.
This part of his conjoins with my disease,
And helps to end me.—See, sons, what things you are!
How quickly nature falls into revolt,
When gold becomes her object!
For this the foolish over-careful fathers
Have broke their sleeps with thought, their brains with care,
Their bones with industry;
For this they have engrossèd and pil'd up
The canker'd heaps of strange-achievéd gold;
For this they have been thoughtful to invest
Their sons with arts, and martial exercises:
When, like the bee, tolling from every flower
The virtuous sweets,
Our thighs pack'd with wax, our mouths with honey,
We bring it to the hive; and, like the bees,
Are murdered for our pains. This bitter taste
Yield his engrossments to the ending father.—

Re-enter WARWICK.

Now, where is he that will not stay so long
Till his friend sickness hath determin'd me?
War. My lord, I found the prince in the next room,
Washing with kindly tears his gentle cheeks;
With such a deep demeanor in great sorrow,
That tyranny, which never quaff'd but blood,
Would, by beholding him, have wash'd his knife
With gentle eye-drops. He is coming hither.
K. Hen. But wherefore did he take away the crown?
Lo, where he comes.—

Re-enter PRINCE HENRY.

Come hither to me, Harry.—
Depart the chamber, leave us here alone.
[*Exeunt all except* K. HENRY *and* P. HENRY.
P. Hen. I never thought to hear you speak again.
K. Hen. Thy wish was father, Harry, to that thought:
I stay too long by thee, I weary thee.
Dost thou so hunger for my empty chair,
That thou wilt needs invest thee with mine honors
Before thy hour be ripe? O foolish youth!
Thou seek'st the greatness that will overwhelm thee.
Stay but a little; for my cloud of dignity

Is held from falling with so weak a wind,
That it will quickly drop: my day is dim.
Thou hast stol'n that, which, after some few hours,
Were thine without offence; and at my death
Thou hast seal'd up my expectation:
Thy life did manifest thou lov'dst me not,
And thou wilt have me die assur'd of it.
Thou hid'st a thousand daggers in thy thoughts,
Which thou hast whetted on thy stony heart,
To stab at half an hour of my life.
What! canst thou not forbear me half an hour?
Then get thee gone, and dig my grave thyself;
And bid the merry bells ring to thine ear,
That thou art crowned, not that I am dead.
Let all the tears that should bedew my hearse,
Be drops of balm to sanctify thy head:
Only compound me with forgotten dust;
Give that which gave thee life unto the worms.
Pluck down my officers, break my decrees;
For now a time is come to mock at form:—
Harry the fifth is crown'd!—Up, vanity!
Down, royal state! all you sage counsellors, hence!
And to the English court assemble now,
From every region, apes of idleness!
Now, neighbor confines, purge you of your scum:
Have you a ruffian that will swear, drink, dance,
Revel the night, rob, murder, and commit
The oldest sins the newest kind of ways?
Be happy, he will trouble you no more;
England shall double gild his treble guilt,—
England shall give him office, honor, might;
For the fifth Harry from curb'd licence plucks
The muzzle of restraint, and the wild dog
Shall flesh his tooth in every innocent.
O my poor kingdom, sick with civil blows!
When that my care could not withhold thy riots,
What wilt thou do when riot is thy care?
O, thou wilt be a wilderness again,
Peopled with wolves, thy old inhabitants!

P. Hen. [*Kneeling.*] O, pardon me, my liege! but for my tears,
The moist impediments unto my speech,
I had forestall'd this dear and deep rebuke,
Ere you with grief had spoke, and I had heard
The course of it so far. There is your crown;
And He that wears the crown immortally,
Long guard it yours! If I affect it more,
Than as your honor, and as your renown,
Let me no more from this obedience rise,—

Which my most true and inward duteous spirit
Teacheth,—this prostrate and exterior bending!
Heaven witness with me, when I here came in,
And found no course of breath within your majesty,
How cold it struck my heart! if I do feign,
O, let me in my present wildness die,
And never live to show th' incredulous world
The noble change that I have purposed!
Coming to look on you, thinking you dead,
(And dead almost, my liege, to think you were,)
I spake unto the crown, as having sense,
And thus upbraided it: "The care on thee depending,
Hath fed upon the body of my father;
Therefore, thou, best of gold, art worst of gold:
Other, less fine in carat, is more precious,
Preserving life in medicine potable;
But thou, most fine, most honor'd, most renown'd,
Hast eat thy bearer up." Thus, my most royal liege,
Accusing it, I put it on my head,
To try with it,—as with an enemy
That had before my face murder'd my father,—
The quarrel of a true inheritor.
But if it did infect my blood with joy,
Or swell my thoughts to any strain of pride;
If any rebel or vain spirit of mine
Did, with the least affection of a welcome,
Give entertainment to the might of it,—
Let heaven forever keep it from my head,
And make me as the poorest vassal is,
That doth with awe and terror kneel to it!
K. Hen. O my son,
Heaven put it in thy mind to take it hence,
That thou might'st win the more thy father's love,
Pleading so wisely in excuse of it!
Come hither, Harry, sit thou by my bed;
And hear, I think, the very latest counsel
That ever I shall breathe. Heaven knows, my son,
By what by-paths, and indirect crook'd ways,
I met this crown; and I myself know well
How troublesome it sat upon my head:
To thee it shall descend with better quiet,
Better opinion, better confirmation.
Yet, though thou stand'st more sure than I could do,
Thou art not firm enough, since griefs are green;
And all thy friends,—which thou must make thy friends,—
Have but their stings and teeth newly ta'en out;
By whose fell working I was first advanc'd,
And by whose power I well might lodge a fear

To be again displac'd: which to avoid,
I cut them off; and had a purpose now
To lead out many to the Holy Land,
Lest rest, and lying still, might make them look
Too near unto my state. Therefore, my Harry,
Be it thy course to busy giddy minds
With foreign quarrels; that action, hence borne out,
May waste the memory of the former days.
More would I, but my lungs are wasted so,
That strength of speech is utterly denied me.
How I came by the crown, O heaven, forgive!
And grant it may with thee in true peace live!
P. Hen. My gracious liege,
You won it, wore it, kept it, gave it me;
Then plain and right must my possession be:
Which I, with more than with a common pain,
'Gainst all the world will rightfully maintain.
K. Hen. Look, look, here comes my John of Lancaster.

Enter PRINCE JOHN OF LANCASTER, WARWICK, Lords, *and others.*

P. John. Health, peace, and happiness, to my royal father!
K. Hen. Thou bring'st me happiness and peace, son John;
But health, alack, with youthful wings is flown
From this bare wither'd trunk: upon thy sight,
My worldly business makes a period.
Where is my lord of Warwick?
P. Hen. My lord of Warwick!
K. Hen. Doth any name particular belong
Unto the lodging where I first did swoon?
War. 'Tis call'd Jerusalem, my noble lord.
K. Hen. Laud be to God!—even there my life must end.
It hath been prophesied to me many years,
I should not die but in Jerusalem;
Which vainly I suppos'd the Holy Land:—
But bear me to that chamber; there I'll lie;
In that Jerusalem shall Harry die. [*Exeunt.*

ACT V.

SCENE I.—Glostershire. *A Hall in* SHALLOW'S *House.*

Enter SHALLOW, FALSTAFF, BARDOLPH, *and* Page.

Shal. By cock and pie, sir, you shall not away to-night.—What, Davy, I say!

Fal. You must excuse me, master Robert Shallow.

Shal. I will not excuse you; you shall not be excused; excuses shall not be admitted; there is no excuse shall serve; you shall not be excused.—Why, Davy!

Enter Davy.

Davy. Here, sir.

Shal. Davy, Davy, Davy, Davy,—let me see, Davy; let me see, Davy;—let me see:—yea, marry; William cook, bid him come hither.—Sir John, you shall not be excused.

Davy. Marry, sir, thus, those precepts cannot be served: and again, sir,—shall we sow the headland with wheat?

Shal. With red wheat, Davy. But for William cook:—are there no young pigeons?

Davy. Yes, sir.—Here is, now, the smith's note for shoeing, and plough iron.

Shal. Let it be cast, and paid.—Sir John, you shall not be excused.

Davy. Now, sir, a new link to the bucket must needs be had: —and, sir, do you mean to stop any of William's wages, about the sack he lost the other day at Hinckley fair?

Shal. He shall answer it.—Some pigeons, Davy; a couple of short-legged hens, a joint of mutton, and any pretty little tiny kickshaws, tell William cook.

Davy. Doth the man of war stay all night, sir?

Shal. Yes, Davy. I will use him well: a friend i' the court is better than a penny in purse. Use his men well, Davy; for they are arrant knaves, and will backbite.

Davy. No worse than they are back-bitten.

Shal. Well conceited, Davy. About thy business, Davy.

Davy. I beseech you, sir, to countenance William Visor of Wincot against Clement Perkes of the hill.

Shal. There are many complaints, Davy, against that Visor: that Visor is an arrant knave, on my knowledge.

Davy. I grant your worship, that he is a knave, sir; but yet, heaven forbid, sir, but a knave should have some countenance at his friend's request. An honest man, sir, is able to speak for himself, when a knave is not. I have served your worship truly, sir, this eight years; and if I cannot once or twice in a quarter bear out a knave against an honest man, I have but a very little credit with your worship. The knave is mine honest friend, sir; therefore, I beseech your worship, let him be countenanced.' •

Shal. Go to; I say, he shall have no wrong. Look about, Davy. [*Exit* Davy.] Where are you, Sir John? Come, come, come, off with your boots.—Give me your hand, master Bardolph.

Bard. I am glad to see your worship.

Shal. I thank thee with all my heart, kind master Bardolph: —[*To the* Page.] and welcome, my tall fellow. Come, Sir John.

Fal. I'll follow you, good master Robert Shallow. [*Exit* SHALLOW.] Bardolph, look to our horses. [*Exeunt* BARDOLPH *and* Page.] If I were sawed into quantities, I should make four dozen of such bearded hermit's staves as master Shallow. It is a wonderful thing, to see the semblable coherence of his men's spirits and his: they, by observing him, do bear themselves like foolish justices; he, by conversing with them, is turned into a justice-like serving-man: their spirits are so married in conjunction with the participation of society, that they flock together in consent, like so many wild geese. If I had a suit to master Shallow, I would humor his men with the imputation of being near their master: if to his men, I would curry with master Shallow, that no man could better command his servants. It is certain, that either wise bearing, or ignorant carriage, is caught, as men take diseases, one of another: therefore, let men take heed of their company. I will devise matter enough out of this Shallow, to keep prince Harry in continual laughter and wearing out of six fashions. O, it is much, that a lie with a slight oath, and a jest with a sad brow, will do with a fellow that never had the ache in his shoulders! O, you shall see him laugh, till his face be like a wet cloak ill laid up!

Shal. [*Within.*] Sir John!

Fal. I come, master Shallow; I come, master Shallow. [*Exit.*

SCENE II.—Westminster. *An Apartment in the Palace.*

Enter WARWICK *and the* Lord Chief Justice.

War. How now, my lord chief justice! whither away?
Ch. Just. How doth the king?
War. Exceeding well; his cares are now all ended.
Ch. Just. I hope, not dead.
War. He's walk'd the way of nature;
And to our purposes he lives no more.
Ch. Just. I would his majesty had call'd me with him:
The service that I truly did his life,
Hath left me open to all injuries.
War. Indeed, I think the young king loves you not.
Ch. Just. I know he doth not; and do arm myself,
To welcome the condition of the time.
War. Here come the heavy issue of dead Harry:
O! that the living Harry had the temper
Of him, the worst of these three gentlemen!
How many nobles then should hold their places,
That must strike sail to spirits of vile sort!
Ch. Just. O heaven! I fear, all will be overturn'd!

Enter PRINCE JOHN, PRINCE HUMPHREY, CLARENCE, WESTMORELAND, *and others.*

P. John. Good morrow, cousin Warwick, good morrow.
P. Humph. Cla. Good morrow, cousin.
P. John. We meet like men that had forgot to speak.
War. We do remember; but our argument
Is all too heavy to admit much talk.
P. John. Well, peace be with him that hath made us heavy!
Ch. Just. Peace be with us, lest we be heavier!
P. Humph. O, good my lord, you have lost a friend, indeed;
And I dare swear, you borrow not that face
Of seeming sorrow,—it is sure your own.
Cla. Well, you must now speak Sir John Falstaff fair;
Which swims against your stream of quality.
Ch. Just. Sweet princes, what I did, I did in honor,
Led by th' impartial conduct of my soul;
And never shall you see that I will beg
A ragged and forestall'd remission.
If truth and upright innocency fail me,
I'll to the king, my master, that is dead,
And tell him who hath sent me after him.
War. Here comes the prince.

Enter KING HENRY V.

Ch. Just. Good morrow, and heaven save your majesty!
King. This new and gorgeous garment, majesty,
Sits not so easy on me as you think.—
Brothers, you mix your sadness with some fear:
This is the English, not the Turkish court;
Not Amurath an Amurath succeeds,
But Harry Harry. Yet be sad, good brothers,
For, to speak truth, it very well becomes you:
Sorrow so royally in you appears,
That I will deeply put the fashion on,
And wear it in my heart: why, then, be sad;
But entertain no more of it, good brothers,
Than a joint burden laid upon us all.
For me, by heaven, I bid you be assur'd,
I'll be your father and your brother too;
Let me but bear your love, I'll bear your cares:
Yet weep that Harry's dead, and so will I;
But Harry lives, that shall convert those tears,
By number, into hours of happiness.
P. John, &c. We hope no other from your majesty.
King. You all look strangely on me:—[*To the Chief Justice.*] and you, most:
You are, I think, assur'd I love you not.

Ch. Just. I am assur'd, if I be measur'd rightly,
Your majesty hath no just cause to hate me.
King. No!
How might a prince of my great hopes forget
So great indignities you laid upon me?
What! rate, rebuke, and roughly send to prison
The immediate heir of England! Was this easy?
May this be wash'd in Lethe, and forgotten?
Ch. Just. I then did use the person of your father;
The image of his power lay then in me:
And, in th' administration of his law,
Whiles I was busy for the commonwealth,
Your highness pleasèd to forget my place,
The majesty and power of law and justice,
The image of the king whom I presented,
And struck me in my very seat of judgment:
Whereon, as an offender to your father,
I gave bold way to my authority,
And did commit you. If the deed were ill,
Be you contented, wearing now the garland,
To have a son set your decrees at naught.
And then imagine me taking your part,
And, in your power, soft silencing your son.
After this cold considerance, sentence me;
And, as you are a king, speak in your state,
What I have done that misbecame my place,
My person, or my liege's sovereignty.
King. You are right, Justice, and you weigh this well;
Therefore still bear the balance, and the sword:
And I do wish your honors may increase,
Till you do live to see a son of mine
Offend you, and obey you, as I did.
So shall I live to see my fathers' words:—
"Happy am I, that have a man so bold,
That dares do justice on my proper son;
And not less happy, having such a son,
That would deliver up his greatness so
Into the hands of justice."
There is my hand.
You shall be as a father to my youth:
My voice shall sound as you do prompt mine ear;
And I will stoop and humble my intents
To your well-practised wise directions.—
And, princes all, believe me, I beseech you;—
My father is gone wild into his grave,
For in his tomb lie my affections;
And with his spirit sadly I survive,
To mock the expectation of the world,

To frustrate prophecies, and to raze out
Rotten opinion, who hath writ me down
After my seeming.
Our coronation done, we will summon,
As I before remember'd, all our state:
And (heaven consigning to my good intents,)
No prince, nor peer, shall have just cause to say,
Heaven shorten Harry's happy life one day. [*Exeunt.*

SCENE III.—Glostershire. *The Garden of* SHALLOW'S *House.*

Enter FALSTAFF, SHALLOW, SILENCE, BARDOLPH, *the* Page, *and* DAVY.

Shal. Nay, you shall see mine orchard; where, in an arbor, we will eat a last year's pippin of my own graffing, with a dish of carraways, and so-forth:—come, cousin Silence;—and then to bed.

Fal. 'Fore heaven, you have here a goodly dwelling, and a rich.

Shal. Barren, barren, barren; beggars all, beggars all, Sir John:—marry, good air.—Spread, Davy; spread, Davy: well said, Davy.

Fal. This Davy serves you for good uses.

Shal. A good varlet, a good varlet, a very good varlet, Sir John.—By the mass, I have drunk too much sack at supper:— A good varlet. Now sit down, now sit down:—come, cousin.

Sil. Ah, sirrah! quoth-a,—we shall [*Singing.*

Do nothing but eat, and make good cheer,
And praise heaven for the merry year;
When flesh is cheap and females dear,
And lusty lads roam here and there
So merrily,
And ever among so merrily.

Fal. There's a merry heart!—Good master Silence,
I'll give you a health for that anon.

Shal. Give master Bardolph some wine, Davy.

Davy. [*To* BARDOLPH, *and pointing to a side table.*] Sweet sir, sit; I'll be with you anon; most sweet sir, sit.—Master page, good master page, sit. What you want in meat, we'll have in drink; but you must bear; the heart's all. [*Exit.*

Shal. Be merry, master Bardolph;—and my little soldier there, be merry.

Sil. [*Singing.*

Be merry, be merry, my wife has all;
For women are shrews, both short and tall:
'Tis merry in hall when beards wag all,
And welcome merry shrove-tide.
Be merry, be merry, &c.

Fal. I did not think master Silence had been a man of this mettle.

Sil. Who, I? I have been merry twice and once, ere now.

Re-enter DAVY.

Davy. There is a dish of leather-coats for you.
[*Setting them before* BARDOLPH.

Shal. Davy,—

Davy. Your worship?—[*To* BARDOLPH.] I'll be with you straight.—[*To* SHALLOW.] A cup of wine, sir?

Sil. [*Singing.*]

A cup of wine, that's brisk and fine,
And drink unto the lover mine;
And a merry heart lives long-a.

Fal. Well said, master Silence.

Sil. And we shall be merry;—now comes in the sweet of the night.

Fal. Health and long life to you, master Silence.

Sil. [*Singing.*]

Fill the cup, and let it come;
I'll pledge you a mile to the bottom.

Shal. Honest Bardolph, welcome: if thou wantest any thing, and wilt not call, beshrew thy heart.—Welcome, my little tiny thief; and welcome, indeed, too.—I'll drink to master Bardolph, and to all the cavaleroes about London.

Davy. I hope to see London once ere I die.

Bard. An I might see you there, Davy,—

Shal. By the mass, you'll crack a quart together,—ha! will you not, master Bardolph?

Bard. Yea, sir, in a pottle-pot.

Shal. I thank thee:—the knave will stick by thee, I can assure thee that: he will not out; he is true bred.

Bard. And I'll stick by him, sir.

Shal. Why, there spoke a king. Lack nothing: be merry. [*Knocking heard.*] Look who's at the door there. Ho! who knocks? [*Exit* DAVY.

Fal. [*To* SILENCE, *who drinks a bumper.*] Why, now you have done me right.

Sil. [*Singing.*]

Do me right,
And dub me knight:
Samingo.

Is't not so?

Fal. 'Tis so.

Sil. Is't so? Why, then, say an old man can do somewhat.

Re-enter DAVY.

Davy. An't please your worship, there's one Pistol come from the court with news.

Fal. From the court? let him come in.—[*Enter* PISTOL.] How now, Pistol!

Pist. Sir John, heaven save you!

Fal. What wind blew you hither, Pistol?

Pist. Not the ill wind which blows no man to good.—Sweet knight, thou art now one of the greatest men in the realm.

Sil. By'r lady, I think he be, but goodman Puff of Barson.

Pist. Puff?
Puff in thy teeth, most recreant coward base!—
Sir John, I am thy Pistol, and thy friend,
And helter-skelter have I rode to thee;
And tidings do I bring, and lucky joys,
And golden times, and happy news of price.

Fal. I pr'ythee now, deliver them like a man of this world.

Pist. A foutra for the world, and worldlings base!
I speak of Africa, and golden joys.

Fal. O base Assyrian knight, what is thy news?
Let king Cophetua know the truth thereof.

Sil. [*Singing.*]

And Robin Hood, Scarlet, and John.

Pist. Shall mongrel curs confront the Helicons?
And shall good news be baffled?
Then, Pistol, lay thy head in Furies' lap.

Shal. Honest gentleman, I know not your breeding.

Pist. Why then, lament therefore.

Shal. Give me pardon, sir:—if, sir, you come with news from the court, I take it there is but two ways,—either to utter them, or to conceal them. I am, sir, under the king, in some authority.

Pist. Under which king, Bezonian? speak, or die.

Shal. Under king Harry.

Pist. Harry the fourth? or fifth?

Shal. Harry the fourth.

Pist. A foutra for thine office!—
Sir John, thy tender lambkin now is king;
Harry the fifth's the man. I speak the truth:
When Pistol lies, do this; [*makes a contemptuous gesture.*] and fig me, like
The bragging Spaniard.

Fal. What! is the old king dead?

Pist. As nail in door: the things I speak are just.

Fal. Away, Bardolph! saddle my horse.—Master Robert Shallow, choose what office thou wilt in the land, 'tis thine.—Pistol, I will double-charge thee with dignities.

Bard. O joyful day!—I would not take a knighthood for my fortune.

Pist. What, I do bring good news?

Fal. Carry master Silence to bed.—Master Shallow, my lord

Shallow, be what thou wilt; I am fortune's steward. Get on thy boots: we'll ride all night.—O sweet Pistol!—Away, Bardolph!—[*Exit* BARD.] Come, Pistol, utter more to me; and, withal, devise something to do thyself good. Boot, boot, master Shallow: I know the young king is sick for me. Let us take any man's horses; the laws of England are at my commandment. Happy are they which have been my friends; and woe unto my lord chief justice!

Pist. Let vultures vile seize on his lungs also!
"Where is the life that late I led?" say they:
Why, here it is;—welcome these pleasant days! [*Exeunt.*

SCENE V.—*A Public Place near* Westminster Abbey.

Enter two Grooms, *strewing rushes.*

1 *Groom.* More rushes, more rushes.

2 *Groom.* The trumpets have sounded twice.

1 *Groom.* It will be two o'clock ere they come from the coronation: despatch, despatch. [*Exeunt* Grooms.

Enter FALSTAFF, SHALLOW, PISTOL, BARDOLPH, *and* Page.

Fal. Stand here by me, master Robert Shallow; I will make the king do you grace: I will leer upon him, as he comes by; and do but mark the countenance that he will give me.

Pist. Heaven bless thy lungs, good knight.

Fal. Come here, Pistol; stand behind me.—[*To* SHALLOW.] O, if I had had time to have made new liveries, I would have bestowed the thousand pound I borrowed of you. But 'tis no matter; this poor show doth better: this doth infer the zeal I had to see him,—

Shal. It doth so.

Fal. It shows my earnestness of affection,—

Shal. It doth so.

Fal. My devotion,—

Shal. It doth, it doth, it doth.

Fal. As it were, to ride day and night; and not to deliberate, not to remember, not to have patience to shift me,—

Shal. It is most certain.

Fal. But to stand stained with travel, and sweating with desire to see him; thinking of nothing else, putting all affairs else in oblivion, as if there were nothing else to be done but to see him.

Pist. 'Tis all in every part.

Shal. 'Tis so, indeed. [*Shouts within and trumpets sound.*

Pist. There roar'd the sea, and trumpet-clangor sounds.

Enter KING *and his train, the* Chief Justice *among them.*

Fal. Heaven save thy grace, king Hal! my royal Hal!

Pist. The heavens thee guard and keep, most royal imp of fame!

Fal. Heaven save thee, my sweet boy!

King. My lord chief justice, speak to that vain man.

Ch. Just. Have you your wits? know you what 'tis you speak?

Fal. My king! my Jove! I speak to thee, my heart!

King. I know thee not, old man: fall to thy prayers;
How ill white hairs become a fool, and jester!
I have long dream'd of such a kind of man,
So surfeit-swell'd, so old, and so profane;
But, being awake, I do despise my dream.
Make less thy body hence, and more thy grace;
Leave gormandizing; know, the grave doth gape
For thee thrice wider than for other men.—
Reply not to me with a fool-born jest:
Presume not that I am the thing I was;
For heaven doth know, so shall the world perceive,
That I have turn'd away my former self;
So will I those that kept me company.
When thou dost hear I am as I have been,
Approach me, and thou shalt be as thou wast,
The tutor and the feeder of my riots:
Till then I banish thee, on pain of death,—
As I have done the rest of my misleaders,—
Not to come near our person by ten mile.
For competence of life I will allow you,
That lack of means enforce you not to evil;
And, as we hear you do reform yourselves,
We will, according to your strength and qualities,
Give you advancement.—[*To* Ch. Just.] Be it your charge, my lord,
To see perform'd the tenor of our word.—
Set on. [*Exeunt* KING *and his train.*

Fal. Master Shallow, I owe you a thousand pound.

Shal. Ay, marry, Sir John; which I beseech you to let me have home with me.

Fal. That can hardly be, master Shallow. Do not you grieve at this; I shall be sent for in private to him: look you, he must seem thus to the world: fear not your advancement; I will be the man yet that shall make you great.

Shal. I cannot perceive how; unless you should give me your doublet, and stuff me out with straw. I beseech you, good Sir John, let me have five hundred of my thousand.

Fal. Sir, I will be as good as my word: this that you heard was but a color.

Shal. A color, I fear, that you will die in, Sir John.

Fal. Fear no colors: go with me to dinner:—come, lieutenant Pistol; come, Bardolph:—I shall be sent for soon at night.

Re-enter PRINCE JOHN, *the* Chief Justice, Officers, *&c.*

Ch. Just. Go, carry Sir John Falstaff to the Fleet:
Take all his company along with him.
Fal. My lord, my lord,—
Ch. Just. I cannot now speak: I will hear you soon.—
Take them away.
[*Exeunt* FAL. SHAL. PIST. BARD. *and* Page, *with* Officers.
P. John. I like this fair proceeding of the king's:
He hath intent his wonted followers
Shall all be very well provided for;
But all are banish'd, till their conversations
Appear more wise and modest to the world.
Ch. Just. And so they are.
P. John. The king hath call'd his parliament, my lord.
Ch. Just. He hath.
P. John. I will lay odds, that, ere this year expire,
We bear our civil swords and native fire
As far as France: I heard a bird so sing,
Whose music, to my thinking, pleas'd the king.
Come, will you hence? [*Exeunt.*

THE HISTORY OF

KING HENRY V.

This play was styled in the earlier editions a "Chronicle History," which it strictly is, in a dramatic form—"for it borrows nothing from mere invention in incident, and scarcely in character." The story, in all its details, is purely historical; and even the comic personages introduced are almost historical in their character, exhibiting, as they do, types or representatives of the classes of the period. The period comprised in this Dramatic History commences about the latter end of the first, and terminates in the eighth year of this king's reign; when he married Katharine of France, and closed up the differences betwixt England and that crown.

PERSONS REPRESENTED.

King Henry the Fifth.
Duke of Gloster, } *Brothers to the* King.
Duke of Bedford, }
Duke of Exeter, *Uncle to the* King.
Duke of York, *Cousin to the* King.
Earls of Salisbury, Westmoreland, *and* Warwick.
Archbishop of Canterbury.
Bishop of Ely.
Earl of Cambridge, }
Lord Scroop, } *Conspirators.*
Sir Thomas Grey, }
Sir Thomas Erpingham, Gower, Fluellen, Macmorris, Jamy, *Officers in* King Henry's *Army.*
Bates, Court, Williams, *Soldiers in the Same.*
Pistol, Nym, Bardolph.
Boy, *Servant to them.* *A* Herald.
Charles the Sixth, *King of* France.
Lewis, *the Dauphin.*
Dukes of Burgundy, Orleans, *and* Bourbon.
The Constable of France.
Rambures, *and* Grandpre, *French Lords.*
Montjoy, *a French Herald.*

Governor of Harfleur.
Embassadors to England.

ISABEL, *Queen of* France.
KATHARINE, *Daughter of* CHARLES *and* ISABEL.
ALICE, *a Lady attending on the Princess* KATHARINE.
Hostess *of the* Boar's Head Tavern *in* Eastcheap; *formerly Mistress* QUICKLY, *now wife to* PISTOL.

Lords, Ladies, Officers, Soldiers, Citizens, Messengers, *and* Attendants.

SCENE,—*In* ENGLAND *and in* FRANCE.

ACT I.

SCENE I.—London. *An Ante-chamber in the* KING'S *Palace.*

Enter the ARCHBISHOP OF CANTERBURY *and the* BISHOP OF ELY.

Cant. My lord, I'll tell you,—that self bill is urg'd,
Which in th' eleventh year of the last king's reign
Was like, and had indeed against us pass'd,
But that the scambling and unquiet time
Did push it out of farther question.
Ely. But how, my lord, shall we resist it now?
Cant. It must be thought on. If it pass against us,
We lose the better half of our possession:
For all the temporal lands, which men devout
By testament have given to the church,
Would they strip from us.
Ely. This would drink deep.
Cant. 'Twould drink the cup and all.
Ely. But what prevention?
Cant. The king is full of grace, and fair regard.
Ely. And a true lover of the holy church.
Cant. The courses of his youth promis'd it not.
The breath no sooner left his father's body,
But that his wildness, mortified in him,
Seem'd to die too; yea, at that very moment,
Consideration like an angel came,
And whipp'd th' offending Adam out of him,
Leaving his body as a paradise,
To envelope and contain celestial spirits.
Never was such a sudden scholar made;
Never came reformation in a flood,
With such a heady current, scouring faults;
Nor never Hydra-headed wilfulness

So soon did lose his seat, and all at once,
As in this king.
Ely. We are blessèd in the change.
Cant. Hear him but reason in divinity,
And, all-admiring, with an inward wish
You would desire the king were made a prelate:
Hear him debate of commonwealth affairs,
You would say, it hath been all-in-all his study:
List his discourse of war, and you shall hear
A fearful battle render'd you in music:
Turn him to any cause of policy,
The Gordian knot of it he will unloose,
Familiar as his garter:—that, when he speaks,
The air, a charter'd libertine, is still,
And the mute wonder lurketh in men's ears,
To steal his sweet and honeyed sentences.
Ely. The strawberry grows underneath the nettle,
And wholesome berries thrive and ripen best,
Neighbor'd by fruit of baser quality:
And so the prince obscur'd his contemplation
Under the veil of wildness; which, no doubt,
Grew like the summer grass, fastest by night,
Unseen, yet crescive* in his faculty.
Cant. It must be so, for miracles are ceas'd.
Ely. But, my good lord,
How now for mitigation of this bill
Urg'd by the commons? Doth his majesty
Incline to it, or no?
Cant. He seems indifferent;
Or, rather, swaying more upon our part,
Than cherishing th' exhibiters against us:
For I have made an offer to his majesty,—
Upon our spiritual convocation,
And in regard of causes now in hand,
Which I have open'd to his grace at large,
As touching France,—to give a greater sum
Than ever at one time the clergy yet
Did to his predecessors part withal.
Ely. How did this offer seem receiv'd, my lord?
Cant. With good acceptance of his majesty;
Save, that there was not time enough to hear
The severals, and unhidden passages
Of his true titles to some certain dukedoms,
And, generally, to the crown and seat of France,
Deriv'd from Edward, his great grandfather.
Ely. What was th' impediment that broke this off?

* *Crescive*—increasing, growing.

Cant. The French embassador upon that instant
Crav'd audience; and the hour, I think, is come,
To give him hearing: is it four o'clock?
Ely. It is.
Cant. Then go we in, to know his embassy;
Which I could, with a ready guess, declare,
Before the Frenchman speak a word of it.
Ely. I'll wait upon you; and I long to hear it. [*Exeunt.*

SCENE II.—London. *A Room of State in the Palace.*

Enter KING HENRY, GLOSTER, BEDFORD, EXETER, WARWICK, WESTMORELAND, *and* Attendants.

K. Hen. Where is my gracious lord of Canterbury?
Exe. Not here in presence.
K. Hen. Send for him, good uncle.
West. Shall we call in th' embassador, my liege?
K. Hen. Not yet, my cousin: we would be resolv'd,
Before we hear him, of some things of weight,
That task our thoughts, concerning us and France.

Enter the ARCHBISHOP OF CANTERBURY *and the* BISHOP OF ELY.

Cant. Heaven and its angels, guard your sacred throne,
And make you long become it!
K. Hen. Sure, we thank you.
My learned lord, we pray you to proceed,
And justly and religiously unfold,
Why the law Salique, that they have in France,
Or should, or should not, bar us in our claim:
And heaven forbid, my dear and faithful lord,
That you should fashion, wrest, or bow your reading,
Or nicely charge your understanding soul
With opening titles miscreate, whose right
Suits not in native colors with the truth;
For heaven doth know how many, now in health,
Shall drop their blood in approbation
Of what your reverence shall incite us to.
Therefore, take heed how you impawn our person,
How you awake the sleeping sword of war:
We charge you in the name of heaven, take heed.
Under this conjuration, speak, my lord;
And we will hear, note, and believe in heart,
That what you speak is in your conscience wash'd,
As pure as sin with baptism.
Cant. Then hear me, gracious sovereign, and you peers,
That owe yourselves, your lives, and services,

To this imperial throne.—There is no bar
To make against your highness' claim to France,
But this, which they produce from Pharamond,—
"No woman shall succeed in Salique land:"
Which Salique land the French unjustly gloze*
To be the realm of France, and Pharamond
The founder of this law, and female bar.
Yet their own authors faithfully affirm,
That the land Salique is in Germany,
Between the floods of Sala and of Elbe;
Where Charles the great, having subdued the Saxons,
There left behind and settled certain French;
Who, holding in disdain the German women
For some dishonest manners of their life,
Establish'd then this law,—to wit, no female
Should be inheritrix in Salique land.
The kings of France hold up this Salique law,
To bar your highness claiming from the female;
And rather choose to hide them in a net,
Than amply to imbar their crooked titles
Usurp'd from you and your progenitors.
K. Hen. May I with right and conscience make this claim?
Cant. The sin upon my head, dread sovereign!
For in the Book of Numbers is it writ,—
When the son dies, let the inheritance
Descend unto the daughter. Gracious lord,
Stand for your own; unwind your bloody flag;
Look back into your mighty ancestors:
Go, my dread lord, to your great grandsire's tomb,
From whom you claim; invoke his warlike spirit,
And your great uncle's, Edward the black prince,
Who on the French ground play'd a tragedy,
Making defeat on the full power of France.
Ely. Awake remembrance of these valiant dead,
And with your puissant arm renew their feats.
Exe. Your brother kings and monarchs of the earth
Do all expect that you should rouse yourself,
As did the former lions of your blood.
West. They know your grace hath cause and means and might.
Cant. O, let our bodies follow, my dear liege,
With blood, and sword, and fire, to win your right:
In aid whereof, we of the spirituality
Will raise your highness such a mighty sum,
As never did the clergy at one time
Bring in to any of your ancestors.
K. Hen. We must not only arm to invade the French,

* Gloze—to palliate by specious exposition.

But lay down our proportions to defend
Against the Scot, who will make road upon us
With all advantages.
Cant. They of those marches, gracious sovereign,
Shall be a wall sufficient to defend
Our inland from the pilfering borderers.
K. Hen. We do not mean the coursing snatchers only
But fear the main intendment of the Scot,
Who hath been still a giddy neighbor to us.
West. There is a saying, very old and true,—
"If that you will France win,
Then with Scotland first begin:"
For once the eagle England being in prey,
To her unguarded nest the weasel Scot
Comes sneaking, and so sucks her princely eggs;
Playing the mouse in absence of the cat,
To spoil and havock more than she can eat.
Exe. It follows, then, the cat must stay at home;
For government, though high, and low, and lower,
Put into parts, doth keep in one concent,*
Congreeing in a full and natural close,
Like music.
Cant. Therefore doth heaven divide
The state of man in divers functions,
Setting endeavor in continual motion;
To which is fixed, as an aim or butt,
Obedience: for so work the honey bees;
Creatures, that by a rule in nature, teach
The act of order to a peopled kingdom.
They have a king, and officers of sorts:
Where some, like magistrates, correct at home;
Others, like merchants, venture trade abroad;
Others, like soldiers, armed in their stings,
Make boot upon the summer's velvet buds;
Which pillage they with merry march bring home
To the tent-royal of their emperor:
Who, busied in his majesty, surveys
The singing masons building roofs of gold;
The civil citizens kneading up the honey;
The poor mechanic porters crowding in
Their heavy burdens at his narrow gate;
The sad-ey'd justice, with his surly hum,
Delivering o'er to executors pale
The lazy yawning drone. I this infer,—
That many things, having full reference
To one concent, may work contrariously.

* *Concent*—consistency, accordance.

Therefore to France, my liege.
Divide your happy England into four;
Whereof take you one quarter into France,
And you withal shall make all Gallia shake.
K. Hen. Call in the messengers sent from the Dauphin.
[*Exit an* Attendant.
Now are we well resolv'd; and, by God's help,
And yours, the noble sinews of our power,
France being ours, we'll bend it to our awe,
Or break it all to pieces: or there we'll sit,
Ruling in large and ample empery,
O'er France, and all her almost kingly dukedoms,
Or lay these bones in an unworthy urn,
Tombless, with no remembrance over them:
Either our history shall with full mouth
Speak freely of our acts, or else our grave,
Like Turkish mute, shall have a tongueless mouth,
Not worshipp'd with a waxen epitaph.

Enter Embassadors of France.

Now are we well prepar'd to know the pleasure
Of our fair cousin Dauphin; for we hear
Your greeting is from him, not from the king.
1 *Emb.* May't please your majesty to give us leave
Freely to render what we have in charge;
Or shall we sparingly show you far off
The Dauphin's meaning and our embassy?
K. Hen. We are no tyrant, but a Christian king;
Unto whose grace our passion is as subject,
As are our wretches fetter'd in our prisons:
Therefore with frank and with uncurbèd plainness
Tell us the Dauphin's mind.
1 *Emb.* Thus, then, in few.
Your highness, lately sending into France,
Did claim some certain dukedoms, in the right
Of your great predecessor, king Edward the third.
In answer of which claim, the prince our master
Says, that you savor too much of your youth;
And bids you be advis'd, there's naught in France
That can be with a nimble galliard won;—
You cannot revel into dukedoms there.
He therefore sends you, meeter for your spirit,
This tun of treasure; and, in lieu of this,
Desires you let the dukedoms that you claim
Hear no more of you. This the Dauphin speaks.
K. Hen. What treasure, uncle?
Exe. Tennis-balls, my liege.
K. Hen. We are glad the Dauphin is so pleasant with us;

His present, and your pains, we thank you for:
When we have match'd our rackets to these balls,
We will, in France, by heaven's grace, play a set,
Shall strike his father's crown into the hazard.
Tell the Dauphin, I will keep my state;
Be like a king, and show my sail of greatness,
When I do rouse me in my throne of France:
To venge me as I may, and to put forth
My rightful hand in a well-hallow'd cause.
So, get you hence in peace; and tell the Dauphin,
His jest will savor but of shallow wit,
When thousands weep, more than did laugh at it.—
Convey them with safe conduct.—Fare you well.
[*Exeunt* Embassadors.

Exe. This was a merry message.

K. Hen. We hope to make the sender blush at it.
Therefore, my lords, omit no happy hour,
That may give fartherance to our expedition;
For we have now no thought in us but France,
Save those to heaven, that run before our business.
Therefore, let our proportions for these wars
Be soon collected, and all things thought upon,
That may with reasonable swiftness add
More feathers to our wings; for, heaven before,
We'll chide this Dauphin at his father's door.
Therefore, let every man now task his thought,
That this fair action may on foot be brought. [*Exeunt.*

ACT II.

SCENE I.—London. *Eastcheap.*

Enter NYM *and* BARDOLPH, *meeting.*

Bard. Well met, corporal Nym.

Nym. Good morrow, lieutenant Bardolph.

Bard. What, are ancient Pistol and you friends yet?

Nym. For my part, I care not; I say little; but when time shall serve, there shall be smiles;—but that shall be as it may. I dare not fight; but I will wink, and hold out mine iron: it is a simple one; but what though? it will toast cheese, and it will endure cold as another man's sword will; and there's an end.

Bard. I will bestow a breakfast to make you friends; and we'll be all three sworn brothers to France: let it be so, good corporal Nym.

Nym. 'Faith, I will live so long as I may, that's the certain of it; and when I cannot live any longer, I will do as I may: that is my rest, that is the rendezvous of it.

Bard. It is certain, corporal, that he is married to Nell Quickly: and, certainly, she did you wrong; for you were troth-plight to her.

Nym. I cannot tell:—things must be as they may: men may sleep, and they may have their throats about them at that time; and, some say, knives have edges. It must be as it may; though patience be a tired mare, yet she will plod. There must be conclusions. Well, I cannot tell.

Bard. Here comes ancient Pistol, and his wife:—good corporal, be patient here.—

Enter PISTOL *and* Hostess.

How now, mine host Pistol!

Pist. Base tike, call'st thou me host?
Now, by this hand, I swear, I scorn the term.

Bard. Good lieutenant,—good corporal,—offer nothing here.

Nym. Pish!

Pist. Pish for thee, Iceland dog! thou cur of Iceland!

Host. Good corporal Nym, show thy valor, and put up your sword.

Nym. Will you shog off? I would have you *solus*.
[*Sheathing his sword.*

Pist. *Solus*, egregious dog? O viper vile!
The *solus* in thy most marvellous face:
The *solus* in thy teeth, and in thy throat,
And in thy hateful lungs, yea, in thy maw, perdy.

Nym. I am not Barbason; you cannot conjure me. I have a humor to knock you indifferently well: If you grow foul with me, Pistol, I will scour you with my rapier, as I may, in fair terms: in good terms, as I may; and that's the humor of it.

Pist. O braggart vile, and cursed furious wight!
The grave doth gape, and doting death is near;
Therefore exhale. [PISTOL *and* NYM *draw.*

Bard. Hear me, hear me what I say:—he that strikes the first stroke, I'll run him up to the hilts, as I am a soldier. [*Draws.*

Pist. An oath of mickle might; and fury shall abate.—
Give me thy fist, thy fore-foot to me give:
Thy spirits are most tall.

Nym. I will cut thy throat, one time or other, in fair terms; that is the humor of it.

Pist. I thee defy again.
O hound of Crete, think'st thou my spouse to get?
I have, and I will hold, the *quondam* Quickly
For the only she; and—*pauca*, there's enough.
Go to.

Enter the Boy.

Boy. Mine host Pistol, you must come to my master,—and you, hostess:—he is very sick, and would to bed.—'Faith, he's very ill.

Bard. Away, you rogue!

Host. By my troth, he'll yield the crow a pudding one of these days: the king has killed his heart.—Good husband, come home presently. [*Exeunt* Hostess *and* Boy.

Bard. Come, shall I make you two friends? We must to France together: why should we keep knives to cut one another's throats?

Pist. Let floods o'erswell, and fiends for food howl on!

Nym. You'll pay me the eight shillings I won of you at betting?

Pist. Base is the slave that pays.

Nym. That now I will have: that's the humor of it.

Pist. As manhood shall compound; push home. [*They draw.*

Bard. By this sword, he that makes the first thrust, I'll kill him; by this sword, I will.

Pist. Sword is an oath, and oaths must have their course.

Bard. Corporal Nym, an thou wilt be friends, be friends: an thou wilt not, why, then, be enemies with me too. Pr'ythee, put up.

Nym. I shall have my eight shillings, I won of you at betting?

Pist. A noble shalt thou have, and present pay;
And liquor likewise will I give to thee,
And friendship shall combine, and brotherhood:
I'll live by Nym, and Nym shall live by me;—
Is not this just?—for I shall sutler be
Unto the camp, and profits will accrue.
Give me thy hand.

Nym. I shall have my noble?

Pist. In cash most justly paid.

Nym. Well then, that's the humor of it.

Re-enter Hostess.

Host. As ever you came of women, come in quickly to Sir John. Ah, poor heart! he is so shaked of a burning quotidian tertian, that it is most lamentable to behold. Sweet men, come to him.

Nym. The king hath run bad humors on the knight, that's the even of it,

Pist. Nym, thou hast spoke the right;
His heart is fracted, and corroborate.

Nym. The king is a good king: but it must be as it may; he passes some humors, and careers.

Pist. Let us condole the knight; for, lambkins we will live.
[*Exeunt.*

SCENE III.—London. *The Boar's Head Tavern in Eastcheap.*

Enter Pistol, Hostess, Nym, Bardolph, *and* Boy.

Host. Pr'ythee, honey-sweet husband, let me bring thee to Staines.

Pist. No; for my manly heart doth yearn.—
Bardolph, be blithe; Nym, rouse thy vaunting veins;
Boy, bristle thy courage up, for Falstaff he is dead,
And we must yearn therefor.

Bard. Would I were with him, wheresome'er he is.

Host. Nay, sure, he's in Arthur's bosom, if ever man went to Arthur's bosom. 'A made a finer end, and went away, an it had been any christom child: 'a parted even just between twelve and one, even at the turning o' the tide: for after I saw him fumble with the sheets, and play with flowers, and smile upon his finger's ends, I knew there was but one way; for his nose was as sharp as a pen, and 'a babbled of green fields.

Bard. Well, the fuel is gone that maintained us.

Nym. Shall we shog? the king will be gone from Southampton.

Pist. Come, let's away.—My love, give me thy lips.
Look to my chattels, and my moveables:
Let senses rule; the word is, "Pitch and pay;"
Trust none;
For oaths are straws, men's faiths are wafer-cakes,
And hold-fast is the only dog, my duck:
Yoke-fellows in arms,
Let us to France; like horse-leeches, my boys,
To suck, to suck, the very blood to suck!

Boy. And that is but unwholesome food, they say.

Pist. Touch her soft mouth, and march.

Bard. [*Kissing her.*] Farewell, hostess.

Nym. I cannot kiss, that is the humor of it; but, adieu.

Pist. Let housewifery appear: keep close, I thee command.

Host. Farewell; adieu. [*Exeunt.*

SCENE IV.—France. *A Room in the* French King's *Palace.*

Flourish. Enter the French King, *attended; the* Dauphin, *the* Duke of Burgundy, *the* Constable, *and others.*

Fr. King. Thus come the English with full power upon us;
And more than carefully it us concerns,
To answer royally in our defences.
For England his approaches makes as fierce,
As waters to the sucking of a gulf.
It fits us, then, to be as provident

As fear may teach us, out of late examples
Left by the fatal and neglected English
Upon our fields.
Dau. My most redoubted father,
It is most meet we arm us 'gainst the foe;
Therefore, I say, 'tis meet we all go forth,
To view the sick and feeble parts of France:
And let us do it with no show of fear;
No, with no more, than if we heard that England
Were busied with a Whitsun morris dance:
For, my good liege, she is so idly king'd,
Her sceptre so fantastically borne
By a vain, giddy, shallow, humorous youth,
That fear attends her not.
Con. O peace, prince Dauphin!
You are too much mistaken in this king:
Question your grace the late embassadors,—
With what great state he heard their embassy,
How well supplied with noble counsellors,
How modest in exception, and, withal,
How terrible in constant resolution,—
And you shall find, his vanities forespent
Were but the outside of the Roman Brutus,
Covering discretion with a coat of folly.
Fr. King. Think we king Harry strong;
And, princes, look you strongly arm to meet him.
The kindred of him hath been flesh'd upon us;
And he is bred out of that bloody strain,
That haunted us in our familiar paths:
Witness our too much memorable shame,
When Cressy battle fatally was struck,
And all our princes captiv'd, by the hand
Of that black name, Edward, black prince of Wales.
This is a stem
Of that victorious stock; and let us fear
The native mightiness and fate of him.

Enter a Messenger.

Mess. Embassadors from Harry king of England
Do crave admittance to your majesty.
Fr. King. We'll give them present audience. Go, and bring them. [*Exeunt* Mess. *and certain* Lords.
You see, this chase is hotly follow'd, friends.
Dau. Turn head, and stop pursuit; for coward dogs
Most spend their mouths, when what they seem to threaten
Runs far before them. Good my sovereign,
Take up the English short; and let them know
Of what a monarchy you are the head:

Self-love, my liege, is not so vile a sin
As self-neglecting.

Re-enter Lords, *with* EXETER *and train.*

Fr. King. From our brother England?
Exe. From him; and thus he greets your majesty.
He wills you, in the name of heaven,
That you divest yourself, and lay apart
The borrow'd glories, that by gift of heaven,
By law of nature and of nations, 'long
To him, and to his heirs; namely, the crown,
And all wide-stretched honors that pertain,
By custom and the ordinance of times,
Unto the crown of France.
Fr. King. Or else what follows?
Exe. Bloody constraint; for if you hide the crown
Even in your hearts, there will he rake for it,
Therefore in fierce tempest is he coming,
In thunder and in earthquake, like a Jove;
And bids you, in the bowels of the Lord,
Deliver up the crown: and to take mercy
On the poor souls, for whom this hungry war
Opens his vasty jaws:
This is his claim, his threat'ning, and my message;
Unless the Dauphin be in presence here,
To whom expressly I bring greeting too.
Fr. King. For us, we will consider of this farther:
To-morrow shall you bear our full intent
Back to our brother England.
Dau. For the Dauphin,
I stand here for him: what to him from England?
Exe. Scorn and defiance; slight regard, contempt,
And any thing that may not misbecome
The mighty sender, doth he prize you at.
Dau. Say, if my father render fair return,
It is against my will; for I desire
Nothing but odds with England: to that end,
As matching to his youth and vanity,
I did present to him the Paris balls.
Exe. He'll make your Paris Louvre shake for it,
Were it the mistress court of mighty Europe.
Fr. King. To-morrow shall you know our mind at full
Exe. Despatch us with all speed, lest that our king
Come here himself to question our delay;
For he is footed in this land already.
Fr. King. You shall be soon despatch'd with fair conditions:
A night is but small breath, and little pause,
To answer matters of this consequence. [*Flourish. Exeunt.*

ACT III.

SCENE I.—France. *Before* Harfleur.

Alarums. Enter KING HENRY, EXETER, BEDFORD, GLOSTER, *and* Soldiers, *with scaling ladders.*

K. Hen. Once more unto the breach, dear friends, once more;
Or close the wall up with our English dead!
In peace, there's nothing so becomes a man,
As modest stillness, and humility:
But when the blast of war blows in our ears,
Then imitate the action of the tiger;
Stiffen the sinews, summon up the blood,
Disguise fair nature with hard-favor'd rage:
Then lend the eye a terrible aspéct;
Let it pry through the portage of the head,
Like the brass cannon; let the brow o'erwhelm it,
As fearfully, as doth a galled rock,
O'erhang and jutty his confounded base,
Swill'd with the wild and wasteful ocean.
Now set the teeth, and stretch the nostril wide;
Hold hard the breath, and bend up every spirit
To his full height!—On, on, you noblest English,
Whose blood is fet* from fathers of war-proof!—
Fathers, that, like so many Alexanders,
Have in these parts from morn till even fought,
And sheath'd their swords for lack of argument.
Dishonor not your mothers;
Be copy now to men of grosser blood,
And teach them how to war!—And you, good yeomen,
Whose limbs were made in England, show us here
The mettle of your pasture; let us swear
That you are worth your breeding; which I doubt not;
For there is none of you so mean and base,
That hath not noble lustre in your eyes.
I see you stand like greyhounds in the slips,
Straining upon the start. The game's afoot:
Follow your spirit: and, upon this charge,
Cry—God for Harry! England! and Saint George!
[*Exeunt. Alarum, and chambers go off.*

* *Fet*—fetched.

SCENE II.—*The Same.*

Forces pass over; then enter NYM, BARDOLPH, PISTOL, *and* BOY.

Bard. On, on, on, on, on! to the breach, to the breach!

Nym. Pray thee, corporal, stay: the knocks are too hot; and for mine own part, I have not a case of lives: the humor of it is too hot, that is the very plain-song of it.

Pist. The plain-song is most just; for humors do abound:
Knocks go and come; heaven's vassals drop and die;
And sword and shield
In bloody field,
Doth win immortal fame.

Boy. Whould I were in an ale-house in London! I would give all my fame for a pot of ale, and safety.

Pist. And I:
If wishes would prevail with me,
My purpose should not fail with me,
But thither would I hie.

Boy. As duly, but not as truly,
As bird doth sing on bough.

Enter FLUELLEN.

Flu. Up to the preach, you dogs! avaunt, you cullions!
[*Driving them forward.*

Pist. Be merciful, great duke, to men of mould!
Abate thy rage, abate thy manly rage!
Abate thy rage, great duke!
Good captain, bate thy rage! use lenity, sweet chuck!

Nym. These be good humors!—your honor wins bad humors.
[*Exeunt* NYM, PISTOL, *and* BARDOLPH, *followed by* FLUELLEN.

Re-enter FLUELLEN, GOWER *following.*

Gow. Captain Fluellen, you must come presently to the mines; the duke of Gloster would speak with you.

Flu. To the mines! tell you the duke, it is not so good to come to the mines; for, look you, the mines is not according to the disciplines of the war: the concavities of it is not sufficient; for, look you, th' athversary (you may discuss unto the duke, look you) is digt himself four yards under the countermines: I think, 'a will blow up all, if there is not better directions.

Gow. The duke of Gloster to whom the order of the siege is given, is altogether directed by an Irishman,—a very valiant gentleman, i' faith.

Flu. It is captain Macmorris, is it not?

Gow. I think it be.

Flu. He is an ass; I will verify as much in his peard: he has no more directions in the true disciplines of the wars, look you, of the Roman disciplines, than is a puppy-dog.

Gow. Here 'a comes; and the Scots captain, captain Jamy, with him.

Flu. Captain Jamy is a marvellous falorous gentleman, that is certain; and of great expedition, and knowledge in the ancient wars, upon my particular knowledge of his directions. He will maintain his argument as well as any military man in the world, in the disciplines of the pristine wars of the Romans.

Enter MACMORRIS *and* JAMY.

Jamy. I say, gude day, captain Fluellen.

Flu. God-den to your worship, goot captain Jamy.

Gow. How now, captain Macmorris! have you quit the mines? have the pioneers given o'er?

Mac. Tish ill done: the work ish give over, the trumpet sound the retreat. By my hand, I swear, and my father's soul, the work ish ill done; it ish give over: I would have blowed up the town in an hour: O, tish ill done, tish ill done; by my hand, tish ill done!

Flu. Captain Macmorris, I peseech you now, will you voutsafe me, look you, a few disputations with you, as partly touching or concerning the disciplines of the war, the Roman wars, in the way of argument, look you, and friendly communication; partly, to satisfy my opinion, and partly, for the satisfaction, look you, of my mind, as touching the direction of the military discipline; that is the point.

Jamy. It sall be very gud, gud feith, gud captains bath: and I sall quit you with gud leve, as I may pick occasion; that sall I, marry.

Mac. It is no time to discourse, so heaven save me: the day is hot, and the weather, and the wars, and the king, and the dukes: it is no time to discourse. The town is beseeched, and the trumpet calls us to the breach; and we talk, and do nothing: 'tis shame for us all; so heaven sa' me, 'tis shame to stand still; it is shame, by my hand: and there is throats to be cut, and works to be done; and there ish nothing done.

Jamy. By the mess, ere theise eyes of mine take themselves to slumber, aile do gud service, or aile ligge i' the grund for it; ay, or go to death; and aile pay it as valorously as I may, that sal I surely do, that is the breff and the long. Marry, I wad full fain heard some question 'tween you tway.

Flu. Captain Macmorris, I think, look you, under your correction, there is not many of your nation—

Mac. Of my nation! What ish my nation? what ish my nation? Who talks of my nation, ish a villain, and a knave, and a rascal.

Flu. Look you, if you take the matter otherwise than is

meant, captain Macmorris, peradventure, I shall think you do not use me with that affability as in discretion you ought to use me, look you; being as goot a man as yourself, both in the disciplines of wars, and in the derivation of my birth, and in other particularities.

Mac. I do not know you so good a man as myself: so heaven save me, I will cut off your head.

Gow. Gentlemen both, you will mistake each other.

Jamy. Au! that's a foul fault. [*A parley sounded.*

Gow. The town sounds a parley.

Flu. Captain Macmorris, when there is more better opportunity to be required, look you, I will be so bold as to tell you, I know the disciplines of wars; and there is an end. [*Exeunt.*

SCENE III.—France. *Before the Gates of* Harfleur.

The Governor *and some* Citizens *on the walls; the English forces below. Enter* KING HENRY *and his train.*

K. Hen. How yet resolves the governor of the town?
This is the latest parle we will admit:
Therefore, to our best mercy give yourselves;
Or, like to men proud of destruction,
Defy us to our worst: for, as I am a soldier,
(A name that, in my thoughts, becomes me best)
If I begin the battery once again,
I will not leave the half-achieved Harfleur,
Till in her ashes she lie buried.
The gates of mercy shall be all shut up;
And the flesh'd soldier,—rough and hard of heart,—
In liberty of bloody hand shall range.
What is it then to me, if impious war,—
Arrayed in flames, like to the prince of fiends,—
Do, with his smirch'd complexion, all fell feats
Enlink'd to waste and desolation?
Therefore, you men of Harfleur,
Take pity of your town, and of your people,
Whiles yet my soldiers are in my command.
What say you? will you yield, and this avoid?
Or, guilty in defence, be thus destroy'd?
Gov. Our expectation hath this day an end:
The Dauphin, whom of succor we entreated,
Returns us, that his powers are yet not ready
To raise so great a siege. Therefore, dread king,
We yield our town and lives to thy soft mercy.
Enter our gates; dispose of us, and ours;
For we no longer are defensive.
K. Hen. Open your gates.—Come, uncle Exeter,

Go you and enter Harfleur; there remain,
And fortify it strongly 'gainst the French:
Use mercy to them all. For us, dear uncle,—
The winter coming on, and sickness growing
Upon our soldiers,—we will retire to Calais.
To-night in Harfleur will we be your guest;
To-morrow for the march are we addrest.
[*Flourish. The* KING, *&c. enter the town.*

SCENE V.—Rouen. *Another Room in the Palace.*

Enter the French King, *the* Dauphin, DUKE OF BOURBON, *the* Constable of France, *and others.*

Fr. King. 'Tis certain, he hath pass'd the river Somme.
Con. And if he be not fought withal, my lord,
Let us not live in France; let us quit all,
And give our vineyards to a barbarous people.
Dau. Shall a few sprays of us,
The emptying of our fathers' luxury,
Our scions, put in wild and savage stock,
Spirt up so suddenly into the clouds,
And overlook their grafters?
Con. Where have they this mettle?
Is not their climate foggy, raw, and dull;
On whom, as in despite, the sun looks pale,
Killing their fruit with frowns? Can sodden water,
A drench for sur-rein'd jades, their barley broth,
Decoct their cold blood to such valiant heat?
And shall our quick blood, spirited with wine,
Seem frosty? O, for honor of our land,
Let us not hang like roping icicles
Upon our houses' thatch, whiles a more frosty people
Sweat drops of gallant youth in our rich fields,—
Poor we may call them, in their native lords!
Fr. King. Where is Montjoy, the herald? speed him hence:
Let him greet England with our sharp defiance.—
Up, princes! and, with spirit of honor, edg'd
More sharper than your swords, hie to the field;
Bar Harry England, that sweeps through our land,
With pennons painted in the blood of Harfleur;
Rush on his host, as doth the melted snow
Upon the valleys, whose low vassal seat
The Alps doth spit and void his rheum upon:
Go down upon him,—you have power enough,—
And in a captive chariot into Rouen
Bring him our prisoner.

Now, forth, lord constable, and princes all,
And quickly bring us word of England's fall. [*Exeunt.*

SCENE VI.—*An English Camp in* Picardy.

Enter GOWER *and* FLUELLEN.

Gow. How now, captain Fluellen! come you from the bridge?

Flu. I assure you, there is very excellent services committed at the pridge.

Gow. Is the duke of Exeter safe?

Flu. The duke of Exeter is as magnanimous as Agamemnon; and a man that I love and honor with my soul, and my heart, and my duty, and my life, and my living, and my uttermost power: he is not any hurt in the 'orld; but keeps the pridge most valiantly, with excellent discipline. There is an ensign there at the pridge,—I think, in my very conscience, he is as valiant a man as Mark Antony; and he is a man of no estimation in the 'orld; but I did see him do as gallant service.

Gow. What do you call him?

Flu. He is called ancient Pistol.

Gow. I know him not.

Flu. Here is the man.

Enter PISTOL.

Pist. Captain, I thee beseech to do me favors:
The duke of Exeter doth love thee well.

Flu. Ay, I praise heaven; and I have merited some love at his hands.

Pist. Bardolph, a soldier, firm and sound of heart
And of buxom valor, hath, by cruel fate,
And giddy Fortune's furious fickle wheel,—
That goddess blind,
That stands upon the rolling restless stone,—

Flu. By your patience, ancient Pistol:—Fortune is painted plind, with a muffler afore her eyes, to signify to you that Fortune is plind; and she is painted also with a wheel, to signify to you, which is the moral of it, that she is turning, and inconstant, and mutability, and variation: and her foot, look you, is fixed upon a spherical stone, which rolls, and rolls, and rolls:—in good truth, the poet makes a most excellent description of it: Fortune, is an excellent moral.

Pist. Fortune is Bardolph's foe, and frowns on him;
For he hath stol'n a pax, and hanged must 'a be,—
Let gallows gape for dog; let man go free,
And let not hemp his wind-pipe suffocate:
But Exeter hath given the doom of death,
For pax of little price.

Therefore, go speak,—the duke will hear thy voice;
And let not Bardolph's vital thread be cut
With edge of penny cord, and vile reproach:
Speak, captain, for his life, and I will thee requite.

Flu. Ancient Pistol, I do partly understand your meaning.

Pist. Why then, rejoice therefore.

Flu. Certainly, ancient, it is not a thing to rejoice at: for if, look you, he were my brother, I would desire the duke to use his good pleasure, and put him to execution; for disciplines ought to be used.

Pist. A figo for thy friendship!

Flu. It is well.

Pist. The fig of Spain! [*Exit.*

Flu. Very good.

Gow. Why, this is an arrant counterfeit rascal; I remember him now; a vile cutpurse.

Flu. I'll assure you, 'a utter'd as prave 'ords at the pridge, as you shall see in a summer's day. But it is very well; what he has spoke to me, that is well, I warrant you, when time is serve.

Gow. Why, 'tis a gull, a fool, a rogue, that now and then goes to the wars, to grace himself, at his return into London, under the form of a soldier. But you must learn to know such slanders of the age, or else you may be marvellously mistook.

Flu. I tell you what, captain Gower; I do perceive, he is not the man that he would gladly make show to the 'orld he is: if I find a hole in his coat, I will tell him my mind. [*Drum heard.*] Hark you, the king is coming; and I must speak with him from the pridge.

Enter KING HENRY, GLOSTER, *and* soldiers.

Flu. Got pless your majesty!

K. Hen. How now, Fluellen! cam'st thou from the pridge?

Flu. Ay, so please your majesty. The duke of Exeter has very gallantly maintained the pridge: the French is gone off, look you; and there is gallant and most prave passages: marry, th' athversary was have possession of the pridge; but he is enforced to retire, and the duke of Exeter is master of the pridge: I can tell your majesty, the duke is a prave man.

K. Hen. What men have you lost, Fluellen?

Flu. The perdition of th' athversary hath been very great, reasonable great: marry, for my part, I think the duke hath lost never a man, but one that is like to be executed for robbing a church,—one Bardolph, if your majesty know the man: his face is all bubukles, and whelks, and knobs, and flames of fire; and his lips plows at his nose, and it is like a coal of fire, sometimes plue, and sometimes red; but his nose is executed, and his fire's out.

K. Hen. We would have all such offenders so cut off:—and we give express charge, that in our marches through the country, there be nothing compelled from the villages, nothing taken but paid for, none of the French upbraided or abused in disdainful language; for when lenity and cruelty play for a kingdom, the gentler gamester is the soonest winner.

Tucket sounds. Enter MONTJOY.

Mont. You know me by my habit.
K. Hen. Well then, I know thee: what shall I know of thee?
Mont. My master's mind.
K. Hen. Unfold it.
Mont. Thus says my king:—Say thou to Harry of England, Though we seemed dead, we did but sleep; advantage is a better soldier than rashness. Tell him, we could have rebuked him at Harfleur, but that we thought not good to bruise an injury, till it were full ripe. To this add defiance: and tell him, for conclusion, he hath betrayed his followers, whose condemnation is pronounced. So far my king and master; so much my office.
K. Hen. What is thy name? I know thy quality.
Mont. Montjoy.
K. Hen. Thou dost thy office fairly. Turn thee back.
And tell thy king,—I do not seek him now;
But could be willing to march on to Calais
Without impeachment: for, to say the sooth,
(Though 'tis no wisdom to confess so much
Unto an enemy of craft and vantage)
My people are with sickness much enfeebled;
My numbers lessen'd; and those few I have,
Almost no better than so many French;
Go, therefore, tell thy master, here I am;
My ransom is this frail and worthless trunk;
My army but a weak and sickly guard:
Yet, heaven before, tell him we will come on,
Though France himself, and such another neighbor,
Stand in our way. There's for thy labor, Montjoy.
Go, bid thy master well advise himself:
If we may pass, we will; if we be hinder'd,
We shall your tawny ground with your red blood
Discolor: and so, Montjoy, fare you well.
The sum of all our answer is but this:
We would not seek a battle, as we are;
Nor, as we are, we say, we will not shun it:
So tell your master.
Mont. I shall deliver so. Thanks to your highness. [*Exit.*
Glo. I hope they will not come upon us now.
K. Hen. We are in God's hand, brother, not in theirs.
March to the bridge; it now draws towards night:—

Beyond the river we'll encamp ourselves;
And on to-morrow bid them march away. [*Exeunt.*

SCENE VII.—*The French Camp, near* Agincourt.

Enter the Constable of France, *the Lord* RAMBURES, *the* DUKE OF ORLEANS, *the* Dauphin, *and others.*

Con. Tut! I have the best armor of the world.—Would it were day!

Orl. You have an excellent armor; but let my horse have his due.

Con. It is the best horse of Europe.

Orl. Will it never be morning?

Dau. My lord of Orleans, and my lord high constable, you talk of horse and armor,—

Orl. You are as well provided of both as any prince in the world.

Dau. What a long night is this!—I will not change my horse with any that treads but on four pasterns. When I bestride him, I soar, I am a hawk: he trots the air; the earth sings when he touches it; the basest horn of his hoof is more musical than the pipe of Hermes.

Orl. He's of the color of the nutmeg.

Dau. And of the heat of the ginger. It is a beast for Perseus: he is pure air and fire; and the dull elements of earth and water never appear in him, but only in patient stillness, while his rider mounts him: he is, indeed, a horse; and all other jades you may call beasts.

Ram. My lord constable, the armor that I saw in your tent to-night,—are those stars, or suns, upon it?

Con. Stars, my lord.

Dau. Some of them will fall to-morrow, I hope.

Con. And yet my sky shall not want.

Dau. That may be, for you bear a many superfluously, and 'twere more honor some were away.

Con. Even as your horse bears your praises; who would trot as well were some of your brags dismounted.

Dau. Would, I were able to load him with his desert!—Will it never be day?—I will trot to-morrow a mile, and my way shall be paved with English faces.

Con. I will not say so, for fear I should be faced out of my way: but I would it were morning; for I would fain be about the ears of the English.

Enter a Messenger.

Mess. My lord high constable, the English lie within fifteen hundred paces of your tents.

Con. Who hath measured the ground?

Mess. The Lord Grandpré.

Con. A valiant and most expert gentleman.—Would it were day!—Alas, poor Harry of England! he longs not for the dawning, as we do.

Orl. What a wretched and peevish fellow is this king of England, to mope with his fat-brained followers so far out of his knowledge!

Con. If the English had any apprehension, they would run away.

Orl. That they lack; for if their heads had any intellectual armor, they could never wear such heavy head-pieces.

Ram. That island of England breeds very valiant creatures; their mastiffs are of unmatchable courage.

Orl. Foolish curs, that run winking into the mouth of a Russian bear, and have their heads crushed like rotten apples! You may as well say, that's a valiant flea, that dare eat his breakfast on the lip of a lion.

Con. Just, just; and the men do sympathize with the mastiffs in robustious and rough coming on, leaving their wits with their wives: and then give them great meals of beef, and iron and steel, they will eat like wolves, and fight like demons.

Orl. Ay, but these English are shrewdly out of beef.

Con. Then shall we find to-morrow they have only stomachs to eat, and none to fight. Now is it time to arm: come, shall we about it?

Orl. It is now two o'clock: but, let me see,—by ten,
We shall have each a hundred Englishmen. [*Exeunt.*

ACT IV.

SCENE I.—France. *The English Camp at* Agincourt.

Enter King Henry, Bedford, *and* Gloster.

K. Hen. Gloster, 'tis true that we are in great danger;
The greater, therefore, should our courage be.—
Good morrow, brother Bedford.—Almighty heaven,
There is some soul of goodness in things evil,
Would men observingly distil it out;
For our bad neighbor makes us early stirrers,
Which is both healthful, and good husbandry:
Besides, they are our outward consciences,
And preachers to us all: admonishing,
That we should 'dress us fairly for our end.

Enter ERPINGHAM.

Good morrow, old Sir Thomas Erpingham:
A good soft pillow for that good white head
Were better than a churlish turf of France.

Erp. Not so, my liege: this lodging likes me better,
Since I may say, Now lie I like a king.

K. Hen. 'Tis good for men to love their present pains,
Upon example; so the spirit is eased,
And when the mind is quicken'd, out of doubt,
The organs, though defunct and dead before,
Break up their drowsy grave, and newly move
With casted slough and fresh legerity.*
Lend me thy cloak, Sir Thomas.—Brothers both,
Commend me to the princes in our camp;
Do my good morrow to them; and, anon,
Desire them all to my pavilion.

Glo. We shall, my liege. [*Exeunt* GLOSTER *and* BEDFORD.

Erp. Shall I attend your grace?

K. Hen. No, my good knight;
Go with my brothers to my lords of England:
I and my bosom must debate a while,
And then I would no other company.

Erp. The Lord in heaven bless thee, noble Harry. [*Exit.*

K. Hen. God-a-mercy, old heart! thou speak'st cheerfully.

Enter PISTOL.

Pist. *Qui va là.*

K. Hen. A friend.

Pist. Discuss unto me; art thou officer?
Or art thou base, common, and popular?

K. Hen. I am a gentleman of a company.

Pist. Trail'st thou the puissant pike?

K. Hen. Even so. What are you?

Pist. As good a gentleman as the emperor.

K. Hen. Then you are a better than the king.

Pist. The king's a bawcock, and a heart of gold,
A lad of life, an imp of fame;
Of parents good, of fist most valiant:
I kiss his dirty shoe, and from my heart-strings
I love the lovely bully.—What's thy name?

K. Hen. Harry *le Roy.*

Pist. *Le Roy!* a Cornish name: art thou of Cornish crew?

K. Hen. No, I am a Welshman.

Pist. Know'st thou Fluellen?

K. Hen. Yes.

* *Legerity*—lightness, nimbleness.

Pist. Tell him, I'll knock his leek about his pate,
Upon St. David's day.

K. Hen. Do not you wear your dagger in your cap that day, lest he knock that about yours.

Pist. Art thou his friend?

K. Hen. And his kinsman too.

Pist. The figo for thee then!

K. Hen. I thank you: heaven be with you!

Pist. My name is Pistol called. [*Exit.*

K. Hen. It sorts well with your fierceness.

Enter FLUELLEN *and* GOWER, *severally.*

Gow. Captain Fluellen!

Flu. So! in the name of heaven, speak lower. It is the greatest admiration in the universal 'orld, when the true and auncient prerogatifes and laws of the wars is not kept: if you would take the pains but to examine the wars of Pompey the Great, you shall find, I warrant you, that there is no tiddle taddle, or pibble pabble, in Pompey's camp; I warrant you, you shall find the ceremonies of the wars, and the cares of it, and the forms of it, and the sobriety of it, and the modesty of it, to be otherwise.

Gow. Why, the enemy is loud; you hear him all night.

Flu. If the enemy is an ass and a fool, and a prating coxcomb, is it meet, think you, that we should also, look you, be an ass, and a fool, and a prating coxcomb,—in your own conscience now?

Gow. I will speak lower.

Flu. I pray you, and beseech you, that you will.
[*Exeunt* GOWER *and* FLUELLEN.

K. Hen. Though it appear a little out of fashion
There is much care and valor in this Welshman.

Enter BATES, COURT, *and* WILLIAMS.

Court. Brother John Bates, is not that the morning which breaks yonder?

Bates. I think it be: but we have no great cause to desire the approach of day.

Will. We see yonder the beginning of the day, but I think we shall never see the end of it.—Who goes there?

K. Hen. A friend.

Will. Under what captain serve you?

K. Hen. Under Sir Thomas Erpingham.

Will. A good old commander, and a most kind gentleman: I pray you, what thinks he of our estate?

K. Hen. Even as men wrecked upon a sand, that look to be washed off the next tide.

Bates. He hath not told his thought to the king?

K. Hen. No; nor it is not meet he should. For, though I

speak it to you, I think the king is but a man, as I am: the violet smells to him, as it doth to me; the element shows to him, as it doth to me; all his senses have but human conditions: his ceremonies laid by, he appears but a man; and though his affections are higher mounted than ours, yet, when they stoop, they stoop with the like wing. Therefore, when he sees reason of fears, as we do, his fears, out of doubt, be of the same relish as ours are; yet, in reason, no man should possess him with any appearance of fear, lest he, by showing it, should dishearten his army.

Bates. He may show what outward courage he will; but I believe, as cold a night as 'tis, he could wish himself in Thames up to the neck;—and so I would he were, and I by him, at all adventures, so we were quit here.

K. Hen. By my troth, I will speak my conscience of the king: I think he would not wish himself any where but where he is.

Bates. Then I would he were here alone; so should he be sure to be ransomed, and a many poor men's lives saved.

K. Hen. I dare say you love him not so ill, to wish him here alone, howsoever you speak this, to feel other men's minds: methinks I could not die any where so contented as in the king's company,—his cause being just, and his quarrel honorable.

Will. That's more than we know.

Bates. Ay, or more than we should seek after; for we know enough, if we know we are the king's subjects: if his cause be wrong, our obedience to the king wipes the crime of it out of us.

Will. But if the cause be not good, the king himself hath a heavy reckoning to make, when all those legs, and arms, and heads, chopped off in a battle, shall join together at the latter day, and cry all. I am afeard there are few die well, that die in a battle; for how can they charitably dispose of any thing, when blood is their argument? Now, if these men do not die well, it will be a black matter for the king that led them to it; whom to disobey were against all proportion of subjection.

K. Hen. So, if a son, that is by his father sent about merchandise, do sinfully miscarry upon the sea, the imputation of his wickedness, by your rule, should be imposed upon his father that sent him: or if a servant, under his master's command, transporting a sum of money, be assailed by robbers, and die in many irreconciled iniquities, you may call the business of the master the author of the servant's condemnation—but this is not so: the king is not bound to answer the particular endings of his soldiers, the father of his son, nor the master of his servant; for they purpose not their death, when they purpose their services. Besides, there is no king, be his cause never so spotless, if it come to the arbitrement of swords, can try it out with all unspotted soldiers: some, peradventure, have on them the guilt of premeditated and contrived murder; some, making the wars their bulwark, that have before gored the gentle bosom of peace with pillage and robbery. Now, if these men have defeated the law, and outrun native punishment, though they can outstrip men, they have no wings to fly from God: war is his beadle, war is his vengeance; so that here men are punished, for before-breach of the king's laws, in now the king's quarrel: where they feared the death, they have borne life away; and where they would be safe, they perish: then, if they die unprovided, no more is the king guilty of their condemnation than he was before guilty of those impieties for the which they are now visited. Every subject's duty is the king's; but every subject's soul is his own. Therefore, should every soldier in the wars do as every sick man in his bed,—wash every mote out of his conscience: and dying so, death is to him advantage; or not dying, the time was blessedly lost, wherein such preparation was gained: and in him that escapes, it were not sin to think, that making heaven so free an offer, he is let out live that day to see his greatness, and to teach others how they should prepare.

Will. 'Tis certain, every man that dies ill, the ill upon his own head,—the king is not to answer it.

Bates. I do not desire he should answer for me; and yet I determine to fight lustily for him.

K. Hen. I myself heard the king say, he would not be ransomed.

Will. Ay, he said so, to make us fight cheerfully: but when our throats are cut, he may be ransomed, and we ne'er the wiser.

K. Hen. If I live to see it, I will never trust his word after.

Will. You pay him then! That's a perilous shot out of an elder gun, that a poor and a private displeasure can do against a monarch! You may as well go about to turn the sun to ice with fanning in his face with a peacock's feather. You'll never trust his word after! come, 'tis a foolish saying.

K. Hen. Your reproof is something too round: I should be angry with you, if the time were convenient.

Will. Let it be a quarrel between us, if you live.

K. Hen. I embrace it.

Will. How shall I know thee again?

K. Hen. Give me any gage of thine, and I will wear it in my bonnet: then, if ever thou darest acknowledge it, I will make it my quarrel.

Will. Here's my glove: give me another of thine.

K. Hen. There.

Will. This will I also wear in my cap: if ever thou come to me and say, after to-morrow, "This is my glove," by this hand, I will take thee a box on the ear.

K. Hen. If ever I live to see it, I will challenge it.

Will. Thou darest as well be hanged.

K. Hen. Well, I will do it, though I take thee in the king's company.

Will. Keep thy word: fare thee well.

Bates. Be friends, you English fools, be friends: we have French quarrels enow, if you could tell how to reckon.

K. Hen. Indeed, the French may lay twenty French crowns to one, they will beat us; for they bear them on their shoulders: but it is no English treason to cut French crowns; and to-morrow the king himself will be a clipper. [*Exeunt* Soldiers.

Upon the king!—let us our lives, our souls,
Our debts, our careful wives, our children, and
Our sins, lay on the king!—we must bear all.
O hard condition! twin-born with greatness,
Subject to the breath of every fool,
Whose sense no more can feel but his own wringing!
What infinite heart's ease must kings neglect,
That private men enjoy!
And what have kings, that privates have not too,
Save ceremony, save general ceremony?
And what art thou, thou idol ceremony?
What kind of god art thou, that suffer'st more
Of mortal griefs, than do thy worshippers?
What are thy rents? what are thy comings-in?
O ceremony, show me but thy worth!
What is thy soul of adoration?
Art thou aught else but place, degree, and form,
Creating awe and fear in other men?
Wherein thou art less happy, being fear'd,
Than they in fearing.
What drink'st thou oft, instead of homage sweet,
But poison'd flattery? O, be sick, great greatness,
And bid thy ceremony give thee cure!
Think'st thou the fiery fever will go out
With titles blown from adulation?
Will it give place to flexure and low bending?
Canst thou, when thou command'st the beggar's knee,
Command the health of it? No, thou proud dream,
That play'st so subtly with a king's repose;
I am a king, that find thee; and I know
'Tis not the balm, the sceptre, and the ball,
The sword, the mace, the crown imperial,
The inter-tissued robe of gold and pearl,
The farced title running 'fore the king,
The throne he sits on, nor the tide of pomp
That beats upon the high shore of this world,—
No, not all these, thrice-gorgeous ceremony,
Not all these, laid in bed majestical,
Can sleep so soundly as the wretched slave,

Who, with a body fill'd, and vacant mind,
Gets him to rest, cramm'd with distressful bread;
Never sees horrid night,
But, like a lackey, from the rise to set,
Sweats in the eye of Phœbus, and all night
Sleeps in Elysium; next day, after dawn,
Doth rise, and help Hyperion to his horse;
And follows so the ever running year
With profitable labor to his grave:
And, but for ceremony, such a wretch,
Winding up days with toil, and nights with sleep,
Had the fore-hand and vantage of a king.
The slave, a member of the country's peace,
Enjoys it; but in gross brain little wots,
What watch the king keeps to maintain the peace,
Whose hours the peasant best advantages.

Enter ERPINGHAM.

Erp. My lord, your nobles, jealous of your absence,
Seek through your camp to find you.
K. Hen. Good old knight,
Collect them all together at my tent:
I'll be before thee.
Erp. I shall do't, my lord. [*Exit.*
K. Hen. O God of battles! steel my soldiers' hearts;
Possess them not with fear; take from them now
The sense of reckoning, if th' opposèd numbers
Pluck their hearts from them!—Not to-day, O Lord,
O, not to-day, think not upon the fault
My father made in compassing the crown!
I Richard's body have interrèd new;
And on it have bestow'd more contrite tears,
Than from it issued forcèd drops of blood:
Five hundred poor I have in yearly pay,
Who twice a day their wither'd hands hold up
Toward heaven, to pardon blood; and I have built
Two chantries, where the sad and solemn priests
Sing still for Richard's soul. More will I do;
Though all that I can do, is nothing worth,
Since that my penitence comes after all,
Imploring pardon.

Enter GLOSTER.

Glo. My liege!
K. Hen. My brother Gloster's voice?—Ay;
I know thy errand, I will go with thee:—
The day, my friends, and all things stay for me. [*Exeunt.*

SCENE II.—*The French Camp.*

Enter Dauphin ORLEANS, RAMBURES, *and others.*

Orl. The sun doth gild our armor; up, my lords!
Dau. *Montez à cheval!*—My horse! *varlet! lacquay!* ha!
Orl. O brave spirit!

Enter Constable.

Dau. Now, my lord constable!
Con. Hark how our steeds for present service neigh!
Dau. Mount them, and make incision in their hides,
That their hot blood may spin in English eyes,
And dout them with superfluous courage, ha!
Ram. What, will you have them weep our horses' blood?
How shall we, then, behold their natural tears?

Enter a Messenger.

Mess. The English are embattled, you French peers.
Con. To horse, you gallant princes! straight to horse!
Do but behold yon poor and starvèd band,
And your fair show will suck away their souls,
Leaving them but the shales and husks of men.
There is not work enough for all our hands:
Scarce blood enough in all their sickly veins,
To give each naked curtle-ax a stain,
That our French gallants shall to-day draw out,
And sheathe for lack of sport: let us but blow on them,
The vapor of our valor will o'erturn them.
For our approach shall so much dare the field,
That England shall crouch down in fear, and yield.

Enter GRANDPRÉ.

Grand. Why do you stay so long, my lords of France?
Yon island carrions, desperate of their bones,
Ill-favor'dly become the morning field:
And their executors, the knavish crows,
Fly o'er them, all impatient for their hour.
Con. They have said their prayers, and they stay for death.
Dau. Shall we go send them dinners, and fresh suits,
And give their fasting horses provender,
And after fight with them?
Con. I stay but for my guard: on, to the field!
I will the banner from a trumpet take,
And use it for my haste. Come, come, away!
The sun is high, and we outwear the day. [*Exeunt.*

SCENE III.—*The English Camp.*

Enter the English host; GLOSTER, BEDFORD, EXETER, SALISBURY, *and* WESTMORELAND.

Glo. Where is the king?
Bed. The king himself is rode to view their battle.
West. Of fighting men they have full threescore thousand.
Exe. There's five to one; besides, they all are fresh.
Sal. Heaven's arm strike with us! 'tis a fearful odds.
Heaven be wi' you, princes all; I'll to my charge:
Bed. Farewell, good Salisbury; and good luck go with thee!
Exe. Farewell, kind lord, fight valiantly to-day:
And yet I do thee wrong, to mind thee of it,
For thou art fram'd of the firm truth of valor.
[*Exit* SALISBURY.
Bed. He is as full of valor, as of kindness;
Princely in both.
West. O, that we now had here

Enter KING HENRY.

But one ten thousand of those men in England,
That do no work to-day!
K. Hen. What's he, that wishes so?
My cousin Westmoreland?—No, my fair cousin:
If we are mark'd to die, we are enough
To do our country loss: and if to live,
The fewer men, the greater share of honor.
I pray thee, wish not one man more.
By Jove, I am not covetous for gold;
Nor care I who doth feed upon my cost;
It yearns me not if men my garments wear;
Such outward things dwell not in my desires:
But, if it be a sin to covet honor,
I am the most offending soul alive.
No, 'faith, my coz, wish not a man from England:
I would not lose so great an honor,
As one man more, methinks, would share from me,
For the best hope I have. O, do not wish one more!
Rather proclaim it, Westmoreland, through my host,
That he which hath no stomach to this fight,
Let him depart: his passport shall be made,
And crowns for convoy put into his purse:
We would not die in that man's company,
That fears his fellowship to die with us.
This day is call'd—the feast of Crispian:
He that outlives this day, and comes safe home,
Will stand a tip-toe when this day is nam'd,

And rouse him at the name of Crispian.
He that shall live this day, and see old age,
Will yearly on the vigil feast his neighbors,
And say—To-morrow is Saint Crispian:
Then will he strip his sleeve, and show his scars,
And say—These wounds I had on Crispin's day.
Old men forget: yet all shall be forgot,
But he'll remember with advantages
What feats he did that day. Then shall our names,
Familiar in their mouths as household words,
Be in their flowing cups freshly remember'd.
This story shall the good man teach his son;
And Crispin Crispian shall ne'er go by,
From this day to the ending of the world,
But we in it shall be remembered,—
We few, we happy few, we band of brothers;
For he, to-day that sheds his blood for me,
Shall be my brother; be he ne'er so vile,
This day shall gentle his condition:
And gentlemen in England, now a-bed,
Shall think themselves accurs'd they were not here;
And hold their manhoods cheap, while any speaks
That fought with us upon Saint Crispin's day.

Re-enter SALISBURY.

Sal. My sovereign lord, bestow yourself with speed:
The French are bravely in their battles set,
And will with all expedience charge on us.
K. Hen. All things are ready, if our minds be so.
West. Perish the man whose mind is backward now!
K. Hen. Thou dost not wish more help from England, coz?
West. Heaven's will! my liege, would you and I alone,
Without more help, could fight this royal battle!
K. Hen. Why, now thou hast unwish'd five thousand men;
Which likes me better than to wish us one.—
You know your places: heaven be with you all!

Tucket. Enter MONTJOY.

Mont. Once more I come to know of thee, king Harry,
If for thy ransom thou wilt now compound,
Before thy most assurèd overthrow:
Besides, in mercy,
The Constable desires thee thou wilt mind
Thy followers of repentance, that their souls
May make a peaceful and a sweet retire
From off these fields, where, wretches, their poor bodies
Must lie and fester.
K. Hen. Who hath sent thee now?

Mont. The Constable of France.

K. Hen. I pray thee, bear my former answer back:
Bid them achieve me, and then sell my bones.
Good heaven! why should they mock poor fellows thus?
The man that once did sell the lion's skin
While the beast liv'd, was kill'd with hunting him.
A many of our bodies shall, no doubt,
Find native graves; upon the which, I trust,
Shall witness live in brass of this day's work:
And those that leave their valiant bones in France,
Dying like men, they shall be fam'd.
Let me speak proudly:—tell the Constable,
We are but warriors for the working-day;
Our gayness and our gilt are all besmirch'd
With rainy marching in the painful field;
There's not a piece of feather in our host,
(Good argument, I hope, we will not fly,)
And time hath worn us into slovenry:
But, by the mass, our hearts are in the trim;
And my poor soldiers tell me, yet ere night
They'll be in fresher robes; or they will pluck
The gay new coats o'er the French soldiers' heads,
And turn them out of service. If they do this,—
As, if heaven please, they shall,—my ransom then
Will soon be levied. Herald, save thou thy labor;
Come thou no more for ransom, gentle herald:
They shall have none, I swear, but these my joints,—
Which, if they have as I will leave 'em them,
Shall yield them little, tell the Constable.

Mont. I shall, king Harry: and so, fare thee well:
Thou never shalt hear herald any more. [*Exit.*

K. Hen. I fear thou'lt once more come again for ransom.

Enter the Duke of York.

York. My lord, most humbly on my knee I beg
The leading of the vaward.

K. Hen. Take it, brave York.—Now, soldiers, march away:—
And how thou pleasest, heaven, dispose the day! [*Exeunt.*

SCENE V.—*The Field of Battle.*

Alarums. Enter Dauphin, Orleans, Bourbon, Constable, Rambures, *and others.*

Orl. O seigneur! le jour est perdu! tout est perdu!

Dau. Mort de ma vie! all is confounded, all!
Reproach and everlasting shame

Sit mocking in our plumes.—*O meschante fortune.*—
Do not run away. [*A short alarum.*
Con. Why, all our ranks are broke.
Dau. O perdurable shame!—let's stab ourselves.
Be these the wretches that we play'd at dice for?
Orl. Is this the king we sent to for his ransom?
Bour. Shame, and eternal shame, nothing but shame!
Let's die in honor: once more back again.
Con. Disorder, that hath spoil'd us, friend us now!
Let us, in heaps, go offer up our lives.
Orl. We are enough, yet living in the field,
To smother up the English in our throngs,
If any order might be thought upon.
Bour. The foul fiend take order now! I'll to the throng:
Let life be short, else shame will be too long. [*Exeunt.*

SCENE VI.—*Another Part of the Field.*

Alarums. Enter KING HENRY *and Forces;* EXETER *and others.*

K. Hen. Well have we done, thrice valiant countrymen:
But all's not done; yet keep the French the field.
Exe. The duke of York commends him to your majesty.
K. Hen. Lives he, good uncle? thrice within this hour
I saw him down; thrice up again, and fighting;
From helmet to the spur all blood he was.
Exe. In which array, brave soldier, doth he lie,
Larding the plain; and by his bloody side,
The noble earl of Suffolk also lies.
K. Hen. For, hearing this, I must perforce compound
With mistful eyes, or they will issue forth.— [*Alarum.*
But hark! what new alarum is this same?—
The French have reinforc'd their scatter'd men:—
Then, every soldier kill his prisoners;
Give the word through. [*Exeunt.*

SCENE VII.—*Another Part of the Field.*

Alarums. Enter FLUELLEN *and* GOWER.

Flu. Kill the poys and the luggage! 'tis expressly against the law of arms: 'tis as arrant a piece of knavery, mark you now, as can be offered: in your conscience now, is it not?

Gow. 'Tis certain, there's not a boy left alive; and the cowardly rascals, that ran from the battle, have done this slaughter: besides, they have burned and carried away all that was in the king's tent: wherefore the king, most worthily, hath caused every soldier to cut his prisoner's throat. O 'tis a gallant king!

Flu. Ay, he was born at Monmouth, captain Gower. What call you the town's name, where Alexander the pig was born?

Gow. Alexander the great.

Flu. Why, I pray you, is not pig, great? The pig, or the great, or the mighty, or the huge, or the magnanimous, are all one reckonings, save the phrase is a little variations.

Gow. I think Alexander the great was born in Macedon: his father was called Philip of Macedon, as I take it.

Flu. I think it is in Macedon where Alexander is porn. I tell you, captain, if you look in the maps of the 'orld, I warrant, you shall find, in the comparisons between Macedon and Monmouth, that the situations, look you, is both alike. There is a river in Macedon; and there is also moreover a river at Monmouth: it is called Wye at Monmouth; but it is out of my prains, what is the name of the other river; but 'tis all one, 'tis alike as my fingers is to my fingers, and there's salmons in both. If you mark Alexander's life well, Harry of Monmouth's life is come after it indifferent well; for there is figures in all things. Alexander, in his rages, and his furies, and his wraths, and his cholers, and his moods, and his displeasures, and his indignations, and also being a little intoxicates in his prains, did, in his ales and his angers, look you, kill his pest friend Clytus.

Gow. Our king is not like him in that: he never killed any of his friends.

Flu. It is not well done, mark you now, to take the tales out of my mouth, ere it is made and finished. I speak but in the figures and comparisons of it; as Alexander killed his friend Clytus, being in his ales and his cups; so also Harry Monmouth, being in his right wits and his good judgments, turned away the fat knight with the great pelly-doublet: he was full of jests, and gipes, and knaveries, and mocks; I have forgot his name.

Gow. Sir John Falstaff.

Flu. That is he:—I'll tell you, there is goot men porn at Monmouth.

Gow. Here comes his majesty.

Alarum. Enter KING HENRY, *with a part of the English forces;* WARWICK, GLOSTER, EXETER, *and others.*

K. Hen. I was not angry since I came to France
Until this instant.—Take a trumpet, herald;
Ride thou unto the horsemen on yon hill:
If they will fight with us, bid them come down,
Or void the field; they do offend our sight.
If they'll do neither, we will come to them,
And make them skirr away, as swift as stones,
Enforcèd from the old Assyrian slings:
Besides, we'll cut the throats of those we have;

And not a man of them that we shall take,
Shall taste our mercy:—go, and tell them so.

Exe. Here comes the herald of the French, my liege.

Glo. His eyes are humbler than they us'd to be.

Enter MONTJOY.

K. Hen. How now! what means this, herald? knowest thou not,
That I have fin'd these bones of mine for ransom?
Com'st thou again for ransom?

Mont. No, great king:
I come to thee for charitable license,
That we may wander o'er this bloody field,
To book our dead, and then to bury them.
O give us leave, great king,
To view the field in safety, and dispose
Of their dead bodies!

K. Hen. I tell thee truly, herald,
I know not if the day be ours, or no;
For yet a many of your horsemen peer,
And gallop o'er the field.

Mont. The day is yours.

K. Hen. Prais'd be heaven, and not our strength for it!—
What is this castle call'd that stands hard by?

Mont. They call it Agincourt.

K. Hen. Then call we this the field of Agincourt,
Fought on the day of Crispin Crispianus.

Flu. Your grandfather of famous memory, an't please your majesty, and your great uncle Edward the plack prince of Wales, as I have read in the chronicles, fought a most prave pattle here in France.

K. Hen. They did, Fluellen.

Flu. Your majesty says very true: if your majesties is remembered of it, the Welshmen did goot service in a garden where leeks did grow, wearing leeks in their Monmouth caps; which your majesty knows, to this hour, is an honorable padge of the service; and I do believe, your majesty takes no scorn to wear the leek upon Saint Tavy's day.

K. Hen. I wear it for a memorable honor;
For I am Welsh, you know, good countryman.

Flu. All the water in Wye cannot wash your majesty's Welsh plood out of your pody, I can tell you that: Got pless it, and preserve it, as long as it pleases his grace, and his majesty too!

K. Hen. Thanks, good my countryman.

Flu. I am your majesty's countryman, I care not who know it; I will confess it to all the 'orld: I need not to be ashamed of your majesty, prais'd be heaven, so long as your majesty is an honest man.

K. Hen. Heaven keep me so!—Our heralds go with him:

Bring me just notice of the numbers dead,
On both our parts.—Call yonder fellow hither.
[*Points to* WILLIAMS. *Exeunt* MONTJOY *and others.*

Exe. Soldier, you must come to the king.

K. Hen. Soldier, why wear'st thou that glove in thy cap?

Will. An't please your majesty, 'tis the gage of one that I should fight withal, if he be alive.

K. Hen. An Englishman?

Will. An't please your majesty, a rascal that swaggered with me, last night; who, if 'a live, and ever dare to challenge this glove, I have sworn to take him a box o' the ear: or, if I can see my glove in his cap, (which he swore, as he was a soldier, he would wear, if alive) I will strike it out soundly.

K. Hen. What think you, captain Fluellen? is it fit this soldier keep his oath?

Flu. He is a craven and a villain else, an't please your majesty, in my conscience.

K. Hen. It may be, his enemy is a gentleman of great sort, quite from the answer of his degree.

Flu. Though he be as goot a gentleman as Lucifer and Belzebub himself, it is necessary, look your grace, that he keep his vow and his oath: if he be perjured, see you now, his reputation is as arrant a villain, and a Jack-sauce, as ever his plack shoe trod upon the ground and earth, in my conscience, la.

K. Hen. Then keep thy vow, sirrah, when thou meet'st the fellow.

Will. So I will, my liege, as I live.

K. Hen. Who servest thou under?

Will. Under captain Gower, my liege.

Flu. Gower is a goot captain, and is good knowledge and literature in the wars.

K. Hen. Call him hither to me, soldier.

Will. I will, my liege. [*Exit.*

K. Hen. Here, Fluellen; wear thou this favor for me, and stick it in thy cap: when Alençon and myself were down together, I plucked this glove from his helm: if any man challenge this, he is a friend to Alençon, and an enemy to our person; if thou encounter any such, apprehend him, an thou dost me love.

Flu. Your grace does me as great honors, as can be desired in the hearts of his subjects: I would fain see the man that shall find himself aggriefed at this glove, that is all; but I would fain see it once.

K. Hen. Knowest thou Gower?

Flu. He is my dear friend, an please you.

K. Hen. Pray thee, go seek him, and bring him to my tent.

Flu. I will fetch him. [*Exit.*

K. Hen. My lord of Warwick, and my brother Gloster,

Follow Fluellen closely at the heels:
The glove, which I have given him for a favor,
May haply purchase him a box o' the ear;
It is the soldier's; I, by bargain, should
Wear it myself. Follow, good cousin Warwick:
If that the soldier strike him, (as, I judge
By his blunt bearing, he will keep his word)
Some sudden mischief may arise of it;
For I do know Fluellen valiant,
And, touch'd with choler, hot as gunpowder,
And quickly will return an injury:
Follow, and see there be no harm between them.—
Go you with me, uncle of Exeter. [*Exeunt.*

SCENE VIII.—*Before* KING HENRY'S *Pavilion.*

Enter GOWER *and* WILLIAMS.

Will. I warrant it is to knight you, captain.

Enter FLUELLEN.

Flu. Captain, I peseech you now, come apace to the king: there is more good toward you, peradventure, than is in your knowledge to dream of.

Will. Sir, know you this glove?

Flu. Know the glove! I know, the glove is a glove.

Will. I know this, and thus I challenge it. [*Strikes him.*

Flu. An arrant traitor, as any's in the universal 'orld, or in France, or in England.

Gow. How now, sir! you villain!

Will. Do you think I'll be forsworn?

Flu. Stand away, captain Gower; I will give treason his payment into plows, I warrant you.

Will. I am no traitor.

Flu. That's a lie in thy throat.—I charge you in his majesty's name, apprehend him: he is a friend of the duke Alençon's.

Enter WARWICK *and* GLOSTER.

War. How now, how now! what's the matter?

Flu. My lord of Warwick, here is a most contagious treason come to light, look you, as you shall desire in a summer's day.— Here is his majesty.

Enter KING HENRY *and* EXETER.

K. Hen. How now! what's the matter?

Flu. My liege, here is a villain and a traitor, that, look your grace, has struck the glove which your majesty is take out of the helmet of Alençon.

Will. My liege, this was my glove; here is the fellow of it; and he that I gave it to in change promised to wear it in his cap: I promised to strike him, if he did: I met this man with my glove in his cap, and I have been as good as my word.

Flu. Your majesty hear now, (saving your majesty's manhood) what an arrant, rascally, beggarly knave it is: I hope your majesty is pear me testimony, and witness, and avouchments, that this is the glove of Alençon, that your majesty is give me, in your conscience, now.

K. Hen. Give me thy glove, soldier: look, here is the fellow of it.
'Twas I, indeed, thou promisedst to strike;
And thou hast given me most bitter terms.

Flu. An please your majesty, let his neck answer for it, if there is any martial law in the 'orld.

K. Hen. How canst thou make me satisfaction?

Will. All offences, my liege, come from the heart: never came any from mine, that might offend your majesty.

K. Hen. It was ourself thou didst abuse.

Will. Your majesty came not like yourself: you appeared to me but as a common man; witness the night, your garments, your lowliness; and what your highness suffered under that shape, I beseech you, take it for your own fault, and not mine: for had you been as I took you for, I made no offence: therefore, I beseech your highness, pardon me.

K. Hen. Here, uncle Exeter, fill this glove with crowns,
And give it to this fellow.—Keep it, fellow;
And wear it for an honor in thy cap,
Till I do challenge it.—Give him the crowns:—
And captain, you must needs be friends with him.

Flu. By this day and this light, the fellow has mettle enough. Hold, there is twelve pence for you, and I pray you to serve Got, and keep you out of prawls, and prabbles, and quarrels, and dissensions; and, I warrant you, it is the better for you.

Will. I will none of your money.

Flu. It is with a goot will; I can tell you, it will serve you to mend your shoes: come, wherefore should you be so pashful? your shoes is not so goot: 'tis a goot silling, I warrant you, or I will change it.

Enter an English Herald.

K. Hen. Now, herald,—are the dead number'd?

Her. Here is the number of the slaughter'd French.
[*Delivers a paper.*

K. Hen. This note doth tell me of ten thousand French,
That in the field lie slain:—
Where is the number of our English dead?
[Herald *presents another paper.*

Edward the duke of York, the earl of Suffolk,
Sir Richard Ketly, Davy Gam, esquire:
None else of name; and of all other men,
But five and twenty.—O heaven, thy arm was here;
And not to us, but to thy arm alone,
Ascribe we all!—When, without stratagem,
But in plain shock and even play of battle,
Was ever known so great and little loss,
On one part and on th' other?—Take it, heaven,
For it is none but thine!

Exe. 'Tis wonderful!

K. Hen. Come, go we in procession to the village:
And be it death proclaimèd through our host,
To boast of this, or take the praise from heaven.

Flu. Is it not lawful, an please your majesty, to tell how many is killed?

K. Hen. Yes, captain; but with this acknowledgment,
That heaven fought for us.

Flu. Yes, my conscience, it did us great goot.

K. Hen. Do we all holy rites:
Let there be sung *Non nobis*, and *Te Deum;*
The dead with charity enclos'd in clay:
We'll then to Calais; and to England then;
Where ne'er from France arriv'd more happy men. [*Exeunt.*

ACT V.

SCENE I.—France. *An English Court of Guard.*

Enter FLUELLEN *and* GOWER.

Gow. Nay, that's right; but why wear you your leek to-day? Saint Davy's day is past.

Flu. There is occasions and causes why and wherefore in all things: I will tell you, as my friend, captain Gower:—the rascally, scald, beggarly, pragging knave, Pistol,—which you and yourself, and all the 'orld, know to be no petter than a fellow, look you now, of no merits,—he is come to me, and prings me pread and salt yesterday, look you, and bid me eat my leek: it was in a place where I could not breed no contentions with him; but I will be so pold as to wear it in my cap till I see him once again, and then I will tell him a little piece of my desires.

Gow. Why, here he comes, swelling like a turkey-cock.

Flu. 'Tis no matter for his swellings, nor his turkey-cocks.—

Enter PISTOL.

Got pless you, ancient Pistol! you scurvy, filthy knave, Got pless you!

Pist. Ha! art thou Bedlam? dost thou thirst, base Trojan,
To have me fold up Parca's fatal web?
Hence! I am qualmish at the smell of leek.

Flu. I peseech you heartily, scurvy knave, at my desires, and my requests, and my petitions, to eat, look you, this leek: because, look you, you do not love it, nor your affections, and your appetites, and your digestions, does not agree with it, I would desire you to eat it.

Pist. Not for Cadwallader and all his goats.

Flu. [*Strikes him.*] There is one goat for you. Will you be so goot, scald knave, as eat it?

Pist. Base Trojan, thou shall die.

Flu. You say very true, scald knave: I will desire you to live in the mean time, and eat your victuals: [*Striking him again.*] come, there is sauce for it. You called me yesterday, mountain-squire, but I will make you to-day a squire of low degree. I pray you, fall to: if you can mock a leek, you can eat a leek.

Gow. Enough, captain: you have astonished him.

Flu. I say, I will make him eat some part of my leek, or I will peat his pate four days.—Pite, I pray you; it is goot for your green wound, and your ploody coxcomb.

Pist. Must I bite?

Flu. Yes, certainly, and out of doubt, and out of question too, and ambiguities.

Pist. By this leek, I will most horribly revenge: I eat,—and eat,—I swear—

Flu. Eat, I pray you: will you have some more sauce to your leek? there is not enough leek to swear by.

Pist. Quiet thy cudgel; thou dost see I eat.

Flu. Much goot do you, scald knave, heartily. Nay, pray you, throw none away; the skin is goot for your proken coxcomb. When you take occasions to see leeks hereafter, I pray you, mock at 'em; that is all.

Pist. Good.

Flu. Ay, leeks is good:—hold you, there is a groat to heal your pate.

Pist. Me a groat!

Flu. Yes, verily and in truth, you shall take it; or I have another leek in my pocket, which you shall eat.

Pist. I take thy groat in earnest of revenge.

Flu. If I owe you any thing, I will pay you in cudgels: you shall be a woodmonger, and buy nothing of me but cudgels.

[*Exeunt* FLUELLEN *and* GOWER.

Pist. Doth fortune play the huswife with me now?
News have I, that my Nell is dead i' the spital.
And there my rendezvous is quite cut off.
Old I do wax; and from my weary limbs
Honor is cudgelled.

To England will I steal, and there I'll steal:
And patches will I get unto these scars,
And swear I got them in the Gallia wars. [*Exit.*

SCENE II.—Troyes in Champagne. *An Apartment in the* French King's *Palace.*

Enter, from one side, KING HENRY, BEDFORD, GLOSTER, EXETER, WARWICK, WESTMORELAND, *and other* Lords; *from the other side, the* French King, *Queen* ISABEL, *the Princess* KATHARINE, Lords, Ladies, *&c.*, *the* DUKE OF BURGUNDY, *and his train.*

K. Hen. Peace to this meeting, wherefore we are met!
Unto our brother France, and to our sister,
Health and fair time of day;—joy and good wishes
To our most fair and princely cousin Katharine;—
And, princes French, and peers, health to you all.
Fr. King. Right joyous are we to behold your face,
Most worthy brother England; fairly met:—
So are you, princes English, every one.
Q. Isa. Happy be the issue, brother England,
Of this good day and of this gracious meeting.
K. Hen. To cry amen to that, thus we appear.
Q. Isa. You English princes all, I do salute you.
Bur. My duty to you both, on equal love,
Great kings of France and England! That I have labor'd,
With all my wits, my pains, and strong endeavors,
To bring your most imperial majesties
Unto this bar and royal interview.
You are assembled: and my speech entreats
That I may know the let, why gentle Peace
Should not expel these inconveniences,
And bless us with her former qualities.
K. Hen. If, duke of Burgundy, you would have peace,
You must buy that peace
With full accord to all our just demands;
Whose tenors and particular effects
You have, enschedul'd briefly, in your hands.
Bur. The king hath heard them; to the which, as yet,
There is no answer made.
K. Hen. Well then, the peace,
Which you before so urg'd, lies in his answer.
Fr. King. I have but with a cursorary eye
O'er-glanc'd the articles: pleaseth your grace
To appoint some of your council presently
To sit with us once more, with better heed
To re-survey them, we will suddenly
Pass our accept, and peremptory answer.
K. Hen. Brother, we shall.—Go, uncle Exeter,—

And brother Clarence,—and you, brother Gloster,—
Warwick,—and Huntington,—go with the king;
And take with you free power to ratify,
Augment, or alter, as your wisdoms best
Shall see advantageable for our dignity,
Any thing in, or out of, our demands;
And we'll consign thereto.—Will you, fair sister,
Go with the princes, or stay here with us?

Q. Isa. Our gracious brother, I will go with them:
Haply a woman's voice may do some good,
When articles, too nicely urg'd, be stood on.

K. Hen. Yet leave our cousin Katharine here with us:
She is our capital demand, compris'd
Within the fore-rank of our articles.

Q. Isa. She hath good leave.

[*Exeunt all except* K. HENRY, KATHARINE, and ALICE.

K. Hen. Fair Katharine, and most fair!
Will you vouchsafe to teach a soldier terms
Such as will enter at a lady's ear,
And plead his love-suit to her gentle heart?

Kath. Your majesty shall mock at me; I cannot speak your England.

K. Hen. O fair Katharine, if you will love me soundly with your French heart, I will be glad to hear you confess it brokenly with your English tongue. Do you like me, Kate?

Kath. *Pardonnez moy*, I cannot tell vat is—like me.

K. Hen. An angel is like you, Kate; and you are like an angel.

Kath. *Que dit-il? que je suis semblable à les anges?*

Alice. *Ouy, vrayment, sauf vostre grace, ainsi dit-il.*

K. Hen. I said so, dear Katharine; and I must not blush to affirm it.

Kath. *O bon Dieu! les langues des hommes sont pleines de tromperie.*

K. Hen. What says she, fair one? that the tongues of men are full of deceits?

Alice. *Ouy*, dat de tongues of de mans is be full of deceits: dat is de princess.

K. Hen. The princess is the better English-woman. I' faith, Kate, my wooing is fit for thy understanding: I am glad thou canst speak no better English; for, if thou couldst, thou wouldst find me such a plain king, that thou wouldst think I had sold my farm to buy my crown. I know no ways to mince it in love, but directly to say—I love you: then, if you urge me farther than to say—Do you in faith? I wear out my suit. Give me your answer; i' faith, do; and so clap hands and a bargain: how say you, lady?

Kath. *Sauf vostre honneur*, me understand well.

K. Hen. Marry, if you would put me to verses, or to dance

for your sake, Kate, why you undid me. If I could win a lady at leap-frog, or by vaulting into my saddle with my armor on my back, under the correction of bragging be it spoken, I should quickly leap into a wife. But, before heaven, Kate, I cannot look greenly, nor gasp out my eloquence, nor I have no cunning in protestation; only downright oaths, which I never use till urged, nor never break for urging. If thou canst love a fellow of this temper, Kate, whose face is not worth sun-burning, that never looks in his glass for love of any thing he sees there,—let thine eye be thy cook. I speak to thee plain soldier: if thou canst love me for this, take me; if not, to say to thee that I shall die, is true,—but for thy love, by the Lord, no; yet I love thee too. And while thou livest, dear Kate, take a fellow of plain and uncoined constancy; for he perforce must do thee right, because he hath not the gift to woo in other places: for these fellows of infinite tongue, that can rhyme themselves into ladies' favors, they do always reason themselves out again. What! a speaker is but a prater; a rhyme is but a ballad. A good limb will fall; a straight back will stoop; a black beard will turn white; a curled pate will grow bald; a fair face will wither; a full eye will wax hollow; but a good heart, Kate, is the sun and the moon; or, rather, the sun, and not the moon,—for it shines bright, and never changes, but keeps his course truly. If thou would have such a one, take me: and take me, take a soldier; take a soldier, take a king: and what sayest thou, then, to my love? speak, my fair, and fairly, I pray thee.

Kath. Is it possible dat I sould love de enemy of France?

K. Hen. No; it is not possible you should love the enemy of France, Kate: but, in loving me, you should love the friend of France; for I love France so well, that I will not part with a village of it; I will have it all mine: and, Kate, when France is mine and I am yours, then yours is France and you are mine.

Kath. I cannot tell vat is dat.

K. Hen. No, Kate? I will tell thee in French; which I am sure will hang upon my tongue like a new-married wife about her husband's neck, hardly to be shook off.—*Quand j'ay la possession de France, et quand vous avez la possession de moy,* (let me see, what then? Saint Dennis be my speed!)—*donc vostre est France, et vous estes mienne.* It is as easy for me, Kate, to conquer the kingdom, as to speak so much more French: I shall never move thee in French, unless it be to laugh at me.

Kath. Sauf vostre honneur, le François que vous parlez, est meilleur que l'Anglois lequel je parle.

K. Hen. No, 'faith, is't not, Kate: but thy speaking of my tongue, and I thine, most truly falsely, must needs be granted to be much at one. But, Kate, dost thou understand thus much English,—Canst thou love me?

Kath. I cannot tell.

K. Hen. How answer you, *la plus belle Katharine du monde, mon très chère et divine déesse?*

Kath. Your *majesté* have *fausse* French enough to deceive de most *sage demoiselle* dat is *en France.*

K. Hen. Now, fie upon my false French! By mine honor, in true English, I love thee, Kate: by which honor I dare not swear, thou lovest me; yet my blood begins to flatter me that thou dost, notwithstanding the poor and untempering effect of my visage. But, in faith, Kate, the elder I wax, the better I shall appear: my comfort is, that old age, that ill layer-up of beauty, can do no more spoil upon my face: thou hast me, if thou hast me, at the worst; and thou shalt wear me, if thou wear me, better and better:—and therefore tell me, most fair Katharine, will you have me? Put off your maiden blushes; avouch the thoughts of your heart with the looks of an empress; take me by the hand, and say—Harry of England, I am thine: which word thou shalt no sooner bless mine ear withal, but I will tell thee aloud—England is thine, Ireland is thine, France is thine, and Henry Plantagenet is thine; who, though I speak it before his face, if he be not fellow with the best king, thou shalt find the best king of good fellows. Come, your answer in broken music,—for thy voice is music, and thy English broken; therefore, queen of all, Katharine, break thy mind to me in broken English,—wilt thou have me?

Kath. Dat is, as it shall please de *roy mon pere.*

K. Hen. Nay, it will please him well, Kate,—it shall please him, Kate.

Kath. Den it shall also content me.

K. Hen. Upon that I kiss your hand, and I call you my queen.

Kath. Laissez, mon seigneur, laissez, laissez: ma foy, je ne veux point que vous abbaissez vostre grandeur, en baisant la main d'une vostre indigne serviteure: excusez moy, je vous supplie, mon très puissant seigneur.

K. Hen. Then I will kiss your lips, Kate.

Kath. Les dames, et damoiselles, pour estre baisées devant leur noces, il n'est pas la coûtume de France.

K. Hen. Madam my interpreter, what says she?

Alice. Dat it is not be de fashion *pour les* ladies of France,—I cannot tell what is, *baiser, en* English.

K. Hen. To kiss.

Alice. Your majesty *entendre* bettre *que moy.*

K. Hen. It is not a fashion for the maids in France to kiss before they are married, would she say?

Alice. Ouy, vrayment.

K. Hen. O Kate, nice customs court'sy to great kings. Dear Kate, you and I cannot be confined within the weak list of a country's fashion: we are the makers of manners, Kate; and the liberty that follows our places stops the mouths of all find-faults,—as I will do yours, for upholding the nice fashion of your country in denying me a kiss: therefore, patiently, and yielding. [*Kissing her.*] You have witchcraft in your lips, Kate: there is more eloquence in a sugar touch of them, than in the tongues of the French council; and they should sooner persuade Harry of England, than a general petition of monarchs.—Here comes your father.

Re-enter the French King *and* Queen, BURGUNDY, BEDFORD, GLOSTER, EXETER, WARWICK, WESTMORELAND, *and other French and English* Lords.

Bur. Heaven save your majesty! My royal cousin,
Teach you our princess English?

K. Hen. I would have her learn, my fair cousin, how perfectly I love her; and that is good English.

Bur. Is she not apt?

K. Hen. Our tongue is rough, coz, and my condition is not smooth; so that, having neither the voice nor the heart of flattery about me, I cannot so conjure up the spirit of love in her, that he will appear in his true likeness.

Bur. I will wink on her to consent, my lord, if you will teach her to know my meaning: for maids, well summered and warm kept, are like flies at Bartholomew-tide, blind, though they have their eyes.

K. Hen. This moral ties me over to time, and a hot summer; and so I shall catch the fly, your cousin, in the latter end, and she must be blind too.

Bur. As love is, my lord, before it loves.

K. Hen. It is so: and you may, some of you, thank love for my blindness, who cannot see many a fair French city, for one fair French maid that stands in my way.

Fr. King. Yes, my lord, you see them perspectively, the cities turned into a maid.

K. Hen. Shall Kate be my wife?

Fr. King. Take her, fair son; and from her blood raise up
Issue to me; that the contending kingdoms
Of France and England, whose very shores look pale
With envy of each other's happiness,
May cease their hatred; and this dear conjunction
Plant neighborhood and christian-like accord
In their sweet bosoms, that never war advance
His bleeding sword 'twixt England and fair France.

K. Hen. Now, welcome, Kate:—and bear me witness all,
That here I kiss her as my sovereign queen. [*Flourish.*
Prepare we for our marriage:—on which day
My lord of Burgundy, we'll take your oath,
And all the peers', for surety of our leagues.—
Then shall I swear to Kate, and you to me;
And may our oaths well kept and prosperous be! [*Exeunt.*

THE HISTORY OF

KING HENRY VI.

PART I.

THE "Chronicle History" of Henry VI. is divided into three parts, forming, together, authentic annals of this monarch's reign; giving a vivid picture of "the contentions of the Houses of York and Lancaster," or the "Wars of the Roses." The chronicles of Hall and Holinshed afforded the poet materials for his labors, and, bating a few errors in dates, the whole of the series may be taken as a faithful historical transcript of the times they are intended to illustrate. The first part of Henry VI. commences with the childhood of Henry, while the kingdom was under the Protectorate of his uncle, the Duke of Gloster, and ends with preparations for the marriage of Henry with Margaret, his future Queen, which took place in the twenty-third year of his reign, 1445.

PERSONS REPRESENTED.

KING HENRY THE SIXTH.
DUKE OF GLOSTER, *Uncle to the* KING, *and Protector.*
DUKE OF BEDFORD, *Uncle to the* KING, *and Regent of France.*
THOMAS BEAUFORT, *Duke of* Exeter, *Great Uncle to the* KING.
HENRY BEAUFORT, *Great Uncle to the* KING; *Bishop of* Winchester, *and afterwards Cardinal.*
JOHN BEAUFORT, *Earl of* Somerset, *afterwards Duke.*
RICHARD PLANTAGENET, *Eldest Son of Richard, late Earl of* Cambridge; *afterwards Duke of* York.
EARLS OF WARWICK, SALISBURY, *and* SUFFOLK.
LORD TALBOT, *afterwards Earl of* Shrewsbury.
JOHN TALBOT, *his Son.*
EDMUND MORTIMER, *Earl of* March.
MORTIMER'S Keepers, *and a* Lawyer.
Sir JOHN FASTOLFE. Sir WILLIAM LUCY. Sir WILLIAM GLANSDALE. Sir THOMAS GARGRAVE.
WOODVILLE, *Lieutenant of the Tower.* Mayor of London.
VERNON, *of the White Rose, or York Faction.*

BASSET, *of the Red Rose, or Lancaster Faction.*

CHARLES, *Dauphin, and afterwards King, of* France.
REIGNIER, *Duke of Anjou, and titular King of* Naples.
DUKES OF BURGUNDY *and* ALENCON. ORLEANS.
Governor of Paris. Master-Gunner of Orleans, *and his* Son.
General of the French Forces in Bourdeaux.
A French Sergeant. *A* Porter. *An old* Shepherd, *Father to* JOAN LA PUCELLE.

MARGARET, *Daughter to* REIGNIER; *afterwards married to* KING HENRY.
COUNTESS OF AUVERGNE.
JOAN LA PUCELLE, *commonly called Joan of Arc.*

Fiends *appearing to* LA PUCELLE, Lords, Warders of the Tower, Heralds, Officers, Soldiers, Messengers, *and several* Attendants *both on the English and French.*

SCENE,—*Partly in* ENGLAND, *and partly in* FRANCE.

ACT I.

SCENE I.—Westminster Abbey.

Dead March. The Corpse of King Henry the Fifth is discovered, lying in state; attended on by the DUKES OF BEDFORD, GLOSTER, *and* EXETER; *the* EARL of WARWICK, *the* BISHOP OF WINCHESTER, Heralds, *&c.*

Bed. Hung be the heavens with black, yield day to night!
Comets, importing change of times and states,
Brandish your crystal tresses in the sky,
And with them scourge the bad revolting stars,
That have consented unto Henry's death!
King Henry the fifth, too famous to live long!
England ne'er lost a king of so much worth.
Glo. England ne'er had a king until his time.
Virtue he had, deserving to command:
His brandish'd sword did blind men with his beams;
His arms spread wider than a dragon's wings.
What should I say? his deeds exceed all speech:
He ne'er lift up his hand, but conquered.
Exe. We mourn in black: why mourn we not in blood?
Henry is dead, and never shall revive.
Win. He was a king, bless'd of the King of kings.
The battles of the Lord of hosts he fought:
The church's prayers made him so prosperous.
Glo. The church! where is it? Had not churchmen pray'd,
His thread of life had not so soon decay'd:
None do you like but an effeminate prince,
Whom, like a school-boy, you may over-awe.

Win. Gloster, whate'er we like, thou art protector,
And lookest to command the prince, and realm.
Thy wife is proud; she holdeth thee in awe,
More than heaven or religious churchmen may.
Glo. Name not religion, for thou lov'st the flesh;
And ne'er throughout the year to church thou go'st,
Except it be to pray against thy foes.
Bed. Cease, cease these jars, and rest your minds in peace!
Let's to the altar:—Heralds, wait on us:—
Instead of gold, we'll offer up our arms;
Since arms avail not, now that Henry's dead.—
Henry the fifth! thy ghost I invocate;
Prosper this realm, keep it from civil broils!
Combat with adverse planets in the heavens!
A far more glorious star thy soul will make,
Than Julius Cæsar, or bright—

Enter a Messenger.

Mess. My honorable lords, health to you all!
Sad tidings bring I to you out of France,
Of loss, of slaughter, and discomfiture:
Guienne, Champaigne, Rheims, Orleans,
Paris, Guysors, Poictiers, are all quite lost.
Bed. What say'st thou, man, before dead Henry's corse?
Speak softly; or the loss of those great towns
Will make him burst his lead, and rise from death.
Exe. How were they lost? what treachery was us'd?
Mess. No treachery; but want of men and money.
Among the soldiers this is muttered,—
That here you maintain several factions;
And, whilst a field should be despatch'd and fought,
You are disputing of your generals:
One would have lingering wars, with little cost;
Another would fly swift, but wanteth wings;
A third man thinks, without expense at all,
By guileful fair words peace may be obtain'd.
Exe. Were our tears wanting to this funeral,
These tidings would call forth her flowing tides.
Bed. Me they concern; regent I am of France.
Give me my steelèd coat! I'll fight for France.
Away with these disgraceful wailing robes!
Wounds will I lend the French, instead of eyes,
To weep their intermissive miseries.

Enter a second Messenger.

2 *Mess.* Lords, view these letters, full of bad mischance.
France is revolted from the English quite,
Except some petty towns of no import:

The Dauphin, Charles, is crownèd king in Rheims;
The bastard of Orleans with him is join'd;
Reignier, duke of Anjou, doth take his part;
The duke of Alençon flieth to his side.
Exe. The Dauphin crowned king! all fly to him!
O, whither shall we fly from this reproach?
Glo. We will not fly, but to our enemies' throats:—
Bedford, if thou be slack, I'll fight it out.
Bed. Gloster, why doubt'st thou of my forwardness?
An army have I muster'd in my thoughts,
Wherewith already France is over-run.

Enter a third Messenger.

3 *Mess.* My gracious lords,—to add to your laments,
Wherewith you now bedew king Henry's hearse,—
I must inform you of a dismal fight
Betwixt the stout lord Talbot and the French.
Win. What! wherein Talbot overcame? is't so?
3 *Mess.* O, no; wherein lord Talbot was o'erthrown:
The circumstance I'll tell you more at large.
The tenth of August last, this dreadful lord,
Retiring from the siege of Orleans,
Having full scarce six thousand in his troop,
By three-and-twenty thousand of the French
Was round encompassed and set upon.
A base Walloon, to win the Dauphin's grace,
Thrust Talbot with a spear into the back;
Whom all France, with their chief assembled strength,
Durst not presume to look once in the face.
Bed. Is Talbot slain? then I will slay myself,
For living idly here in pomp and ease,
Whilst such a worthy leader, wanting aid,
Unto his dastard foe-men is betray'd.
3 *Mess.* O no, he lives; but is took prisoner,
And lord Scales with him, and lord Hungerford:
Most of the rest slaughter'd, or took, likewise.
Bed. His ransom there is none but I shall pay:
I'll hale the Dauphin headlong from his throne;
His crown shall be the ransom of my friend:
Farewell, my masters; to my task will I;
Bonfires in France forthwith I am to make,
To keep our great Saint George's feast withal:
Ten thousand soldiers with me I will take,
Whose bloody deeds shall make all Europe quake.
3 *Mess.* So you had need; for Orleans is besieg'd;
The English army is grown weak and faint:
The earl of Salisbury craveth supply,
And hardly keeps his men from mutiny,
Since they, so few, watch such a multitude.

Exe. Remember, lords, your oaths to Henry sworn,
Either to quell the Dauphin utterly,
Or bring him in obedience to your yoke.
Bed. I do remember it; and here take my leave,
To go about my preparation. [*Exit.*
Glo. I'll to the Tower, with all the haste I can,
To view th' artillery and munition;
And then I wil proclaim young Harry king. [*Exit.*
Exe. To Eltham will I, where the young king is,
Being ordain'd his special governor;
And for his safety there I'll best devise. [*Exit.*
Win. Each hath his place and function to attend:
I am left out; for me nothing remains.
But long I will not be Jack-out-of-office:
The king from Eltham I intend to steal,
And sit at chiefest stern of public weal. [*Exit.*

SCENE II.—France. *Before* Orleans.

Enter CHARLES, *the Dauphin, with his forces;* ALENÇON, REIGNIER, *and others.*

Char. Mars his true moving, even as in the heavens,
So in the earth, to this day is not known:
Late did he shine upon the English side;
Now we are victors, upon us he smiles.
What towns of any moment but we have?
At pleasure here we lie, near Orleans;
Otherwhiles, the famish'd English, like pale ghosts,
Faintly besiege us one hour in a month.
Alen. They want their porridge, and their fat bull-beeves:
Either they must be dieted like mules,
And have their provender tied to their mouths,
Or piteous they will look, like drownèd mice.
Reig. Let's us raise the siege: why live we idly here?
Talbot is taken, whom we wont to fear:
Remaineth none but mad-brain'd Salisbury;
And he may well in fretting spend his gall,—
Nor men, nor money, hath he to make war.
Char. Sound, sound alarum! we will rush on them.
Now for the honor of the forlorn French!
Him I forgive my death, that killeth me,
When he sees me go back one foot, or fly. [*Exeunt.*

Alarums; Excursions; afterwards a Retreat. Re-enter CHARLES, ALENÇON, REIGNIER, *and others.*

Char. Who ever saw the like? what men have I?—

Dogs! cowards! dastards!—I would ne'er have fled,
But that they left me 'midst my enemies.
Reig. Salisbury is a desperate homicide;
He fighteth as one weary of his life.
The other lords, like lions wanting food,
Do rush upon us as their hungry prey.
Alen. Froissart, a countryman of ours, records,
England all Olivers and Rowlands bred,
During the time Edward the third did reign.
More truly now may this be verified;
For none but Samsons, and Goliasses,
It sendeth forth to skirmish. One to ten!
Lean raw-bon'd rascals! who would e'er suppose
They had such courage and audacity?
Char. Let's leave this town; for they are hair-brain'd slaves,
And hunger will enforce them to be more eager:
Of old I know them; rather with their teeth
The walls they'll tear down, than forsake the siege,
Reig. I think, by some odd gimmals,* or device,
Their arms are set like clocks, still to strike on;
Else ne'er could they hold out so as they do.
By my consent, we'll e'en let them alone.
Alen. Be it so.

Enter ORLEANS.

Orl. Where's the prince Dauphin? I have news for him.
Char. Orleans, thrice welcome to us.
Orl. Methinks your looks are sad, your cheer appall'd:
Hath the late overthrow wrought this offence?
Be not dismay'd, for succor is at hand:
A holy maid hither with me I bring,
Which, by a vision sent to her from heaven,
Ordainèd is to raise this tedious siege,
And drive the English forth the bounds of France.
The spirit of deep prophecy she hath,
Exceeding the nine sibyls of old Rome:
What's past and what's to come she can descry.
Speak, shall I call her in? Believe my words,
For they are certain and unfallible.
Char. Go, call her in. [*Exit.* ORLEANS.] But first, to try her skill,
Reignier, stand thou as Dauphin in my place:
Question her proudly; let thy looks be stern:
By this means shall we sound what skill she hath. [*Retires.*

Re-enter ORLEANS, *with* LA PUCELLE.

Reig. Fair maid, is't thou wilt do these wond'rous feats?

* *Gimmals*—machinery, clockwork.

Puc. Reignier, is't thou that thinkest to beguile me?
Where is the Dauphin?—Come, come from behind;
I know thee well though never seen before.
Be not amaz'd, there's nothing hid from me:
In private will I talk with thee apart.—
Stand back, you lords, and give us leave awhile.
Reig. She takes upon her bravely at first dash.
Puc. Dauphin, I am by birth a shepherd's daughter,
My wit untrain'd in any kind of art.
Heaven and our Lady gracious hath it pleas'd
To shine on my contemptible estate:
Lo, whilst I waited on my tender lambs,
And to sun's parching heat display'd my cheeks,
God's mother deigned to appear to me,
And, in a vision full of majesty,
Will'd me to leave my base vocation,
And free my country from calamity:
Her aid she promis'd, and assured success:
In complete glory she reveal'd herself;
And, whereas I was black and swart before,
With these clear rays which she infus'd on me,
That beauty am I bless'd with, which you may see.
Ask me what question thou canst possible,
And I will answer unpremeditated:
My courage try by combat, if thou dar'st,
And thou shalt find that I exceed my sex.
Resolve on this,—thou shalt be fortunate,
If thou receive me for thy warlike mate.
Char. Thou hast astonish'd me with thy high terms:
Only this proof I'll of thy valor make,—
In single combat thou shalt buckle with me;
And if thou vanquishest, thy words are true;
Otherwise, I renounce all confidence.
Puc. I am prepar'd: here is my keen-edg'd sword,
Deck'd with five flower-de-luces on each side;
The which at Touraine, in Saint Katharine's church-yard,
Out of a great deal of old iron I chose forth.
Char. Then come, o' heaven's name; I fear no woman.
Puc. And, while I live, I'll ne'er fly from a man. [*They fight.*
Char. Stay, stay thy hands! thou art an Amazon,
And fightest with the sword of Deborah.
Puc. The virgin helps me, else I were too weak.
Char. Whoe'er helps thee, 'tis thou that must help me:
Impatiently I burn with thy desire;
My heart and hands thou hast at once subdued,
Excellent Pucelle, if thy name be so,
Let me thy servant, and not sovereign, be:
'Tis the French Dauphin sueth to thee thus.

Puc. I must not yield to any rites of love,
For my profession's sacred, from above:
When I have chased all thy foes from hence,
Then will I think upon a recompense.
Char. Mean time look gracious on thy prostrate thrall.
Reig. My lord, methinks, is very long in talk. Shall we disturb him, since he keeps no mean?
Alen. He may mean more than we poor men do know.
Reig. My lord, where are you? what devise you on?
Shall we give over Orleans, or no?
Puc. Why, no, I say, distrustful recreants!
Fight till the last gasp; I will be your guard.
Char. What she says, I'll confirm: we'll fight it out.
Puc. Assign'd am I to be the English scourge.
This night the siege assuredly I'll raise:
Expect Saint Martin's summer, halcyon days,
Since I have entered into these wars.
Glory is like a circle in the water,
Which never ceaseth to enlarge itself,
Till by broad spreading, it disperse to naught.
With Henry's death the English circle ends;
Dispersèd are the glories it included.
Now am I like that proud insulting ship,
Which Cæsar and his fortune bare at once.
Char. Was Mahomet inspirèd with a dove?
Thou with an eagle art inspirèd, then.
Helen, the mother of great Constantine,
Nor yet St. Philip's daughters, were like thee.
Bright star of Venus, fall'n down on the earth,
How may I reverently worship thee enough?
Alen. Leave off delays, and let us raise the siege.
Reig. Woman, do what thou canst to save our honors;
Drive them from Orleans, and be immortaliz'd.
Char. Presently we'll try:—come, let's away about it:—
No prophet will I trust, if she prove false. [*Exeunt.*

SCENE IV.—France. *Before* Orleans.

Enter, on the walls, the Master-Gunner *and his* Son.

M. Gun. Sirrah, thou know'st how Orleans is besieg'd,
And how the English have the suburbs won.
Son. Father, I know; and oft have shot at them,
Howe'er, unfortunate, I miss'd my aim.
M. Gun. But now thou shalt not. Be thou rul'd by me:
Chief master-gunner am I of this town;
Something I must do to procure me grace.
The prince's espials have informed me

How the English, in the suburbs close intrench'd.
Wont, through a secret gate of iron bars
In yonder tower, to overpeer the city;
And thence discover, how, with most advantage,
They may vex us with shot, or with assault.
To intercept this inconvenience,
A piece of ordnance 'gainst it I have plac'd;
And even these three days have I watch'd, if I
Could see them.
Now do thou watch, for I can stay no longer.
If thou spy'st any, run and bring me word;
And thou shalt find me at the governor's. [*Exit.*
Son. Father, I warrant you; take you no care;
I'll never trouble you, if I may spy them.

Enter in an upper chamber of a tower. the LORDS SALISBURY *and* TALBOT; *Sir* WILLIAM GLANSDALE, *Sir* THOMAS GARGRAVE, *and others.*

Sal. Talbot, my life, my joy, again return'd!
How wert thou handled, being prisoner?
Or by what means got'st thou to be releas'd?
Discourse, I pr'ythee, on this turret's top.
Tal. The duke of Bedford had a prisoner,
Call'd the brave Lord Ponton de Santrailles;
For him I was exchang'd and ransomed.
Sal. Yet tell'st thou not how thou wert entertain'd.
Tal. With scoffs, and scorns, and contumelious taunts.
In open market-place produc'd they me,
To be a public spectacle to all:
Here, said they, is the terror of the French,
The scarecrow that affrights our children so.
Then broke I from the officers that led me,
And with my nails digg'd stones out of the ground,
To hurl at the beholders of my shame:
My grisly countenance made others fly;
None durst come near for fear of sudden death.
In iron walls they deem'd me not secure;
So great fear of my name 'mongst them was spread,
That they suppos'd I could rend bars of steel,
And spurn in pieces posts of adamant:
Wherefore a guard of chosen shot I had,
That walk'd about me every minute-while;
And if I did but stir out of my bed,
Ready they were to shoot me to the heart.
Sal. I grieve to hear what torments you endur'd;
But we will be reveng'd sufficiently.
Now it is supper-time in Orleans:
Here, through this grate, I can count every one,

And view the Frenchmen how they fortify:
Let us look in; the sight will much delight thee.—
Sir Thomas Gargrave, and Sir William Glansdale,
Let me have your express opinions,
Where is best place to make our battery next.
Gar. I think, at the north gate; for there stand lords.
Glan. And I, here, at the bulwark of the bridge.
Tal. For aught I see, this city must be famish'd,
Or with light skirmishes enfeebled.
[*Shot from the town.* SALISBURY *and Sir* THOMAS GARGRAVE *fall.*
Sal. O Lord, have mercy on us, wretched sinners!
Gar. O Lord, have mercy on me, woful man!
Tal. What chance is this, that suddenly hath cross'd us?—
[*Thunder heard*; *afterwards an alarum.*
What stir is this? What tumult's in the heavens?
Whence cometh this alarum, and the noise?

Enter a Messenger.

Mess. My lord, my lord, the French have gather'd head:
The Dauphin, with one Joan la Pucelle join'd,—
A holy prophetess, new risen up,—
Is come with a great power to raise the siege.
[SALISBURY *lifts himself up and groans.*
Tal. Hear, hear, how dying Salisbury doth groan!
It irks his heart he cannot be reveng'd.—
Frenchmen, I'll be a Salisbury to you:—
Convey me Salisbury into his tent,
And then we'll try what these dastard Frenchmen dare.
[*Exeunt, bearing out the bodies.*

SCENE V.—Orleans. *Before one of the Gates.*

Alarum. Skirmishings. Enter TALBOT, *pursuing the Dauphin; drives him in, and exit: then enter* LA PUCELLE, *driving Englishmen before her, and exit after them. Then re-enter* TALBOT.

Tal. Where is my strength, my valor, and my force?
Our English troops retire, I cannot stay them;
A woman clad in armor chaseth them.
Here, here she comes.—

Re-enter LA PUCELLE.

I'll have a bout with thee;
Blood will I draw on thee,—thou art a witch,—
And straightway give thy soul to him thou serv'st.
Puc. Come, come, 'tis only I that must disgrace thee.
[*They fight.*

Tal. My breast I'll burst with straining of my courage,
And from my shoulders crack my arms asunder,
But I will chastise this high-minded wanton. [*They fight again.*

Puc. [*Retiring.*] Talbot, farewell; thy hour is not yet come:
I must go victual Orleans forthwith.
O'ertake me, if thou canst; I scorn thy strength.
Go, go, cheer up thy hunger-starved men;
Help Salisbury to make his testament:
This day is ours, as many more shall be.
[LA PUCELLE *enters the town, with* Soldiers.

Tal. My thoughts are whirlèd like a potter's wheel;
I know not where I am, nor what I do:
A witch by fear, not force, like Hannibal,
Drives back our troops, and conquers as she lists:
So bees with smoke, and doves with noisome stench,
Are from their hives and houses driven away.
They call'd us, for our fierceness, English dogs;
Now, like to whelps, we crying run away. [*A short alarum.*
Hark, countrymen! either renew the fight,
Or tear the lions out of England's coat;
Renounce your soil, give sheep in lions' stead:
Sheep run not half so timorous from the wolf,
Or horse or oxen from the leopard,
As you fly from your oft-subduèd slaves.
[*Alarum. Another skirmish.*
It will not be:—retire into your trenches:
You all consented unto Salisbury's death,
For none would strike a stroke in his revenge.—
Pucelle is enter'd into Orleans,
In spite of us or aught that we could do.
O, would I were to die with Salisbury!
The shame hereof will make me hide my head.
[*Alarum. Retreat. Exeunt* TALBOT *and his forces, &c.*

SCENE VI.—*The Same.*

Flourish. Enter on the walls, LA PUCELLE, CHARLES, REIGNIER, ALENÇON, *and* Soldiers.

Puc. Advance our waving colors on the walls;
Rescu'd is Orleans from the English wolves:—
Thus Joan la Pucelle hath perform'd her word.

Char. Divinest creature, bright Astrea's daughter,
How shall I honor thee for this success?
Thy promises are like Adonis' gardens,
That one day bloom'd, and fruitful were the next.—

France, triumph in thy glorious prophetess!
Recover'd is the town of Orleans:
More blessèd hap did ne'er befall our state.
Reig. Why ring not out the bells throughout the town?
Dauphin, command the citizens make bonfires,
And feast and banquet in the open streets,
To celebrate the joy that heaven hath given us.
Alen. All France will be replete with mirth and joy,
When they shall hear how we have play'd the men.
Char. 'Tis Joan, not we, by whom the day is won;
For which I will divide my crown with her;
And all the priests and friars in my realm
Shall in procession sing her endless praise.
A statelier pyramis to her I'll rear,
Than Rhodope's, of Memphis, ever was:
In memory of her when she is dead,
Her ashes, in an urn more precious
Than the rich-jewel'd coffer of Darius,
Transported shall be at high festivals
Before the kings and queens of France.
No longer on Saint Dennis will we cry,
But Joan la Pucelle shall be France's saint.
Come in, and let us banquet royally,
After this golden day of victory. [*Flourish. Exeunt.*

ACT II.

SCENE I.—Orleans. *Before one of the Gates.*

Enter to the Gate a French Sergeant *and two* Sentinels.

Serg. Sirs, take your places, and be vigilant.
If any noise, or soldier, you perceive,
Near to the walls, by some apparent sign
Let us have knowledge at the court of guard.
1 *Sent.* Sergeant, you shall. [*Exit* Sergeant.
Thus are poor servitors
(When others sleep upon their quiet beds)
Constrain'd to watch in darkness, rain, and cold.

Enter TALBOT, BEDFORD, BURGUNDY, *and forces, with scaling ladders; their drums beating a dead march.*

Tal. Lord regent, and redoubted Burgundy,—
By whose approach the regions of Artois,
Walloon, and Picardy, are friends to us,—
This happy night the Frenchmen are secure,

Having all day carous'd and banqueted:
Embrace we, then, this opportunity,
As fitting best to quittance their deceit,
Contriv'd by art and baleful sorcery.

Bed. Coward of France!—how much he wrongs his fame,
Despairing of his own arm's fortitude,
To join with witches and the help of fiends!

Bur. Traitors have never other company.—
But what's that Pucelle, whom they term so pure?

Tal. A maid, they say.

Bed. A maid! and be so martial!

Bur. Pray heaven she prove not masculine ere long;
If underneath the standard of the French
She carry armor, as she hath begun.

Tal. Well, let them practise and converse with spirits:
Heaven is our fortress, in whose conquering name
Let us resolve to scale their flinty bulwarks.

Bed. Ascend, brave Talbot; we will follow thee.

Tal. Not all together: better far, I guess,
That we do make our entrance several ways;
That, if it chance the one of us do fail,
The other yet may rise against their force.

Bed. Agreed: I'll to yon corner.

Bur. And I to this

Tal. And here will Talbot mount, or make his grave.—
Now, Salisbury, for thee, and for the right
Of English Henry, shall this night appear
How much in duty I am bound to both.

[*The English scale the walls, crying,* "St. George a Talbot!" *and all enter the town.*

1 *Sent.* Arm! arm! the enemy doth make assault!

The French leap over the walls. Enter, several ways, ORLEANS, ALENÇON, *and* REIGNIER, *half ready and half unready.*

Alen. How now, my lords! what, all unready so?

Orl. Unready! ay, and glad we scap'd so well.

Reig. 'Twas time, I trow, to wake and leave our beds,
Hearing alarums at our chamber doors.

Alen. Of all exploits, since first I followed arms,
Ne'er heard I of a warlike enterprise
More venturous or desperate than this.

Orl. I think this Talbot be a fiend of darkness.

Reig. If he is not, the heavens, sure, favor him.

Alen. Here cometh Charles: I marvel how he sped.

Orl. Tut! holy Joan was his defensive guard.

Enter CHARLES *and* LA PUCELLE.

Char. Is this thy cunning, thou deceitful dame?

Didst thou at first, to flatter us withal,
Make us partakers of a little gain,
That now our loss might be ten times so much?
Puc. Wherefore is Charles impatient with his friend?
At all times will you have my power alike?
Sleeping or waking, must I still prevail,
Or will you blame and lay the fault on me?—
Improvident soldiers! had your watch been good,
This sudden mischief never could have fallen.
Char. Duke of Alençon, this was your default,
That, being captain of the watch to-night,
Did look no better to that weighty charge.
Alen. Had all your quarters been as safely kept,
As that whereof I had the government,
We had not been thus shamefully surpris'd.
Orl. Mine was secure.
Reig. And so was mine, my lord.
Char. And, for myself, most part of all this night,
Within her quarter, and mine own precinct,
I was employ'd in passing to and fro,
About relieving of the sentinels:
Then how, or which way, should they first break in?
Puc. Question, my lords, no farther of the case,
How, or which way: 'tis sure they found some place
But weekly guarded, where the breach was made
And now there rests no other shift but this,—
To gather our soldiers, scatter'd and dispers'd,
And lay new platforms to endamage them.

Alarum. Enter an English Soldier, *crying,* "A Talbot! a Talbot!" *They fly, leaving their clothes behind.*

Sold. I'll be so bold to take what they have left.
The cry of Talbot serves me for a sword;
For I have loaden me with many spoils,
Using no other weapon but his name. [*Exit.*

SCENE II.—Orleans. *Within the Town.*

Enter Talbot, Bedford, Burgundy, *a* Captain, *and others.*

Bed. The day begins to break, and night is fled,
Whose pitchy mantle over-veil'd the earth,
Here sound retreat, and cease our hot pursuit. [*Retreat sounded.*
Tal. Bring forth the body of old Salisbury,
And here advance it in the market-place,
The middle centre of this cursed town.—
Now have I paid my vow unto his soul;
For every drop of blood was drawn from him,

There hath at least five Frenchmen died to-night.
And that hereafter ages may behold
What ruin happen'd in revenge of him,
Within their chiefest temple I'll erect
A tomb, wherein his corse shall be interr'd:
Upon the which, that every one may read,
Shall be engrav'd the sack of Orleans,
The treacherous manner of his mournful death,
And what a terror he had been to France.
But, lords, in all our bloody massacre,
I muse we met not with the Dauphin's grace,
His new-come champion, virtuous Joan of Arc,
Nor any of his false confederates.

Bed. 'Tis thought, lord Talbot, when the fight began,
Rous'd on the sudden from their drowsy beds,
They did, amongst the troops of armèd men,
Leap o'er the walls for refuge in the field.

Enter a Messenger.

Mess. All hail, my lords! Which of this princely train
Call ye the warlike Talbot, for his acts
So much applauded through the realm of France?

Tal. Here is the Talbot: who would speak with him?

Mess. The virtuous lady, countess of Auvergne,
With modesty admiring thy renown,
By me entreats, great lord, thou wouldst vouchsafe
To visit her poor castle where she lies,
That she may boast she hath beheld the man
Whose glory fills the world with loud report.

Bur. Is it even so? Nay, then, I see our wars
Will turn unto a peaceful comic sport,
When ladies crave to be encounter'd with.—
You may not, my lord, despise her gentle suit.

Tal. Ne'er trust me, then; for when a world of men
Could not prevail with all their oratory,
Yet hath a woman's kindness over-rul'd:—
And therefore tell her I return great thanks,
And in submission will attend on her.—
Will not your honors bear me company?

Bed. No, truly; it is more than manners will:
And I have heard it said, unbidden guests
Are often welcomest when they are gone.

Tal. Well then, alone, since there's no remedy,
I mean to prove this lady's courtesy.—
Come hither, captain. [*Whispers.*] You perceive my mind.

Capt. I do, my lord, and mean accordingly. [*Exeunt.*

SCENE III.—Auvergne. *Court of the Castle.*

Enter the COUNTESS *and her* Porter.

Count. Porter, remember what I gave in charge;
And when you have done so, bring the keys to me.
Port. Madam, I will. [*Exit.*
Count. The plot is laid: if all things fall out right,
I shall as famous be by this exploit,
As Scythian Thomyris by Cyrus' death.
Great is the rumor of this dreadful knight,
And his achievements of no less account:
Fain would mine eyes be witness with mine ears,
To give their censure of these rare reports.

Enter Messenger *and* TALBOT.

Mess. Madam, according as your ladyship desir'd,
By message crav'd, so is lord Talbot come.
Count. And he is welcome. What! is this the man?
Mess. Madam, it is.
Count. Is this the scourge of France?
Is this the Talbot, so much fear'd abroad,
That with his name the mothers still their babes?
I see report is fabulous and false:
I thought I should have seen some Hercules,
A second Hector, for his grim aspéct,
And large proportión of his strong-knit limbs.
Alas, this is a child, a silly dwarf!
It cannot be, this weak and writhled* shrimp
Should strike such terror to his enemies.
Tal. Madam, I have been bold to trouble you;
But since your ladyship is not at leisure,
I'll sort some other time to visit you. [*Going.*
Count. What means he now?—Go ask him, whither he goes.
Mess. Stay, my lord Talbot; for my lady craves
To know the cause of your abrupt departure.
Tal. Marry, for that she's in a wrong belief,
I go to certify her, Talbot's here.

Re-enter Porter *with keys.*

Count. If thou be he, then art thou prisoner.
Tal. Prisoner to whom?
Count. To me, blood-thirsty lord;
And for that cause I train'd thee to my house.
Long time thy shadow hath been thrall to me,
For in my gallery thy picture hangs:

* *Writhled*—shrunk up, withered.

But now the substance shall endure the like,
And I will chain these legs and arms of thine,
That hast by tyranny, these many years,
Wasted our country, slain our citizens,
And sent our sons and husbands captivate.
Tal. Ha, ha, ha!
Count. Laughest thou, wretch? thy mirth shall turn to moan.
Tal. I laugh to see your ladyship so fond,
To think that you have aught but Talbot's shadow,
Whereon to practise your severity.
Count. Why, art not thou the man?
Tal. I am, indeed.
Count. Then have I substance, too.
Tal. No, no, I am but shadow of myself:
You are deceiv'd, my substance is not here;
For what you see, is but the smallest part
And least proportion of humanity:
I tell, you, madam, were the whole frame here,
It is of such a spacious lofty pitch,
Your roof were not sufficient to contain it.
Count. This is a riddling merchant for the nonce;
He will be here, and yet he is not here:
How can these contrarieties agree?
Tal. That will I show you presently.

He winds a horn. Drums strike up; then a peal of ordnance. The gates being forced, enter Soldiers.

How say you, madam? are you now persuaded,
That Talbot is but shadow of himself?
These are his substance, sinews, arms, and strength,
With which he yoketh your rebellious necks,
Razeth your cities, and subverts your towns,
And in a moment makes them desolate.
Count. Victorious Talbot! pardon my abuse:
I find thou art no less than fame hath bruited,
And more than may be gather'd by thy shape.
Let my presumption not provoke thy wrath;
For I am sorry, that with reverence
I did not entertain thee as thou art.
Tal. Be not dismay'd, fair lady; nor misconstrue
The mind of Talbot, as you did mistake
The outward composition of his body.
What you have done hath not offended me:
No other satisfaction do I crave,
But only, (with your patience) that we may
Taste of your wine, and see what cates you have;
For soldiers' stomachs always serve them well.

Count. With all my heart; and think me honored
To feast so great a warrior in my house. [*Exeunt.*

Shakspeare in the following scene has given the origin of the two badges of the Houses of *York* and *Lancaster*. Whether this is historically correct is not fully established.

SCENE IV.—London. *The Temple Garden.*

Enter the EARLS OF SOMERSET, SUFFOLK, *and* WARWICK; RICHARD PLANTAGENET, VERNON, *and another* Lawyer.

Plan. Great lords and gentlemen, what means this silence?
Dare no man answer in a case of truth?
Suf. Within the Temple hall we were too loud;
The garden here is more convenient.
Plan. Then say at once, if I maintain'd the truth
Or else was wrangling Somerset in the error?
Suf. 'Faith, I have been a truant in the law,
And never yet could frame my will to it;
And, therefore, frame the law unto my will.
Som. Judge you, my lord of Warwick, then, between us.
War. Between two hawks, which flies the higher pitch;
Between two dogs, which hath the deeper mouth;
Between two blades, which bears the better temper;
Between two horses, which doth bear him best;
Between two girls, which hath the merriest eye;—
I have, perhaps, some shallow spirit of judgment:
But in these nice sharp quillets of the law,
Good faith, I am no wiser than a daw.
Plan. Tut, tut! here is a mannerly forbearance:
The truth appears so naked on my side,
That any purblind eye may find it out.
Som. And on my side it is so well apparell'd,
So clear, so shining, and so evident,
That it will glimmer through a blind man's eye.
Plan. Since you are tongue-tied, and so loath to speak,
In dumb significants proclaim your thoughts:
Let him that is a true-born gentleman,
And stands upon the honor of his birth,
If he suppose that I have pleaded truth,
From off this brier pluck a white rose with me.
Som. Let him that is no coward, nor no flatterer,
But dare maintain the party of the truth,
Pluck a red rose from off this thorn with me.
War. I love no colors; and, without all color
Of base insinuating flattery,
I pluck this white rose with Plantagenet.

Suf. I pluck this red rose with young Somerset;
And say withal, I think he held the right.
Ver. Stay, lords and gentlemen, and pluck no more,
Till you conclude, that he, upon whose side
The fewest roses are cropp'd from the tree,
Shall yield the other in the right opinion.
Som. Good master Vernon, it is well objected:
If I have fewest, I subscribe in silence.
Plan. And I.
Ver. Then, for the truth and plainness of the case,
I pluck this pale and maiden blossom here,
Giving my verdict on the white rose side.
Som. Prick not your finger as you pluck it off,
Lest, bleeding, you do paint the white rose red,
And fall on my side so, against your will.
Ver. If I, my lord, for my opinion bleed,
Opinion shall be surgeon to my hurt,
And keep me on the side where still I am.
Som. Well, well, come on: who else?
Law. [*To* SOMERSET.] Unless my study and my books be false,
The argument you held, was wrong in you;
In sign whereof, I pluck a white rose too.
Plan. Now, Somerset, where is your argument?
Som. Here, in my scabbard; meditating that,
Shall dye your white rose in a bloody red.
Plan. Meantime, your cheeks do counterfeit our roses;
For pale they look with fear, as witnessing
The truth on our side.
Som. No, Plantagenet,
'Tis not for fear, but anger, that thy cheeks
Blush for pure shame to counterfeit our roses.
And yet thy tongue will not confess thy error.
Plan. Hath not thy rose a canker, Somerset?
Som. Hath not thy rose a thorn, Plantagenet?
Plan. Ay, sharp and piercing, to maintain his truth;
Whiles thy consuming canker eats his falsehood.
Som. Well, I'll find friends to wear my bleeding roses,
That shall maintain what I have said is true,
Where false Plantagenet dare not be seen.
Plan. Now, by this maiden blossom in my hand,
I scorn thee and thy faction, peevish boy.
Suf. Turn not thy scorns this way, Plantagenet.
Plan. Proud Poole, I will; and scorn both him and thee.
Suf. I'll turn my part thereof into thy throat.
Som. Away, away, good William De-la-Poole!
We grace the yeoman, by conversing with him.
War. Now, by heaven's will, thou wrong'st him, Somerset;
His grandfather was Lionel, duke of Clarence,

Third son to the third Edward, king of England.
Spring crestless yeomen from so deep a root?
Plan. He bears him on the place's privilege,
Or durst not, for his craven heart, say thus.
Som. By him that made me, I'll maintain my words
On any plot of ground in Christendom.
Was not thy father, Richard earl of Cambridge,
For treason executed in our late king's day?
And, by his treason, stand'st not thou attainted,
Corrupted, and exempt from ancient gentry?
His trespass yet lives in thy blood;
And, till thou be restor'd, thou art a yeoman.
Plan. My father was attached, not attainted;
Condemn'd to die for treason, but no traitor;
And that I'll prove on better men than Somerset,
Were growing time once ripen'd to my will.
For your partaker Poole, and you yourself,
I'll note you in my book of memory,
To scourge you for this apprehension:
Look to it well, and say you are well warn'd.
Som. Ay, thou shalt find us ready for thee still;
And know us, by these colors, for thy foes,—
For these my friends, in spite of thee, shall wear.
Plan. And, by my soul, this pale and angry rose,
As cognizance of my blood-drinking hate,
Will I for ever, and my faction, wear,
Until it wither with me to my grave,
Or flourish to the height of my degree.
Suf. Go forward, and be chok'd with thy ambition!
And so, farewell, until I meet thee next. [*Exit.*
Som. Have with thee, Poole.—Farewell, ambitious Richard. [*Exit.*
Plan. How I am brav'd, and must perforce endure it!
War. This blot, that they object against your house,
Shall be wip'd out in the next parliament,
Call'd for the truce of Winchester and Gloster:
And if thou be not then created York,
I will not live to be accounted Warwick.
Meantime, in signal of my love to thee,
Against proud Somerset, and William Poole,
Will I upon thy party wear this rose:
And here I prophesy,—this brawl to-day,
Grown to this faction, in the Temple garden,
Shall send, between the red rose and the white,
A thousand souls to death and deadly night.
Plan. Good master Vernon, I am bound to you,
That you on my behalf would pluck a flower.
Ver. In your behalf still will I wear the same.

Law. And so will I.
Plan. Thanks, gentle sir.
Come, let us four to dinner: I dare say
This quarrel will drink blood another day. [*Exeunt.*

ACT III.

SCENE I—London. *The* Parliament-House.

Flourish. Enter KING HENRY, EXETER, GLOSTER, WARWICK, SOMERSET, *and* SUFFOLK; *the* BISHOP OF WINCHESTER, RICHARD PLANTAGENET, *and others.* GLOSTER *offers to put up a bill;* WINCHESTER *snatches it, and tears it.*

Win. Com'st thou with deep premeditated lines,
With written pamphlets studiously devis'd,
Humphrey of Gloster? If thou canst accuse,
Or aught intend'st to lay unto my charge,
Do it without invention, suddenly;
As I, with sudden and extemporal speech,
Purpose to answer what thou canst object.
Glo. Presumptuous priest! this place commands my patience,
Or thou should'st find thou hast dishonor'd me.
Think not, although in writing I preferr'd
The manner of thy vile outrageous crimes,
That therefore I have forg'd, or am not able
Verbatim to rehearse the method of my pen:
No, prelate; such is thy audacious wickedness,
Thy lewd, pestiferous, and dissentious pranks,
As very infants prattle of thy pride.
Thou art a most pernicious usurer;
Froward by nature, enemy to peace;
And for thy treachery, what's more manifest,—
In that thou laid'st a trap to take my life,
As well at London bridge, as at the Tower?
Beside, I fear me, if thy thoughts were sifted,
The king, thy sovereign, is not quite exempt
From envious malice of thy swelling heart.
Win. Gloster, I do defy thee.—Lords, vouchsafe
To give me hearing what I shall reply.
If I were covetous, ambitious, or perverse,
As he will have me, how am I so poor?
Or how haps it, I seek not to advance
Or raise myself, but keep my wonted calling?
And for dissension, who preferreth peace
More than I do,—except I be provok'd?
No, my good lords, it is not that offends;

It is not that that hath incens'd the duke:
It is, because no one should sway but he;
No one but he should be about the king;
And that engenders thunder in his breast,
And makes him roar these accusations forth.
But he shall know, I am as good—

Glo. As good!

Win. Ay, lordly sir; for what are you, I pray,
But one imperious in another's throne?

Glo. Am I not protector, saucy priest?

Win. And am not I a prelate of the church?

Glo. Yes, as an outlaw in a castle keeps,
And useth it to patronage his theft.

Win. Unreverent Gloster!

Glo. Thou art reverent
Touching thy spiritual function, not thy life.

Win. Rome shall remedy this.

War. Roam thither then.

Som. My lord, it were your duty to forbear.

War. Ay, see the bishop be not overborne.

Som. Methinks my lord should be religious,
And know the office that belongs to such.

War. Methinks his lordship should be humbler;
It fitteth not a prelate so to plead.

Som. Yes, when his holy state is touch'd so near.

War. State holy, or unhallow'd, what of that?
Is not his grace protector to the king?

Plan. [*Aside.*] Plantagenet, I see, must hold his tongue,
Lest it be said, "Speak, sirrah, when you should;
Must your bold verdict enter talk with lords?"
Else would I have a fling at Winchester.

K. Hen. Uncles of Gloster, and of Winchester,
The special watchmen of our English weal,
I would prevail, if prayers might prevail,
To join your hearts in love and amity.
O, what a scandal is it to our crown,
That two such noble peers as ye should jar!
Believe me, lords, my tender years can tell,
Civil dissension is a viperous worm,
That gnaws the bowels of the commonwealth.—

[*A noise within;* "Down with the tawny coats!"

What tumult's this?

War. An uproar, I dare warrant,
Begun through malice of the bishop's men.

[*A noise again within;* "Stones! Stones!"

Enter the Mayor of London, *attended.*

May. O, my good lords, and virtuous Henry,

Pity the city of London, pity us!
The bishop and the duke of Gloster's men,
Forbidden late to carry any weapon,
Have fill'd their pockets full of pebble-stones,
And banding themselves in contrary parts,
Do pelt so fast at one another's pate,
That many have their giddy brains knock'd out:
Our windows are broke down in every street,
And we, for fear, compell'd to shut our shops.

Enter, skirmishing, the serving-men of GLOSTER *and* WINCHESTER, *with bloody pates.*

K. Hen. We charge you, on allegiance to ourself,
To hold your slaught'ring hands, and keep the peace.—
Pray, uncle Gloster, mitigate this strife.
1 *Serv.* Nay, if we be
Forbidden stones, we'll fall to it with our teeth.
2 *Serv.* Do what ye dare, we are as resolute. [*Skirmish again.*
Glo. You of my household, leave this peevish broil,
And set this unaccustom'd fight aside.
3 *Serv.* My lord, we know your grace to be a man
Just and upright; and, for your royal birth,
Inferior to none but to his majesty:
And, ere that we will suffer such a prince,
So kind a father of the commonweal,
To be disgraced by an inkhorn mate,
We, and our wives, and children, all will fight,
And have our bodies slaughter'd by thy foes.
1 *Serv.* Ay, and the very parings of our nails
Shall pitch a field, when we are dead. [*Skirmish again.*
Glo. Stay, stay, I say!
And, if you love me, as you say you do,
Let me persuade you to forbear a while.
K. Hen. O, how this discord doth afflict my soul!—
Can you, my lord of Winchester, behold
My sighs and tears, and will not once relent?
Who should be pitiful, if you be not?
Or who should study to prefer a peace,
If holy churchmen take delight in broils?
War. Yield, my lord protector;—yield, Winchester;—
Except you mean, with obstinate repulse,
To slay your sovereign, and destroy the realm.
You see what mischief, and what murder too,
Hath been enacted through your enmity;
Then, be at peace, except ye thirst for blood.
Win. He shall submit, or I will never yield.
Glo. Compassion on the king commands me stoop;

Or I would see his heart out, ere the priest
Should ever get that privilege of me.
War. Behold, my lord of Winchester, the duke
Hath banish'd moody discontented fury,
As by his smoothed brows it doth appear:
Why look you still so stern, and tragical?
Glo. Here, Winchester, I offer thee my hand.
K. Hen. Fie, uncle Beaufort! I have heard you preach,
That malice was a great and grievous sin;
And will not you maintain the thing you teach,
But prove a chief offender in the same?
War. Sweet king!—the bishop hath a kindly gird.—
For shame, my lord of Winchester, relent!
What, shall a child instruct you what to do?
Win. Well, duke of Gloster, I will yield to thee;
Love for thy love, and hand for hand I give.
Glo. [*Aside.*] Ay, but I fear me, with a hollow heart.—
See here, my friends, and loving countrymen;
This token serveth for a flag of truce,
Betwixt ourselves, and all our followers:
So help me heaven, as I dissemble not!
Win. [*Aside.*] So help me heaven, as I intend it not!
K. Hen. O loving uncle, kind duke of Gloster,
How joyful am I made by this contract!—
Away, my masters! trouble us no more;
But join in friendship, as your lords have done.
[*Exeunt* Mayor, *serving-men*, *&c.*
War. Accept this scroll, most gracious sovereign,
Which in the right of Richard Plantagenet
We do exhibit to your majesty.
Glo. Well urg'd, my lord of Warwick:—for, sweet prince,
An if your grace mark every circumstance,
You have great reason to do Richard right.
K. Hen. And those circumstances, uncle, are of force:
Therefore, my loving lords, our pleasure is,
That Richard be restorèd to his blood.
War. Let Richard be restorèd to his blood;
So shall his father's wrongs be recompens'd.
Win. As will the rest, so willeth Winchester.
K. Hen. If Richard will be true, not that alone,
But all the whole inheritance I give,
That doth belong unto the house of York,
From whence you spring by lineal descent.
Plan. Thy humble servant vows obedience,
And humble service, till the point of death.
K. Hen. Stoop, then, and set your knee against my foot;
And, in reguerdon of that duty done,
I girt thee with the valiant sword of York:

Rise, Richard, like a true Plantagenet,
And rise created princely duke of York.
Plan. And so thrive Richard as thy foes may fall!
And as my duty springs, so perish they
That grudge one thought against your majesty!
All. Welcome, high prince, the mighty duke of York!
Som. [*Aside.*] Perish, base prince, ignoble duke of York!
Glo. Now will it best avail your majesty,
To cross the seas, and to be crown'd in France.
The presence of a king engenders love
Amongst his subjects, and his loyal friends,
As it disanimates his enemies.
K. Hen. When Gloster says the word, king Henry goes;
For friendly counsel cuts off many foes.
Glo. Your ships already are in readiness.
[*Flourish. Exeunt all except* EXETER.
Exe. Ay, we may march in England, or in France,
Not seeing what is likely to ensue.
And now I fear that fatal prophecy,
Which, in the time of Henry, nam'd the fifth,
Was in the mouth of every sucking babe,—
That Henry born at Monmouth, should win all;
And Henry born at Windsor, should lose all:
Which is so plain, that Exeter doth wish
His days may finish ere the hapless time. [*Exit.*

SCENE II.—France. *Before* Rouen.

Enter LA PUCELLE *disguised, and* Soldiers *dressed like countrymen, with sacks upon their backs.*

Puc. These are the city gates, the gates of Rouen,
Through which our policy must make a breach:
Take heed, be wary how you place your words;
Talk like the vulgar sort of market-men,
That come to gather money for their corn.
If we have entrance, (as I hope we shall)
And that we find the slothful watch but weak,
I'll by a sign give notice to our friends,
That Charles the Dauphin may encounter them.
1 *Sold.* Our sacks shall be a mean to sack the city,
And we be lords and rulers over Rouen;
Therefore we'll knock. [*Knocks.*
Guard. [*Within.*] *Qui est là?*
Puc. Paisans, pauvres gens de France,—
Poor market-folks, that come to sell their corn.
Guard. [*Opening the gates.*] Enter, go in; the market-bell is rung.

Puc. Now, Rouen, I'll shake thy bulwarks to the ground.
[LA PUCELLE, *&c. enter the city.*

Enter CHARLES, ORLEANS, ALENÇON, *and forces.*

Char. Saint Dennis bless this happy stratagem!
And once again we'll sleep secure in Rouen.
Orl. Here enter'd Pucelle, and her practisants;
Now she is there, how will she specify
Where is the best and safest passage in?
Alen. By thrusting out a torch from yonder tower;
Which, once discern'd, shows that her meaning is,—
No way to that, for weakness, which she enter'd.

Enter LA PUCELLE *on a battlement, holding out a torch burning.*

Puc. Behold, this is the happy wedding torch,
That joineth Rouen unto her countrymen,
But burning fatal to the Talbotites!
Orl. See, noble Charles, the beacon of our friend;
The burning torch in yonder turret stands.
Char. Now shine it like a comet of revenge,
A prophet to the fall of all our foes!
Alen. Defer no time, delays have dangerous ends;
Enter, and cry "The Dauphin!" presently,
And then do execution on the watch.
[*They enter the town. Exit* LA PUCELLE *from the battlement.*

Alarum. Enter, from the town, TALBOT, *and English* Soldiers.

Tal. France, thou shalt rue this treason with thy tears,
If Talbot but survive thy treachery.—
Pucelle, that witch, that cursed sorceress,
Hath wrought this wicked mischief unawares,
That hardly we escap'd the pride of France.
[*Exeunt into the town.*

Alarum: Excursions. Enter, from the town, BEDFORD, *brought in sick in a chair, with* TALBOT, BURGUNDY, *and the English forces. Then, enter on the walls,* LA PUCELLE, CHARLES, ORLEANS, ALENÇON, *and others.*

Puc. Good morrow, gallants! Want ye corn for bread?
I think the duke of Burgundy will fast,
Before he'll buy again at such a rate:
'Twas full of darnel;—do you like the taste?
Bur. Scoff on, vile fiend and shameless wanton!
I trust ere long to choke thee with thine own,
And make thee curse the harvest of that corn.
Char. Your grace may starve, perhaps, before that time.

Bed. O, let no words, but deeds, revenge this treason!
Puc. What will you do, good grey-beard? break a lance,
And run a tilt at death within a chair?
Tal. Foul fiend of France, and hag of all despite,
Becomes it thee to taunt his valiant age,
And twit with cowardice a man half dead?
Damsel, I'll have a bout with you again,
Or else let Talbot perish with this shame.
Puc. Are you so hot, sir?—Yet, Pucelle, hold thy peace;
If Talbot do but thunder, rain will follow.—
[TALBOT, *and the rest, consult together.*
Heaven speed the parliament! who shall be the speaker?
Tal. Dare ye come forth, and meet us in the field?
Puc. Belike your lordship takes us, then, for fools
To try if that our own be ours, or no.
Tal. I speak not to that railing Hecate,
But unto thee, Alençon, and the rest;
Will ye, like soldiers, come and fight it out?
Alen. Signior, no.
Tal. Signior, hang!—base muleteers of France!
Like peasant foot-boys do they keep the walls,
And dare not take up arms like gentlemen.
Puc. Away, captains! let's get us from the walls;
For Talbot means no goodness, by his looks.—
Heaven be wi' you, my lord! we came but to tell you
That we are here. [*Exeunt* LA PUCELLE, *&c. from the walls.*
Tal. And there will we be too, ere it be long,
Or else reproach be Talbot's greatest fame!—
Vow, Burgundy, by honor of thy house,
Either to get the town again, or die;
And I,—as sure as English Henry lives,
And as his father here was conqueror;
As sure as in this late-betrayèd town
Great Cœur-de-lion's heart was buried,—
So sure I swear to get the town or die.
Bur. My vows are equal partners with thy vows.
Tal. But, ere we go, regard this dying prince,
The valiant duke of Bedford.—Come, my lord,
We will bestow you in some better place,
Fitter for sickness, and for crazy age.
Bed. Lord Talbot, do not so dishonor me:
Here will I sit before the walls of Rouen,
And will be partner of your weal or woe.
Bur. Courageous Bedford, let us now persuade you.
Bed. Not to be gone from hence; for once I read,
That stout Pendragon, in his litter, sick,
Came to the field, and vanquishèd his foes:

Methinks I should revive the soldiers' hearts,
Because I ever found them as myself.
Tal. Undaunted spirit in a dying breast!—
Then, be it so:—heavens keep old Bedford safe!—
And now no more ado, brave Burgundy,
But gather we our forces out of hand,
And set upon our boasting enemy.
[*Exeunt into the town,* BURGUNDY, TALBOT, *and forces, leaving* BEDFORD, *and others.*

Alarum: Excursions; in one of which, enter Sir JOHN FASTOLFE, *and a* Captain.

Cap. Whither away, Sir John Fastolfe, in such haste?
Fast. Whither away! to save myself by flight:
We are like to have the overthrow again.
Cap. What! will you fly, and leave lord Talbot?
Fast. Ay,
All the Talbots in the world, to save my life. [*Exit.*
Cap. Cowardly knight! ill fortune follow thee!
[*Exit into the town.*

Retreat: Excursions. Re-enter, from the town, LA PUCELLE, ALENÇON, CHARLES, *&c., and exeunt, flying.*

Bed. Now, quiet soul, depart when heaven please,
For I have seen our enemies' overthrow.
What is the trust or strength of foolish man?
They, that of late were daring with their scoffs,
Are glad and fain by flight to save themselves.
[*Dies, and is carried off in his chair.*

Alarum. Re-enter TALBOT, BURGUNDY, *and others.*

Tal. Lost, and recover'd in a day again!
This is a double honor, Burgundy:
Yet heavens have glory for this victory!
Bur. Warlike and martial Talbot, Burgundy
Enshrines thee in his heart; and there erects
Thy noble deeds, as valor's monument.
Tal. Thanks, gentle duke. But where is Pucelle now?
I think her old familiar is asleep:
Rouen hangs her head for grief,
That such a valiant company are fled.
Now we will take some order in the town,
Placing therein some expert officers;
And then depart to Paris to the king,
For there young Henry, with his nobles, lies.
Bur. What wills lord Talbot, pleaseth Burgundy.
Tal. But yet, before we go, let's not forget
The noble duke of Bedford, late deceas'd,

But see his exequies fulfill'd in Rouen:
A braver soldier never couchèd lance,
A gentler heart did never sway in courts;
But kings and mightiest potentates must die,
For that's the end of human misery. [*Exeunt.*

SCENE III.—*The Plains near* Rouen.

Enter CHARLES, ORLEANS, ALENÇON, LA PUCELLE, *and forces.*

Puc. Dismay not, princes, at this accident,
Nor grieve that Rouen is so recovered:
Care is no cure, but rather corrosive,
For things that are not to be remedied.
Let frantic Talbot triumph for a while,
And like a peacock sweep along his tail;
We'll pull his plumes, and take away his train,
If Dauphin and the rest will be but rul'd.
Char. We have been guided by thee hitherto,
And of thy cunning had no diffidence:
One sudden foil shall never breed distrust.
Orl. Search out thy wit for secret policies,
And we will make thee famous through the world.
Alen. We'll set thy statue in some holy place,
And have thee reverenc'd like a blessed saint:
Employ thee, then, sweet virgin, for our good.
Puc. Then thus it must be; this doth Joan devise:
By fair persuasions, mix'd with sugar'd words,
We will entice the duke of Burgundy
To leave the Talbot, and to follow us.
Char. Ay, marry, sweeting, if we could do that,
France were no place for Henry's warriors;
Nor should that nation boast it so with us,
But be extirpèd from our provinces.
Alen. For ever should they be expuls'd from France,
And not have title of an earldom here.
Puc. Your honors shall perceive how I will work,
To bring this matter to the wishèd end. [*Drums heard.*
Hark! by the sound of drum you may perceive
Their powers are marching unto Paris-ward.

An English march. Enter, and pass over, TALBOT *and his forces.*

There goes the Talbot, with his colors spread,
And all the troops of English after him.

A French march. Enter the DUKE OF BURGUNDY *and his forces.*

Now in the rearward comes the duke and his:

Fortune in favor makes him lag behind.
Summon a parley; we will talk with him.
[*Trumpets sound a parley.*
Char. A parley with the duke of Burgundy!
Bur. Who craves a parley with the Burgundy?
Puc. The princely Charles of France, thy countryman.
Bur. What say'st thou, Charles? for I am marching hence.
Char. Speak, Pucelle, and enchant him with thy words.
Puc. Brave Burgundy, undoubted hope of France!
Stay, let thy humble handmaid speak to thee.
Bur. Speak on; but be not over-tedious.
Puc. Look on thy country, look on fertile France,
And see the cities and the towns defac'd
By wasting ruin of the cruel foe!
As looks the mother on her lowly babe,
When death doth close his tender dying eyes,
See, see, the pining malady of France;
Behold the wounds, the most unnatural wounds,
Which thou thyself hast given her woful breast!
O, turn thy edgèd sword another way;
Strike those that hurt, and hurt not those that help!
One drop of blood, drawn from thy country's bosom,
Should grieve thee more than streams of foreign gore:
Return thee, therefore, with a flood of tears,
And wash away thy country's stained spots.
Bur. Either she hath bewitch'd me with her words,
Or nature makes me suddenly relent.
Puc. Besides, all French and France exclaims on thee,
Doubting thy birth and lawful progeny.
Whom join'st thou with, but with a lordly nation,
That will not trust thee but for profit's sake?
When Talbot hath set footing once in France,
And fashion'd thee that instrument of ill,
Who then but English Henry will be lord,
And thou be thrust out, like a fugitive?
Call we to mind,—and mark but this for proof,
Was not the duke of Orleans thy foe?
And was he not in England prisoner?
But when they heard he was thine enemy,
They set him free, without his ransom paid,
In spite of Burgundy and all his friends.
See, then, thou fight'st against thy countrymen,
And join'st with them will be thy slaughter-men.
Come, come, return; return, thou wand'ring lord;
Charles, and the rest, will take thee in their arms.
Bur. I am vanquished; these haughty words of hers
Have batter'd me like roaring cannon-shot,
And made me almost yield upon my knees.

Forgi.e me, country, and sweet countrymen!
And, lords, accept this hearty kind embrace:
My forces and my power of men are yours:—
So, farewell, Talbot; I'll no longer trust thee.
Puc. Done like a Frenchman,—turn, and turn again!
Char. Welcome, brave duke! thy friendship makes us fresh.
Orl. And doth beget new courage in our breasts.
Alen. Pucelle hath bravely played her part in this,
And doth deserve a coronet of gold.
Char. Now let us on, my lords, and join our powers;
And seek how we may prejudice the foe. [*Exeunt.*

SCENE IV.—Paris. *A Room in the Palace.*

Enter KING HENRY, GLOSTER, *and other* Lords, VERNON, BASSET, *&c.* *To them* TALBOT, *and some of his officers.*

Tal. My gracious prince, and honorable peers,
Hearing of your arrival in this realm,
I have a while given truce unto my wars,
To do my duty to my sovereign:
In sign whereof, this arm,—that hath reclaim'd
To your obedience fifty fortresses,
Twelve cities, and seven walled towns of strength,
Beside five hundred prisoners of esteem,—
Lets fall his sword before your highness' feet,
And with submissive loyalty of heart,
Ascribes the glory of his conquest got,
First to high heaven, and next unto your grace.
K. Hen. Is this the lord Talbot, uncle Gloster,
That hath so long been resident in France?
Glo. Yes, if it please your majesty, my liege.
K. Hen. Welcome, brave captain, and victorious lord!
When I was young, (as yet I am not old)
I do remember how my father said,
A stouter champion never handled sword.
Long since we were resolvèd of your truth,
Your faithful service, and your toil in war;
Yet never have you tasted our reward,
Or been reguerdon'd with so much as thanks,
Because, till now, we never saw your face:
Therefore, stand up; and, for these good deserts,
We here create you earl of Shrewsbury;
And in our coronation take your place. [*Flourish. Exeunt.*

ACT IV.

SCENE I.—Paris. *A Room of State.*

Enter KING HENRY, GLOSTER, EXETER, YORK, SUFFOLK, SOMERSET, WINCHESTER, WARWICK, TALBOT, *the* Governor of Paris, *and others.*

Glo. Lord bishop, set the crown upon his head.
Win. God save king Henry, of that name the sixth!
Glo. Now governor of Paris, take your oath,— [Governor *kneels.*
That you elect no other king but him;
Esteem none friends, but such as are his friends,
And none your foes, but such as shall pretend
Malicious practices against his state:
This shall ye do, so help you righteous heaven.
[*Exeunt* Governor *and his train.*

Enter Sir JOHN FASTOLFE.

Fast. My gracious sovereign, as I rode from Calais,
To haste unto your coronation,
A letter was deliver'd to my hands,
Writ to your grace from the duke of Burgundy.
Tal. Shame to the duke of Burgundy and thee!
I vow'd, base knight, when I did meet thee next,
To tear the garter from thy craven's leg, [*Plucking it off.*
(Which I have done,) because unworthily
Thou wast installèd in that high degree.—
Pardon me, princely Henry, and the rest:
This dastard, at the battle of Patay,
When but in all I was six thousand strong,
And that the French were almost ten to one,—
Before we met, or that a stroke was given,
Like to a trusty squire, did run away:
In which assault we lost twelve hundred men;
Myself, and divers gentlemen beside,
Were there surpris'd, and taken prisoners.
Then judge, great lords, if I have done amiss;
Or whether that such cowards ought to wear
This ornament of knighthood, yea, or no?
Glo. To say the truth, this fact was infamous,
And ill beseeming any common man,
Much more a knight, a captain, and a leader.
Tal. When first this order was ordain'd, my lords,
Knights of the garter were of noble birth,
Valiant and virtuous, full of haughty courage,

Such as were grown to credit by the wars;
Not fearing death, nor shrinking for distress,
But always resolute in most extremes.
He, then, that is not furnish'd in this sort,
Doth but usurp the sacred name of knight,
Profaning this most honorable order;
And should (if I were worthy to be judge)
Be quite degraded, like a hedge-born swain
That doth presume to boast of gentle blood.

K. Hen. Stain to thy countrymen! thou hear'st thy doom:
Be packing, therefore, thou that wast a knight;
Henceforth we banish thee on pain of death.— [*Exit* FASTOLFE.
And now, my lord protector, view the letter
Sent from our uncle duke of Burgundy.

Glo. [*Viewing the superscription.*] What means his grace, he hath chang'd his style?
No more but, plain and bluntly,—"To the king?
Hath he forgot he is his sovereign?
Or doth this churlish superscription
Pretend some alteration in good will?
What's here? [*Reads.*] "I have, upon especial cause,
Mov'd with compassion of my country's wreck,
Together with the pitiful complaints
Of such as your oppression feeds upon,—
Forsaken your pernicious faction,
And join'd with Charles, the rightful king of France."
O, monstrous treachery! Can this be so,—
That in alliance, amity, and oaths,
There should be found such false dissembling guile?

K. Hen. What! doth my uncle Burgundy revolt?

Glo. He doth, my lord; and is become your foe.

K. Hen. Is that the worst this letter doth contain?

Glo. It is the worst, and all, my lord, he writes.

K. Hen. Why then, lord Talbot, there, shall talk with him,
And give him chastisement for this abuse:—
How say you, my lord? are you not content?

Tal. Content, my liege! Yes, but that I am prevented,
I should have begg'd I might have been employ'd.

K. Hen. Then gather strength, and march unto him straight:
Let him perceive how ill we brook his treason,
And what offence it is to flout his friends.

Tal. I go, my lord; in heart desiring still
You may behold confusion of your foes. [*Exit.*

Enter VERNON *and* BASSET.

Ver. Grant me the combat, gracious sovereign!

Bas. And me, my lord, grant me the combat too!

York. This is my servant: hear him, noble prince!
Som. And this is mine: sweet Henry, favor him!
K. Hen. Be patient, lords; and give them leave to speak.—
Say, gentlemen, what makes you thus exclaim?
And wherefore crave you combat? or with whom?
Ver. With him, my lord; for he hath done me wrong.
Bas. And I with him; for he hath done me wrong.
K. Hen. What is that wrong whereof you both complain?
First let me know, and then I'll answer you.
Bas. Crossing the sea from England into France,
This fellow, here, with envious carping tongue,
Upbraided me about the rose I wear;
Saying, the sanguine color of the leaves
Did represent my master's blushing cheeks,
When stubbornly he did repugn the truth
About a certain question in the law,
Argu'd betwixt the duke of York and him;
With other vile and ignominious terms:
In confutation of which rude reproach,
And in defence of my lord's worthiness,
I crave the benefit of law of arms.
Ver. And that is my petition, noble lord:
For though he seem, with forgèd quaint conceit,
To set a gloss upon his bold intent,
Yet know, my lord, I was provok'd by him;
And he first took exceptions at this badge,
Pronouncing, that the paleness of this flower
Bewray'd the faintness of my master's heart.
York. Will not this malice, Somerset, be left?
Som. Your private grudge, my lord of York, will out,
Though ne'er so cunningly you smother it.
K. Hen. Good lord, what madness rules in brain-sick men,
When, for so slight and frivolous a cause,
Such factious emulations shall arise!—
Good cousins both, of York and Somerset,
Quiet yourselves, I pray, and be at peace.
York. Let this dissension first be tried by fight,
And then your highness shall command a peace.
Som. The quarrel toucheth none but us alone;
Betwixt ourselves let us decide it, then.
York. There is my pledge; accept it, Somerset.
Ver. Nay, let it rest where it began at first.
Bas. Confirm it so, mine honorable lord.
Glo. Confirm it so! Confounded be your strife!
And perish ye, with your audacious prate!
Presumptuous vassals, are you not asham'd,
With this immodest clamorous outrage
To trouble and disturb the king and us?—

And you, my lords,—methinks you do not well
To bear with their perverse objections;
Much less to take occasion from their mouths,
To raise a mutiny betwixt yourselves:
Let me persuade you take a better course.
Exe. It grieves his highness:—good my lords, be friends.
K. Hen. Come hither, you that would be combatants:
Henceforth I charge you, as you love our favor,
Quite to forget this quarrel and the cause.—
And you, my lords, remember where we are;
In France, amongst a fickle wavering nation:
If they perceive dissension in our looks,
And that within ourselves we disagree,
How will their grudging stomachs be provok'd
To wilful disobedience, and rebel?
Beside, what infamy will there arise,
When foreign princes shall be certified,
That for a toy, a thing of no regard,
King Henry's peers, and chief nobility,
Destroy'd themselves, and lost the realm of France
O, think upon the conquest of my father;
My tender years; and let us not forego
That for a trifle, that was bought with blood!
Let me be umpire in this doubtful strife.
I see no reason, if I wear this rose, [*Putting on a red rose.*
That any one should therefore be suspicious
I more incline to Somerset, than York:
Both are my kinsmen, and I love them both:
Therefore, as we hither came in peace,
So let us still continue peace and love.—
Cousin of York, we institute your grace
To be our regent in these parts of France:—
And, good my lord of Somerset, unite
Your troops of horsemen with his bands of foot;
And like true subjects, sons of your progenitors,
Go cheerfully together, and digest
Your angry choler on your enemies.
Ourself, my lord protector, and the rest,
After some respite, will return to Calais;
From thence to England; where I hope ere long
To be presented by your victories,
With Charles, Alençon, and that traitorous rout.
[*Flourish. Exeunt* KING HENRY, GLO. SOM. WIN. SUF. *and* BASSET.
War. My lord of York, I promise you, the king
Prettily, methought, did play the orator.
York. And so he did; but yet I like it no
In that he wears the badge of Somerset.

War. Tush! that was but his fancy, blame him not;
I dare presume, sweet prince, he thought no harm.
York. An if I wist he did,—But let it rest;
Other affairs must now be managed.
[*Exeunt* YORK, WARWICK, *and* VERNON.
Exe. Well didst thou, Richard, to suppress thy voice;
For, had the passions of thy heart burst out,
I fear we should have seen decipher'd there,
More rancorous spite, more furious raging broils,
Than yet can be imagin'd or suppos'd.
But howsoe'er, no simple man that sees
This jarring discord of nobility,
This shouldering of each other in the court,
This factious bandying of their favorites,
But that it doth presage some ill event.
'Tis much, when sceptres are in children's hands;
But more, when envy breeds unkind division:
There comes the ruin, there begins confusion. [*Exit.*

SCENE III.—*Plains in* Gascony.

Enter YORK, *with forces; to him, a* Messenger.

York. Are not the speedy scouts return'd again,
That dogg'd the mighty army of the Dauphin?
Mess. They are return'd, my lord; and give it out,
That he is march'd to Bourdeaux with his power,
To fight with Talbot: as he march'd along,
By your espials were discovered
Two mightier troops than that the Dauphin led;
Which join'd with him, and made their march for Bourdeaux.
York. A plague upon that villain Somerset,
That thus delays my promisèd supply
Of horsemen, that were levied for this siege!
Renownèd Talbot doth expect my aid;
And I am louted by a traitor villain,
And cannot help the noble chevalier:
God comfort him in this necessity!
If he miscarry, farewell wars in France.

Enter Sir WILLIAM LUCY.

Lucy. Thou princely leader of our English strength,
Never so needful on the earth of France,
Spur to the rescue of the noble Talbot,
Who now is girdled with a waist of iron,
And hemm'd about with grim destruction.
To Bourdeaux, warlike duke! to Bourdeaux, York!
Else, farewell Talbot, France, and England's honor.

York. O heaven, that Somerset,—who in proud heart
Doth stop my cornets,*—were in Talbot's place!
So should we save a valiant gentleman,
By forfeiting a traitor and a coward.
Mad ire, and wrathful fury, make me weep
That thus we die, while remiss traitors sleep.
Lucy. O, send some succor to the distress'd lord!
York. He dies, we lose; I break my warlike word;
We mourn, France smiles; we lose, they daily get;
All 'long of this vile traitor Somerset.
Lucy. Then heaven take mercy on brave Talbot's soul
And on his son, young John; whom two hours since
I met in travel toward his warlike father.
This seven years did not Talbot see his son;
And now they meet where both their lives are done.
York. Alas, what joy shall noble Talbot have,
To bid his young son welcome to his grave?
Away! vexation almost stops my breath,
That sunder'd friends greet in the hour of death.—
Lucy, farewell: no more my fortune can,
But curse the cause I cannot aid the man.—
Maine, Blois, Poictiers, and Tours, are won away,
'Long all of Somerset and his delay. [*Exit with forces.*
Lucy. Thus, while the vulture of sedition
Feeds in the bosom of such great commanders,
Sleeping neglection doth betray to loss
The conquest of our scarce-cold conqueror,
That ever-living man of memory,
Henry the fifth:—whiles they each other cross,
Lives, honors, lands, and all, hurry to loss. [*Exit.*

SCENE V.—*The English Camp near* Bourdeaux.

Enter TALBOT *and* JOHN *his Son.*

Tal. O young John Talbot! I did send for thee
To tutor thee in stratagems of war,
That Talbot's name might be in thee reviv'd,
When sapless age, and weak unable limbs,
Should bring thy father to his drooping chair.
But,—O, malignant and ill-boding stars!—
Now thou art come unto a feast of death,
A terrible and unavoided danger:
Therefore, dear boy, mount on my swiftest horse;
And I'll direct thee how thou shalt escape,
By sudden flight: come, dally not, begone.

* *Cornets*—cavalry soldiers.

John. Is my name Talbot? and am I your son!
And shall I fly? O, if you love my mother,
Dishonor not her honorable name;
The world will say he is not Talbot's blood,
That basely fled when noble Talbot stood.
Tal. Fly to revenge my death, if I be slain.
John. He that flies so will ne'er return again.
Tal. If we both stay, we both are sure to die.
John. Then let me stay; and, father, do you fly;
Your loss is great, so your regard should be;
My worth unknown, no loss is known in me.
Upon my death the French can little boast;
In yours they will, in you all hopes are lost.
Flight cannot stain the honor you have won;
But mine it will, that no exploit have done:
You fled for vantage, every one will swear;
But if I bow, they'll say it was for fear.
There is no hope that ever I will stay,
If, the first hour, I shrink and run away.
Here, on my knee, I beg mortality,
Rather than life preserv'd with infamy.
Tal. Shall all thy mother's hopes lie in one tomb?
Upon my blessing, I command thee go.
John. To fight I will, but not to fly the foe.
Tal. Part of thy father may be sav'd in thee.
John. No part of him but will be shame in me.
Tal. Thou never hadst renown, nor canst not lose it.
John. Yes, your renownèd name: shall flight abuse it?
Tal. Thy father's charge shall clear thee from that stain.
John. You cannot witness for me, being slain.
If death be so apparent, then both fly.
Tal. And leave my followers here, to fight, and die?
My age was never tainted with such shame.
John. And shall my youth be guilty of such blame?
No more can I be sever'd from your side,
Than can yourself yourself in twain divide:
Stay, go, do what you will, the like do I;
For live I will not, if my father die.
Tal. Then here I take my leave of thee, fair son,
Born to eclipse thy life this afternoon.
Come, side by side together live and die;
And soul with soul from France to heaven fly. [*Exeunt.*

SCENE VII.—*Another Part of the Field.*

Alarum. Excursions. Enter TALBOT, *wounded, supported by a* Servant.

Tal. Where is my other life?—mine own is gone;—
O, where's young Talbot? where is valiant John?—
Triumphant death, smear'd with captivity,
Young Talbot's valor makes me smile at thee.—
When he perceiv'd me shrink, and on my knee,
His bloody sword he brandish'd over me
And, like a hungry lion, did commence
Rough deeds of rage, and stern impatience;
But when my angry guardant stood alone,
Tendering my ruin, and assail'd of none,
Dizzy-ey'd fury, and great rage of heart,
Suddenly made him from my side to start
Into the clust'ring battle of the French;
And in that sea of blood my boy did drench
His overmounting spirit; and there died
My Icarus, my blossom, in his pride.
Serv. O, my dear lord, lo, where your son is borne!

Enter Soldiers, *bearing the body of* JOHN TALBOT.

Tal. Thou antick, death, which laugh'st us here to scorn,
Anon, from thy insulting tyranny,
Coupled in bonds of perpetuity,
Two Talbots wingèd through the lither sky,
In thy despite, shall 'scape mortality.—
O thou, whose wounds become hard-favor'd death,
Speak to thy father, ere thou yield thy breath!
Brave death by speaking, whether he will or no;
Imagine him a Frenchman, and thy foe.—
Poor boy! he smiles, methinks, as who should say,
Had death been French, then death hath died to-day.—
Come, come, and lay him in his father's arms:
My spirit can no longer bear these harms.
Soldiers, adieu! I have what I would have,
Now my old arms are young John Talbot's grave. [*Dies.*

Alarums. Exeunt Soldiers *and* Servant, *leaving the two bodies. Enter* CHARLES, ALENÇON, BURGUNDY, ORLEANS, LA PUCELLE, *and forces.*

Char. Had York and Somerset brought rescue in,
We should have found a bloody day of this.
Orl. How the young whelp of Talbot's, raging wood,
Did flesh his puny sword in Frenchmen's blood!
Puc. Once I encounter'd him, and thus I said,

"Thou maiden youth, be vanquish'd by a maid:"
But, with a proud majestical high scorn,
He answered thus,—"Young Talbot was not born
To be the pillage of a giglot wench:"
So, rushing in the bowels of the French,
He left me proudly, as unworthy fight.
Bur. Doubtless, he would have made a noble knight:—
See, where he lies inhersed in the arms
Of the most bloody nurser of his harms!
Orl. Hew them to pieces, hack their bones asunder,
Whose life was England's glory, Gallia's wonder.
Char. O, no, forbear! for that which we have fled
During the life, let us not wrong it dead.

Enter Sir William Lucy, *attended; a French* Herald *preceding.*

Lucy. Herald, conduct me to the Dauphin's tent,
To know who hath obtain'd the glory of the day.
Char. On what submissive message art thou sent?
Lucy. Submission, Dauphin! 'tis a mere French word;
We English warriors wot not what it means.
I come to know what prisoners thou hast ta'en,
And to survey the bodies of the dead.
Char. For prisoners ask'st thou?
But tell me whom thou seek'st.
Lucy. Where is the great Alcides of the field,
Valiant lord Talbot, earl of Shrewsbury?
Puc. Him, that thou magnifiest with these titles,
Stinking, and fly-blown, lies here at our feet.
Lucy. Is Talbot slain,—the Frenchmen's only scourge,
Your kingdom's terror and black Nemesis?
O, were mine eye-balls into bullets turn'd,
That I, in rage, might shoot them at your faces!
O, that I could but call these dead to life!
It were enough to fright the realm of France:
Were but his picture left among you here,
It would amaze the proudest of you all.
Give me their bodies, that I may bear them hence,
And give them burial as beseems their worth.
Puc. I think this upstart is old Talbot's ghost,
He speaks with such a proud commanding spirit.
Char. Go, take their bodies hence.
Lucy. I'll bear them hence:
But from their ashes shall be rear'd
A phœnix that shall make all France afeard.
Char. So we be rid of them, do with 'em what thou wilt.—
And now to Paris, in this conquering vein:
All will be ours, now bloody Talbot's slain. [*Exeunt.*

ACT V.

SCENE I.—London. *A Room in the Palace.*

Enter KING HENRY, GLOSTER, *and* EXETER.

K. Hen. Have you perus'd the letters from the pope,
The emperor, and the earl of Armagnac?
Glo. I have, my lord; and their intent is this:—
They humbly sue unto your excellence,
To have a godly peace concluded of,
Between the realms of England and of France.
K. Hen. How doth your grace affect their motion?
Glo. Well, my good lord; and as the only means
To stop effusion of our Christian blood,
And 'stablish quietness on every side.
K. Hen. Ay, marry, uncle; for I always thought,
It was both impious and unnatural,
That such immanity* and bloody strife
Should reign among professors of one faith.
Glo. Beside, my lord, the sooner to effect
And surer bind this knot of amity,
The earl of Armagnac,—near knit to Charles,
A man of great authority in France,—
Proffers his only daughter to your grace
In marriage, with a large and sumptuous dowry.
K. Hen. Marriage, uncle! alas, my years are young;
And fitter is my study and my books.
Yet, call th' embassadors; and, as you please,
So let them have their answers every one:
I shall be well content with any choice,
Tends to God's glory, and my country's weal.

Enter a Legate, *and two* Embassadors, *with* WINCHESTER, *now* CARDINAL BEAUFORT, *and habited accordingly.*

Exe. [*Aside.*] What, is my lord of Winchester install'd,
And call'd unto a cardinal's degree?
Then, I perceive that will be verified,
Henry the fifth did sometime prophesy,
"If once he come to be a cardinal,
He'll make his cap co-equal with the crown."
K. Hen. My lords embassadors, your several suits
Have been consider'd and debated on.
Your purpose is both good and reasonable;
And therefore are we certainly resolv'd
To draw conditions of a friendly peace;

* *Immanity*—savageness, barbarity.

Which, by my lord of Winchester, we mean
Shall be transported presently to France.

Glo. And for the proffer of my lord, your master,
I have inform'd his highness so at large,
As,—liking of the lady's virtuous gifts,
Her beauty, and the value of her dower,—
He doth intend she shall be England's queen.

K. Hen. [*To the* Emb.] In argument and proof of which contract,
Bear her this jewel, pledge of my affection.—
And so, my lord protector, see them guarded,
And safely brought to Dover; where, inshipp'd,
Commit them to the fortune of the sea.

[*Exeunt* KING HENRY *and train;* GLOSTER, EXETER, *and* Embassadors.

Win. Now, Winchester will not submit, I trow,
Or be inferior to the proudest peer.
Humphrey of Gloster, thou shalt well perceive,
That, neither in birth, or for authority,
The bishop will be overborne by thee:
I'll either make thee stoop, and bend thy knee,
Or sack this country with a mutiny. [*Exit*

SCENE III.—France. *Before* Angiers.

Alarum. Excursions. Enter LA PUCELLE.

Puc. The regent conquers, and the Frenchmen fly.—
Now help, ye charming spells and periapts;*
And ye choice spirits that admonish me,
And give me signs of future accidents,— [*Thunder.*
You speedy helpers, that are substitutes
Under the lordly monarch of the north,
Appear, and aid me in this enterprise!

Enter Fiends.

This speedy and quick appearance argues proof
Of your accustom'd diligence to me.
Now, ye familiar spirits, that are cull'd
Out of the powerful legions under earth,
Help me this once, that France may get the field.—

[*They walk about, and speak not*

O, hold me not with silence over-long.
Where I was wont to feed you with my blood,
I'll lop a member off, and give it you,
In earnest of a farther benefit;
So you do condescend to help me now.—

[*They hang their heads.*

Periapt—an amulet.

No hope to have redress?—My body shall
Pay recompense, if you will grant my suit.—
[*They shake their heads.*
Cannot my body, nor blood-sacrifice,
Entreat you to your wonted fartherance?
Then take my soul,—my body, soul, and all,
Before that England give the French the foil. [*They depart.*
See, they forsake me! Now the time is come,
That France must vail her lofty-plumèd crest,
And let her head fall into England's lap.
My ancient incantations are too weak,
And fiends too strong for me to buckle with:
Now, France, thy glory droopeth to the dust. [*Exit.*

Alarum. Enter French and English, fighting; LA PUCELLE *and* YORK *fight hand to hand:* LA PUCELLE *is taken. The French fly.*

York. Damsel of France, I think I have you fast:
Unchain your spirits now with spelling charms,
And try if they can gain your liberty.—
See, how the ugly witch doth bend her brows,
As if, with Circe, she would change my shape.
Puc. Chang'd to a worser shape thou canst not be.
York. O, Charles the Dauphin is a proper man;
No shape but his can please your dainty eye.
Puc. A plaguing mischief light on Charles, and thee!
And may ye both be suddenly surpris'd
By bloody hands, in sleeping on your beds!
York. Fell banning hag, enchantress, hold thy tongue!
Puc. I pr'ythee, give me leave to curse awhile.
York. Curse, miscreant, when thou comest to the stake.
[*Exeunt.*

Alarum. Enter SUFFOLK, *leading in Lady* MARGARET.

Suf. Be what thou wilt, thou art my prisoner. [*Gazes on her.*
O fairest beauty, do not fear, nor fly,
For I will touch thee but with reverent hands
And lay them gently on thy tender side.
Who art thou? say, that I may honor thee.
Mar. Margaret my name, and daughter to a king,
The king of Naples,—whosoe'er thou art.
Suf. An earl I am, and Suffolk am I call'd.
Be not offended, nature's miracle,
Thou art allotted to be ta'en by me:
So doth the swan her downy cygnets save,
Keeping them prisoners underneath her wings.
Yet if this servile usage once offend,

Go, and be free again, as Suffolk's friend.

[*She turns away as going.*

O, stay!—I have no power to let her pass;
My hand would free her, but my heart says—no.
As plays the sun upon the glassy streams,
Twinkling another counterfeited beam,
So seems this gorgeous beauty to mine eyes.
Fain would I woo her, yet I dare not speak:
I'll call for pen and ink, and write my mind:—
Fie, De-la-Poole! disable not thyself;
Hast not a tongue? is she not here thy prisoner?
Wilt thou be daunted at a woman's sight?
Ay, beauty's princely majesty is such,
Confounds the tongue, and makes the senses rough.
Mar. Say, earl of Suffolk,—if thy name be so,—
What ransom must I pay before I pass?
For, I perceive, I am thy prisoner.
Suf. [*Aside.*] How canst thou tell she will deny thy suit,
Before thou make a trial of her love?
Mar. Why speak'st thou not? what ransom must I pay?
Suf. [*Aside.*] She's beautiful, and therefore to be woo'd;
She is a woman, therefore to be won.
Mar. Wilt thou accept of ransom, yea, or no?
Suf. [*Aside.*] Fond man! remember, that thou hast a wife.
Mar. I were best to leave him, for he will hot hear.
Suf. [*Aside.*] There all is marr'd; there lies a cooling card.
Mar. He talks at random: sure, the man is mad.
Suf. [*Aside.*] And yet a dispensation may be had.
Mar. And yet I would that you would answer me.
Suf. [*Aside.*] I'll win this lady Margaret. For whom?
Why, for my king: tush, that's a wooden thing!
Mar. [*Overhearing him.*] He talks of wood: it is some carpenter.
Suf. [*Aside.*] Yet so my fancy may be satisfied,
And peace established between these realms.
But there remains a scruple in that, too;
For though her father be the king of Naples,
Duke of Anjou and Maine, yet is he poor,
And our nobility will scorn the match.
Mar. Hear ye, captain,—are you not at leisure?
Suf. [*Aside.*] It shall be so, disdain they ne'er so much:
Henry is youthful, and will quickly yield.—
Madam, I have a secret to reveal,
Mar. [*Aside.*] What though I be enthrall'd? he seems a knight,
And will not any way dishonor me.
Suf. Lady, vouchsafe to listen what I say.
Mar. [*Aside.*] Perhaps, I shall be rescu'd by the French;
And then I need not crave his courtesy.

Suf. Sweet madam, give me hearing in a cause—
Say, gentle princess, would you not suppose
Your bondage happy, to be made a queen?
Mar. To be a queen in bondage is more vile
Than is a slave in base servility;
For princes should be free.
Suf. And so shall you,
If happy England's royal king be free.
Mar. Why, what concerns his freedom unto me?
Suf. I'll undertake to make thee Henry's queen;
To put a golden sceptre in thy hand,
And set a precious crown upon thy head,
If thou wilt condescend to be my—
Mar. What?
Suf. His love.
Mar. I am unworthy to be Henry's wife.
Suf. No, gentle madam; I unworthy am
To woo so fair a dame to be his wife,
And have no portion in the choice myself.
How say you, madam,—are you so content?
Mar. An if my father please, I am content.
Suf. Then, call our captains, and our colors forth!—
[*Troops come forward.*
And, madam, at your father's castle walls
We'll crave a parley, to confer with him.

A parley sounded. Enter REIGNIER, *on the walls.*

Suf. See, Reignier, see thy daughter prisoner?
Reig. To whom?
Suf. To me.
Reig. Suffolk, what remedy?
I am a soldier, and unapt to weep,
Or to exclaim on fortune's fickleness.
Suf. Yes, there is remedy enough, my lord:
Consent (and, for thy honor, give consent)
Thy daughter shall be wedded to my king;
Whom I with pain have woo'd and won thereto,
And this her easy-held imprisonment
Hath gain'd thy daughter princely liberty.
Reig. Speaks Suffolk as he thinks?
Suf. Fair Margaret knows
That Suffolk doth not flatter, face, or feign.
Reig. Upon thy princely warrant, I descend
To give thee answer of thy just demand.
Suf. And here I will expect thy coming.
[*Exit* REIGNIER *from the walls.*

Trumpets sound. Enter REIGNIER, *below.*

Reig. Welcome, brave earl, into our territories:
Command in Anjou what your honor pleases.
Suf. Thanks, Reignier, happy for so sweet a child,
Fit to be made companion with a king:
What answer makes your grace unto my suit?
Reig. Since thou dost deign to woo her little worth
To be the princely bride of such a lord,
Upon condition I may quietly
Enjoy mine own, the county Maine, and Anjou,
Free from oppression or the stroke of war,
My daughter shall be Henry's, if he please.
Suf. That is her ransom,—I deliver her;
And those two counties, I will undertake,
Your grace shall well and quietly enjoy.
Reig. And I again, in Henry's royal name,
As deputy unto that gracious king,
Give thee her hand, for sign of plighted faith.
Suf. Reignier of France, I give thee kingly thanks,
Because this is in traffic of a king:—
[*Aside.*] And yet, methinks, I could be well content
To be mine own attorney in this case.—
[*To* REIG.] I'll over, then, to England with this news,
And make this marriage to be solemniz'd.
So, farewell, Reignier: set this diamond safe
In golden palaces, as it becomes.
Reig. I do embrace thee, as I would embrace
The Christian prince, king Henry, were he here.
Mar. Farewell, my lord: good wishes, praise, and prayers,
Shall Suffolk ever have of Margaret. [*Going.*
Suf. Farewell, sweet madam: but hark you, Margaret,—
No princely commendations to my king?
Mar. Such commendations as become his servant, say to him.
Suf. Words sweetly plac'd, and modestly directed.
But, madam, I must trouble you again,—
No loving token to his majesty?
Mar. Yes, my good lord,—a pure unspotted heart,
Never yet taint with love, I send the king.
Suf. And this withal. [*Kisses her.*
Mar. That for thyself: I will not so presume,
To send such peevish tokens to a king.
[*Exeunt* REIGNIER *and* MARGARET.
Suf. O, wert thou for myself!—But Suffolk, stay;
Thou may'st not wander in that labyrinth;
There Minotaurs, and ugly treasons, lurk.
Solicit Henry with her wond'rous praise:
Bethink thee on her virtues that surmount
Mad natural graces that extinguish art;

Repeat their semblance often on the seas,
That, when thou com'st to kneel at Henry's feet,
Thou may'st bereave him of his wits with wonder. [*Exit.*

SCENE IV.—*Camp of the* Duke of York, *in* Anjou.

Enter York, Warwick, *and others.*

York. Bring forth that sorceress, condemn'd to burn.

Enter La Pucelle, *guarded; and a* Shepherd.

Shep. Ah, Joan, this kills thy father's heart outright!
Have I sought every country far and near,
And, now it is my chance to find thee out,
Must I behold thy timeless cruel death?
Ah, Joan, sweet daughter Joan, I'll die with thee!
Puc. Decrepit miser! base ignoble wretch!
I am descended of a gentler blood:
Thou art no father, nor no friend, of mine.
Shep. Out, out!—My lords, an please you, 'tis not so.
War. Graceless! wilt thou deny thy parentage?
York. This argues what her kind of life hath been,—
Wicked and vile; and so her death concludes.
Shep. Fie, Joan, that thou wilt be so obstacle!
Heaven knows, thou art a collop of my flesh;
And for thy sake have I shed many a tear:
Deny me not, I pr'ythee, gentle Joan.
Puc. Peasant, avaunt!—You have suborn'd this man,
Of purpose to obscure my noble birth.
Shep. Kneel down and take my blessing, good my girl.
Wilt thou not stoop? Now cursed be the time
Of thy nativity!
When thou didst keep my lambs a-field,
I wish some ravenous wolf had eaten thee!
Dost thou deny thy father, cursed girl?
O, burn her, burn her! hanging is too good. [*Exit.*
York. Take her away; for she hath lived too long,
To fill the world with vicious qualities.
Puc. First, let me tell you whom you have condemn'd:
Not me begotten of a shepherd swain,
But issu'd from the progeny of kings;
Virtuous, and holy; chosen from above,
By inspiration of celestial grace,
To work exceeding miracles on earth.
I never had to do with wicked spirits:
But you,—that are polluted with your lusts,
Stain'd with the guiltless blood of innocents,
Corrupt and tainted with a thousand vices,—
Because you want the grace that others have,

You judge it straight a thing impossible
To compass wonders, but by help of demons.
York. Away with her to execution!
Puc. Will nothing turn your unrelenting hearts?—
Then lead me hence;—
May never glorious sun reflex his beams
Upon the country where you make abode;
But darkness and the gloomy shade of death
Environ you, till mischief and despair
Drive you to break your necks, or hang yourselves!
[*Exit, guarded.*
York. Break thou in pieces, and consume to ashes,
Thou foul accursed minister of darkness.

Enter CARDINAL BEAUFORT, *attended.*

Car. Lord regent, I do greet your excellence
With letters of commission from the king.
For know, my lords, the states of Christendom,
Mov'd with remorse of these outrageous broils,
Have earnestly implor'd a general peace
Betwixt our nation and the aspiring French;
And here at hand the Dauphin, and his train,
Approacheth to confer about some matter.
York. Is all our travail turn'd to this effect?
Shall we at last conclude effeminate peace?
Have we not lost most part of all the towns,
By treason, falsehood, and by treachery,
Our great progenitors had conquered?—
O, Warwick, Warwick! I foresee with grief
The utter loss of all the realm of France.
War. Be patient, York: if we conclude a peace,
It shall be with such strict and severe covenants,
As little shall the Frenchmen gain thereby.

Enter CHARLES, *attended;* ALENÇON, ORLEANS, REIGNIER, *and others.*

Char. Since, lords of England, it is thus agreed,
That peaceful truce shall be proclaimed in France,
We come to be informèd by yourselves
What the conditions of that league must be.
York. Speak, Winchester; for boiling choler chokes
The hollow passage of my prison'd voice,
By sight of these our baleful enemies.
Car. Charles, and the rest, it is enacted thus:—
That, in regard king Henry gives consent,
Of mere compassion, and of lenity,
To ease your country of distressful war,
And suffer you to breathe in fruitful peace,—
You shall become true liegemen to his crown:

And, Charles, upon condition thou wilt swear
To pay him tribute, and submit thyself,
Thou shalt be plac'd as viceroy under him,
And still enjoy thy regal dignity.
Char. 'Tis known already that I am possess'd
With more than half the Gallian territories,
And therein reverenc'd for their lawful king:
Shall I, for lucre of the rest unvanquish'd,
Detract so much from that prerogative,
As to be call'd but viceroy of the whole?
No, lord embassador; I'll rather keep
That which I have, than, coveting for more,
Be cast from possibility of all.
York. Insulting Charles! hast thou by secret means
Used intercession to obtain a league,
And, now the matter grows to compromise,
Stand'st thou aloof upon comparison?
Either accept the title thou usurp'st,
Of benefit proceeding from our king,
And not of any challenge of desert,
Or we will plague thee with incessant wars.
Reig. [*Aside to* CHAR.] My lord, you do not well in obstinacy
To cavil in the course of this contract:
If once it be neglected, ten to one,
We shall not find like opportunity.
Alen. [*Aside to* CHAR.] To say the truth, it is your policy
To save your subjects from such massacre,
And ruthless slaughters, as are daily seen
By our proceeding in hostility;
And therefore take this compact of a truce,
Although you break it when your pleasure serves.
War. How say'st thou, Charles? shall our condition stand?
Char. It shall; only reserv'd, you claim no interest
In any of our towns of garrison.
York. Then swear allegiance to his majesty;
As thou art knight, never to disobey,
Nor be rebellious to the crown of England,—
Thou, nor thy nobles, to the crown of England.
[CHARLES, *and his Nobles, give tokens of fealty.*
So, now dismiss your army when ye please;
Hang up your ensigns, let your drums be still,
For here we entertain a solemn peace. [*Exeunt.*

SCENE V.—London. *A Room in the Palace.*

Enter KING HENRY, *in conference with* SUFFOLK; GLOSTER *and* EXETER *following.*

K. Hen. Your wondrous rare description, noble earl,
Of beauteous Margaret hath astonish'd me:
Her virtues, gracèd with external gifts,
Do breed love's settled passions in my heart:
And like as rigor of tempestuous gusts
Provokes the mightiest hulk against the tide,
So am I driven, by breath of her renown,
Either to suffer shipwreck, or arrive
Where I may have fruition of her love.
Suf. Tush, my good lord,—this superficial tale
Is but a preface of her worthy praise;
The chief perfections of that lovely dame
Would make a volume of enticing lines,
Able to ravish any dull conceit:
And, which is more, she is not so divine,
So full replete with choice of all delights,
But, with as humble lowliness of mind,
She is content to be at your command,
To love and honor Henry as her lord.
K. Hen. My lord protector, give consent,
That Margaret may be England's royal queen,
Glo. So should I give consent to flatter sin.
You know, my lord, your highness is betroth'd
Unto another lady of esteem:
How shall we, then, dispense with that contract,
And not deface your honor with reproach?
Suf. As doth a ruler with unlawful oaths;
Or one that, at a triumph having vow'd
To try his strength, forsaketh yet the lists
By reason of his adversary's odds:
A poor earl's daughter is unequal odds,
And therefore may be broke without offence.
Glo. Why, what, I pray, is Margaret more than that?
Her father is no better than an earl,
Although in glorious titles he excel.
Suf. Yes, my good lord, her father is a king,
The king of Naples and Jerusalem;
And of such great authority in France,
As his alliance will confirm our peace,
And keep the Frenchmen in allegiance.
Glo. And so the earl of Armagnac may do,
Because he is near kinsman unto Charles.

Exe. Beside, his wealth doth warrant liberal dower;
Where Reignier sooner will receive, than give.
Suf. A dower, my lords! disgrace not so your king,
That he should be so abject, base, and poor,
To choose for wealth, and not for perfect love.
Henry is able to enrich his queen,
And not to seek a queen to make him rich:
So worthless peasants bargain for their wives,
As market-men for oxen, sheep, or horse.
Marriage is a matter of more worth,
Than to be dealt in by attorneyship;
Not whom we will, but whom his grace affects,
Must be companion of his nuptial ties:
And therefore, lords, since he affects her most,
It most of all these reasons bindeth us,
In our opinions she should be preferr'd.
For what is wedlock forcèd, but a curse,
An age of discord and continual strife?
Whereas the contrary bringeth bliss,
And is a pattern of celestial peace.
Whom should we match with Henry, being a king,
But Margaret, that is daughter to a king?
Her peerless feature, joinèd with her birth,
Approves her fit for none but for a king:
Her valiant courage and undaunted spirit
(More than in women commonly is seen)
Will answer our hope in issue of a king.
Then yield, my lords; and here conclude with me
That Margaret shall be queen, and none but she.
K. Hen. Whether it be through force of your report,
My noble lord of Suffolk, or for that
My tender youth was never yet attaint
With any passion of inflaming love,
I cannot tell; but this I am assur'd,
I feel such sharp dissension in my breast,
Such fierce alarums both of hope and fear,
As I am sick with working of my thoughts.
Take, therefore, shipping; post, my lord, to France;
Agree to any covenants, and procure
That lady Margaret do vouchsafe to come
To cross the seas to England, and be crown'd
King Henry's faithful and anointed queen:
For your expenses and sufficient charge,
Among the people gather up a tenth.
Be gone, I say; for, till you do return,
I rest perplexèd with a thousand cares.-
And you, good uncle, banish all offence:
If you do censure me by what you were,

Not what you are, I know it will excuse
This sudden execution of my will.
And so, conduct me where, from company,
I may revolve and ruminate my grief. [*Exit.*

Glo. Ay, grief, I fear me, both at first and last.
[*Exeunt* GLOSTER *and* EXETER.

Suf. Thus Suffolk hath prevail'd; and thus he goes,
As did the youthful Paris once to Greece,
With hope to find the like event in love,
But prosper better than the Trojan did.
Margaret shall now be queen, and rule the king;
But I will rule both her, the king, and realm. [*Exit.*

THE HISTORY OF

KING HENRY VI.

PART II.

THE Second Part of Henry VI. appears to be an enlargement and improvement of an older play written by the author, in the earlier period of his dramatic career. That play was printed under the title of "The first part of the Contention betwixt the two famous houses of Yorke and Lancaster, with the death of the goode Duke Humphrey: And the banishment and death of the Duke of Suffolke, and the Tragicall end of the proud Cardinal of Winchester, with the notable Rebellion of Jack Cade: And the Duke of Yorke's first claim unto the Crowne." This enumeration of the leading transactions of the Play are all strictly in accordance with historical facts, and the chief personages in the action are marked with strong and distinct accuracy in the delineation. About ten years are comprised in the action of the play. It opens with the marriage of Henry and Margaret, 1445, and closes with the first battle fought at St. Albans, and won by the York faction, in 1455.

PERSONS REPRESENTED.

KING HENRY THE SIXTH.
HUMPHREY, DUKE OF GLOSTER, *his Uncle.*
CARDINAL BEAUFORT, *Bishop of Winchester Great Uncle to the* KING.
RICHARD PLANTAGENET, *Duke of York.*
EDWARD *and* RICHARD, *his Sons.*
DUKE OF SOMERSET, DUKE OF SUFFOLK, DUKE OF BUCKINGHAM, LORD CLIFFORD, YOUNG CLIFFORD, *his Son*, — *Of the* KING'S *Party.*
EARL OF SALISBURY, EARL OF WARWICK, — *Of the York Faction.*
LORD SCALES, *Governor of the Tower.* LORD SAY, Sir HUMPHREY STAFFORD, *and* WILLIAM STAFFORD, *his Brother.* Sir JOHN STANLEY.
WALTER WHITMORE.

A Sea-captain, Master, *and* Master's Mate.
Two Gentlemen, *prisoners with* SUFFOLK. VAUX.
HUME *and* SOUTHWELL, *Priests.*
BOLINGBROKE, *a Conjurer. A* Spirit *raised by him.*
THOMAS HORNER, *an Armorer.* PETER, *his Man.*
Clerk of Chatham. Mayor of St. Albans.
SIMPCOX, *an Impostor. Two* Murderers.
JACK CADE, *a Rebel.*
GEORGE, JOHN, DICK, SMITH, *the Weaver*, MICHAEL, *&c.*, CADE'S *Followers.*
ALEXANDER IDEN, *a Kentish Gentleman.*

MARGARET, *Queen to* KING HENRY.
ELEANOR, DUCHESS OF GLOSTER.
MARGERY JOURDAIN, *a Witch.* Wife *to* SIMPCOX.

Lords, Ladies, *and* Attendants; Herald; Petitioners, Aldermen, *a* Beadle, Sheriff, *and* Officers; Citizens, Prentices, Falconers, Guards, Soldiers, Messengers, *&c.*

SCENE,—*In various Parts of* ENGLAND.

ACT I.

SCENE I.—London. *A Room of State in the Palace.*

Flourish of Trumpets: then Hautboys. Enter, on one side, KING HENRY, DUKE OF GLOSTER, SALISBURY, WARWICK, *and* CARDINAL BEAUFORT; *on the other,* QUEEN MARGARET, *led in by* SUFFOLK; YORK, SOMERSET, BUCKINGHAM, *and others, following.*

Suf. As by your high imperial majesty
I had in charge at my depart from France,
As procurator to your excellence,
To marry princess Margaret for your grace;
So, in the famous ancient city, Tours,
In presence of the kings of France and Sicil,
The dukes of Orleans, Calaber, Bretaigne, and Alençon,
Seven earls, twelve barons, and twenty reverend bishops,
I have perform'd my task, and was espous'd:
And humbly now, upon my bended knee,
In sight of England and her lordly peers,
Deliver up my title in the queen
To your most gracious hands, that are the substance
Of that great shadow I did represent;
The happiest gift that ever marquess gave,
The fairest queen that ever king receiv'd.
K. Hen. Suffolk, arise.—Welcome, queen Margaret:
I can express no kinder sign of love,
Than this kind kiss.—O Lord, that lends me life,

Lend me a heart replete with thankfulness!
For thou hast given me, in this beauteous face,
A world of earthly blessings to my soul,
If sympathy of love unite our thoughts.

Q. Mar. Great king of England, and my gracious lord,
The mutual conference that my mind hath had,
By day, by night, waking and in my dreams,
In courtly company or at my beads,
With you, mine alder-liefest* sovereign,
Makes me the bolder to salute my king
With ruder terms, such as my wit affords,
And over-joy of heart doth minister.

K. Hen. Her sight did ravish; but her grace in speech,
Her words y-clad with wisdom's majesty,
Makes me from wondering fall to weeping joys;
Such is the fulness of my heart's content.—
Lords, with one cheerful voice welcome my love.

All. [*Kneeling.*] Long live queen Margaret, England's happiness!

Q. Mar. We thank you all. [*Flourish.*

Suf. My lord protector, so it please your grace,
Here are the articles of contracted peace,
Between our sovereign, and the French king Charles,
For eighteen months concluded by consent.

Glo. [*Reads.*] "*Imprimis*, It is agreed between the French king, Charles, and William De-la-Poole, marquess of Suffolk, embassador for Henry king of England,—that the said Henry shall espouse the lady Margaret, daughter unto Reignier king of Naples, Sicilia, and Jerusalem; and crown her queen of England ere the thirtieth of May next ensuing. *Item*, That the duchy of Anjou and the county of Maine shall be released and delivered to the king her father"—

K. Hen. Uncle, how now!

Glo. Pardon me, my gracious lord;
Some sudden qualm hath struck me at the heart,
And dimm'd mine eyes, that I can read no farther.

K. Hen. Uncle of Winchester, I pray, read on.

Car. [*Reads.*] "*Item*, It is farther agreed between them, that the duchies of Anjou and Maine shall be released and delivered over to the king her father; and she sent over of the king of England's own proper costs and charges, without having any dowry."

K. Hen. They please us well.—Lord marquess, kneel down:
We here create thee the first duke of Suffolk,
And girt thee with the sword.—Cousin of York,
We here discharge your grace from being regent

* *Alder-liefest*—most dearly beloved.

I' the parts of France, till term of eighteen months
Be full expir'd.—Thanks, uncle Winchester,
Gloster, York, Buckingham, Somerset,
Salisbury, and Warwick;
We thank you all for this great favor done,
In entertainment to my princely queen.
Come, let us in; and with all speed provide
To see her coronation be perform'd.

[*Exeunt* KING, QUEEN, *and* SUFFOLK.

Glo. Brave peers of England, pillars of the state,
To you duke Humphrey must unload his grief,—
Your grief, the common grief of all the land.
What! did my brother Henry spend his youth,
His valor, coin, and people, in the wars?
Did he so often lodge in open field,
In winter's cold, and summer's parching heat,
To conquer France, his true inheritance?
And did my brother Bedford toil his wits,
To keep by policy what Henry got?
Have you yourselves, Somerset, Buckingham,
Brave York, Salisbury, and victorious Warwick,
Receiv'd deep scars in France and Normandy?
Or hath mine uncle Beaufort and myself,
With all the learnèd council of the realm,
Studied so long, sat in the council-house
Early and late, debating to and fro
How France and Frenchmen might be kept in awe?
And hath his highness in his infancy
Been crowned in Paris, in despite of foes?
And shall these labors, and these honors, die?
Shall Henry's conquest, Bedford's vigilance,
Your deeds of war, and all our counsel, die?
O peers of England, shameful is this league!
Fatal this marriage! cancelling your fame,
Blotting your names from books of memory,
Razing the characters of your renown,
Defacing monuments of conquer'd France,
Undoing all, as all had never been!

Car. Nephew, what means this passionate discourse,
This peroration with such circumstance?
For France, 'tis ours; and we will keep it still.

Glo. Ay, uncle, we will keep it, if we can;
But now it is impossible we should.
Suffolk, the new-made duke that rules the roast,
Hath given the duchies of Anjou and Maine
Unto the poor king Reignier, whose large style
Agrees not with the leanness of his purse.

Sal. These counties were the keys of Normandy:—
But wherefore weeps Warwick, my valiant son?
War. For grief that they are past recovery:
For, were there hope to conquer them again,
My sword should shed hot blood, mine eyes no tears.
Anjou and Maine! myself did win them both;
Those provinces these arms of mine did conquer:
And are the cities, that I got with wounds,
Deliver'd up again with peaceful words?
York. For Suffolk's duke, may he be suffocate,
That dims the honor of this warlike isle!
France should have torn and rent my very heart,
Before I would have yielded to this league.
I never read but England's kings have had
Large sums of gold, and dowries, with their wives;
And our king Henry gives away his own,
To match with her that brings no vantages.
Glo. A proper jest, and never heard before,
That Suffolk should demand a whole fifteenth,
For costs and charges in transporting her!
She should have stay'd in France, and starv'd in France,
Before—
Car. My lord of Gloster, now you grow too hot:
It was the pleasure of my lord the king.
Glo. My lord of Winchester, I know your mind;
'Tis not my speeches that you do mislike,
But 'tis my presence that doth trouble ye.
Rancor will out: proud prelate, in thy face
I see thy fury: if I longer stay,
We shall begin our ancient bickerings.—
Lordlings, farewell; and say, when I am gone,
I prophesied France will be lost ere long. [*Exit.*
Car. So, there goes our protector in a rage.
'Tis known to you he is mine enemy;
Nay, more, an enemy unto you all;
And no great friend, I fear me, to the king.
Consider, lords, he is the next of blood,
And heir-apparent to the English crown:
Had Henry got an empire by his marriage,
And all the wealthy kingdoms of the west,
There's reason he should be displeas'd at it.
Look to it, lords; let not his smoothing words
Bewitch your hearts; be wise, and circumspect.
What though the common people favor him,
Calling him "Humphrey, the good duke of Gloster;"
Clapping their hands, and crying with loud voice—
"Heaven maintain your royal excellence!"
With—"Heaven preserve the good duke Humphrey!"

I fear me, lords, for all this flattering gloss,
He will be found a dangerous protector.
Buck. Why should he, then, protect our sovereign,
He being of age to govern of himself?—
Cousin of Somerset, join you with me,
And all together, with the duke of Suffolk,
We'll quickly hoist duke Humphrey from his seat.
Car. This weighty business will not brook delay;
I'll to the duke of Suffolk presently. [*Exit.*
Som. Cousin of Buckingham, though Humphrey's pride
And greatness of his place be grief to us,
Yet let us watch the haughty cardinal:
His insolence is more intolerable
Than all the princes in the land beside:
If Gloster be displac'd, he'll be protector.
Buck. Or thou, or I, Somerset, will be protector,
Despite duke Humphrey, or the cardinal.
[*Exeunt* BUCKINGHAM *and* SOMERSET.
Sal. Pride went before, ambition follows him.
While these do labor for their own preferment,
Behoves it us to labor for the realm.
I never saw but Humphrey, duke of Gloster,
Did bear him like a noble gentleman.
Oft have I seen the haughty cardinal,—
More like a soldier, than a man o' the church,
As stout, and proud, as he were lord of all.
War. So heaven help Warwick, as he loves the land,
And common profit of his country.
York. And so says York, for he hath greatest cause.
Sal. Then let's make haste away, and look unto the main.
War. Unto the main! O father, Maine is lost;
That Maine, which by main force Warwick did win,
And would have kept, so long as breath did last!
Main chance, father, you meant; but I meant Maine,—
Which I will win from France, or else be slain.
[*Exeunt* WARWICK *and* SALISBURY.
York. Anjou and Maine are given to the French;
Paris is lost; the state of Normandy
Stands on a tickle point, now they are gone:
Suffolk concluded on the articles;
The peers agreed; and Henry was well pleas'd
To change two dukedoms for a duke's fair daughter.
I cannot blame them all: what is't to them?
'Tis thine they give away, and not their own.
Pirates may make cheap pennyworths of their pillage,
And York must sit, and fret, and bite his tongue,
While his own lands are bargain'd for, and sold.
A day will come when York shall claim his own;

And therefore I will take the Nevils' parts,
And make a show of love to proud duke Humphrey,
And, when I spy advantage, claim the crown,
For that's the golden mark I seek to hit:
Nor shall proud Lancaster usurp my right,
Nor hold the sceptre in his childish fist,
Nor wear the diadem upon his head,
Whose church-like humors fit not for a crown.
Then, York, be still awhile, till time do serve:
Watch thou and wake, when others be asleep,
To pry into the secrets of the state;
Till Henry, surfeiting in joys of love,
With his new bride and England's dear-bought queen,
And Humphrey with the peers be fall'n at jars:
Then will I raise aloft the milk-white rose,
With whose sweet smell the air shall be perfum'd;
And in my standard bear the arms of York,
To grapple with the house of Lancaster;
And, force perforce, I'll make him yield the crown,
Whose bookish rule hath pull'd fair England down. [*Exit.*

SCENE II.—London. *A Room in the* DUKE OF GLOSTER'S *House.*

The Duke of Gloster, saddened at the growing discontents in the kingdom, confers with his duchess, a haughty, ambitious woman. She narrates her dream, which seems to promise her a queenly dignity. The duchess sends to a certain Margery Jourdain and one Roger Bolingbroke, a conjurer, to consult with them, and then proceeds with the duke to join King Henry and the court, at St. Alban's.

SCENE III.—London. *A Room in the Palace.*

Enter PETER *and other* Petitioners.

1 *Pet.* My masters, let's stand close: my lord protector will come this way by and by, and then we may deliver our supplications in the quill.

2 *Pet.* Marry, the Lord protect him, for he's a good man!

1 *Pet.* Here 'a comes, methinks, and the queen with him. I'll be the first, sure.

Enter SUFFOLK *and* QUEEN MARGARET.

2 *Pet.* Come back, fool! this is the duke of Suffolk, and not my lord protector.

Suf. How now, fellow! would'st any thing with me?

1 *Pet.* I pray, my lord, pardon me; I took ye for my lord protector.

Q. Mar. [*Glancing at the superscriptions.*] "To my lord protector!" are your supplications to his lordship? Let me see them: what is thine?

1 *Pet.* Mine is, an't please your grace, against John Goodman, my lord cardinal's man, for keeping my house, and lands, and wife and all, from me.

Suf. That is wrong, indeed.—What's your's?—What's here? [*Reads.*] "Against the duke of Suffolk, for enclosing the commons of Melford."—How now, sir knave!

2 *Pet.* Alas, sir, I am but a poor petitioner of our whole township.

Peter. [*Presenting his Petition.*] Against my master, Thomas Horner, for saying that the duke of York was rightful heir to the crown.

Q. Mar. What say'st thou? Did the duke of York say he was rightful heir to the crown?

Pet. That my master was? No, forsooth: my master said that he was; and that the king was a usurper.

Suf. Who is there? [*Enter* Servants.]—Take this fellow in, and send for his master with a pursuivant presently:—we'll hear more of your matter before the king.

[*Exeunt* Servants *with* PETER.

Q. Mar. And as for you, that love to be protected
Under the wings of our protector's grace,
Begin your suits anew, and sue to him. [*Tears the Petitions.*
Away, base cullions!—Suffolk, let them go.

All. Come, let's be gone. [*Exeunt* Petitioners.

Q. Mar. My lord of Suffolk, say, is this the guise,
Is this the fashion in the court of England?
Is this the government of Britain's isle,
And this the royalty of Albion's king?
What, shall king Henry be a pupil still,
Under the surly Gloster's governance?
Am I a queen in title and in style,
And must be made a subject to a duke?
I tell thee, Poole, when in the city Tours
Thou ran'st a tilt in honor of my love,
And stol'st away the ladies' hearts of France,
I thought king Henry had resembled thee
In courage, courtship, and proportion:
But all his mind is bent to holiness,
To number *Ave-Maries* on his beads:
His champions are the prophets and apostles;
His weapons, holy saws of sacred writ;
His study is his tilt-yard, and his loves
Are brazen images of canoniz'd saints.
I would the college of the cardinals
Would choose him pope, and carry him to Rome,

And set the triple crown upon his head:—
That were a state fit for his holiness.
Suf. Madam, be patient: as I was cause
Your highness came to England, so will I
In England work your grace's full content.
Q. Mar. Beside the high protector, have we Beaufort,
The imperious churchman; Somerset, Buckingham,
And grumbling York: and not the least of these,
But can do more in England than the king.
Suf. And he of these that can do most of all,
Cannot do more in England than the Nevils:
Salisbury, and Warwick, are no simple peers.
Q. Mar. Not all these lords do vex me half so much,
As that proud dame, the lord protector's wife.
She sweeps it through the court with troops of ladies,
More like an empress than duke Humphrey's wife:
Strangers in court do take her for the queen:
She bears a duke's revénues on her back,
And in her heart she scorns our poverty.
Shall I not live to be aveng'd on her?
Suf. Madam, myself have lim'd a bush for her,
And plac'd a quire of such enticing birds,
That she will 'light to listen to the lays,
And never mount to trouble you again
So, let her rest: and, madam, list to me;
For I am bold to counsel you in this.
Although we fancy not the cardinal,
Yet must we join with him and with the lords,
Till we have brought duke Humphrey in disgrace.
As for the duke of York, this late complaint
Will make but little for his benefit.
So, one by one, we'll weed them all at last,
And you yourself shall steer the happy helm.

Enter KING HENRY, YORK, *and* SOMERSET; DUKE *and* DUCHESS OF GLOSTER, CARDINAL BEAUFORT, BUCKINGHAM, SALISBURY, *and* WARWICK.

K. Hen. For my part, noble lords, I care not which;
Or Somerset, or York, all's one to me.
York. If York have ill demean'd himself in France,
Then let him be denied the regentship.
Som. If Somerset be unworthy of the place,
Let York be regent; I will yield to him.
War. Whether your grace be worthy, yea or no,
Dispute not that: York is the worthier.
Car. Ambitious Warwick, let thy betters speak.
War. The cardinal's not my better in the field.
Buck. All in this presence are thy betters, Warwick.

War. Warwick may live to be the best of all.
Sal. Peace, son!—and show some reason, Buckingham,
Why Somerset should be preferr'd in this.
Q. Mar. Because the king, forsooth, will have it so.
Glo. Madam, the king is old enough himself
To give his censure: these are no women's matters.
Q. Mar. If he be old enough, what needs your grace
To be protector of his excellence?
Glo. Madam, I am protector of the realm;
And, at his pleasure, will resign my place.
Suf. Resign it, then, and leave thine insolence.
Since thou wert king, (as who is king but thou?)
The commonwealth hath daily run to wreck;
The Dauphin hath prevail'd beyond the seas;
And all the peers and nobles of the realm
Have been as bondmen to thy sovereignty.
Car. The commons hast thou rack'd; the clergy's bags
Are lank and lean with thy extortions.
Som. Thy sumptuous buildings, and thy wife's attire,
Have cost a mass of public treasury.
Buck. Thy cruelty in execution
Upon offenders, hath exceeded law,
And left thee to the mercy of the law.
Q. Mar. Thy sale of offices and towns in France,—
If they were known, as the suspect is great,—
Would make thee quickly hop without thy head.
[*Exit* GLOSTER. *The* QUEEN *drops her fan.*
Give me my fan: what, minion! can you not?
[*Giving the* DUCHESS *a box on the ear.*
I cry you mercy, madam, was it you?
Duch. Was't I! yea, I it was, proud Frenchwoman:
Could I come near your beauty with my nails,
I'd set my ten commandments in your face.
K. Hen. Sweet aunt, be quiet; 'twas against her will.
Duch. Against her will! Good king, look to't in time;
She'll hamper thee, and dandle thee like a baby:
She shall not strike dame Eleanor unreveng'd. [*Exit.*
Buck. Lord Cardinal, I will follow Eleanor,
And listen after Humphrey, how he proceeds:
She's tickled now; her fume can need no spurs,
She'll gallop fast enough to her destruction. [*Exit* BUCKINGHAM.

Re-enter GLOSTER.

Glo. Now, lords, my choler being over-blown
I come to talk of commonwealth affairs.
As for your spiteful false objections,
Prove them, and I lie open to the law:
But heaven in mercy so deal with my soul,

As I in duty love my king and country!
But, to the matter that we have in hand:—
I say, my sovereign, York is meetest man
To be your regent in the realm of France.
Suf. Before we make election, give me leave
To show some reason, of no little force,
That York is most unmeet of any man.
York. I'll tell thee, Suffolk, why I am unmeet:
First, for I cannot flatter thee in pride;
Next, if I be appointed for the place,
My lord of Somerset will keep me here,
Without discharge, money, or furniture,
Till France be won into the Dauphin's hands:
Last time I danc'd attendance on his will,
Till Paris was besieg'd, famish'd, and lost.
War. That can I witness; and a fouler fact
Did never traitor in the land commit.
Suf. Peace, headstrong Warwick!
War. Image of pride, why should I hold my peace?

Enter Servants *of* SUFFOLK, *bringing in* HORNER *and* PETER.

Suf. Because here is a man accus'd of treason:
Pray heaven the duke of York excuse himself!
York. Doth any one accuse York for a traitor?
K. Hen. What mean'st thou, Suffolk? tell me, what are these?
Suf. Please it your majesty, this is the man
That doth accuse his master of high treason:
His words were these,—that Richard, duke of York,
Was rightful heir unto the English crown,
And that your majesty was a usurper.
K. Hen. Say, man, were these thy words?

Hor. An't shall please your majesty, I never said nor thought any such matter: heaven is my witness, I am falsely accused by the villain.

Pet. [*Holding up his hands.*] By these ten bones, my lords, he did speak them to me in the garret one night, as we were scouring my lord of York's armor.

York. Base villain and mechanical,
I'll have thy head for this thy traitor's speech.—
I do beseech your royal majesty,
Let him have all the rigor of the law.

Hor. Alas, my lord, hang me, if ever I spake the words. My accuser is my prentice; and when I did correct him for his fault the other day, he did vow upon his knees he would be even with me: I have good witness of this; therefore I beseech your majesty, do not cast away an honest man for a villain's accusation.

K. Hen. Uncle, what shall we say to this in law?
Glo. This doom, my lord, if I may judge:

Let Somerset be regent o'er the French,
Because in York this breeds suspicion;
And let these have a day appointed them
For single combat in convenient place,
For he hath witness of his servant's malice:
This is the law, and this duke Humphrey's doom.

K. Hen. Then be it so.—My lord of Somerset,
We make your grace lord regent o'er the French.

Som. I humbly thank your royal majesty.

Hor. And I accept the combat willingly.

Pet. Alas, my lord, I cannot fight; for heaven's sake, pity my case! the spite of man prevaileth against me. Have mercy upon me! I shall never be able to fight a blow.

Glo. Sirrah, or you must fight, or else be hang'd.

K. Hen. Away with them to prison; and the day
Of combat shall be the last of the next month.—
Come, Somerset, we'll see thee sent away. [*Exeunt.*

SCENE IV.—London. *The* DUKE OF GLOSTER'S *Garden.*

Enter MARGERY JOURDAIN, HUME, SOUTHWELL, *and* BOLINGBROKE.

Hume. Come, my masters, the duchess, I tell you, expects performance of your promises.

Boling. Master Hume, we are therefore provided: will her ladyship behold and hear our exorcisms?

Hume. Ay, what else? fear you not her courage.

Boling. I have heard her reported to be a woman of an invincible spirit: but it shall be convenient, master Hume, that you be by her aloft, while we be busy below; and so, I pray you, go and leave us. [*Exit* HUME.] Mother Jourdain, be you prostrate, and grovel on the earth;—John Southwell, read you;—and let us to our work.

Enter DUCHESS *above; and presently,* HUME.

Duch. Well said, my masters; and welcome all.
To this gear; the sooner the better.

Boling. Patience, good lady; wizards know their times.
Deep night, dark night, the silent of the night,
The time of night when Troy was set on fire;
The time when screech-owls cry, and bandogs howl,
And spirits walk, and ghosts break up their graves,—
That time best fits the work we have in hand.
Madam, sit you, and fear not: whom we raise,
We will make fast within a hallow'd verge.

[*Here they perform the ceremonies appertaining, and make the Circle;* BOLINGBROKE, *or* SOUTHWELL, *reads,* Conjuro te, &c. *It thunders and lightens terribly; then the* Spirit *riseth.*

Spir. Adsum.

M. Jourd. Asmath,
By the Eternal, at whose name and power
Thou tremblest, answer that I shall ask;
For, till thou speak, thou shalt not pass from hence.

Spir. Ask what thou wilt:—that I had said and done!

Boling. [*Reads from a paper.*] "First, of the king: what shall of him become?"

Spir. The duke yet lives, that Henry shall depose;
But him outlive, and die a violent death.

[*As the* Spirit *speaks,* SOUTHWELL *writes the answers.*

Boling. [*Reads.*] "What fates await the duke of Suffolk?"

Spir. By water shall he die, and take his end.

Boling. [*Reads.*] "What shall befall the duke of Somerset?"

Spir. Let him shun castles;
Safer shall he be upon the sandy plains,
Than where castles mounted stand.—
Have done, for more I hardly can endure.

Boling. Descend to darkness, and the burning lake!
False fiend, avoid!

[*Thunder and lightning.* Spirit *descends.*

Enter YORK *and* BUCKINGHAM, *hastily, with their* Guards, *and others.*

York. Lay hands upon these traitors, and their trash.—
Beldam, I think we watch'd you at an inch.—
What, madam, are you there? the king and commonweal
Are deeply indebted for this piece of pains:
My lord protector will, I doubt it not,
See you well guerdon'd for these good deserts.

Duch. Not half so bad as thine to England's king,
Injurious duke, that threat'st where is no cause.

Buck. True, madam, none at all:—what call you this?

[*Showing her the papers that have been seized.*

Away with them! let them be clapp'd up close,
And kept asunder.—You, madam, shall with us.—
Stafford, take her to thee.—
We'll see your trinkets here all forthcoming.—
All, away!

[*Exeunt, above,* DUCHESS *and* HUME *guarded. Exeunt, below,* SOUTHWELL, BOLINGBROKE, *&c. guarded.*

York. Lord Buckingham, methinks, you watch'd her well:
A pretty plot, well chosen to build upon!
Now, pray, my lord, let's see the fiend's writ.
What have we here?
[*Reads.*] "The duke yet lives, that Henry shall depose;
But him outlive, and die a violent death."
Well, to the rest:

[*Reads.*] "Tell me, what fate awaits the duke of Suffolk?—
By water shall he die, and take his end."—
"What shall betide the duke of Somerset?—
Let him shun castles;
Safer shall he be upon the sandy plains,
Than where castles mounted stand."—
Come, come, my lords;
These oracles are hardly attain'd,
And hardly understood.
The king is now in progress towards Saint Albans;
With him, the husband of this lovely lady:
Thither go these news, as fast as horse can carry them,-
A sorry breakfast for my lord protector.
Buck. Your grace shall give me leave, my lord of York,
To be the post, in hope of his reward.
York. At your pleasure, my good lord.—Who's within there, ho!

Enter a Servant.

Invite my lords of Salisbury, and Warwick,
To sup with me to-morrow night.—Away! [*Exeunt.*

ACT II.

SCENE I.—Saint Albans.

Enter KING HENRY, QUEEN MARGARET, GLOSTER, CARDINAL, *and* SUFFOLK, *with* Falconers *hollaing.*

Q. Mar. Believe me, lords, for flying at the brook,
I saw not better sport these seven years' day:
Yet, by your leave, the wind was very high;
And, ten to one, old Joan had not gone out.
K. Hen. But what a point, my lord, your falcon made,
And what a pitch she flew above the rest!—
To see how heaven in all its creatures works!
Yea, man and birds, are fain of climbing high.
Suf. No marvel, an it like your majesty,
My lord protector's hawks do tower so well;
They know their master loves to be aloft,
And bears his thoughts above his falcon's pitch.
Glo. My lord, 'tis but a base, ignoble mind,
That mounts no higher than a bird can soar.
Car. I thought as much: he'd be above the clouds.
Glo. Ay, my lord cardinal; how think you by that?
Were it not good your grace could fly to heaven?
K. Hen. The treasury of everlasting joy!
Car. Thy heaven is on earth; thine eyes and thoughts

Beat on a crown, the treasure of thy heart;
Pernicious protector, dangerous peer,
That smooth'st it so with king and commonweal!
Glo. What, cardinal, is your priesthood grown peremptory?
Good uncle, hide such malice;
With such holiness can you do it?
Suf. No malice, sir; no more than well becomes
So good a quarrel, and so bad a peer.
Glo. As who, my lord?
Suf. Why, as you, my lord,
An't like your lordly lord-protectorship.
Glo. Why, Suffolk, England knows thine insolence.
Q. Mar. And thy ambition, Gloster.
K. Hen. I pr'ythee, peace,
Good queen, and whet not on these furious peers;
For blessèd are the peacemakers on earth.
Car. Let me be blessèd for the peace I make,
Against this proud protector with my sword!
Glo. [*Aside to* CAR.] 'Faith, holy uncle, would 'twere come to that!
Car. [*Aside to* GLO.] Marry, when thou dar'st.
Glo. [*Aside to* CAR.] Make up no factious numbers for the matter;
In thine own person answer thy abuse.
Car. [*Aside to* GLO.] Ay, where thou dar'st not peep: an if thou dar'st,
This evening on the east side of the grove.
K. Hen. How now, my lords!
Car. Believe me, cousin Gloster,
Had not your man put up the fowl so suddenly,
We had had more sport.—[*Aside to* GLO.] Come with thy two-hand sword.
Glo. True, uncle.
Car. Are you advis'd?—[*Aside to* GLO.] the east side of the grove.
Glo. [*Aside to* CAR.] Cardinal, I am with you.
K. Hen. Why, how now, uncle Gloster!
Glo. Talking of hawking; nothing else, my lord.—
[*Aside to* CAR.] Priest, I'll shave your crown
For this, or all my fence shall fail.
Car. [*Aside to* GLO.] Protector, see to't well, protect yourself.
K. Hen. The winds grow high; so do your stomachs, lords.
How irksome is this music to my heart!
When such strings jar, what hope of harmony?
I pray, my lords, let me compound this strife.

Enter a Townsman *of St. Albans, crying,* "A Miracle!"

Glo. What means this noise?
Fellow, what miracle dost thou proclaim?

Towns. A miracle! a miracle!
Suf. Come to the king, and tell him what miracle.
Towns. Forsooth, a blind man at St. Alban's shrine,
Within this half hour, hath receiv'd his sight;
A man that ne'er saw in his life before.
K. Hen. Now, heaven be prais'd, that to believing souls
Gives light in darkness, comfort in despair!

Enter the Mayor of Saint Albans, *and his brethren; and* SIMPCOX, *borne between two persons in a chair; his* Wife *and a multitude following.*

Car. Here come the townsmen on procession,
To present your highness with the man.
K. Hen. Great is his comfort in this earthly vale,
Although by his sight his sin be multiplied.
Glo. Stand by, my masters:—bring him near the king;
His highness' pleasure is to talk with him.
K. Hen. Good fellow, tell us here the circumstance,
That we for thee may glorify the Lord.
What, hast thou been long blind, and now restor'd?
Simp. Born blind, an't please your grace.
Wife. Ay, indeed, was he.
Suf. What woman is this?
Wife. His wife, an't like your worship.
Glo. Hadst thou been his mother, thou could'st have better told.
K. Hen. Where wert thou born?
Simp. At Berwick in the north, an't like your grace.
K. Hen. Poor soul! Heaven's goodness hath been great to thee:
Let never day nor night unhallow'd pass,
But still remember what the Lord hath done.
Q. Mar. Tell me, good fellow, cam'st thou here by chance,
Or of devotion, to this holy shrine?
Simp. Of pure devotion; being call'd
A hundred times, and oft'ner, in my sleep,
By good Saint Alban; who said,—"Simpcox, come;
Come, offer at my shrine, and I will help thee."
Wife. Most true, forsooth; and many time and oft
Myself have heard a voice to call him so.
Car. What, art thou lame?
Simp. Ay, pray heaven help me!
Suf. How cam'st thou so?
Simp. A fall off a tree.
Wife. A plum-tree, master.
Glo. How long hast thou been blind?
Simp. O, born so, master.
Glo. What, and would'st climb a tree?

Simp. But that in all my life, when I was a youth.

Wife. Too true; and bought his climbing very dear.

Glo. 'Mass, thou lov'dst plums well, that would'st venture so.

Simp. Alas, good master, my wife desir'd some damsons,
And made me climb, with danger of my life.

Glo. A subtle knave! but yet it shall not serve.—
Let me see thine eyes:—wink now;—now open them:—
In my opinion yet thou seest not well.

Simp. Yes, master, clear as day, I thank heaven and Saint Alban.

Glo. Say'st thou me so? What color is this cloak of?

Simp. Red, master; red as blood.

Glo. Why, that's well said. What color is my gown of?

Simp. Black, forsooth; coal-black, as jet.

K. Hen. Why then, thou know'st what color jet is of?

Suf. And yet, I think, jet did he never see.

Glo. But cloaks, and gowns, before this day, a many.

Wife. Never, before this day, in all his life.

Glo. Tell me, sirrah, what's my name?

Simp. Alas, master, I know not.

Glo. What's his name?

Simp. I know not.

Glo. Nor his?

Simp. No, indeed, master.

Glo. What's thine own name?

Simp. Saunder Simpcox, an if it please you, master.

Glo. Then, Saunder, sit there, the lyingest knave in Christendom. If thou hadst been born blind, thou might'st as well have known all our names, as thus to name the several colors we do wear. Sight may distinguish of colors; but suddenly to nominate them all, it is impossible.—My lords, Saint Alban here hath done a miracle; and would ye not think that cunning to be great, that could restore this cripple to his legs again?

Simp. O, master, that you could!

Glo. My masters of Saint Albans, have you not beadles in your town, and things called whips?

May. Yes, my lord, if it please your grace.

Glo. Then send for one presently.

May. Sirrah, fetch the beadle hither straight.

[*Exit an* Attendant.

Glo. Now fetch me a stool hither by and by. [*A stool brought out.*] Now, sirrah, if you mean to save yourself from whipping, leap me over this stool, and run away.

Simp. Alas, master, I am not able to stand alone:
You go about to torture me in vain.

Re-enter Attendant, *and a* Beadle *with a whip.*

Glo. Well, sir, we must have you find your legs.—Sirrah beadle, whip him till he leap over that same stool.

Bead. I will, my lord.—Come on, sirrah; off with your doublet quickly.

Simp. Alas, master, what shall I do? I am not able to stand.

After the Beadle *hath hit him once, he leaps over the stool, and runs away; and the people follow and cry,* "A Miracle!"

K. Hen. O heaven, seest thou this, and bear'st so long?
Q. Mar. It made me laugh to see the villain run.
Glo. Follow the knave; and take this drab away.
Wife. Alas, sir, we did it for pure need.
Glo. Let them be whipp'd through every market town,
Till they come to Berwick, from whence they came.
[*Exeunt* Mayor, Beadle, Wife, *&c.*
Car. Duke Humphrey has done a miracle to-day.
Suf. True; he made the lame to leap, and fly away.
Glo. But you have done more miracles than I;
You made in a day, my lord, whole towns to fly.

Enter BUCKINGHAM.

K. Hen. What tidings with our cousin Buckingham?
Buck. Such as my heart doth tremble to unfold.
A sort of naughty persons, lewdly bent,—
Under the countenance and confederacy
Of lady Eleanor, the protector's wife,
The ringleader and head of all this rout,—
Have practis'd dangerously against your state,
Dealing with witches, and with conjurers:
Whom we have apprehended in the fact;
Raising up wicked spirits from under ground,
Demanding of king Henry's life and death,
And other of your highness' privy council,
As more at large your grace shall understand.
Car. [*Aside to* GLO.] And so, my lord protector, by this means
Your lady is forthcoming yet at London.
This news, I think, hath turn'd your weapon's edge;
'Tis like, my lord, you will not keep your hour.
Glo. Ambitious churchman, leave to afflict my heart:
Sorrow and grief have vanquish'd all my powers;
And, vanquish'd as I am, I yield to thee,
Or to the meanest groom.
K. Hen. O heaven, what mischiefs work the wicked ones,
Heaping confusion on their own heads thereby!
Q. Mar. Gloster, see here the tainture of thy nest;
And look thyself be faultless, thou wert best.
Glo. Madam, for myself, to heaven I do appeal,
How I have lov'd my king, and commonweal:
And, for my wife, I know not how it stands;

Sorry I am to hear what I have heard:
Noble she is; but if she have forgot
Honor and virtue, and convers'd with such
As, like to pitch, defile nobility,
I give her, as a prey, to law and shame,
That hath dishonor'd Gloster's honest name.
K. Hen. Well, for this night, we will repose us here:
To-morrow toward London back again,
To look into this business thoroughly,
And call these foul offenders to their answers;
And poise the cause in justice' equal scales,
Whose beam stands sure, whose rightful cause prevails.
[*Flourish. Exeunt.*

The Duke of York obtains assurances from Warwick and Salisbury of their aid and support, to enable him to seize the crown as his inheritance, in right of his descent from Edward, third son of the Duke of Clarence, whose issue, Edmund Mortimer, the rightful heir to the throne on the death of Richard II., was displaced by Bolingbroke, afterward Henry IV., the founder of the house of Lancaster.

SCENE III.—London. *A Hall of Justice.*

Trumpets sounded. Enter KING HENRY, QUEEN MARGARET, GLOSTER, YORK, SUFFOLK, *and* SALISBURY; *the* DUCHESS OF GLOSTER, MARGERY, JOURDAIN, SOUTHWELL, HUME, *and* BOLINGBROKE, *under guard.*

K. Hen. Stand forth, dame Eleanor Cobham, Gloster's wife:
In sight of heaven and us, your guilt is great:
Receive the sentence of the law.
[*To* JOURD, *&c.*] You four, from hence to prison back again;
From thence unto the place of execution:
The witch in Smithfield shall be burn'd to ashes,
And you three shall be strangled on the gallows.—
You, madam, for you are more nobly born,
Despoilèd of your honor in your life,
Shall, after three days' open penance done,
Live in your country here, in banishment,
With Sir John Stanley, in the Isle of Man.
Duch. Welcome is banishment; welcome were my death.
Glo. Eleanor, the law, thou seest, hath judged thee:
I cannot justify whom the law condemns.—
[*Exeunt the* DUCHESS *and the other Prisoners, guarded.*
Mine eyes are full of tears, my heart of grief.
Ah, Humphrey, this dishonor in thine age
Will bring thy head with sorrow to the ground!
I beseech your majesty, give me leave to go;
Sorrow would solace, and mine age would ease.

K. Hen. Stay, Humphrey duke of Gloster: ere thou go,
Give up thy staff: Henry will to himself
Protector be; and heaven shall be my hope,
My stay, my guide, and lantern to my feet:
And go in peace, Humphrey; no less belov'd,
Than when thou wert protector to thy king.
Q. Mar. I see no reason why a king of years
Should be to be protected like a child.—
Heaven and king Henry govern England's helm!—
Give up your staff, sir, and the king his realm.
Glo. My staff! here, noble Henry, is my staff:
As willingly do I the same resign,
As e'er thy father Henry made it mine;
And even as willingly at thy feet I leave it,
As others would ambitiously receive it.
Farewell, good king: when I am dead and gone,
May honorable peace attend thy throne. [*Exit.*
Q. Mar. Why, now is Henry king, and Margaret queen;
And Humphrey, duke of Gloster, scarce himself,
That bears so shrewd a maim; two pulls at once,—
His lady banish'd, and a limb lopp'd off:
This staff of honor raught, there let it stand,
Where it best fits to be,—in Henry's hand.
Suf. Thus droops this lofty pine, and hangs his sprays;
Thus Eleanor's pride dies in her youngest days.
York. Lords, let him go.—Please it your majesty,
This is the day appointed for the combat;
And ready are the appellant and defendant,
The armorer and his man, to enter the lists,
So please your highness to behold the fight.
Q. Mar. Ay, good my lord; for purposely therefore
Left I the court, to see this quarrel tried.
K. Hen. See the lists and all things fit:
Here let them end it; and God defend the right!
York. I never saw a fellow worse bested,
Or more afraid to fight, than is the appellant,
The servant of this armorer, my lords.

Enter, on one side, HORNER, *and his* Neighbors, *drinking to him so much that he is drunk; and he enters bearing his staff with a sand-bag fastened to it; a drum before him: on the other side,* PETER, *with a drum and a similar staff; accompanied by* Prentices *drinking to him.*

1 *Neigh.* Here, neighbor Horner, I drink to you in a cup of sack: and fear not, neighbor, you shall do well enough.

2 *Neigh.* And here, neighbor, here's a cup of charneco.

3 *Neigh.* And here's a pot of good double beer, neighbor: drink, and fear not your man.

Hor. Let it come, i' faith, and I'll pledge you all; and a fig for Peter!

1 *Pren.* Here, Peter, I drink to thee: and be not afraid.

2 *Pren.* Be merry, Peter, and fear not thy master: fight for credit of the prentices.

Peter. I thank you all: drink, and pray for me, I pray you; for, I think, I have taken my last draught in this world.—Here, Robin, an if I die, I give thee my apron: and, Will, thou shalt have my hammer:—and here, Tom, take all the money that I have.—O Lord bless me, for I am never able to deal with my master, he hath learnt so much fence already.

Sal. Come, leave your drinking, and fall to blows.—Sirrah, what's thy name?

Peter. Peter, forsooth.

Sal. Peter! what more?

Peter. Thump.

Sal. Thump! then see thou thump thy master well.

Hor. Masters, I am come hither, as it were, upon my man's instigation, to prove him a knave, and myself an honest man: and touching the duke of York, I will take my death, I never meant him any ill, nor the king, nor the queen: and therefore, Peter, have at thee with a downright blow!

York. Despatch:—this knave's tongue begins to double.—
Sound, trumpets, alarum to the combatants.

[*Alarum. They fight, and* PETER *strikes down his Master.*

Hor. Hold, Peter, hold! I confess, I confess treason. [*Dies.*

York. Take away his weapon.—Fellow, thank heaven, and the good wine in thy master's way.

Peter. O, have I overcome mine enemies in this presence?
O Peter, thou hast prevail'd in right!

K. Hen. Go, take hence that traitor from our sight;
For, by his death, we do perceive his guilt:
And heaven in justice hath reveal'd to us
The truth and innocence of this poor fellow,
Which he had thought to have murder'd wrongfully.—
Come, fellow, follow us for thy reward. [*Exeunt.*

ACT III.

SCENE I.—*The* Abbey *at* Bury.

Sennet. Enter to the Parliament, KING HENRY, QUEEN MARGARET, CARDINAL BEAUFORT, SUFFOLK, YORK, BUCKINGHAM, *and others.*

K. Hen. I muse my lord of Gloster is not come:
'Tis not his wont to be the hindmost man,
Whate'er occasion keeps him from us now.

Q. Mar. Can you not see? or will you not observe
The strangeness of his alter'd countenance?
With what a majesty he bears himself;
How insolent of late he is become,
How proud, how peremptory, and unlike himself?
We know the time since he was mild and affable;
And, if we did but glance a far-off look,
Immediately he was upon his knee,
That all the court admir'd him for submission;
But meet him now, and, be it in the morn,
When every one will give the time of day,
He knits his brow, and shows an angry eye,
And passeth by with stiff unbowèd knee,
Disdaining duty that to us belongs.
The reverent care I bear unto my lord
Made me collect these changes in the duke.
My lord of Suffolk,—Buckingham,—and York,—
Reprove my allegation, if you can,
Or else conclude my words effectual.
Suf. Well hath your highness seen into this duke;
And had I first been put to speak my mind,
I think I should have told your grace's tale.
Smooth runs the water where the brook is deep;
And in his simple show he harbors treason.
The fox barks not when he would steal the lamb.
No, no, my sovereign; Gloster is a man
Unsounded yet, and full of deep deceit.
Car. Did he not, contrary to form of law,
Devise strange deaths for small offences done?
York. And did he not, in his protectorship,
Levy great sums of money through the realm
For soldiers' pay in France, and never sent it?
By means whereof the towns each day revolted.
Buck. Tut! these are petty faults to faults unknown,
Which time will bring to light in smooth duke Humphrey.
K. Hen. My lords, at once:—the care you have of us,
To mow down thorns that would annoy our foot,
Is worthy praise: but shall I speak my conscience?
Our kinsman Gloster is as innocent
From meaning treason to our royal person,
As is the sucking lamb, or harmless dove:
The duke is virtuous, mild, and too well given,
To dream on evil, or to work my downfall.
Q. Mar. Ah, what's more dangerous than this fond affiance!
Seems he a dove? his feathers are but borrow'd,
For he's disposèd as the hateful raven:
Is he a lamb? his skin is surely lent him,
For he's inclin'd as is the ravenous wolf.

Who cannot steal a shape, that means deceit?
Take heed, my lord; the welfare of us all
Hangs on the cutting short that fraudful man.

Enter SOMERSET.

Som. All health unto my gracious sovereign!
K. Hen. Welcome, lord Somerset. What news from France?
Som. That all your interest in those territories
Is utterly bereft you; all is lost.
K. Hen. Cold news, lord Somerset: but heaven's will be done!
York. [*Aside.*] Cold news for me; for I had hope of France,
As firmly as I hope for fertile England.
Thus are my blossoms blasted in the bud,
And caterpillars eat my leaves away:
But I will remedy this gear ere long,
Or sell my title for a glorious grave.

Enter GLOSTER.

Glo. All happiness unto my lord the king!
Pardon, my liege, that I have stay'd so long.
Suf. Nay, Gloster, know, that thou art come too soon,
Unless thou wert more loyal than thou art:
I do arrest thee of high treason here.
Glo. Well, Suffolk, yet thou shalt not see me blush,
Nor change my countenance for this arrest:
A heart unspotted is not easily daunted.
The purest spring is not so free from mud,
As I am clear from treason to my sovereign:
Who can accuse me? wherein am I guilty?
York. 'Tis thought, my lord, that you took bribes of France,
And, being protector, stayed the soldiers' pay;
By means whereof his highness hath lost France.
Glo. Is it but thought so? What are they that think it?
I never robb'd the soldiers of their pay,
Nor ever had one penny bribe from France.
So help me heaven, as I have watch'd the night,—
Ay, night by night,—in studying good for England!
Car. It serves you well, my lord, to say so much.
Glo. I say no more than truth.
York. In your protectorship you did devise
Strange tortures for offenders, never heard of,
That England was defam'd by tyranny.
Glo. Why, 'tis well known that, whiles I was protector,
Pity was all the fault that was in me;
For I should melt at an offender's tears,
And lowly words were ransom for their fault.
Suf. My lord, these faults are easy, quickly answer'd:
But mightier crimes are laid unto your charge,
Whereof you cannot easily purge yourself.

I do arrest you in his highness' name;
And here commit you to my lord cardinal
To keep, until your farther time of trial.
K. Hen. My lord of Gloster, 'tis my special hope,
That you will clear yourself from all suspects:
My conscience tells me you are innocent.
Glo. Ah, gracious lord, these days are dangerous!
Virtue is chok'd with foul ambition,
And charity chas'd hence by rancor's hand;
Foul subornation is predominant,
And equity exil'd your highness' land.
I know their complot is to have my life;
I shall not want false witness to condemn me,
Nor store of treasons to augment my guilt;
The ancient proverb will be well effected,—
A staff is quickly found to beat a dog.
Car. My liege, his railing is intolerable:
If those that care to keep your royal person
From treason's secret knife, and traitors' rage,
Be thus upbraided, chid, and rated at,
And the offender granted scope of speech,
'Twill make them cool in zeal unto your grace.—
Sirs, take away the duke, and guard him sure.
Glo. Ah, thus king Henry throws away his crutch,
Before his limbs be firm to bear his body!
Thus is the shepherd beaten from thy side,
And wolves are gnarling who shall gnaw thee first.
Ah, that my fear were false! ah, that it were!
For, good king Henry, thy decay I fear.
[*Exeunt* Attendants *with* GLOSTER.
K. Hen. My lords, what to your wisdoms seemeth best,
Do, or undo, as if ourself were here.
Q. Mar. What, will your highness leave the parliament?
K. Hen. Ay, Margaret, my heart is drown'd with grief,
Whose flood begins to flow within mine eyes;
My body round engirt with misery,—
For what's more miserable than discontent?—
Ah, uncle Humphrey, in thy face I see
The map of honor, truth, and loyalty!
His fortunes I will weep; and, 'twixt each groan,
Say—"Who's a traitor, Gloster he is none." [*Exit.*
Q. Mar. Free lords, cold snow melts with the sun's hot beams.
Henry my lord is cold in great affairs,
Too full of foolish pity.
This Gloster should be quickly rid the world,
To rid us from the fear we have of him.
Car. That he should die is worthy policy;
But yet we want a color for his death:
'Tis meet he be condemn'd by course of law.

Suf. But, in my mind, that were no policy:
The king will labor still to save his life;
The commons haply rise to save his life.
York. So that, by this, you would not have him die.
Suf. Ah, York, no man alive so fain as I!
York. 'Tis York that hath more reason for his death.
Suf. Seeing the deed is meritorious,
And to preserve my sovereign from his foe,—
Say but the word, and I will be his priest.
Car. But I would have him dead, my lord of Suffolk,
Ere you can take due orders for a priest:
Say, you consent, and censure well the deed,
And I'll provide his executioner,—
I tender so the safety of my liege.
Suf. Here is my hand; the deed is worthy doing.
Q. Mar. And so say I.
York. And I: and now we three have spoke it,
It skills not greatly who impugns our doom.

Enter a Messenger.

Mess. Great lords, from Ireland am I come amain,
To signify that rebels there are up,
And put the Englishmen unto the sword:
Send succors, lords, and stop the rage betime,
Before the wound do grow incurable;
For, being green, there is great hope of help.
Car. A breach that craves a quick expedient stop!
What counsel give you in this weighty cause?
York. That Somerset be sent as regent thither:
'Tis meet, that lucky ruler be employ'd;
Witness the fortune he hath had in France.
Som. If York, with all his far-fet policy,
Had been the regent there instead of me,
He never would have stay'd in France so long.
York. No, not to lose it all, as thou hast done:
I rather would have lost my life betimes,
Than bring a burden of dishonor home,
By staying there so long, till all were lost.
Show me one scar character'd on thy skin:
Men's flesh preserv'd so whole do seldom win.
Q. Mar. Nay then, this spark will prove a raging fire,
If wind and fuel be brought to feed it with:—
No more, good York;—sweet Somerset, be still:—
Thy fortune, York, hadst thou been regent there,
Might happily have prov'd far worse than his.
York. What, worse than naught? nay then, a shame take all.
Som. And, in the number, thee, that wishest shame.

Car. My lord of York, try what your fortune is.
The uncivil kernes of Ireland are in arms,
And temper clay with blood of Englishmen:
To Ireland will you lead a band of men,
Collected choicely, from each county some,
And try your hap against the Irishmen?
York. I will, my lord, so please his majesty.
Suf. Why, our authority is his consent,
And what we do establish, he confirms:
Then, noble York, take thou this task in hand.
York. I am content: provide me soldiers, lords,
Whiles I take order for mine own affairs.
Suf. A charge, lord York, that I will see perform'd.
But now return we to the false duke Humphrey.
Car. No more of him; for I will deal with him,
That henceforth, he shall trouble us no more:
And so break off; the day is almost spent.
Lord Suffolk, you and I must talk of that event.
York. My lord of Suffolk, within fourteen days
At Bristol I expect my soldiers;
For there I'll ship them all for Ireland.
Suf. I'll see it truly done, my lord of York.
[*Exeunt all except* YORK.
York. Now, York, or never, steel thy fearful thoughts,
And change misdoubt to resolution:
Be that thou hop'st to be; or what thou art
Resign to death,—it is not worth the enjoying.
Whiles I in Ireland nourish a mighty band,
I will stir up in England some black storm;
And this fell tempest shall not cease to rage
Until the golden circuit on my head,
Like to the golden sun's transparent beams,
Do calm the fury of this mad-bred flaw.
And, for a minister of my intent,
I have seduc'd a headstrong Kentishman,
John Cade of Ashford,
To make commotion, as full well he can,
Under the title of John Mortimer.
That fellow here shall be my substitute;
For that John Mortimer, which now is dead,
In face, in gait, in speech, he doth resemble:
By this I shall perceive the commons' mind,
How they affect the house and claim of York.
Say, he be taken, rack'd, and tortured,
I know no pain they can inflict upon him
Will make him say I mov'd him to those arms.
Say, that he thrive, (as 'tis great like he will,)
Why, then from Ireland come I with my strength,

And reap the harvest which that rascal sow'd;
For, Humphrey being dead, as he shall be,
And Henry put apart, the next for me. [*Exit.*

SCENE II.—Bury. *A Room in the Palace.*

Enter certain Murderers, *hastily.*

1 *Mur.* Run to my lord of Suffolk; let him know
We have despatch'd the duke, as he commanded.
2 *Mur.* O that it were to do!—What have we done?
Didst ever hear a man so penitent?
1 *Mur.* Here comes my lord.

Enter SUFFOLK.

Suf. Now, sirs, have you despatch'd this thing?
1 *Mur.* Ay, my good lord, he's dead.
Suf. Why, that's well said. Go, get you to my house;
I will reward you for this venturous deed.
The king and all the peers are here at hand:—
Have you laid fair the bed? are all things well,
According as I gave directions?
1 *Mur.* 'Tis, my good lord.
Suf. Away! be gone. [*Exeunt* Murderers.

Trumpets sounded. Enter KING HENRY, QUEEN MARGARET, CARDINAL BEAUFORT, SOMERSET, Lords, *and others.*

K. Hen. Go, call our uncle to our presence straight;
Say, we intend to try his grace to-day,
If he be guilty, as 'tis published.
Suf. I'll call him presently, my noble lord. [*Exit.*
K. Hen. Lords, take your places; and, I pray you all,
Proceed no straiter 'gainst our uncle Gloster,
Than from true evidence, of good esteem,
He be approv'd in practice culpable.
Q. Mar. Heaven forbid any malice should prevail,
That faultless may condemn a nobleman!
Pray heaven he may acquit him of suspicion!
K. Hen. I thank thee, Margaret; these words content me much.—

Re-enter SUFFOLK.

How now! why look'st thou pale? why tremblest thou?
Where is our uncle? what's the matter, Suffolk?
Suf. Dead in his bed, my lord; Gloster is dead.
Q. Mar. Marry, heaven forefend!
Car. Heaven's secret judgment:—I did dream to-night
The duke was dumb, and could not speak a word.
[*The* KING *swoons.*

Q. Mar. How fares my lord?—Help, lords! the king is dead.
Run, go, help, help!—O Henry, ope thine eyes!
Suf. He doth revive again:—Madam, be patient.
K. Hen. O heavenly Father!
Q. Mar. How fares my gracious lord?
Suf. Comfort, my sovereign! gracious Henry, comfort!
K. Hen. What! doth my lord of Suffolk comfort me?
Came he right now to sing a raven's note,
Whose dismal tune bereft my vital powers;
And thinks he, that the chirping of a wren,
By crying comfort from a hollow breast,
Can chase away the first-conceivèd sound?
Hide not thy poison with such sugar'd words:
Lay not thy hands on me; forbear, I say;
Their touch affrights me as a serpent's sting.
Thou baleful messenger, out of my sight!
Upon thy eye-balls murderous tyranny
Sits in grim majesty, to fright the world.
Look not upon me, for thine eyes are wounding:—
Yet do not go away:—come, basilisk,
And kill the innocent gazer with thy sight;
For in the shade of death I shall find joy,—
In life, but double death, now Gloster's dead.
Q. Mar. Why do you rate my lord of Suffolk thus?
Although the duke was enemy to him,
Yet he, most Christian-like, laments his death.
K. Hen. Ah, woe is me for Gloster, wretched man!
Q. Mar. Be woe for me, more wretched than he is.
What! dost thou turn away, and hide thy face?
I am no loathsome leper; look on me.
What, art thou, like the adder, waxen deaf?
Be poisonous too, and kill thy forlorn queen.
Is all thy comfort shut in Gloster's tomb?

Noise within. Enter WARWICK *and* SALISBURY. *The* Commons *press to the door*

War. It is reported, mighty sovereign,
That good duke Humphrey traitorously is murder'd
By Suffolk and the cardinal Beaufort's means.
The commons, like an angry hive of bees
That want their leader, scatter up and down,
And care not who they sting in his revenge.
Myself have calm'd their spleenful mutiny,
Until they hear the order of his death.
K. Hen. That he is dead, good Warwick, 'tis too true;
But how he died, heaven knows, not Henry:
Enter his chamber, view his breathless corse,
And comment then upon his sudden death.

War. That shall I do, my liege.—Stay, Salisbury,
With the rude multitude, till I return.

WARWICK *goes into an inner chamber.* SALISBURY *retires to the* Commons *at the door.*

K. Hen. O thou that judgest all things, stay my thoughts,—
My thoughts, that labor to persuade my soul
Some violent hands were laid on Humphrey's life!
If my suspect be false, forgive me, heaven;
For judgment only doth belong to thee.
Fain would I go to chafe his paly lips
With twenty thousand kisses, and to drain
Upon his face an ocean of salt tears;
To tell my love unto his dumb deaf trunk,
And with my fingers feel his hand unfeeling:
But all in vain are these mean obsequies;
And to survey his dead and earthy image,
What were it but to make my sorrow greater?

The doors of the inner chamber are thrown open, and GLOSTER *is discovered dead in his bed;* WARWICK *and others standing by it.*

War. Come hither, gracious sovereign, view this body.
K. Hen. That is to see how deep my grave is made;
For with his soul fled all my worldly solace,
For seeing him, I see my life in death.
War. As surely as my soul intends to live
With that dread King, that took our state upon him
To free us from his Father's wrathful curse,
I do believe that violent hands were laid
Upon the life of this thrice-famèd duke.
Suf. A dreadful oath, sworn with a solemn tongue!
What instance gives lord Warwick for his vow?
War. See, how the blood is settled in his face.
His eye-balls farther out than when he liv'd,
Staring full ghastly like a strangled man;
His hair uprear'd, his nostrils stretch'd with struggling;
His hands abroad display'd, as one that grasp'd
And tugg'd for life, and was by strength subdued:
It cannot be but he was murder'd here;
The least of all these signs were probable.
Suf. Why, Warwick, who should do the duke to death?
Myself and Beaufort had him in protection;
And we, I hope, sir, are no murderers.
War. But both of you were vow'd duke Humphrey's foes;
And you, forsooth, had the good duke to keep;
'Tis like, you would not feast him like a friend;
And 'tis well seen he found an enemy.

Q. Mar. Then you, belike, suspect these noblemen
As guilty of duke Humphrey's timeless death.
War. Who finds the heifer dead, and bleeding fresh,
And sees fast by a butcher with an axe,
But will suspect 'twas he that made the slaughter?
Who finds the partridge in the puttock's * nest,
But may imagine how the bird was dead,
Although the kite soar with unbloodied beak?
Even so suspicious is this tragedy.
Q. Mar. Are you the butcher, Suffolk? where's your knife?
Is Beaufort termed a kite? where are his talons?
Suf. I wear no knife, to slaughter sleeping men;
But here's a vengeful sword, rusted with ease,
That shall be scoured in his rancorous heart,
That slanders me with murder's crimson badge:—
Say, if thou dar'st, proud lord of Warwickshire,
That I am faulty in duke Humphrey's death.
[*Exeunt* CARDINAL, SOMERSET, *and others.*
War. What dares not Warwick, if false Suffolk dare him?
Q. Mar. He dares not calm his contumelious spirit,
Nor cease to be an arrogant controller,
Though Suffolk dare him twenty thousand times.
War. Madam, be still,—with reverence may I say;
For every word you speak in his behalf
Is slander to your royal dignity.
Suf. Blunt-witted lord, ignoble in demeanor!
War. But that the guilt of murder bucklers thee,
And I should rob the deathsman of his fee,
And that my sovereign's presence makes me mild,
I would, false murderous coward, on thy knee
Make thee beg pardon for thy passed speech,
Pernicious bloodsucker of sleeping men.
Suf. Thou shalt be waking while I shed thy blood,
If from this presence thou dar'st go with me.
War. Away even now, or I will drag thee hence:
Unworthy though thou art, I'll cope with thee,
And do some service to duke Humphrey's ghost.
[*Exeunt* SUFFOLK *and* WARWICK.
K. Hen. What stronger breast-plate than a heart untainted!
Thrice is he arm'd that hath his quarrel just;
And he but naked, though lock'd up in steel,
Whose conscience with injustice is corrupted. [*A noise within.*
Q. Mar. What noise is this?

Re-enter SUFFOLK *and* WARWICK, *with their weapons drawn.*

K. Hen. Why, how now, lords! your wrathful weapons drawn

* *Puttock*—kite, or hawk.

Here in our presence! dare you be so bold?—
Why, what tumultuous clamor have we here?
Suf. The traitorous Warwick, with the men of Bury,
Set all upon me, mighty sovereign.
Sal. [*To the* Commons *at the door.*] Sirs, stand apart; the king shall know your mind.— [*Advancing.*
Dread lord, the commons send you word by me,
Unless false Suffolk straight be done to death,
Or banished fair England's territories,
They will by violence tear him from your palace,
And torture him with grievous lingering death.
They say, by him the good duke Humphrey died;
They say, in him they fear your highness' death;
And mere instinct of love and loyalty,—
Free from a stubborn opposite intent,
As being thought to contradict your liking,—
Makes them thus forward in his banishment.
Commons. [*Within.*] An answer from the king, my lord of Salisbury!
Suf. 'Tis like the commons, rude unpolish'd hinds,
Could send such message to their sovereign:
But you, my lord, were glad to be employ'd,
To show how quaint an orator you are:
But all the honor Salisbury hath won,
Is, that he was the lord embassador,
Sent from a sort of tinkers to the king.
Commons. [*Within.*] An answer from the king, or we will all break in!
K. Hen. Go, Salisbury, and tell them all from me,
I thank them for their tender loving care;
And had I not been cited so by them,
Yet did I purpose as they do entreat;
For, sure, my thoughts do hourly prophesy
Mischance unto my state by Suffolk's means;
And therefore,—by His majesty I swear,
Whose far unworthy deputy I am,—
He shall not breathe infection in this air
But three days longer, on the pain of death. [*Exit* SALISBURY.
Q. Mar. O Henry, let me plead for gentle Suffolk!
K. Hen. Ungentle queen, to call him gentle Suffolk!
No more, I say: if thou dost plead for him,
Thou wilt but add increase unto my wrath.
Had I but said, I would have kept my word;
But when I swear, it is irrevocable.—
If after three days' space, thou here be'st found
On any ground that I am ruler of,
The world shall not be ransom for thy life.—

Come, Warwick, come, good Warwick, go with me;
I have great matters to impart to thee.
[*Exeunt* KING HENRY, WARWICK, Lords, *&c.*

Q. Mar. Mischance and sorrow go along with you!
Heart's discontent, and sour affliction,
Be playfellows to keep you company!
And threefold vengeance tend upon your steps!

Suf. Cease, gentle queen, these execrations,
And let thy Suffolk take his heavy leave.

Q. Mar. Fie, coward woman, and soft-hearted wretch!
Hast thou not spirit to curse thine enemies?

Suf. A plague upon them! wherefore should I curse them?
Would curses kill, as doth the mandrake's groan,
I would invent as bitter-searching terms,
As curst, as harsh, and horrible to hear,
Deliver'd strongly through my fixed teeth,
With full as many signs of deadly hate,
As lean-fac'd Envy in her loathsome cave:
My tongue should stumble in mine earnest words;
Mine eyes should sparkle like the beaten flint;
My hair be fix'd on end, as one distract;
Ay, every joint should seem to curse and ban:
And even now my burden'd heart would break,
Should I not curse them. Poison be their drink!
Gall, worse than gall, the daintiest that they taste!
Their sweetest shade, a grove of cypress trees!
Their chiefest prospect, murdering basilisks!
Their softest touch, as smart as lizards' stings!
Their music, frightful as the serpent's hiss,
And boding screech-owls make the concert full!

Q. Mar. Enough, sweet Suffolk; thou torment'st thyself.

Suf. You bade me ban, and will you bid me leave?
Now, by the ground that I am banish'd from,
Well could I curse away a winter's night,
Though standing naked on a mountain top,
Where biting cold would never let grass grow,
And think it but a minute spent in sport.

Q. Mar. O, let me entreat thee, cease! Give me thy hand,
That I may dew it with my mournful tears;
Nor let the rain of heaven wet this place,
To wash away my woful monuments.
O, could this kiss be printed in thy hand [*Kisses his hand.*
That thou might'st think upon these by the seal,
Through whom a thousand sighs are breath'd for thee!
So, get thee gone, that I may know my grief;
Go; speak not to me; even now be gone.

Suf. Thus is poor Suffolk ten times banished,
Once by the king, and three times thrice by thee.

Enter VAUX.

Q. Mar. Whither goes Vaux so fast? what news, I pr'ythee?
Vaux. To signify unto his majesty
That cardinal Beaufort is at point of death;
And I am sent to tell his majesty
That even now he cries aloud for him.
Q. Mar. Go tell this heavy message to the king. [*Exit* VAUX.
Ah me! what is this world! what news are these!
But wherefore grieve I at an hour's poor loss,
Omitting Suffolk's exile, my soul's treasure?
Now get thee hence: the king, thou know'st, is coming;
If thou be found by me, thou art but dead.
To France, sweet Suffolk: let me hear from thee;
For wheresoe'er thou art in this world's globe,
I'll have an Iris that shall find thee out.
Suf. I go.
Q. Mar. And take my heart with thee.
Suf. A jewel, lock'd into the wofull'st cask
That ever did contain a thing of worth.
Even as a splitted bark, so sunder we:
This way fall I to death.
Q. Mar. This way for me. [*Exeunt, severally.*

SCENE III.—London. CARDINAL BEAUFORT'S *Bedchamber.*

Enter KING HENRY, SALISBURY, WARWICK, *and others. The* CARDINAL *in bed;* Attendants *with him.*

K. Hen. How fares my lord? speak, Beaufort, to thy sovereign.
Car. If thou be'st death, I'll give thee England's treasure,
Enough to purchase such another island,
So thou wilt let me live, and feel no pain.
K. Hen. Ah, what a sign it is of evil life,
Where death's approach is seen so terrible!
War. Beaufort, it is thy sovereign speaks to thee.
Car. Bring me unto my trial when you will.
Died he not in his bed? where should he die?
Can I make men live, whe'r they will or no?
O, torture me no more! I will confess.—
Alive again? then show me where he is:
I'll give a thousand pound to look upon him.—
He hath no eyes, the dust hath blinded them.—
Comb down his hair; look, look! it stands upright,
Like lime-twigs set to catch my wingèd soul!—
Give me some drink; and bid the apothecary
Bring the strong poison that I bought of him.

K. Hen. O thou eternal mover of the heavens,
Look with a gentle eye upon this wretch!
O, beat away the busy meddling fiend,
That lays strong siege unto this wretch's soul,
And from his bosom purge this black despair!
War. See how the pangs of death do make him grin!
Sal. Disturb him not, let him pass peaceably.
K. Hen. Peace to his soul, if heaven's good pleasure be!—
Lord cardinal, if thou think'st on heaven's bliss,
Hold up thy hand, make signal of thy hope.—
He dies, and makes no sign: O heaven, forgive him!
War. So bad a death argues a monstrous life.
K. Hen. Forbear to judge, for we are sinners all.—
Close up his eyes, and draw the curtain close;
And let us all to meditation. [*Exeunt.*

ACT IV.

SCENE I.—Kent. *The Sea-shore near* Dover.

Firing heard at Sea. Then enter from a boat, a Captain, *a* Master, *a* Master's-Mate, Walter Whitmore, *and others; with them* Suffolk, *disguised; and other* Gentlemen, *prisoners.*

In this scene the Duke of Suffolk is murdered by Walter Whitmore and his associates.

SCENE II.—Blackheath.

Enter George Bevis *and* John Holland.

Geo. Come, and get thee a sword, though made of a lath: they have been up these two days.

John. They have the more need to sleep now, then.

Geo. I tell thee, Jack Cade, the clothier, means to dress the commonwealth, and turn it, and set a new nap upon it.

John. So he had need, for 'tis threadbare. Well, I say, it was never merry world in England, since gentlemen came up.

Geo. O miserable age! Virtue is not regarded in handicraftsmen.

John. The nobility think scorn to go in leather aprons.

Geo. Nay, more, the king's council are no good workmen.

John. True; and yet it is said,—labor in thy vocation; which is as much to say, as,—let the magistrates be laboring men; and therefore should we be magistrates.

Geo. Thou hast hit it; for there's no better sign of a brave mind, than a hard hand.

John. I see them! I see them! There's Best's son, the tanner of Wingham,—

Geo. He shall have the skins of our enemies to make dog's leather of.

John. And Dick the butcher,—

Geo. Then is sin struck down like an ox, and iniquity's throat cut like a calf.

John. And Smith the weaver,—

Geo. Their thread of life is spun.

John. Come, come, let's fall in with them.

Drum. *Enter* CADE, DICK *the Butcher*, SMITH *the Weaver, and others in great number.*

Cade. We John Cade, so termed of our supposed father,—

Dick. [*Aside.*] Or rather, of stealing a cade of herrings.

Cade. For our enemies shall fall before us,—inspired with the spirit of putting down kings and princes,—Command silence.

Dick. Silence!

Cade. My father was a Mortimer,—

Dick. [*Aside.*] He was an honest man, and a good bricklayer.

Cade. My mother a Plantagenet,—

Dick. [*Aside.*] I knew her well; she was a nurse.

Cade. My wife descended of the Lacies,—

Dick. [*Aside.*] She was, indeed, a pedler's daughter, and sold many laces.

Smith. [*Aside.*] But now of late, not able to travel with her furred pack, she washes bucks here at home.

Cade. Therefore am I of an honorable house.

Dick. [*Aside.*] Ay, by my faith, the field is honorable; and there was he born, under a hedge; for his father had never a house, but the cage.

Cade. Valiant I am.

Smith. [*Aside.*] 'A must needs; for beggary is valiant.

Cade. I am able to endure much.

Dick. [*Aside.*] No question of that; for I have seen him whipped three market days together.

Cade. I fear neither sword nor fire.

Smith. [*Aside.*] He need not fear the sword; for his coat is of proof.

Dick. [*Aside.*] But methinks he should stand in fear of fire, being burnt i' the hand for stealing of sheep.

Cade. Be brave, then; for your captain is brave, and vows reformation. There shall be in England seven half-penny loaves sold for a penny: the three-hooped pot shall have ten hoops; and I will make it felony, to drink small beer: all the realm shall be in common; and in Cheapside shall my palfrey go to grass: and, when I am king, (as king I will be)—

All. Heaven save your majesty!

Cade. I thank you, good people:—there shall be no money; all shall eat and drink on my score; and I will apparel them all in one livery, that they may agree like brothers, and worship me their lord.

Dick. The first thing we do, let's kill all the lawyers.

Cade. Nay, that I mean to do. Is not this a lamentable thing, that of the skin of an innocent lamb should be made parchment? that parchment, being scribbled o'er, should undo a man? Some say, the bee stings: but I say, 'tis the bee's wax; for I did but seal once to a thing, and I was never mine own man since.—How now! who's there?

Enter some, bringing in the Clerk of Chatham.

Smith. The clerk of Chatham: he can write and read, and cast accounts.

Cade. O monstrous!

Smith. We took him setting of boys' copies.

Cade. Here's a villain!

Smith. H'as a book in his pocket, with red letters in't.

Cade. Nay, then, he is a conjurer.

Dick. Nay, he can make obligations, and write court-hand.

Cade. I am sorry for't: the man is a proper man, of mine honor; unless I find him guilty, he shall not die.—Come hither, sirrah, I must examine thee: what is thy name?

Clerk. Emmanuel.

Dick. They use to write it on the top of letters.—'Twill go hard with you.

Cade. Let me alone.—Dost thou use to write thy name? or hast thou a mark to thyself, like an honest plain-dealing man?

Clerk. Sir, I thank heaven, I have been so well brought up, that I can write my name.

All. He hath confessed: away with him! he's a villain, and a traitor.

Cade. Away with him, I say! hang him with his pen and ink-horn about his neck. [*Exeunt some with the* Clerk.

Enter Michael.

Mich. Where's our general?

Cade. Here I am, thou particular fellow.

Mich. Fly, fly, fly! Sir Humphrey Stafford and his brother are hard by, with the king's forces.

Cade. Stand, villain, stand, or I'll fell thee down. He shall be encountered with a man as good as himself: he is but a knight, is 'a?

Mich. No.

Cade. To equal him, I will make myself a knight presently. [*Kneels.*] Rise up Sir John Mortimer. [*Rises.*] Now have at him.

Enter Sir Humphrey Stafford *and* William *his Brother, with drum and forces.*

Staf. Rebellious hinds, the filth and scum of Kent,
Mark'd for the gallows, lay your weapons down;
Home to your cottages, forsake this groom:—
The king is merciful, if you revolt.
W. Staf. But angry, wrathful, and inclin'd to blood,
If you go forward; therefore yield, or die.
Cade. As for these silken-coated slaves, I pass not:
It is to you, good people, that I speak,
O'er whom, in time to come, I hope to reign;
For I am rightful heir unto the crown.
Staf. Villain, thy father was a plasterer;
And thou thyself a shearman,—art thou not?
Cade. And Adam was a gardener.
W. Staf. And what of that?
Cade. Marry, this:—Edmund Mortimer, earl of March,
Married the duke of Clarence' daughter,—did he not?
Staf. Ay, sir.
Cade. By her he had two children at one birth.
W. Staf. That's false.
Cade. Ay, there's the question; but I say, 'tis true:
The elder of them, being put to nurse,
Was by a beggar-woman stol'n away;
And, ignorant of his birth and parentage,
Became a bricklayer when he came to age:
His son am I; deny it, if you can.
Dick. Nay, 'tis too true; therefore he shall be king.

Smith. Sir, he made a chimney in my father's house, and the bricks are alive at this day to testify it; therefore deny it not.

Staf. And will you credit this base drudge's words,
That speaks he knows not what?
All. Ay, marry, will we; therefore get ye gone.
W. Staf. Jack Cade, the duke of York hath taught you this.

Cade. [*Aside.*] He lies, for I invented it myself.—Go to, sirrah: tell the king from me, that, for his father's sake, Henry the fifth, I am content he shall reign; but I'll be protector over him.

Dick. And farthermore, we'll have the lord Say's head, for selling the dukedom of Maine.

Cade. And good reason; for thereby is England maimed, and fain to go with a staff, but that my puissance holds it up. Fellow kings, I tell you that that lord Say hath injured the commonwealth: and more than that, he can speak French; and therefore he is a traitor.

Staf. O, gross and miserable ignorance!

Cade. Nay, answer, if you can:—the Frenchmen are our

enemies; go to, then, I ask but this,—can he that speaks with the tongue of an enemy be a good counsellor, or no?

All. No, no; and therefore we'll have his head.

W. Staf. Well, seeing gentle words will not prevail,
Assail them with the army of the king.

Staf. Herald, away; and throughout every town,
Proclaim them traitors that are up with Cade;
That those which fly before the battle ends,
May, even in their wives' and children's sight,
Be hang'd up for example at their doors:—
And you, that be the king's friends, follow me.
[*Exeunt the two* STAFFORDS *and forces.*

Cade. And you, that love the commons, follow me.
Now show yourselves men: 'tis for liberty.
We will not leave one lord, one gentleman:
Spare none but such as go in clouted shoon;
For they are thrifty honest men, and such
As would (but that they dare not) take our parts.

Dick. They are all in order, and march toward us.

Cade. But then are we in order, when we are most out of order. Come, march forward! [*Exeunt.*

SCENE III.—*Another part of* Blackheath.

Alarums. The two Parties enter and fight, and both the STAFFORDS *are slain.*

Cade. Where's Dick, the butcher of Ashford?

Dick. Here, sir.

Cade. They fell before thee like sheep and oxen, and thou behavedst thyself as if thou hadst been in thine own slaughter-house: therefore, thus will I reward thee,—the Lent shall be as long again as it is; and thou shalt have a license to kill for a hundred lacking one.

Dick. I desire no more.

Cade. And, to speak truth, thou deservest no less. This monument of the victory will I bear; [*Puts on Sir* H. STAFFORD'S *armor.*] and the bodies shall be dragged at my horse' heels, till I do come to London, where we will have the mayor's sword borne before us.

Dick. If we mean to thrive and do good, break open the jails, and let out the prisoners.

Cade. Fear not that, I warrant thee.—Come, let's march towards London. [*Exeunt.*

SCENE IV.—London. *A Room in the Palace.*

Enter KING HENRY, *reading a Supplication; the* DUKE OF BUCKINGHAM *and* LORD SAY *with him: at a distance,* QUEEN MARGARET *mourning over* SUFFOLK'S *head.*

Q. Mar. Oft have I heard that grief softens the mind,
And makes it fearful and degenerate;
Think therefore on revenge, and cease to weep.
But who can cease to weep, and look on this?
Here may his head lie on my throbbing breast:
But where's the body that I should embrace?

Buck. What answer makes your grace to the rebels' supplication?

K. Hen. I'll send some holy bishop to entreat;
For heaven forbid so many simple souls
Should perish by the sword! And I myself,
Rather than bloody war shall cut them short,
Will parley with Jack Cade their general:
But stay, I'll read it over once again.

Q. Mar. Ah, barbarous villains! hath this lovely face
Rul'd, like a wandering planet, over me,
And could it not enforce them to relent,
That were unworthy to behold the same?

K. Hen. Lord Say, Jack Cade hath sworn to have thy head.

Say. Ay, but I hope your highness shall have his.

K. Hen. How now, madam!
Still lamenting and mourning for Suffolk's death?
I fear me, love, if that I had been dead,
Thou wouldest not have mourn'd so much for me.

Q. Mar. No, my love; I should not mourn, but die for thee.

Enter a Messenger.

K. Hen. How now: what news? why com'st thou in such haste?

Mess. The rebels are in Southwark; fly, my lord!
Jack Cade proclaims himself lord Mortimer,
Descended from the duke of Clarence' house;
And calls your grace usurper openly,
And vows to crown himself in Westminster.
His army is a ragged multitude
Of hinds and peasants, rude and merciless:
Sir Humphrey Stafford and his brother's death
Hath given them heart and courage to proceed:
All scholars, lawyers, courtiers, gentlemen,
They call false caterpillars, and intend their death.

K. Hen. O graceless men! they know not what they do.

Buck. My gracious lord, retire to Killingworth,
Until a power be rais'd to put them down.
Q. Mar. Ah, were the duke of Suffolk now alive,
These Kentish rebels would be soon appeas'd!
K. Hen. Lord Say, the traitors hate thee;
Therefore away with us to Killingworth.
Say. So might your grace's person be in danger;
The sight of me is odious in their eyes:
And therefore in this city will I stay,
And live alone as secret as I may.

Enter a second Messenger.

2 *Mess.* Jack Cade hath gotten London bridge; the citizens
Fly and forsake their houses:
The rascal people, thirsting after prey,
Join with the traitor; and they jointly swear
To spoil the city, and your royal court.
Buck. Then linger not, my lord; away, take horse.
K. Hen. Come, Margaret; heaven, our hope, will succor us.
Q. Mar. My hope is gone, now Suffolk is deceas'd.
K. Hen. [*To* LORD SAY.] Farewell, my lord: trust not the Kentish rebels.
Buck. Trust nobody, for fear you be betray'd.
Say. The trust I have is in mine innocence,
And therefore am I bold and resolute. [*Exeunt.*

SCENE VI.—London. *Cannon Street.*

Enter JACK CADE *and his followers. He strikes his staff on London stone.*

Cade. Now is Mortimer lord of this city. And here, sitting upon London-stone, I charge and command, that, of the city's cost, the conduit run nothing but claret wine this first year of our reign. And now, henceforward, it shall be treason for any that calls me other than lord Mortimer.

Enter a Soldier *running.*

Sold. Jack Cade! Jack Cade!
Cade. Knock him down there. [*They kill him.*
Smith. If this fellow be wise, he'll never call you Jack Cade more: I think he hath a very fair warning.
Dick. My lord, there's an army gathered together in Smithfield.
Cade. Come then, let's go fight with them: but first, go and set London-bridge on fire; and, if you can, burn down the Tower too. Come, let's away. [*Exeunt.*

SCENE VII.—London. *Smithfield.*

Alarum. Enter, on one side, CADE *and his company; on the other,* Citizens, *and the* King's *forces, headed by* MATTHEW GOUGH. *They fight; the* Citizens *are routed, and* MATTHEW GOUGH *is slain.*

Cade. So, sirs:—Now go some and pull down the Savoy; others to the inns of court; down with them all.

Dick. I have a suit unto your lordship.

Cade. Be it a lordship, thou shalt have it for that word.

Dick. Only, that the laws of England may come out of your mouth.

John. [*Aside.*] Mass, 'twill be sore law, then; for he was thrust in the mouth with a spear, and 'tis not whole yet.

Cade. I have thought upon it, it shall be so. Away, burn all the records of the realm: my mouth shall be the parliament of England.

John. [*Aside.*] Then we are like to have biting statutes, unless his teeth be pulled out.

Cade. And henceforward all things shall be in common.

Enter a Messenger.

Mess. My lord, a prize, a prize! here's the lord Say, which sold the towns in France; he that made us pay one and twenty fifteens, and one shilling to the pound, the last subsidy.

Enter GEORGE BEVIS, *with the* LORD SAY.

Cade. Well, he shall be beheaded for it ten times.—Ah, thou say, thou serge, nay, thou buckram lord! now art thou within point-blank of our jurisdiction regal. What canst thou answer to my majesty, for giving up of Normandy unto the dauphin of France? Be it known unto thee, by these presence, even the presence of lord Mortimer, that I am the besom that must sweep the court clean of such dirt as thou art. Thou hast most traitorously corrupted the youth of the realm in erecting a grammar-school: and whereas, before, our fore-fathers had no other books but the score and the tally, thou hast caused printing to be used; and, contrary to the king, his crown, and dignity, thou hast built a paper-mill. It will be proved to thy face, that thou hast men about thee, that usually talk of a noun, and a verb, and such abominable words, as no Christian ear can endure to hear. Thou hast appointed justices of peace, to call poor men before them about matters they were not able to answer. Moreover, thou hast put them in prison; and because they could not read, thou hast hanged them; when, indeed, only for that cause they have been most worthy to live. Thou dost ride on a footcloth, dost thou not?

Say. What of that?

Cade. Marry, thou oughtest not to let thy horse wear a cloak, when honester men than thou go in their hose and doublets.

Say. You men of Kent,—

Dick. What say you of Kent?

Say. Nothing but this,—'tis *bona terra, mala gens.*

Cade. Away with him, away with him! he speaks Latin.

Say. Great men have reaching hands; oft have I struck
Those that I never saw, and struck them dead.

Geo. O monstrous coward! what, to come behind folks?

Say. These cheeks are pale for watching for your good.

Cade. Give him a box o' the ear, and that will make 'em red again.

Say. Long sitting, to determine poor men's causes,
Hath made me full of sickness and diseases.

Cade. Ye shall have a hempen caudle, then, and the help of hatchet.

Dick. Why dost thou quiver, man?

Say. The palsy, and not fear, provoketh me.

Cade. Nay, he nods at us, as who should say, I'll be even with you: I'll see if his head will stand steadier on a pole, or no. Take him away, and behead him.

Say. Tell me, wherein have I offended most?
Have I affected wealth, or honor? speak.
Are my chests fill'd up with extorted gold?
Is my apparel sumptuous to behold?
Whom have I injur'd, that ye seek my death?
These hands are free from guiltless blood-shedding,
This breast from harboring foul deceitful thoughts.
O, let me live!

Cade. [*Aside.*] I feel remorse in myself with his words; but I'll bridle it: he shall die, an it be but for pleading so well for his life.—Away with him! he has a familiar * under his tongue. Go, take him away, I say, and strike off his head presently; and then break into his son-in-law's house, Sir James Cromer, and strike off his head, and bring them both upon two poles hither.

All. It shall be done.

Say. Ah, countrymen! if when you make your prayers,
Heaven should be so obdurate as yourselves,
How would it fare with your departed souls?
And therefore yet relent, and save my life.

Cade. Away with him! and do as I command ye.

[*Exeunt some, with* LORD SAY.

The proudest peer in the realm shall not wear a head on his shoulders, unless he pay me tribute.

Dick. My lord, when shall we go to Cheapside, and take up commodities upon our bills?

* *Familiar*—an evil spirit.

Cade. Marry, presently.
All. O, brave!

Re-enter Rebels with the heads of LORD SAY *and his Son-in-law.*

Cade. But is not this braver?—Let them kiss one another, for they loved well, when they were alive. Now part them again, lest they consult about the giving up of some more towns in France. Soldiers, defer the spoil of the city until night: for with these borne before us, instead of maces, will we ride through the streets; and at every corner have them kiss.—Away!
[*Exeunt.*

SCENE VIII.—Southwark.

Alarum. Enter CADE *and all his rabblement.*

Cade. Up Fish street! down Saint Magnus' corner! kill and knock down! throw them into Thames!—[*A parley sounded, then a retreat.*] What noise is this I hear? Dare any be so bold to sound retreat or parley, when I command them kill?

Enter BUCKINGHAM *and Old* CLIFFORD, *with forces.*

Buck. Ay, here they be that dare, and will disturb thee.
Know, Cade, we come embassadors from the king
Unto the commons whom thou hast misled:
And here pronounce free pardon to them all,
That will forsake thee, and go home in peace.
Clif. What say ye, countrymen? will ye relent,
And yield to mercy, whilst 'tis offer'd you;
Or let a rebel lead you to your deaths?
Who loves the king, and will embrace his pardon,
Fling up his cap, and say—God save his majesty!
Who hateth him, and honors not his father,
Henry the fifth, that made all France to quake,
Shake he his weapon at us, and pass by.
All. God save the king! God save king!
Cade. What, Buckingham, and Clifford, are ye so brave?—And you, base peasants, do ye believe him? will you needs be hanged with your pardons about your necks? Hath my sword therefore broke through London Gates, that you should leave me at the White Hart in Southwark? I thought ye would never have given out these arms, till you had recovered your ancient freedom: but you are all recreants and dastards, and delight to live in slavery to the nobility. Let them break your backs with burdens, take your houses over your heads: for me, I will make shift for one; and so, heaven's curse 'light upon you all!
All. We'll follow Cade, we'll follow Cade!
Clif. Is Cade the son of Henry the fifth,
That thus you do exclaim, you'll go with him?

Will he conduct you through the heart of France,
And make the meanest of you earls and dukes?
Alas, he hath no home, no place to fly to;
Nor knows he how to live, but by the spoil,
Unless by robbing of your friends, and us.
Were't not a shame, that whilst you live at jar,
The fearful French, whom you late vanquished,
Should make a start o'er seas, and vanquish you?
Methinks already in this civil broil,
I see them lording it in London streets.
Better ten thousand base-born Cades miscarry,
Than you should stoop unto a Frenchman's mercy.
To France, to France, and get what you have lost;
Spare England, for it is your native coast:
Henry hath money, you are strong and manly;
Heaven on our side, doubt not of victory.

All. A Clifford! a Clifford! we'll follow the king, and Clifford.

Cade. [*Aside.*] Was ever feather so lightly blown to and fro, as this multitude? the name of Henry the fifth hales them to a hundred mischiefs, and makes them leave me desolate. I see them lay their heads together, to surprise me: my sword make way for me, for here is no staying.—Heavens and honor be witness, that no want of resolution in me, but only my followers' base and ignominious treasons, makes me betake me to my heels. [*Exit.*

Buck. What! is he fled? go some, and follow him;
And he, that brings his head unto the king,
Shall have a thousand crowns for his reward.—
[*Exeunt some of them.*
Follow me, soldiers: we'll devise a mean
To reconcile you all unto the king. [*Exeunt.*

Cade's rebellion is suppressed by the king's forces, and Cade is slain. The Duke of York gathers an army in Ireland, and lands in England, expecting to be assisted by Cade and the insurgents, in his attempt to depose King Henry.

ACT V.

SCENE I.—Kent. *Fields between* Dartford *and* Blackheath.

The KING'S *Camp on one side: on the other, enter* YORK *attended, with drum and colors; his forces at some distance.*

York. From Ireland thus comes York, to claim his right,
And pluck the crown from feeble Henry's head:
Ring, bells, aloud; burn, bonfires, clear and bright;
To entertain great England's lawful king.

Enter BUCKINGHAM.

[*Aside.*] Whom have we here? Buckingham, to disturb me?
The king hath sent him, sure: I must dissemble.
Buck. York, if thou meanest well, I greet thee well.
York. Humphrey of Buckingham, I accept thy greeting.
Art thou a messenger, or come of pleasure?
Buck. A messenger from Henry, our dread liege,
To know the reason of these arms in peace;
Or why thou,—being a subject as I am,—
Against thy oath and true allegiance sworn,
Should'st raise so great a power without his leave,
Or dare to bring thy force so near the court.
York. [*Aside.*] Scarce can I speak, my choler is so great:
O, I could hew up rocks, and fight with flint,
I am so angry at these abject terms;
I am far better born than is the king;
More like a king, more kingly in my thoughts;
But I must make fair weather yet awhile,
Till Henry be more weak, and I more strong.—
[*Aloud.*] Buckingham, I pr'ythee, pardon me,
That I have given no answer all this while;
My mind was troubled with deep melancholy.
The cause why I have brought this army hither,
Is, to remove proud Somerset from the king,
Seditious to his grace, and to the state.
Buck. That is too much presumption on thy part:
But if thy arms be to no other end,
The king hath yielded unto thy demand;
The duke of Somerset is in the Tower.
York. Upon thine honor, is he prisoner?
Buck. Upon mine honor, he is prisoner.
York. Then, Buckingham, I do dismiss my powers.—
Soldiers, I thank you all; disperse yourselves;
Meet me to-morrow in St. George's field,
You shall have pay, and every thing you wish.—
And let my sovereign, virtuous Henry,
Command my eldest son,—nay, all my sons,
As pledges of my fealty and love;
I'll send them all, as willing as I live:
Lands, goods, horse, armor, any thing I have,
Is his to use, so Somerset may die.
Buck. York, I commend this kind submission:
We twain will go into his highness' tent.

Enter KING HENRY, *attended.*

K. Hen. Buckingham, doth York intend no harm to us,
That thus he marcheth with thee arm in arm?

York. In all submission and humility,
York doth present himself unto your highness.
K. Hen. Then what intend these forces thou dost bring?
York. To heave the traitor Somerset from hence;
And fight against that monstrous rebel, Cade,
Who since I heard to be discomfited.

Enter IDEN, *with* CADE's *head*.

Iden. If one so rude, and of so mean condition,
May pass into the presence of a king,
Lo, I present your grace a traitor's head,
The head of Cade, whom I in combat slew.
K. Hen. The head of Cade!—Great heaven, how just art thou!—
O, let me view his visage, being dead,
That living wrought me such exceeding trouble.—
Tell me, my friend, art thou the man that slew him?
Iden. I was, an't like your majesty.
K. Hen. How art thou call'd? and what is thy degree?
Iden. Alexander Iden, that's my name;
A poor esquire of Kent, that loves his king.
Buck. So please it you, my lord, 'twere not amiss
He were created knight for his good service.
K. Hen. Iden, kneel down. [*He kneels*.] Rise up a knight.
We give thee for reward a thousand marks;
And will, that thou henceforth attend on us.
Iden. May Iden live to merit such a bounty,
And never live but true unto his liege!
K. Hen. See, Buckingham! Somerset comes with the queen:
Go, bid her hide him quickly from the duke.

Enter QUEEN MARGARET *and* SOMERSET.

Q. Mar. For thousand Yorks he shall not hide his head,
But boldly stand, and front him to his face.
York. How now! is Somerset at liberty?
Then, York, unloose thy long-imprison'd thoughts,
And let thy tongue be equal with thy heart.
Shall I endure the sight of Somerset?—
False king! why hast thou broken faith with me,
Knowing how hardly I can brook abuse?
King did I call thee? no, thou art not king;
Not fit to govern and rule multitudes,
Which dar'st not, no, nor canst not rule a traitor.
That head of thine doth not become a crown;
Thy hand is made to grasp a palmer's staff,
And not to grace an awful princely sceptre.
That gold must round engirt these brows of mine;
Whose smile and frown, like to Achilles' spear,

Is able with the change to kill and cure.
Here is a hand to hold a sceptre up,
And with the same to act controlling laws.
Give place: by heaven, thou shalt rule no more
O'er him whom heaven created for thy ruler.
Som. O monstrous traitor!—I arrest thee, York,
Of capital treason 'gainst the king and crown:
Obey, audacious traitor; kneel for grace.
York. Would'st have me kneel? first let me ask of these,
If they can brook I bow a knee to man.—
Sirrah, call in my sons to be my bail: [*Exit an* Attendant.
I know, ere they will have me go to ward,
They'll pawn their swords for my enfranchisement.
Q. Mar. Call hither Clifford; bid him come amain,
To say, if that the base-born sons of York
Shall be the surety for their traitor father.
York. O, blood-bespotted Neapolitan,
Outcast of Naples, England's bloody scourge!
The sons of York, thy betters in their birth,
Shall be their father's bail; and bane to those
That for my surety will refuse the boys!
See where they come: I'll warrant they'll make it good.
Q. Mar. And here comes Clifford, to deny their bail.

Enter EDWARD *and* RICHARD PLANTAGENET, *with forces at one side; at the other, with forces also, Old* CLIFFORD *and his Son.*

Clif. [*Kneeling.*] Health and all happiness to my lord the king!
York. I thank thee, Clifford: say, what news with thee?
Nay, do not fright us with an angry look:
We are thy sovereign, Clifford, kneel again;
For thy mistaking so, we pardon thee.
Clif. This is my king, York, I do not mistake
But thou mistak'st me much, to think I do:—
To Bedlam with him! is the man grown mad?
K. Hen. Ay, Clifford; a bedlam and ambitious humor
Makes him oppose himself against his king.
Clif. He is a traitor; let him to the Tower,
And chop away that factious pate of his.
Q. Mar. He is arrested, but will not obey;
His sons, he says, shall give their words for him.
York. Will you not, sons?
Edw. Ay, noble father, if our words will serve.
Rich. And if words will not, then our weapons shall.
Clif. Why, what a brood of traitors have we here!
York. Look in a glass, and call thy image so:
I am thy king, and thou a false-heart traitor.—

Call hither to the stake my two brave bears,
That with the very shaking of their chains
They may astonish these fell lurking curs:
Bid Salisbury, and Warwick, come to me.

Drums. Enter WARWICK *and* SALISBURY, *with forces.*

Clif. Are thèse thy bears? we'll bait thy bears to death,
And manacle the bear-ward in their chains,
If thou dar'st bring them to the baiting-place.
Rich. Oft have I seen a hot o'erweening cur
Run back and bite, because he was withheld;
Who, being suffer'd with the bear's fell paw,
Hath clapp'd his tail between his legs, and cried:
And such a piece of service will you do,
If you oppose yourselves to match lord Warwick.
Clif. Hence, heap of wrath, foul indigested lump,
As crooked in thy manners as thy shape!
York. Nay, we shall heat you thoroughly anon.
Clif. Take heed, lest by your heat you burn yourselves.
K. Hen. Why, Warwick, hath thy knee forgot to bow?—
Old Salisbury,—shame to thy silver hair,
Thou mad misleader of thy brain-sick son!
What, wilt thou on thy death-bed play the ruffian,
And seek for sorrow with thy spectacles?—
O, where is faith? O, where is loyalty?
If it be banish'd from the frosty head,
Where shall it find a harbor in the earth?—
Wilt thou go dig a grave to find out war,
And shame thine honorable age with blood?
Why art thou old, and want'st experience?
Or wherefore dost abuse it, if thou hast it?
For shame! in duty bend thy knee to me,
That bows unto the grave with mickle age.
Sal. My lord, I have consider'd with myself
The title of this most renownèd duke;
And in my conscience do repute his grace
The rightful heir to England's royal seat.
K. Hen. Hast thou not sworn allegiance unto me?
Sal. I have.
K. Hen. Canst thou dispense with heaven for such an oath?
Sal. It is great sin to swear unto a sin;
But greater sin to keep a sinful oath.
Who can be bound by any solemn vow
To do a murderous deed, to rob a man,
To reave the orphan of his patrimony,
To wring the widow from her custom'd right;
And have no other reason for this wrong,
But that he was bound by a solemn oath?

Q. Mar. A subtle traitor needs no sophister.
K. Hen. Call Buckingham, and bid him arm himself.
York. Call Buckingham, and all the friends thou hast;
I am resolv'd for death, or dignity.
Clif. The first I warrant thee, if dreams prove true.
War. You were best to go to bed and dream again,
To keep thee from the tempest of the field.
Clif. I am resolv'd to bear a greater storm,
Than any thou canst conjure up to-day;
And that I'll write upon thy burgonet,
Might I but know thee by thy household badge.
War. Now, by my father's badge, old Nevil's crest,
The rampant bear chain'd to the ragged staff,
This day I'll wear aloft my burgonet,
(As on a mountain-top the cedar shows,
That keeps his leaves in spite of any storm)
Even to affright thee with the view thereof.
Clif. And from thy burgonet I'll rend thy bear,
And tread it underfoot with all contempt,
Despite the bear-ward that protects the bear.
Y. Clif. And so to arms, victorious father,
To quell the rebels, and their 'complices. [*Exeunt severally.*

SCENE II.—Saint Albans.

Alarums. Excursions. Enter WARWICK.

War. Clifford of Cumberland, 'tis Warwick calls!
And if thou dost not hide thee from the bear,
Now,—when the angry trumpet sounds alarm,
And dead men's cries do fill the empty air,—
Clifford, I say, come forth and fight with me!
Proud northern lord, Clifford of Cumberland,
Warwick is hoarse with calling thee to arms.

Enter YORK.

How now, my noble lord! what, all a-foot?
York. The deadly-handed Clifford slew my steed
But match to match I have encounter'd him,
And made a prey for carrion kites and crows
Even of the bonny beast he lov'd so well.

Enter Old CLIFFORD.

War. Of one or both of us the time is come.
York. Hold, Warwick, seek thee out some other chace,
For I myself must hunt this deer to death.
War. Then, nobly, York; 'tis for a crown thou fight'st.—
As I intend, Clifford, to thrive to-day,
It grieves my soul to leave thee unassail'd. [*Exit.*

Clif. What seest thou in me, York? why dost thou pause?
York. With thy brave bearing should I be in love,
But that thou art so fast mine enemy.
Clif. Nor should thy prowess want praise and esteem
But that 'tis shown ignobly, and in treason.
York. So let it help me now against thy sword,
As I in justice and true right express it.
Clif. My soul and body on the action both!
York. A dreadful lay!—address thee instantly.
[*They fight, and* CLIFFORD *falls and dies.*
York. Thus war hath given thee peace, for thou art still.
Peace with his soul, heaven, if it be thy will! [*Exit.*

Enter Young CLIFFORD.

Y. Clif. Shame and confusion! all is on the rout;
Fear frames disorder, and disorder wounds
Where it should guard. O war!
Whom angry heavens do make their minister,
Throw in the frozen bosoms of our part
Hot coals of vengeance!—Let no soldier fly:
He that is truly delicate to war,
Hath no self-love; nor he, that loves himself,
Hath not essentially, but by circumstance,
The name of valor.— [*Seeing his father's body.*
O, let the vile world end,
And the premisèd flames of the last day
Knit earth and heaven together!
Now let the general trumpet blow his blast,
Particularities and petty sounds
To cease!—Wast thou ordain'd, dear father,
To lose thy youth in peace, and to achieve
The silver livery of advised age,
And, in thy reverence, and thy chair-days, thus
To die in ruffian battle?—Even at this sight,
My heart is turn'd to stone: and while 'tis mine,
It shall be stony. York not our old men spares;
No more will I their babes: tears virginal
Shall be to me even as the dew to fire;
And beauty, that the tyrant oft reclaims,
Shall to my flaming wrath be oil and flax.
Come, thou new ruin of old Clifford's house:
[*Taking up the body.*
As did Æneas old Anchises bear,
So bear I thee upon my manly shoulders;
But then, Æneas bare a living load,
Nothing so heavy as these woes of mine. [*Exit.*

Enter RICHARD PLANTAGENET *and* SOMERSET, *fighting:* SOMERSET *is killed.*

Rich. So, lie thou there;—
For underneath an ale-house' paltry sign,
The Castle in Saint Albans, Somerset
Hath made the wizard famous in his death.
Sword, hold thy temper; heart, be wrathful still:
Priests pray for enemies, but princes kill. [*Exit.*

Alarums: Excursions. Enter KING HENRY, QUEEN MARGARET, *and others, retreating.*

Q. Mar. Away, my lord! you are slow; for shame, away!
K. Hen. Can we outrun the heavens? good Margaret, stay.
Q. Mar. What are you made of? you'll nor fight, nor fly
Now is it manhood, wisdom, and defence,
To give the enemy way; and to secure us
By what we can, which can no more but fly. [*Alarum afar off.*
If you be ta'en, we then should see the bottom
Of all our fortunes: but if we haply scape,
(As well we may, if not through your neglect)
We shall to London get: where you are lov'd;
And where this breach, now in our fortunes made,
May readily be stopp'd.

Re-enter Young CLIFFORD.

Y. Clif. But that my heart's on future mischief set,
I would speak blasphemy ere bid you fly:
But fly you must; uncurable discomfit
Reigns in the hearts of all our present parts.
Away, for your relief! and we will live
To see their day, and them our fortune give:
Away, my lord, away! [*Exeunt.*

SCENE III.—*Field near* Saint Albans.

Alarum: Retreat. Flourish; then enter YORK, RICHARD PLANTAGENET, WARWICK, *and* Soldiers, *with drum and colors.*

York. Of Salisbury, who can report of him,—
That winter lion, who in rage forgets
Agèd contusions and all brush of time,
And, like a gallant in the brow of youth,
Repairs him with occasion? this happy day
Is not itself, nor have we won one foot,
If Salisbury be lost.
Rich. My noble father,
Three times to-day I holp him to his horse,

Three times bestrid him, thrice I led him off,
Persuaded him from any farther act:
But still, where danger was, still there I met him;
And like rich hangings in a homely house,
So was his will in his old feeble body.
But, noble as he is, look where he comes.

Enter SALISBURY.

Sal. Now, by my sword, well hast thou fought to-day;
By the mass, so did we all.—I thank you, Richard·
Heaven knows how long it is I have to live;
And it hath pleas'd him, that three times to-day
You have defended me from imminent death.—
Well, lords, we have not got that which we have:
'Tis not enough our foes are this time fled,
Being opposites of such repairing nature.

York. I know our safety is to follow them;
For, as I hear, the king has fled to London,
To call a present court of parliament.
Let us pursue him, ere the writs go forth:—
What says lord Warwick? shall we after them?

War. After them! nay, before them, if we can.
Now, by my hand, lords, 'twas a glorious day:
Saint Alban's battle, won by famous York,
Shall be eterniz'd in all age to come.—
Sound, drums and trumpets:—and to London all;
And more such days as these to us befall' [*Exeunt.*

THE HISTORY OF

KING HENRY VI.

PART III.

THE third part of Henry VI. continues the series of events involved in the contentions of the houses of York and Lancaster, with consecutive exactness. It opens immediately after the first battle of St. Albans in 1455, and details the struggles of the York faction with Henry; the death of Richard, Duke of York; the subsequent usurpation of the crown by his eldest son, who assumed the throne with the title of Edward IV., and the action closes with the murder of Henry VI., 1471, embracing a history of sixteen years. Shakspeare has painted the leading characters in this part of Henry VI. with great power and fidelity. King Henry's meek and almost saint-like forbearance forms a beautiful contrast to the Amazonian courage and fiery qualities of his Queen. Warwick, the haughty, imperious "king-maker," is also drawn with a strong master hand; but in the character of Richard, Duke of Gloster, the poet exhibits the full power of his genius. Intending to make Gloster the subject of a distinct Historical Drama, Shakspeare ingeniously develops the future Richard III. in all his moral and physical deformity, and prepares us for the tissue of crimes which form the principal incidents of the succeeding drama.

PERSONS REPRESENTED.

KING HENRY THE SIXTH.
EDWARD, *Prince of Wales, his Son.*
LEWIS XI., *King of France.*
DUKE OF SOMERSET,
DUKE OF EXETER,
EARL OF OXFORD,
EARL OF NORTHUMBERLAND,
EARL OF WESTMORELAND,
LORD CLIFFORD,
} *on King Henry's side.*
RICHARD PLANTAGENET, *Duke of York.*

EDWARD, *Earl of March, afterwards* KING EDWARD IV., } *his Sons.*
EDMUND, *Earl of Rutland,*
GEORGE, *afterwards Duke of Clarence,*
RICHARD, *afterwards Duke of Glocester,*
DUKE OF NORFOLK, } *of the Duke of York's party.*
MARQUESS OF MONTAGUE,
EARL OF WARWICK,
EARL OF PEMBROKE,
LORD HASTINGS,
LORD STAFFORD,
Sir JOHN MORTIMER, } *Uncles to the Duke of York.*
Sir HUGH MORTIMER,
HENRY, *Earl of Richmond, a Youth.*
LORD RIVERS, *Brother to Lady Grey.*
Sir WILLIAM STANLEY.
Sir JOHN MONTGOMERY.
Sir JOHN SOMERVILLE.
Tutor to Rutland.
Mayor of York.
Lieutenant to the Tower.
A Nobleman. *Two* Keepers. *A* Huntsman.
A Son *that has killed his Father.*
A Father *that has killed his Son.*

QUEEN MARGARET.
LADY GREY, *afterwards Queen to* EDWARD IV.
BONA, *Sister to the French Queen.*

Soldiers, *and other* Attendants *on King Henry and King Edward,* Messengers, Watchmen, *&c.*

SCENE,—*During part of the Third Act, in* FRANCE; *during the rest of the Play, in* ENGLAND.

ACT I.

SCENE I.—London. *The Parliament House.*

Drums. Some Soldiers *of* YORK'S *party break in. Then, enter the* DUKE OF YORK, EDWARD, RICHARD, NORFOLK, MONTAGUE, WARWICK, *and others, with white roses in their hats.*

War. I wonder how the king escap'd our hands.
York. While we pursued the horsemen of the north,
He slily stole away, and left his men:
Whereat the great lord of Northumberland,
Whose warlike ears could never brook retreat,
Cheer'd up the drooping army; and himself,
Lord Clifford, and lord Stafford, all a-breast,
Charg'd our main battle's front, and, breaking in,
Were by the swords of common soldiers slain.
Edw. Lord Stafford's father, duke of Buckingham,
Is either slain, or wounded dangerous;

I cleft his beaver with a downright blow:
That this is true, father, behold his blood.
[*Showing his bloody sword.*
Mont. And brother, here's the earl of Wiltshire's blood,
[*To* YORK, *showing his.*
Whom I encounter'd as the battles join'd.
Rich. Speak thou for me, and tell them what I did.
[*Throwing down the Duke of Somerset's head.*
York. Richard hath best deserv'd of all my sons.—
But, is your grace dead, my lord of Somerset?
Norf. Such hope have all the line of John of Gaunt!
Rich. Thus do I hope to shake king Henry's head.
War. And so do I.—Victorious prince of York,
Before I see thee seated in that throne
Which now the house of Lancaster usurps,
I vow by heaven these eyes shall never close.
This is the palace of the fearful king,
And this the regal seat: possess it, York;
For this is thine, and not king Henry's heirs'.
York. Assist me, then, sweet Warwick, and I will;
For hither we have broken in by force.
Norf. We'll all assist you, he that flies shall die.
York. Thanks, gentle Norfolk:—stay by me, my lords;—
And, soldiers, stay, and lodge by me this night.
War. And when the king comes, offer him no violence,
Unless he seek to thrust you out by force. [*The* Soldiers *retire.*
York. The queen, this day, here holds her parliament,
But little thinks we shall be of her council:
By words or blows here let us win our right.
Rich. Arm'd as we are, let's stay within this house.
War. The bloody parliament shall this be call'd,
Unless Plantagenet, duke of York, be king,
And bashful Henry depos'd, whose cowardice
Hath made us by-words to our enemies.
York. Then leave me not, my lords; be resolute;
I mean to take possession of my right.
War. Neither the king, nor he that loves him best,
The proudest he that holds up Lancaster,
Dare stir a wing, if Warwick shake his bells.
I'll plant Plantagenet, root him up who dares:—
Resolve thee, Richard; claim the English crown.
[WARWICK *leads* YORK *to the throne, who seats himself.*

Flourish. Enter KING HENRY, CLIFFORD, NORTHUMBERLAND, WESTMORELAND, EXETER, *and others, with red roses in their hats.*

K. Hen. My lords, look where the sturdy rebel sits,
Even in the chair of state! belike he means

(Back'd by the power of Warwick, that false peer)
To aspire unto the crown, and reign as king.—
Earl of Northumberland, he slew thy father;
And thine, lord Clifford; and you both have vow'd revenge
On him, his sons, his favorites, and his friends.
North. If I be not, heavens be reveng'd on me!
Clif. The hope thereof makes Clifford mourn in steel.
West. What, shall we suffer this? let's pluck him down:
My heart for anger burns; I cannot brook it.
K. Hen. Be patient, gentle earl of Westmoreland.
Clif. Patience is for poltroons, such as he:
He durst not sit there, had your father liv'd.
My gracious lord, here in the parliament
Let us assail the family of York.
North. Well hast thou spoken, cousin: be it so.
K. Hen. Ah, know you not the city favors them,
And they have troops of soldiers at their beck?
Exe. But when the duke is slain, they'll quickly fly.
K. Hen. Far be the thought of this from Henry's heart,
To make a shambles of the parliament-house!
Cousin of Exeter, frowns, words, and threats,
Shall be the war that Henry means to use.
[*They advance to the* DUKE.
Thou factious duke of York, descend my throne,
And kneel for grace and mercy at my feet;
I am thy sovereign.
York. I am thine.
Exe. For shame, come down: he made thee duke of York.
York. 'Twas my inheritance, as the earldom was.
Exe. Thy father was a traitor to the crown.
War. Exeter, thou art a traitor to the crown
In following this usurping Henry.
Clif. Whom should he follow but his natural king?
War. True, Clifford; and that's Richard, duke of York.
K. Hen. And shall I stand, and thou sit in my throne?
York. It must and shall be so: content thyself.
War. Be duke of Lancaster; let him be king.
West. He is both king and duke of Lancaster;
And that the lord of Westmoreland shall maintain.
War. And Warwick shall disprove it. You forget
That we are those which chas'd you from the field,
And slew your fathers, and with colors spread,
March'd through the city to the palace gates.
North. Yes, Warwick, I remember it to my grief;
And, by his soul, thou and thy house shall rue it.
West. Plantagenet, of thee, and these thy sons,
Thy kinsmen, and thy friends, I'll have more lives
Than drops of blood were in my father's veins.

Clif. Urge it no more: lest that, instead of words,
I send thee, Warwick, such a messenger
As shall revenge his death before I stir.
War. Poor Clifford! how I scorn his worthless threats.
York. Will you we show our title to the crown?
If not, our swords shall plead it in the field.
K. Hen. What title hast thou, traitor, to the crown?
Thy father was, as thou art, duke of York;
Thy grandfather, Roger Mortimer, earl of March:
I am the son of Henry the fifth,
Who made the Dauphin and the French to stoop,
And seiz'd upon their towns and provinces.
War. Talk not of France, sith thou hast lost it all.
K. Hen. The lord protector lost it, and not I:
When I was crown'd, I was but nine months old.
Rich. You are old enough now,'and yet, methinks, you lose.—
Father, tear the crown from the usurper's head.
Edw. Sweet father, do so; set it on your head.
Mont. [*To* YORK.] Good brother, as thou lov'st and honor'st arms,
Let's fight it out, and not stand cavilling thus.
Rich. Sound drums and trumpets, and the king will fly.
York. Sons, peace!
K. Hen. Peace thou! and give king Henry leave to speak.
War. Plantagenet shall speak first: hear him, lords;
And be you silent and attentive too,
For he that interrupts him shall not live.
K. Hen. Think'st thou, that I will leave my kingly throne,
Wherein my grandsire and my father sat?
No; first shall war unpeople this my realm;
Ay, and their colors,—often borne in France,
And now in England, to our heart's great sorrow,—
Shall be my winding-sheet.—Why faint you, lords?
My title's good, and better far than his.
War. Prove it, Henry, and thou shalt be king.
K. Hen. Henry the fourth by conquest got the crown.
York. 'Twas by rebellion against his king.
K. Hen. [*Aside.*] I know not what to say; my title's weak.—
[*Aloud.*] Tell me, may not a king adopt an heir?
York. What then?
K. Hen. An if he may, then am I lawful king;
For Richard, in the view of many lords,
Resign'd the crown to Henry the fourth,
Whose heir my father was, and I am his.
York. He rose against him, being his sovereing,
And made him to resign his crown perforce.
Henry of Lancaster, resign thy crown.—
What mutter you, or what conspire you, lords?

War. Do right unto this princely duke of York;
Or I will fill the house with armèd men,
And o'er the chair of state, where now he sits,
Write up his title with usurping blood.
[*He stamps, and the* Soldiers *show themselves.*
K. Hen. My lord of Warwick, hear me but one word:—
Let me for this my life-time reign as king.
York. Confirm the crown to me, and to mine heirs,
And thou shalt reign in quiet while thou liv'st.
K. Hen. I am content: Richard Plantagenet,
Enjoy the kingdom after my decease.
Clif. What wrong is this unto the prince your son!
War. What good is this to England, and himself!
West. Base, fearful, and despairing Henry!
Clif. How hast thou injur'd both thyself and us!
West. I cannot stay to hear these articles.
North. Nor I.
Clif. Come, cousin, let us tell the queen these news.
West. Farewell, faint-hearted and degenerate king,
In whose cold blood no spark of honor bides.
North. Be thou a prey unto the house of York,
And die in bands, for this unmanly deed!
Clif. In dreadful war may'st thou be overcome;
Or live in peace, abandon'd, and despis'd!
[*Exeunt* NORTHUMBERLAND, CLIFFORD, *and* WESTMORELAND.
War. Turn this way, Henry, and regard them not.
Exe. They seek revenge, and therefore will not yield.
K. Hen. Ah, Exeter!
War. Why should you sigh, my lord?
K. Hen. Not for myself, lord Warwick, but my son,
Whom I unnaturally shall disinherit.
But, be it as it may:—I here entail
The crown to thee, and to thine heirs for ever;
Conditionally, that here thou take an oath
To cease this civil war, and, whilst I live,
To honor me as thy king and sovereign,
And neither by treason, nor hostility,
To seek to put me down, and reign thyself.
York. This oath I willingly take, and will perform.
[*Coming from the throne.*
War. Long live king Henry!—Plantagenet, embrace him.
K. Hen. And long live thou, and these thy forward sons!
York. Now York and Lancaster are reconcil'd.
Exe. Accurs'd be he that seeks to make them foes!
[*Sennet.** *The* Lords *come forward.*
York. Farewell, my gracious lord; I'll to my castle.

**Sennet*, a flourish of trumpets.

War. And I'll keep London with my soldiers.
Norf. And I to Norfolk with my followers.
Mont. And I unto the sea, from whence I came.
[*Exeunt* YORK *and his sons*, WARWICK, NORFOLK, MONTAGUE, Soldiers, *and* Attendants.
K. Hen. And I, with grief and sorrow, to the court.
Exe. Here comes the queen, whose looks bewray her anger:
I'll steal away. [*Going*.
K. Hen. Exeter, so will I. [*Going*.

Enter QUEEN MARGARET *and the* PRINCE OF WALES.

Q. Mar. Nay, go not from me; I will follow thee.
K. Hen. Be patient, gentle queen, and I will stay.
Q. Mar. Who can be patient in such extremes?
Ah, wretched man would I had died a maid,
And never seen thee, never borne thee son,
Seeing thou hast prov'd so unnatural a father!
Hath he deserv'd to lose his birth-right thus?
Hadst thou but lov'd him half so well as I,
Thou wouldst have left thy dearest heart-blood there,
Rather than have made that savage duke thine heir,
And disinherited thine only son.
Prince. Father, you cannot disinherit me·
If you be king, why should not I succeed?
K. Hen. Pardon me, Margaret;—pardon me, sweet son:—
The earl of Warwick, and the duke, enforc'd me.
Q. Mar. Enforc'd thee! art thou king, and wilt be forc'd?
I shame to hear thee speak. Ha, timorous wretch!
Thou hast undone thyself, thy son, and me;
And given unto the house of York such head,
As thou shalt reign but by their sufferance.
To entail him and his heirs unto the crown,
What is it, but to make thy sepulchre,
And creep into it far before thy time?
Warwick is chancellor, and the lord of Calais;
Stern Faulconbridge commands the narrow seas;
The duke is made protector of the realm;
And yet shalt thou be safe? such safety finds
The trembling lamb, environed with wolves.
Had I been there, which am a silly woman,
The soldiers should have toss'd me on their pikes,
Before I would have granted to that act.
But thou preferr'st thy life before thine honor·
And seeing thou dost, I here divorce myself,
Until that act of parliament be repeal'd,
Whereby my son is disinherited.
The northern lords, that have forsworn thy colors,
Will follow mine, if once they see them spread;

And spread they shall be, to thy foul disgrace,
And utter ruin of the house of York.
Thus do I leave thee.—Come, son, let's away;
Our army is ready; come, we'll after them.
K. Hen. Stay, gentle Margaret, and hear me speak.
Q. Mar. Thou hast spoke too much already: get thee gone.
K. Hen. Gentle son Edward, thou wilt stay with me?
Q. Mar. Ay, to be murder'd by his enemies.
Prince. When I return with victory from the field,
I'll see your grace: till then, I'll follow her.
Q. Mar. Come, son, away; we may not linger thus.
[*Exeunt* QUEEN MARGARET *and the* PRINCE.
K. Hen. Poor queen! how love to me, and to her son,
Hath made her break out into terms of rage!
Reveng'd may she be on that hateful duke,
Whose haughty spirit, wingèd with desire,
Will cost my crown, and like an empty eagle,
Tire on the flesh of me, and of my son!
The loss of those three lords torments my heart:
I'll write unto them, and entreat them fair:—
Come, cousin, you shall be the messenger.
Exe. And I, I hope, shall reconcile them all. [*Exeunt.*

Urged on by his sons, Edward and Richard, the Duke of York determines to call in the aid of Warwick and the leading adherents of the Lancastrian party, to rise against King Henry. Queen Margaret with an army of 20,000 men moves towards Sandal Castle to meet the insurgents.

SCENE IV.—*The Plains near Sandal Castle.*

Alarum. Enter YORK.

York. The army of the queen hath got the field:
My uncles both are slain in rescuing me;
And all my followers to the eager foe
Turn back, and fly, like ships before the wind,
Or lambs pursu'd by hunger-starved wolves.
My sons,—heaven knows what hath bechanced them,
But this I know,—they have demean'd themselves
Like men born to renown by life or death.
Three times did Richard make a lane to me;
And thrice cried,—"Courage, father! fight it out!"
And full as oft came Edward to my side,
With purple faulchion, painted to the hilt
In blood of those that had encounter'd him:
And when the hardiest warriors did retire,
Richard cried,—"Charge! and give no foot of ground!"
And cried,—"A crown, or else a glorious tomb!

A sceptre, or an earthly sepulchre!"
With this, we charg'd again: but, out, alas!
We bodg'd again: as I have seen a swan
With bootless labor swim against the tide,
And spend her strength with over-matching waves.
[*A short alarum within.*
Ah, hark! the fatal followers do pursue;
And I am faint, and cannot fly their fury:
And were I strong, I would not shun their fury:
The sands are number'd that make up my life;
Here must I stay, and here my life must end.

Enter QUEEN MARGARET, CLIFFORD, NORTHUMBERLAND, *and* Soldiers.

Come, bloody Clifford,—rough Northumberland,—
I dare your quenchless fury to more rage:
I am your butt, and I abide your shot.
North. Yield to our mercy, proud Plantagenet.
Clif. Ay, to such mercy as his ruthless arm,
With downright payment, show'd unto my father.
York. My ashes, as the phœnix, may bring forth
A bird that will revenge upon you all:
And in that hope I throw mine eyes to heaven,
Scorning whate'er you can afflict me with.
Why come you not? what! multitudes, and fear?
Clif. So cowards fight when they can fly no farther;
So doves do peck the falcon's piercing talons;
So desperate thieves, all hopeless of their lives,
Breathe out invectives 'gainst the officers.
York. O Clifford, but bethink thee once again,
And in thy thought o'er-run my former time;
And, if thou canst for blushing, view this face,
And bite thy tongue, that slanders him with cowardice,
Whose frown hath made thee faint and fly ere this.
Clif. I will not bandy with thee word for word,
But buckle with thee blows, twice two for one. [*Draws.*
Q. Mar. Hold, valiant Clifford! for a thousand causes
I would prolong awhile the traitor's life.—
Wrath makes him deaf:—speak thou, Northumberland.
North. Hold, Clifford! do not honor him so much
To prick thy finger, though to wound his heart.
[*They lay hands on* YORK, *who struggles.*
Clif. Ay, ay, so strives the woodcock with the gin.
North. So doth the coney struggle in the net.
[YORK *is taken prisoner.*
York. So triumph thieves upon their conquer'd booty;
So true men yield, with robbers so o'er-match'd.
North. What would your grace have done unto him now?

Q. Mar. Brave warriors, Clifford and Northumberland,
Come, make him stand upon this molehill here,
That raught at mountains with outstretchèd arms,
Yet parted but the shadow with his hand.—
What! was it you that would be England's king?
York cannot speak, unless he wear a crown.—
A crown for York!—and, lords, bow low to him:—
Hold you his hands, whilst I do set it on.—
[*Putting a paper crown on his head.*
Ay, marry, sir, now looks he like a king.
Ay, this is he that took king Henry's chair;
And this is he was his adopted heir.—
Off with the crown; and, with the crown, his head;
And, whilst we breathe, take time to do him dead.
Clif. That is my office, for my father's sake.
Q. Mar. Nay, stay; let's hear the orisons he makes.
York. She-wolf of France,—but worse than wolves of France,—
Whose tongue more poisons than the adder's tooth!
I would assay, proud queen, to make thee blush:
To tell thee whence thou cam'st, of whom deriv'd,
Were shame enough to shame thee, wert thou not shameless.
Thou art as opposite to every good,
As the antipodes are unto us.
O tiger's heart, wrapp'd in a woman's hide!
How could'st thou drain the life-blood of the child,
To bid the father wipe his eyes withal,
And yet be seen to bear a woman's face?
Women are soft, mild, pitiful, and flexible;
Thou stern, obdurate, flinty, rough, remorseless.
Bidd'st thou me rage? why, now thou hast thy wish:
Would'st have me weep? why, now thou hast thy will:
These tears are my sweet Rutland's obsequies;
And every drop cries vengeance for his death,
'Gainst thee, fell Clifford, and thee, false French-woman.
North. Beshrew me, but his passions move me so,
That hardly can I check my eyes from tears.
York. That face of his the hungry cannibals
Would not have touch'd, would not have stain'd with blood:
But you are more inhuman, more inexorable,—
O, ten times more,—than tigers of Hyrcania.
See, ruthless queen, a hapless father's tears:
This cloth thou dipp'dst in blood of my sweet boy,
And I with tears do wash the blood away.
Keep thou the napkin, and go boast of this:
[*Giving back the handkerchief.*
And if thou tell'st the heavy story right,
Upon my soul, the hearers will shed tears;

Yea, even my foes will shed fast-falling tears,
And say,—"Alas, it was a piteous deed!"—
There, take the crown, and, with the crown, my curse;
[*Giving back the paper crown.*
And, in thy need, such comfort come to thee,
As now I reap at thy too cruel hand!—
Hard-hearted Clifford, take me from the world:
My soul to heaven, my blood upon your head!
North. Had he been slaughter-man to all my kin,
I should not, for my life, but weep with him,
To see how inly sorrow gripes his soul.
Q. Mar. What, weeping-ripe, my lord Northumberland
Think but upon the wrong he did us all,
And that will quickly dry thy melting tears.
Clif. Here's for my oath, here's for my father's death.
[*Stabbing him.*
Q. Mar. And here's to right our gentle-hearted king.
[*Stabbing him.*
York. Open thy gate of mercy, gracious heaven!
My soul flies through these wounds to seek out thee. [*Dies.*
Q. Mar. Off with his head, and set it on York gates;
So York may overlook the town of York. [*Flourish. Exeunt.*

ACT II.

The Earl of Warwick now takes the command of the rebel forces and, with the Princes Edward and Richard, marches against King Henry, who meets them before the city of York.

SCENE II.—*Before* York.

Flourish. Enter KING HENRY, QUEEN MARGARET, *the* PRINCE OF WALES, CLIFFORD, *and* NORTHUMBERLAND, *with forces.*

Q. Mar. Welcome, my lord, to this brave town of York.
Yonder's the head of that arch-enemy,
That sought to be encompass'd with your crown:
Doth not the object cheer your heart, my lord?
K. Hen. Ay, as the rocks cheer them that fear their wreck;—
To see this sight, it irks my very soul.—
Withhold revenge, dear heaven! 'tis not my fault,
Nor wittingly have I infring'd my vow.
Clif. My gracious liege, this too much lenity
And harmful pity, must be laid aside.
Ambitious York did level at thy crown;
Thou smiling, while he knit his angry brows:
He, but a duke, would have his son a king,

And raise his issue like a loving sire;
Thou, being a king, bless'd with a goodly son,
Didst yield consent to disinherit him,
Which argued thee a most unloving father.
Look on the boy;
And let his manly face, which promiseth
Successful fortune, steel thy melting heart
To hold thine own, and leave thine own with him.

K. Hen. Full well hath Clifford play'd the orator,
Inferring arguments of mighty force.
But, Clifford, tell me, didst thou never hear
That things ill got had ever bad success?
I'll leave my son my virtuous deeds behind;
And would my father had left me no more!
For all the rest is held at such a rate,
As brings a thousand-fold more care to keep,
Than in possession any jot of pleasure.
Ah, cousin York! would thy best friends did know,
How it doth grieve me that thy head is here!

Q. Mar. My lord, cheer up your spirits: our foes are nigh,
And this soft courage makes your followers faint.
You promis'd knighthood to our forward son:
Unsheathe your sword, and dub him presently.—
Edward, kneel down.

K. Hen. Edward Plantagenet, arise a knight;
And learn this lesson,—Draw thy sword in right.

Prince. My gracious father, by your kingly leave,
I'll draw it as apparent to the crown,
And in that quarrel use it to the death.

Clif. Why, that is spoken like a toward prince.

Enter a Messenger.

Mess. Royal commanders, be in readiness:
For with a band of thirty thousand men
Comes Warwick, backing of the duke of York;
And in the towns, as they do march along,
Proclaims him king, and many fly to him.

Clif. I would your highness would depart the field:
The queen hath best success when you are absent.

Q. Mar. Ay, good my lord, and leave us to our fortune.

K. Hen. Why, that's my fortune too; therefore I'll stay.

North. Be it with resolution, then, to fight.

Prince. My royal father, cheer these noble lords,
And hearten those that fight in your defence:
Unsheathe your sword, good father; cry, "Saint George!"

March. Enter EDWARD, GEORGE, RICHARD, WARWICK, NORFOLK, MONTAGUE, *and* Soldiers.

Edw. Now, perjur'd Henry! wilt thou kneel for grace,

And set thy diadem upon my head;
Or bide the mortal fortune of the field?
Q. Mar. Go, rate thy minions, proud insulting boy!
Becomes it thee to be thus bold in terms,
Before thy sovereign, and thy lawful king?
Edw. I am his king, and he should bow his knee;
I was adopted heir by his consent:
Since when, his oath is broke; for, as I hear,
You, that are king, though he do wear the crown,
Have caus'd him, by new act of parliament,
To blot out me, and put his own son in.
Clif. And reason too:
Who should succeed the father, but the son?
Rich. Are you there, butcher?—O, I cannot speak!
Clif. Ay, crook-back, here I stand to answer thee,
Or any he the proudest of thy sort.
Rich. 'Twas you that kill'd young Rutland, was it not?
Clif. Ay, and old York, and yet not satisfied.
Rich. For heaven's sake, lords, give signal to the fight.
War. What say'st thou, Henry, wilt thou yield the crown?
Q. Mar. Why, how now, long-tongu'd Warwick! dare you speak?
When you and I met at Saint Albans last,
Your legs did better service than your hands.
War. Then 'twas my turn to fly, and now 'tis thine.
Clif. You said so much before, and yet you fled.
War. 'Twas not your valor, Clifford, drove me thence.
North. No, nor your manhood, that durst make you stay.
Rich. Northumberland, I hold thee reverently.—
Break off the parley; for scarce I can refrain
The execution of my big-swoln heart
Upon that Clifford, that cruel child-killer.
Clif. I slew thy father,—call'st thou him a child?
Rich. Ay, like a dastard, and a treacherous coward,
As thou didst kill our tender brother Rutland;
But ere sun-set I'll make thee curse the deed.
K. Hen. Have done with words, my lords, and hear me speak.
Q. Mar. Defy them, then, or else hold close thy lips.
K. Hen. I pr'ythee, give no limits to my tongue:
I am a king, and privileg'd to speak.
Clif. My liege, the wound that bred this meeting here,
Cannot be cur'd by words; therefore be still.
Rich. Then, executioner, unsheathe thy sword:
By him that made us all, I am resolv'd,
That Clifford's manhood lies upon his tongue.
Edw. Say, Henry, shall I have my right, or no?
A thousand men have broke their fasts to-day,
That ne'er shall dine, unless thou yield the crown.

War. If thou deny, their blood upon thy head;
For York in justice puts his armor on.
Prince. If that be right, which Warwick says is right,
There is no wrong, but every thing is right.
Rich. Well I wot, thou hast thy mother's tongue.
Q. Mar. But thou art neither like thy sire, nor dam;
But like a foul mis-shapen stigmatick,*
Mark'd by the destinies to be avoided,
As venom toads, or lizards' dreadful stings.
Rich. Iron of Naples, hid with English gilt,
Whose father bears the title of a king,
(As if a channel should be call'd the sea)
Sham'st thou not, knowing whence thou art extraught,
To let thy tongue detect thy base-born heart?
Edw. A wisp of straw were worth a thousand crowns,
To make this shameless callat know herself.—
Geo. Know thou [*To* Queen.], since we have begun to strike,
We'll never leave, till we have hewn thee down,
Or bath'd thy growing with our heated bloods.
Edw. And in this resolution I defy thee;
Not willing any longer conference,
Since thou deny'st the gentle king to speak.—
Sound trumpets!—let our bloody colors wave!—
And either victory, or else a grave.
Q. Mar. Stay, Edward.
Edw. No, wrangling woman, we'll no longer stay:
These words will cost ten thousand lives to-day. [*Exeunt.*

The rival factions meet between Towton and Saxton, in Yorkshire.

SCENE V.

Alarum. Enter King Henry.

K. Hen. This battle fares like to the morning's war,
When dying clouds contend with growing light,
What time the shepherd, blowing of his nails,
Can neither call it perfect day, nor night.
Now sways it this way, like a mighty sea
Forc'd by the tide to combat with the wind;
Now sways it that way, like the self-same sea
Forc'd to retire by fury of the wind:
Sometime the flood prevails, and then the wind;
Now one the better, then another best;
Both tugging to be victors, breast to breast
Yet neither conqueror, nor conquered:
So is the equal poise of this fell war.

* *Stigmatick*—one deformed, or criminal.

Here on this molehill will I sit me down.
To whom heaven will, there be the victory!
For Margaret my queen, and Clifford too,
Have chid me from the battle; swearing both,
They prosper best of all when I am thence.
Would I were dead! if heaven's good will were so;
For what is in this world but grief and woe?
O heaven! methinks it were a happy life,
To be no better than a homely swain;
To sit upon a hill, as I do now,
To carve out dials quaintly, point by point,
Thereby to see the minutes how they run;—
How many make the hour full complete;
How many hours bring about the day;
How many days will finish up the year;
How many years a mortal man may live.
When this is known, then to divide the times,—
So many hours must I tend my flock;
So many hours must I take my rest;
So many hours must I contemplate;
So many hours must I sport myself;
So many days my ewes have been with young;
So many weeks ere the poor fools will yean;
So many years ere I shall shear the fleece:
So minutes, hours, days, months, and years,
Pass'd over to the end they were created,
Would bring white hairs unto a quiet grave.
Ah, what a life were this! how sweet! how lovely!
Gives not the hawthorn bush a sweeter shade
To shepherds, looking on their silly sheep,
Than doth a rich embroider'd canopy
To kings, that fear their subjects' treachery?
O, yes, it doth; a thousand fold it doth.
And to conclude,—the shepherd's homely curds,
His cold thin drink out of his leather bottle,
His wonted sleep under a fresh tree's shade,
All which secure and sweetly he enjoys,
Is far beyond a prince's delicates,
His viands sparkling in a golden cup,
His body couchèd in a curious bed,
When care, mistrust, and treason wait on him.

Alarum. Enter a Son *that has killed his Father, with the dead body.*

O piteous spectacle! O bloody times!
While lions war, and battle for their dens,
Poor harmless lambs abide their enmity.—
Weep, wretched man, I'll aid thee, tear for tear;

And let our hearts and eyes, like civil war,
Be blind with tears, and break o'ercharg'd with grief.

Enter a Father *who has killed his Son, with the body in his arms.*

Woe above woe! grief more than common grief!
O, that my death would stay these ruthful deeds!—
O, pity, pity, gentle heaven, pity!—
The red rose and the white are on his face,
The fatal colors of our striving houses:
The one his purple blood right well resembles;
The other his pale cheeks, methinks, presenteth:
Wither one rose, and let the other flourish;
If you contend, a thousand lives must wither.

Son. How will my mother, for a father's death,
Take on with me, and ne'er be satisfied!

Fath. How will my wife, for slaughter of my son,
Shed seas of tears, and ne'er be satisfied!

K. Hen. How will the country, for these woful chances,
Misthink the king, and not be satisfied!

Son. Was ever son so rued a father's death?

Fath. Was ever father so bemoan'd a son?

K. Hen. Was ever king so griev'd for subjects' woe?
Much is your sorrow; mine, ten times so much.

Son. I'll bear thee hence, where I may weep my fill.
[*Exit with the body.*

Fath. These arms of mine shall be thy winding-sheet;
My heart, sweet boy, shall be thy sepulchre,—
For from my heart thine image ne'er shall go;
My sighing breast shall be thy funeral bell;
And so obsequious will thy father be,
E'en for the loss of thee, having no more,
As Priam was for all his valiant sons.
I'll bear thee hence; and let them fight that will,
For I have murder'd where I should not kill.
[*Exit with the body.*

K. Hen. Sad-hearted men, much overgone with care,
Here sits a king more woful than you are.

Alarums: Excursions. Enter QUEEN MARGARET, PRINCE OF WALES, *and* EXETER.

Prince. Fly, father, fly! for all your friends are fled,
And Warwick rages like a chafèd bull:
Away! for death doth hold us in pursuit.

Q. Mar. Mount you, my lord; towards Berwick post amain:
Edward and Richard, like a brace of greyhounds
Having the fearful flying hare in sight,
With fiery eyes sparkling for very wrath,
And bloody steel grasp'd in their ireful hands,
Are at our backs; and therefore hence amain.

Exe. Away! for vengeance comes along with them:
Nay, stay not to expostulate; make speed;
Or else come after: I'll away before.
K. Hen. Nay, take me with thee, good sweet Exeter:
Not that I fear to stay, but love to go
Whither the queen intends. Forward; away! [*Exeunt.*

The Yorkists are victorious, and Edward is declared king. He creates his brothers George and Richard, dukes of Clarence and Gloster; and proceeds to London to his coronation. King Henry escapes to Scotland, but in returning to England is made prisoner.

ACT III.

SCENE I.—London. *A Room in the Palace.*

Enter KING EDWARD, GLOSTER, CLARENCE, *and* LADY GREY.

K. Edw. Brother of Gloster, at Saint Alban's field
This lady's husband, Sir John Grey, was slain,
His lands then seiz'd on by the conqueror:
Her suit is now, to repossess those lands;
Which we in justice cannot well deny,
Because in quarrel of the house of York
The worthy gentleman did lose his life.
Glo. Your highness shall do well to grant her suit;
It were dishonor to deny it her.
K. Edw. It were no less: but yet I'll make a pause.
Glo. [*Aside to* CLAR.] Yea, is it so?
K. Edw. Widow, we will consider of your suit;
And come some other time to know our mind.
L. Grey. Right gracious lord, I cannot brook delay:
May it please your highness to resolve me now;
And what your pleasure is, shall satisfy me.
K. Edw. How many children hast thou, widow? tell me.
L. Grey. Three, my most gracious lord.
K. Edw. 'Twere pity, they should lose their father's lands.
L. Grey. Be pitiful, dread lord, and grant it then.
K. Edw. Lords, give us leave: I'll try this widow's wit.
Glo. [*Aside, retiring with* CLARENCE.] Ay, good leave have you; for you will have leave.
K. Edw. Now tell me, madam, do you love your children?
L. Grey. Ay, full as dearly as I love myself.
K. Edw. And would you not do much, to do them good?
L. Grey. To do them good I would sustain some harm.
K. Edw. Then, get your husband's lands to do them good.
L. Grey. Therefore I came unto your majesty.

K. Edw. I'll tell you how these lands are to be got.
L. Grey. So shall you bind me to your highness' service.
K. Edw. What service wilt thou do me, if I give them?
L. Grey. What you command, that rests in me to do.
K. Edw. But you will take exceptions to my boon.
L. Grey. No, gracious lord, except I cannot do it.
K. Edw. Ay, but thou canst do what I mean to ask.
L. Grey. Why then, I will do what your grace commands.
Why stops my lord? shall I not hear my task?
K. Edw. An easy task: 'tis but to love a king.
L. Grey. That's soon perform'd, because I am a subject.
K. Edw. Why then, thy husband's lands I freely give thee.
L. Grey. I take my leave with many thousand thanks.
Glo. [*Aside.*] The match is made; she seals it with a court'sy.
K. Edw. But stay thee; 'tis the fruits of love I mean.
L. Grey. The fruits of love I mean, my loving liege.
K. Edw. Ay, but, I fear me, in another sense.
What love, think'st thou, I sue so much to get?
L. Grey. My love till death, my humble thanks, my prayers;
That love which virtue begs, and virtue grants.
K. Edw. No, by my troth, I did not mean such love.
L. Grey. Why, then you mean not as I thought you did.
K. Edw. But now you partly may perceive my mind.
L. Grey. My mind will never grant what I perceive
Your highness aims at, if I aim aright.
K. Edw. Why then, thou shalt not have thy husband's lands.
L. Grey. Why then, mine honesty shall be my dower;
For by that loss I will not purchase them.
K. Edw. Therein thou wrong'st thy children mightily.
L. Grey. Herein your highness wrongs both them and me.
But, mighty lord, this merry inclination
Accords not with the sadness of my suit:
Please you dismiss me, either with ay, or no.
K. Edw. Ay, if thou wilt say ay to my request;
No, if thou dost say no to my demand.
L. Grey. Then, no, my lord. My suit is at an end.
Glo. [*Aside to* CLAR.] The widow likes him not, she knits her brows.
Clar. [*Aside to* GLO.] He is the bluntest wooer in Christendom.
K. Edw. [*Aside.*] Her looks do argue her replete with modesty;
Her words do show her wit incomparable;
All her perfections challenge sovereignty:
One way or other, she is for a king;
And she shall be my love, or else my queen.—
Say, that king Edward take thee for his queen?
L. Grey. 'Tis better said than done, my gracious lord:

I am a subject fit to jest withal,
But far unfit to be a sovereign.
K. Edw. Sweet widow, by my state I swear to thee,
I speak no more than what my soul intends.
L. Grey. I know I am too mean to be your queen,
And yet too good to be your mistress.
K. Edw. You cavil, widow: I did mean, my queen.
L. Grey. 'Twill grieve your grace, my sons should call you father.
K. Edw. No more, than when my daughters call thee mother.
Answer no more, for thou shalt be my queen.
Brothers, you muse what chat we two have had.
Glo. The widow likes it not, for she looks very sad.
K. Edw. You'd think it strange if I should marry her.
Clar. To whom, my lord?
K. Edw. Why, Clarence, to myself.
Glo. That would be ten days' wonder, at the least.
Clar. That's a day longer than a wonder lasts.
Glo. By so much is the wonder in extremes.
K. Edw. Well, jest on, brothers: I can tell you both,
Her suit is granted for her husband's lands.

Enter a Nobleman.

Nob. My gracious lord, Henry your foe is taken,
And brought your prisoner to your palace gate.
K. Edw. See that he be convey'd unto the Tower:
And go we, brothers, to the man that took him,
To question of his apprehension.—
Widow, go you along:—lords, use her honorably.
[*Exeunt* KING EDWARD, LADY GREY, CLARENCE, *and* Nobleman.
Glo. Ay, Edward will use women honorably.—
'Would he were wasted, marrow, bones, and all,
That from his loins no hopeful branch may spring,
To cross me from the golden time I look for!
And yet, between my soul's desire and me,
Is Clarence, Henry, and his son young Edward,
And all the unlook'd-for issue of their bodies,
To take their rooms, ere I can place myself:
A cold premeditation for my purpose!
Why then, I do but dream on sovereignty;
Like one that stands upon a promontory,
And spies a far-off shore where he would tread,
Wishing his foot were equal with his eye;
And chides the sea that sunders him from thence,
Saying—he'll lade it dry to have his way:
So do I wish the crown, being so far off;
And so I chide the means that keep me from it;

And so I say—I'll cut the causes off,
Flattering me with impossibilities.—
My eye's too quick, my heart o'erweens too much,
Unless my hand and strength could equal them.
Well, say there is no kingdom, then, for Richard;
What other pleasure can the world afford?
I'll make my heaven in a lady's lap,
And deck my body in gay ornaments,
And witch sweet ladies with my words and looks.
O miserable thought! and more unlikely,
Than to accomplish twenty golden crowns!
Why, love forswore me ere that I was born.
And, for I should not deal in her soft laws,
She did corrupt frail nature with some bribe,
To shrink mine arm up like a wither'd shrub;
To make an envious mountain on my back,
Where sits deformity to mock my body;
To shape my limbs of an unequal size;
To disproportion me in every part.
And am I, then, a man to be belov'd?
O monstrous fault, to harbor such a thought
Then, since this earth affords no joy to me,
But to command, to check, to o'erbear such
As are of better person than myself,
I'll make my heaven to dream upon the crown,
Until my mis-shap'd trunk that bears this head,
Be round impalèd with a glorious crown.
Why, I can smile, and murder while I smile;
And cry, content, to that which grieves my heart;
And wet my cheeks with artificial tears,
And frame my face to all occasions.
Can I do this, and cannot get a crown?
Tut! were it farther off, I'll pluck it down. [*Exit.*

Queen Margaret seeks refuge at the court of France. Warwick is empowered by King Edward to crave a league of amity with King Lewis, and to ask the hand of the French king's sister, the Lady Bona, for his sovereign Edward IV. The French king accedes to the match—but news having arrived at the French king's court that Edward has married the Lady Elizabeth Grey, he indignantly casts off allegiance to Edward, and offers to lead any force the French king and Queen Margaret can send against England.

ACT IV.

King Edward, by his marriage with Lady Elizabeth Grey, excites the enmity of his brother Clarence, and the Duke of Somerset. Warwick levies an army of French and other forces, and proceeds to England to make war on King Edward. Clarence and Somerset join the Earl of Warwick. Edward, with his army, meets the rebellious lords near the town of Warwick.

SCENE II.—*A Plain in* Warwickshire.

Enter WARWICK *and* OXFORD, *with French and other forces.*

War. Trust me, my lord, all hitherto goes well·
The common people by numbers swarm to us.—
But see where Somerset and Clarence come!

Enter CLARENCE *and* SOMERSET.

Speak suddenly, my lords,—are we all friends?
Clar. Fear not that, my lord.
War. Then, gentle Clarence, welcome unto Warwick;—
And welcome, Somerset;—I hold it cowardice,
To rest mistrustful where a noble heart
Hath pawn'd an open hand in sign of love;
Else might I think that Clarence, Edward's brother,
Were but a feigned friend to our proceedings:
But welcome, sweet Clarence; my daughter shall be thine.
And now what rests, but in night's coverture,
Thy brother being carelessly encamp'd,
His soldiers lurking in the towns about,
And but attended by a simple guard,
We may surprise and take him at our pleasure?
Our scouts have found the adventure very easy:
You, that will follow me to this attempt,
Applaud the name of Henry with your leader.
[*They all cry*, "Henry!"
Why, then, let's on our way in silent sort:
For Warwick and his friends, God and Saint George! [*Exeunt.*

SCENE III.—EDWARD'S *Camp near* Warwick.

Enter certain Watchmen, *to guard the* KING'S *tent.*

1 *Watch.* Come on, my masters, each man take his stand:
The king, by this, is set him down to sleep.
2 *Watch.* What, will he not to bed!
1 *Watch.* Why, no; for he hath made a solemn vow
Never to lie and take his natural rest,
Till Warwick or himself be quite suppressed.

2 Watch. To-morrow then, belike, shall be the day,
If Warwick be so near as men report.

3 Watch. But say, I pray, what nobleman is that,
That with the king here resteth in his tent?

1 Watch. 'Tis the lord Hastings, the king's chiefest friend.

3 Watch. O, is it so? But why commands the king,
That his chief followers lodge in towns about him,
While he himself keeps in the cold field?

2 Watch. 'Tis the more honor, because more dangerous.

3 Watch. Ay, but give me worship and quietness;
I like it better than a dangerous honor.
If Warwick knew in what estate he stands,
'Tis to be doubted, he would waken him.

1 Watch. Unless our halberts did shut up his passage.

2 Watch. Ay, wherefore else guard we his royal tent,
But to defend his person from night-foes?

Enter WARWICK, CLARENCE, OXFORD, SOMERSET, *and forces.*

War. This is his tent; and see, where stand his guard.
Courage, my masters! honor now, or never
But follow me, and Edward shall be ours.

1 Watch. Who goes there?

2 Watch. Stay, or thou diest.

[WARWICK, *and the rest, cry all*—"Warwick! Warwick!" *and set upon the* Guard; *who fly, crying*—"Arm! Arm!" WARWICK, *and the rest, following them.*

Drums beating, and Trumpets sounding, re-enter WARWICK, *and the rest, bringing the* KING *out in his gown, sitting in a chair.* GLOSTER *and* HASTINGS *fly.*

Som. What are they that fly there?

War. Richard, and Hastings: let them go; here's the duke.

K. Edw. The duke! why, Warwick, when we parted last,
Thou call'dst me king!

War. Ay, but the case is alter'd:
When you disgrac'd me in my embassade,
Then I degraded you from being king,
And come now to create you duke of York.
Alas, how should you govern any kingdom,
That know not how to use embassadors;
Nor how to be contented with one wife;
Nor how to use your brothers brotherly;
Nor how to study for the people's welfare;
Nor how to shroud yourself from enemies?

K. Edw. Yea, brother of Clarence, art thou here too?
Nay, then, I see that Edward needs must down.—
Yet, Warwick, in despite of all mischance,

Of thee thyself, and all thy complices,
Edward will always bear himself as king:
Though Fortune's malice overthrow my state,
My mind exceeds the compass of her wheel.
War. Then, for his mind, be Edward England's king:
[*Takes off his crown.*
But Henry now shall wear the English crown,
And be true king indeed; thou but the shadow.—
My lord of Somerset, at my request,
See that forthwith duke Edward be convey'd
Unto my brother, archbishop of York.
When I have fought with Pembroke and his fellows,
I'll follow you, and tell what answer
Lewis, and the lady Bona, send to him.—
Now, for a while farewell, good duke of York.
K. Edw. What fates impose, that men must needs abide;
It boots not to resist both wind and tide.
[*Exit, led out;* SOMERSET *with him.*
Oxf. What now remains, my lords, for us to do,
But march to London with our soldiers?
War. Ay, that's the first thing that we have to do;
To free king Henry from imprisonment,
And see him seated in the regal throne. [*Exeunt.*

SCENE VI.—*A Room in the Tower.*

Enter KING HENRY, CLARENCE, WARWICK, SOMERSET, *young* RICHMOND, OXFORD, MONTAGUE, Lieutenant of the Tower, *and* Attendants.

K. Hen. Master lieutenant, now that heaven and friends
Have shaken Edward from the regal seat,
And turn'd my captive state to liberty,
My fear to hope, my sorrows unto joys,—
At our enlargement what are thy due fees?
Lieu. Subjects may challenge nothing of their sovereigns;
But if a humble prayer may prevail,
I then crave pardon of your majesty.
K. Hen. For what, lieutenant? for well using me?
Nay, be thou sure, I'll well requite thy kindness,
For that it made my imprisonment a pleasure;
Ay, such a pleasure as incaged birds
Conceive, when, after many moody thoughts,
At last, by notes of household harmony,
They quite forget their loss of liberty.—
Warwick, chiefly I thank heaven and thee;
It was the author, thou the instrument.
Therefore, that I may conquer fortune's spite,

By living low, where fortune cannot hurt me,
And that the people of this blessed land
May not be punish'd with my thwarting stars,—
Warwick, although my head still wear the crown,
I here resign my government to thee,
For thou art fortunate in all thy deeds.
War. Your grace hath still been fam'd for virtuous;
And now may seem as wise as virtuous,
By spying and avoiding fortune's malice,
For few men rightly temper with the stars:
Yet in this one thing let me blame your grace,
For choosing me when Clarence is in place.
Clar. No, Warwick, thou art worthy of the sway,
To whom the heavens, in thy nativity,
Adjudg'd an olive branch, and laurel crown,
As likely to be blest in peace, and war;
And therefore I yield thee my free consent,
War. And I choose Clarence only for protector.
K. Hen. Warwick and Clarence, give me both your hands:
Now join your hands, and with your hands your hearts,
That no dissension hinder government:
I make you both protectors of this land;
While I myself will lead a private life,
And in devotion spend my latter days,
To sin's rebuke, and my Creator's praise.
War. What answers Clarence to his sovereign's will?
Clar. That he consents, if Warwick yield consent;
For on thy fortune I repose myself.
War. Why then, though loth, yet must I be content:
We'll yoke together, like a double shadow
To Henry's body, and supply his place;
I mean, in bearing weight of government,
While he enjoys the honor, and his ease.
And, Clarence, now then, it is more than needful,
Forthwith that Edward be pronounc'd a traitor,
And all his lands and goods be confiscate.
Clar. What else? and that succession be determin'd.
War. Ay, therein Clarence shall not want his part.
K. Hen. But, with the first of all your chief affairs,
Let me entreat, (for I command no more)
That Margaret your queen, and my son Edward,
Be sent for, to return from France with speed;
For, till I see them here, by doubtful fear
My joy of liberty is half eclips'd.
Clar. It shall be done, my sovereign, with all speed.
K. Hen. My lord of Somerset, what youth is that,
Of whom you seem to have so tender care?
Som. My liege, it is young Henry, earl of Richmond.

K. Hen. Come hither, England's hope. If secret powers
[*Lays his hand on his head*
Suggest but truth to my divining thoughts,
This pretty lad will prove our country's bliss.
His looks are full of peaceful majesty;
His head by nature fram'd to wear a crown,
His hand to wield a sceptre; and himself
Likely in time to bless a regal throne.
Make much of him, my lords; for this is he,
Must help you more than you are hurt by me.

Enter a Messenger.

War. What news, my friend?
Mess. That Edward is escaped from your brother,
And fled, as he hears since, to Burgundy.
War. Unsavory news! but how made he escape?
Mess. He was convey'd by Richard duke of Gloster,
And the lord Hastings, who attended him
In secret ambush on the forest side,
And from the bishop's huntsmen rescued him;
For hunting was his daily exercise.
War. My brother was too careless of his charge.—
But let us hence, my sovereign, to provide
A salve for any sore that may betide.
[*Exeunt* KING HENRY, WARWICK, CLARENCE,
Lieutenant, *and* Attendants.
Som. My lord, I like not of this flight of Edward's;
For doubtless Burgundy will yield him help,
And we shall have more wars before't be long.
As Henry's late presaging prophecy
Did glad my heart with hope of this young Richmond,
So doth my heart misgive me, in these conflicts
What may befal him, to his harm and ours:
Therefore, lord Oxford, to prevent the worst,
Forthwith we'll send him hence to Brittany,
Till storms be past of civil enmity.
Oxf. Ay, for if Edward repossess the crown,
'Tis like that Richmond with the rest shall down.
Som. It shall be so; he shall to Brittany.
Come, therefore, let's about it speedily. [*Exeunt.*

SCENE VII.—*Before* York.

Enter KING EDWARR, GLOSTER, HASTINGS, *and forces.*

K. Edw. Now, brother Richard, lord Hastings, and the rest,
Yet thus far fortune maketh us amends,
And says, that once more I shall interchange

My wanèd state for Henry's regal crown.
Well have we pass'd, and now repass'd the seas,
And brought desired help from Burgundy:
What then remains, we being thus arriv'd
From Ravenspurg haven before the gates of York,
But that we enter, as into our dukedom?
Glo. The gates made fast!—Brother, I like not this;
For many men that stumble at the threshold,
Are well foretold that danger lurks within.
K. Edw. Tush, man! abodements must not now affright us:
By fair or foul means we must enter in,
For hither will our friends repair to us.
Hast. My liege, I'll knock once more to summon them.

Enter on the walls, the Mayor of York *and* Aldermen.

May. My lords, we were forewarned of your coming,
And shut the gates for safety of ourselves;
For now we owe allegiance unto Henry.
K. Edw. But, master mayor, if Henry be your king,
Yet Edward, at the least, is duke of York.
May. True, my good lord; I know you for no less.
K. Edw. Why, and I challenge nothing but my dukedom,
As being well content with that alone.
Glo. [*Aside.*] But when the fox hath once got in his nose,
He'll soon find means to make the body follow.
Hast. Why, master mayor, why stand you in a doubt?
Open the gates; we are king Henry's friends.
May. Ay, say you so? the gates shall then be open'd.
[*Exit with* Aldermen, *above.*
Glo. A wise stout captain, and soon persuaded.
Hast. The good old man would fain that all were well,
So 'twere not 'long of him; but, being enter'd,
I doubt not, I, but we shall soon persuade
Both him and all his brothers unto reason.

Re-enter the Mayor *and* Aldermen, *below.*

K. Edw. So, master mayor: these gates must not be shut,
But in the night, or in the time of war.
What! fear not, man, but yield me up the keys; [*Takes his keys.*
For Edward will defend the town and thee,
And all those friends that deign to follow me.

Drum. *Enter* Montgomery *and forces, marching.*

Glo. Brother, this is Sir John Montgomery,
Our trusty friend, unless I be deceiv'd.
K. Edw. Welcome, Sir John! but why come you in arms?
Mont. To help king Edward in his time of storm,
As every loyal subject ought to do.

K. Edw. Thanks, good Montgomery; but we now forget
Our title to the crown, and only claim
Our dukedom, till heaven please to send the rest.
Mont. Then fare you well, for I will hence again:
I came to serve a king, and not a duke.—
Drummer, strike up, and let us march away. [*A march begun.*
K. Edw. Nay, stay, Sir John, a while; and we'll debate,
By what safe means the crown may be recover'd.
Mont. What talk you of debating? in few words,—
If you'll not here proclaim yourself our king,
I'll leave you to your fortune, and be gone
To keep them back that come to succor you
Why shall we fight, if you pretend no title?
Glo. Why, brother, wherefore stand you on nice points?
K. Edw. When we grow stronger, then we'll make our claim:
Till then, 'tis wisdom to conceal our meaning.
Hast. Away with scrupulous wit! now arms must rule.
Glo. And fearless minds climb soonest unto crowns.
Brother, we will proclaim you out of hand;
The bruit thereof will bring you many friends.
K. Edw. Then be it as you will; for 'tis my right,
And Henry but usurps the diadem.
Mont. Ay, now my sovereign speaketh like himself;
And now will I be Edward's champion.
Hast. Sound, trumpet; Edward shall be here proclaim'd.—
Come, fellow-soldier, make thou proclamation.
[*Gives him a paper. Flourish.*
Sold. [*Reads.*] "Edward the fourth, by the grace of God king of England and France, and lord of Ireland," &c.
Mont. And whosoe'er gainsays king Edward's right,
By this I challenge him to single fight.
[*Throws down his gauntlet.*
All. Long live Edward the fourth!
K. Edw. Thanks, brave Montgomery;—and thanks unto you all:
If fortune serve me, I'll requite this kindness.
Now, for this night, let's harbor here in York
And when the morning sun shall raise his car
Above the border of this horizon,
We'll forward towards Warwick, and his mates.
Come on, brave soldiers; doubt not of the day;
And, that once gotten, doubt not of large pay. [*Exeunt.*

King Edward and his forces march to London, King Henry is captured, and confined in the Tower. Warwick heads an army at Coventry, where he is met by Edward, Gloster, and forces.

ACT V.

SCENE I.—Coventry.

Enter, upon the walls, WARWICK, *the* Mayor of Coventry, *two* Messengers, *and others.*

War. Where is the post that came from valiant Oxford?
How far hence is thy lord, mine honest fellow?
1 *Mess.* By this at Dunsmore, marching hitherward.
War. How far off is our brother Montague?
Where is the post that came from Montague?
2 *Mess.* By this at Daintry, with a puissant troop.

Enter Sir JOHN SOMERVILLE.

War. Say, Somerville, what says my loving son?
And, by thy guess, how nigh is Clarence now?
Som. At Southam I did leave him with his forces,
And do expect him here some two hours hence. [*Drum heard.*
War. Then Clarence is at hand, I hear his drum.
Som. It is not his, my lord; here Southam lies:
The drum your honor hears marcheth from Warwick.
War. Who should that be? belike, unlook'd-for friends.
Som. They are at hand, and you shall quickly know.

March. Flourish. Enter KING EDWARD, GLOSTER, *and forces.*

K. Edw. Go, trumpet, to the walls, and sound a parle.
Glo. See how the surly Warwick mans the wall!
War. O, unbid spite! is sportful Edward come?
Where slept our scouts, or how are they seduc'd,
That we could hear no news of his repair?
K. Edw. Now, Warwick, wilt thou ope the city gates
Speak gentle words, and humbly bend thy knee?
Call Edward king, and at his hands beg mercy,
And he shall pardon thee these outrages.
War. Nay, rather, wilt thou draw thy forces hence,
Confess who set thee up and pluck'd thee down?
Call Warwick patron, and be penitent,
And thou shalt still remain the duke of York.
Glo. I thought, at least, he would have said the king;
Or did he make the jest against his will?
War. Is not a dukedom, sir, a goodly gift?
Glo. Ay, by my faith, for a poor earl to give:
I'll do thee service for so good a gift.
War. 'Twas I that gave the kingdom to thy brother.
K. Edw. Why then, 'tis mine, if but by Warwick's gift.
War. Thou art no Atlas for so great a weight:

And, weakling, Warwick takes his gift again;
And Henry is my king, Warwick his subject.
K. Edw. But Warwick's king is Edward's prisoner:
And, gallant Warwick, do but answer this,—
What is the body, when the head is off?
Glo. Alas, that Warwick had no more forecast,
But, whiles he thought to steal the single ten,
The king was slily finger'd from the deck!
You left poor Henry at the bishop's palace,
And ten to one, you'll meet him in the Tower.
K. Edw. 'Tis even so; yet you are Warwick still.
Glo. Come, Warwick, take the time; kneel down, kneel down:
Nay, when? strike now, or else the iron cools.
War. I had rather chop this hand off at a blow,
And with the other fling it at thy face,
Than bear so low a sail, to strike to thee.
K. Edw. Sail how thou canst, have wind and tide thy friend;
This hand, fast wound about thy coal-black hair,
Shall, whiles thy head is warm, and new cut off,
Write in the dust this sentence with thy blood,—
"Wind-changing Warwick now can change no more."

Enter OXFORD, *with forces, drum, and colors.*

War. O cheerful colors! see where Oxford comes.
Oxf. Oxford, Oxford, for Lancaster!
[*He and his forces enter the city.*
Glo. The gates are open, let us enter too.
K. Edw. So other foes may set upon our backs.
Stand we in good array; for they, no doubt,
Will issue out again and bid us battle:
If not, the city being but of small defence,
We'll quickly rouse the traitors in the same.
War. O, welcome, Oxford! for we want thy help.

Enter MONTAGUE, *with forces, drum, and colors.*

Mont. Montague, Montague, for Lancaster!
[*He and his forces enter the city.*
Glo. Thou and thy brother both shall buy this treason,
Even with the dearest blood your bodies bear.
K. Edw. The harder match'd, the greater victory:
My mind presageth happy gain, and conquest.

Enter SOMERSET, *with forces, drum, and colors.*

Som. Somerset, Somerset, for Lancaster!
[*He and his forces enter the city.*
Glo. Two of thy name, both dukes of Somerset
Have sold their lives unto the house of York;
And thou shalt be the third, if this sword hold.

Enter CLARENCE, *with forces, drum, and colors.*

War. And lo, where George of Clarence sweeps along,
Of force enough to bid his brother battle;
With whom an upright zeal to right prevails,
More than the nature of a brother's love!—
[GLOSTER *and* CLARENCE *whisper.*
Come, Clarence, come; thou wilt, if Warwick call.
Clar. Father of Warwick, know you what this means?
[*Taking the red rose out of his hat.*
Look here, I throw my infamy at thee:
I will not ruinate my father's house,
Who gave his blood to lime the stones together,
And set up Lancaster. Why, trow'st thou, Warwick,
That Clarence is so harsh, so blunt, unnatural,
To bend the fatal instruments of war
Against his brother, and his lawful king?
And so, proud-hearted Warwick, I defy thee,
And to my brother turn my blushing cheeks.—
Pardon me, Edward, I will make amends;—
And, Richard, do not frown upon my faults,
For I will henceforth be no more unconstant.
K. Edw. Now welcome more, and ten times more belov'd,
Than if thou never hadst deserv'd our hate.
Glo. Welcome, good Clarence; this is brother-like.
War. O passing traitor, perjur'd, and unjust!
K. Edw. What, Warwick, wilt thou leave the town, and fight?
Or shall we beat the stones about thine ears?
War. Alas, I am not coop'd here for defence!
I will away towards Barnet presently,
And bid thee battle, Edward, if thou dar'st.
K. Edw. Yes, Warwick, Edward dares, and leads the way.—
Lords, to the field; Saint George, and victory! [*March. Exeunt.*

SCENE II.—*A Field of Battle near* Barnet.

Alarums and Excursions. Enter KING EDWARD, *bringing in* WARWICK *wounded.*

K. Edw. So, lie thou there: die thou, and die our fear;
Now, Montague, sit fast; I seek for thee,
That Warwick's bones may keep thine company. [*Exit.*
War. Ah, who is nigh? come to me, friend or foe,
And tell me who is victor, York or Warwick?
Why ask I that? my mangled body shows,
My blood, my want of strength, my sick heart shows,
That I must yield my body to the earth,
And, by my fall, the conquest to my foe.

These eyes, that now are dimm'd with death's black veil,
Have been as piercing as the mid-day sun,
To search the secret treasons of the world:
The wrinkles in my brows, now fill'd with blood,
Were liken'd oft to kingly sepulchres;
For who liv'd king, but I could dig his grave?
And who durst smile when Warwick bent his brow?
Lo, now my glory smear'd in dust and blood!
My parks, my walks, my manors that I had,
Even now forsake me; and, of all my lands,
Is nothing left me, but my body's length!
Why, what is pomp, rule, reign, but earth and dust?
And, live we how we can, yet die we must.

Enter OXFORD *and* SOMERSET.

Som. Ah, Warwick, Warwick! wert thou as we are,
We might recover all our loss again:
The queen from France hath brought a puissant power;
Even now we heard the news: ah, could'st thou fly!
War. Why, then I would not fly.—Ah, Montague
If thou be there, sweet brother, take my hand,
And with thy lips keep in my soul awhile!
Thou lov'st me not; for, brother, if thou didst,
Thy tears would wash this cold congealèd blood,
That glues my lips, and will not let me speak.
Come quickly, Montague, or I am dead.
Som. Ah, Warwick! Montague hath breath'd his last;
And to the last gasp, cried out for Warwick,
And said—"Commend me to my valiant brother."
War. Sweet rest his soul!—Fly, lords, and save yourselves;
For Warwick bids you all farewell, to meet in heaven. [*Dies.*
Oxf. Away, away, to meet the queen's great power.
Exeunt, bearing off WARWICK'S *body.*

SCENE IV.—*Plains near* Tewksbury.

March. *Enter* QUEEN MARGARET, PRINCE EDWARD, SOMERSET, OXFORD, *and* Soldiers.

Q. Mar. Great lords, wise men ne'er sit and wail their loss.
But cheerly seek how to redress their harms.
Say, Warwick was our anchor; what of that?
And Montague our top-mast; what of him?
Our slaughter'd friends the tackles; what of these?
Why, is not Oxford here another anchor?
And Somerset another goodly mast?
The friends of France our shrouds and tacklings?
And, though unskilful, why not Ned and I

For once allow'd the skilful pilot's charge?
We will not from the helm to sit and weep;
But keep our course, though the rough wind say no,
From shelves and rocks that threaten us with wreck.
Why, courage, then! what cannot be avoided,
'Twere childish weakness to lament, or fear.
Prince. Methinks a woman of this valiant spirit,
Should, if a coward heard her speak these words,
Infuse his breast with magnanimity.
Oxf. Women and children of so high a courage,
And warriors faint! why, 'twere perpetual shame.—
O brave young prince! thy famous grandfather
Doth live again in thee: long may'st thou live
To bear his image, and renew his glories!
Som. And he, that will not fight for such a hope,
Go home to bed, and, like the owl by day,
If he arise, be mock'd and wonder'd at.
Q. Mar. Thanks, gentle Somerset;—sweet Oxford, thanks.
Prince. And take his thanks, that yet hath nothing else.

Enter a Messenger.

Mess. Prepare you, lords, for Edward is at hand,
Ready to fight; therefore be resolute.
Oxf. I thought no less: it is his policy
To haste thus fast, to find us unprovided.
Som. But he's deceiv'd; we are in readiness.
Q. Mar. This cheers my heart, to see your forwardness.
Oxf. Here pitch our battle; hence we will not budge.

Flourish and march. Enter, at a distance, KING EDWARD, CLARENCE, GLOSTER, *and forces.*

K. Edw. Brave followers, yonder stands the thorny wood,
Which, by the heavens' assistance, and your strength,
Must by the roots be hewn up yet ere night.
I need not add more fuel to your fire,
For well I wot ye blaze to burn them out:
Give signal to the fight, and to it, lords.
Q. Mar. Lords, knights, and gentlemen, what I should say,
My tears gainsay; for every word I speak,
Ye see, I drink the water of mine eyes.
Therefore, no more but this:—Henry, your sovereign,
Is prisoner to the foe; his state usurp'd,
His realm a slaughterhouse, his subjects slain,
His statutes cancell'd, and his treasure spent;
And yonder is the wolf that makes this spoil.
You fight in justice: then, in heaven's name, lords,
Be valiant, and give signal to the fight. [*Exeunt both armies.*

SCENE V.—*Another part of the Plains.*

Alarums: Excursions: and afterwards a retreat. Then enter KING EDWARD, CLARENCE, GLOSTER, *and forces; with* QUEEN MARGARET, OXFORD, *and* SOMERSET, *prisoners.*

K. Edw. Now, here a period of tumultuous broils.
Away with Oxford to Hammes' castle straight:
For Somerset, off with his guilty head.
Go, bear them hence; I will not hear them speak.
Oxf. For my part, I'll not trouble thee with words.
Som. Nor I, but stoop with patience to my fortune.
[*Exeunt* OXFORD *and* SOMERSET, *guarded.*
Q. Mar. So part we sadly in this troublous world,
To meet with joy in sweet Jerusalem.
K. Edw. Is proclamation made, that who finds Edward
Shall have a high reward, and he his life?
Glo. It is: and lo, where youthful Edward comes.

Enter Soldiers, *with* PRINCE EDWARD.

K. Edw. Bring forth the gallant, let us hear him speak.
Edward, what satisfaction canst thou make,
For bearing arms, for stirring up my subjects,
And all the trouble thou hast turn'd me to?
Prince. Speak like a subject, proud ambitious York!
Suppose, that I am now my father's mouth;
Resign thy chair, and where I stand kneel thou,
Whilst I propose the self-same words to thee,
Which, traitor, thou would'st have me answer to.
K. Edw. Peace, wilful boy, or I will charm your tongue.
Clar. Untutor'd lad, thou art too malapert.
Prince. I know my duty; you are all undutiful:
Lascivious Edward,—and thou perjur'd George,—
And thou mis-shapen Dick,—I tell ye all,
I am your better, traitors as ye are;—
And thou usurp'st my father's right and mine.
K. Edw. Take that, the likeness of this railer here.
[*Stabs him.*
Glo. Sprawl'st thou? take that, to end thy agony.
[*Stabs him.*
Clar. And there's for twitting me with perjury. [*Stabs him.*
Q. Mar. O, kill me too!
Glo. Marry, and shall. [*Offers to kill her.*
K. Edw. Hold, Richard, hold! for we have done too much.
Glo. Why should she live, to fill the world with words?
K. Edw. What, doth she swoon? use means for her recovery.
Glo. Clarence, excuse me to the king, my brother;

I'll hence to London on a serious matter:
Ere ye come there, be sure to hear some news.
Clar. What? what?
Glo. The Tower, the Tower! [*Exit.*
Q. Mar. O, Ned, sweet Ned! speak to thy mother, boy!
Canst thou not speak?—O traitors! murderers!—
They that stabb'd Cæsar shed no blood at all,
Did not offend, nor were not worthy blame,
If this foul deed were by to equal it:
He was a man; this, in respect, a child,—
And men ne'er spend their fury on a child.
Butchers and villains! bloody cannibals!
How sweet a plant have you untimely cropp'd.
You have no children, butchers! if you had,
The thought of them would sure have stirr'd remorse.
K. Edw. Away with her; go, bear her hence perforce.
Q. Mar. Nay, never bear me hence, despatch me here;
Here sheathe thy sword, I'll pardon thee my death.
What, wilt thou not?—then, Clarence, do it thou.
Clar. By heaven, I will not do thee so much ease.
Q. Mar. Good Clarence, do; sweet Clarence, do thou do it.
Clar. Didst thou not hear me swear I would not do it?
Q. Mar. Ay, but thou usest to forswear thyself:
'Twas sin before, but now 'tis charity.
What, wilt thou not? Where is that fiendish butcher,
Hard-favor'd Richard? Richard, where art thou?
Thou art not here: murder is thy alms-deed;
Petitioners for blood thou ne'er put'st back.
K. Edw. Away, I say; I charge ye, bear her hence.
Q. Mar. So come to you and yours, as to this prince!
[*Exit, led out forcibly.*
K. Edw. Where's Richard gone?
Clar. To London, all in post; and, as I guess,
To make a bloody supper in the Tower.
K. Edw. He's sudden, if a thing comes in his head.
Now march we hence: discharge the common sort
With pay and thanks, and let's away to London,
And see our gentle queen how well she fares;
By this, I hope, she hath a son for me. [*Exeunt.*

SCENE VI.—London. *A Room in the Tower.*

KING HENRY *is discovered sitting with a book in his hand*, *the* Lieutenant *attending.* *Enter* GLOSTER.

Glo. Good day, my lord. What, at your book so hard?
K. Hen. Ay, my good lord:—my lord, I should say, rather;
'Tis sin to flatter, good was little better:

Good Gloster and good evil one were like,
And both preposterous; therefore, not good lord.
Glo. Sirrah, leave us to ourselves: we must confer.
[*Exit* Lieutenant.
K. Hen. So flies the reckless shepherd from the wolf;
So first the harmless sheep doth yield his fleece,
And next his throat unto the butcher's knife.—
What scene of death hath Roscius now to act?
Glo. Suspicion always haunts the guilty mind;
The thief doth fear each bush an officer.
K. Hen. The bird that hath been limèd in a bush,
With trembling wings misdoubteth every bush;
And I, the hapless male to one sweet bird,
Have now the fatal object in my eye,
Where my poor young was lim'd, was caught, and kill'd.
Glo. Why, what a peevish fool was that of Crete,
That taught his son the office of a fowl!
And yet, for all his wings, the fool was drown'd.
K. Hen. I, Dædalus; my poor boy, Icarus;
Thy father, Minos, that denied our course;
The sun, that sear'd the wings of my sweet boy,
Thy brother Edward; and thyself, the sea,
Whose envious gulf did swallow up his life.
Ah, kill me with thy weapon, not with words!
My breast can better brook thy dagger's point,
Than can my ears that tragic history.
But wherefore dost thou come? is't for my life?
Glo. Think'st thou I am an executioner?
K. Hen. A persecutor, I am sure, thou art:
If murdering innocents be executing,
Why, then thou art an executioner.
Glo. Thy son I kill'd for his presumption.
K. Hen. Hadst thou been kill'd, when first thou didst presume,
Thou hadst not liv'd to kill a son of mine.
And thus I prophesy,—that many a thousand,
Which now mistrust no parcel of my fear,
And many an old man's sigh, and many a widow's,
And many an orphan's water-standing eye,—
Men for their sons', wives for their husbands' fate,
And orphans for their parents' timeless death,—
Shall rue the hour that ever thou wast born.
The owl shriek'd at thy birth,—an evil sign;
The night-crow cried, aboding luckless time;
Dogs howl'd, and hideous tempest shook down trees;
The raven rook'd her on the chimney's top,
And chattering pies in dismal discord sung.
Teeth hadst thou in thy head when thou wast born,
To signify, thou cam'st to bite the world:

And, if the rest be true which I have heard,
Thou cam'st—

Glo. I'll hear no more:—Die, prophet, in thy speech: [*Stabs him.*
For this, amongst the rest, was I ordain'd.

K. Hen. Ay, and for much more slaughter after this.
O, heaven forgive my sins, and pardon thee! [*Dies.*

Glo. What, will the aspiring blood of Lancaster
Sink in the ground? I thought it would have mounted.
See how my sword weeps for the poor king's death!
O, may such purple tears be always shed
From those that wish the downfall of our house!— [*Stabs him again.*
For I have neither pity, love, nor fear.—
Indeed, 'tis true, that Henry told me of;
That I was born with teeth,
And so I was; which plainly signified
That I should snarl, and bite, and play the dog.
Then, since the heavens have shap'd my body so,
Let fiends make crook'd my mind to answer it.
I have no brother, I am like no brother;
And this word "love," which greybeards call divine,
Be resident in men like one another,
And not in me: I am myself alone.—
Clarence, beware; thou keep'st me from the light:
But I will sort a pitchy day for thee;
For I will buz abroad such prophecies,
That Edward shall be fearful of his life;
And then, to purge his fear, I'll be thy death.
King Henry, and the prince his son, are gone:
Clarence, thy turn is next, and then the rest;
Counting myself but bad, till I be best.—
I'll throw thy body in another room,
And triumph, Henry, in thy day of doom. [*Exit with the body.*

SCENE VII.—London. *A Room in the Palace.*

KING EDWARD *is discovered sitting on his throne;* QUEEN ELIZABETH *with the infant Prince,* CLARENCE, GLOSTER, HASTINGS, *and others, near him.*

K. Edw. Once more we sit in England's royal throne,
Re-purchas'd with the blood of enemies.
Come hither, Bess, and let me kiss my boy.—
Young Ned, for thee, thine uncles and myself,
Have in our armors watch'd the winter's night;
Went all a-foot in summer's scalding heat,

That thou might'st repossess the crown in peace:
And of our labors thou shalt reap the gain.
Glo. [*Aside.*] I'll blast his harvest, if your head were laid;
For yet I am not look'd on in the world.
This shoulder was ordain'd so thick, to heave;
And heave it shall some weight, or break my back:—
Work thou the way, and that shall execute.
K. Edw. Clarence, and Gloster, love my lovely queen;
And kiss your princely nephew, brothers both.
Clar. The duty, that I owe unto your majesty,
I seal upon the lips of this sweet babe.
K. Edw. Thanks, noble Clarence; worthy brother, thanks.
Glo. And, that I love the tree from whence thou sprang'st,
Witness the loving kiss I give the fruit.—
[*Aside.*] To say the truth, so Judas kiss'd his master,
And cried—all hail! when as he meant—all harm.
K. Edw. Now am I seated as my soul delights,
Having my country's peace, and brothers' loves.
Clar. What will your grace have done with Margaret?
Reignier, her father, to the king of France
Hath pawn'd the Sicils and Jerusalem,
And hither have they sent it for her ransom.
K. Edw. Away with her, and waft her hence to France.—
And now what rests, but that we spend the time
With stately triumphs, mirthful comic shows,
Such as befit the pleasure of the court?
Sound drums and trumpets!—farewell, sour annoy!
For here, I hope, begins our lasting joy. [*Exeunt.*

LIFE AND DEATH OF

KING RICHARD III.

UNDER the title of "The Life and Death of King Richard III.," Shakspeare has given the leading incidents in the last fourteen years of the life of Richard, Duke of Gloster, in almost continuous succession, from the close of the Third Part of Henry VI. In the fuller and more perfect development of Richard's character in this dramatic chronicle, the poet rises to his greatest powers of original sustained conception. The Richard of Shakspeare is incorporated in our minds, as a real picture of the man, notwithstanding the sceptical doubts, thrown by later historians and commentators, as to the faithfulness of the poet's delineation. From this vivid individualism of character may be ascribed the great popularity of this Play, during a period of two hundred and fifty years. It has been, and still is, the most in favor, in the representation, of all his series of Historical Dramas; and that success is not, alone, attributable to the version prepared by Colley Cibber, in the early part of the last century, which still is used in representation; but previous to the adoption of that compiled alteration of Richard III., the Play, as originally given by Shakspeare, held possession of the stage, when most of the poet's other dramas had sunk into disuse.

PERSONS REPRESENTED.

KING EDWARD THE FOURTH.
EDWARD, *Prince of Wales; afterwards* KING EDWARD V., } *Sons to the* KING.
RICHARD, *Duke of York,* } *Sons to the* KING.
GEORGE, *Duke of Clarence,* } *Brothers to the* KING.
RICHARD, *Duke of Gloster; afterwards* KING RICHARD III., } *Brothers to the* KING.
A young Son of CLARENCE.
HENRY, *Earl of Richmond; afterwards* KING HENRY VII.
CARDINAL BOUCHIER, *Archbishop of Canterbury.*
THOMAS ROTHERHAM, *Archbishop of York.*
JOHN MORTON, *Bishop of Ely.*
DUKE OF BUCKINGHAM.
DUKE OF NORFOLK. EARL OF SURREY, *his Son.*

EARL RIVERS, *Brother to* KING EDWARD'S *Queen :* MARQUESS OF DORSET, *and* LORD GREY, *her Sons.*
EARL OF OXFORD. LORD HASTINGS.
LORD STANLEY. LORD LOVEL.
Sir THOMAS VAUGHAN. Sir RICHARD RATCLIFF.
Sir WILLIAM CATESBY. Sir JAMES TYRREL.
Sir JAMES BLOUNT. Sir WALTER HERBERT.
Sir ROBERT BRAKENBURY, *Lieutenant of the Tower.*
CHRISTOPHER URSWICK, *a Priest. Another* Priest.
Lord Mayor of London. Sheriff of Wiltshire.

ELIZABETH, *Queen of* KING EDWARD IV.
MARGARET, *Widow of* KING HENRY VI.
DUCHESS OF YORK, *Mother to* KING EDWARD IV., CLARENCE, *and* GLOSTER.
LADY ANNE, *Widow of* EDWARD, *Prince of Wales, Son to* KING HENRY VI.; *afterwards married to the* DUKE OF GLOSTER.
LADY MARGARET PLANTAGENET, *a young Daughter of* CLARENCE.

Lords, *and other* Attendants; *two* Gentlemen, *a* Pursuivant, Scrivener, Citizens, Murderers, Messengers, Ghosts, Soldiers, *&c.*

SCENE,—ENGLAND.

ACT I.

SCENE I.—London. *A Street.*

Enter GLOSTER.

Glo. Now is the winter of our discontent
Made glorious summer by this sun of York;
And all the clouds, that lower'd upon our house,
In the deep bosom of the ocean buried.
Now are our brows bound with victorious wreaths;
Our bruised arms hung up for monuments;
Our stern alarums chang'd to merry meetings,
Our dreadful marches to delightful measures.
Grim-visag'd war hath smooth'd his wrinkled front;
And now,—instead of mounting barbed steeds,
To fright the souls of fearful adversaries,—
He capers nimbly in a lady's chamber,
To the lascivious pleasing of a lute.
But I,—that am not shap'd for sportive tricks,
Nor made to court an amorous looking-glass;
I, that am rudely stamp'd, and want love's majesty,
To strut before a wanton ambling nymph;
I, that am curtail'd of this fair proportion,
Cheated of feature by dissembling nature,
Deform'd, unfinish'd, sent before my time
Into this breathing world, scarce half made up,
And that so lamely and unfashionable,

That dogs bark at me, as I halt by them;—
Why I, in this weak piping time of peace,
Have no delight to pass away the time,
Unless to see my shadow in the sun,
And descant on mine own deformity:
And therefore,—since I cannot prove a lover,
To entertain these fair well-spoken days,—
I am determined to prove a villain,
And hate the idle pleasures of these days.
Plots have I laid, inductions dangerous,
By drunken prophecies, libels, and dreams,
To set my brother Clarence and the king
In deadly hate the one against the other:
And, if king Edward be as true and just,
As I am subtle, false, and treacherous,
This day should Clarence closely be mew'd up,
About a prophecy, which says—that G
Of Edward's heirs the murderer shall be.
Dive, thoughts, down to my soul: here Clarence comes.

Enter CLARENCE, *guarded, and* BRAKENBURY.

Brother, good day: what means this armèd guard,
That waits upon your grace?
Clar. His majesty,
Tendering my person's safety, hath appointed
This conduct to convey me to the Tower.
Glo. Upon what cause?
Clar. Because my name is George.
Glo. Alack, my lord, that fault is none of yours·
He should, for that, commit your godfathers:
O, belike his majesty hath some intent
That you should be new christen'd in the Tower.
But what's the matter, Clarence? may I know?
Clar. Yea, Richard, when I know; for I protest
As yet I do not: but, as I can learn,
He hearkens after prophecies and dreams;
And from the cross-row plucks the letter G,
And says a wizard told him, that by G
His issue disinherited should be;
And, for my name of George begins with G,
It follows in his thought that I am he.
These, as I learn, and such like toys as these,
Have mov'd his highness to commit me now.
Glo. Why, this it is, when men are rul'd by women:
'Tis not the king that sends you to the Tower;
My Lady Grey, his wife, Clarence, 'tis she
That tempers him to this extremity.
We are not safe, Clarence; we are not safe.

Clar. By heaven, I think there is no man secure,
But the queen's kindred, and night-walking heralds
That trudge betwixt the king and mistress Shore.
Heard you not, what a humble suppliant
Lord Hastings was to her for his delivery?
Glo. Humbly complaining to her deity
Got my lord chamberlain his liberty.
I'll tell you what,—I think it is our way,
If we will keep in favor with the king,
To be her men, and wear her livery:
The jealous o'er-worn widow and herself,
Since that our brother dubb'd them gentlewomen,
Are mighty gossips in this monarchy.
Brak. I beseech your graces both to pardon me:
His majesty hath straitly given in charge
That no man shall have private conference,
Of what degree soever, with your brother.
Glo. Even so; an please your worship, Brakenbury,
You may partake of anything we say.
Brak. I beseech your grace to pardon me; and withal,
Forbear your conference with the noble duke.
Clar. We know thy charge, Brakenbury, and will obey.
Glo. We are the queen's abjects, and must obey.—
Brother, farewell: I will unto the king;
And whatsoe'er you will employ me in,—
Were it to call king Edward's widow, sister,—
I will perform it to enfranchise you.
Meantime, this deep disgrace in brotherhood
Touches me deeper than you can imagine.
Clar. I know it pleaseth neither of us well.
Glo. Well, your imprisonment shall not be long;
I will deliver you, or else lie for you:
Meantime, have patience.
Clar. I must perforce: farewell.
[*Exeunt* CLARENCE, BRAKENBURY, *and* Guard.
Glo. Go, tread the path that thou shalt ne'er return,
Simple, plain Clarence!—I do love thee so,
That I will shortly send thy soul to heaven,
If heaven will take the present at our hands.—
But who comes here? the new-deliver'd Hastings?

Enter HASTINGS.

Hast. Good time of day unto my gracious lord!
Glo. As much unto my good lord chamberlain!
Well are you welcome to this open air.
How hath your lordship brook'd imprisonment?
Hast. With patience, noble lord, as prisoners must:

But I shall live, my lord, to give them thanks,
That were the cause of my imprisonment.
Glo. No doubt, no doubt; and so shall Clarence too;
For they that were your enemies are his,
And have prevail'd as much on him, as you.
Hast. More pity, that the eagles should be mew'd,
While kites and buzzards prey at liberty.
Glo. What news abroad?
Hast. No news so bad abroad, as this at home;—
The king is sickly, weak, and melancholy,
And his physicians fear him mightily.
Glo. Now, by Saint Paul, this news is bad indeed.
O, he hath kept an evil diet long,
And over-much consum'd his royal person:
'Tis very grievous to be thought upon.
What, is he in his bed?
Hast. He is.
Glo. Go you before, and I will follow you. [*Exit* HASTINGS.
He cannot live, I hope; and must not die,
Till George be pack'd with posthorse up to heaven.
I'll in to urge his hatred more to Clarence,
With lies well steel'd with weighty arguments;
And, if I fail not in my deep intent,
Clarence hath not another day to live:
Which done, heaven take king Edward to his mercy,
And leave the world for me to bustle in!
For then I'll marry Warwick's youngest daughter:
What though I kill'd her husband, and her father?
The readiest way to make the wench amends,
Is to become her husband, and her father:
The which will I; not all so much for love,
As for another secret close intent,
By marrying her, which I must reach unto.
But yet I run before my horse to market:
Clarence still breathes; Edward still lives and reigns:
When they are gone, then must I count my gains. [*Exit.*

SCENE II.—London. *Another Street.*

Enter the corse of King Henry the Sixth, borne in an open coffin, Gentlemen *bearing halberds to guard it; and* LADY ANNE *as mourner.*

Anne. Set down, set down your honorable load,—
Whilst I awhile obsequiously lament
Th' untimely fall of virtuous Lancaster.—
Thou bloodless remnant of that royal blood!
Be it lawful that I invocate thy ghost,

To hear the lamentations of poor Anne.
Lo, in these windows, that let forth thy life,
I pour the helpless balm of my poor eyes:—
O, cursed be the hand that made these holes!
Cursed the heart, that had the heart to do it!
Cursed the blood, that let this blood from hence!
If ever he have child, abortive be it,
And be it heir to his unhappiness!
If ever he have wife, let her be made
More miserable by the death of him,
Than I am made by my young lord, and thee!—
Come, now toward Chertsey with your holy load.
[*The bearers take up the corse and advance.*

Enter GLOSTER.

Glo. Stay, you that bear the corse, and set it down.
Anne. What black magician conjures up this fiend,
To stop devoted charitable deeds?
Glo. Villains, set down the corse; or, by Saint Paul,
I'll make a corse of him that disobeys!
1 *Gent.* My lord, stand back, and let the coffin pass.
Glo. Unmanner'd dog! stand thou, when I command:
Advance thy halberd higher than my breast,
Or, by Saint Paul, I'll strike thee to my foot,
And spurn upon thee, beggar, for thy boldness.
[*The bearers set down the coffin.*
Anne. Avaunt, thou dreadful minister of wrath!
Thou hadst but power over his mortal body,—
His soul thou canst not have; therefore, begone.
Glo. Sweet saint, for charity, be not so curst.
Anne. Foul devil, for heaven's sake hence, and trouble us not.
Glo. Lady, you know no rules of charity.
Anne. Villain, thou know'st no law of God nor man:
No beast so fierce but knows some touch of pity.
Glo. But I know none, and therefore am no beast.
Anne. O wonderful, when devils tell the truth!
Glo. More wonderful, when angels are so angry.—
Vouchsafe, divine perfection of a woman,
Of these supposed evils, to give me leave,
By circumstance, but to acquit myself.
Anne. Vouchsafe, diffus'd infection of a man,
For these known evils, but to give me leave,
By circumstance, to curse thy cursed self.
Glo. Fairer than tongue can name thee, let me have
Some patient leisure to excuse myself.
Anne. Fouler than heart can think thee, thou canst make
No excuse current, but to hang thyself.
Glo. By such despair, I should accuse myself.

Anne. And by despairing, shalt thou stand excus'd;
For doing worthy vengeance on thyself,
That didst unworthy slaughter upon others.
Glo. Say, that I slew them not?
Anne. Then say they were not slain.
Glo. I did not kill your husband.
Anne. Why, then he is alive.
Glo. Nay, he is dead; and slain by Edward's hand.
Anne. In thy foul throat thou liest: queen Margaret saw
Thy murderous faulchion smoking in his blood;
The which thou once didst bend against her breast.
But that thy brothers beat aside the point.
Glo. I was provoked by her sland'rous tongue,
That laid their guilt upon my guiltless shoulders.
Anne. Thou wast provoked by thy bloody mind,
That never dreamt on aught but butcheries:
Didst thou not kill this king?
Glo. I grant ye.
Anne. O, he was gentle, mild, and virtuous!
Glo. The fitter for the King of heaven, that hath him.
Anne. He is in heaven, where thou shalt never come.
Glo. Let him thank me, that holp to send him thither;
For he was fitter for that place than earth.
Anne. And thou unfit for any place.
Glo. Yes, one place else, if you will hear me name it.
Anne. Some dungeon.
Glo. Your bed-chamber.
Anne. Ill rest betide the chamber where thou liest.
Glo. So will it, madam, till I lie in yours.
Anne. I hope so.
Glo. I know so.—But, gentle lady Anne,—
To leave this keen encounter of our wits,
And fall somewhat into a slower method,—
Is not the causer of the timeless deaths
Of these Plantagenets, Henry and Edward,
As blameful as the executioner?
Anne. Thou wast the cause, and most accurs'd effect.
Glo. Your beauty was the cause of that effect;
Your beauty, that did haunt me in my sleep,
To undertake the death of all the world,
So I might live one hour in your sweet bosom.
Anne. If I thought that, I tell thee, homicide,
These nails should rend that beauty from my cheeks.
Glo. These eyes could not endure that beauty's wreck;
You should not blemish it, if I stood by·
As all the world is cheerèd by the sun,
So I by that; it is my day, my life.
Anne. Black night o'ershade thy day, and death thy life!

Glo. Curse not thyself, fair creature; thou art both.
Anne. I would I were, to be reveng'd on thee.
Glo. It is a quarrel most unnatural,
To be reveng'd on him that loveth thee.
Anne. It is a quarrel just and reasonable,
To be reveng'd on him that kill'd my husband.
Glo. He that bereft thee, lady, of thy husband,
Did it to help thee to a better husband.
Anne. His better doth not breathe upon the earth.
Glo. He lives that loves thee better than he could.
Anne. Name him.
Glo. Plantagenet.
Anne. Why, that was he.
Glo. The salf-same name, but one of better nature.
Anne. Where is he?
Glo. Here.
Anne. Out of my sight! thou dost infect mine eyes.
Glo. Thine eyes, sweet lady, have infected mine.
Anne. Would they were basilisks, to strike thee dead!
Glo. I would they were, that I might die at once;
For now they kill me with a living death.
I never sued to friend, nor enemy;
My tongue could never learn sweet smoothing words;
But, now thy beauty is propos'd my fee,
My proud heart sues, and prompts my tongue to speak.
[*She looks scornfully at him.*
If thy revengeful heart cannot forgive,
Lo, here I lend thee this sharp-pointed sword;
Which if thou please to hide in this true breast,
And let the soul forth that adoreth thee,
I lay it naked to the deadly stroke,
And humbly beg the death upon my knee.
[*He lays his breast open.*
Nay, do not pause; for I did kill king Henry,—
[*She offers at it with his sword.*
But 'twas thy beauty that provoked me.
Nay, now despatch; 'twas I that stabb'd young Edward,—
[*She again offers at his breast.*
But 'twas thy heavenly face that set me on.
[*She lets fall the sword.*
Take up the sword again, or take up me.
Anne. Arise, dissembler: though I wish thy death,
I will not be thy executioner.
Glo. Then bid me kill myself, and I will do it.
Anne. I have already.
Glo. That was in thy rage:
Speak it again, and, even with the word,
This hand, which for thy love, did kill thy love,

Shall, for thy love, kill a far truer love:
To both their deaths shalt thou be accessary.
Anne. I would I knew thy heart.
Glo. 'Tis figur'd in my tongue.
Anne. I fear me both are false.
Glo. Then never man was true.
Anne. Well, well, put up your sword.
Glo. Say, then, my peace is made.
Anne. That shalt thou know hereafter.
Glo. But shall I live in hope?
Anne. All men, I hope, live so.
Glo. Vouchsafe to wear this ring.
Anne. To take, is not to give. [*She puts on the ring.*
Glo. Look, how my ring encompasseth thy finger,
Even so thy breast encloseth my poor heart;
Wear both of them, for both of them are thine.
And if thy poor devoted servant may
But beg one favor at thy gracious hand,
Thou dost confirm his happiness for ever.
Anne. What is it?
Glo. That it may please you leave these sad designs
To him that hath most cause to be a mourner,
And presently repair to Crosby-place;
Where,—after I have solemnly interr'd
At Chertsey monastery, this noble king,
And wet his grave with my repentant tears,—
I will with all expedient duty see you:
For divers unknown reasons, I beseech you,
Grant me this boon.
Anne. With all my heart; and much it joys me too,
To see you are become so penitent.—
Tressel, and Berkley, go along with me.
Glo. Bid me farewell.
Anne. 'Tis more than you deserve;
But since you teach me how to flatter you,
Imagine I have said farewell already.
[*Exeunt* LADY ANNE, TRESSEL, *and* BERKLEY.
Rich. Sirs, take up the corse.
Gent. Towards Chertsey, noble lord?
Glo. No, to White-Friars; there attend my coming.
[*Exeunt the rest with the corse.*
Was ever woman in this humor woo'd?
Was ever woman in this humor won?
I'll have her;—but I will not keep her long.
What! I, that kill'd her husband, and his father,
To take her in her heart's extremest hate;
With curses in her mouth, tears in her eyes,
The bleeding witness of her hatred by;

Having heaven, her conscience, and these bars against me,
And I no friends to back my suit withal,
But the plain devil, and dissembling looks,
And yet to win her,—all the world to nothing!
Ha!
Hath she forgot already that brave prince,
Edward, her lord, whom I, some three months since,
Stabb'd in my angry mood at Tewksbury?
And will she yet abase her eyes on me,
On me, whose all not equals Edward's moiety?
On me, that halt, and am mis-shapen thus?
My dukedom to a beggarly denier,
I do mistake my person all this while:
Upon my life, she finds, although I cannot,
Myself to be a marvellous proper man.
I'll be at charges for a looking-glass;
And entertain a score or two of tailors,
To study fashions to adorn my body:
Since I am crept in favor with myself,
I will maintain it with some little cost.
But, first, I'll turn yon fellow to his grave;
And then return lamenting to my love.—
Shine out, fair sun, till I have bought a glass,
That I may see my shadow as I pass. [*Exit.*

SCENE III.—London. *A Room in the Palace.*

Enter QUEEN ELIZABETH, RIVERS, *and* GREY.

Riv. Have patience, madam: there's no doubt, his majesty
Will soon recover his accustom'd health.
Grey. In that you brook it ill, it makes him worse:
Therefore, for heaven's sake, entertain good comfort,
And cheer his grace with quick and merry words.
Q. Eliz. If he were dead, what would betide on me?
Grey. No other harm, but loss of such a lord.
Q. Eliz. The loss of such a lord includes all harms.
Grey. The heavens have bless'd you with a goodly son,
To be your comforter when he is gone.
Q. Eliz. Ah, he is young; and his minority
Is put unto the trust of Richard Gloster,
A man that loves not me, nor none of you.
Riv. Is it concluded he shall be protector?
Q. Eliz. It is determin'd, not concluded yet:
But so it must be, if the king miscarry.
Grey. Here come the lords of Buckingham and Stanley.

Enter BUCKINGHAM *and* STANLEY.

Buck. Good time of day unto your royal grace!

Stan. Heaven make your majesty joyful as you have been!
Q. Eliz. Saw you the king to-day, my lord of Stanley?
Stan. But now, the duke of Buckingham, and I,
Are come from visiting his majesty.
Q. Eliz. What likelihood of his amendment, lords?
Buck. Madam, good hope; his grace speaks cheerfully.
Q. Eliz. Heaven grant him health! Did you confer with him?
Buck. Ay, madam: he desires to make atonement
Between the duke of Gloster and your brothers,
And between them and my lord chamberlain;
And sent to warn them to his royal presence.
Q. Eliz. Would all were well!—But that will never be:
I fear our happiness is at the height.

Enter GLOSTER, HASTINGS, *and* DORSET.

Glo. They do me wrong, and I will not endure it:—
Who are they, that complain unto the king,
That I, forsooth, am stern, and love them not?
By holy Paul, they love his grace but lightly,
That fill his ears with such dissentious rumors.
Because I cannot flatter, and speak fair,
Smile in men's faces, smooth, deceive, and cog,
Duck with French nods and apish courtesy,
I must be held a rancorous enemy.
Cannot a plain man live, and think no harm,
But thus his simple truth must be abus'd
By silken, sly, insinuating Jacks?
Grey. To whom in all this presence speaks your grace!
Glo. To thee, that hast nor honesty, nor grace.
When have I injur'd thee? when done thee wrong?—
Or thee?—or thee?—or any of your faction?
A plague upon you all! His royal grace,
(Whom heaven preserve better than you would wish!)
Cannot be quiet scarce a breathing-while,
But you must trouble him with lewd complaints.
Q. Eliz. Brother of Gloster, you mistake the matter.
Glo. I cannot tell:—the world is grown so bad,
That wrens make prey where eagles dare not perch:
Since every Jack became a gentleman,
There's many a gentle person made a Jack.
Q. Eliz. Come, come, we know your meaning, brother Gloster;
You envy my advancement, and my friends':
God grant, we never may have need of you!
Glo. Meantime, heaven grants that we have need of you:
Our brother is imprison'd by your means,
Myself disgrac'd, and the nobility
Held in contempt; while great promotions

Are daily given, to ennoble those
That scarce, some two days since, were worth a noble.
Q. Eliz. By Him that rais'd me to this careful height
From that contented hap which I enjoy'd,
I never did incense his majesty
Against the duke of Clarence, but have been
An earnest advocate to plead for him.
Glo. You may deny that you were not the mean
Of my lord Hastings' late imprisonment.
Riv. She may, my lord; for—
Glo. She may, lord Rivers,—why, who knows not so?
She may do more, sir, than denying that:
She may help you to many fair preferments;
And then deny her aiding hand therein,
And lay those honors on your high desert.
What may she not? She may,—ay, marry, may she,—
Riv. What, marry, may she?
Glo. What, marry, may she! marry with a king,
A bachelor, a handsome stripling too;
I wis, your grandam had a worser match.
Q. Eliz. My lord of Gloster, I have too long borne
Your blunt upbraidings, and your bitter scoffs:
By heaven, I will acquaint his majesty
Of those gross taunts that oft I have endur'd.
I had rather be a country servant-maid,
Than a great queen, with this condition,—
To be so baited, scorn'd, and stormed at:

Enter QUEEN MARGARET, *behind.*

Small joy have I in being England's queen.
Q. Mar. [*Apart.*] And lessen'd be that small, heaven, I beseech him!—
Thy honor, state, and seat, is due to me.
Glo. What! threat you me with telling of the king?
Tell him, and spare not: look, what I have said
I will avouch in presence of the king:
I dare adventure to be sent to the Tower.
'Tis time to speak,—my pains are quite forgot.
Q. Mar. [*Apart.*] Out, false one! I remember them too well:
Thou kill'dst my husband Henry in the Tower,
And Edward, my poor son, at Tewksbury.
Glo. Ere you were queen, ay, or your husband king,
I was a pack-horse in his great affairs;
A weeder-out of his proud adversaries,
A liberal rewarder of his friends:
To royalize his blood, I spilt mine own.
Q. Mar. [*Apart.*] Ay, and much better blood than his, or thine.

Glo. In all which time, you, and your husband Grey,
Were factious for the house of Lancaster;—
And, Rivers, so were you:—was not your husband
In Margaret's battle at St. Albans slain?
Let me put in your minds, if you forget,
What you have been ere this, and what you are;
Withal, what I have been, and what I am.
Q. Mar. [*Apart.*] A murd'rous villain, and so still thou art.
Glo. Poor Clarence did forsake his father, Warwick;
Ay, and forswore himself,—which heaven pardon!—
Q. Mar. [*Apart.*] Which heaven revenge!
Glo. To fight on Edward's party, for the crown;
And for his meed, poor lord, he is mew'd up.
I would to heaven my heart were flint, like Edward's;
Or Edward's soft and pitiful, like mine:
I am too childish-foolish for this world.
Riv. My lord of Gloster, in those busy days,
Which here you urge to prove us enemies,
We follow'd then our lord, our sovereign king:
So should we you, if you should be our king.
Glo. If I should be!—I had rather be a pedler.
Far be it from my heart, the thought thereof!
Q. Eliz. As little joy, my lord, as you suppose
You should enjoy, were you this country's king,—
As little joy you may suppose in me,
That I enjoy, being the queen thereof.
Q. Mar. [*Apart.*] As little joy enjoys the queen thereof;
For I am she, and altogether joyless.
I can no longer hold me patient.— [*Advancing.*
Hear me, you wrangling pirates, that fall out
In sharing that which you have pill'd* from me!
Which of you trembles not, that looks on me?
If not, that, I being queen, you bow like subjects,
Yet that, by you depos'd, you quake like rebels?—
Ah, gentle villain, do not turn away!
Glo. Foul wrinkled witch, what mak'st thou in my sight?
Q. Mar. But repetition of what thou hast marr'd;
That will I make, before I let thee go.
Glo. Wert thou not banished, on pain of death?
Q. Mar. I was; but I do find more pain in banishment,
Than death can yield me here by my abode.
A husband, and a son, thou ow'st to me,—
And thou, a kingdom,—all of you, allegiance:
This sorrow that I have, by right is yours;
And all the pleasures you usurp are mine.
Glo. The curse my noble father laid on thee,

* *Pill*—to pillage, to rob.

When thou did'st crown his warlike brows with paper,
And with thy scorns drew'st rivers from his eyes;
And then, to dry them, gav'st the duke a clout
Steep'd in the faultless blood of pretty Rutland;
His curses, then from bitterness of soul
Denounc'd against thee, are all fallen upon thee;
And heaven, not we, hath plagu'd thy bloody deed.
Q. Eliz. So just is heaven, to right the innocent.
Hast. O, 'twas the foulest deed to slay that babe,
And the most merciless, that e'er was heard of!
Riv. Tyrants themselves wept when it was reported.
Dors. No man but prophesied revenge for it.
Buck. Northumberland, then present, wept to see it.
Q. Mar. What, were you snarling all, before I came,
Ready to catch each other by the throat,
And turn you all your hatred now on me?
Did York's dread curse prevail so much with heaven,
That Henry's death, my lovely Edward's death,
Their kingdom's loss, my woful banishment,
Could all but answer for that peevish brat?
Can curses pierce the clouds, and enter heaven?—
Why, then, give way, dull clouds, to my quick curses!—
Though not by war, by surfeit die your king,
As ours by murder, to make him a king!
Edward, thy son, that now is prince of Wales,
For Edward, my son, that was prince of Wales,
Die in his youth by like untimely violence!
Thyself a queen, for me that was a queen,
Outlive thy glory, like my wretched self!
Long may'st thou live to wail thy children's loss;
And see another, as I see thee now,
Deck'd in thy rights, as thou art stall'd in mine!
Long die thy happy days before thy death;
And, after many lengthen'd hours of grief,
Die neither mother, wife, nor England's queen!-
Rivers, and Dorset, you were standers by,—
And so wast thou, lord Hastings,—when my son
Was stabb'd with bloody daggers: heaven, I pray him,
That none of you may live his natural age,
But by some unlook'd accident cut off!
Glo. Have done thy charm, thou hateful wither'd hag!
Q. Mar. And leave out thee? stay, dog, for thou shalt hear me.
If heaven have any grievous plague in store,
Exceeding those that I can wish upon thee,
O, let them keep it till thy sins be ripe,
And then hurl down their indignation
On thee, the troubler of the poor world's peace!
Thou rag of honor! thou detested—

Q. Eliz. Thus have you breath'd your curse against yourself.
Q. Mar. Poor painted queen, vain flourish of my fortune!
Why strew'st thou sugar on that bottled spider?
Buck. Peace, peace, for shame, if not for charity.
Q. Mar. O princely Buckingham, I'll kiss thy hand,
In sign of league and amity with thee:
Now fair befall thee, and thy noble house!
Thy garments are not spotted with our blood,
Nor thou within the compass of my curse.
Buck. Nor no one here; for curses never pass
The lips of those that breathe them in the air.
Q. Mar. I will not think but they ascend the sky,
And there awake heaven's gentle-sleeping peace.
O Buckingham, take heed of yonder dog!
Look, when he fawns, he bites; and when he bites,
His venom tooth will rankle to the death:
Have not to do with him, beware of him.
Glo. What doth she say, my lord of Buckingham?
Buck. Nothing that I respect, my gracious lord.
Q. Mar. What, dost thou scorn me for my gentle counsel?
O, but remember this another day,
When he shall split thy very heart with sorrow,
And say, poor Margaret was a prophetess!—
Live each of you the subjects of his hate,
And he to yours, and all of you to heaven's. [*Exit.*
Hast. My hair doth stand on end to hear her curses.
Riv. And so doth mine: I muse why she's at liberty.
Glo. I cannot blame her:
She hath had too much wrong; and I repent
My part thereof, that I have done to her.
Q. Eliz. I never did her any, to my knowledge.
Glo. Yet you have all the vantage of her wrong.
I was too hot to do somebody good,
That is too cold in thinking of it now.

Enter CATESBY.

Cates. Madam, his majesty doth call for you,—
And for your grace,—and you, my noble lords.
Q. Eliz. Catesby, I come.—Lords, will you go with me?
Riv. We wait upon your grace.
[*Exeunt all except* GLOSTER.

Glo. I do the wrong, and first begin to brawl.
The secret mischiefs that I set abroach,
I lay unto the grievous charge of others.
Clarence,—whom I, indeed, have cast in darkness,—
I do beweep to many simple gulls;
And seem a saint, when most I play the devil.—
But soft! here come my executioners.—

Enter two Murderers.

How now, my hardy, stout resolved mates!
Are you now going to despatch this thing?
1 *Murd.* We are, my lord; and come to have the warrant,
That we may be admitted where he is.
Glo. Well thought upon; I have it here about me:
[*Gives the warrant.*
When you have done, repair to Crosby place.
But, sirs, be sudden in the execution,
Withal obdurate; do not hear him plead;
For Clarence is well-spoken, and perhaps
May move your hearts to pity, if you mark him.
1 *Murd.* Tut, tut, my lord, we will not stand to prate;
Talkers are no good doers: be assur'd
We go to use our hands, and not our tongues.
Glo. Your eyes drop mill-stones, when fool's eyes fall tears:
I like you, lads;—about your business straight;
Go, go, despatch.
1 *Murd.* We will, my noble lord. [*Exeunt.*

SCENE IV.—London. *A Room in the Tower.*

Enter CLARENCE *and* BRAKENBURY.

Brak. Why looks your grace so heavily to-day?
Clar. O, I have pass'd a miserable night,
So full of fearful dreams, of ugly sights,
That, as I am a Christian faithful man,
I would not spend another such a night,
Though 'twere to buy a world of happy days,—
So full of dismal terror was the time!
Brak. What was your dream, my lord? I pray you, tell me.
Clar. Methought that I had broken from the Tower,
And was embark'd to cross to Burgundy;
And, in my company, my brother Gloster;
Who from my cabin tempted me to walk
Upon the hatches: thence we look'd toward England,
And cited up a thousand heavy times,
During the wars of York and Lancaster,
That had befall'n us. As we pac'd along
Upon the giddy footing of the hatches,
Methought that Gloster stumbled; and, in falling,
Struck me, that thought to stay him, over-board,
Into the tumbling billows of the main.
O Lord! methought what pain it was to drown!
What dreadful noise of water in mine ears!
What sights of ugly death within mine eyes!

Methought I saw a thousand fearful wrecks;
A thousand men that fishes gnaw'd upon;
Wedges of gold, great anchors, heaps of pearl,
Inestimable stones, unvalued jewels,
All scatter'd in the bottom of the sea:
Some lay in dead men's skulls; and in those holes
Where eyes did once inhabit, there were crept
(As 'twere in scorn of eyes) reflecting gems,
That woo'd the slimy bottom of the deep,
And mock'd the dead bones that lay scatter'd by.
Brak. Had you such leisure in the time of death,
To gaze upon these secrets of the deep?
Clar. Methought I had; and often did I strive
To yield the ghost: but still the envious flood
Stopt in my soul, and would not let it forth
To find the empty, vast, and wandering air;
But smother'd it within my panting bulk,
Which almost burst to belch it in the sea.
Brak. Awak'd you not with this sore agony?
Clar. No, no, my dream was lengthen'd after life;
O, then began the tempest to my soul!
I pass'd, methought, the melancholy flood,
With that grim ferryman which poets write of,
Unto the kingdom of perpetual night.
The first that there did greet my stranger soul,
Was my great father-in-law, renownèd Warwick;
Who cried aloud, "What scourge for perjury
Can this dark monarchy afford false Clarence?"
And so he vanish'd: then came wandering by
A shadow like an angel, with bright hair
Dabbled in blood; and he shriek'd out aloud,
"Clarence is come,—false, fleeting, perjur'd Clarence,—
That stabb'd me in the field by Tewksbury;—
Seize on him, Furies! take him to your torments!"
With that, methought, a legion of foul fiends
Environ'd me, and howlèd in mine ears
Such hideous cries, that, with the very noise,
I trembling wak'd, and, for a season after,
Could not believe but that I was in hell,—
Such terrible impression made my dream.
Brak. No marvel, lord, though it affrighted you;
I am afraid, methinks, to hear you tell it.
Clar. O Brakenbury, I have done these things,
That now give evidence against my soul,
For Edward's sake; and see how he requites me!—
O heaven! if my deep prayers cannot appease thee,
But thou wilt be aveng'd on my misdeeds,
Yet execute thy wrath on me alone:

O, spare my guiltless wife and my poor children!
I pray thee, gentle keeper, stay by me;
My soul is heavy, and I fain would sleep.
Brak. I will, my lord: Heaven give your grace good rest.
[CLARENCE *sleeps.*
Sorrow breaks seasons and reposing hours,
Makes the night morning, and the noon-tide night.
Princes have but their titles for their glories,
An outward honor for an inward toil;
And, for unfelt imaginations,
They often feel a world of restless cares:
So that, between their titles, and low name,
There's nothing differs but the outward fame.

The Duke of Clarence is murdered at the instigation of his brother Gloster.

ACT II.

King Edward falls into the fatal sickness which terminates his life.

SCENE II.—*Another Room in the Palace.*

Enter the DUCHESS OF YORK, *with a* Son *and* Daughter *of* CLARENCE.

Son. Good grandam, tell us, is our father dead?
Duch. No, boy.
Daugh. Why do you weep so oft, and beat your breast,
And cry—"O Clarence, my unhappy son!"
Son. Why do you look on us, and shake your head,
And call us—orphans, wretches, cast-aways,
If that our noble father be alive?
Duch. My pretty cousins, you mistake me both,
I do lament the sickness of the king,
As loath to lose him, not your father's death;
It were lost sorrow to wail one that's lost.
Son. Then you conclude, my grandam, he is dead.
The king mine uncle is to blame for this:
Heaven will revenge it; whom I will importune
With earnest prayers all to that effect.
Daugh. And so will I.
Duch. Peace, children, peace! the king doth love you well:
Incapable and shallow innocents,
You cannot guess who caus'd your father's death.
Son. Grandam, we can; for my good uncle Gloster
Told me, the king, provok'd to it by the queen,
Devis'd impeachments to imprison him:
And when my uncle told me so, he wept,

And pitied me, and kindly kiss'd my cheek;
Bade me rely on him, as on my father,
And he would love me dearly as his child.
Duch. Ah, that deceit should steal such gentle shape,
And with a virtuous visor hide deep vice!
He is my son; ay, and therein my shame.
Son. Think you my uncle did dissemble, grandam?
Duch. Ay, boy.
Son. I cannot think it.—Hark! what noise is this?

Enter QUEEN ELIZABETH, *distractedly;* RIVERS *and* DORSET *following her.*

Q. Eliz. Ah, who shall hinder me to wail and weep,
To chide my fortune, and torment myself?
I'll join with black despair against my soul,
And to myself become an enemy.
Duch. What means this scene of rude impatience?
Q. Eliz. Edward, my lord, thy son, our king, is dead.
Why grow the branches when the root is gone?
Why wither not the leaves that want their sap?
If you will live, lament; if die, be brief,
That our swift-winged souls may catch the king's;
Or, like obedient subjects, follow him
To his new kingdom of ne'er changing night.
Duch. Ah, so much interest have I in thy sorrow,
As I had title in thy noble husband!
Clarence and Edward. O, what cause have I,
To over-go thy woes, and drown thy cries!
Son. Ah, aunt, you wept not for our father's death!
How can we aid you with our kindred tears?
Daugh. Our fatherless distress was left unmoan'd;
Your widow-dolor likewise be unwept!
Q. Eliz. Give me no help in lamentation;
Ah, for my husband, for my dear lord, Edward!
Chil. Ah, for our father, for our dear lord Clarence!
Duch. Alas, for both, both mine, Edward and Clarence!
Q. Eliz. What stay had I but Edward? and he's gone.
Chil. What stay had we but Clarence? and he's gone.
Duch. What stays had I but they? and they are gone.
Q. Eliz. Was never widow had so dear a loss!
Chil. Were never orphans had so dear a loss!
Duch. Was never mother had so dear a loss!
Alas, I am the mother of these griefs!
Their woes are parcell'd, mine are general.
Alas, you three, on me, threefold distress'd,
Pour all your tears! I am your sorrow's nurse,
And I will pamper it with lamentation.
Dor. Comfort, dear mother: heaven is much displeas'd

That you take with unthankfulness his doing:
In common worldly things, 'tis call'd ungrateful,
With dull unwillingness to repay a debt,
Which with a bounteous hand was kindly lent;
Much more to be thus opposite with heaven,
For it requires the royal debt it lent you.
Riv. Madam, bethink you, like a careful mother,
Of the young prince your son: send straight for him;
Let him be crown'd; in him your comfort lives:
Drown desperate sorrow in dead Edward's grave,
And plant your joys in living Edward's throne.

Enter GLOSTER, BUCKINGHAM, STANLEY, HASTINGS, RATCLIFF, *and others.*

Glo. Sister, have comfort: all of us have cause
To wail the dimming of our shining star;
But none can cure their harms by wailing them.—
Madam, my mother, I do cry you mercy;
I did not see your grace:—humbly on my knee
I crave your blessing.
Duch. Heaven bless thee; and put meekness in thy breast,
Love, charity, obedience, and true duty!
Glo. Amen; and make me die a good old man!—
[*Aside.*] That is the butt-end of a mother's blessing;
I marvel that her grace did leave it out.
Buck. You cloudy princes, and heart-sorrowing peers,
Though we have spent our harvest of this king,
We are to reap the harvest of his son.
Me seemeth good, that, with some little train,
Forthwith from Ludlow the young prince be fetch'd
Hither to London, to be crown'd our king.
Glo. Be it so; and go we to determine
Who they shall be that straight shall post to Ludlow.
Madam,—and you my mother,—will you go
To give your censures in this business?
[*Exeunt all except* BUCKINGHAM *and* GLOSTER.
Buck. My lord, whoever journeys to the prince,
For heaven's sake, let not us two stay at home;
For, by the way, I'll sort occasion,
As index to the story we late talk'd of,
To part the queen's proud kindred from the prince.
Glo. My other self, my counsel's consistory,
My oracle, my prophet!—My dear cousin,
I, as a child, will go by thy direction.
Towards Ludlow then, for we'll not stay behind. [*Exeunt.*

SCENE IV.—London. *A Room in the Palace.*

Enter the ARCHBISHOP OF YORK, *the young* DUKE OF YORK, QUEEN ELIZABETH, *and the* DUCHESS OF YORK.

Arch. Last night, I hear, they lay at Northampton;
At Stony-Stratford will they be to-night:
To-morrow, or next day, they will be here.
Duch. I long with all my heart to see the prince:
I hope he is much grown since last I saw him.
Q. Eliz. But I hear, no; they say my son of York
Hath almost overta'en him in his growth.
York. Ay, mother, but I would not have it so.
Duch. Why, my young cousin? it is good to grow.
York. Grandam, one night, as we did sit at supper,
My uncle Rivers talk'd how I did grow
More than my brother: "Ay," quoth my uncle Gloster,
"Small herbs have grace, great weeds do grow apace:"
And since, methinks, I would not grow so fast,
Because sweet flowers are slow, and weeds make haste.
Duch. 'Good faith, 'good faith, the saying did not hold
In him who did object the same to thee:
He was the wretched'st thing when he was young,
So long a-growing, and so leisurely,
That, if his rule were true, he should be gracious.
Arch. And so, no doubt he is, my gracious madam.
Duch. I hope he is; but yet let mothers doubt.
York. Now, by my troth, if I had been remember'd,
I could have given my uncle's grace a flout,
To touch his growth nearer than he touch'd mine.
Duch. How, my young York? I pr'ythee, let me hear it.
York. Marry, they say my uncle grew so fast,
That he could gnaw a crust at two hours old:
'Twas full two years ere I could get a tooth.
Grandam, this would have been a biting jest.
Duch. I pr'ythee, pretty York, who told thee this?
York. Grandam, his nurse.
Duch. His nurse! why, she was dead ere thou wast born.
York. If 'twere not she, I cannot tell who told me.
Q. Eliz. A parlous boy:—go to, you are too shrewd.
Arch. Good madam, be not angry with the child.
Q. Eliz. Pitchers have ears.
Arch. Here comes a messenger.

Enter a Messenger.

What news?
Mess. Such news, my lord, as grieves me to report.
Q. Eliz. How doth the prince?

Mess. Well, madam, and in health.
Duch. What is thy news?
Mess. Lord Rivers and lord Grey are sent to Pomfret,
With them Sir Thomas Vaughan, prisoners.
Duch. Who hath committed them?
Mess. The mighty dukes,
Gloster and Buckingham.
Q. Eliz. For what offence?
Mess. The sum of all I can, I have disclos'd;
Why or for what the nobles were committed,
Is all unknown to me, my gracious lady.
Q. Eliz. Ah me, I see the ruin of my house!
The tiger now hath seiz'd the gentle hind;
Insulting tyranny begins to jut
Upon the innocent and awless throne:
Welcome, destruction, blood, and massacre!
I see, as in a map, the end of all.
Come, come, my boy; we will to sanctuary.—
Madam, farewell.
Duch. Stay, I will go with you.
Q. Eliz. You have no cause.
Arch. [*To the* QUEEN.] My gracious lady, go:
And thither bear your treasure and your goods.
Come, I'll conduct you to the sanctuary. [*Exeunt.*

ACT III.

SCENE I.—London. *A Street.*

The trumpets sound. Enter the PRINCE OF WALES, GLOSTER, BUCKINGHAM, CATESBY, CARDINAL BOURCHIER, *and others.*

Buck. Welcome, sweet prince, to London, to your chamber.
Glo. Welcome, dear cousin, my thoughts' sovereign:
The weary way hath made you melancholy.
Prince. No, uncle; but our crosses on the way
Have made it tedious, wearisome, and heavy:
I want more uncles here to welcome me.
Glo. Sweet prince, the untainted virtue of your years
Hath not yet div'd into the world's deceit:
No more can you distinguish of a man,
Than of his outward show; which, heaven knows,
Seldom or never jumpeth with the heart.
Those uncles which you want were dangerous;
Your grace attended to their sugar'd words,
But look'd not on the poison of their hearts:
Heaven keep you from them, and from such false friends!

Prince. Heaven keep me from false friends! but they were none.
Glo. My lord, the mayor of London comes to greet you.

Enter the Lord Mayor *and his train.*

May. Heaven bless your grace with health and happy days!
Prince. I thank you, good my lord;—and thank you all.—
[*Exeunt* Mayor, *&c.*
I thought my mother, and my brother York,
Would long ere this have met us on the way.

Enter HASTINGS.

Welcome, my lord: what, will our mother come?
Hast. On what occasion, heaven knows, not I,
The queen your mother, and your brother York,
Have taken sanctuary: the tender prince
Would fain have come with me to meet your grace,
But by his mother was perforce withheld.
Buck. Fie, what an indirect and peevish course
Is this of hers!—Lord cardinal, will your grace
Persuade the queen to send the duke of York
Unto his princely brother presently?
If she deny,—lord Hastings, go with him,
And from her jealous arms pluck him perforce.
Card. My lord of Buckingham, if my weak oratory
Can from his mother win the duke of York,
Anon expect him here; but if she be obdurate
To mild entreaties, heaven forbid
We should infringe the holy privilege
Of blessed sanctuary! not for all this land
Would I be guilty of so great a sin.
Buck. You are too senseless-obstinate, my lord,
Too ceremonious and traditional.
Card. My lord, you shall o'er-rule my mind for once.—
Come on, lord Hastings, will you go with me?
Hast. I go, my lord.
Prince. Good lords, make all the speedy haste you may.—
[*Exeunt* CARDINAL *and* HASTINGS.
Say, uncle Gloster, if our brother come,
Where shall we sojourn till our coronation?
Glo. Where it seems best unto your royal self.
If I may counsel you, some day or two
Your highness shall repose you at the Tower:
Then where you please, and shall be thought most fit
For your best health and recreation.
Prince. I do not like the Tower, of any place.—
Did Julius Cæsar build that place, my lord?
Buck. He did, my gracious lord, begin that place;
Which, since, succeeding ages have re-edified.

Prince. Is it upon record, or else reported
Successively from age to age, he built it?
Buck. Upon record, my gracious lord.
Prince. But say, my lord, it were not register'd,
Methinks the truth should live from age to age,
As 'twere retail'd to all posterity,
Even to the general all-ending day.
Glo. [*Aside.*] So wise so young, they say, do never live long.
Prince. What say you, uncle?
Glo. I say, without charácters fame lives long.—
Prince. That Julius Cæsar was a famous man;
With what his valor did enrich his wit,
His wit set down to make his valor live:
Death makes no conquest of this conqueror;
For now he lives in fame, though not in life.—
I'll tell you what, my cousin Buckingham,—
Buck. What, my gracious lord?
Prince. And if I live until I be a man,
I'll win our ancient right in France again,
Or die a soldier, as I liv'd a king.
Glo. [*Aside.*] Short summers lightly have a forward spring.
Buck. Now, in good time, here comes the duke of York.

Enter YORK, HASTINGS, *and the* CARDINAL.

Prince. Richard of York! how fares our loving brother?
York. Well, my dread lord; so must I call you now.
Prince. Ay, brother,—to our grief, as it is yours:
Too late he died that might have kept that title,
Which by his death hath lost much majesty.
Glo. How fares our cousin, noble lord of York?
York. I thank you, gentle uncle. O, my lord,
You said that idle weeds are fast in growth:
The prince my brother hath outgrown me far.
Glo. He hath, my lord.
York. And therefore is he idle?
Glo. O, my fair cousin, I must not say so.
York. Then he is more beholden to you than I.
Glo. He may command me as my sovereign;
But you have power in me as in a kinsman.
York. I pray you, uncle, give me this dagger.
Glo. My dagger, little cousin? with all my heart.
Prince. A beggar, brother?
York. Of my kind uncle, that I know will give;
And, being but a toy, which is no grief to give.
Glo. A greater gift than that I'll give my cousin.
York. A greater gift! O, that's the sword to it.
Glo. Ay, gentle cousin, were it light enough.

York. O, then, I see, you'll part but with light gifts;
In weightier things you'll say a beggar, nay.
Glo. It is too weighty for your grace to wear.
York. I weigh it lightly, were it heavier.
Glo. What, would you have my weapon, little lord?
York. I would, that I might thank you as you call me.
Glo. How?
York. Little.
Prince. My lord of York will still be cross in talk:—
Uncle, your grace knows how to bear with him.
York. You mean, to bear me, not to bear with me:—
Uncle, my brother mocks both you and me;
Because that I am little, like an ape,
He thinks that you should bear me on your shoulders.
Glo. My lord, will't please you pass along?
Myself and my good cousin Buckingham
Will to your mother, to entreat of her
To meet you at the Tower, and welcome you.
York. What, will you go into the Tower, my lord?
Prince. My lord protector needs will have it so.
York. I shall not sleep in quiet at the Tower.
Glo. Why, what should you fear?
York. Marry, my uncle Clarence' angry ghost:
My grandam told me he was murder'd there.
Prince. I fear no uncles dead.
Glo. Nor none that live, I hope.
Prince. An if they live, I hope, I need not fear.
But come, my lord; and, with a heavy heart,
Thinking on them, go I unto the Tower.
[*Sennet. Exeunt* PRINCE, YORK, HASTINGS, CARDINAL, *and* Attendants.
Buck. Think you, my lord, this little prating York
Was not incensed by his subtle mother
To taunt and scorn you thus opprobriously?
Glo. No doubt, no doubt: O, 'tis a parlous boy;
Bold, quick, ingenious, forward, capable:
He's all the mother's, from the top to toe.
Buck. Well, let them rest.—Come hither, Catesby.
Thou art sworn as deeply to effect what we intend,
As closely to conceal what we impart:
Thou know'st our reasons urg'd upon the way;—
What think'st thou? is it not an easy matter
To make William lord Hastings of our mind,
For the instalment of this noble duke
In the seat royal of this famous isle?
Cate. He for his father's sake so loves the prince,
That he will not be won to aught against him.
Buck. What think'st thou, then, of Stanley? not he?

Cate. He will do all in all as Hastings doth.
Buck. Well then, no more but this: go, gentle Catesby,
And, as it were far off, sound thou lord Hastings,
How he doth stand affected to our purpose;
And summon him to-morrow to the Tower,
To sit about the coronation.
If thou dost find him tractable to us,
Encourage him, and tell him all our reasons:
If he be leaden, icy, cold, unwilling,
Be thou so too; and so break off the talk,
And give us notice of his inclination:
For we to-morrow hold divided councils,
Wherein thyself shalt highly be employ'd.
Glo. Commend me to lord William: tell him, Catesby,
His ancient knot of dangerous adversaries
To-morrow are let blood at Pomfret castle.
Buck. Good Catesby, go, effect this business soundly.
Cate. My good lords both, with all the heed I can.
Glo. Shall we hear from you, Catesby, ere we sleep?
Cate. You shall, my lord.
Glo. At Crosby-place, there shall you find us both.
[*Exit* CATESBY.
Buck. Now, my lord, what shall we do, if we perceive
Lord Hastings will not yield to our complots?
Glo. Chop off his head, man;—somewhat we will do:—
And, look, when I am king, claim thou of me
The earldom of Hereford, and all the moveables
Whereof the king, my brother, was possess'd.
Buck. I'll claim that promise at your grace's hand.
Glo. And look to have it yielded with all kindness.
Come, let us sup betimes, that afterwards
We may digest our complots in some form. [*Exeunt.*

Catesby sounds Hastings, but finds him firm in his allegiance to young Edward. Gloster orders the execution of the lords Rivers, Grey, and Vaughan.

SCENE IV.—London. *A Room in the Tower.*

BUCKINGHAM, STANLEY, HASTINGS, *the* BISHOP OF ELY, RATCLIFF, LOVEL, *and others, sitting at a table: Officers of the Council attending.*

Hast. Now, noble peers, the cause why we are met
Is to determine of the coronation:
In heaven's name, speak,—when is the royal day?
Buck. Are all things ready for that royal time?
Stan. They are; and wants but nomination.

Ely. To-morrow, then, I judge a happy day.
Buck. Who knows the lord protector's mind herein?
Who is most inward with the noble duke?
Ely. Your grace, we think, should soonest know his mind.
Buck. We know each other's faces; for our hearts,
He knows no more of mine, than I of yours;
Nor I of his, my lord, than you of mine.—
Lord Hastings, you and he are near in love.
Hast. I thank his grace, I know he loves me well;
But, for his purpose in the coronation,
I have not sounded him, nor he deliver'd
His gracious pleasure any way therein:
But you, my honorable lords, may name the time;
And in the duke's behalf I'll give my voice,
Which, I presume, he'll take in gentle part.
Ely. In happy time, here comes the duke himself.

Enter GLOSTER.

Glo. My noble lords and cousins, all, good morrow.
I have been long a sleeper; but, I trust,
My absence doth neglect no great design,
Which by my presence might have been concluded.
Buck. Had you not come upon your cue, my lord,
William lord Hastings had pronounc'd your part,—
I mean, your voice, for crowning of the king.
Glo. Than my lord Hastings, no man might be bolder;
His lordship knows me well, and loves me well.—
Cousin of Buckingham, a word with you. [*Takes him aside.*
Catesby hath sounded Hastings in our business,
And finds the testy gentleman so hot,
That he will lose his head ere give consent
His master's child, as worshipfully he terms it,
Shall lose the royalty of England's throne.
Buck. Withdraw yourself awhile; I'll go with you.
[*Exeunt* GLOSTER *and* BUCKINGHAM.
Stan. We have not yet set down this day of triumph.
To-morrow, in my judgment, is too sudden;
For I myself am not so well provided
As else I would be, were the day prolong'd.
Ely. Where is my lord, the duke of Gloster?
Hast. His grace looks cheerfully and smooth this morning;
There's some conceit or other likes him well,
When that he bids good-morrow with such spirit.
I think there's never a man in Christendom
Can lesser hide his love or hate than he;
For by his face straight shall you know his heart.
Stan. What of his heart perceive you in his face,
By any livelihood he show'd to-day?

Hast. Marry, that with no man here he is offended;
For, were he, he had shown it in his looks.

Re-enter GLOSTER *and* BUCKINGHAM.

Glo. I pray you all, tell me what they deserve,
That do conspire my death with devilish plots
Of cursed witchcraft, and that have prevail'd
Upon my body with their deadly charms?
Hast. The tender love I bear your grace, my lord,
Makes me most forward in this princely presence
To doom th' offenders: whosoe'er they be,
I say, my lord, they have deserved death.
Glo. Then, be your eyes the witness of their evil:
Look how I am bewitch'd; behold mine arm
Is like a blasted sapling wither'd up:
And this is Edward's wife, that monstrous witch,
Consorted with that vile mistress Shore,
That by their witchcraft thus have marked me.
Hast. If they have done this deed, my noble lord,—
Glo. If! thou protector of this vile wanton,
Talk'st thou to me of "ifs?"—Thou art a traitor:—
Off with his head!—now, by Saint Paul I swear,
I will not dine until I see the same.—
Lovel, and Ratcliff, look that it be done:—
The rest, that love me, rise, and follow me.
[*Exeunt Council, with* GLOSTER *and* BUCKINGHAM.
Hast. Woe, woe, for England! not a whit for me;
For I, too fond, might have prevented this.
O Margaret, Margaret, now thy heavy curse
Is lighted on poor Hastings' wretched head!
Rat. Come, come, despatch; the duke would be at dinner:
Make a short shrift; he longs to see your head.
Hast. O momentary grace of mortal men,
Which we more hunt for than the grace of God!
Who builds his hope in air of your good looks,
Lives like a drunken sailor on a mast;
Ready, with every nod, to tumble down
Into the fatal bowels of the deep.
Lov. Come, come, despatch; 'tis bootless to exclaim.
Hast. O bloody Richard!—miserable England!
I prophesy the fearfull'st time to thee,
That ever wretched age had look'd upon.
Come, lead me to the block; bear him my head:
They smile at me, who shortly shall be dead. [*Exeunt.*

Hastings is beheaded. Gloster, pursuing his designs to seize the crown, makes friends with the mayor and citizens of London. He sends Buckingham to Guildhall, there to meet the citizens in council, and urge the supposed illegitimacy of Edward

the Fourth's children, and the legal claims of Gloster to the crown. Buckingham is directed afterwards to meet Gloster at Baynard's Castle, with the mayor and citizens, where Richard will be found closeted "with reverend fathers of the church and well learned bishops."

SCENE VII.—London. *The Court of Baynard's Castle.*

Enter GLOSTER *and* BUCKINGHAM, *meeting.*

Glo. How now, how now! what say the citizens?
Buck. Now, by my faith, my lord,
The citizens are mum, say not a word.
Glo. Touch'd you the bastardy of Edward's children?
Buck. I did; with his contract with lady Lucy,
And his contract by deputy in France·
Withal I did infer your lineaments,—
Being the right idea of your father,
Both in your form and nobleness of mind;
Laid open all your victories in Scotland,
Your discipline in war, wisdom in peace,
Your bounty, virtue, fair humility;
Indeed, left nothing fitting for your purpose
Untouch'd, or slightly handled, in discourse:
And when my oratory drew toward end,
I bade them that did love their country's good,
Cry—"God save Richard, England's royal king!"
Glo. And did they so?
Buck. No, so heaven help me, they spake not a word;
But, like dumb statuas, or breathing stones,
Star'd each on other, and look'd deadly pale.
Which when I saw, I reprehended them;
And ask'd the mayor what meant this wilful silence:
His answer was,—the people were not us'd
To be spoke to, but by the recorder.
Then he was urg'd to tell my tale again,—
"Thus saith the duke, thus hath the duke inferr'd;"
But nothing spoke in warrant from himself.
When he had done, some followers of mine own,
At lower end of the hall, hurl'd up their caps,
And some ten voices cried, "God save king Richard!"
And thus I took the vantage of those few,—
"Thanks, gentle citizens and friends," quoth I;
"This general applause, and cheerful shout,
Argues your wisdom, and your love to Richard:"
And even here brake off, and came away.
Glo. What tongueless blocks were they! would they not speak?
Will not the mayor, then, and his brethren, come?

Buck. The mayor is here at hand. Intend some fear;
Be not you spoke with, but by mighty suit;
And look you get a prayer-book in your hand,
And stand between two churchmen, good my lord;
For on that ground I'll make a holy descant:
And be not easily won to our requests.
Glo. I go; and if you plead as well for them,
As I can say nay to thee for myself,
No doubt we bring it to a happy issue.
Buck. Go, go, up to the leads; the lord mayor knocks.—
[*Exit* GLOSTER.

Enter the Lord Mayor, Aldermen, *and* Citizens.

Welcome, my lord: I dance attendance here;
I think the duke will not be spoke withal.—

Enter, from the Castle, CATESBY.

Now, Catesby,—what says your lord to my request?
Cate. He doth entreat your grace, my noble lord,
To visit him to-morrow or next day:
He is within, with two right reverend fathers,
Divinely bent to meditation;
And in no worldly suit would he be mov'd,
To draw him from his holy exercise.
Buck. Return, good Catesby, to the gracious duke;
Tell him, myself, the mayor and aldermen,
In deep designs, in matter of great moment,
No less importing than our general good,
Are come to have some conference with his grace.
Cate. I'll signify so much unto him straight. [*Exit.*
Buck. Ah, ha, my lord, this prince is not an Edward!
Happy were England, would this virtuous prince
Take on his grace the sovereignty thereof:
But, sure, I fear, we shall not win him to it.
May. Marry, heaven defend his grace should say us nay!
Buck. I fear he will. Here Catesby comes again.—

Re-enter CATESBY.

Now, Catesby, what says his grace?
Cate. He wonders to what end you have assembled
Such troops of citizens to come to him:
His grace not being warn'd thereof before,
He fears, my lord, you mean no good to him.
Buck. Sorry I am my noble cousin should
Suspect me, that I mean no good to him:
By heaven, we come to him in perfect love;
And so once more return, and tell his grace. [*Exit* CATESBY.
When holy and devout religious men

Are at their beads, 'tis much to draw them thence,—
So sweet is zealous contemplation.

Enter GLOSTER, *in a gallery above, between two* Bishops. CATESBY *returns.*

May. See, where his grace stands 'tween two clergymen!
Buck. Two props of virtue for a Christian prince,
To stay him from the fall of vanity:
And, see, a book of prayer in his hand.
Famous Plantagenet, most gracious prince,
Lend favorable ear to our requests;
And pardon us the interruption
Of thy devotion, and right Christian zeal.
Glo. My lord, there needs no such apology:
I do beseech your grace to pardon me,
Who, earnest in the service of heaven,
Deferr'd the visitation of my friends.
But, leaving this, what is your grace's pleasure?
Buck. Even that, I hope, which pleaseth heaven,
And all good men of this ungovern'd isle.
Glo. I do suspect I have done some offence,
That seems disgracious in the city's eye;
And that you come to reprehend my ignorance.
Buck. You have, my lord: would it might please your grace,
On our entreaties to amend your fault.
Glo. Else wherefore breathe I in a Christian land?
Buck. Know, then, it is your fault that you resign
The supreme seat, the throne majestical,
The sceptred office of your ancestors,
Your state of fortune and your due of birth,
The lineal glory of your royal house,
To the corruption of a blemish'd stock:
Which to recover, we heartily solicit
Your gracious self to take on you the charge
And kingly government of this your land;—
Not as protector, steward, substitute,
Or lowly factor for another's gain;
But as successively, from blood to blood,
Your right of birth, your empery, your own.
For this, consorted with the citizens,
Your very worshipful and loving friends,
In this just suit come I to move your grace.
Glo. I cannot tell, if to depart in silence,
Or bitterly to speak in your reproof,
Best fitteth my degree, or your condition:
If, not to answer,—you might haply think
Tongue-tied ambition, not replying, yielded
To bear the golden yoke of sovereignty,

Which fondly you would here impose on me;
If to reprove you for this suit of yours,
So season'd with your faithful love to me,
Then, on the other side, I check'd my friends.
Your love deserves my thanks; but my desert,
Unmeritable, shuns your high request.
The royal tree hath left us royal fruit,
Which, mellow'd by the stealing hours of time,
Will well become the seat of majesty,
And make, no doubt, us happy by his reign.
On him I lay, that you would lay on me,—
The right and fortune of his happy stars;
Which heaven defend that I should wring from him!
Buck. My lord, this argues conscience in your grace;
But the respects thereof are nice and trivial,
All circumstances well considered.
Pray, my good lord, take to your royal self
This proffer'd benefit of dignity;
If not to bless us and the land withal,
Yet to draw forth your noble ancestry
From the corruption of abusing time,
Into a lineal true-derived course.
May. Do, good my lord; your citizens entreat you.
Buck. Refuse not, mighty lord, this proffer'd love.
Cate. O, make them joyful, grant their lawful suit!
Glo. Alas, why would you heap those cares on me?
I am unfit for state and majesty:—
I do beseech you, take it not amiss;
I cannot, nor I will not, yield to you.
Buck. If you refuse it,—as, in love and zeal,
Loath to depose the child, your brother's son;
As well we know your tenderness of heart,—
Yet know, whe'r you accept our suit or no,
Your brother's son shall never reign our king;
But we will plant some other in the throne,
To the disgrace and downfall of your house:
And, in this resolution, here we leave you.—
Come, citizens, we will entreat no more.
[*Exit* BUCKINGHAM; *the* Mayor, Aldermen, *and* Citizens, *retiring*.
Cate. Call them again, sweet prince, accept their suit:
If you deny them, all the land will rue it.
Glo. Will you enforce me to a world of cares?
Call them again. [CATESBY *goes to the* Mayor, *&c.*, *and then exit.*
I am not made of stone,
But penetrable to your kind entreaties,
Albeit against my conscience, and my soul.—

Re-enter Buckingham *and* Catesby; *the* Mayor, *&c., coming forward.*

Cousin of Buckingham,—and sage, grave men,—
Since you will buckle fortune on my back,—
To bear her burden, whether I will or no,
I must have patience to endure the load:
But if black scandal, or foul-fac'd reproach,
Attend the sequel of your imposition,
Your mere enforcement shall acquittance me
From all the impure blots and stains thereof;
For heaven knows, and you may partly see,
How far I am from the desire of this.
May. Heaven bless your grace! we see it, and will say it.
Glo. In saying so, you shall but say the truth.
Buck. Then I salute you with this royal title,—
Long live king Richard, England's worthy king.
All. Amen.
Buck. To-morrow may it please you to be crown'd?
Glo. Even when you please, for you will have it so.
Buck. To-morrow, then, we will attend your grace:
And so, most joyfully, we take our leave.
Glo. [*To the* Bishops.] Come, let us to our holy work again.—
Farewell, my cousin;—farewell, gentle friends. [*Exeunt.*

ACT IV.

Gloster is crowned king, under the title of Richard III. The young princes, Edward V. and his brother the Duke of York, are separated from their mother, and confined in the Tower. Richard having married the Lady Anne, she is crowned with him.

SCENE II.—*A Room of State in the Palace.*

Sennet. Richard, *as king upon his throne;* Buckingham, Catesby, *a* Page, *and others.*

K. Rich. Stand all apart.—Cousin of Buckingham,—
Buck. My gracious sovereign?
K. Rich. Give me thy hand. Thus high, by thy advice,
And thy assistance, is king Richard seated:—
But shall we wear these glories for a day?
Or shall they last, and we rejoice in them?
Buck. Still live they, and forever let them last!
K. Rich. Ah, Buckingham, now do I play the touch,
To try if thou be current gold indeed:—
Young Edward lives;—think now what I would speak.

Buck. Say on, my loving lord.
K. Rich. Why, Buckingham, I say, I would be king.
Buck. Why, so you are, my thrice-renowned liege.
K. Rich. Ha! am I king? 'Tis so:—but Edward lives.
Buck. True, noble prince.
K. Rich. O bitter consequence,
That Edward still should live,—"true, noble prince!"—
Cousin, thou wast not wont to be so dull:—
Shall I be plain?—I wish the youngsters dead;
And I would have it suddenly perform'd.
What say'st thou now? speak suddenly, be brief.
Buck. Your grace may do your pleasure.
K. Rich. Tut, tut! thou art all ice, thy kindness freezes:
Say, have I thy consent that they shall die?
Buck. Give me some little breath, some pause, dear lord,
Before I positively speak in this:
I will resolve you herein presently. [*Exit.*
Cate. [*Aside to another.*] The king is angry: see, he gnaws his lip.
K. Rich. [*Descends from his throne.*] I will converse with iron-witted fools,
And unrespective boys: none are for me,
That look into me with considerate eyes:—
High-reaching Buckingham grows circumspect.—
Boy!—
Page. My lord?
K. Rich. Know'st thou not any, whom corrupting gold
Will tempt into a close exploit of death?
Page. I know a discontented gentleman,
Whose humble means match not his haughty spirit:
Gold were as good as twenty orators,
And will, no doubt, tempt him to any thing.
K. Rich. What is his name?
Page. His name, my lord, is Tyrrel.
K. Rich. I partly know the man: go, call him hither, boy.— [*Exit* Page.
The deep-revolving witty Buckingham
No more shall be the neighbor to my counsels:
Hath he so long held out with me untir'd,
And stops he now for breath?—well, be it so.

Enter STANLEY.

How now, lord Stanley! what's the news?
Stan. Know, my loving lord,
The marquis Dorset, as I hear, is fled
To Richmond, in the parts where he abides.
K. Rich. Come hither, Catesby:—rumor it abroad,
That Anne, my wife, is very grievous sick;

I will take order for her keeping close:
Enquire me out some mean poor gentleman,
Whom I will marry straight to Clarence' daughter:—
The boy is foolish, and I fear not him.—
Look, how thou dream'st!—I say again, give out
That Anne my queen is sick, and like to die:
About it; for it stands me much upon,
To stop all hopes whose growth may damage me.—

[*Exit* CATESBY.

I must be married to my brother's daughter,
Or else my kingdom stands on brittle glass:—
Murder her brothers, and then marry her!
Uncertain way of gain! But I am in
So far in blood, that sin will pluck on sin:
Tear-falling pity dwells not in this eye.—

Re-enter Page, *with* TYRREL.

Is thy name Tyrrel?

Tyr. [*Kneeling.*] James Tyrrel, and your most obedient subject.

K. Rich. Art thou, indeed?

Tyr. Prove me, my gracious lord.

K. Rich. Dar'st thou resolve to kill a friend of mine?

Tyr. Please you; but I had rather kill two enemies.

K. Rich. Why, then thou hast it: two deep enemies,
Foes to my rest, and my sweet sleep's disturbers,
Are they that I would have thee deal upon:—
Tyrrel, I mean those princes in the Tower.

Tyr. Let me have open means to come to them,
And soon I'll rid you from the fear of them.

K. Rich. Thou sing'st sweet music. Hark, come hither, Tyrrel:
Go, by this token.—Rise, and lend thine ear: *Whispers.*
There is no more but so:—say it is done,
And I will love thee, and prefer thee for it.

Tyr. I will despatch it straight. [*Exit.*

Re-enter BUCKINGHAM.

Buck. My lord, I have consider'd in my mind
The late demand that you did sound me in.

K. Rich. Well, let that rest. Dorset is fled to Richmond.

Buck. I hear the news, my lord.

K. Rich. Stanley, he is your wife's son:—well, look to it.

Buck. My lord, I claim the gift, my due by promise,
For which your honor and your faith is pawn'd;
Th' earldom of Hereford, and the moveables,
Which you have promised I shall possess.

K. Rich. Stanley, look to your wife: if she convey
Letters to Richmond, you shall answer it.

Buck. What says your highness to my just request?
K. Rich. I do remember me,—Henry the sixth
Did prophesy that Richmond should be king,
When Richmond was a little peevish boy.
A king!—perhaps—
Buck. My lord,—
K. Rich. How chance, the prophet could not at that time
Have told me, I being by, that I should kill him?
Buck. My lord, your promise for the earldom,—
K. Rich. Richmond!—When last I was at Exeter,
The mayor in courtesy show'd me the castle,
And call'd it—Rouge-mont: at which name I started,
Because a bard of Ireland told me once,
I should not live long after I saw Richmond.
Buck. My lord,—
K. Rich. Ay, what's o'clock?
Buck. I am thus bold to put your grace in mind
Of what you promis'd me.
K. Rich. Well, but what's o'clock?
Buck. Upon the stroke of ten.
K. Rich. Well, let it strike.
Buck. Why let it strike?
K. Rich. Because that, like a Jack, thou keep'st the stroke
Betwixt thy begging and my meditation.
I am not in the giving vein to-day.
Buck. Why, then resolve me whether you will, or no.
K. Rich. Thou troublest me; I am not in the vein.
[*Exeunt* KING RICHARD *and train.*
Buck. And is it thus? repays he my deep service
With such contempt? made I him king for this?
O, let me think on Hastings, and be gone
To Brecknock, while my fearful head is on. [*Exit.*

Young Edward and his brother York are murdered in the Tower, by order of Gloster. Buckingham levies an army in Wales, to march against Richard. The Earl of Richmond receives aid from the discontented nobles, who desert Gloster.

SCENE IV.—*Before the Palace.*

Enter QUEEN MARGARET.

Q. Mar. [*Apart.*] Plantagenet doth quit Plantagenet,
Edward for Edward pays a dying debt.
Q. Eliz. Wilt thou, O heaven! fly from such gentle lambs,
And throw them in the entrails of the wolf?
When didst thou sleep, when such a deed was done?
Q. Mar. [*Apart.*] When holy Harry died, and my sweet son.
Duch. Dead life, blind sight, poor mortal living ghost,

Woe's scene, world's shame, grave's due by life usurp'd,
Brief abstract and record of tedious days,
Rest thy unrest on England's lawful earth, [*Sitting down.*
Unlawfully made drunk with innocent blood!
Q. Eliz. Ah, that thou would'st as soon afford a grave,
As thou canst yield a melancholy seat!
Then would I hide my bones, not rest them here.
Ah, who hath any cause to mourn but we? [*Sitting down by her.*
Q. Mar. [*Coming forward.*] If ancient sorrow be most reverent,
Give mine the benefit of seniory,
And let my griefs frown on the upper hand.
If sorrow can admit society, [*Sitting down with them.*
Tell o'er your woes again by viewing mine:—
I had an Edward, till a Richard kill'd him;
I had a husband, till a Richard kill'd him:
Thou hadst an Edward, till a Richard kill'd him;
Thou hadst a Richard, till a Richard kill'd him.
Duch. I had a Richard too, and thou didst kill him;
I had a Rutland too, thou holp'st to kill him.
Q. Mar. Thou hadst a Clarence too, and Richard kill'd him.
Duch. O Harry's wife, triumph not in my woes!
Heaven witness with me, I have wept for thine.
Q. Eliz. O, thou didst prophesy the time would come,
That I should wish for thee to help me curse
That bottled spider, that foul hunch-back'd toad!
Q. Mar. I call'd thee then, vain flourish of my fortune;
I call'd thee then, poor shadow, painted queen;
The presentation of but what I was.
Where is thy husband now? where be thy brothers?
Where be thy two sons? wherein dost thou joy?
Who sues, and kneels, and says—God save the queen?
Where be the bending peers that flatter'd thee?
Where be the thronging troops that follow'd thee?
Thou didst usurp my place, and dost thou not
Usurp the just proportion of my sorrow?
Now thy proud neck bears half my burden'd yoke;
From which, even here, I slip my wearied head,
And leave the burden of it all on thee.
Farewell, York's wife, and queen of sad mischance:—
These English woes shall make me smile in France.
Q. Eliz. O thou, well skill'd in curses, stay a while,
And teach me how to curse mine enemies!
My words are dull; O, quicken them with thine!
Q. Mar. Thy woes will make them sharp, and pierce like mine. [*Exit.*
Duch. Why should calamity be full of words?
Q. Eliz. Poor breathing orators of miseries!

Let them have scope: though what they do impart
Help nothing else, yet do they ease the heart.
Duch. If so, then be not tongue-tied: go with me,
And in the breath of bitter words let's smother
My guilty son, that thy two sweet sons smother'd. [*Drum heard.*
I hear his drum:—be copious in exclaims.

Enter KING RICHARD, *and his train, marching.*

K. Rich. Who intercepts me in my expedition?
Duch. O, she that might have intercepted thee,
By strangling thee when thou wast born,
From all the slaughters, wretch, that thou hast done!
Q. Eliz. Hid'st thou that forehead with a golden crown,
Where should be branded, if that right were right,
The slaughter of the prince that ow'd that crown,
And the dire death of my poor sons and brothers?
Tell me, thou villain-slave, where are my children?
Duch. Where is thy brother Clarence?
And little Ned Plantagenet, his son?
Q. Eliz. Where is the gentle Rivers, Vaughan, Grey?
Duch. Where is kind Hastings?
K. Rich. A flourish, trumpets! strike alarum, drums!
Let not the heavens hear these tell-tale women
Rail on the Lord's anointed: strike, I say!— [*Flourish. Alarums.*
Either be patient, and entreat me fair,
Or with the clamorous report of war
Thus will I drown your exclamations.
Duch. Art thou my son?
K. Rich. Madam, I have a touch of your condition,
That cannot brook the accent of reproof.
Duch. O, let me speak!
K. Rich. Do, then; but I'll not hear.
Duch. I will be mild and gentle in my words.
K. Rich. And brief, good mother; for I am in haste.
Duch. Art thou so hasty? I have stay'd for thee,
Heaven knows, in torment and in agony.
K. Rich. And came I not at last to comfort you?
Duch. No!
A grievous burden was thy birth to me;
Tetchy and wayward was thy infancy;
Thy school-days frightful, desperate, wild, and furious;
Thy prime of manhood daring, bold, and venturous:
Thy age confirm'd, proud, subtle, sly, and bloody,
More mild, but yet more harmful, kind in hatred:
No comfortable hour canst thou name,
That ever grac'd me in thy company.
K. Rich. If I be so disgracious in your eye,

Let me march on, and not offend you, madam.—
Strike up the drum!
Duch. I pr'ythee, hear me speak.
K. Rich. You speak too bitterly.
Duch. Hear me a word;
For I shall never speak to thee again.
K. Rich. So.
Duch. Either thou wilt die, by heaven's just ordinance,
Ere from this war thou turn a conqueror;
Or I with grief and extreme age shall perish,
And never look upon thy face again.
Therefore take with thee my most heavy curse;
Which, in the day of battle, tire thee more
Than all the complete armor that thou wear'st!
Bloody thou art, bloody will be thy end;
Shame serves thy life, and doth thy death attend. [*Exit.*
Q. Eliz. Though far more cause, yet much less spirit to curse
Abides in me; I say amen to her. [*Going.*
K. Rich. Stay, madam; I must talk a word with you.
Q. Eliz. I have no more sons of the royal blood,
For thee to slaughter: for my daughters, Richard,—
They shall be praying nuns, not weeping queens;
And therefore level not to hit their lives.
K. Rich. You have a daughter call'd Elizabeth,
Virtuous and fair, royal and gracious.
Q. Eliz. And must she die for this?
K. Rich. Madam, so thrive I in my enterprise,
And dangerous success of bloody wars,
As I intend more good to you and yours,
Than ever you or yours by me were harm'd!
Q. Eliz. What good is cover'd with the face of heaven,
To be discover'd, that can do me good?
K. Rich. Th' advancement of your children, gentle lady.
Q. Eliz. Up to some scaffold, there to lose their heads?
K. Rich. No, to the dignity and height of honor,
The high imperial type of this earth's glory.
Q. Eliz. Flatter my sorrow with report of it;
Tell me what state, what dignity, what honor,
Canst thou demise to any child of mine?
K. Rich. Even all I have; ay, and myself and all,
Will I withal endow a child of thine;
So in the Lethe of thy angry soul
Thou drown the sad remembrance of those wrongs,
Which thou supposest I have done to thee.
Q. Eliz. Be brief, lest that the process of thy kindness
Last longer telling than thy kindness' date.
K. Rich. Then know, that with my soul I love thy daughter,
And do intend to make her queen of England.

Q. Eliz. Well then, who dost thou mean shall be her king?
K. Rich. Even he that makes her queen: who else should be?
Q. Eliz. What, thou?
K. Rich. I, even I: what think you of it, madam?
Q. Eliz. How canst thou woo her?
K. Rich. That I would learn of you,
As one being best acquainted with her humor.
Q. Eliz. And wilt thou learn of me?
K. Rich. Madam, with all my heart.
Q. Eliz. Send to her, by the man that slew her brothers,
A pair of bleeding hearts; thereon engrave
Edward and York; then haply will she weep:
Therefore present to her,—as sometime Margaret
Did to thy father, steep'd in Rutland's blood,—
A handkerchief; which, say to her, did drain
The purple sap from her sweet brother's body,
And bid her wipe her weeping eyes withal.
If this inducement move her not to love,
Send her a letter of thy noble deeds;
Tell her thou mad'st away her uncle Clarence,
Her uncle Rivers; ay, and, for her sake,
Mad'st quick conveyance with her good aunt Anne.
K. Rich. You mock me, madam; this is not the way
To win your daughter.
Q. Eliz. There is no other way;
Unless thou couldst put on some other shape,
And not be Richard that hath done all this.
K. Rich. Say, that I did all this for love of her?
Q. Eliz. Nay, then indeed, she cannot choose but hate thee,
Having bought love with such a bloody spoil.
K. Rich. Look, what is done cannot be now amended:
Men shall deal unadvisedly sometimes,
Which after-hours give leisure to repent.
If I did take the kingdom from your sons,
To make amends I'll give it to your daughter.
I swear—
Q. Eliz. What canst thou swear by?
K. Rich. The time to come.
Q. Eliz. That thou hast wrongèd in the time o'erpast.
The children live, whose parents thou hast slaughter'd,
Ungovern'd youth, to wail it in their age;
The parents live, whose children thou hast butcher'd,
Old barren plants, to wail it with their age.
Swear not by time to come; for that thou hast
Misus'd ere us'd, by times ill-us'd o'er-past.
K. Rich. As I intend to prosper and repent,
So thrive I in my dangerous attempt
Of hostile arms! myself myself confound!

Heaven and fortune bar me happy hours!
Day, yield me not thy light, nor, night, thy rest!
Be opposite all planets of good luck
To my proceeding, if, with pure heart's love,
Immaculate devotion, holy thoughts,
I tender not thy beauteous princely daughter!
In her consists my happiness and thine;
Without her, follows to myself and thee,
Herself, the land, and many a Christian soul,
Death, desolation, ruin, and decay:
It cannot be avoided, but by this;
It will not be avoided, but by this.
Therefore, dear mother, (I must call you so)
Be the attorney of my love to her:
Plead what I will be, not what I have been;
Not my deserts, but what I will deserve:
Urge the necessity and state of times,
And be not peevish found in great designs.

Q. Eliz. Shall I be tempted thus?

K. Rich. Ay, if thou art tempted to do good.

Q. Eliz. Shall I forget myself, to be myself?

K. Rich. Ay, if your self's remembrance wrong yourself.

Q. Eliz. Shall I go win my daughter to thy will?

K. Rich. And be a happy mother by the deed.

Q. Eliz. I go.—Write to me very shortly,
And you shall understand from me her mind.

K. Rich. Bear her my true love's kiss; and so, farewell.
[*Kissing her.* *Exit* Q. ELIZABETH.
Relenting fool, and shallow, changing woman!

Enter RATCLIFF; CATESBY *following.*

How now! what news?

Rat. Most mighty sovereign, on the western coast
Rideth a puissant navy; to the shore
Throng many doubtful hollow-hearted friends,
Unarm'd, and unresolv'd to beat them back:
'Tis thought that Richmond is their admiral;
And there they hull, expecting but the aid
Of Buckingham to welcome them ashore.

K. Rich. Some light-foot friend post to the duke of Norfolk:—
Ratcliff, thyself,—or Catesby; where is he?

Cate. Here, my good lord.

K. Rich. Catesby, fly to the duke.

Cate. I will, my lord, with all convenient haste.

K. Rich. Ratcliff, come hither:—post to Salisbury:
When thou com'st thither,—Dull, unmindful villain,
[*To* CATESBY.
Why stay'st thou here, and go'st not to the duke?

Cate. First, mighty liege, tell me your highness' pleasure,
What from your grace I shall deliver to him.
K. Rich. O, true, good Catesby:—bid him levy straight
The greatest strength and power he can make,
And meet me suddenly at Salisbury.
Cate. I go. [*Exit.*
Rat. What, may it please you, shall I do at Salisbury?
K. Rich. Why, what wouldst thou do there, before I go?
Rat. Your highness told me I should post before.

Enter STANLEY.

K. Rich. My mind is chang'd.—Stanley, what news with you?
Stan. None good, my liege, to please you with the hearing;
Nor none so bad, but well may be reported.
K. Rich. Heyday, a riddle! neither good nor bad
What need'st thou run so many miles about,
When thou may'st tell thy tale the nearest way?
Once more, what news?
Stan. Richmond is on the seas.
K. Rich. There let him sink, and be the seas on him!
White-liver'd runagate, what doth he there?
Stan. I know not, mighty sovereign, but by guess.
K. Rich. Well, as you guess?
Stan. Stirr'd up by Dorset, Buckingham, and Morton,
He makes for England, here, to claim the crown.
K. Rich. Is the chair empty? is the sword unsway'd?
Is the king dead? the empire unpossess'd?
What heir of York is there alive, but we?
And who is England's king, but great York's heir?
Then, tell me, what makes he upon the seas?
Stan. Unless for that, my liege, I cannot guess.
K. Rich. Unless for that he comes to be your liege,
You cannot guess wherefore the Welshman comes.
Thou wilt revolt, and fly to him, I fear.
Stan. No, mighty liege; therefore, mistrust me not.
K. Rich. Where is thy power, then, to beat him back?
Where be thy tenants and thy followers?
Are they not now upon the western shore,
Safe-conducting the rebels from their ships?
Stan. No, my good lord, my friends are in the north.
K. Rich. Cold friends to me: What do they in the north,
When they should serve their sovereign in the west?
Stan. They have not been commanded, mighty king
Pleaseth your majesty to give me leave,
I'll muster up my friends, and meet your grace,
Where and what time your majesty shall please.
K. Rich. Ay, ay, thou wouldst be gone to join with Richmond:
But I'll not trust thee.

Stan. Most mighty sovereign,
You have no cause to hold my friendship doubtful:
I never was, nor never will be false.
K. Rich. Go, then, and muster men. But leave behind
Your son, George Stanley: look your heart be firm,
Or else his head's assurance is but frail.
Stan. So deal with him, as I prove true to you. [*Exit.*

Enter a Messenger.

Mess. My gracious sovereign, now in Devonshire,
As I by friends am well advertised,
Sir Edward Courtney, and the haughty prelate,
Bishop of Exeter, his elder brother,
With many more confederates, are in arms.

Enter a second Messenger.

2 *Mess.* In Kent, my liege, the Guildfords are in arms:
And every hour more competitors
Flock to the rebels, and their power grows strong.

Enter a third Messenger.

3 *Mess.* My lord, the army of great Buckingham—
K. Rich. Out on ye, owls! nothing but songs of death?
[*He strikes him.*
There, take thou that, till thou bring better news.
3 *Mess.* The news I have to tell your majesty
Is, that by sudden floods and fall of waters,
Buckingham's army is dispers'd and scatter'd;
And he himself wander'd away alone,
No man knows whither.
K. Rich. I cry thee mercy:
There is my purse, to cure that blow of thine.
Hath any well-advised friend proclaim'd
Reward to him that brings the traitor in?
3 *Mess.* Such proclamation hath been made, my lord.

Enter a fourth Messenger.

4 *Mess.* Sir Thomas Lovel, and lord marquess Dorset,
'Tis said, my liege, in Yorkshire are in arms:
But this good comfort bring I to your highness,—
The Bretagne navy is dispers'd by tempest:
Richmond, in Dorsetshire, sent out a boat
Unto the shore, to ask those on the banks,
If they were his assistants, yea, or no;
Who answer'd him, they came from Buckingham
Upon his party: he, mistrusting them,
Hois'd sail, and made his course again for Bretagne.
K. Rich. March on, march on, since we are up in arms;

If not to fight with foreign enemies,
Yet to beat down these rebels here at home.

Enter CATESBY.

Cate. My liege, the duke of Buckingham is taken,—
That is the best news: that the earl of Richmond
Is with a mighty power landed at Milford,
Is colder news, but yet they must be told.
K. Rich. Away towards Salisbury! while we reason here,
A royal battle might be won and lost:—
Some one take order, Buckingham be brought
To Salisbury; the rest march on with me. [*Exeunt.*

ACT V.

SCENE I.—Salisbury. *An open Place.*

The Duke of Buckingham is executed by order of Richard.

SCENE II.—*A Plain near* Tamworth.

Enter, with drum and colors, RICHMOND, OXFORD, *Sir* JAMES BLUNT, *Sir* WALTER HERBERT, *and others, with forces, marching.*

Richm. Fellows in arms, and my most loving friends,
Bruis'd underneath the yoke of tyranny,
Thus far into the bowels of the land
Have we march'd on without impediment;
And here receive we from our father Stanley
Lines of fair comfort and encouragement.
The wretched, bloody, and usurping boar,
That spoil'd your summer fields, and fruitful vines,
Is now even in the centre of this isle,
Near to the town of Leicester, as we learn:
From Tamworth thither is but one day's march.
In heaven's name, cheerly on, courageous friends,
To reap the harvest of perpetual peace
By this one bloody trial of sharp war.
Oxf. Every man's conscience is a thousand swords,
To fight against that bloody homicide.
Herb. I doubt not but his friends will turn to us.
Blunt. He hath no friends but what are friends for fear,
Which in his dearest need will fly from him.
Richm. All for our vantage. Then, in heaven's name, march:
True hope is wift, and flies with swallow's wings;
Kings it makes gods, and meaner creatures kings. [*Exeunt.*

SCENE III.—Bosworth Field.

Enter KING RICHARD *and forces; the* DUKE OF NORFOLK, EARL OF SURREY, *and others.*

K. Rich. Here pitch our tent, even here in Bosworth field.—
My lord of Surrey, why look you so sad?
Sur. My heart is ten times lighter than my looks.
K. Rich. My lord of Norfolk,—
Nor. Here, most gracious liege.
K. Rich. Norfolk, we must have knocks; ha! must we not?
Nor. We must both give and take, my loving lord.
K. Rich. Up with my tent! here will I lie to-night;
[Soldiers *begin to set up the* KING'S *tent.*
But where to-morrow?—Well, all's one for that.—
Who hath descried the number of the traitors?
Nor. Six or seven thousand is their utmost power.
K. Rich. Why, our battalia trebles that account:
Besides, the king's name is a tower of strength,
Which they upon the adverse faction want.—
Up with the tent!—Come, noble gentlemen,
Let us survey the vantage of the ground;—
Call for some men of sound direction:—
Let's lack no discipline, make no delay;
For, lords, to-morrow is a busy day. [*Exeunt.*

Enter, on the other side of the field, RICHMOND, *Sir* WILLIAM BRANDON, OXFORD, *and other* Lords. *Some of the* Soldiers *pitch* RICHMOND'S *tent.*

Richm. The weary sun hath made a golden set,
And, by the bright track of his fiery car,
Gives token of a goodly day to-morrow.—
Sir William Brandon, you shall bear my standard.—
Give me some ink and paper in my tent:
I'll draw the form and model of our battle,
Limit each leader to his several charge,
And part in just proportion our small power.—
My lord of Oxford,—you, Sir William Brandon,—
And you, Sir Walter Herbert,—stay with me.—
The earl of Pembroke keeps his regiment:—
Good captain Blunt, bear my good night to him,
And by the second hour in the morning
Desire the earl to see me in my tent:
Yet one thing more, good captain, do for me,—
Where is lord Stanley quarter'd, do you know?
Blunt. Unless I have mista'en his colors much,
(Which, well I am assur'd, I have not done)

His regiment lies half a mile at least
South from the mighty power of the king.
Richm. If without peril it be possible,
Sweet Blunt, make some good means to speak with him,
And give him from me this most needful note.
Blunt. Upon my life, my lord, I'll undertake it;
And so, God give you quiet rest to-night!
Richm. Good night, good captain Blunt. — Come, gentlemen,
Let us consult upon to-morrow's business:
In to my tent, the air is raw and cold.
[*They withdraw into the tent.*

Enter, to his tent, KING RICHARD, NORFOLK, RATCLIFF, *and* CATESBY.

K. Rich. What is't o'clock?
Cate. It's supper-time, my lord; it's nine o'clock.
K. Rich. I will not sup to-night.—
Give me some ink and paper.—
What, is my beaver easier than it was?
And all my armor laid into my tent?
Cate. It is, my liege; and all things are in readiness.
K. Rich. Good Norfolk, hie thee to thy charge;
Use careful watch, choose trusty sentinels.
Nor. I go, my lord.
K. Rich. Stir with the lark to-morrow, gentle Norfolk.
Nor. I warrant you, my lord. [*Exit.*
K. Rich. Ratcliff,—
Rat. My lord?
K. Rich. Send out a pursuivant at arms
To Stanley's regiment; bid him bring his power
Before sun-rising, lest his son George fall
Into the blind cave of eternal night.—
Fill me a bowl of wine.—Give me a watch.—
Saddle white Surrey for the field to-morrow.—
Look that my staves be sound, and not too heavy.—
Ratcliff,—
Rat. My lord?
K. Rich. Saw'st thou the melancholy lord Northumberland?
Rat. Thomas the earl of Surrey, and himself,
Went through the army, cheering up the soldiers.
K. Rich. So, I am satisfied.—Give me a bowl of wine:
I have not that alacrity of spirit,
Nor cheer of mind, that I was wont to have.—
Set it down.—Is ink and paper ready?
Rat. It is, my lord.
K. Rich. Bid my guard watch; leave me.

Ratcliff, about the mid of night, come to my tent
And help to arm me.—Leave me, I say.
[KING RICHARD *retires into his tent. Exeunt* RATCLIFF *and* CATESBY.

RICHMOND'S *tent opens, and discovers him and his officers, &c.*

Enter STANLEY.

Stan. Fortune and victory sit on thy helm!
Richm. All comfort that the dark night can afford,
Be to thy person, noble father-in-law!
Tell me, how fares our loving mother?
Stan. I, by attorney, bless thee from thy mother,
Who prays continually for Richmond's good.
Prepare thy battle early in the morning,
And put thy fortune to the arbitrement
Of bloody strokes, and mortal-staring war.
I, as I may, (that which I would I cannot)
With best advantage will deceive the time,
And aid thee in this doubtful shock of arms:
But on thy side I may not be too forward,
Lest, being seen, thy brother, tender George,
Be executed in his father's sight.
Farewell: the leisure and the fearful time
Cuts off the ceremonious vows of love,
And ample interchange of sweet discourse,
Which so long sunder'd friends should dwell upon:
Heaven give us leisure for these rites of love!
Once more, adieu: be valiant, and speed well!
Richm. Good lords, conduct him to his regiment:
I'll strive, with troubled thoughts, to take a nap,
Lest leaden slumber bear me down to-morrow,
When I should mount with wings of victory:
Once more, good night, kind lords and gentlemen.
[*Exeunt* Officers, *&c., with* STANLEY.
O Thou, whose captain I account myself,
Look on my forces with a gracious eye;
Put in their hands thy bruising irons of wrath,
That they may crush down with a heavy fall
Th' usurping helmets of our adversaries!
Make us thy ministers of chastisement,
That we may praise thee in thy victory!
To thee I do commend my watchful soul,
Ere I let fall the windows of mine eyes:
Sleeping and waking, O, defend me still! [*Sleeps.*

The Ghost of PRINCE EDWARD, *son to Henry the Sixth, rises between the two tents.*

Ghost. [*To* KING R.] Let me sit heavy on thy soul to-morrow!

Think, how thou stabb'dst me in my prime of youth
At Tewksbury: despair, therefore, and die!—
Be cheerful, Richmond; for the wrongèd souls
Of butcher'd princes fight in thy behalf:
King Henry's issue, Richmond, comforts thee.

The Ghost of KING HENRY THE SIXTH *rises.*

Ghost. [*To* KING R.] When I was mortal, my anointed body
By thee was punchèd full of deadly holes:
Think on the Tower, and me: despair and die,—
Harry the sixth bids thee despair and die!—
[*To* RICHMOND.] Virtuous and holy, be thou conqueror!
Harry, that prophesied thou should'st be king,
Doth comfort thee in sleep: live, and flourish!

The Ghost of CLARENCE *rises.*

Ghost. [*To* KING R.] Let me sit heavy on thy soul to-morrow!
I, that was wash'd to death with fulsome wine,
Poor Clarence, by thy guile betray'd to death!
To-morrow in the battle think on me,
And fall thy edgeless sword: despair, and die!
[*To* RICHMOND.] Thou offspring of the house of Lancaster,
The wrongèd heirs of York do pray for thee:
Good angels guard thy battle! Live, and flourish!

The Ghosts of RIVERS, GREY, *and* VAUGHAN *rise.*

Gh. of Riv. [*To* KING R.] Let me sit heavy on thy soul to-morrow!
Rivers, that died at Pomfret! Despair, and die!
Gh. of Grey. [*To* KING R.] Think upon Grey, and let thy soul despair,
Gh. of Vaugh. [*To* KING R.] Think upon Vaughan, and with guilty fear
Let fall thy lance: despair, and die!
All Three. [*To* RICHMOND.] Awake! and think our wrongs in Richard's bosom
Will conquer him!—Awake, and win the day!

The Ghost of HASTINGS *rises.*

Ghost. [*To* KING R.] Bloody and guilty, guiltily awake,
And in a bloody battle end thy days!
Think on lord Hastings: despair, and die!—
[*To* RICHMOND.] Quiet untroubled soul, awake, awake!
Arm, fight, and conquer, for fair England's sake.

The Ghosts of the two young PRINCES *rise.*

Ghosts. Dream on thy cousins smother'd in the Tower:
Let us be lead within thy bosom, Richard,

And weigh thee down to ruin, shame, and death!
Thy nephews' souls bid thee despair, and die!—
Sleep, Richmond, sleep in peace, and wake in joy;
Good angels guard thee from the boar's annoy!
Edward's unhappy sons do bid thee flourish.

The Ghost of QUEEN ANNE *rises.*

Ghost. Richard, thy wife, that wretched Anne thy wife,
Now fills thy sleep with perturbations:
To-morrow in the battle think on me,
And fall thy edgeless sword: despair, and die!—
[*To* RICHMOND.] Thou quiet soul, sleep thou a quiet sleep;
Dream of success and happy victory:
Thy adversary's wife doth pray for thee.

The Ghost of BUCKINGHAM *rises.*

Ghost. [*To* KING R.] The first was I that help'd thee to the crown;
The last was I that felt thy tyranny:
O, in the battle think on Buckingham,
And die in terror of thy guiltiness!
Dream on, dream on, of bloody deeds and death:
Fainting, despair; despairing, yield thy breath!—
[*To* RICHMOND.] I died for hope ere I could lend thee aid:
But cheer thy heart, and be thou not dismay'd:
God and good angels fight on Richmond's side;
And Richard falls in height of all his pride.
[*The Ghosts vanish.* KING RICHARD *starts out of his dream.*

K. Rich. Give me another horse!—bind up my wounds!—
Have mercy, heaven!—Soft! I did but dream.—
O coward conscience, how dost thou afflict me!—
The lights burn blue.—It is now dead midnight.
Cold fearful drops stand on my trembling flesh.
What, do I fear myself? there's none else by:
Richard loves Richard; that, is, I am I.
Is there a murderer here? No;—yes, I am:
Then fly. What, from myself? Great reason why,
Lest I revenge. What, myself upon myself?
Alack, I love myself. Wherefore? for any good
That I myself have done unto myself?
O, no! alas, I rather hate myself
For hateful deeds committed by myself!
I am a villain: yet I lie, I am not.
Fool, of thyself speak well:—fool, do not flatter.
My conscience hath a thousand several tongues,
And every tongue brings in a several tale,
And every tale condemns me for a villain.

Perjury, perjury, in the high'st degree;
Murder, stern murder, in the dir'st degree;
All several sins, all us'd in each degree,
Throng to the bar, crying all,—Guilty! guilty!
I shall despair.—There is no creature loves me;
And if I die, no soul shall pity me:—
Nay, wherefore should they,—since that I myself
Find in myself no pity to myself?
Methought the souls of all that I had murder'd
Came to my tent; and every one did threat
To-morrow's vengeance on the head of Richard.

Enter RATCLIFF.

Rat. My lord,—
K. Rich. Who's there?
Rat. Ratcliff, my lord; 'tis I. The early village cock
Hath twice done salutation to the morn;
Your friends are up, and buckle on their armor.
K. Rich. O Ratcliff, I have dream'd a fearful dream!—
What think'st thou?—will our friends prove all true?
Rat. No doubt, my lord.
K. Rich. O Ratcliff, I fear, I fear,
Rat. Nay, good my lord, be not afraid of shadows.
K. Rich. By Saint Paul, shadows to-night
Have struck more terror to the soul of Richard,
Than can the substance of ten thousand soldiers,
Armed in proof, and led by shallow Richmond.
It is not yet near day. Come, go with me;
Under our tents I'll play the eaves-dropper,
To hear if any mean to shrink from me.
[*Exeunt* KING RICHARD *and* RATCLIFF.

Enter OXFORD, *and others.*

Lords. Good morrow, Richmond!
Richm. [*Waking.*] Cry mercy, lords, and watchful gentlemen,
That you have ta'en a tardy sluggard here.
Lords. How have you slept, my lord?
Richm. The sweetest sleep, and fairest-boding dreams
That ever enter'd in a drowsy head,
Have I since your departure had, my lords.
Methought their souls, whose bodies Richard murder'd,
Came to my tent, and cried on victory:
I promise you, my heart is very jocund
In the remembrance of so fair a dream.
How far into the morning is it, lords?
Lords. Upon the stroke of four.
Richm. Why, then 'tis time to arm, and give direction.—
[*He advances to the troops.*

More than I have said, loving countrymen,
The leisure and enforcement of the time
Forbids to dwell on: yet remember this,—
Heaven and our good cause fight upon our side;
The prayers of holy saints and wrongèd souls,
Like high-rear'd bulwarks, stand before our faces;
Richard except, those whom we fight against
Had rather have us win, than him they follow:
For what is he they follow? truly, gentlemen,
A bloody tyrant and a homicide;
One rais'd in blood, and one in blood establish'd;
One that made means to come by what he hath,
And slaughter'd those that were the means to help him;
A base foul stone, made precious by the foil
Of England's chair, where he is falsely set;
One that is an enemy to heaven.
Then, if you fight against such enemy,
Heaven will, in justice, ward you as his soldiers;
If you do fight to put a tyrant down,
You sleep in peace, the tyrant being slain;
Then, in the name of heaven and all your rights,
Advance your standards, draw your willing swords.
For me, the ransom of my bold attempt
Shall be this cold corse on the earth's cold face;
But if I thrive, the gain of my attempt
The least of you shall share his part thereof.
Sound drums and trumpets boldly and cheerfully;
God and Saint George! Richmond and victory! [*Exeunt.*

Re-enter KING RICHARD, RATCLIFF, Attendants, *and forces.*

K. Rich. What said Northumberland, as touching Richmond?
Rat. That he was never trained up in arms.
K. Rich. He said the truth: and what said Surrey then?
Rat. He smil'd, and said, the better for our purpose.
K. Rich. He was i' the right; and so, indeed, it is.
[*Clock strikes.*
Tell the clock there.—Give me a calendar.—
Who saw the sun to-day?
Rat. Not I, my lord.
K. Rich. Then he disdains to shine; for by the book,
He should have brav'd the east an hour ago:
A black day will it be to somebody.—
Ratcliff,—
Rat. My lord?
K. Rich. The sun will not be seen to-day;
The sky doth frown and lower upon our army.
I would these dewy tears were from the ground.
Not shine to-day! Why, what is that to me,

More than to Richmond? for the self-same heaven
That frowns on me, looks sadly upon him.

Enter NORFOLK.

Nor. Arm, arm, my lord, the foe vaunts in the field.
K. Rich. Come, bustle, bustle;—caparison my horse;—
Call up lord Stanley, bid him bring his power:
I will lead forth my soldiers to the plain,
And thus my battle shall be ordered:—
My forward shall be drawn out all in length,
Consisting equally of horse and foot;
Our archers shall be placèd in the midst:
John duke of Norfolk, Thomas earl of Surrey,
Shall have the leading of this foot and horse.
They thus directed, we will follow
In the main battle; whose puissance on either side
Shall be well winged with our chiefest horse.
This, and Saint George to boot!—What think'st thou, Norfolk?
Nor. A good direction, warlike sovereign.—
This found I on my tent this morning. [*Giving a scroll.*
K. Rich. [*Reads.*] "Jocky of Norfolk, be not too bold,
For Dickon thy master is bought and sold."
A thing devisèd by the enemy.—
Go, gentlemen, every man to his charge:
Let not our babbling dreams affright our souls;
Conscience is but a word that cowards use,
Devis'd at first to keep the strong in awe:
Our strong arms be our conscience, swords our law.
March on, join bravely, let us to't pell-mell;—
Remember whom you are to cope withal;—
A sort of vagabonds, rascals, and run-aways,
A scum of Bretagnes, and base lackey peasants,
Whom their o'er-cloyed country vomits forth
To desperate ventures and assur'd destruction.
And who doth lead them, but a paltry fellow,
Long kept in Bretagne at our mother's cost?
A milk-sop, one that never in his life
Felt so much cold as over shoes in snow?
Let's whip these stragglers o'er the seas again;
Lash hence these over-weening rags of France,
These famish'd beggars, weary of their lives;
Who, but for dreaming on this fond exploit,
For want of means, poor rats, had hang'd themselves:
If we be conquer'd, let men conquer us,
And not these dastard Bretagnes; whom our fathers
Have in their own land beaten, bobb'd, and thump'd,
And, on record, left them the heirs of shame. [*Drum afar off.*
Hark! I hear their drum.

Fight, gentlemen of England! fight, bold yeomen!
Draw, archers, draw your arrows to the head!
Spur your proud horses hard, and ride in blood!

Enter a Messenger.

What says lord Stanley? will he bring his power?
Mess. My lord, he doth deny to come.
K. Rich. Off with his son George's head!
Nor. My lord, the enemy is pass'd the marsh:
After the battle let George Stanley die.
K. Rich. A thousand hearts are great within my bosom:
Advance our standards, set upon our foes;
Our ancient word of courage, fair Saint George,
Inspire us with the spleen of fiery dragons!
Upon them! Victory sits on our helms. [*Exeunt.*

SCENE IV.—*Another Part of the Field.*

Alarum: Excursions. Enter NORFOLK *and forces; to him* CATESBY.

Cate. Rescue, my lord of Norfolk, rescue, rescue!
The king enacts more wonders than a man,
Daring an opposite to every danger:
His horse is slain, and all on foot he fights,
Seeking for Richmond in the throat of death.
Rescue, fair lord, or else the day is lost!

Alarum. Enter KING RICHARD.

K. Rich. A horse! a horse! my kingdom for a horse!
Cate. Withdraw, my lord; I'll help you to a horse.
K. Rich. Slave, I have set my life upon a cast,
And I will stand the hazard of the die.
I think there be six Richmonds in the field;
Five have I slain to-day, instead of him.—
A horse! a horse! my kingdom for a horse!

Alarums. Enter from opposite sides KING RICHARD *and* RICHMOND; *they fight, and exeunt fighting. Retreat and flourish. Then re-enter* RICHMOND, *with* STANLEY *bearing the crown, and divers other* Lords, *and forces.*

Richm. Heaven and your arms be prais'd, victorious friends;
The day is ours, the bloody Richard's dead.
Stan. Courageous Richmond, well hast thou acquit thee.
Lo, here, this long-usurped royalty,
From the dead temples of this bloody wretch
Have I pluck'd off, to grace thy brows withal:
Wear it, enjoy it, and make much of it.

Richm. But, tell me, is young George Stanley living?
Stan. He is, my lord, and safe in Leicester town;
Whither, if you please, we may withdraw us.
Richm. What men of name are slain on either side?
Stan. John duke of Norfolk, Walter lord Ferrers,
Sir Robert Brakenbury, and Sir William Brandon.
Richm. Inter their bodies as becomes their births:
Proclaim a pardon to the soldiers fled,
That in submission will return to us:
Now we'll unite the white rose and the red:—
Smile heaven upon this fair conjunction,
That long hath frown'd upon their enmity!—
What traitor hears me, and says not amen?
England hath long been mad, and scarr'd herself;
The brother blindly shed the brother's blood,
The father rashly slaughter'd his own son,
The son, compell'd, been butcher to the sire:
All this divided York and Lancaster,
Divided in their dire division,
O, now, let Richmond and Elizabeth,
The true succeeders of each royal house,
By heaven's fair ordinance conjoin together!
And let their heirs (heaven, if thy will be so)
Enrich the time to come with smooth-fac'd peace,
With smiling plenty, and fair prosperous days
Abate the edge of traitors, gracious Lord,
That would reduce these bloody days again,
And make poor England weep in streams of blood!
Let them not live to taste this land's increase,
That would with treason wound this fair land's peace
Now civil wounds are stopp'd, peace lives again:
That she may long live here, heaven say amen! [*Exeunt.*

THE HISTORY OF

KING HENRY VIII.

The History of King Henry VIII. closes the series of Shakspeare's "Chronicle Plays." It comprises a period of twelve years, commencing in 1521, and ending with the christening of Elizabeth, in 1533. Shakspeare has deviated from the truth of history by placing the birth of Queen Elizabeth after Queen Katharine's death, which latter event did not take place until 1536. One great merit of this History, however, is its faithful and powerful delineation of the characters of Queen Katharine and Cardinal Wolsey. The poet has drawn his materials in these portraitures from the most authentic sources. The very language, at times, of these personages is literally rendered in the dialogue, as found in the Life of Wolsey by his secretary, Cavendish—and in the chronicles of Holinshed, Stowe, and Hall. Henry VIII., however, is not given with the same historic fidelity. The more repulsive features of his character are softened, in compliment perhaps, to Queen Elizabeth, or rather to her memory; we yet have a very graphic picture of "bluff King Hal." He stands boldly out in the group of leading characters—and contrasts admirably with the noble-minded Katharine, and the ambitious Wolsey. The play is deeply interesting in a historical point of view, forming, as it does, a picture of the immediate causes which led to the establishment of Protestantism in the British dominions, as the religion of the State.

PERSONS REPRESENTED.

King Henry the Eighth.
Cardinal Wolsey.
Cardinal Campeius.
Capucius, *Embassador from the Emperor*, Charles V.
Cranmer, *Archbishop of Canterbury*.
Duke of Norfolk.
Earl of Surrey.
Duke of Suffolk.
Duke of Buckingham.
Lord Chamberlain.
Lord Chancellor.

GARDINER, *Bishop of Winchester.*
BISHOP OF LINCOLN. LORD ABERGAVENNY. LORD SANDS.
Sir HENRY GUILFORD.
Sir THOMAS LOVELL.
Sir ANTHONY DENNY.
Sir NICHOLAS VAUX.
Secretaries *to* WOLSEY.
CROMWELL, *Servant to* WOLSEY.
GRIFFITH, *Gentleman-Usher to* QUEEN KATHARINE.
Three other Gentlemen. Garter, *King at Arms.*
DOCTOR BUTTS, *Physician to the* KING.
Surveyor *to the* DUKE OF BUCKINGHAM.
BRANDON, *and a* Sergeant at Arms.
Door-keeper *of the Council-Chamber.* Porter, *and his* Man.
Page *to* GARDINER. *A* Crier.

QUEEN KATHARINE, *Wife to* KING HENRY; *afterwards divorced.*
ANNE BULLEN, *her Maid of Honor; afterwards* QUEEN.
An Old Lady, *Friend to* ANNE BULLEN.
PATIENCE, *Woman to* QUEEN KATHARINE.

Several Lords *and* Ladies *in the Dumb Shows;* Women *attending upon the* QUEEN; Spirits, *which appear to her;* Scribes, Officers, Guards, *and other* Attendants.

SCENE,—*Chiefly in* LONDON *and* WESTMINSTER; *once, at* KIMBOLTON.

ACT I.

SCENE I.—London. *An Ante-chamber in the Palace.*

Enter, on one side, the DUKE OF NORFOLK; *on the other, the* DUKE OF BUCKINGHAM *and* LORD ABERGAVENNY.

Buck. Good morrow, and well met. How have you done,
Since last we saw in France?
Nor. I thank your grace,
Healthful; and ever since a fresh admirer
Of what I saw there.
Buck. An untimely ague
Stay'd me a prisoner in my chamber, when
Those suns of glory, those two lights of men,
Met in the vale of Andren.
Nor. 'Twixt Guynes and Arde: *
I was then present, saw them salute on horseback;
Beheld them, when they lighted, how they clung
In their embracement, as they grew together;
Which had they, what four thron'd ones could have weigh'd
Such a compounded one?

*The meeting between Henry VIII. and Francis I.—celebrated in history as the "*Field of the Cloth of Gold*,"—is vividly described by Norfolk.

Buck. All the whole time
I was my chamber's prisoner.
Nor. Then you lost
The view of earthly glory: men might say,
Till this time, pomp was single; but now married
To one above itself. Each following day
Became the next day's master, till the last
Made former wonders it's: to-day the French
All clinquant, all in gold, like heathen gods,
Shone down the English; and to-morrow they
Made Britain, India: every man that stood
Show'd like a mine. Their dwarfish pages were
As cherubins, all gilt: the madams too,
Not us'd to toil, did almost sweat to bear
The pride upon them, that their very labor
Was to them as a painting: now this mask
Was cried incomparable; and the ensuing night
Made it a fool, and beggar. The two kings,
Equal in lustre, were now best, now worst,
As presence did present them; him in eye,
Still him in praise: and, being present both,
'Twas said they saw but one; and no discerner
Durst wag his tongue in censure. When these suns
(For so they phrase them) by their heralds challeng'd
The noble spirits to arms, they did perform
Beyond thought's compass; that former fabulous story,
Being now seen possible enough, got credit,
That Bevis was believ'd.
Buck. O, you go far.
Nor. As I belong to worship, all was royal;
To the disposing of it naught rebell'd;
Order gave each thing view; the office did
Distinctly his full function.
Buck. Who did guide,
I mean, who set the body and the limbs
Of this great sport together, as you guess?
Nor. One, certes, that promises no element
In such a business.
Buck. I pray you, who, my lord?
Nor. All this was order'd by the good discretion
Of the right reverend cardinal of York.
Buck. The foul fiend speed him! no man's pie is freed
From his ambitious finger. What had he
To do in these fierce vanities?
Nor. Surely, sir,
There's in him stuff that puts him to these ends;
For, being not propp'd by ancestry, whose grace
Chalks successors their way; nor call'd upon

For high feats done to the crown; neither allied
To eminent assistants; but, spider-like,
Out of his self-drawing web, he gives us note,
The force of his own merit makes his way;
A gift that heaven gives for him, which buys
A place next to the king.
Aber. I cannot tell
What heaven hath given him,—let some graver eye
Pierce into that; but I can see his pride
Peep through each part of him.
Buck. Upon this French going-out, why took he upon him,
Without the privity o' the king, to appoint
Who should attend on him? He makes up the file
Of all the gentry; for the most part such
To whom as great a charge as little honor
He meant to lay upon.
Aber. I do know
Kinsmen of mine, three at the least, that have
By this so sicken'd their estates, that never
They shall abound as formerly.
Buck. O, many
Have broke their backs with laying manors on them
For this great journey. What did this vanity,
But minister communication of
A most poor issue?
Nor. Grievingly I think,
The peace between the French and us not values
The cost that did conclude it.
Buck. Every man,
After the hideous storm that follow'd, was
A thing inspir'd; and, not consulting, broke
Into a general prophecy,—that this tempest,
Dashing the garment of this peace, aboded
The sudden breach on't.
Nor. Which is budded out;
For France hath flaw'd the league, and hath attach'd
Our merchants' goods at Bourdeaux.
Aber. A proper title of a peace; and purchas'd
At a superfluous rate!
Buck. Why, all this business
Our reverend cardinal carried.
Nor. 'Like it your grace,
The state takes notice of the private difference
Betwixt you and the cardinal. I advise you,
(And take it from a heart that wishes towards you
Honor and plenteous safety) that you read
The cardinal's malice and his potency
Together; to consider farther, that

What his high hatred would effect, wants not
A minister in his power. You know his nature,
That he's revengeful; and I know his sword
Hath a sharp edge: it's long, and, 't may be said,
It reaches far; and where 'twill not extend,
Thither he darts it.—Bosom up my counsel,
You'll find it wholesome.—Lo, where comes that rock
That I advise your shunning.

Enter CARDINAL WOLSEY, (*the Purse borne before him,*) *certain of the* Guard, *and two* Secretaries, *with papers. The* CARDINAL *in his passage fixeth his eye on* BUCKINGHAM, *and* BUCKINGHAM *on him, both full of disdain.*

Wol. The duke of Buckingham's surveyor, ha?
Where's his examination?
1 *Secr.* Here, so please you.
Wol. Is he in person ready?
1 *Secr.* Ay, please your grace.
Wol. Well, we shall then know more; and Buckingham
Shall lessen this big look. [*Exeunt* WOLSEY *and train.*
Buck. This butcher's cur is venom-mouth'd, and I
Have not the power to muzzle him; therefore best
Not wake him in his slumber. A beggar's book
Ou -worths a noble's blood.
Nor. What, are you chaf'd?
Ask heaven for temperance; that's th' appliance only,
Which your disease requires.
Buck. I read in's looks
Matter against me; and his eye revil'd
Me, as his abject object: at this instant
He bores me with some trick: he's gone t' the king;
I'll follow, and out-stare him.
Nor. Stay, my lord,
And let your reason with your choler question
What 'tis you go about: to climb steep hills,
Requires slow pace at first: anger is like
A full-hot horse, who being allow'd his way,
Self-mettle tires him. Not a man in England
Can advise me like you: be to yourself,
As you would to your friend.
Buck. I'll to the king;
And from a mouth of honor quite cry down
This Ipswich fellow's insolence; or proclaim
There's difference in no persons.
Nor. Be advis'd;
Heat not a furnace for your foe so hot
That it do singe yourself: be advis'd:
I say again, there is no English soul

More stronger to direct you than yourself,
If with the sap of reason you would quench,
Or but allay, the fire of passion.
Buck. Sir,
I am thankful to you; and I'll go along
By your prescription: but this top-proud fellow,
I do know
To be corrupt and treasonous.
Nor. Say not, treasonous.
Buck. To the king I'll say't; and make my vouch as strong
As shore of rock. Attend. This holy fox,
Only to show his pomp as well in France
As here at home, suggests the king our master
To this last costly treaty, th' interview,
That swallow'd so much treasure, and like a glass
Did break i' the rinsing.
Nor. Faith, and so it did.
Buck. Pray, give me favor, sir. This cunning cardinal
The articles o' the combination drew,
As himself pleas'd; and they were ratified.
Let the king know,
(As soon he shall by me) that the cardinal
Does buy and sell his honor as he pleases,
And for his own advantage.
Nor. I am sorry
To hear this of him; and could wish he were
Something mistaken in't.
Buck. No, not a syllable:
I do pronounce him in that very shape
He shall appear in proof.

Enter BRANDON; *a* Sergeant at Arms *before him, and two or three of the* Guard.

Bran. Your office, sergeant; execute it.
Serg. Sir,
My lord the duke of Buckingham, and earl
Of Hereford, Stafford, and Northampton, I
Arrest thee of high treason, in the name
Of our most sovereign king.
Buck. Lo, you, my lord,
The net has fall'n upon me! I shall perish
Under device and practice.
Bran. I am sorry
To see you ta'en from liberty, to look on
The business present: 'tis his highness' pleasure,
You shall to the Tower.
Buck. It will help me nothing
To plead mine innocence; for that dye is on me,

Which makes my whit'st part black. The will of heaven
Be done in this and all things!—I obey.—
O my lord Aberga'ny, fare you well!

Bran. Nay, he must bear you company.—[*To* ABER.] The king
Is pleas'd you shall to the Tower, till you know
How he determines farther.

Aber. As the duke said,
The will of heaven be done, and the king's pleasure
By me obey'd!

Bran. Here is a warrant from
The king to attach lord Montacute; and the bodies
Of the duke's confessor, John de la Car,
One Gilbert Peck, his chancellor,—

Buck. So, so;
These are the limbs o' the plot:—no more, I hope.

Bran. A monk o' the Chartreux.

Buck. O, Nicholas Hopkins?

Bran. He.

Buck. My surveyor is false; the o'er-great cardinal
Hath show'd him gold; my life is spann'd already:
I am the shadow of poor Buckingham,
Whose figure even this instant cloud puts on,
By darkening my clear sun.—My lord, farewell. [*Exeunt.*

SCENE II.—*The Council-Chamber.*

Cornets. Enter KING HENRY, CARDINAL WOLSEY, *the* Lords of the Council, *Sir* THOMAS LOVELL, Officers, Attendants. *The* KING *enters leaning on the* CARDINAL'S *shoulder.*

K. Hen. My life itself, and the best heart of it,
Thanks you for this great care: I stood i' the level
Of a full charg'd confederacy, and give thanks
To you that chok'd it.—Let be call'd before us
That gentleman of Buckingham's: in person
I'll hear him his confessions justify;
And point by point the treasons of his master
He shall again relate.

[*The* KING *takes his state. The* Lords of the Council *take their several places. The* CARDINAL *places himself under the* KING'S *feet, on his right side.*

A noise within, crying "Room for the Queen!" *Enter the* QUEEN, *ushered by the* DUKES OF NORFOLK *and* SUFFOLK: *she kneels. The* KING *riseth from his state, takes her up, kisses, and placeth her by him.*

Q. Kath. Nay, we must longer kneel: I am a suitor.

K. Hen. Arise, and take place by us:—half your suit
Never name to us; you have half our power:
The other moiety, ere you ask, is given;
Repeat your will, and take it.
Q. Kath. Thank your majesty.
That you would love yourself, and in that love
Not unconsider'd leave your honor, nor
The dignity of your office, is the point
Of my petition.
K. Hen. Lady mine, proceed.
Q. Kath. I am solicited, not by a few,
And those of true condition, that your subjects
Are in great grievance: there have been commissions
Sent down among them, which hath flaw'd the heart
Of all their loyalties:—wherein, although,
My good lord cardinal, they vent reproaches
Most bitterly on you, as putter-on
Of these exactions, yet the king our master,
(Whose honor heaven shield from soil!) even he escapes not
Language unmannerly; yea, such which breaks
The sides of loyalty, and almost appears
In loud rebellion.
Nor. Not almost appears,—
It doth appear; for, upon these taxations,
The clothiers all, not able to maintain
The many to them 'longing, have put off
The spinsters, carders, fullers, weavers, who,
Unfit for other life, compell'd by hunger
And lack of other means, in desperate manner
Daring th' event to the teeth, are all in uproar,
And danger serves among them.
K. Hen. Taxation!
Wherein? and what taxation?—My lord cardinal,
You that are blam'd for it alike with us,
Know you of this taxation?
Wol. Please you, sir,
I know but of a single part, in aught
Pertains to the state; and front but in that file
Where others tell steps with me.
Q. Kath. No, my lord,
You know no more than others; bnt you frame
Things that are known alike; which are not wholesome
To those which would not know them, and yet must
Perforce be their acquaintance. These exactions,
Whereof my sovereign would have note, they are
Most pestilent to the hearing; and, to bear them,
The back is sacrifice to the load. They say

They are devis'd by you; or else you suffer
Too hard an exclamation.
K. Hen. Still exaction!
The nature of it? In what kind, let's know,
Is this exaction?
Q. Kath. I am much too venturous
In tempting of your patience; but am bolden'd
Under your promis'd pardon. The subjects' grief
Comes through commissions, which compel from each
The sixth part of his substance, to be levied
Without delay; and the pretence for this
Is nam'd, your wars in France: this makes bold mouths
Tongues spit their duties out, and cold hearts freeze
Allegiance in them; their curses now
Live where their prayers did: and it's come to pass,
This tractable obedience is a slave
To each incensèd will. I would your highness
Would give it quick consideration, for
There is no primer business.
K. Hen. By my life,
This is against our pleasure.
Wol. And for me,
I have no farther gone in this, than by
A single voice; and that not pass'd me but
By learnèd approbation of the judges. If I am
Traduc'd by ignorant tongues, which neither know
My faculties nor person, yet will be
The chronicles of my doing,—let me say,
'Tis but the fate of place, and the rough brake
That virtue must go through. We must not stint
Our necessary actions, in the fear
To cope malicious censurers; which ever,
As ravenous fishes, do a vessel follow
That is new trimm'd, but benefit no farther
Than vainly longing. What we oft do best,
By sick interpreters, once weak ones, is
Not ours, or not allow'd; what worst, as oft,
Hitting a grosser quality, is cried up
For our best act. If we shall stand still,
In fear our motion will be mock'd or carp'd at,
We should take root here where we sit, or sit
State statues only.
K. Hen. Things done well,
And with a care, exempt themselves from fear;
Things done without example, in their issue
Are to be fear'd. Have you a precedent
Of this commission? I believe, not any.
We must not rend our subjects from our laws,

And stick them in our will. Sixth part of each?
A trembling contribution! Why, we take
From every tree, lop, bark, and part o' the timber;
And, though we leave it with a root, thus hack'd,
The air will drink the sap. To every county
Where this is question'd, send our letters, with
Free pardon to each man that has denied
The force of this commission: pray, look to't;
I put it to your care.
Wol. [*To the* Secretary.] A word with you.
Let there be letters writ to every shire,
Of the king's grace and pardon. The griev'd commons
Hardly conceive of me; let it be nois'd,
That through our intercession this revokement
And pardon comes: I shall anon advise you
Farther in the proceeding. [*Exit* Secretary.

Enter Surveyor.

Q. Kath. I am sorry that the duke of Buckingham
Is run in your displeasure.
K. Hen. It grieves many:
The gentleman is learn'd, and a most rare speaker;
To nature none more bound; his training such,
That he may furnish and instruct great teachers,
And never seek for aid out of himself. Yet see,
When these so noble benefits shall prove
Not well dispos'd, the mind growing once corrupt,
They turn to vicious forms, ten times more ugly
Than ever they were fair. Sit by us; you shall hear
(This was his gentleman in trust) of him
Things to strike honor sad.—Bid him recount
The fore-recited practices; whereof
We cannot feel too little, hear too much.
Wol. Stand forth, and with bold spirit relate what you,
Most like a careful subject, have collected
Out of the duke of Buckingham.
K. Hen. Speak freely.
Surv. First, it was usual with him, every day
It would infect his speech,—that if the king
Should without issue die, he'd carry it so
To make the sceptre his: these very words
I've heard him utter to his son-in-law,
Lord Aberga'ny; to whom by oath he menac'd
Revenge upon the cardinal.
Wol. Please your highness, note
This dangerous conception in this point.
Not friended by his wish, to your high person

His will is most malignant; and it stretches
Beyond you, to your friends.
Q. Kath. My learn'd lord cardinal,
Deliver all with charity.
K. Hen. Speak on:
How grounded he his title to the crown,
Upon our fall? to this point hast thou heard him
At any time speak aught?
Surv. He was brought to this
By a vain prophecy of Nicholas Hopkins.
K. Hen. What was that Hopkins?
Surv. Sir, a Chartreux friar,
His confessor; who fed him every minute
With words of sovereignty.
K. Hen. How know'st thou this?
Surv. Not long before your highness sped to France,
The duke being at the Rose, within the parish
Saint Lawrence Poultney, did of me demand
What was the speech among the Londoners
Concerning the French journey: I replied,
Men fear'd the French would prove perfidious,
To the king's danger. Presently the duke
Said, 'twas the fear, indeed; and that he doubted
'Twould prove the verity of certain words
Spoke by a holy monk; "that oft," says he,
"Hath sent to me, wishing me to permit
John de la Car, my chaplain, a choice hour
To hear from him a matter of some moment:
Whom after, under the confession's seal,
He solemnly had sworn, that, what he spoke,
My chaplain to no creature living, but
To me, should utter, with demure confidence
This pausingly ensu'd,—Neither the king, nor's heirs,
(Tell you the duke) shall prosper: bid him strive
To gain the love o' the commonalty: the duke
Shall govern England."
Q. Kath. If I know you well,
You were the duke's surveyor, and lost your office
On the complaint o' the tenants: take good heed
You charge not in your spleen a noble person,
And spoil your nobler soul: I say, take heed;
Yes, heartily beseech you.
K. Hen. Let him on.—
Go forward.
Surv. On my soul, I'll speak but truth.
I told my lord the duke, by foul illusions
The monk might be deceiv'd; and that 'twas dangerous for him
To ruminate on this so far, until

It forg'd him some design, which, being believ'd,
It was much like to do: he answered, "Tush!
It can do me no damage;" adding farther,
That, had the king in his last sickness fail'd,
The cardinal's and Sir Thomas Lovell's heads
Should have gone off.
K. Hen. Ha! what, so rank? Ah, ha!
There's mischief in this man:—canst thou say farther?
Surv. I can, my liege.
K. Hen. Proceed.
Surv. Being at Greenwich,
After your highness had reprov'd the duke
About Sir William Blomer,—
K. Hen. I remember
Of such a time:—being my sworn servant,
The duke retain'd him his.—But on; what hence?
Surv. "If," quoth he, "I for this had been committed,
As, to the Tower, I thought,—I would have play'd
The part my father meant to act upon
Th' usurper Richard; who, being at Salisbury,
Made suit to come in's presence: which if granted,
As he made semblance of his duty, would
Have put his knife into him."
K. Hen. A giant traitor!
Wol. Now, madam, may his highness live in freedom,
And this man out of prison?
Q. Kath. Heaven mend all!
K. Hen. There's something more would out of thee; what say'st?
Surv. After "the duke his father," with "the knife,"
He stretch'd him, and, with one hand on his dagger,
Another spread on's breast, mounting his eyes,
He did discharge a horrible oath; whose tenor
Was,—were he evil us'd, he would out-go
His father, by as much as a performance
Does an irresolute purpose.
K. Hen. There's his period,
To sheathe his knife in us. He is attach'd;
Call him to present trial: if he may
Find mercy in the law, 'tis his; if none,
Let him not seek 't of us. By day and night,
He's traitor to the height! [*Exeunt.*

SCENE IV.—*The Presence Chamber in* York-Place.

Hautboys. A small table under a state for the CARDINAL, *a longer table for the guests. Enter, on one side,* ANNE BULLEN, *and divers* Lords, Ladies, *and* Gentlemen, *as guests; on the other, enter Sir* HENRY GUILFORD.

Guild. Ladies, a general welcome from his grace
Salutes ye all; this night he dedicates
To fair content and you: none here, he hopes,
In all this noble bevy, has brought with her
One care abroad; he would have all as merry,
As, first, good company, good wine, good welcome,
Can make good people.—

Enter Lord Chamberlain, LORD SANDS, *and Sir* THOMAS LOVELL.

O, my lord, you're tardy:
The very thought of this fair company
Clapp'd wings to me.

Cham. You are young, Sir Harry Guilford.

Sands. Sir Thomas Lovell, had the cardinal
But half my lay-thoughts in him, some of these
Should find a running banquet ere they rested.
They are a sweet society of fair ones.

Lov. O, that your lordship were but now confessor
To one or two of these!

Sands. I would I were;
They should find easy penance.

Cham. Sweet ladies, will it please you sit?—Sir Harry,
Place you that side; I'll take the charge of this:
His grace is entering.—Nay, you must not freeze;
Two women plac'd together makes cold weather:—
My lord Sands, you are one will keep them waking;
Pray, sit between these ladies.

Sands. By my faith,
And thank your lordship.—By your leave, sweet ladies.
[*Seats himself between* ANNE BULLEN *and another* Lady.
If I chance to talk a little wild, forgive me;
I had it from my father.

Anne. Was he mad, sir?

Sands. O, very mad, exceeding mad, in love too:
But he would bite none; just as I do now,
He would kiss you twenty with a breath. [*Kisses her.*

Cham. Well said, my lord.—
So, now you are fairly seated.—Gentlemen,
The penance lies on you, if these fair ladies
Pass away frowning.

Sands. For my little cure,
Let me alone.

Hautboys. Enter CARDINAL WOLSEY, *attended, and takes his state.*

Wol. You're welcome, my fair guests: that noble lady,
Or gentleman, that is not freely merry,
Is not my friend. This, to confirm my welcome;
And to you all, good health. [*Drinks.*
Sands. Your grace is noble:—
Let me have such a bowl may hold my thanks,
And save me so much talking.
Wol. My lord Sands,
I am beholden to you: cheer your neighbors.—
Ladies, you are not merry:—gentlemen,
Whose fault is this?
Sands. The red wine first must rise
In their fair cheeks, my lord; then, we shall have them
Talk us to silence.
Anne. You are a merry gamester,
My lord Sands.
[*Drum and trumpets within; chambers discharged.*
Wol. What's that?
Cham. Look out there, some of you. [*Exit a* Servant.
Wol. What warlike voice,
And to what end, is this?—Nay, ladies, fear not;
By all the laws of war you're privileg'd.

Re-enter Servant.

Cham. How now! what is't?
Serv. A noble troop of strangers,—
For so they seem: they've left their barge, and landed:
And hither make, as great ambassadors
From foreign princes.
Wol. Good lord chamberlain,
Go, give them welcome; you can speak the French tongue;
And, pray, receive them nobly, and conduct them
Into our presence, where this heaven of beauty
Shall shine at full upon them.—Some attend him.—

[*Exit* Chamberlain, *attended. All arise, and tables removed.*

You have now a broken banquet; but we'll mend it.
A good digestion to you all: and, once more,
I shower a welcome on ye;—welcome all.

Hautboys. Enter the KING, *and others, as Maskers, habited like shepherds, ushered by the* Lord Chamberlain. *They pass directly before the* CARDINAL, *and gracefully salute him.*

A noble company! what are their pleasures?

Cham. Because they speak no English, thus they pray'd
To tell your grace,—that, having heard by fame
Of this so noble and so fair assembly
This night to meet here, they could do no less,
Out of the great respect they bear to beauty,
But leave their flocks; and, under your fair conduct,
Crave leave to view these ladies, and entreat
An hour of revels with them.
Wol. Say, lord chamberlain,
They have done my poor house grace; for which I pay them
A thousand thanks, and pray them take their pleasures.

[Ladies *chosen for the dance. The* KING *chooses* ANNE BULLEN.

K. Hen. The fairest hand I ever touch'd. O beauty,
Till now I never knew thee! [*Music. Dance.*
Wol. My lord,—
Cham. Your grace?
Wol. Pray tell them thus much from me.
There should be one amongst them, by his person,
More worthy this place than myself; to whom,
If I but knew him, with my love and duty
I would surrender it.
Cham. I will, my lord.
[*Goes to the Maskers, and returns.*
Wol. What say they?
Cham. Such a one, they all confess,
There is, indeed; which they would have your grace
Find out, and he will take it.
Wol. Let me see, then.—
[*Comes from his state.*
By all your good leaves, gentlemen;—here I'll make
My royal choice.
K. Hen. [*Unmasking.*] You have found him, cardinal:
You hold a fair assembly; you do well, lord:
You are a churchman, or, I'll tell you, cardinal,
I should judge now unhappily.
Wol. I am glad
Your grace is grown so pleasant.
K. Hen. My lord chamberlain,
Pr'ythee, come hither: what fair lady's that?
Cham. An't please your grace, Sir Thomas Bullen's daughter,—
The viscount Rochford—one of her highness' women.
K. Hen. By heaven, she is a dainty one!—Sweetheart,
I were unmannerly to take you out,
And not to kiss you.—A health, gentlemen!
Let it go round.
Wol. Sir Thomas Lovell, is the banquet ready
I' the privy chamber?
Lov. Yes, my lord.

Wol. Your grace,
I fear, with dancing is a little heated.
K. Hen. I fear, too much.
Wol. There's fresher air, my lord,
In the next chamber.
K. Hen. Lead in your ladies, every one:—sweet partner,
I must not yet forsake you:—let's be merry:—
Good my lord cardinal, I have half a dozen healths
To drink to these fair ladies, and a measure
To lead them once again; and then let's dream
Who's best in favor.—Let the music knock it.
[*Exeunt with trumpets.*

ACT II.

SCENE I.—London. *A Street.*

The Duke of Buckingham is brought to trial. He is found guilty on the charge of "high treason," and is condemned to suffer death.

Enter BUCKINGHAM *from his arraignment; tipstaves before him; the axe with the edge towards him; halberts on each side: with him Sir* THOMAS LOVELL, *Sir* NICHOLAS VAUX, *Sir* WILLIAM SANDS, *and common people.*

2 *Gent.* Let's stand close, and behold him.
Buck. All good people,
You that thus far have come to pity me,
Hear what I say, and then go home and lose me.
I have this day receiv'd a traitor's judgment,
And by that name must die: yet, heaven bear witness,
And if I have a conscience let it sink me,
Even as the axe falls, if I be not faithful!
The law I bear no malice for my death;
It has done, upon the premises, but justice:
But those that sought it I could wish more Christians:
Be what they will, I heartily forgive them:
Yet let them look they glory not in mischief,
Nor build their evils on the graves of great men;
For then my guiltless blood must cry against them.
For farther life in this world I ne'er hope,
Nor will I sue, although the king have mercies
More than I dare make faults. You few that lov'd me,
And dare be bold to weep for Buckingham,
His noble friends and fellows, whom to leave
Is only bitter to him, only dying,
Go with me, like good angels, to my end;
And, as the long divorce of steel falls on me,

Make of your prayers one sweet sacrifice,
And lift my soul to heaven.—Lead on, o' heaven's name.

Lov. I do beseech your grace, for charity,
If ever any malice in your heart
Were hid against me, now to forgive me frankly.

Buck. Sir Thomas Lovell, I as free forgive you,
As I would be forgiven: I forgive all;
There cannot be those numberless offences
'Gainst me, that I can not take peace with: no black envy
Shall mark my grave. Commend me to his grace;
And, if he speak of Buckingham, pray, tell him
You met him half in heaven: my vows and prayers
Yet are the king's; and, till my soul forsake,
Shall cry for blessings on him: may he live
Longer than I have time to tell his years!
Ever belov'd and loving may his rule be!
And when old time shall lead him to his end,
Goodness and he fill up one monument!

Lov. To the water side I must conduct your grace;
Then give my charge up to Sir Nicholas Vaux,
Who undertakes you to your end.

Vaux. Prepare there!
The duke is coming: see, the barge be ready;
And fit it with such furniture as suits
The greatness of his person.

Buck. Nay, Sir Nicholas,
Let it alone; my state now will but mock me.
When I came hither, I was lord high constable,
And duke of Buckingham; now, poor Edward Bohun:
Yet I am richer than my base accusers,
That never knew what truth meant: I now seal it;
And with that blood will make them one day groan for't.
Yet, you that hear me,
This from a dying man receive as certain:—
Where you are liberal of your loves and counsels,
Be sure you be not loose; for those you make friends,
And give your hearts to, when they once perceive
The least rub in your fortunes, fall away
Like water from ye, never found again
But where they mean to sink ye. All good people,
Pray for me! I must now forsake ye: the last hour
Of my long weary life is come upon me.
Farewell:
And when you would say something that is sad,
Speak how I fell.—I have done; and God forgive me!

[*Exeunt* BUCKINGHAM *and train.*

SCENE II.—*An Ante-chamber in the Palace.*

Enter the DUKES OF NORFOLK, SUFFOLK, *and the* Lord Chamberlain.

Nor. Well met, my lord chamberlain.
Cham. Good day to both your graces.
Suf. How is the king employ'd?
Cham. I left him private,
Full of sad thoughts and troubles.
Nor. What's the cause?
Cham. It seems, the marriage with his brother's wife
Has crept too near his conscience.
Suf. No, his conscience
Has crept too near another lady.
Nor. 'Tis so:
This is the cardinal's doing, the king-cardinal:
That blind priest, like the eldest son of fortune,
Turns what he list. The king will know him one day.
Suf. Pray heaven he do! he'll never know himself else.
Nor. How holily he works in all his business!
And with what zeal! for, now he has crack'd the league
Between us and the emperor, the queen's great nephew,
He dives into the king's soul, and there scatters
Dangers, doubts, wringing of the conscience,
Fears, and despairs,—and all these for his marriage:
And, out of all these, to restore the king,
He counsels a divorce; a loss of her,
That, like a jewel, has hung twenty years
About his neck, yet never lost her lustre:
Of her, that loves him with that excellence
That angels love good men with; even of her,
That, when the greatest stroke of fortune falls,
Will bless the king: and is not this course pious?
Cham. Heaven keep me from such counsel! 'Tis most true,
These news are every where; every tongue speaks them,
And every true heart weeps for't: all that dare
Look into these affairs, see this main end,—
The French king's sister. Heaven will one day open
The king's eyes, that so long have slept upon
This bold bad man.
Suf. And free us from his slavery.
Nor. We had need pray,
And heartily, for our deliverance;
Or this imperious man will work us all
From princes into pages: all men's honors
Lie like one lump before him, to be fashion'd
Into what pitch he please.

Suf. For me, my lords,
I love him not, nor fear him; there's my creed.
Nor. Let's in;
And with some other business put the king
From these sad thoughts, that work too much upon him:—
My lord, you'll bear us company?
Cham. Excuse me;
The king hath sent me otherwhere: besides,
You'll find a most unfit time to disturb him:
Health to your lordships.
Nor. Thanks, my good lord chamberlain.
[*Exit* Lord Chamberlain.

NORFOLK *opens a folding-door. The* KING *is discovered sitting, and reading pensively.*

Suf. How sad he looks! sure, he is much afflicted.
K. Hen. Who is there, ha?
Nor. Pray heaven he be not angry.
K. Hen. Who's there, I say? How dare you thrust yourselves
Into my private meditations?
Who am I, ha?
Nor. A gracious king that pardons all offences
Malice ne'er meant; our breach of duty this way
Is business of estate; in which we come
To know your royal pleasure.
K. Hen. You are too bold:
Go to; I'll make ye know your times of business:
Is this an hour for temporal affairs, ha?—

Enter WOLSEY *and* CAMPEIUS.

Who's there? my good lord cardinal?—O, my Wolsey,
The quiet of my wounded conscience;
Thou art a cure fit for a king.—[*To* CAMPEIUS.] You're welcome,
Most learnèd reverend sir, into our kingdom:
Use us, and it.—[*To* WOLSEY.] My good lord, have great care
I be not found a talker.
Wol. Sir, you cannot.
I would your grace would give us but an hour
Of private conference.
K. Hen. [*To* NORFOLK *and* SUFFOLK.] We are busy; go.
Nor. [*Aside to* SUF.] This priest has no pride in him.
Suf. [*Aside to* NOR.] Not to speak of;
I would not be so sick though for his place:
But this cannot continue.
Nor. [*Aside to* SUF.] If it do,
I'll venture one have-at-him.

Suf. [*Aside to* Nor.] I another.

[*Exeunt* Norfolk *and* Suffolk.

Wol. Your grace has given a precedent of wisdom
Above all princes, in committing freely
Your scruple to the voice of Christendom:
Who can be angry now? what envy reach you?
The Spaniard, tied by blood and favor to her,
Must now confess, if they have any goodness,
The trial just and noble. All the clerks,—
I mean the learnèd ones,—in Christian kingdoms
Have their free voices: Rome, the nurse of judgment,
Invited by your noble self, hath sent
One general tongue unto us, this good man,
This just and learnèd priest, Cardinal Campeius,—
Whom once more I present unto your highness.

K. Hen. And once more in mine arms I bid him welcome,
And thank the holy conclave for their loves:
They have sent me such a man I would have wish'd for.

Cam. Your grace must needs deserve all strangers' loves,
You are so noble. To your highness' hand
I tender my commission;—by whose virtue,
(The court of Rome commanding) you, my lord
Cardinal of York, are join'd with me, their servant,
In the impartial judging of this business.

K. Hen. Two equal men. The queen shall be acquainted
Forthwith for what you come.—Where's Gardiner?

Wol. I know your majesty has always lov'd her
So dear in heart, not to deny her that
A woman of less place might ask by law,—
Scholars, allow'd freely to argue for her.

K. Hen. Ay, and the best, she shall have; and my favor
To him that does best: heaven forbid else. Cardinal,
Pr'ythee, call Gardiner to me, my new secretary:
I find him a fit fellow. [*Exit* Wolsey.

Re-enter Wolsey, *with* Gardiner.

Wol. [*Aside to* Gard.] Give me your hand: much joy and favor to you;
You are the king's now.

Gard. [*Aside to* Wol.] But to be commanded
For ever by your grace, whose hand has rais'd me.

K. Hen. Come hither, Gardiner. [*They converse apart.*

Cam. My lord of York, was not one doctor Pace
In this man's place before him?

Wol. Yes, he was.

Cam. Was he not held a learnèd man?

Wol. Yes, surely.

Cam. Believe me, there's an ill opinion spread, then,
Even of yourself, lord cardinal.
Wol. How! of me?
Cam. They will not stick to say, you envied him;
And fearing he would rise, he was so virtuous,
Kept him a foreign man still; which so griev'd him,
That he ran mad and died.
Wol. Heaven's peace be with him!
That's Christian care enough: for living murmurers
There's places of rebuke. He was a fool;
For he would needs be virtuous: that good fellow,
If I command him, follows my appointment:
I will have none so near else. Learn this, brother,
We live not to be grip'd by meaner persons.
K. Hen. Deliver this with modesty to the queen.
[*Exit* GARDINER.
The most convenient place that I can think of,
For such receipt of learning, is Black-Friars;
There ye shall meet about this weighty business:—
My Wolsey, see it furnish'd.—O my lord,
Would it not grieve an honest man to leave
So sweet a wife? But, conscience, conscience,—
O, 'tis a tender place! and I must leave her. [*Exeunt.*

SCENE III.—*An Ante-chamber in the* QUEEN'S *Apartments.*

Enter ANNE BULLEN *and an* Old Lady.

Anne. Not for that neither: here's the pang that pinches:—
His highness having liv'd so long with her, and she
So good a lady, that no tongue could ever
Pronounce dishonor of her,—by my life,
She never knew harm-doing;—O, now, after
So many courses of the sun enthron'd,
Still growing in a majesty and pomp,—the which
To leave, a thousand-fold more bitter than
'Tis sweet at first t' acquire,—after this process,
To give her the avaunt! it is a pity
Would move a monster.
Old L. Hearts of most hard temper
Melt and lament for her.
Anne. O, heaven's will! much better
She ne'er had known pomp: though it be temporal,
Yet, if that quarrel, fortune, do divorce
It from the bearer, 'tis a sufferance panging
As soul and body's severing.
Old L. Alas, poor lady!
She's a stranger now again.

Anne. So much the more
Must pity drop upon her. Verily,
I swear, 'tis better to be lowly born,
And range with humble livers in content,
Than to be perk'd up in a glistering grief,
And wear a golden sorrow.
Old L. Our content
Is our best having.
Anne. By my troth, I would not be a queen.
Old L. Beshrew me, I would; and so would you,
For all this spice of your hypocrisy.
Anne. Nay, good troth,—
Old L. Yes, troth, and troth;—you would not be a queen?
Anne. No, not for all the riches under heaven.
Old L. 'Tis strange: a three-pence bowed would hire me,
Old as I am, to queen it: but, I pray you,
What think you of a duchess? have you limbs
To bear that load of title?
Anne. No, in truth.
I swear again, I would not be a queen
For all the world.

Enter the Lord Chamberlain.

Cham. Good morrow, ladies. What were't worth to know
The secret of your conference?
Anne. My good lord,
Not your demand; it values not your asking:
Our mistress' sorrows we were pitying.
Cham. It was a gentle business, and becoming
The action of good women: there is hope
All will be well.
Anne. Now, I pray heaven, amen!
Cham. You bear a gentle mind, and heavenly blessings
Follow such creatures. That you may, fair lady,
Perceive I speak sincerely, and high note's
Ta'en of your many virtues, the king's majesty
Commends his good opinion of you to you, and
Does purpose honor to you no less flowing
Than marchioness of Pembroke; to which title
A thousand pound a-year, annual support,
Out of his grace he adds.
Anne. I do not know
What kind of my obedience I should tender;
More than my all is nothing: nor my prayers
Are not words duly hallow'd, nor my wishes
More worth than empty vanities: yet prayers and wishes
Are all I can return. Beseech your lordship,
Vouchsafe to speak my thanks and my obedience,

As from a blushing handmaid, to his highness;
Whose health and royalty I pray for.
Cham. Lady,
I shall not fail to approve the fair conceit
The king hath of you.—[*Aside.*] I have perus'd her well;
Beauty and honor in her are so mingled,
That they have caught the king: and who knows yet,
But from this lady may proceed a gem
To lighten all this isle?—[*To her.*] I'll to the king,
And say, I spoke with you.
Anne. My honor'd lord.
[*Exit* Lord Chamberlain.
Old L. Why, this it is; see, see!
I have been begging sixteen years in court,
(Am yet a courtier beggarly) nor could
Come pat betwixt too early and too late,
For any suit of pounds; and you, O fate!
A very fresh-fish here, (fie, fie, fie upon
This compell'd fortune!) have your mouth fill'd up,
Before you open it.
Anne. This is strange to me.
Old L. How tastes it? is it bitter? forty pence, no.
There was a lady once, ('tis an old story)
That would not be a queen, that would she not,
For all the mud in Egypt:—have you heard it?
Anne. Come, you are pleasant.
Old L. With your theme, I could
O'ermount the lark. The marchioness of Pembroke!
A thousand pounds a-year, for pure respect!
No other obligation! By my life,
That promises more thousands: honor's train
Is longer than his foreskirt. By this time,
I know, your back will bear a duchess:—say,
Are you not stronger than you were?
Anne. Good lady,
Make yourself mirth with your particular fancy,
And leave me out on't. Would I had no being,
If this salute my blood a jot: it faints me,
To think what follows.
The queen is comfortless, and we forgetful
In our long absence: pray, do not deliver
What here you've heard, to her.
Old L. What do you think me?
[*Exeunt.*

SCENE IV.—*A Hall in* Black-Friars.

Trumpets, sennet, and cornets. Enter two Vergers, *with short silver wands; next them, two* Scribes, *in the habit of doctors; after them, the* Archbishop of Canterbury, *alone; after him, the* Bishops of Lincoln, Ely, Rochester, *and* Saint Asaph; *next them, with some small distance, follows a* Gentleman, *bearing the Purse, with the Great Seal, and a cardinal's hat; then two* Priests, *bearing each a silver cross; then a* Gentleman-Usher *bare-headed, accompanied with a* Sergeant at Arms, *bearing a silver mace; then two* Gentlemen, *bearing two great silver pillars; after them, side by side, the two* Cardinals Wolsey *and* Campeius; *two* Noblemen *with the sword and mace. Then enter the* King *and* Queen, *and their trains. The* King *takes place under the cloth of state; the two* Cardinals *sit under him as judges. The* Queen *takes place at some distance from the* King. *The* Bishops *place themselves on each side the court, in manner of a consistory; below them, the* Scribes. *The* Lords *sit next the* Bishops. *The* Crier *and the rest of the* Attendants *stand in convenient order about the Hall.*

Wol. Whilst our commission from Rome is read,
Let silence be commanded.
K. Hen. What's the need?
It hath already publicly been read,
And on all sides th' authority allow'd;
You may, then, spare that time.
Wol. Be't so.—Proceed.
Scribe. Say, Henry king of England, come into the court.
Crier. Henry king of England, &c.
K. Hen. Here.
Scribe. Say, Katharine queen of England, come into the court.
Crier. Katharine, queen of England, &c.
[*The* Queen *makes no answer, rises out of her chair, goes about the court, comes to the* King, *and kneels at his feet; then speaks.*
Q. Kath. Sir, I desire you do me right and justice;
And to bestow your pity on me: for
I am a most poor woman, and a stranger,
Born out of your dominions; having here
No judge indifferent, nor no more assurance
Of equal friendship and proceeding. Alas, sir,
In what have I offended you? what cause
Hath my behavior given to your displeasure,
That thus you should proceed to put me off,
And take your good grace from me? Heaven witness,
I have been to you a true and humble wife,

At all times to your will conformable;
Ever in fear to kindle your dislike,
Yea, subject to your countenance,—glad or sorry
As I saw it inclin'd. When was the hour
I ever contradicted your desire,
Or made it not mine too? Or which of your friends
Have I not strove to love, although I knew
He were mine enemy? what friend of mine
That had to him deriv'd your anger, did I
Continue in my liking? nay, gave notice
He was from thence discharg'd. Sir, call to mind
That I have been your wife, in this obedience,
Upward of twenty years; if, in the course
And process of this time, you can report,
And prove it too, against mine honor aught,
My bond to wedlock, or my love and duty,
Against your sacred person, in God's name,
Turn me away; and let the foul'st contempt
Shut door upon me, and so give me up
To the sharp'st kind of justice. Please you, sir,
The king, your father, was reputed for
A prince most prudent, of an excellent
And unmatch'd wit and judgment: Ferdinand,
My father, king of Spain, was reckon'd one
The wisest prince that there had reign'd by many
A year before: it is not to be question'd
That they had gather'd a wise council to them
Of every realm, that did debate this business,
Who deem'd our marriage lawful: wherefore I humbly
Beseech you, sir, to spare me, till I may
Be by my friends in Spain advis'd; whose counsel
I will implore: if not, i' the name of heaven,
Your pleasure be fulfill'd!

Wol. You have here, lady,
(And of your choice) these reverend fathers; men
Of singular integrity and learning,
Yea, the elect o' the land, who are assembled
To plead your cause: it shall be therefore bootless
That longer you desire the court; as well
For your own quiet, as to rectify
What is unsettled in the king.

Cam. His grace
Hath spoken well and justly: therefore, madam,
It's fit this royal session do proceed;
And that, without delay, their arguments
Be now produc'd and heard.

Q. Kath. Lord cardinal,—
To you I speak.

Wol. Your pleasure, madam?
Q. Kath. Sir,
I am about to weep; but, thinking that
We are a queen, (or long have dream'd so) certain
The daughter of a king, my drops of tears
I'll turn to sparks of fire.
Wol. Be patient yet.
Q. Kath. I will, when you are humble; nay, before,
Or God will punish me. I do believe,
Induc'd by potent circumstances, that
You are mine enemy; and make my challenge
You shall not be my judge: for it is you
Have blown this coal betwixt my lord and me,—
Therefore I say again,
I utterly abhor, yea, from my soul
Refuse you for my judge; whom, yet once more,
I hold my most malicious foe, and think not
At all a friend to truth.
Wol. I do profess
You speak not like yourself; who ever yet
Have stood to charity, and display'd th' effects
Of disposition gentle, and of wisdom
O'ertopping woman's power. Madam, you do me wrong:
I have no spleen against you; nor injustice
For you, or any: how far I have proceeded,
Or how far farther shall, is warranted
By a commission from the consistory,—
Yea, the whole consistory of Rome. You charge me
That I have blown this coal: I do deny it:
The king is present: if it be known to him
That I gainsay my deed, how may he wound,
And worthily, my falsehood! yea, as much
As you have done my truth. If he know
That I am free of your report, he knows
I am not of your wrong. Therefore in him
It lies to cure me: and the cure is, to
Remove these thoughts from you: the which before
His highness shall speak in, I do beseech
You, gracious madam, to unthink your speaking,
And to say so no more.
Q. Kath. My lord, my lord,
I am a simple woman, much too weak
To oppose your cunning. You are meek and humble-mouth'd;
You sign your place and calling, in full seeming,
With meekness and humility; but your heart
Is cramm'd with arrogancy, spleen, and pride.
You have, by fortune and his highness' favors,
Gone slightly o'er low steps, and now are mounted

Where powers are your retainers; and your words,
Domestics to you, serve your will as't please
Yourself pronounce their office. I must tell you,
You tender more your person's honor than
Your high profession spiritual: that again
I do refuse you for my judge; and here,
Before you all, appeal unto the pope,
To bring my whole cause 'fore his holiness,
And to be judg'd by him.

[*She courtsies to the* KING, *and offers to depart.*

Cam. The queen is obstinate,
Stubborn to justice, apt to accuse it, and
Disdainful to be tried by't: 'tis not well.
She's going away.

K. Hen. Call her again.

Crier. Katharine, queen of England, come into the court.

Grif. Madam, you are call'd back.

Q. Kath. What need you note it? Pray you, keep your way:
When you are call'd, return.—Now, the Lord help!
They vex me past my patience!—Pray you, pass on:
I will not tarry; no, nor ever more
Upon this business my appearance make
In any of their courts.

[*Exeunt* QUEEN, GRIFFITH, *and her other* Attendants.

K. Hen. Go thy ways, Kate:
That man o' the world who shall report he has
A better wife, let him in nought be trusted,
For speaking false in that: thou art, alone,
(If thy rare qualities, sweet gentleness,
Thy meekness saint-like, wife-like government,—
Obeying in commanding—and thy parts
Sovereign and pious else, could speak thee out)
The queen of earthly queens:—she's noble born;
And, like her true nobility, she has
Carried herself towards me.

Cam. So please your highness,
The queen being absent, 'tis a needful fitness
That we adjourn this court till farther day:
Meanwhile must be an earnest motion
Made to the queen, to call back her appeal
She intends unto his holiness. [*They rise to depart.*

K. Henry. [*aside.*] I may perceive,
These cardinals trifle with me: I abhor
This dilatory sloth and tricks of Rome.
My learn'd and well beloved servant, Cranmer,
Pr'ythee, return! with thy approach, I know,
My comfort comes along.—Break up the court:
I say, set on. [*Exeunt, in manner as they entered.*

ACT III.

SCENE I.—London. *The Palace at* Bridewell. *A Room in the* QUEEN'S *Apartment.*

The QUEEN, *and some of her women, at work.*

Q. Kath. Take thy lute, wench: my soul grows sad with troubles;
Sing, and disperse them, if thou canst: leave working.

SONG.

Orpheus with his lute made trees,
And the mountain-tops that freeze,
Bow themselves, when he did sing:
To his music, plants and flowers
Ever sprung; as sun and showers
There had made a lasting spring.

Every thing that heard him play,
Even the billows of the sea,
Hung their heads, and then lay by.
In sweet music is such art,
Killing care and grief of heart
Fall asleep, or hearing, die.

Enter a Gentleman.

Q. Kath. How now!
Gent. An't please your grace, the two great cardinals
Wait in the presence.
Q. Kath. Would they speak with me?
Gent. They will'd me say so, madam.
Q. Kath. Pray their graces
To come near. [*Exit* Gent.] What can be their business
With me, a poor weak woman, fallen from favor?
I do not like their coming, now I think on't.
They should be good men; their affairs as righteous;
But all hoods make not monks.

Enter WOLSEY *and* CAMPEIUS.

Wol. Peace to your highness!
Q. Kath. Your graces find me here part of a housewife;
I would be all, against the worst may happen.
What are your pleasures with me, reverend lords?
Wol. May it please you, noble madam, to withdraw
Into your private chamber, we shall give you
The full cause of our coming.
Q. Kath. Speak it here;
There's nothing I have done yet, o' my conscience
Deserves a corner: would all other women
Could speak this with as free a soul as I do!

My lords, I care not (so much I am happy
Above a number) if my actions
Were tried by every tongue, every eye saw them,
Envy and base opinion set against them,
I know my life so even. If your business
Seek me out, and that way I am wife in,
Out with it boldly: truth loves open dealing.
Wol. Tanta est erga te mentis integritas, regina serenissima,—
Q. Kath. O, good my lord, no Latin;
I am not such a truant since my coming,
As not to know the language I have liv'd in;
A strange tongue makes my cause more strange, suspicious;
Pray, speak in English; here are some will thank you,
If you speak truth, for their poor mistress' sake,—
Believe me, she has had much wrong: lord cardinal,
The willing'st sin I ever yet committed
May be absolv'd in English.
Wol. Noble lady,
I am sorry my integrity should breed
(And service to his majesty and you)
So deep suspicion, where all faith was meant.
We come not by the way of accusation,
To taint that honor every good tongue blesses,
Nor to betray you any way to sorrow,—
You have too much, good lady; but to know
How you stand minded in the weighty difference
Between the king and you; and to deliver,
Like free and honest men, our just opinions,
And comforts to your cause.
Cam. Most honor'd madam,
My lord of York,—out of his noble nature,
Zeal and obedience he still bore your grace,—
Forgetting, like a good man, your late censure
Both of his truth and him, (which was too far)—
Offers, as I do, in a sign of peace,
His service and his counsel.
Q. Kath. [*Aside.*] To betray me.—
My lords, I thank you both for your good wills;
Ye speak like honest men: (pray heaven, ye prove so!)
But how to make ye suddenly an answer,
In such a point of weight, so near mine honor,
(More near my life, I fear,) with my weak wit,
And to such men of gravity and learning,
In truth, I know not. I was set at work
Among my maids; full little, heaven knows, looking
Either for such men, or such business.
For her sake that I have been, (for I feel
The last fit of my greatness,) good your graces,

Let me have time and counsel for my cause:
Alas, I am a woman, friendless, hopeless!
Wol. Madam, you wrong the king's love with these fears:
Your hopes and friends are infinite.
Q. Cath. In England
But little for my profit: can you think, lords,
That any Englishman dare give me counsel?
Or be a known friend, 'gainst his highness' pleasure,
And live a subject? Nay, forsooth, my friends,
They that must weigh out my afflictions,
They that my trust must grow to, live not here:
They are, as all my other comforts, far hence,
In mine own country, lords.
Cam. I would your grace
Would leave your griefs, and take my counsel.
Q. Kath. How, sir?
Cam. Put your main cause into the king's protection;
He's loving, and most gracious: 'twill be much
Both for your honor better, and your cause;
For if the trial of the law o'ertake you,
You'll part away disgrac'd.
Wol. He tells you rightly
Q. Kath. Ye tell me what ye wish for both,—my ruin:
Is this your Christian counsel? out upon ye!
Heaven is above all yet; there sits a Judge
That no king can corrupt.
Cam. Your rage mistakes us.
Q. Kath. The more shame for ye! holy men I thought ye,
Upon my soul, two reverend cardinal virtues;
But cardinal sins, and hollow hearts, I fear ye:
Mend them, for shame, my lords. Is this your comfort?
The cordial that ye bring a wretched lady,—
A woman lost among ye, laugh'd at, scorn'd?
I will not wish ye half my miseries;
I have more charity: but say, I warn'd ye,
Take heed, for heaven's sake, take heed, lest at once
The burden of my sorrows fall upon ye.
Wol. Madam, this is a mere distraction;
You turn the good we offer into envy.
Q. Kath. Ye turn me into nothing: woe upon ye,
And all such false professors! Would ye have me
Put my sick cause into his hands that hates me?
I am old, my lords,
And all the fellowship I hold now with him
Is only my obedience. What can happen
To me above this wretchedness? all your studies
Make me a curse like this.
Cam. Your fears are worse.

Q. Kath. Have I liv'd thus long—(let me speak myself,
Since virtue finds no friends,)—a wife, a true one?
A woman (I dare say without vain-glory)
Never yet branded with suspicion?
Have I with all my full affections
Still met the king? lov'd him next heaven? obey'd him?
Been, out of fondness, superstitious to him?
Almost forgot my prayers to content him?
And am I thus rewarded? 'tis not well, lords.
Bring me a constant woman to her husband,
One that ne'er dream'd a joy beyond his pleasure;
And to that woman, when she has done most,
Yet will I add an honor,—a great patience.

Wol. Madam, you wander from the good we aim at.

Q. Kath. My lord, I dare not make myself so guilty,
To give up willingly that noble title
Your master wed me to: nothing but death
Shall e'er divorce my dignities.

Wol. Pray, hear me.

Q. Kath. Would I had never trod this English earth,
Or felt the flatteries that grow upon it!
Ye have angels' faces, but heaven knows your hearts.
What will become of me now, wretched lady!
I am the most unhappy woman living.—
[*To her women.*] Alas, poor wenches, where are now your fortunes!
Shipwreck'd upon a kingdom, where no pity,
No friends, no hope; no kindred weep for me;
Almost no grave allow'd me:—like the lily,
That once was mistress of the field and flourish'd,
I'll hang my head and perish.

Wol. If your grace
Could but be brought to know our ends are honest,
You'd feel more comfort.

Q. Kath. Do what ye will, my lords; and, pray, forgive me,
If I have us'd myself unmannerly;
You know I am a woman, lacking wit
To make a seemly answer to such persons.
Pray, do my service to his majesty:
He has my heart yet; and shall have my prayers
While I shall have my life. Come, reverend fathers,
Bestow your counsels on me: she now begs,
That little thought, when she set footing here,
She should have bought her dignities so dear. [*Exeunt.*

SCENE II.—*Ante-chamber to the* KING'S *Apartment.*

Enter the DUKE OF NORFOLK, *the* DUKE OF SUFFOLK, *the* EARL OF SURREY, *and the* Lord Chamberlain.

Nor. If you will now unite in your complaints,
And force them with a constancy, the cardinal
Cannot stand under them.
Cham. If you cannot
Bar his access to the king, never attempt
Anything on him; for he hath a witchcraft
Over the king in's tongue.
Nor. O, fear him not;
His spell in that is out: the king hath found
Matter against him, that for ever mars
The honey of his language. No, he's settled,
Not to come off, in his displeasure.
Sur. Sir,
I should be glad to hear such news as this
Once every hour.
Nor. Believe it, this is true:
In the divorce his contrary proceedings
Are all unfolded; wherein he appears,
As I would wish mine enemy.
Sur. How came
His practices to light?
Suf. Most strangely.
Sur. O, how, how?
Suf. The cardinal's letter to the pope miscarried,
And came to the eye o' the king: wherein was read,
How that the cardinal did entreat his holiness
To stay the judgment o' the divorce; for if
It did take place, "I do," quoth he, "perceive
My king is tangled in affection to
A creature of the queen's, lady Anne Bullen."
The cardinal! [*They stand aside.*

Enter WOLSEY *and* CROMWELL.

Nor. Observe, observe, he's moody.
Wol. The packet, Cromwell, gave it you the king?
Crom. To his own hand, in his bedchamber.
Wol. Look'd he o' th' inside of the paper?
Crom. Presently
He did unseal them: and the first he view'd,
He did it with a serious mind; a heed
Was in his countenance. You he bade
Attend him here this morning.
Wol. Is he ready
To come abroad?
Crom. I think, by this he is.

Wol. Leave me awhile.— [*Exit* CROMWELL.
It shall be to the duchess of Alençon,
The French king's sister: he shall marry her.—
Anne Bullen? No; I'll no Anne Bullens for him:
There's more in't than fair visage.—Bullen!
No, we'll no Bullens.—Speedily I wish
To hear from Rome.—The marchioness of Pembroke!
Nor. He's discontented.
Suf. May be, he hears the king
Does whet his anger to him.
Sur. Sharp enough,
Lord, for thy justice!
Wol. The late queen's gentlewoman, a knight's daughter,
To be her mistress' mistress! the queen's queen!—
This candle burns not clear: 'tis I must snuff it;
Then, out it goes.—What though I know her virtuous
And well-deserving? yet I know her for
A spleeny Lutheran; and not wholesome to
Our cause. Again, there is sprung up
A heretic, an arch one, Cranmer; one
Hath crawl'd into the favor of the king,
And is his oracle. [*Remains aloof, meditating.*
Nor. He is vex'd at something.
Suf. I would 'twere something that would fret the string,
The master-cord on's heart!
Suf. The king, the king!

Enter the KING, *reading a schedule; and* LOVELL.

K. Hen. What piles of wealth hath he accumulated
To his own portion! and what expence by the hour
Seems to flow from him! How, i' the name of thrift,
Does he rake this together?—Now, my lords,
Saw you the cardinal?
Nor. [*Advancing.*] My lord, we have
Stood here observing him: some strange commotion
Is in his brain: he bites his lip, and starts;
Stops on a sudden, looks upon the ground,
Then lays his finger on his temple; straight
Springs out into fast gait; then stops again,
Strikes his breast hard; and anon he casts
His eye against the moon: in most strange postures
We have seen him set himself.
K. Hen. It may well be;
There is a mutiny in's mind. This morning
Papers of state he sent me to peruse,
As I requir'd; and wot you what I found
There, on my conscience, put unwittingly?
Forsooth, an inventory, thus importing,—

The several parcels of his plate, his treasure,
Rich stuffs, and ornaments of household; which
I find at such proud rate, that it out-speaks
Possession of a subject.

Nor. It's heaven's will:
Some spirit put this paper in the packet,
To bless your eye withal.

K. Hen. If we did think
His contemplation were above the earth,
And fix'd on spiritual object, he should still
Dwell in his musings: but I am afraid
His thinkings are below the moon, not worth
His serious considering.

[*He takes his seat, and whispers* LOVELL, *who goes to* WOLSEY.

Wol. Heaven forgive me!—
Ever heaven bless your highness.

K. Hen. Good my lord,
You are full of heavenly stuff, and bear the inventory
Of your best graces in your mind; the which
You were now running o'er: you have scarce time
To steal from spiritual leisure a brief span,
To keep your earthly audit: sure, in that
I deem you an ill husband, and am glad
To have you therein my companion.

Wol. Sir,
For holy offices I have a time; a time
To think upon the part of business which
I bear i' the state: and nature does require
Her times of preservation, which perforce
I, her frail son, amongst my brethren mortal,
Must give my tendance to.

K. Hen. You have said well.

Wol. And ever may your highness yoke together,
As I will lend you cause, my doing well
With my well saying!

K. Hen. 'Tis well said again;
And 'tis a kind of good deed to say well:
And yet words are no deeds. My father lov'd you:
He said he did; and with his deed did crown
His word upon you. Since I had my office,
I have kept you next my heart; have not alone
Employ'd you where high profits might come home,
But par'd my present havings, to bestow
My bounties upon you.

Wol. [*Aside.*] What should this mean?

K. Hen. Have I not made you
The prime man of the state? I pray you, tell me,

If what I now pronounce you have found true:
And, if you may confess it, say withal,
If you are bound to us, or no. What say you?
Wol. My sovereign, I confess, your royal graces,
Shower'd on me daily, have been more than could
My studied purposes requite; which went
Beyond all man's endeavors:—my endeavors
Have ever come too short of my desires,
Yet fil'd with my abilities: mine own ends
Have been mine so, that evermore they pointed
To the good of your most sacred person, and
The profit of the state. For your great graces
Heap'd upon me, poor undeserver, I
Can nothing render but allegiant thanks;
My prayers to heaven for you; my loyalty
Which ever has and ever shall be growing,
Till death, that winter, kill it.
K. Hen. Fairly answer'd;
A loyal and obedient subject is
Therein illustrated: the honor of it
Does pay the act of it; as, i' the contrary,
The foulness is the punishment. I presume,
That as my hand has open'd bounty to you,
My heart dropp'd love, my power rain'd honor, more
On you than any; so your hand and heart,
Your brain, and every function of your power,
Should, notwithstanding that your bond of duty,
As 'twere in love's particular, be more
To me, your friend, than any.
Wol. I do profess,
That for your highness' good I ever labor'd
More than mine own; that am, have, and will be,
Though all the world should crack their duty to you,
And throw it from their soul; though perils did
Abound, as thick as thought could make them, and
Appear in forms more horrid, yet my duty,
As doth a rock against the chiding flood,
Should the approach of this wild river break,
And stand unshaken yours.
K. Hen. 'Tis nobly spoken:—
Take notice, lords, he has a loyal breast,
For you have seen him open't.—Read o'er this;
[*Giving him papers.*
And after, this: and then to breakfast, with
What appetite you have.
[*Exit, frowning upon* CARDINAL WOLSEY: *the* NOBLES *throng after him, smiling and whispering.*

Wol. What should this mean?
What sudden anger's this? how have I reap'd it?
He parted frowning from me, as if ruin
Leap'd from his eyes: so looks the chafed lion
Upon the daring huntsman that has gall'd him;
Then makes him nothing. I must read this paper;
I fear, the story of his anger.—'Tis so;
This paper has undone me:—'Tis th' account
Of all that world of wealth I have drawn together
For mine own ends; indeed, to gain the popedom,
And fee my friends in Rome. O negligence,
Fit for a fool to fall by! what cross devil
Made me put this main secret in the packet
I sent the king?—Is there no way to cure this?
No new device to beat this from his brains?
I know 'twill stir him strongly; yet I know
A way, if it take right, in spite of fortune
Will bring me off again.—What's this—"To the Pope?"
The letter, as I live, with all the business
I writ to his holiness. Nay then, farewell!
I have touch'd the highest point of all my greatness;
And, from that full meridian of my glory,
I haste now to my setting: I shall fall
Like a bright exhalation in the evening,
And no man see me more.

Re-enter the DUKES OF NORFOLK *and* SUFFOLK, *the* EARL OF SURREY, *and the* Lord Chamberlain.

Nor. Hear the king's pleasure, cardinal: who commands you
To render up the great seal presently
Into our hands; and to confine yourself
To Asher-house, my lord of Winchester's,
Till you hear farther from his highness.
Wol. Stay,—
Where's your commission, lords? words cannot carry
Authority so weighty.
Suf. Who dare cross them,
Bearing the king's will from his mouth expressly?
Wol. Till I find more than will or words to do it,
(I mean your malice,) know, officious lords,
I dare and must deny it. Now I feel
Of what coarse metal ye are moulded,—envy:
How eagerly ye fellow my disgraces,
As if it fed ye! and how sleek and wanton
Ye appear in every thing may be my ruin!
Follow your envious courses, men of malice;
You have Christian warrant for them, and, no doubt,
In time will find their fit rewards. That seal,

You ask with such a violence, the king
(Mine and your master) with his own hand gave me;
Bade me enjoy it, with the place and honors,
During my life; and to confirm his goodness,
Tied it by letters patent:—now, who'll take it?

Sur. The king, that gave it.

Wol. It must be himself, then.

Sur. Thou art a proud traitor, priest.

Wol. Proud lord, thou liest:
Within these forty hours Surrey durst better
Have burnt that tongue than said so.

Sur. Thy ambition,
Thou scarlet sin, robb'd this bewailing land
Of noble Buckingham, my father-in-law:
The heads of all thy brother cardinals
(With thee and all thy best parts bound together)
Weigh'd not a hair of his. Plague of your policy!
You sent me deputy for Ireland;
Far from his succor, from the king, from all
That might have mercy on the fault thou gav'st him;
Whilst your great goodness, out of holy pity,
Absolv'd him with an axe.

Wol. This, and all else
This talking lord can lay upon my credit,
I answer is most false. The duke by law
Found his deserts: how innocent I was
From any private malice in his end,
His noble jury and foul cause can witness.
If I lov'd many words, lord, I should tell you,
You have as little honesty as honor;
That I, in the way of loyalty and truth
Toward the king, my ever royal master,
Dare mate a sounder man than Surrey can be,
And all that love his follies.

Sur. By my soul,
Your long coat, priest, protects you; thou should'st feel
My sword i' the life-blood of thee else.—My lords,
Can ye endure to hear this arrogance?
And from this fellow? If we live thus tamely,
To be thus jaded by a piece of scarlet,
Farewell nobility; let his grace go forward,
And dare us with his cap, like larks.

Wol. All goodness
Is poison to thy stomach.

Sur. Yes, that goodness
Of gleaning all the land's wealth into one,
Into your own hands, cardinal, by extortion;
The goodnesss of your intercepted packets,

You writ to the pope, against the king: your goodness,
Since you provoke me, shall be most notorious.
Wol. How much, methinks, I could despise this man,
But that I am bound in charity against it.
Suf. Lord cardinal, the king's farther pleasure is,—
Because all those things you have done of late,
By your power legatine, within this kingdom,
Fall into the compass of a *præmunire*,—
That therefore such a writ be sued against you;
To forfeit all your goods, lands, tenements,
Chattels, and whatsoever, and to be
Out of the king's protection:—this is my charge.
Nor. And so we'll leave you to your meditations
How to live better. For your stubborn answer
About the giving back the great seal to us,
The king shall know it, and, no doubt, shall thank you.
So fare you well, my little good lord cardinal.
[*Exeunt all except* WOLSEY.
Wol. So, farewell to the little good you bear me.
Farewell, a long farewell, to all my greatness!
This is the state of man: to-day he puts forth
The tender leaves of hope; to-morrow blossoms,
And bears his blushing honors thick upon him:
The third day comes a frost, a killing frost;
And,—when he thinks, good easy man, full surely
His greatness is a ripening,—nips his root,
And then he falls, as I do. I have ventur'd,
Like little wanton boys that swim on bladders,
This many summers in a sea of glory;
But far beyond my depth: my high blown pride
At length broke under me; and now has left me,
Weary and old with service, to the mercy
Of a rude stream, that must for ever hide me.
Vain pomp and glory of this world, I hate ye:
I feel my heart new open'd. O, how wretched
Is that poor man that hangs on princes' favors!
There is, betwixt that smile we would aspire to,
That sweet aspect of princes, and their ruin,
More pangs and fears than wars or women have:
And when he falls, he falls like Lucifer,
Never to hope again.—

Enter CROMWELL, *amazedly.*

Why, how now, Cromwell!
Crom. I have no power to speak, sir.
Wol. What, amaz'd
At my misfortunes? can thy spirit wonder
A great man should decline? Nay, an you weep,
I am fallen indeed.

Crom. How does your grace?
Wol. Why, well;
Never so truly happy, my good Cromwell.
I know myself now; and I feel within me
A peace above all earthly dignities,
A still and quiet conscience. The king has cur'd me,
I humbly thank his grace; and from these shoulders,
These ruin'd pillars, out of pity, taken
A load would sink a navy,—too much honor:
O, 'tis a burden, Cromwell, 'tis a burden
Too heavy for a man that hopes for heaven!
Crom. I am glad your grace has made that right use of it.
Wol. I hope I have: I am able now, methinks,
(Out of a fortitude of soul I feel)
To endure more miseries, and greater far,
Than my weak-hearted enemies dare offer.–
What news abroad?
Crom. The heaviest, and the worst,
Is your displeasure with the king.
Wol. God bless him!
Crom. The next is, that Sir Thomas More is chosen
Lord Chancellor in your place.
Wol. That's somewhat sudden:
But he's a learnèd man. May he continue
Long in his highness' favor, and do justice
For truth's sake, and his conscience; that his bones,
When he has run his course and sleeps in blessings,
May have a tomb of orphans' tears wept on them!
What more?
Crom. That Cranmer is return'd with welcome,
Install'd lord archbishop of Canterbury.
Wol. That's news indeed!
Crom. Last, that the lady Anne,
Whom the king hath in secrecy long married,
This day was view'd in open, as his queen,
Going to chapel; and the voice is now
Only about her coronation.
Wol. There was the weight that pulled me down. O Cromwell,
The king has gone beyond me: all my glories
In that one woman I have lost for ever:
No sun shall ever usher forth mine honors,
Or gild again the noble troops that waited
Upon my smiles. Go, get thee from me, Cromwell;
I am a poor fallen man, unworthy now
To be thy lord and master: seek the king;
(That sun, I pray, may never set!) I have told him
What, and how true thou art: he will advance thee;
Some little memory of me will stir him,

(I know his noble nature) not to let
Thy hopeful service perish too: good Cromwell,
Neglect him not; make use now, and provide
For thine own future safety.
Crom. O my lord,
Must I, then, leave you? must I needs forego
So good, so noble, and so true a master?
Bear witness, all that have not hearts of iron,
With what a sorrow Cromwell leaves his lord.
The king shall have my service; but my prayers,
For ever and for ever, shall be yours.
Wol. Cromwell, I did not think to shed a tear
In all my miseries; but thou hast forc'd me,
Out of thy honest truth, to play the woman.
Let's dry our eyes: and thus far hear me, Cromwell;
And,—when I am forgotten, as I shall be,
And sleep in dull cold marble, where no mention
Of me more must be heard of,—say, I taught thee,
Say, Wolsey,—that once trod the ways to glory,
And sounded all the depths and shoals of honor,—
Found thee a way, out of his wreck, to rise in;
A sure and safe one, though thy master miss'd it.
Mark but my fall, and that that ruin'd me.
Cromwell, I charge thee, fling away ambition:
By that sin fell the angels; how can man, then,
The image of his Maker, hope to win by't?
Love thyself last: cherish those hearts that hate thee:
Corruption wins not more than honesty.
Still in thy right hand carry gentle peace,
To silence envious tongues. Be just, and fear not:
Let all the ends thou aim'st at be thy country's,
Thy God's, and truth's; then if thou fall'st, O Cromwell,
Thou fall'st a blessed martyr!
Serve the king; and,—pr'ythee, lead me in:
There take an inventory of all I have,
To the last penny; 'tis the king's: my robe,
And my integrity to heaven, is all
I dare now call mine own. O Cromwell, Cromwell!
Had I but serv'd my God with half the zeal
I serv'd my king, he would not in mine age
Have left me naked to mine enemies.
Crom. Good sir, have patience.
Wol. So I have. Farewell
The hopes of court! my hopes in heaven do dwell. [*Exeunt.*

ACT IV.

King Henry, having obtained his divorce from Katharine, marries Anne Bullen, who is crowned Queen of England. Katharine is removed to Kimbolton, where she lives in retirement, until her death.

SCENE II.—Kimbolton.

Enter KATHARINE, *Dowager, sick; led between* GRIFFITH *and* PATIENCE.

Grif. How does your grace?
Kath. O Griffith, sick to death!
My limbs, like loaden branches, bow to the earth,
Willing to leave their burden. Reach a chair:—
So,—now, methinks, I feel a little ease.
Didst thou not tell me, Griffith, as thou led'st me,
That the great child of honor, Cardinal Wolsey,
Was dead?
Grif. Yes, madam; but I think your grace,
Out of the pain you suffer'd, gave no ear to't.
Kath. Pry'thee, good Griffith, tell me how he died:
If well, he stepp'd before me, happily,
For my example.
Grif. Well, the voice goes, madam:
For after the stout earl Northumberland
Arrested him at York, and brought him forward
(As a man sorely tainted) to his answer,
He fell sick suddenly, and grew so ill,
He could not sit his mule.
Kath. Alas, poor man!
Grif. At last, with easy roads, he came to Leicester;
Lodg'd in the abbey; where the reverend abbot,
With all his convent, honorably receiv'd him;
To whom he gave these words,—"O father abbot,
An old man, broken with the storms of state,
Is come to lay his weary bones among ye;
Give him a little earth for charity!"
So went to bed; where eagerly his sickness
Pursu'd him still: and, three nights after this,
About the hour of eight, (which he himself
Foretold should be his last) full of repentance,
Continual meditations, tears, and sorrows,
He gave his honors to the world again,
His blessed part to heaven, and slept in peace.
Kath. So may he rest; his faults lie gently on him!
Yet thus far, Griffith, give me leave to speak him,

And yet with charity. He was a man
Of an unbounded stomach, ever ranking
Himself with princes; one, that, by suggestion,
Tied all the kingdom: simony was fair play;
His own opinion was his law: i' the presence
He would say untruths; and be ever double,
Both in his words and meaning. He was never,
But where he meant to ruin, pitiful:
His promises were, as he then was, mighty;
But his performance, as he is now, nothing.
Of his own body he was ill, and gave
The clergy ill example.

Grif. Noble madam,
Men's evil manners live in brass; their virtues
We write in water. May it please your highness
To hear me speak his good now?

Kath. Yes, good Griffith;
I were malicious else.

Grif. This cardinal,
Though from a humble stock, undoubtedly
Was fashion'd to much honor from his cradle.
He was a scholar, and a ripe and good one;
Exceeding wise, fair spoken, and persuading:
Lofty and sour to them that lov'd him not;
But, to those men that sought him, sweet as summer.
And though he were unsatisfied in getting,
(Which was a sin) yet in bestowing, madam,
He was most princely: ever witness for him
Those twins of learning, that he rais'd in you,
Ipswich, and Oxford! one of which fell with him,
Unwilling to outlive the good that did it;
The other, though unfinish'd, yet so famous,
So excellent in art, and still so rising,
That Christendom shall ever speak his virtue.
His overthrow heap'd happiness upon him;
For then, and not till then, he felt himself,
And found the blessedness of being little:
And, to add greater honors to his age
Than man could give him, he died fearing God.

Kath. After my death I wish no other herald,
No other speaker of my living actions,
To keep mine honor from corruption,
But such an honest chronicler as Griffith.
Whom I most hated living, thou hast made me,
With thy religious truth and modesty,
Now in his ashes honor: peace be with him!—
Patience, be near me still; and set me lower:
I have not long to trouble thee.—Good Griffith,

Cause the musicians play me that sad note
I nam'd my knell, whilst I sit meditating
On that celestial harmony I go to. [*Sad and solemn music.*
Grif. She is asleep: good wench, let's sit down quiet,
For fear we wake her:—softly, gentle Patience.

The Vision. Enter, solemnly tripping one after another, six Personages, clad in white robes, wearing on their heads garlands of bays, and golden vizards on their faces; branches of bays, or palm, in their hands. They first congee unto her, then dance; and, at certain changes, the first two hold a spare garland over her head; at which, the other four make reverend court'sies: then, the two that held the garland deliver the same to the other next two, who observe the same order in their changes, and holding the garland over her head: which done, they deliver the same garland to the last two, who, likewise observe the same order: at which (as it were by inspiration) she makes in her sleep signs of rejoicing, and holdeth up her hands to heaven: and so in their dancing they vanish, carrying the garland with them. The music continues.

Kath. Spirits of peace, where are ye? Are ye all gone,
And leave me here in wretchedness behind ye?
Grif. Madam, we are here.
Kath. It is not you I call for:
Saw ye none enter, since I slept?
Grif. None, madam.
Kath. No? Saw you not, even now, a blessed troop
Invite me to a banquet; whose bright faces
Cast thousand beams upon me, like the sun?
They promis'd me eternal happiness;
And brought me garlands, Griffith, which I feel
I am not worthy yet to wear: I shall, assuredly.
Grif. I am most joyful, madam, such good dreams
Possess your fancy.
Kath. Bid the music leave,
They are harsh and heavy to me. [*Music ceases.*
Pat. [*Aside to* GRIF.] Do you note
How much her grace is alter'd on the sudden?
How long her face is drawn? How pale she looks,
And of an earthly cold? Mark her eyes!
Grif. [*Aside to* PAT.] She is going: pray, pray.
Pat. [*Aside to* GRIF.] Heaven comfort her!

Enter a Messenger.

Mess. An't like your grace,—
Kath. You are a saucy fellow:
Deserve we no more reverence?

Grif. You are to blame,
Knowing she will not lose her wonted greatness,
To use so rude behavior: go to, kneel.
Mess. I humbly do entreat your highness' pardon;
My haste made me unmannerly. There is staying
A gentleman, sent from the king, to see you.
Kath. Admit him entrance, Griffith: but this fellow
Let me ne'er see again. [*Exeunt* GRIFFITH *and* Messenger.

Re-enter GRIFFITH *with* CAPUCIUS.

If my sight fail not,
You should be lord embassador from the emperor,
My royal nephew, and your name Capucius.
Cap. Madam, the same,—your servant.
Kath. O my lord,
The times and titles now are alter'd strangely
With me, since first you knew me. But, I pray you,
What is your pleasure with me?
Cap. Noble lady,
First, mine own service to your grace; the next,
The king's request that I would visit you;
Who grieves much for your weakness, and by me
Sends you his princely commendations,
And heartily entreats you take good comfort.
Kath. O, my good lord, that comfort comes too late;
'Tis like a pardon after execution:
That gentle physic, given in time, had cur'd me;
But now I am past all comforts here, but prayers.
How does his highness?
Cap. Madam, in good health.
Kath. So may he ever do! and ever flourish,
When I shall dwell with worms, and my poor name
Banish'd the kingdom!—Patience, is that letter,
I caus'd you write, yet sent away?
Pat. No, madam.
[*Giving it to* KATHARINE.
Kath. Sir, I most humbly pray you to deliver
This to my lord the king.
Cap. Most willingly, madam.
Kath. In which I have commended to his goodness
The model of our chaste loves, his young daughter,—
The dews of heaven fall thick in blessings on her!—
Beseeching him to give her virtuous breeding;
(She is young, and of a noble modest nature,—
I hope, she will deserve well) and a little
To love her for her mother's sake, that lov'd him,
Heaven knows how dearly. My next poor petition
Is, that his noble grace would have some pity

Upon my wretched women, that so long
Have follow'd both my fortunes faithfully:
The last is, for my men;—they are the poorest,
But poverty could never draw them from me;—
That they may have their wages duly paid them,
And something over to remember me by:
If heaven had pleas'd to have given me longer life,
And able means, we had not parted thus.
These are the whole contents:—and, good my lord,
By that you love the dearest in this world,
As you wish Christian peace to souls departed,
Stand these poor people's friend, and urge the king
To do me this last right.

Cap. By heaven, I will,
Or let me lose the fashion of a man!

Kath. I thank you, honest lord. Remember me
In all humility unto his highness:
Say, his long trouble now is passing
Out of this world; tell him, in death I bless'd him,
For so I will.—Mine eyes grow dim.—Farewell,
My lord.—Griffith, farewell.—Nay, Patience,
You must not leave me yet: I must to bed;
Call in more women.—When I am dead, good wench,
Let me be us'd with honor: strew me over
With maiden flowers, that all the world may know
I was a chaste wife to my grave: embalm me,
Then lay me forth: although unqueen'd, yet like
A queen, and daughter to a king, inter me.
I can no more. [*Exeunt, leading* KATHARINE.

ACT V.

Cranmer is made Archbishop of Canterbury and Primate of all England, and is especially favored by the King. These honors, and the strong Protestant tendencies of the Archbishop, excite the hatred of Gardiner, Bishop of Winchester, who creates a strong court party against Cranmer, who is arraigned before the council on the charge of holding heretical opinions dangerous to the state.

SCENE II.—*The Council-chamber.*

Enter the LORD CHANCELLOR, *the* DUKE OF SUFFOLK, *the* DUKE OF NORFOLK, EARL OF SURREY, Lord Chamberlain, GARDINER, *and* CROMWELL. *The* CHANCELLOR *places himself at the upper end of the table on the left hand; a seat being left void above him, as for the* ARCHBISHOP OF CANTERBURY. *The rest seat themselves in order on each side.* CROMWELL *at the lower end, as secretary.*

Chan. Speak to the business, master secretary:
Why are we met in council?
Crom. Please your honors,
The chief cause concerns his grace of Canterbury.
Gar. Has he had knowledge of it?
Crom. Yes.
Nor. Who waits there?
D. Keep. Without, my noble lords?
Gar. Yes.
D. Keep. My lord archbishop;
And has done half an hour, to know your pleasures.
Chan. Let him come in.
D. Keep. Your grace may enter now.
[CRANMER *approaches the Council-table.*
Chan. My good lord archbishop, I am very sorry
To sit here at this present, and behold
That chair stand empty: but we all are men,
In our own natures frail, and capable
Of our flesh; few are angels: out of which frailty,
And want of wisdom, you, that best should teach us,
Have misdemean'd yourself, and not a little,
Toward the king first, then his laws, in filling
The whole realm, by your teaching and your chaplains,
(For so we are inform'd) with new opinions,
Divers and dangerous; which are heresies,
And, not reform'd, may prove pernicious.
Gar. Which reformation must be sudden too,
My noble lords; for those that tame wild horses
Pace them not in their hands to make them gentle,
But stop their mouths with stubborn bits, and spur them,
Till they obey the manage. If we suffer
(Out of our easiness and childish pity
To one man's honor) this contagious sickness,
Farewell all physic: and what follows then?
Commotions, uproars, with a general taint
Of the whole state: as, of late days, our neighbors,
The upper Germany, can dearly witness,
Yet freshly pitied in our memories.
Cran. My good lords, hitherto, in all the progress
Both of my life and office, I have labor'd,
And with no little study, that my teachings
And the strong course of my authority,
Might go one way, and safely; and the end
Was ever, to do well: nor is there living
(I speak it with a single heart, my lords,)
A man that more detests, more stirs against,
Both in his private conscience and his place,
Defacers of a public peace, than I do.

Pray heaven, the king may never find a heart
With less allegiance in it! Men, that make
Envy and crooked malice nourishment,
Dare bite the best. I do beseech your lordships,
That, in this case of justice, my accusers,
Be what they will, may stand forth face to face,
And freely urge against me.

Suf. Nay, my lord,
That cannot be: you are a counsellor,
And, by that virtue, no man dare accuse you.

Gar. My lord, because we have business of more moment,
We will be short with you. 'Tis his highness' pleasure,
And our consent, for better trial of you,
From hence you be committed to the Tower;
Where, being but a private man again,
You shall know many dare accuse you boldly,
More than, I fear, you are provided for.

Cran. Ah, my good lord of Winchester, I thank you;
You are always my good friend; if your will pass,
I shall both find your lordship judge and juror,
You are so merciful: I see your end,—
'Tis my undoing: love and meekness, lord,
Become a churchman better than ambition:
Win straying souls with modesty again,
Cast none away. That I shall clear myself,
Lay all the weight ye can upon my patience,
I make as little doubt, as you do conscience,
In doing daily wrongs. I could say more,
But reverence to your calling makes me modest.

Gar. My lord, my lord, you are a sectary;
That's the plain truth: your painted gloss discovers,
To men that understand you, words and weakness.

Crom. My lord of Winchester, you are a little,
By your good favor, too sharp; men so noble,
However faulty, yet should find respect
For what they have been: 'tis a cruelty
To load a falling man.

Gar. Good master secretary,
I cry your honor mercy; you may, worst
Of all this table, say so.

Crom. Why, my lord?

Gar. Do not I know you for a favorer
Of this new sect? ye are not sound.

Crom. Not sound?

Gar. Not sound, I say.

Crom. Would you were half so honest!
Men's prayers then would seek you, not their fears.

Gar. I shall remember this bold language.

Crom. Do.
Remember your bold life too.
Chan. This is too much;
Forbear, for shame, my lords.
Gar. I have done.
Crom. And I.
Chan. Then thus for you, my lord:—it stands agreed,
I take it, by all voices, that forthwith
You be convey'd to the Tower a prisoner;
There to remain, till the king's farther pleasure
Be known unto us:—are you all agreed, lords?
All. We are.
Cran. Is there no other way of mercy,
But I must needs to the Tower, my lords?
Gar. What other
Would you expect? You are strangely troublesome.—
Let some o' the guard be ready there.

Enter Guard.

Cran. For me?
Must I go like a traitor thither?
Gar. Receive him,
And see him safe i' the Tower.
Cran. Stay, good my lords,
I have a little yet to say. Look there, my lords;
By virtue of that ring, I take my cause
Out of the gripes of cruel men, and give it
To a most noble judge, the king my master.
Chan. This is the king's ring.
Sur. 'Tis no counterfeit.
Suf. 'Tis the right ring, by heaven: I told ye all,
When we first put this dangerous stone a rolling,
'Twould fall upon ourselves.
Nor. Do you think, my lords,
The king will suffer but the little finger
Of this man to be vex'd?
Chan. 'Tis now too certain:
How much more is his life in value with him!
Would I were fairly out on't.
Crom. My mind misgave me,
In seeking tales and informations
Against this man,
Ye blew the fire that burns ye.—Now have at ye!

Enter the KING, *frowning on them; he takes his seat.*

Gar. Dread sovereign, how much are we bound to heaven
In daily thanks, that gave us such a prince;
Not only good and wise, but most religious:

One that, in all obedience, makes the church
The chief aim of his honor; and, to strengthen
That holy duty, out of dear respect,
His royal self in judgment comes to hear
The cause betwixt her and this great offender.

K. Hen. You were ever good at sudden commendations,
Bishop of Winchester. But know, I come not
To hear such flattery now, and in my presence;
They are too thin and base to hide offences.
To me you cannot reach: you play the spaniel,
And think with wagging of your tongue to win me:
But, whatsoe'er thou tak'st me for, I'm sure
Thou hast a cruel nature and a bloody.—
[*To* CRANMER.] Good man, sit down. Now let me see the proudest,
He that dares most, but wag his finger at thee:
By all that's holy, he had better starve,
Than but once think this place becomes thee not.

Sur. May it please your grace,—

K. Hen. No, sir, it does not please me.
I had thought, I had had men of some understanding
And wisdom of my council; but I find none.
Was it discretion, lords, to let this man,
This good man, (few of you deserve that title)
This honest man, wait like a dirty footboy
At chamber door? and one as great as you are?
Why, what a shame was this! Did my commission
Bid ye so far forget yourselves? I gave ye
Power, as he was a counsellor to try him,
Not as a groom: there's some of ye, I see,
More out of malice than integrity,
Would try him to the utmost, had ye mean;
Which ye shall never have while I live.

Chan. Thus far,
My most dread sovereign, may it like your grace
To let my tongue excuse all. What was purpos'd
Concerning his imprisonment, was rather
(If there be faith in men) meant for his trial,
And fair purgation to the world, than malice,—
I'm sure, in me.

K. Hen. Well, well, my lords, respect him;
Take him, and use him well, he's worthy of it.
I will say thus much for him,—if a prince
May be beholden to a subject, I
Am, for his love and service, so to him.
Make me no more ado, but all embrace him:
Be friends, for shame, my lords!—My lord of Canterbury,
I have a suit which you must not deny me;

That is, a fair young maid that yet wants baptism,
You must be godfather, and answer for her.
Cran. The greatest monarch now alive may glory
In such an honor: how may I deserve it,
That am a poor and humble subject to you?
K. Hen. Come, come, my lord, you'd spare your spoons:
You shall have two noble partners with you;
The old duchess of Norfolk, and lady marquess Dorset:
Will these please you?—
Once more, my lord of Winchester, I charge you,
Embrace and love this man.
Gar. With a true heart
And brother-love I do it.
Cran. And let heaven
Witness, how dear I hold this confirmation.
K. Hen. Good man, those joyful tears show thy true heart:
The common voice, I see, is verified
Of thee, which says thus, "Do my lord of Canterbury
A shrewd turn, and he is your friend for ever."—
Come, lords, we trifle time away; I long
To have this young one made a Christian.
As I have made ye one, lords, one remain;
So I grow stronger, you more honor gain. [*Exeunt.*

We close our selections with the christening of the Princess Elizabeth; afterwards so famous in English History, as "Good Queen Bess." As Shakspeare produced this Dramatic History in the latter period of that Queen's reign, he takes occasion to convey to her most courtly eulogy, by putting into the speeches of Cranmer prophetic visions of the greatness and glory of Elizabeth's reign.

SCENE IV.—*The Palace.*

Enter trumpets, sounding; then two Aldermen, Lord Mayor, Garter, CRANMER, DUKE OF NORFOLK, *with his Marshal's staff,* DUKE OF SUFFOLK, *two* Noblemen *bearing great standing bowls for the christening gifts; then, four* Noblemen *bearing a canopy, under which the* DUCHESS OF NORFOLK, *godmother, bearing the child richly habited in a mantle, &c. Train borne by a* Lady; *then follows the* MARCHIONESS OF DORSET, *the other godmother, and* Ladies. *The troop pass once about the stage, and* Garter *speaks.*

Gart. Heaven, from thy endless goodness, send prosperous life, long, and ever happy, to the high and mighty princess of England, Elizabeth!

Flourish. Enter KING *and train.*

Cran. [*Kneeling.*] And to your royal grace, and the good queen,

My noble partners, and myself, thus pray;—
All comfort, joy, in this most gracious lady,
Heaven ever laid up to make parents happy
May hourly fall upon ye!

K. Hen. Thank you, good lord archbishop:
What is her name?

Cran. Elizabeth.

K. Hen. Stand up, lord.—
[*The* KING *kisses the child.*
With this kiss take my blessing: heaven protect thee!
Into whose hand I give thy life.

Cran. Amen.

K. Hen. My noble gossips, ye have been too prodigal:
I thank ye heartily; so shall this lady,
When she has so much English.

Cran. Let me speak, sir,
For heaven now bids me; and the words I utter
Let none think flattery, for they'll find them truth.
This royal infant, (heaven still move about her!)
Though in her cradle, yet now promises
Upon this land a thousand thousand blessings,
Which time shall bring to ripeness: she shall be
(But few now living can behold that goodness)
A pattern to all princes living with her,
And all that shall succeed: Seba was never
More covetous of wisdom, and fair virtue,
Than this pure soul shall be: all princely graces,
That mould up such a mighty piece as this is,
With all the virtues that attend the good,
Shall still be doubled on her: truth shall nurse her,
Holy and heavenly thoughts still counsel her:
She shall be lov'd and fear'd: her own shall bless her;
Her foes shake like a field of beaten corn,
And hang their heads with sorrow: good grows with her:
In her days every man shall eat in safety,
Under his own vine, what he plants; and sing
The merry songs of peace to all his neighbors:
God shall be truly known; and those about her
From her shall read the perfect ways of honor,
And by those claim their greatness, not by blood.
Nor shall this peace sleep with her: but as when
The bird of wonder dies, the maiden phœnix,
Her ashes new create another heir,
As great in admiration as herself;
So shall she leave her blessedness to one,
(When heaven shall call her from this cloud of darkness)
Who, from the sacred ashes of her honor,
Shall star-like rise, as great in fame as she was,

And so stand fix'd: peace, plenty, love, truth, terror,
That were the servants to this chosen infant,
Shall then be his, and like a vine grow to him:
Wherever the bright sun of heaven shall shine,
His honor and the greatness of his name
Shall be, and make new nations: he shall flourish,
And, like a mountain cedar, reach his branches
To all the plains about him:—our children's children
Shall see this, and bless heaven.

K. Hen. Thou speakest wonders.

Cran. She shall be, to the happiness of England,
An aged princess; many days shall see her,
And yet no day without a deed to crown it.
Would I had known no more! but she must die,—
She must, the saints must have her,—yet a virgin;
A most unspotted lily shall she pass
To the ground, and all the world shall mourn her.

K. Hen. O lord archbishop,
Thou hast made me now a man!
This oracle of comfort has so pleased me,
That when I am in heaven I shall desire
To see what this child does, and praise my Maker.—
I thank ye all.—To you, my good lord mayor,
And your good brethren, I am much beholden;
I have received much honor by your presence,
And ye shall find me thankful.—Lead the way, lords:—
Ye must all see the queen, and she must thank ye;
She will be sick else. This day, no man think
He has business at his house; for all shall stay:
This little one shall make it holiday. [*Exeunt.*

THE END.

Gillespie's Land Surveying: Theoretical and Practical. By W. M. GILLESPIE, LL. D., Professor of Civil Engineering in Union College. With 400 Engravings, and a Map, showing the Variations of the Needle in the United States. 8vo. 424 pages.

——— **Levelling, Topography, and Higher Surveying.** Edited by CADY STALEY, A. M., C. E. 8vo. 171 pages.

Graham's English Synonymes. Classified and Explained. With Practical Exercises, and Illustrative Authorities. Edited by HENRY REED, LL. D. 12mo. 344 pages.

Guizot's History of Civilization in Europe.

Greene's History of the Middle Ages.

Haswell's Book-Keeping by Double Entry, Explained and Practically Illustrated in a Complete Record of Mercantile and Financial Transactions, including Rules and numerous Examples in Commercial Calculations. Designed for Schools, the Counting-House, and Private Instruction. In two parts. 8vo.

Huxley & Youmans's Elements of Physiology and Hygiene: for Schools and Academies. With numerous Illustrations. 12mo.

Keightley's Mythology. 18mo.

Kœppen's Historical Geography. 2 vols., 12mo.

Krusi's Drawing. Inventive Course, in Four Series. Now ready, Synthetic Series, Manual, 1 vol, 8vo., 44 pages. Drawing-Book, 4 parts, 16 pages.

Latham's Hand-Book of English Literature. 12mo. 398 pages.

Lockyer's Elements of Astronomy. Embracing the latest Discoveries, richly illustrated, and accompanied with Arago's Celestial Charts, and Colored Delineations of the Solar, Stellar, and Nebular Spectra. By J. NORMAN LOCKYER. American edition, specially adapted to the Schools of the United States. 12mo. 312 pages.

Lyell's Principles of Geology. 2 vols., 8vo. New and revised edition. 843 pages.

Marsh's Book-Keeping by Single Entry. New edition. Printed in colors. 8vo. 142 pages.

——— **Book-Keeping by Double Entry.** Printed in colors. 8vo. 220 pages. Blanks to each of above.

☞ SEE END OF THIS VOLUME.

www.ingramcontent.com/pod-product-compliance
Lightning Source LLC
LaVergne TN
LVHW021317110826
845150LV00003B/595